Hong Kong & Macau

Steve Fallon

LONELY PLANET PUBLICATIONS
Melbourne • Oakland • London • Paris

Hong Kong & Macau
10th edition – January 2002
First published – May 1978

Published by
Lonely Planet Publications Pty Ltd ABN 36 005 607 983
90 Maribyrnong St, Footscray, Victoria 3011, Australia

Lonely Planet offices
Australia Locked Bag 1, Footscray, Victoria 3011
USA 150 Linden St, Oakland, CA 94607
UK 10a Spring Place, London NW5 3BH
France 1 rue du Dahomey, 75011 Paris

Photographs
Many of the images in this guide are available for licensing from
Lonely Planet Images.
W www.lonelyplanetimages.com

Front cover photograph
The Bank of China Building, Hong Kong, China (Dennis Johnson)

ISBN 1 86450 230 4

Although the authors
and Lonely Planet try
to make the informa-
tion as accurate as
possible, we accept
no responsibility for
any loss, injury or
inconvenience sus-
tained by anyone
using this book.

Contents – Text

Contents – Maps

The Author

Steve Fallon

A native of Boston, Massachusetts, Steve graduated from Georgetown University with a Bachelor of Science in modern languages and then taught English at the University of Silesia near Katowice in Poland. After he had worked for several years for a Gannett newspaper and earned a master's degree in journalism, his fascination with the 'new' Asia took him to Hong Kong, where he lived for over a dozen years, working for a variety of publications and opening and running a travel bookshop. Steve lived in Budapest for 2½ years from where he wrote *Hungary* and *Slovenia* before moving to London in 1994. He has written or contributed to a number of other Lonely Planet titles.

From the Author

A number of people helped in the research of this book, but first and foremost stands Neva Shaw, amusing, erudite, full of tales and – OK, OK, already – gorgeous. If Hong Kong had royalty, La Shaw would be queen. Other friends who helped with topics as diverse as Hong Kong history, politics, the economy and what's hot and what's not on the outlying islands included Diane Stormont, Bernard Cheung Ming-on and Marilyn Hood. I'd also like to thank colleague Dani Valent for doing such a cracking good job on the *Hong Kong Condensed* guide. When I grow up, I want to be just like her.

Rocky Dang of Phoenix Services Agency took time to assist me with the Getting There & Away chapter and Ian Findlay-Brown of Asian Art News and Johnson Chang Tsong-zung of Hanart TZ Gallery helped with the special section Contemporary Art. Thanks, too, to staff at the Macau Government Tourist Office, specifically Kathy Iong Mei Va, Alorino Noruega and João Novikoff and, at the Hong Kong Tourism Board in London, Liam Fitzpatrick and Jo Hodson.

Margaret Leung and her team at Get Smart, including KK Chung and Miko Ismael, were hospitable, helpful and formidable dining companions. Miko guided me through the complex warren that is the Hong Kong public transport system, and I am very grateful.

Friends who offered mirth, inspiration, sustenance and/or a pint or three along the way included Paul Bayfield, Andy Chworowsky, Simon Elegant, Pat Elliott-Shercore, Nichole Garnaut, Akira Nagata, Joe Spitzer and Lilian Tang – not to mention the Friday night denizens of the Foreign Correspondents' Club. A special *dziękuję* goes to Jolanta Kazoń Podwitz, who travelled all the way up from Down Under and was as rude, wonderful and unforgettable as she was 15 years before at the age of, say, about 14.

5

As always I'd like to dedicate these efforts to my partner, Michael Rothschild, who doesn't allow a day to slip by without giving our old hometown a passing thought, but also to Michael Moles, thinker, doctor, soldier and (maybe) spy, whose life's journey came to an end as I flew out of the territory. Never forgotten.

Thanks

Many thanks to the travellers who used the last edition and wrote to us with helpful hints, useful advice and interesting anecdotes.

Jackie Ashe, Joanne Basso, Nick Baughan, Roger Beard, Marshall Berdan, Rikki Bewley, Richard Brooks, Helene Buckley, Thierry Carquet, Nicole Carr, Annfielde Chan, Clifford Chan, Juliette Chrisman, Louisa Chui, Nicole Clark, Robert Clements, Laura Cloniger Smith, Simon Coffey, Judith A Coopy, Andrew Correia, Luuk Damhuis, Jennifer Davidson, Barry Dawkins, K de Bruijn, Ellen DeRogatis, Jesse Engdahl, Ruby Foon, Michael Francis, Dave Gand, Paul W Gioffi, Harriet Grabow, Richard E Graves, Martin Gray, Kath Green, Ken Haley, Angus Hardern, Jennifer Henderson, Sally Hopkins, Mary Ann & Douglas Irvin, Ross & Helga Ivers, Arved Jalast, James Jarvis, Barry Jones, Eldon Kendrew, Louis King, Klaudia Krammer, Sandra Lachlan, Jackie Lam, Torng Lih, Mei Ling Chua, Aimee Linnett, Keith Lyons, Kevin Martin, Andreas Matthias, Gabriela Maya, John McBeath, Angus McIntyre, Paul Medcalf, David Mercer, Maurice Montenegro, Desmond Mow, Dr David C New, Roger Nicholl, Merilee Nonce, K L Onisiforou, Rupert Osborne, Lluis Pages, Robin Parker, Wendy Potter, Paul & Linda Przibilla, Juan Recio, David Reece, Sam Ribet, Caroline Ross, Frank Ross, Bojan Rotovnik, Jeff Salyer, Craig Scott, Gloria Ser, Danny Shaw, Gideon Sheps, Laura Short, Greg Slade, James Smith, Brian Souter, Jan Sperling, Rachael Stead, Donna Stewart, Samo Stritof, Eva & Donal Stuart-Tsang, Laurence Svirchev, Thomas Tang, Dr Joseph Y S Ting, Henry To, Barbara van Duynen Montijn, Derek Van Pelt, Elin Vigrestad, Michael Voytinsky, Tse Wai Man, Andrea Maree Wheeler, Peter White, Joanne Williams, Nev & Margaret Williams, Timothy Windever, Lucille Wong, L H Woo, Clayton Wood, Rodney & Alison Woodcock, Oliver Zoellner

This Book

The 1st edition of this book was researched and written by Carol Clewlow, and since then it has undergone several incarnations under the influence of a number of people. The 2nd edition was updated by Jim Hart, the 3rd and 4th editions were updated by Alan Samalgalski, and the 5th, 6th, 7th and 8th editions rewritten and updated by Robert Storey. Damian Harper updated the 9th edition and Steve Fallon revamped this 10th edition.

From the Publisher

The coordinating cartographer/designer of this edition was Barbara Benson in the Melbourne office. She was assisted by Chris Thomas, Chris Tsismetzis, Clare Capell and Corinne Waddell; thanks to Kusnandar for his help with climate charts. Editing was coordinated by Michael Day with Kyla Gillzan taking the reins at layout stage. They had the invaluable assistance of Craig MacKenzie, Yvonne Byron and Anastasia Safioleas.

The Language chapter was handled by Emma Koch. Charles Qin assisted with Chinese script. Matt King coordinated illustrations. Mark Germanchis overcame tricky layout issues and the cover was designed by Simon Bracken. Glenn Beanland and Fiona Croydon supplied all the photographs from LPI.

The whole process was overseen by Jocelyn Harewood (editing) and Meredith Mail, Jack Gavran and Chris Love (design).

Also, we thank Yvonne Cheung from MTR (Mass Transit Rail), Kitty Lun and David Chan for their help with 'which way is up?' and the following galleries for supplying art for the Contemporary Art special section – Hanart TZ, Plum Blossoms and J Gallery.

Foreword

ABOUT LONELY PLANET GUIDEBOOKS

The story begins with a classic travel adventure: Tony and Maureen Wheeler's 1972 journey across Europe and Asia to Australia. Useful information about the overland trail did not exist at that time, so Tony and Maureen published the first Lonely Planet guidebook to meet a growing need.

From a kitchen table, then from a tiny office in Melbourne (Australia), Lonely Planet has become the largest independent travel publisher in the world, an international company with offices in Melbourne, Oakland (USA), London (UK) and Paris (France).

Today Lonely Planet guidebooks cover the globe. There is an ever-growing list of books and there's information in a variety of forms and media. Some things haven't changed. The main aim is still to help make it possible for adventurous travellers to get out there – to explore and better understand the world.

At Lonely Planet we believe travellers can make a positive contribution to the countries they visit – if they respect their host communities and spend their money wisely. Since 1986 a percentage of the income from each book has been donated to aid projects and human rights campaigns.

Updates Lonely Planet thoroughly updates each guidebook as often as possible. This usually means there are around two years between editions, although for more unusual or more stable destinations the gap can be longer. Check the imprint page (following the colour map at the beginning of the book) for publication dates.

Between editions up-to-date information is available in two free newsletters – the paper *Planet Talk* and email *Comet* (to subscribe, contact any Lonely Planet office) – and on our Web site at www.lonelyplanet.com. The *Upgrades* section of the Web site covers a number of important and volatile destinations and is regularly updated by Lonely Planet authors. *Scoop* covers news and current affairs relevant to travellers. And, lastly, the *Thorn Tree* bulletin board and *Postcards* section of the site carry unverified, but fascinating, reports from travellers.

Correspondence The process of creating new editions begins with the letters, postcards and emails received from travellers. This correspondence often includes suggestions, criticisms and comments about the current editions. Interesting excerpts are immediately passed on via newsletters and the Web site, and everything goes to our authors to be verified when they're researching on the road. We're keen to get more feedback from organisations or individuals who represent communities visited by travellers.

Lonely Planet gathers information for everyone who's curious about the planet – and especially for those who explore it first-hand. Through guidebooks, phrasebooks, activity guides, maps, literature, newsletters, image library, TV series and Web site we act as an information exchange for a worldwide community of travellers.

Research Authors aim to gather sufficient practical information to enable travellers to make informed choices and to make the mechanics of a journey run smoothly. They also research historical and cultural background to help enrich the travel experience and allow travellers to understand and respond appropriately to cultural and environmental issues.

Authors don't stay in every hotel because that would mean spending a couple of months in each medium-sized city and, no, they don't eat at every restaurant because that would mean stretching belts beyond capacity. They do visit hotels and restaurants to check standards and prices, but feedback based on readers' direct experiences can be very helpful.

Many of our authors work undercover, others aren't so secretive. None of them accept freebies in exchange for positive write-ups. And none of our guidebooks contain any advertising.

Production Authors submit their manuscripts and maps to offices in Australia, USA, UK or France. Editors and cartographers – all experienced travellers themselves – then begin the process of assembling the pieces. When the book finally hits the shops, some things are already out of date, we start getting feedback from readers and the process begins again ...

WARNING & REQUEST

Things change – prices go up, schedules change, good places go bad and bad places go bankrupt – nothing stays the same. So, if you find things better or worse, recently opened or long since closed, please tell us and help make the next edition even more accurate and useful. We genuinely value all the feedback we receive. A well-travelled team reads and acknowledges every letter, postcard and email and ensures that every morsel of information finds its way to the appropriate authors, editors and cartographers for verification.

Everyone who writes to us will find their name listed in the next edition of the appropriate guidebook. They will also receive the latest issue of *Planet Talk*, our quarterly printed newsletter, or *Comet*, our monthly email newsletter. Subscriptions to both newsletters are free. The very best contributions will be rewarded with a free guidebook.

We may edit, reproduce and incorporate your comments in all Lonely Planet products, such as guidebooks, Web sites and digital products, so let us know if you don't want your comments reproduced or your name acknowledged.

Send all correspondence to the Lonely Planet office closest to you:

Australia: Locked Bag 1, Footscray, Victoria 3011
USA: 150 Linden St, Oakland, CA 94607
UK: 10a Spring Place, London NW5 3BH

Or email us at: talk2us@lonelyplanet.com.au

For news, views and updates see our Web site: www.lonelyplanet.com

HOW TO USE A LONELY PLANET GUIDEBOOK

The best way to use a Lonely Planet guidebook is any way you choose. At Lonely Planet we believe the most memorable travel experiences are often those that are unexpected, and the finest discoveries are those you make yourself. Guidebooks are not intended to be used as if they provide a detailed set of infallible instructions!

Contents All Lonely Planet guidebooks follow roughly the same format. The Facts about the Destination chapters or sections give background information ranging from history to weather. Facts for the Visitor gives practical information on issues like visas and health. Getting There & Away gives a brief starting point for researching travel to and from the destination. Getting Around gives an overview of the transport options when you arrive.

The peculiar demands of each destination determine how subsequent chapters are broken up, but some things remain constant. We always start with background, then proceed to sights, places to stay, places to eat, entertainment, getting there and away, and getting around information – in that order.

Heading Hierarchy Lonely Planet headings are used in a strict hierarchical structure that can be visualised as a set of Russian dolls. Each heading (and its following text) is encompassed by any preceding heading that is higher on the hierarchical ladder.

Entry Points We do not assume guidebooks will be read from beginning to end, but that people will dip into them. The traditional entry points are the list of contents and the index. In addition, however, some books have a complete list of maps and an index map illustrating map coverage.

There may also be a colour map that shows highlights. These highlights are dealt with in greater detail in the Facts for the Visitor chapter, along with planning questions and suggested itineraries. Each chapter covering a geographical region usually begins with a locator map and another list of highlights. Once you find something of interest in a list of highlights, turn to the index.

Maps Maps play a crucial role in Lonely Planet guidebooks and include a huge amount of information. A legend is printed on the back page. We seek to have complete consistency between maps and text, and to have every important place in the text captured on a map. Map key numbers usually start in the top left corner.

Although inclusion in a guidebook usually implies a recommendation we cannot list every good place. Exclusion does not necessarily imply criticism. In fact there are a number of reasons why we might exclude a place – sometimes it is simply inappropriate to encourage an influx of travellers.

Introduction

Hong Kong – a pulsating, superlative-ridden fusion of West and East – is an exercise in controlled chaos, a densely populated place 'that shouldn't be but is'. Hong Kong is simply like no other city on earth.

The vast majority of Hong Kong's people are Chinese – the long-awaited handover of the territory to the People's Republic of China proceeded smoothly in 1997. The Chinese world, with its noise, activity, unfamiliar food and language, is everywhere. Intruding into this sphere are familiar icons too: monolithic skyscrapers wedged between squatter huts, Christian churches next to Taoist and Buddhist temples, minimalist fusion restaurants beside noodle shops and food stalls. The meeting of these two worlds shakes an invigorating cocktail of colour and aroma, taste and sensation.

Hong Kong has something for everyone. Shoppers will trip over themselves trying to reach the huge malls of Central, Admiralty, Causeway Bay and Kowloon, and the factory outlets in the New Territories. Travellers with a sense of romance can gaze by night at the lights across Victoria Harbour or from atop the Peak. Aficionados of modern architecture will appreciate Hong Kong's arresting Central district. Easily reached beaches and secluded walks await those who yearn for more space.

Hong Kong has a surprising number of natural retreats. Much of Lantau Island, a short ferry ride away, is designated country park. The New Territories cuts a huge swathe to the north and, while it is becoming urbanised, still offers dramatic scenery, bracing hikes and one of the region's most important wetlands.

Gastronomes will be spoiled for choice in the city's eclectic eateries, and not just when selecting Chinese and other Asian dishes – a revolution in the restaurant scene has turned Hong Kong into a veritable atlas of world food. Hong Kong's pubs and bars colour the spectrum from the alternative and the chic to the oh-so refined, and its clubs and discos offer an energetic mix of moods and rhythms.

Then there's Macau, an hour by ferry to the west, a charming, less frenetic city that returned to Chinese sovereignty in 1999 after some 450 years under Portuguese rule. Here, Portuguese and Chinese influences have combined to create a unique 'Macanese' culture, and the pastel-coloured Catholic churches and civic buildings, narrow streets, traditional shops and splendid Portuguese and Macanese food give Macau more a Mediterranean than southern Chinese feel. Macau brims not just with atmosphere but sights as well, and a host of new museums make the region much more than just a charming diversion.

Finally, the two Special Economic Zones just over the border in the mainland – the 'anything goes' cowboy town of Shenzhen and leafy Zhuhai – offer an interesting contrast to their southern neighbours. Visiting them also gives travellers a glimpse at the direction in which China is heading.

Hong Kong remains every bit the 'moveable feast' that was Paris to Hemingway. Arrive with your eyes and ears open, your taste buds and olfactory senses primed, and your fingers at the ready to see and hear, touch, smell and taste the essence of Hong Kong and its Pearl River delta neighbours.

11

Facts about Hong Kong

HISTORY

Strictly speaking, the story of Hong Kong as it is today – the Special Administrative Region (SAR) of Hong Kong – begins on 1 July 1997, when China resumed control of the territory after more than a century and a half of British rule. But like everything else here, it's not that simple. A lot was going on in these parts long before that wintry morning in 1841 when a contingent of British marines clambered ashore and planted the Union flag on the western part of Hong Kong Island, claiming it for the crown.

Early Inhabitants

Hong Kong has supported human life since at least the Stone Age. Archaeological evidence suggests that as far back as the Neolithic period (about 4000 BC) nomadic gatherers, hunters and fisherfolk lived along the coast, shifting their camps from bay to bay. They appear to have had a relatively rich diet, subsisting on small mammals, shellfish and fish harvested far offshore, and iron-rich vegetables.

Finds uncovered at cremation pits in the territory indicate that the inhabitants of these settlements were warlike. The remnants of Bronze Age habitations unearthed on Lamma and Lantau, and at some 20 other sites, as well as the geometric rock carvings that can still be seen at various locations along Hong Kong's coastline, also suggest that these people practised some form of cosmology.

The Five Great Clans

Just when the area that is now Hong Kong became an integral part of the Chinese empire is difficult to say. Salvage anthropologists believe the indigenous population, the Yue, a people possibly of Malay stock who migrated from South-East Asia, were interacting in some way with dynastic China by the time of the Qin (221–207 BC). What is certain, however, is that by the Han dynasty (200 BC–AD 220) imperial rule had been extended over the region that now incorporates Hong Kong. The discovery of a number of Han sites here, including the tomb of a senior Han warrior at Lei Cheng Uk in central Kowloon, confirms this view.

The first of Hong Kong's mighty Five Clans, Han Chinese whose descendants enjoy political clout even today, began settling in walled villages in the fertile plains and valleys of what are now the New Territories around the 12th century AD. The first and most powerful of the arrivals were the Tang, who initially settled around Kam Tin. The hamlet of Kat Hing Wai (*wai* means 'protective wall', *tin* means 'field'), which is probably the most visited of the remaining traditional walled villages in the New Territories, formed part of this cluster.

Over the next 600 years or so, the Tang were followed by the Hau, who spread around what is present-day Sheung Shui, and the Pang from central Jiangsu province, who settled around what is now the area around Fanling. These three clans were followed by the Liu in the 15th century and the Man a century later.

The Cantonese-speaking newcomers called themselves Punti, the English transliteration for *bun dei*, meaning 'indigenous' or 'local' – something they clearly were not. They looked down on the true original inhabitants, many of whom had been shunted off the land and had become boat people. It is probable that the fisherfolk called the Tanka, or 'egg people', a derogatory term used in Cantonese for boat-dwellers, emerged from this persecuted group as they, too, speak Cantonese. The Tanka in turn feuded with the Hoklo boat people, a rival fishing community originating from the coastal regions of present-day Fujian province who retained their own language.

An Imperial Outpost

Clinging to the southern edge of Canton (now Guangdong) province, the peninsula and islands that became Hong Kong counted only as a remote pocket in a neglected corner of the Chinese empire. Among the scattered communities of farmers and fisherfolk were pirates, who hid from the authorities among the rocky islands that afforded easy access to the nearby Pearl River.

Hong Kong's first recorded brush with imperial China was in the 13th century and was as brief as it was tragic. In 1277, as the Mongol hoards swept across China, a group of loyal retainers of the Song dynasty (AD 960–1279) smuggled the boy emperor, Wang Wei, south to the remote fringes of the empire. The Song court reigned, if only nominally, from Hong Kong for a brief moment of history.

Little Wong Wei drowned when Mongol ships defeated the tattered remnants of the imperial fleet in a battle on the Pearl River, but his legacy endured in the name of the peninsula north of Hong Kong Island: Kowloon. The word means 'nine dragons' in Cantonese and is derived from the eight peaks that once surrounded the peninsula; according to the ancient tenets of fung shui, these hills are home to the lucky dragons believed to emerge at dawn to frolic in the harbour. The drowned Dragon Emperor is the ninth of these dragons.

The Punti flourished until the struggle that saw the moribund Ming dynasty (1368–1644) overthrown. The victorious Qing (1644–1911), angered by the resistance put up by southerners loyal to the *ancien régime* and determined to solve the endemic problem of piracy, ordered a forced evacuation inland in the 1660s. The resulting devastation and famine decimated a thriving population of more than 20,000 to little more than 2000.

These turbulent times saw the birth of the Triads, which would degenerate over the centuries into Hong Kong's own version of the Mafia. They were originally founded as patriotic secret societies dedicated to overthrowing the Qing dynasty and restoring the Ming. Today's Triad societies – the Hong Kong police estimate there are more than 50 in the territory – still mouth an oath of allegiance to the Ming, but their loyalty is to the

dollar rather than the vanquished Son of Heaven.

More than four generations passed before the population was able to recover to its mid-17th century levels, boosted in part by the influx of the Hakka, Cantonese for 'guest people'. These hardy migrants from north-eastern China were resented by the southerners for their aggression, studiousness and self-sufficiency. Most are now assimilated into the Cantonese-speaking mainstream of Hong Kong, but some retain their distinctive language, songs and folklore. Hakka women can be recognised in the New Territories by their distinctive spliced-bamboo hats with wide brims and black cloth fringes.

Outer Barbarians

Regular trade between China and the West began in 1557 when Portuguese navigators won permission to set up a base within a walled enclave in Macau, 65km west of Hong Kong. Jesuit priests arrived in 1582, and their scientific and technical knowledge so aroused the interest of the imperial court that a few of the clerics were permitted to live in Peking (now Beijing).

For centuries, the Pearl River estuary had been an important trading artery centred on the port of Canton (now Guangzhou). Arab traders had entered – and sacked – the settlement as early as the 8th century AD. Guangzhou was thousands of kilometres south of Beijing, and the Cantonese view that the 'mountains are high and the emperor is far away' was not enthusiastically disputed in the imperial capital. The Ming emperors regarded their cousins to the south as akin to witches and sorcerers, their language as unintelligible and their culinary predilections as downright disgusting. It was therefore fitting that Guangzhou should trade with the 'outer barbarians', or foreign traders.

Dutch traders came on the heels of the Portuguese and were in turn followed by the French. British ships had begun arriving as early as 1685 from the East India Company concessions along the coast of India, and by 1712 the company had established 'factories', offices and residences housing 'factors' (or managers), in Guangzhou to trade for tea, silk and porcelain. By the end of the century, the flags of more than a dozen nations, including Britain, would be flying over the buildings at 13 Factories Street (now a street market).

In 1757 an imperial edict awarded the *co hong*, a local merchants' guild, the monopoly on China's trade with the outsiders. Numerous restrictions were placed on Western traders: it was illegal for foreigners to learn Chinese or to deal with anyone except the co hong; they could only reside in Guangzhou and only from November to May; they were restricted to Shamian Island on Guangzhou's Pearl River; and they had to leave their wives and families behind in Macau. The traders complained about the tight restrictions but, nevertheless, trade flourished.

Opium & War

While the West had developed a voracious demand for Chinese products, especially tea, the Chinese were largely self-sufficient, for the most part disdaining Western manufactured goods. The West's ensuing trade deficit was reversed, however, when the British discovered a commodity that the Chinese craved: opium. In 1773 they unloaded a thousand chests at Guangzhou, each containing almost 70kg of opium from India.

Addiction swept China like wildfire, pulling mandarins and coolies alike into its narcotic embrace, and opium sales skyrocketed. The British, with a virtually inexhaustible supply of the drug from the poppy fields of India, developed the trade aggressively, and opium formed the basis of most of their transactions with China by the start of the 19th century.

LPP

Enjoying a quiet smoke

Alarmed by the drain of silver out of the country to pay for the opium and the spread of addiction, Emperor Dao Guang issued an edict in 1799 totally banning trade in the drug. But in Guangzhou the co hong and corrupt officials helped ensure that the trade continued, and fortunes were amassed on both sides. Imports of the drug increased further after 1834, when the British East India Company lost its monopoly on China trade and other firms rushed in, supplying opium from as far afield as Turkey and the Levant.

All that was supposed to change in 1839 with the arrival of Lin Zexu, governor of Hunan and Hubei and a mandarin of great integrity, with orders from Beijing to stamp out the opium trade. It took Lin a week to surround the British in Guangzhou, cut off their food supplies and demand the surrender of all opium in their possession. The British held out for six weeks until they were ordered by Captain Charles Elliot, Britain's chief superintendent of trade, to turn over more than 20,000 chests of opium. Lin then had this 'foreign mud' publicly burned.

Elliott suspended all trade with China while he awaited instructions from London. This, along with other such incidents, was a ruse for hawkish elements in the British government to win support for military action against China. The foreign secretary, Lord Palmerston, goaded on by prominent Scottish merchants in Guangzhou, William Jardine and James Matheson, ordered the Royal Navy in Guangzhou to force a settlement in Sino-British commercial relations. An expeditionary force under Rear Admiral George Elliot, a cousin of Captain Charles Elliot, was sent to extract reparations and secure favourable trade arrangements.

What would become known as the First Opium War began in June 1840 when British forces besieged Guangzhou before sailing north and occupying or blockading a number of ports and cities along the Yangzi River and the coast as far as Shanghai. To the emperor's great alarm, the force threatened Beijing, and he sent his envoy Qi Shan to negotiate with the Elliots. In exchange for the Britons' withdrawal from northern China Qi agreed to the Convention of Chuenpi (now Chuanbi), which ceded Hong Kong Island to Britain.

Though neither side accepted the Chuanbi terms, a couple of subsequent events would see the cession of Hong Kong signed and sealed. In February 1841, Captain Elliot attacked the Bogue forts at Humen, took control of the Pearl River and laid siege to Guangzhou, withdrawing only after having extracted considerable financial reparations and other concessions from the merchants there. Six months later a powerful British force sailed north and seized Amoy (now Xiamen), Ningpo (now Ningbo), Shanghai and other ports. With the strategic city of Nanking (now Nanjing) under immediate threat, the Chinese were forced to accept Britain's terms.

The Treaty of Nanking abolished the monopoly system of trade, opened five ports to British residence and foreign trade, exempted British nationals from all Chinese laws and, most important of all (in hindsight if not at the time), ceded the island of Hong Kong to the British 'in perpetuity'. The treaty, signed in 1842 and ratified the following year, set the scope and character of the unequal relationship between China and the West that the Chinese later would call 'national humiliations'.

British Hong Kong

'Albert is so amused at my having got the island of Hong Kong', wrote Queen Victoria to King Leopold of Belgium in 1841. While the queen's husband may have seen the funny side of her owning an apparently useless lump of rock off the southern coast of China, Foreign Secretary Lord Palmerston was less amused. 'A barren island with hardly a house upon it!' he raged in a letter to Captain Elliot, the man responsible for the deal. 'It will never be a mart for trade.'

Palmerston got it wrong on both counts. Even in the 1840s Hong Kong was not quite the backwater portrayed by the foreign secretary. At the time, Hong Kong contained about 20 dozen villages and settlements with a population of some 3650 on land and another 2000 living on fishing boats. While the mountainous terrain lacked fertile land

and water, it did offer one distinct advantage for the British trading fleet: a deep, sheltered harbour.

The place was familiar to British seamen, who had been using the fine harbour to anchor vessels carrying opium since the 1820s. They called the island Hong Kong, after the Cantonese name *Heung Gong*, or 'fragrant harbour'.

The British merchants in Guangzhou and the Royal Navy sided with Lord Palmerston; a small barren island with nary a house on it was not the type of sweeping concession that a British victory was supposed to achieve. The *Canton Press* newspaper caustically observed that 'we now only require houses, inhabitants, and commerce to make this settlement one of the most valuable of our possessions'.

Growing Pains

What would later be called the Second Opium War broke out in 1856 when Chinese soldiers boarded the British merchant ship *Arrow* to search for pirates. French troops supported the British in this war, while Russia and the USA lent naval support. The war was brought to an end two years later by the Treaty of Tientsin (now Tianjin), which permitted the British to establish diplomatic representation in China.

Despite warnings from the Chinese, the British tried to capitalise on this agreement three years later by sending a flotilla carrying the first 'British envoy and minister plenipotentiary' up the Pei Ho River to Beijing. The armada was fired upon by the Chinese and sustained heavy losses. Using this as an excuse, a combined British and French force invaded China and marched on Beijing. The victorious British forced the Chinese to the Convention of Peking in 1860, which ratified the Treaty of Tientsin and ceded the Kowloon Peninsula and Stonecutters Island to Britain. Britain was now in complete control of Victoria Harbour.

Within 40 years, Hong Kong was growing in population, and the British army felt it needed more land to protect the colony. Hong Kong made its move when the Qing dynasty was at its nadir, fending off concession demands from other European countries as well as Japan and dealing with home-grown unrest such as the Taiping Rebellion (1851–65).

The government petitioned China for a land extension and in June 1898 the Second Convention of Peking presented Britain with a larger-than-expected slice of territory running north to the Shumchun (or Shenzhen) River and 235 islands, increasing the colony's size by 90 percent. But instead of annexing the 'New Territories', the British agreed to sign a 99-year lease, beginning on 1 July 1898 and ending at midnight on 30 June 1997.

A Sleepy Backwater

While the 'hongs' – Hong Kong's major trading houses – prospered from the China trade, the colony hardly thrived in its early decades. Fever and typhoons threatened life and property, and at first the colony attracted a fair number of criminals.

Gradually though, Hong Kong began to shape itself into a more substantial community; the territory saw its population leap from 33,000 in 1851 to more than 300,000 by the end of the century. Gas and electrical power companies were set up, ferries, trams and the Kowloon-Canton Railway provided a decent transport network, and land was reclaimed. Nonetheless, in the years leading up to WWII, Hong Kong lived in the shadow of Shanghai, which had become Asia's premier trade and financial centre – not to mention its style capital.

Hong Kong also became a beacon for China's regular outflow of refugees. One of the earliest waves was sparked by the Chinese Revolution of 1911, which ousted the decaying Qing dynasty and ushered in several decades of strife, rampaging warlords and mass starvation. The civil war in China kept the numbers of refugees entering the colony high, but the stream became a flood after Japan invaded China in 1937: As many as 700,000 mainland Chinese sought shelter in Hong Kong over the next two years.

Hong Kong's status as a British colony would only offer the refugees a temporary haven, however. The day after its attack on the US naval base at Pearl Harbor on 7 December 1941, Japan's military machine swept down from Guangzhou and into Hong Kong. After more than two weeks of fierce but futile resistance, the British forces surrendered on Christmas Day, beginning nearly four years of Japanese occupation.

Conditions were harsh, with indiscriminate massacres of mostly Chinese civilians. European civilians were incarcerated at Stanley Prison on Hong Kong Island. Many Hong Kong Chinese fled to Macau, administered by neutral Portugal. In the latter years of the war Japan actually started deporting people from Hong Kong in a bid to ease the severe food shortages there. The population, numbering approximately 1.6 million in 1941, was reduced to about 650,000 by the end of the war.

The Road to Boomtown

After Japan's withdrawal from Hong Kong, and subsequent surrender in August 1945, the colony looked set to resume its sleepy routine. But events both at home and on the mainland forced the colony in a new direction.

Just before WWII Hong Kong had begun to shift from entrepôt trade servicing China to home-grown manufacturing. The turmoil on the mainland, leading to the defeat of the Nationalists and takeover by the Communists in 1949, unleashed a torrent of refugees – both rich and poor – into Hong Kong. By 1947, the population had once again reached the level it had been at the start of the war and, by the end of 1950, it mushroomed to 2.3 million. When Beijing sided with North Korea that year and went to war against the forces of the USA and the United Nations, the subsequent embargo on all Western trade with China threatened to strangle the colony economically.

But on a paltry, war-torn foundation, both local and foreign businesses built an immense manufacturing (notably textiles and garments) and financial services centre that transformed Hong Kong into one of the world's great economic success stories.

Much of the success depended on the enormous pool of cheap labour from China.

Working conditions in those early years of Hong Kong's economic revolution were often Dickensian: 16-hour days, unsafe working conditions, low wages and child labour were all common. Refugee workers endured, and some even earned their way out of poverty and into prosperity. The Hong Kong government, after coming under international pressure, eventually began to establish and enforce labour standards and the situation gradually improved.

Hong Kong was a haven in comparison with life on Taiwan and the mainland, but trouble flared up in the 1950s and 60s due to social discontent and the poor working conditions. Feuding between Communist and Nationalist supporters in Hong Kong led to riots in 1957 and again in 1962. The 1966 riots, ostensibly over a 10-cent fare increase on the Star Ferry, demonstrated the frustration many local people had with the colonial government.

When the Communists came to power in China in 1949, many people were sure that Hong Kong would be overrun. Even without force, the Chinese could simply have ripped down the fence on the border and sent the masses to settle on Hong Kong territory. In 1962 China actually staged what looked like a trial run for this, sending 70,000 people across the frontier in a couple of weeks. But though the Chinese continued to denounce the 'unequal treaties' that had created a British colony on their own soil, they recognised Hong Kong's importance to the national economy.

At the height of the so-called Cultural Revolution in 1967, when the ultra-leftist Red Guards were calling the shots in China, Hong Kong's stability again looked precarious. Riots rocked the colony, bringing with them a wave of bombings, looting and arson attacks. A militia of 300 armed Chinese crossed the border, killing five policemen and penetrating 3km into the New Territories before pulling back. The governor at the time, David Trench, kept an aircraft on standby at Kai Tak Airport in case he and his family would need to flee.

Property values in Hong Kong plunged, as did China's foreign exchange earnings, as trade and tourism ground to a halt. However the bulk of the population – and, importantly, the Hong Kong police – stood firm with the colonial authorities. By the end of the 1960s China, largely due to the intervention of premier Chou Enlai, had come to its senses and order had been restored. The time for China to recover Hong Kong was not yet ripe.

A Society in Transition

As China went back into its cage, Hong Kong got on with the business of making money, which included improving the territory's infrastructure. In 1972, the Cross-Harbour Tunnel between Causeway Bay and Hung Hom opened, ending the reliance on ferry transport between Hong Kong Island and Kowloon. The next year, the first 'New Town' – Sha Tin – was completed, paving the way towards better housing for millions of Hong Kong people.

By 1979 the colony had its own subway, with the opening of the first line of the Mass Transit Railway (MTR).

The stock market collapsed in 1973, but Hong Kong's economy resumed its upward trend later in the decade. At the same time, many of Hong Kong's neighbours, including Taiwan, South Korea and Singapore, began to mimic the colony's success. Just as their cheap labour was threatening to undermine the competitive edge of Hong Kong manufacturers, China began to emerge from its self-imposed isolation. Deng Xiaoping, who took control of China in the mayhem following Mao Zedong's death in 1976, opened up the country to tourism and foreign investment in 1978.

Deng's so-called Open Door policy, designed to pull China into the 20th century, revived Hong Kong's role as the gateway to the mainland. Hong Kong companies gradually began moving their factories over the border, and foreign firms came in droves seeking out Hong Kong businesses for their China contacts and expertise. Investment in China grew and trade in Hong Kong skyrocketed as it became the trans-shipment point for China's exports, and later on, imports. Underpinning the boom was the drive to rake in as much profit as possible ahead of 1997, when Hong Kong's unpredictable new master was due to take over.

The 1997 Question

In reality, few people gave much thought to Hong Kong's future until the late 1970s, when the British and Chinese governments met for the first time to decide what would happen in – and after – 1997. Britain was legally bound to hand back only the New Territories but, with nearly half of Hong Kong's population living there by that time, it would have been an untenable division.

In Beijing's eyes, Hong Kong remained the last remnant of foreign imperialism on the mother soil. (Macau was a somewhat different story, having never been formally ceded to Portugal.) As both China's economy and confidence grew stronger, the British presence in Hong Kong became intolerable.

It was Deng Xiaoping who decided that the time was ripe to recover Hong Kong, forcing the British to the negotiating table. In December 1984, after more than two years of closed-door wrangling, the two parties announced that the UK had agreed to hand back the entire colony at midnight on 30 June 1997. The decision laid to rest political jitters that had seen the Hong Kong dollar collapse and subsequently pegged to the US dollar in 1983, but there was considerable resentment that the fate of 5.5 million people had been decided without their input and that Whitehall had decided against providing Hong Kong people with full British passports and right of abode in the UK.

Despite soothing words from China, Britain and the Hong Kong government, over the next 13 years the population of Hong Kong suffered considerable anxiety at the possible political and economic consequences of the handover. Tens of thousands of people immigrated to Canada, the USA, Australia, Britain and New Zealand – or at least managed to secure a foreign passport.

'One Country, Two Systems'

The agreement signed by China and Britain, enshrined in a document known as the Sino-British Joint Declaration on the Question of Hong Kong, pledged to allow Hong Kong to retain its pre-handover social, economic and legal systems for 50 years after 1997. Hong Kong as a 'British-administered territory' would disappear and re-emerge as a Special Administrative Region (SAR) of China. The Hong Kong SAR would be permitted to retain its capitalist system after 1997, while across the border the Chinese would continue with a system that it labelled socialist. The Chinese catch phrase for this was 'one country, two systems'.

In 1988, the details of this rather unorthodox system of government were spelled out in *The Basic Law for Hong Kong*, the SAR's future constitution. The Basic Law, ratified by the National People's Congress in Beijing in 1990, confirmed that Hong Kong people would govern Hong Kong. It preserved Hong Kong's English common law judicial system and guaranteed the right of property and ownership. It also included the rights of assembly, free speech, association, travel and movement, correspondence, choice of occupation, academic research, religious belief and the right to strike. The SAR would enjoy a high degree of autonomy except in foreign affairs and matters of defence.

As China's own constitution has lofty guarantees of individual freedoms and respect for human rights, few Hong Kong Chinese had faith in the Basic Law. The guarantees were seen as empty promises and many felt the Basic Law provided Beijing with the means to interfere in Hong Kong's internal affairs to preserve public order, public morals and national security. Hong Kong's fledgling democratic movement denounced the Joint Declaration as the new 'unequal treaty' and the Basic Law as a 'basic flaw'.

Although Hong Kong under the British had never been anything more than a benignly ruled oligarchy, Whitehall had nevertheless promised to introduce democratic reforms prior to the handover. But it soon became apparent that British and Chinese definitions of democracy differed considerably.

Beijing made it abundantly clear that it also would not allow Hong Kong to establish its own democratically elected government. The chief executive was to be chosen by a Beijing-appointed panel of delegates; the people would elect some lower officials. In the face of opposition from Beijing, planned elections for 1988 were postponed until 1991 after a rigged referendum was interpreted to demonstrate acceptance of a 'slower pace of democracy'.

Tiananmen & Its Aftermath

The concern of many Hong Kong people over their future turned to outright fear on 4 June 1989, when Chinese troops used tanks and machine guns to mow down pro-democracy demonstrators in Beijing's Tiananmen Square. The massacre of students and their supporters horrified Hong Kong people, many of whom had donated funds and equipment to the demonstrators. Up to one million Hong Kong people – one in six of the population – braved a typhoon to march in sorrow and anger. As the Chinese authorities spread out to hunt down activists, an underground smuggling operation, codenamed Yellow Bird, was set up in Hong Kong to spirit them to safety overseas.

The Tiananmen massacre, still marked every year with a candlelight vigil in Victoria Park on Hong Kong Island, was a watershed for Hong Kong. Sino-British relations deteriorated, confidence in Hong Kong plummeted. The stock market fell 22% in one day, and a great deal of capital left the territory for destinations overseas. The Hong Kong dollar wobbled, but the link held firm.

The Hong Kong government sought to rebuild confidence by launching a new airport and shipping port – with an estimated price tag of HK$160 billion, the world's most expensive infrastructure project of the day, it was designed to lure foreign investors. But China had already signalled its intentions loud and clear.

Hong Kong-based Chinese officials who had spoken out against the Tiananmen killings were yanked from their posts or sought asylum in the USA and Europe.

Local Hong Kong people with money and skills made a mad dash to emigrate to any country that would take them. At its height in 1990, more than 1000 people were emigrating each week, especially to Canada and Australia. Tiananmen hardened the resolve of those people who either could not leave or chose not to, giving rise to the territory's first official political parties.

Democracy & the Last Governor

Hong Kong was never as politically apathetic as was generally thought in the 1970s and 80s. The word 'party' may have been anathema to the refugees who had fled from the Communists or Nationalists in the 1930s and 40s, but not necessarily to their sons and daughters.

Born and bred in the territory, these first generation Hong Kong youths were trickling into the universities and colleges by the 1970s and becoming politically active. Like student activists everywhere they were idealistic and passionate, agitating successfully for Chinese to be recognised as an official language alongside English. They opposed colonialism, expressed pride in their Chinese heritage and railed against the benign dictatorship of the Hong Kong government. But they were split between those who supported the Chinese Communist Party and those who mistrusted it.

This generation, the first to consider themselves 'Hong Kong people' rather than refugees from China, formed the pressure groups emerging in the 1980s to debate Hong Kong's future. By the end of the decade they were coalescing into nascent political parties and preparing for the 1991 elections.

The first party to emerge was the United Democratic Party, led by outspoken democrats Martin Lee and Szeto Wah. The pair, initially courted by China for their anti-colonial positions and appointed to the committee that drafted the Basic Law, infuriated Beijing by publicly burning copies of the proto-constitution in protest over the Tiananmen massacre. China denounced them as subversives and continues to demonise them.

Sino-British relations worsened with the arrival in 1992 of Chris Patten, Hong

Kong's 28th – and last – British governor. Patten lost no time in putting the British plans for limited democracy back on track and even widened their scope slightly.

His legislative reforms were not particularly radical – he lowered the voting age from 21 to 18 and broadened the franchise for the indirectly elected segment of Hong Kong's complicated electoral system. Hong Kong residents were largely sceptical at first, with many wondering why Britain had chosen to wait until this late date to start experiments in democracy.

China reacted badly, first levelling daily verbal attacks on the governor, then threatening the post-1997 careers of any pro-democracy politicians or officials. When these tactics failed, it targeted Hong Kong's economy. Negotiations on certain business contracts straddling 1997 suddenly came to a halt, and Beijing scared off foreign investors by boycotting all talks on the new airport program.

Sensing that it had alienated even its supporters in Hong Kong, China backed down and in 1994 gave its blessing to the new airport at Chek Lap Kok. It remained hostile to direct elections, however, and vowed to disband the democratically elected legislature after 1997.

In August 1994, China adopted a resolution to terminate the terms of office of Hong Kong's three tiers of elected bodies (district boards, municipal councils and the legislature). A Provisional Legislative Council was elected by Beijing, which included pro-Beijing councillors defeated by democratic ones in the existing Legislative Council. The rival chamber met over the border in Shenzhen, as it had no authority in Hong Kong until the transfer of power.

As for the executive branch of power, no-one was fooled by the pseudo-election choreographed by China in 1996 to select Hong Kong's first post-colonial leader. But Tung Chee Hwa (1937–), the Shanghai-born shipping magnate destined to become chief executive, won approval by retaining Patten's right-hand woman, Anson Chan, as his chief secretary and Sir Donald Tsang as financial secretary.

China agreed to a low-key entry into Hong Kong and PLA troops were trucked straight to their barracks in Stanley, Kowloon Tong and Bonham Rd in the Mid-Levels. On the night of 30 June 1997 the handover celebrations held at the purpose-built Convention Centre in Wan Chai were watched by millions around the world. Prince Charles was stoic and Chris Patten wept while Chinese Premier Jiang Zemin beamed.

Post-1997 Hong Kong

The Hong Kong SAR started out on a positive footing. While the predicted political storm failed to appear, other slip-ups and disasters – economic recession, a plague and an ill-fated launch for the new airport – helped to sandbag the new SAR in its early years.

The financial crisis that rocked Thailand and then South Korea before spreading across South-East Asia began to be felt in Hong Kong at the end of 1997. A strain of

How Now to Kowtow

Although the Basic Law guarantees religious freedom in the Hong Kong SAR, in early 2001 the Chief Executive Tung Chee Hwa, following the lead of the mainland, branded the Falun Gong a 'vicious cult', a move that would limit the group's activities in Hong Kong.

The Falun Gong, a group that claims not to be a religion at all but a system for 'improving and elevating the mind, body and spirit' through simple tai chi-style exercises and *qigong* breathing, emerged in China in 1992. Adherents there claim that continued persecution by the Chinese authorities (some 100 members have died while in police custody) led to the public suicide of five Falun Gong members by self-immolation in Tiananmen Square in January 2001.

Word on the street was that Tung's bosses in Beijing had given him carte blanche, affirming that he was in charge in Hong Kong and could make his own decision. Mr Tung obviously decided a kowtow (and a kiss and a lick) was in everyone's interest – especially his own, since he is seeking a second five-year term in 2002 and needs China's backing.

deadly avian flu, which many people feared would become a world-wide epidemic, saw Hong Kong slaughtering more than one million chickens. Then came the Chek Lap Kok-up of 1998, when the much trumpeted new airport opened to a litany of disasters. Hong Kong was making world headlines again – but for all the wrong reasons.

Meanwhile, Chief Executive Tung Chee Hwa's popularity was declining. His claim at the SAR inauguration ceremony that 'now we are masters of our own house' rang hollow. He was seen increasingly as Beijing's puppet, often dictatorial but strangely weak and indecisive in times of crisis. Opinion poll after opinion poll showed that, if given the choice, Hong Kong people would have preferred to see Chief Secretary Anson Chan, dubbed the 'conscience of Hong Kong', at the helm.

When Tung surprised Hong Kong by extending Chan's posting past her official retirement age, confidence surged – only to sink when the chief secretary announced she could take no more and would resign in mid-2001. Chan was coy, but she did admit that 'certain people' had tried to drive a wedge between her and the chief executive. Her departure raised fears of an impending 'Singapore-isation' of Hong Kong, with a strongman in charge of a rubber-stamping legislature, and of the hardline 'one country' side of the equation coming to dominate the pluralistic 'two systems' side.

GEOGRAPHY

Hong Kong measures 1098 sq km, an increase of 3% of the total surface in the past decade or so due to land reclamation. The territory is divided into four main areas: Hong Kong Island, Kowloon, the New Territories and the outlying islands.

Hong Kong Island covers 80 sq km, or just over 7% of the total land area. It lies on the southern side of Victoria Harbour, and contains the main business district. Towering above the skyscrapers of Central is the Peak, Hong Kong's premier scenic outlook and residential address. Other important neighbourhoods on the island include, from west to east: Sheung Wan, the Mid-Levels,

Wan Chai, Happy Valley, Causeway Bay and Quarry Bay.

Kowloon is a peninsula on the northern side of the harbour. The southern tip, an area called Tsim Sha Tsui (pronounced 'chim sha choy') is a major tourist area and where most of the budget hotels are located. Kowloon proper only includes the land south of Boundary St, but land reclamation and encroachment into the New Territories gives it an area of about 47 sq km, or just over 4% of the total. Besides Tsim Sha Tsui, which is often called 'Tsimsy' (pronounced 'chimsy') locally, other Kowloon districts include Hung Hom, Yau Ma Tei, Mong Kok and Kowloon Tong.

The New Territories occupies 796 sq km, or more than 72% of Hong Kong's land area, and spreads out like a fan between Kowloon and the mainland Chinese border. What was once the territory's rural hinterland has become in large part a network of 'New Towns' such as Tsuen Wan, Tuen Mun, Yuen Long, Tai Po and Sha Tin, which upwards of 50% of Hong Kong's population call home.

The outlying islands refer to the territory's 234 islands, apart from Hong Kong Island and Stonecutters Island off the western shore of the Kowloon Peninsula, which has been absorbed by land reclamation. Officially, they are part of the New Territories and their 175 sq km make up just under 16% of Hong Kong's total land area. While many of the islands are no more than large rocks, the largest – Lantau – is nearly twice the size of Hong Kong Island itself.

GEOLOGY

Hong Kong is what geologists call an anticline – a series of steep slopes. The slopes run north-east to south-west. The mountains on both the mainland and the islands consist mainly of volcanic rock while some of the lower hills are granite. Apart from the mudflats around Deep Bay formed by sediment deposited by the Pearl River, Hong Kong's soil is generally acidic and of low fertility. Over-development and deforestation has caused much erosion, and slope engineering in the built-up areas is extensive.

CLIMATE

Hong Kong lies on the northern edge of the tropical zone; its climate and vegetation can thus be called sub-tropical. A powerful Arctic wind blows across the great land mass of Asia in a north-easterly direction in winter, while in summer monsoons blow from the south-west, bringing humid tropical air. There are three, rather than four, seasons but these are not always so well defined.

What those living in the Northern Hemisphere would call autumn and early winter (October to late January/early February) is the dry season and the best time to visit Hong Kong. During the first three months skies are invariably clear, the sun is shining and the temperature cool – though there is still a risk of typhoons in October.

In January and part of February northerly winds can cause the thermometer to dip below 10°C and occasionally bring frost on high ground, but the mean temperature for those months is around 16°. It rarely rains during these months, but it's cold enough to wear a warm sweater or coat.

'Spring', running from late February/early March to May is generally a ghastly time of year. It's warmish and humid and a low cloud ceiling often leaves the mountains shrouded in mist. Worse, a thick fog can rapidly descend on the airport and harbour, disrupting air traffic and ferry services. It rains infrequently at this time, but when it does it's usually a depressing drizzle that can last for days.

The rainy season – roughly May to September – is a mixed bag, with fine though humid days punctuated by rainy days and typhoons. Big thunderstorms become more frequent as June approaches and the summer monsoon season starts. July and

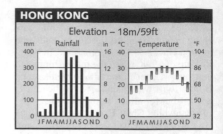

August are sunny, hot and humid, with occasional showers. Approximately 80% of the annual 2215mm of rain falls between May and September, with August being the wettest month. The average mean temperature in July is 29°C.

September brings just a hint of cooler weather, but it's the month when Hong Kong is most likely to be hit by anything from a tropical storm to a severe typhoon, which can be devastating if it scores a direct hit. Winds can reach speeds of up to 220km/h and rain may last days on end. You can't go outside during a bad typhoon, and businesses shut down (see the boxed text Typhoon! in the Kowloon chapter). When a typhoon approaches the territory, warnings are broadcast continuously on the TV and radio. You can also contact the Royal Observatory (☎ 2926 8200) or its special typhoon hotline (☎ 2926 8200) for updates. Daily weather reports in English are available on ☎ 187 8966 and online at 🆆 www.weather.org.hk.

ECOLOGY & ENVIRONMENT

Until recently, Hong Kong's laissez faire stance towards business and economic growth put measures to control waste, water, air and noise pollution very much in the back seat. And the attitude was not just that of the government and big business.

Now that has all begun to change. According to opinion polls, the environment – not politics – is the greatest issue of concern for Hong Kong residents post-1997.

The first major step taken to deal with the causes rather than just treat the symptoms of Hong Kong's environmental problems came in 1989 with the formation of the Environmental Protection Department. The

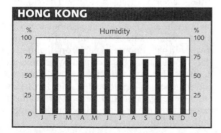

EPD was set up as an advisory and regulatory body to deal with the 18,000 tonnes of domestic, industrial and construction waste generated daily in Hong Kong. Three large landfills in the New Territories now absorb all Hong Kong municipal solid waste.

An aggressive public service campaign was implemented to remind locals not to treat the roads, waterways and parks as rubbish bins. Most recently, the department has resurrected – and modernised for the cyber generation – one Laap Saap (meaning 'garbage') Cheung, a particularly effective cartoon character used in anti-litter campaigns in the mid-1970s and early 80s. This, as well as the increased use of private trash collectors and more recycling, which amounted to 35% of total municipal waste in 1999, appears to be having some effect: Hong Kong looks cleaner than ever before, at least on the surface.

Water pollution has been one of Hong Kong's most serious ecological problems over the years. Victoria Harbour remains in a pitiful state, suffering from the effects of years of industrial and sewage pollution. Steps are being taken and the harbour's *E. coli* bacteria count has stabilised, though it is still very high by world standards. Factories and farms in the New Territories must now by law have their own sewage disposal systems and are fined heavily for dumping untreated industrial or animal waste into freshwater rivers or streams. A great deal of damage has already been done, of course. But the percentage of rivers in the 'good' and 'excellent' categories increased from 27% in 1986 to 65% in 2000.

The quality of the water at Hong Kong's 36 gazetted beaches must be rated 'fair' or 'good' to allow public use, but many beaches here fall below the World Health Organisation's levels for safe swimming due to pollution. Since 1998 water has been tested at each beach every two weeks during the swimming season (April to October) and judgements made based upon the level of *E. coli* bacteria present in the sample. The list of beaches deemed safe enough for swimming are listed in the newspapers and on the EPD's Web site (W www.info.gov.hk/epd).

Another of Hong Kong's most serious problems is air pollution. Smoke-belching factories, ceaseless construction and a high proportion of diesel vehicles have made for dangerous levels of particulate matter and nitrogen dioxide, especially in Central, Causeway Bay and Mong Kok. Case numbers of asthma and bronchial infection have soared in recent years, and doctors blame it on poor air quality. Travellers with respiratory conditions should take this into consideration if planning to stay for a prolonged period, especially in summer. An hourly update of Hong Kong's air pollution index can be found on the EPD's Web site.

Arguably the most annoying form of pollution in Hong Kong is the noise created by traffic, industry and commerce. The aircraft noise problem ended for most people in Hong Kong when the airport was moved from Kai Tak in Kowloon to Chek Lap Kok north of Lantau Island, but traffic noise has worsened. A short section of road has been resurfaced with a porous, low-noise 'skin' as an experiment, but up to one million people remain affected and building insulation is being considered.

Laws governing the use of construction machinery appear strict on paper, but this being Hong Kong, there's usually a way around things. General construction is allowed to continue between the hours of 7pm and 7am as long as builders secure a permit.

FLORA & FAUNA
Flora

The Hong Kong countryside is very lush. Take a close look and you'll see many of the estimated 2900 species of indigenous and introduced plants, flowers and trees, including Hong Kong's own flower, the bauhinia (*Bauhinia blakeana*; see the boxed text A Sterile Hybrid). Hong Kong's beaches and coastal areas are also home to a wide variety of plant life, including creeping beach vitex *(Vitex trifolia),* rattlebox *(Croatalaria retusa),* beach naupaka *(Scaevola sericea)* and screw pine *(Pandanus tectorius).*

Centuries of felling and burning trees for fuel have left only about 12% of Hong Kong's land area forested. Most of the stands of pine, eucalyptus, banyan, casuarina and palm that you'll see in the New Territories and the outlying islands owe their origins to post-war reafforestation programs.

Fauna

Hong Kong is home to a wide variety of animal life. While the constant creation and expansion of New Towns has decreased the number of larger animals, there are smaller mammals, amphibians, reptiles, birds and insects in large numbers.

One of the largest natural habitats for wildlife in Hong Kong is the Mai Po Marsh, which is listed with the inner area of Deep Bay as a 'Wetland of International Importance' under the Ramsar Convention of 1995. Mai Po is a 500-hectare network of ponds and mudflats that attract almost 70,000 waterfowl every winter. Roughly 300 species of bird have been spotted in the area among the shrimp ponds and dwarf mangroves. For more information, see the boxed text A Wetlands for Hong Kong in the New Territories chapter). There are also sanctuaries in the wetland areas of Tin Shui Wai, Kam Tin and Kwu Yung around Mai Po.

Wooded areas throughout Hong Kong are habitats for warblers, flycatchers, robins, bulbuls and tits. Occasionally you'll see sulphur-crested cockatoos, even on Hong Kong Island, and flocks of domestic budgerigars (parakeets) which have managed to fly the coop.

The areas around some of Hong Kong's reservoirs shelter a large number of long-tailed macaques and rhesus monkeys, both of which are non-native species. Common smaller mammals include woodland and house shrews and bats. Occasionally spotted are leopard and civet cats, the black and white Chinese porcupine, masked palm civets, ferret badgers and barking deer.

Wild boars, some weighing over 100kg, are sometimes seen routing crops in rural areas of the New Territories. An interesting creature is the Chinese pangolin, a scaly mammal resembling an armadillo that rolls itself up into an impenetrable ball when threatened. Unfortunately, it is in danger of becoming extinct because the Chinese use its flesh to make a medicinal tonic.

Frogs, lizards and snakes, including the deadly red-necked keelback, which has not one but *two* sets of fangs, can be seen in the New Territories and the outlying islands. Hong Kong is also home to an incredible variety of insects. There are some 200 species of butterfly and moth alone, including the giant silkworm moth with a

A Sterile Hybrid

Hong Kong can look and feel like an artificial place – concrete jungles sprouting on reclaimed land; parks and gardens landscaped to within an inch of their lives; foreign residents spending 'just a year or two' in the territory before moving on – so what better symbol for the new SAR than the *Bauhinia blakeana*? Unique to Hong Kong, it's a sterile tree with purple blossoms.

The story goes that priests from the French Mission (now the Court of Final Appeal, in Central) discovered the tree near the seashore in the late 19th century. As no identical tree could be found anywhere else in the world, it was declared a new species of bauhinia (of which there are 250 to 300) and named after Sir Henry Blake, governor of Hong Kong from 1898 to 1903.

The *Bauhinia blakeana*, also known as the Hong Kong Orchid Tree, has spreading branches and broad, heart-shaped leaves. Its delicately scented flowers have five magenta-coloured petals, and white stamens; it is in blossom from early November to March. The tree does not produce seeds and can only be propagated by air-layering, cutting or grafting. Thus all *Bauhinia blakeana* today are direct descendants of that single tree discovered by the priests.

You'll see examples of the *Bauhinia blakeana* throughout the territory, but specific locations include Victoria Park on Hong Kong Island, the Kowloon Walled City Park, Penfold Park in the centre of the Sha Tin Racecourse in the New Territories and along Yu Tong Rd in Tung Chung on Lantau Island.

wingspan of over 20cm. One favourite arachnid is the enormous woodland spider.

Hong Kong waters are rich in sea life, including sharks; most gazetted beaches are equipped with shark nets. Hong Kong is also visited by four species of whale and 11 species of dolphin, including Chinese white dolphins, which are actually pink in colour (see the boxed text Seeing Pink Dolphins in the Outlying Islands chapter for more information), and the finless porpoise. Endangered green turtles call on Sham Wan beach on Lamma (and more recently Shek O on Hong Kong Island) to lay eggs; see the Green Turtles & Eggs boxed text in the Outlying Islands chapter.

Hong Kong waters support some 50 species of coral. A walk along the more secluded beaches of the outlying islands can turn up cowries, limpets, cone shells, helmet shells, turban shells and bearded ark shells. Cone shells should be approached with caution, especially if spotted alive underwater: The barb sac of this creature contains a potentially deadly venom, so don't touch live shells.

Country Parks

Although Hong Kong may at first appear a hopelessly built-up and urbanised enclave, some 38% of the territory's total land area has been designated as protected country parks. These 23 parks – for the most part in the New Territories and outlying islands, but encompassing the slopes of Hong Kong Island too – comprise upland, woodlands, coastlines, marshes and all of Hong Kong's 17 freshwater reservoirs. In addition, there are three protected marine parks and one marine reserve. The areas are off-limits to development and private motor vehicles; hikers, campers, birdwatchers and other nature lovers all benefit from this protection.

GOVERNMENT & POLITICS

The government of the Hong Kong SAR is a complicated hybrid of a quasi-presidential system glued awkwardly onto a quasi-parliamentary model. It is not what could be called a democratic system, although democratic elements exist within its structure.

The executive branch of government is led by the chief executive, currently Shanghai business tycoon Tung Chee Hwa, who assumed office for a five-year term on 1 July 1997. The chief executive selects the 13 members of the Executive Council, which serves effectively as the cabinet and advises on policy matters. The top three policy secretaries are the chief secretary for the administration of government, the financial secretary and the secretary for justice. Council members are usually civil servants, but Tung appears to be politicising such posts by appointing policy secretaries from outside the bureaucracy.

The Legislative Council is responsible for passing legislation proposed by the Executive Council, approves public expenditure and, in theory, monitors the administration. The pre-handover Legislative Council was shadowed by a Beijing-appointed Provisional Legislature, which was installed on 1 July 1997. This provisional body served until May 1998, when a new Legislative Council was elected partially by the people of Hong Kong, partially by the business constituencies and partially by powerbrokers in Beijing.

The pro-democracy camp won two thirds of the popular vote, but due to the rules of appointment they took only one-third of the seats. In subsequent elections in 2000 they again dominated the popular vote, but remained a minority in the house.

This is because only 20 seats (out of a total of 60) in the Legislative Council are returned through direct election. Ten are returned by a Selection Committee dominated by pro-Beijing functionaries and institutions and the other 30 by narrowly defined, occupationally based 'functional constituencies'. With two or three exceptions (eg, the education functional constituency, which permits every member of the teaching profession to vote), 'corporate voting' is the rule, enfranchising only a few powerful and conservative members of each functional constituency. The number of directly elected seats in the Legislative Council is set to increase to 30 in 2004, when the 10 Selection Committee seats will be abolished.

The judiciary is headed by the chief justice and is, according to the Basic Law, independent of the executive and the legislative branches. The most significant change to the legal system after the handover was the replacement of the Privy Council with a Court of Final Appeal (CFA), which is now the highest court in the land and has the power of final adjudication.

The government's decision to challenge a CFA ruling in 1999 permitting residency rights for the China-born offspring of parents who became Hong Kong citizens after 1997 caused the greatest damage to the credibility of the SAR administration since the change in sovereignty.

It appealed to the standing committee of the National People's Congress, China's rubber-stamp parliament, to 'reinterpret' the relevant clauses of the Basic Law, which the NPC dutifully did. When it discovered that 1.6 million people on the mainland would be eligible for right of abode according to the law, the NPC ruled according to what the law drafters 'meant' but had somehow failed to write into law.

The 18 District Boards, created in 1982 and restructured in 1997, are meant to give Hong Kong residents a degree of control in their local areas. These boards consist of government officials and elected representatives, but they have little power.

The Hong Kong Civil Service employs 188,000 people, representing 5% of the total workforce. Expatriate civil servants once numbered in the thousands, but there are few such employees left outside the judiciary and police force. The Basic Law limits senior positions in major government departments to 'Chinese citizens who are permanent residents of the Hong Kong SAR with no right of abode in any foreign country'.

Although the stated aim of the Basic Law is 'full democracy', it supplies no definition for this. Furthermore, the law requires a political review of all democratic reforms in 2007. Changes to the system can only be made with the agreement of the chief executive and a two-thirds majority of the legislature. With the democratic camp in the minority in the Legislative Council, many are pessimistic about the prospects of installing genuine democracy in Hong Kong.

Nevertheless, party politics have become firmly rooted in Hong Kong society. The United Democrats, formed in 1990, have evolved into the Democratic Party. Martin Lee remains leader though he plans to retire, and it remains to be seen how well the party can handle the change. Many of Hong Kong's most internationally prominent pro-democracy advocates, such as Emily Lau and Margaret Ng, prefer to remain independent rather than submit to a party whip. This could fragment the democratic movement in coming years.

Ranged against the Democratic Party is the Democratic Alliance for the Betterment of Hong Kong (DAB). What one wag dubbed 'the Communist Party in drag', DAB is not opposed to democracy per se and supports elections, but it also advocates a 'softly-softly' approach to avoid alienating Beijing, which means cooperating with Beijing's representative in Hong Kong, Chief Executive Tung Chee Hwa.

A third and much smaller grouping consists of the inaccurately named Liberal Party, a staunchly pro-business group, many of whose members were colonial appointees in the days when the British coopted the business sector into the ruling structure. They quickly changed horses but are not fully trusted by Beijing, which ordered the formation of a rival 'red capitalist' party. The Beijing-friendly Hong Kong Progressive Alliance, which served faithfully in the provisional legislature and election committee, has more or less dwindled away.

ECONOMY

Although it holds out its much vaunted laissez faire economic policies as a capitalist's dream, considerable sections of the Hong Kong economy, including transport and power generation, are dominated by a handful of cartels and monopolistic franchises. Nonetheless, Hong Kong's economy is by far the freest in Asia, enjoying low taxes, a modern and efficient port and airport, excellent world-wide communications and strict anti-corruption laws.

Hong Kong has moved from labour- to capital-intensive industries in recent decades. Telecommunications, banking, insurance, tourism and retail sales have pushed manufacturing into the background, and most manual labour is now performed across the border in southern China. The shift from manufacturing to services has been accompanied by a dramatic increase in wages but there has not been a corresponding expansion of the welfare state.

Hong Kong has a very small agricultural base. Only 2.4% of the total land area is under cultivation and less than 1% of the population – just over 22,000 people – is engaged in agriculture or fishing. Most of the food is imported from the mainland.

Indeed, Hong Kong depends on imports for virtually all its requirements, even water (50% of its water is pumped from China). To pay for these imports Hong Kong has to generate foreign exchange through exports, tourism and overseas investments.

China is now Hong Kong's largest overall trading partner, although almost as many exports are destined for the USA as the mainland. And Hong Kong is now the largest foreign investor in mainland China, accounting for just over half of the national total of US$156 billion.

Hong Kong's gross domestic product grew an average 5% per annum between 1989 and 1997, putting its GDP on a par with the four leading economies of Western Europe. The Asia-wide economic crisis of 1997 pushed it into recession, but a recovery became apparent in 1999 when GDP grew by 1.9%. It achieved phenomenal growth of over 10% in 2000. In terms of purchasing power, Hong Kong's annual per capita GDP of US$23,100 ranks second in Asia after Japan. By comparison China's amounted to just $3800.

Hong Kong people get to keep most of their earnings. The maximum personal income tax is 15%, company profits tax is 16.5% and there are no capital gains or transfer taxes. These attractive tax conditions attract dynamic businesses and professionals to Hong Kong, but a recent slowdown in property prices (land premiums account for 17% of revenues) has slashed government income and is raising concern about the narrowness of the tax base. Generous personal tax allowances mean only 37% of the working population pay any salaries tax at all and only 0.3% pay the full 15%.

Although unemployment in Hong Kong rose during the Asian crisis and remains high (by Hong Kong standards) at about 4.5%, the territory has traditionally suffered from a labour shortage. Most of the menial work (domestic, construction etc) is performed by imported labour, chiefly from the Philippines. The labour shortage is most acute in the hi-tech and financial fields, prompting the government to consider relaxing restrictions on importing talent from the mainland, a move deeply unpopular with Hong Kong's working class.

POPULATION & PEOPLE

Hong Kong's population is 6.975 million, with an annual growth rate of between 1.5% and 2%. It is also expected that each year up to 55,000 *legal* immigrants from China will move into the territory. Hong Kong, once a very 'young' society, is now ageing. The median age rose from 30 in 1989 to 36 in 2000.

Almost half the population (48%) lives in the New Territories, followed by Kowloon (31%), Hong Kong Island (20.6%) and the outlying islands (1.2%). The overall population density is 6480 people per sq km, but this figure is deceiving as the density varies from area to area.

About 95% of Hong Kong's population is ethnic Chinese, most of whom can trace their origins to Guangdong province in southern China. Approximately 60% were born in the colony.

Hong Kong has a community of foreigners, but this figure is deceiving as well since many 'foreign passport holders' are Hong Kong Chinese. In any case, of the 386,700 people so described, the three largest groups are Filipinos at 136,100, Indonesians at 53,400 and Americans at 35,100. Canadians are up there with 33,400 but British and Australians fall well behind at 22,300 and 21,800 respectively.

According to the Basic Law, Hong Kong SAR passports can only be issued to 'Chinese citizens who are Hong Kong permanent residents'. So race is the deciding factor, not place of birth. This also poses a problem for other nationalities, such as Hong Kong's long-standing Indian community, whose members number about 22,000. They are issued Documents of Identity for Visa Purposes (or DIs) and are in effect stateless.

EDUCATION

Hong Kong's education system is based on the British model. Education is free and compulsory for nine years (generally from ages five to 15). At secondary level, students begin to specialise – some go on to university or college preparatory programs, while others select vocational education combined with apprenticeships.

An ongoing debate in Hong Kong concerns the medium of instruction at secondary level. While primary school classes are taught almost exclusively in Cantonese (with the exception of international schools), more than 20% of secondary schools use English, with the rest – about 300 schools in total – teaching in the vernacular.

The official reason has always been that the schools considered English a useful language for success in life, but most parents sent their children to so-called Anglo-Chinese schools in order for them to secure a place at Hong Kong University – the most prestigious tertiary institution in the territory – where lectures are in English. When the post-handover government insisted that government-assisted schools make the switch, all hell broke loose. Eventually a compromise was reached and those schools fulfilling certain requirements are allowed to teach in English.

At the tertiary level, education is competitive but, with the advent of so many new universities, not as fierce as it once was. About 18% of the eligible age group now have the chance of securing a university placement – double the figure in 1990. For further details, see the Universities section in the Hong Kong Facts for the Visitor chapter.

ARTS

The epithet 'cultural desert' can in no way be used for Hong Kong at the start of the third millennium. There are both philharmonic and Chinese orchestras, Chinese and modern dance troupes, a ballet company, several theatre groups and numerous art schools and organisations. Government funds also allow local venues to bring in top international performers, and the number of international arts festivals hosted here seems to grow each year.

Local street-opera troupes occasionally pop up around the city. Both local and mainland Chinese opera troupes can also sometimes be seen in more formal settings.

At one time Hong Kong was scorned for having the worst museums in the British Empire. That's all changed, and the territory now counts 20 museums showcasing everything from tea ware and military history to film and outer space. Six of them, including the new world-class Hong Kong Heritage Museum near Sha Tin, have extensive art collections.

Dance

Hong Kong has three professional dance companies. The Hong Kong Dance Company focuses on Chinese traditional and folk dancing as well as full-length dance dramas based on local and Chinese themes. The City Contemporary Dance Company stages modern dance performances that include new commissions and past works, often choreographed by locals. Both companies frequently work with artists from China, and sometimes with those from other Asian countries. Founded in 1979, the Hong Kong Ballet regularly performs both classical and modern pieces, and tours overseas each year.

The lion dance is one Chinese tradition that lives on in Hong Kong. Dancers and martial artists take position under an elaborately painted costume of a mythical Chinese lion. To the accompaniment of banging cymbals and, if in a remote location like one of the outlying islands, sometimes exploding firecrackers (which are illegal in Hong Kong), the lion leaps its way around the crowd, giving the dancers a chance to demonstrate their acrobatic skills. The lion's mouth and eyes open and close and a beard hangs down from the lion's lower jaw; the longer the beard, the more venerable the school that performs the dance.

Lion dances are most commonly seen in late January or February during the Chinese New Year. Lion dance troupes are also hired for the opening ceremonies of new buildings and businesses and sometimes weddings.

Music

Traditional Music Whereas Western music uses a seven-tone diatonic scale, traditional Chinese music employs five tones. Think of it as playing just the black keys on a piano and you'll get the idea. For a good many Westerners it is *not* an acquired taste.

In any case, you won't hear much of it on the streets of Hong Kong, except perhaps the sound of the doleful *dida*, a clarinet-like instrument played in a funeral procession, the hollow-sounding drums *(goo)* and crashing gongs *(loh)* and cymbals *(bat)* at temple ceremonics and lion dances or the *yi woo* (*erhu* in Mandarin), a two-stringed fiddle favoured by beggars for its plaintive sound. The best place to hear this kind of music in full orchestration is by attending a concert given by the Hong Kong Chinese Orchestra or a Chinese opera (see the Theatre section).

Classical Music Western classical music is very popular in Hong Kong. The territory city boasts philharmonic, sinfonietta and chamber orchestras, and the Hong Kong Chinese Orchestra often combines Western orchestration with traditional Chinese instruments. Overseas performers of world repute frequently make it to Hong Kong and the number of foreign performances soars during the Hong Kong Arts Festival held in February/March each year.

Popular Music Hong Kong's home-grown music scene is dominated by 'Canto-pop'. Original compositions often blend Western rock or pop with traditional Chinese melodies or rhythms. There is an entire constellation of local stars that, while perhaps known in Asia, are all but unheard of in the West. Many younger Hong Kongers pay homage to their favourite stars by crooning their tunes at karaoke bars, among Hong Kong's most popular music venues.

Architecture

Over the years Hong Kong has played host to scores of Chinese temples, walled villages, Qing-dynasty forts, Victorian mansions and Edwardian hotels. But in Hong Kong's ceaseless cycle of deconstruction and rebuilding few structures have survived the wrecking ball. Enthusiasts of modern architecture, on the other hand, will have a field day; see the special section Contemporary Architecture.

About the only examples of pre-colonial Chinese architecture left in urban Hong Kong are Tin Hau temples dating from the early to mid-19th century, including those at Tin Hau near Causeway Bay, Shau Kei Wan and Aberdeen. Museums in Chai Wan and Tsuen Wan have preserved a few buildings left over from Hakka villages that predate the arrival of the British. But for anything more substantial, you have to go to the New Territories or the outlying islands, where walled villages, fortresses and 18th-century temples can be found.

Colonial architecture is also in fairly short supply. Most of what is left can be seen on Hong Kong Island, including, in Central, the Legislative Council building (formerly the Supreme Court), built in 1912, and the former Government House, built in 1856. In Sheung Wan there's the Western Market (1906) and the Old Pathological Institute (now the Hong Kong Museum of Medical Sciences); and in Stanley the old police station (1859) and Murray House (1848). The Hong Kong Antiquities & Monuments Office (☎ 2721 2326, fax 2721 6216), itself housed in a 1920 British schoolhouse at 136 Nathan Rd in Tsim Sha Tsui, has information and exhibits on current preservation efforts. It's open from 9.30am to 5pm on Monday and Wednesday to Saturday, and from 1pm to 5pm on Sunday.

Painting & Sculpture

Painting in Hong Kong falls into three broad categories: classical Chinese, Western and modern local. Local artists dedicated to preserving such classical Chinese disciplines as calligraphy and landscape painting have usually spent years studying in China, and their work tends to reflect current trends in classical painting there. While Hong Kong does not have a great deal of home-grown Western art, the Hong Kong Museum of Art in Tsim Sha Tsui has both a permanent collection and temporary exhibits from abroad.

Hong Kong modern art, including painting and sculpture, has gone through many phases – from the dynamic to the moribund – since it first arrived on the scene after WWII. For more information see the special section Contemporary Art.

Film

Hong Kong is something of an Eastern Hollywood, churning out about 150 films each year, the third highest after Hollywood and Bombay. The figures are deceiving, however: Up to half of the films made here go directly into video format, to be pirated and sold as VCDs or DVDs in the markets of Mong Kok and Shenzhen for HK$20 a pop. Quality films are *very* few and far between, but even the mindless action flicks, nonsense comedies and sickening romances can be loads of fun.

Modern Hong Kong cinema arrived with the films of Bruce Lee – who first appeared in *The Big Boss* (1971) – and the emergence of kung fu as a film genre. The 'chop sockey' trend continued through the 1970s and into the early 1980s, when bullet-riddled action films took over.

Three directors stand out during this period. Jackie Chan made many kung fu films in the late 1970s, including *Snake in the Eagle's Shadow* (1978) and *Drunken Master* (1978), but he later moved on to police-related stories (such as *The Protector* in 1985 and the highly popular *Police Story* series). King Hu directed several stylish Mandarin kung fu films in the early 1970s, and the films of today still take his work as

a reference point for action design. Michael Hui, along with his brother Sam Hui, produced many popular social comedies, including *Private Eyes* (1976) and *The Pilferers' Progress* (1977; directed by John Woo).

Overall, however, it was an uphill battle for the local product at this time, with market share declining in the face of foreign competition. The upturn came in the mid-1980s, with John Woo's *A Better Tomorrow* series. Also prominent were the historical action films by Tsui Hark, including the *Once Upon a Time in China* series based on the exploits of the hero Wong Fei Hung, and featuring great action design and a stirring score.

The new wave of Hong Kong films in the 1990s attracted fans worldwide, particularly John Woo's blood-soaked epics *Hardboiled* and *The Killer*. Woo was courted by Hollywood, and achieved international success directing films such as *Face/Off* and *Mission Impossible 2*.

Other stars to make it in Hollywood include Hong Kong superstar Jackie Chan, whose blend of kung fu and self-effacing comedy is beloved the world over. He starred in *Crime Story* and Stanley Tong's *Rumble in the Bronx* (a better-than-average action flick), while Lamma native Chow Yun Fat featured in *The Replacement Killers* and *Anna & the King*. Jet Li, star of *Lethal Weapon 4* and *Romeo Must Die*, is another Hong Kong boy who has made a splash overseas. Wong Kar Wai, director of the cult favourite *Chung King Express* received the Palme d'Or at the Cannes Film Festival in 1997 for his film *Happy Together*.

But by the time of the handover all was not well with the Hong Kong film industry; only 92 films were made in 1998 against some 200 in the years of the early 90s. The economic downturn was partly to blame but, more importantly, local box offices were taking a beating from the proliferation of pirated VCDs and DVDs. With the price of a pirated version half that of a normal cinema ticket, moviegoers were staying home. At the same time Hong Kong people seemed to lose their confidence in local films, preferring Hollywood blockbusters, with all their high-tech special effects.

In just a few short years, however, the industry has rebounded and at the start of the third millennium seems to have entered a new, more mature phase. Wong Kar Wai's sublime *In the Mood For Love* (2000), a complicated tale of infidelity and obsession, raised Hong Kong film to a new level and earned its star, Tony Leung Chiu Wai, the Best Actor award at Cannes. A film that took the world by storm, the Oscar award-winning martial arts epic *Crouching Tiger, Hidden Dragon* (2000), may have been shot by Taiwan director Ang Lee, but most of the cast are Hong Kong talent.

Directors to watch out for include Peter Chan Ho-sun *(Comrades, Almost a Love Story, The Love Letter, He's a Woman, She's a Man)*; Fruit Chan *(Made in Hong Kong)*; Andy Lau *(Young and Dangerous, A Man Called Hero)*; Chan Muk Sing *(Gen-Y Cops series)*; and Stanley Kwan *(New York Stories)*.

Excellence in Hong Kong films is recognised each April with the presentation of the Hong Kong Film Awards, the territory's own 'Oscars'. The annual 16-day Hong Kong International Film Festival held in March/April brings in more than 200 films and is now one of the world's major film festivals.

One of the best sources for information on Hong Kong movies is *Hong Kong Babylon: An Insiders Guide to the Hollywood of the East* by Frederic Dannen & Barry Long, a rollicking ride through the Byzantine world of the local film industry.

For information about the new Hong Kong Film Archive in Sai Wan Ho, see that section in the Hong Kong Island chapter.

Theatre

Nearly all theatre in Hong Kong is Western in form, if not content. Most productions are staged in Cantonese, and a large number are new plays by Hong Kong writers. The plays often provide an insightful and sometimes humorous look at contemporary Hong Kong life. The Hong Kong Repertory Theatre tends to stage larger-scale productions of both original works on Chinese themes or translated Western plays. More experimental troupes are the Chung Ying Theatre Company and Zuni Icosahedron.

English-language theatre in Hong Kong is mostly the domain of expatriate amateurs, and plays are more often than not scripted by local writers. One of the more popular venues is the Star Alliance Theatre at the Fringe Club in Central. The Hong Kong Cultural Centre in Tsim Sha Tsui and the Hong Kong Academy for Performing Arts in Wan Chai also host foreign productions, ranging from grandiose Western musicals such as *Les Misérables* to minimalist Japanese *kyogen* theatre.

Chinese Opera

Chinese opera *(kek)* is a world away from its Western counterpart but the themes are pretty much the same: mortal heroes battle overwhelmingly powerful supernatural foes; legendary spirits defend the world against evil; lovers seek escape from domineering and disapproving parents.

Foreigners will find that Chinese opera performances take some getting used to. Both male and female performers sing in an almost reedy falsetto designed to pierce through crowd noise, and the instrumental accompaniment often takes the form of drumming, gonging and other nonmelodic punctuation. Performances can last as long as five or six hours, and the audience makes an evening of it – eating, chatting amongst themselves and changing seats while laughing at the funny parts and crying at the sad bits.

There are three types of Chinese opera performed in Hong Kong. The Beijing opera *(ging kek)* is a highly refined style which uses almost no scenery but a variety of traditional props. This is where you'll find the most acrobatics and swordplay. The Cantonese variety *(yuet kek)* is more 'music hall' style, usually with a 'boy meets girl' theme, and often incorporating modern and foreign references. The most traditional is Chiu Chow opera *(chiu kek)*, now the least performed of the three in Hong Kong. It is staged almost as it was in the Ming dynasty, with stories from the legends and folklore of the Chiu Chow (Chaozhou in

Mandarin), an ethnic group from the easternmost region of Guangdong province.

Much of the meaning in a Chinese opera is derived from costumes, props and body language, so a little homework beforehand may make things easier to understand and enjoy. An excellent introduction to the mysterious world of Chinese opera is offered by Chen Kaige's wonderful film *Farewell My Concubine*. The Hong Kong Heritage Museum (see the New Territories chapter) has an entire hall dedicated to Cantonese opera, including costumes, make-up, sets and videos of classic performances.

The best time to see Cantonese opera is during the Hong Kong International Cantonese Opera Festival in December. There are also performances during the Hong Kong Arts Festival in February/March and the biannual Festival of Asian Arts and the Festival of Chinese Arts in October/November. Outdoor Performances are staged in Victoria Park on Hong Kong Island during Mid-Autumn Festival.

Puppet Theatre Puppetry is the oldest of the Chinese theatre arts. Styles include rod, shadow and glove puppets. The rod puppets, visible only from waist up, are fixed to a long pole with short sticks for hand movements. The puppets are made from camphor wood and the main characters have larger heads than the rest of the cast. Shadow puppets are made from leather and perform from behind a silken screen. Shadow and glove puppet performances are accompanied musically by the two-stringed *yi woo* (*erhu* in Mandarin) and zither-like *jang*. Most performances relate tales of past dynasties. Live puppet shows are somewhat rare these days, but they are sometimes broadcast on television. The Law Uk Folk Museum in Chai Wan (see the Hong Kong Island chapter) has a large collection of rod puppets, props and sets.

SOCIETY & CONDUCT

It's difficult – and dangerous – to generalise about a city and a society of almost 7 million people, but we'll give it a go anyway. The most common preconceptions about Hong Kong people in the past were that they were rapacious, money-grabbing and, in the case of service staff, discourteous to the point of being rude.

The word *gwai-lo*, meaning 'ghost person' (*gwai-po* is reserved for white women, *hak-gwai* for a 'black ghost') was used regularly and contemptuously. And although Caucasians have 'possessed' this word and use it jocularly among themselves, it was – and remains – a deeply pejorative word in Hong Kong.

OK, so there might still be greed, but the rudeness seems to have all but disappeared, and everyone – from tourists to long-term Western residents to locals themselves – remarks on it. Some people say it's because the Asian economic crisis and subsequent recession had Hong Kong people eating humble pie for the first time in decades. Others say that when many Hong Kong Chinese people awoke on 1 July 1997 they realised something for the first time: they were different from their cousins on the mainland. Chinese, yes. Yet, somehow, different…

Not only could the gwai-los stay, they were encouraged to do so (legally, of course). Otherwise, Hong Kong would just become another spot on the backside of China, not the cosmopolitan place it was and, hopefully, will remain.

All this is not to make excuses for the colonial government or to suggest many people would like to see its return. On the contrary; until the arrival of 'our hero' Chris Patten the Hong Kong government was a patronising, pseudo-democracy that at times could be as despotic, arbitrary and archaic as any tin-pot dictatorship. Most Britons would be shocked if they understood fully just how unenlightened *their* colonial government was. Homosexuality, for example, was outlawed (yes, banned) until – wait for it – 1991.

Hong Kong is Chinese, an essential part of China. Everyone has known that since 1841; it just took a while to settle the matter. But it is now Chinese with an international flavour.

[continued on page 36]

Contemporary Art

Sailing Boats, Lui Shou-kwan
(Hanart TZ Gallery)

The Universe Is My Mind, Irene Chou
(Hanart TZ Gallery)

Riding with the Clouds, Chu Hing-wah
(Hanart TZ Gallery)

Smooth #4, David Chan
(J Gallery)

Growing Up, Luis Chan (Hanart TZ Gallery)

C ontemporary Hong Kong art differs enormously from that produced in mainland China, and for good reason. Those artists coming of age in Hong Kong after WWII were largely (though not entirely) the offspring of refugees, distanced from the memories of economic deprivation, war and hunger. They were the products of a cultural fusion and sought new ways to reflect a culture that blended two worlds.

In general Chinese are interested in traditional forms and painting processes – not composition and colour. Brush strokes and the utensils used to produce them are of vital importance and interest. In traditional Chinese art, change for the sake of change was never the philosophy or the trend; Chinese artists would compare their work with that of the master and judge it accordingly.

The influential Lingnan School of Painting, founded by the watercolourist Chao Shao-an (1905–98) in the 1930s, attempted to redress the situation. It combined traditional Chinese, Japanese and Western artistic traditions to produce a unique and rather decorative style, and basically dominated what art market there was in Hong Kong for the next two decades.

WWII brought great changes not only to China but to Hong Kong, and the post-war generation of artists was characterised by an intense search for identity – Hong Kong rather than Chinese. It also set the stage for the golden age of modern Hong Kong art to come.

The late 1950s and early '60s saw the formation of several avant-garde groups, including the influential Modern Literature and Art Association, which counted Lui Shou-kwan, Wucius Wong, Jackson Yu and Irene Chou among its earliest members. Very structural but at the same time spontaneous, the association spawned a whole generation of new talent obsessed with romanticism and naturalism. The Circle Art Group, founded by Hon Chee Fun in 1963, was influenced by Abstract Expressionism and characterised by its spontaneous brush work.

The year 1975 was a watershed for Hong Kong art. Both Lui Shou-kwan and his contemporary, the important expatriate painter Douglas Bland, died. Soon a whole new generation returned from studying abroad, less concerned with naturalism or cultural identity.

Today, like young artists in urban centres everywhere, Hong Kong painters are concerned with finding their orientation in a great metropolis through personal statement. They are overwhelmingly unfussed with orthodox Chinese culture and, judging from their work, still not overly concerned with their Hong Kong identity.

Of course, Hong Kong's artists form a society that is hardly typical of society as a whole. Artists here have always fought against a deep-seated apathy to art in a community that makes business and financial success the ultimate achievement. Even the most successful artists were 'Sunday painters' – Wucius Wong taught at what was then the Hong Kong Polytechnic, Chu Hung-Wah worked in a psychiatric hospital.

Title page: *Sunflowers at Night I*, Victor Lai (Plum Blossoms)

It's a matter of taste (as it always is when it comes to art), but the following artists – both established and new – are among the most interesting and accessible in the world of Hong Kong contemporary art. The best place to view the works of these and other modern Hong Kong painters is the Contemporary Hong Kong Art Gallery in the **Hong Kong Museum of Art** in Tsim Sha Tsui. There are no galleries specialising exclusively in local art, though **Hanart TZ Gallery** and **Plum Blossom** in Central stage exhibits from time to time as does the **Hong Kong Visual Arts Centre** and the **Montblanc Gallery** at the Fringe Club, both also in Central. **Para/Site Artspace** in Sheung Wan is the territory's most important artists' cooperative.

The best sources of up-to-date information on contemporary Hong Kong and other Asian art are the bimonthly *Asian Art News* and its sister-publication, the quarterly **World Sculpture News**. The two-volume *Hong Kong Artists* is a hefty and substantial reference work.

Gaylord Chan (1925–) He is a very individualistic painter who cannot be placed in any one school or movement. His work is characterised by highly enigmatic and haunting shapes in bold primary colours. *Homing*, for example, shows a torso-like form with a tiny and secret chest of drawers in the centre. Have a look, too, at his *The Story of Eyes*, somewhat reminiscent of a Nepalese temple, and the anthropomorphic *Yellow Ribbons*.

Luis Chan (1905–95) He was the first Hong Kong Chinese artist to paint in the Western style and one of the few to evolve continuously from the 1960s onward, producing everything from psychedelic landscapes *(New Territories)* to colourful naive forms epitomised in *Reptiles* and the amusing *Conversation in Two Parts*, a *tête à tête* involving a chicken, a gull and a grotesque figure. Chan never travelled beyond China and Macau and is praised for his humour and ability to catch the pulse of Hong Kong street life.

David Chan (1950–) He studied under Lui Shou-kwan in the 60s and experiments with calligraphy, but his work is too graphic to call him a calligrapher as such (eg, *Smooth #4*). He is interested in the repetition of forms; the acrylic 'characters' are not to be read as words but taken as one single unit. His enigmatic *(Fragrant The Taste of the Scent of Flowers)* is particularly powerful.

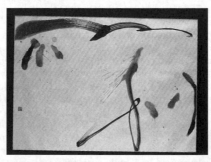

Left: *Smooth #5*, David Chan (J Gallery).

Irene Chou (1924–) This artist started painting under the influence of the Lingnan School and studied under Lui Shou-kwan. She is an intensely personal artist. Chou has never painted people or even buildings, but bits and pieces of nature which she has explored through her own body. Landscapes take on long, geodesic lines that appear like biomorphic nerves or hair; somewhere in her paintings (eg, *The Fire, Internal Landscapes*) is at least one enigmatic sphere that suggests a seed or catalyst of some sort. Have a look at *My Inner World III*, with what looks like molten steel issuing from the 'nerves' and that ever-present sphere.

Chu Hing-wah (1935–) He is another highly individualistic painter who defies characterisation. There's a certain sadness and feeling of alienation in much of his work, such as the four lone figures in *10.30 in the Evening*. He has experimented with many techniques, including pointillism.

Victor Lai (1961–) He is a figurative artist much influenced by Francis Bacon and the German Expressionists. His work is characterised by broad, almost dripping brushstrokes *(Sunflowers, Figure with Mandolin and Lemon)*.

Holly Lee (1956–) She specialises in digital art. Her work, satirising Barbie as a beauty icon and putting familiar faces on Chinese icons (eg, *The God of Wealth*), has been shown at the Hong Kong Heritage Museum in the New Territories.

Lui Shou-kwan (1919–75) He is the most influential of all painters to emerge from the Hong Kong art scene. He began his career as a landscape artist, but slowly turned to abstract forms, especially involving the lotus, using mostly Chinese black ink and red paste (eg, *Painting #0-64*).

Ellen Pau (1961–) She is at the forefront of video art in Hong Kong and one of the founding members of Videotage, which has produced some cutting-edge work (eg, *City Vibrant, Drained*). Like many of her predecessors, Ellen too has kept her day job and works as a hospital radiographer.

Wucius Wong (1936–) This elder statesman of contemporary Hong Kong art was originally inspired by traditional Chinese landscape painting. By analysing, isolating and then playing with brushstrokes in the 1960s, he developed his characteristic 'grids' laid over water *(River Thoughts)*, mountains *(Beyond Solitude #1)* and sky *(Soaring Clouds #3)*, in oil paintings that somehow look like watercolours. His dark, monochromatic colour schemes give his work a gloomy, though infinite, feel.

[continued from page 32]

This was thanks, to some degree, to more than a century and a half under the ying gwok yahn (British). Was that too high a price to pay to produce one of the most dynamic and vibrant societies on the face of the earth? We humbly submit that it was not.

Traditional Culture

While Hong Kong can appear at first glance as Western as a Big Mac, many old Chinese traditions persist. Whether people still believe in all of them or, as in some cases, just go through the motions to please parents, neighbours or co-workers is hard to say. But during your visit you'll encounter many examples of traditional Chinese culture.

Superstitions One of the most important words in traditional Hong Kong Chinese culture is *joss*, meaning 'luck'. But the Hong Kong Chinese are too astute to leave something as important as luck to chance. Gods have to be appeased, bad spirits blown away and sleeping dragons soothed to keep joss on your side. No house, wall or shrine is built until an auspicious date for the start of construction is chosen and the most favourable location is selected. Incense must be burnt, gifts presented and prayers said to appease the spirits inhabiting the construction site.

Numbers Southern Chinese – and by extension Hong Kong – culture embraces a wealth of guidelines on controlling the amount of good or bad luck in one's life. One of the most prevalent is the belief in the power of numbers. In the Cantonese language many words share the same pronunciation: their difference is marked by one of six tones (more or less). This gives rise to numerous homonyms. For example, the word for three sounds similar to the word for life, nine is similar to eternity and the ever-popular number eight to prosperity. Lowest on the list is four, which has the same pronunciation as the word for death.

Companies or home buyers will shell out extra money for an address that contains one or more number eights. Each year the Hong Kong government draws in millions of dollars for charity by auctioning off automobile licence plates that feature lucky numbers. Dates and prices are affected too. The Bank of China Tower was officially opened on 8 August 1988, a rare union of the prosperous numbers. Parties were held throughout the territory on that day, and some pregnant women asked their doctors to induce birth. August is always a busy month for weddings.

A few buildings around the city are missing their 4th or 14th floors, but overall people seem able to live with the number four, despite its ominous overtones. In fact, you might spot the Chinese-owned Rolls-Royce on the streets of Hong Kong that has the vehicle registration number '4'.

Foods Some foods are considered lucky. Birthdays celebrants eat noodles, as the strands symbolise longevity. Sea moss, which in Cantonese has the same sound as 'prosperity', is always an auspicious ingredient. Peach juice is believed to be an elixir, while garlic and ginger can protect babies against evil.

As the God of Longevity rides on the back of the deer (just as Jesus rode the ass into Jerusalem) parts of the unfortunate creature are used in Chinese medicine to cure ailments and prolong life. Similarly, the long life of the tortoise can be absorbed through a soup made from its flesh. The carp, which can live for up to 40 years, is among the most prized possessions in a wealthy household's fish pond.

Fung Shui The Cantonese word *fung shui* (*feng shui* in Mandarin) literally means 'wind-water'. Westerners call it geomancy, the art (or science if you prefer) of manipulating or judging the environment to produce good fortune. If you want to build a house or find a suitable site for a grave, you call in a geomancer. The Chinese warn that violating the principles of good fung shui can have dire consequences. Therefore, fung shui masters are consulted before an apartment block is built, a highway laid down, telephone poles erected or trees chopped down.

Trees may have a spirit living inside, and for this reason some villages and temples in the New Territories still have fung shui groves to provide a place for the good spirits to live. Even if they don't do their job, they are havens for such birds as warblers, flycatchers, robins, bulbuls and tits. Attempts to cut down fung shui groves to construct new buildings have sometimes led to massive protests and even violent confrontations.

Businesses that are failing may call in a geomancer. Sometimes the solution is to move a door or window or place an aquarium full of goldfish near the entrance. If this doesn't do the trick, it might be necessary to move an ancestor's grave. The location of an ancestor's grave is a serious matter; if it's in a bad spot or facing the wrong way, there is no telling what trouble the spirit might cause.

If a fung shui master is not consulted, and the family of the deceased suddenly runs into a spate of bad luck, then it's time to see a Taoist priest, who knows how to deal with the troublesome ghosts. While we were researching this book, such a priest was called into the offices of Hong Kong's leading English newspaper to exorcise ghosts harassing staff in the loo. Construction of Hong Kong's underground Mass Transit Railway (MTR) began with an invocation by a group of Taoist priests who paid respects to the spirits of the earth whose domain was about to be violated.

Zodiac Astrology has a long history in China and is integrated with religious beliefs. As in the Western system of astrology there are 12 zodiac signs, but their representations are all animals. Your sign is based on the year of your birth (according to the lunar calendar) rather than the time of year you were born, though the exact day and time of birth is also carefully considered in charting an astrological path.

It is said that the animal year chart originated from when Buddha commanded all the beasts of the earth to assemble before

Everybody's Kung Fu Fighting?

Whilst often mistakenly thought of as being a style of martial art in itself, kung fu is actually a generic description that encompasses the hundreds of Chinese styles that have evolved since about AD 500.

Seen every morning in parks throughout Asia, tai chi ch'uan (taijiquan), or simply tai chi, is the most visible and commonly practiced form of kung fu today. Not only is tai chi a terrific form of exercise, promoting health and well-being, it can also form a solid foundation to any martial arts practice. Its various forms are often characterised by deep, powerful stances, soft and flowing hand techniques and relaxed breathing. During the cultural revolution in China last century, where all teachings outside Maoist philosophy were suppressed, the practice of innocuous-looking tai chi forms were allowed, helping kung fu to live on.

The visibility of this ancient art on the ground is elusive to say the least. Many well-connected instructors from around the world have honed their skills under Hong Kong masters, but the average enthusiast may struggle just to find one, let alone convince him to impart his knowledge. Martial arts in China, traditionally passed down through patriarchal family lines, were seldom taught to outsiders. In ancient times these skills were far too valuable to spread indiscriminately. Today, the right introductions and a fistful of dollars might win entrance to some schools, but by and large it's a closed society, wary of outsiders and protective of its arcane teachings.

For the adventurous visitor in Kong Kong, there may be little chance of partaking in any serious kung fu training, but an early-morning tai chi constitutional may be just the thing. If that sounds too sedate, an armchair adrenaline fix can always be found via the latest Jackie Chan or Jet Li kung fu feature at a local cinema. The more culturally minded should keep an eye out for the occasional tour of theatrical kung fu, or wushu, performers. In an age where traditional culture is rapidly losing currency, witnessing displays of true kung fu is an increasingly rare and humbling experience.

Rodney Zandbergs

him. Only 12 animals came and they were rewarded by having their names given to a specific year. Buddha also decided to name each year in the order in which the animals arrived – the first was the rat, then the ox, tiger, rabbit and so on.

Being born or married in a particular year is believed to determine one's fortune. In this era of modern birth-control techniques and abortion, Chinese parents will often carefully manipulate the birth times of their children. The year of the dragon sees the biggest jump in the birth rate, closely followed by the year of the tiger. A girl born in the year of the pig could have trouble finding a husband.

Five Elements Many festivals are held throughout the year in accordance with the lunar calendar. Some festivals only occur at the end of the 12-year astrological cycle, while others take place once every 60 years. This is because each of the 12 animals is influenced at different times by the five elements: metal, wood, earth, water and fire. The full cycle thus takes 60 years and at the end of this time there is a 'super festival'.

The elements belong to a cycle of creation and destruction whereby wood creates fire, fire creates earth (ie, ash), earth creates metal (ore), metal creates water (through condensation) and water creates wood (through growth). Conversely, earth destroys water (by damming it), water destroys fire, fire destroys metal (by melting), metal destroys wood (axe), and wood destroys earth (by breaking it up with roots).

If you are born in a metal year, it might be bad news to marry someone who is born in a wood year. However, each element is subdivided into 12 more degrees, so you can be of a very weak metal nature and marry someone of a strong wood nature, and live happily ever after.

Fortune Telling If you're interested in having your destiny laid out before you, you'll not be short of choice in Hong Kong. You can go to a temple and consult the gods and spirits or have your palm or face read. Wong Tai Sin Temple in Kowloon (see that chapter)

is one of the best places to get your fortune told, as many of the seers speak English.

The most common method of divination in Hong Kong is using so-called fortune sticks. The altar of a temple, be it Buddhist or Taoist, is usually flanked by stacks of narrow wooden sticks called *chim* in bamboo canisters. The routine is to ask the spirits or gods a question and shake the canister until one stick falls out. Each stick bears a numeral, which corresponds to a printed slip of paper in a set held by the temple keeper. That slip of paper should be taken to the temple's fortune-teller, who can interpret its particular meaning for you. The fortune-teller will also study your face and ask your date and time of birth.

If you are asking a simple 'yes' or 'no' question (eg, 'will I ever be happy in this mortal life?') you can turn to two clam-shaped pieces of wood called *bui* (shell). The way they fall when thrown in the air in front of the altar indicates the gods' answer to your query. One side of each piece of wood is *yin* (*yeung* in Cantonese), or male; the other side is *yang* (*yam*), which is female. If both pieces land with the same side up, the answer is negative. But if they fall with different sides up, it indicates a balance of yin and yang, denoting an affirmative answer.

Palm-readers usually examine both the lines and features of the hand. Palms are thought to be emotional; their lines change according to your life experiences and can reveal the past and what the future may hold. Readings for men are taken from the left palm, those for women from the right.

Palmists will sometimes examine your facial features: There are eight basic facial shapes but 48 recognised eye patterns that reveal character and fortune. Clues are also provided by the shape of your ears, nose, mouth, lips and eyebrows. For example, people with small earlobes are less likely to become wealthy. As with the fortune-stick seers, you will also probably be asked to provide the date and time of your birth. Palmists can be found near street markets, including Temple St in Yau Ma Tei (see the Kowloon chapter).

At Temple St you'll also find fortune tellers with birds who will pick the answer to your question from a stack of papers. The dumb clucks don't speak English.

Dos & Don'ts

There aren't many unusual rules of etiquette or codes of conduct to follow in Hong Kong; generally, common sense will take you as far as you'll need to go. But on matters of identity, appearance, gift-giving and the big neighbour to the north, local people might see things a little different than you do.

For pointers on how to conduct yourself at the table see Table Etiquette in the special section Chinese Food.

Clothing Hong Kong is a very fashion-conscious city. Still, it's also very cosmopolitan so you can really get away with wearing just about anything. Revealing clothing – short shorts, miniskirts and low-cut tops – is OK, but save the bikini for the beach. Topless or nude bathing is a definite no-no.

There is one exception to this tolerance: thongs or flip-flops. Thongs are OK to wear in hotel rooms, but most definitely not in the hotel's lobby or outdoors (except around a swimming pool or beach). Sandals, on the other hand, are perfectly acceptable.

For formal affairs – a wedding or an important cocktail party, say – many Chinese women will don a *cheongsam* (see the

The Wardrobe of Suzie Wong

Neon-coloured Indian saris are beautiful things when fastidiously wrapped and tucked, and Japanese kimonos can be like bright cocoons from which a chrysalis coyly peaks. And what's so wrong with a sarong with a bright blue Polynesian lagoon as backdrop?

But there's nothing quite like a cheongsam, the close-fitting sheath that is as Chinese as a bowl of wonton noodle soup. It lifts where it should and never pulls where it ought not to. And those thigh-high slits up the sides – well, they're enough to give any man apoplexy. It's sensuous and never lewd, revealing without showing too much.

Reach into any Hong Kong Chinese girl's or woman's closet and you're bound to find at least one cheongsam (*qipao* in Mandarin), the closest thing the territory has to national dress. It's there for formal occasions like Chinese New Year gatherings, work (most receptionists at Hong Kong's hangar-sized dim sum restaurants wear them, as do many nightclub hostesses), school – cotton cheongsam are still the uniform at several colleges and secondary schools – or for the 'big day'. Modern Hong Kong brides may take their vows in white just as their sisters around the world do, but when they're slipping off for the honeymoon, they slip on a red cheongsam.

It's difficult to imagine that this bedazzling dress started life as a man's garment. During the Qing dynasty, the Manchus ordered Han Chinese to emulate their way of dress – elite men wore a loose 'long robe' (*changpao*) with a 'riding jacket' (*makwa*) while women wore trousers under a long garment. By the 1920s, modern women in the international port of Shanghai had taken to wearing the androgynous changpao, which released them from layers of confining clothing. From this evolved the cheongsam as we know it today.

The 'bourgeois' cheongsam dropped out of favour in China when the Communists came to power in 1949 and was banned outright during the Cultural Revolution, but the 1950s and 60s was the outfit's heyday in Hong Kong. This was the era of Suzie Wong (the cheongsam is still called a 'Suzie Wong dress' in London) and, though hemlines rose and dropped, collars stiffened and more darts were added to give it more of a Marilyn Monroe-style fit, the cheongsam remained essentially the same: elegant, sexy and very Chinese.

And Chinese they remain: Western women seldom look 'right' in a cheongsam. Unless you look like Nicole Kidman (and we're not just talking face here) and have a cheongsam-inspired dress like that red and white floral number La Kidman wore to Cannes in May 2001, eschew the cheongsam for the little black cocktail dress. What's good for the goose isn't always good for the gander.

boxed text The Wardrobe of Suzie Wong), the traditional dress that makes them all look fantastic and is oh-so Hong Kong.

China Please, do us all a favour and don't rag on about China. Very few Hong Kong Chinese people have the attitude of 'my country, right or wrong' and do not always support what the mainland announces, denounces or legislates. Remember that you are in China while in the Hong Kong SAR and despite their problems with some aspects of the motherland (China is always a mother, never a father), most Hong Kong people are proud of China's successes since the birth of the republic in 1912. You needn't be, but just don't dwell on its failures. Everyone here knows all about those already. That's why they (or their parents or their grandparents) 'voted with their feet' and found their way to Hong Kong.

Colours Most colours are symbolic to the Chinese, and they often convey a message. Red is normally a happy colour – it symbolises good luck, virtue and wealth, and brides wear red. Messages written in red ink, however, convey anger, hostility or unfriendliness. If you want to give someone your address or telephone number, write in any colour but red.

White – or anything undyed – is the colour of death and it is appropriate to give white flowers only at funerals. Colour symbols can be a little obscure. The expression 'to wear a green hat' in Cantonese means 'cuckolded'; you won't see many men wearing them in Hong Kong.

Gifts If invited to someone's home – a rare privilege among the Hong Kong Chinese, who live in small flats and prefer to entertain at restaurants – it's a good idea to bring some sort of gift, such as flowers or chocolates. More and more Hong Kong Chinese are drinking wine (particularly red), and a bottle of brandy always goes down a treat.

Money is given at weddings and to children and the unmarried at Chinese New Year, when it is called *laisee*. The money should be placed in one of the little red

CLINT CURÉ

Try to resist opening a gift in front of the giver.

envelopes sold in stationery shops all over Hong Kong. It is usually given in paired amounts: HK$20, HK$200 etc.

A Chinese person with perfect manners is supposed to refuse any gift you offer at least once, maybe twice. You are supposed to insist and they will then 'reluctantly' accept. To accept a gift too readily is considered greedy and will cause the recipient to lose face. If you receive a gift-wrapped present, it is customary not to open it in front of the giver unless asked to do so. If you open it immediately, you will also look greedy.

Face Much is made of the Chinese concept of 'face', which is roughly equivalent to status or respect. Owning nice clothes, a big house or flat in a prime location, or an expensive car all help to 'gain face'. This is not necessarily unique to the Chinese – Westerners and other Asians too buy and wear ridiculously expensive clothing and jewellery to impress those around them. However, getting into a loud argument in front of others with, say, a shopkeeper, is not the way to gain face; they will do their utmost not to knuckle under and lose face themselves. If you want to help people gain face – and get some in return – treat them with respect and show consideration for their culture.

Identity Hong Kong is name card crazy, and cards make a good impression. If you don't have any of your own, they can be printed cheaply at print shops throughout the territory (Sheung Wan is a good place to start); expect to pay about HK$300 for 200 cards. You might come across Express Card machines at train stations or the airport that can produce customised cards in less than 10 minutes. For HK$35 you get 50 cards.

You will notice that Hong Kong Chinese always hand business cards – or any piece of paper – with two hands, sometimes accompanied by a slight lowering of the head. Using just one hand may be interpreted as rudeness.

RELIGION
Traditional Chinese Beliefs
Buddhism and Taoism, entwined with elements of Confucianism, ancient animist beliefs and ancestor worship, are the dominant religions in Hong Kong. The number of active Buddhists in Hong Kong is estimated at between 650,000 to 700,000, though the figure probably includes a good number of Taoists as well.

On a daily level the Chinese are much less concerned with the high-minded philosophies and asceticism of Buddha, Confucius or Laozi, the founder of Taoism, than they are with the pursuit of worldly success, the appeasement of the dead and the spirits, and the seeking of hidden knowledge about the future.

Visits to temples are usually made to ask the gods' blessings or favours for specific things: a relative's health, the birth of a son, the success of a business, even a lucky day at the racing track. Fung shui and the Chinese zodiac also play key roles in choosing dates for funerals, and sites for graves and ancestral shrines.

Integral parts of Chinese religion are death, the afterlife and ancestor worship. Chinese funerals are usually lavish and drawn-out events. A grave site is chosen on the side of a hill with a good view for the deceased. The body can only be buried on a special day and this day is signalled by the clash of cymbals and the moan of the clarinet-like *dida*.

A heavy wooden coffin, its end panels shaped like clovers, is carried by grief-stricken mourners (sometimes they're professional keeners). Many wear Ku Klux Klan-like outfits of coarse hemp, secured around the waist with a rope and with white or undyed hoods. A fine spread of roast pig and other foods to be offered to the gods accompanies the funeral. Paper offerings – from 'hell money' and model cars to replicas of takeaway chips and hairdryers to help the deceased in the next world – are ready for burning.

Hong Kong has about 600 temples, monasteries and shrines, most of which are Buddhist or Taoist. More than 40 of the temples are public ones maintained by the Chinese Temples Committee of the Home Affairs Bureau, which derives some of its income from donations by worshippers. Temples are usually dedicated to one or two deities, whose images can be found in the main hall. Side halls house images of subsidiary gods, or *bodhisattvas*. Since Buddhism and Taoism are both accepted as traditional Chinese religions, deities from each faith are often honoured within the same temple. The majority of temples are tiny, but there are some enormous ones such as the Po Lin Monastery on Lantau Island, the Temple of Ten Thousand Buddhas at Sha Tin and Wong Tai Sin in Kowloon.

Other Religions
Many other faiths are practised in Hong Kong apart from traditional Chinese ones. There are 527,000 Christians, about 57% of whom are Protestant and 43% Catholic. Due to the zeal of lay Christians and missionaries, the number of independent Protestant churches has steadily risen since the 1970s and now includes around 1300 congregations in more than 50 denominations.

The Roman Catholic Church established its first mission in Hong Kong in 1841, when the British took possession. The present bishop, John Baptist Wu, was made cardinal in 1988. The majority of services at the 59 parishes are conducted in Cantonese, though a few churches provide services in English.

Hong Kong is also home to 80,000 Muslims. More than half are Chinese, with the rest either locally born non-Chinese or residents from Pakistan, India, Malaysia,

Indonesia, the Middle East or Africa. Four principal mosques are used daily for prayers. The oldest is the Jamia Masjid on Shelley St in the Mid-Levels, which was established in the late 19th century and rebuilt in 1915. Over in Kowloon stands the Kowloon Mosque and Islamic Centre, a white marble structure that has become a Tsim Sha Tsui landmark.

There are around 12,000 Hindus in Hong Kong. The Jewish community, which can trace its roots back to the time of the British arrival, numbers about 1000. There's both an Orthodox and a Reformed synagogue on Robinson Rd in the Mid-Levels.

Places of Worship

The following places either offer services themselves, or will tell you when and where services are held. You should also check the *Yellow Pages* for a more comprehensive list of Hong Kong churches and other places of worship.

Anglican (Church of England; ☎ 2523 4157) St John's Cathedral, 4–8 Garden Rd, Central

Baha'i (☎ 2367 6407) Flat C-6, 11th floor, Hankow Centre, Middle Rd, Tsim Sha Tsui

Christian Scientist (☎ 2524 2701) 31 MacDonnell Rd, Central

Hindu (☎ 2572 5284) 1B Wong Nai Chung Rd, Happy Valley

The Gods & Goddesses of South China

Chinese religion is polytheistic, meaning it worships many divinities. Most every household has its house, kitchen and/or door gods. Trades have their own deities too. Students worship Man Cheung, the deified scholar, while shopkeepers pray to Tsai Shin, God of Riches. Every profession has its own god or goddess, and temples throughout Hong Kong and Macau are dedicated to individual ones. The following are profiles of some of the most important local divinities.

Kwan Tai Kwan Tai (Kuantdi in Mandarin), a real-life Han dynasty soldier born in the 2nd century AD, is worshipped as the red-cheeked God of War. Naturally soldiers pray to Kwan Tai, but he is worshipped not just for his prowess in battle but for his righteousness, integrity and loyalty too. The life of Kwan Tai, who can avert war and protect people from its horrors, is recounted in an old Chinese legend called *The Story of the Three Kingdoms*. He is also the patron of restaurants, pawn shops and literature, as well as the Hong Kong police force and secret societies such as the Triads. Kwan Tai temples are at Tai O on Lantau Island and on Hollywood Road in Sheung Wan, Hong Kong Island.

Kwun Yam Kwun Yam (Guanyin in Mandarin) is the Buddhist equivalent of Tin Hau (see later). As the Goddess of Mercy, she exudes tenderness and compassion for the unhappy lot of mortals. You'll find Kwun Yum temples at Repulse Bay and Stanley on Hong Kong Island and on Cheung Chau. There are a couple of important temples dedicated to Kwun Yam in Macau (where her name is spelled Kun Iam) as well as a 20m statue atop an ecumenical centre (see the Macau Peninsula chapter for details).

Pak Tai Some Chinese deities keep an eye on certain areas only, and Cheung Chau is Pak Tai's domain. Like Kwan Tai (above), Pak Tai is a military protector of the state, a guardian of peace and order. There are many stories and legends about his origins. On Cheung Chau, Pak Tai is revered as a saviour, having intervened to end a plague that struck the island at the end of the 18th century. The island's oldest temple is dedicated to him and is the focus of the annual Cheung Chau Bun Festival (see the Outlying Islands chapter for details). There's also a Pak Tai temple on Coloane Island in Macau.

Tam Kung Tam Kung is worshipped only on a small stretch of the southern Chinese coast. One theory suggests that he is the deification of the last emperor of the Southern Song dynasty (AD 1127–1279), who drowned when Mongol ships routed the tattered remnants of the imperial fleet

Jewish (☎ 2801 5440) Jewish Community
Centre, Ohel Leah Synagogue, 70 Robinson
Rd, Mid-Levels
Methodist (☎ 2570 8709) North Point
Methodist Church, 11 Cheung Hong St,
North Point
Mormon (☎ 2559 3325) Church of Jesus Christ
of the Latter-Day Saints, 7 Castle Rd,
Mid-Levels
Muslim (☎ 2575 2218) Islamic Union, 40 Oi
Kwan Rd, Wan Chai
Quaker (☎ 9192 3477) Society of Friends, St
John's Cathedral Annexe, 3 Garden Rd, Central
Roman Catholic (☎ 2552 3992) St Joseph's,
37 Garden Rd, Central
Sikh (☎ 2574 9837) 371 Queen's Rd East,
Wan Chai

LANGUAGE

Hong Kong's two official languages are
English and Cantonese. Cantonese is a
southern Chinese dialect spoken in Guangdong province and parts of Guangxi
province on the mainland, as well as in
Hong Kong and Macau. While China
counts about eight main dialects, around
70% of the population speaks the Beijing
dialect (commonly known as Mandarin in
English), which is the official language of
the People's Republic of China (PRC).

Cantonese is used in Hong Kong in
everyday life by the vast majority of the
population, but English remains the primary

The Gods & Goddesses of South China

in a battle on the Pearl River. Temples dedicated to Tam Kung can be seen at Shau Kei Wan on Hong
Kong Island and Coloane Village in Macau.

Tin Hau Not surprisingly, the Queen of Heaven, whose duties include protecting seafarers, is one
of the most popular gods in coastal Hong Kong and in Macau, where she goes under the pseudo-
nym A-Ma. Followers of Tin Hau (Tianhou in Mandarin) number some 250,000 fisherfolk in Hong
Kong, and there are almost 60 temples dedicated to her. The most famous of these is Tai Miu (literally, 'great temple') at Joss House Bay in the New Territories. It is thought have been first built in
the 13th century by two brothers in thanks to the goddess for having spared their lives during a
storm at sea. Other important temples dedicated to the Queen of Heaven include those on Cheung Chau and Lamma Islands, In Yau Ma Tei in Kowloon and in Causeway Bay and Stanley on Hong
Kong Island.

The Tin Hau cult is based on the worship of Lin Moniang (AD 960–87), the 'mute maiden' of Fujian who never cried as a child and who was born after Kwun Yam (Guanyin), the Goddess of Mercy,
gave her parents a magic pill. The stories of her strengths and miracles are legion, but they always
involve her saving herself and/or others from shipwreck and drowning.

Tou Tei Tou Tei (Toudei in Mandarin) is the earth god who rules over anything from a one-room
flat or shop to a section of a village or town. Shrines to Tou Tei are usually small and inconspicuous
but always a delight. There's a very good example of one on Cheung Chau.

Wong Tai Sin Like Pak Tai, Wong Tai Sin's jurisdiction is limited to a specific area – in this case
the large housing settlement of that name in New Kowloon. Wong Tai Sin began his life as a humble shepherd in Zhejiang province. When he was 15 an immortal taught him how to make a herbal
potion that could cure all illnesses. He is thus worshipped both by the sick and those trying to avoid
illness. Wong Tai Sin spent 40 years in seclusion, performing such miracles as turning white boulders into sheep. He is a favourite god of businesspeople.

Wong Tai Sin's popularity in Hong Kong soared after a man and his son brought an image of the
god from Guangdong province in 1915. They installed it in a small temple in Wan Chai, where the
faithful began to visit it regularly. A temple complex was built in Kowloon in 1921 to accommodate
the growing number of followers and today it is the territory's largest and most active temple.

language of commerce, banking and international trade, and is also used in the law courts. However, there has been a sharp decline in the level of English-speaking proficiency in recent years. Those Hong Kong Chinese who speak excellent English are usually also the wealthiest, and many of them have emigrated. Many secondary schools in Hong Kong that had previously taught all lessons in English made the transition to Cantonese under governmental pressure in 1998.

On the other hand, the ability to speak Mandarin is on the increase. Until recently, the younger generation usually didn't bother to learn Mandarin, preferring English as a second language. The new political realities are changing those attitudes.

For a Cantonese native speaker, Mandarin is far easier to learn than English but it's also the last thing that many school children want to do.

Short-term English-speaking visitors can get along fine in Hong Kong without a word of Cantonese, especially in the tourist areas. Street signs and public transport information are in both English and Cantonese, so there's no problem getting around.

Most expatriates in Hong Kong never learn the local language aside from 'taxi' or 'restaurant' Cantonese. Any effort on your part to learn a few words will be rewarded one hundred-fold.

For more on what to say and how to say it in Cantonese, see the Language section at the back of this book.

Facts for the Visitor

HIGHLIGHTS

The trip on the Peak Tram to Victoria Peak has been practically mandatory for visitors since it opened in 1888. It's fascinating to take a 30-minute ride on a sampan through one of Hong Kong's fishing harbours (Cheung Chau's is best). Equally interesting is a ride on Hong Kong Island's trams. Exploring the outlying islands by ferry is one of Hong Kong's best-kept secrets – the walks are truly excellent. Hong Kong has some amazingly good beaches, such as Cheung Sha on Lantau. No hiker could resist the MacLehose, Lantau or Hong Kong trails – all offer some of the world's most breathtaking views. Amusement park enthusiasts will find Ocean Park hard to beat. Party animals can eat, drink and dance the night away in Lan Kwai Fong, Soho and Wan Chai. Brunch at a dim sum restaurant is one of the great pleasures of this region and, of course, Hong Kong is famous for shopping, though there aren't as many bargains as there once were.

And then there are those who insist that the highlight of their visit to Hong Kong was Macau. (See the Macau chapters of this book for details.)

SUGGESTED ITINERARIES
One Day

If you have only one day, you can catch a tram up the Peak for a good view of the city and stretch your legs on a summit circuit before lunching at the Peak Cafe. Back down at sea level, you could do some shopping at Pacific Place and watch the sun go down from Cyrano's, a bar on the 56th floor of the Island Shangri-La Hotel.

Two Days

If you have two days, you could also take the Star Ferry to Tsim Sha Tsui and visit the Art, Space or History museums, have a yum cha brunch at Wan Loong Court in the Kowloon Hotel then browse along Nathan Rd until you're hungry enough for afternoon tea at the Peninsula Hotel. A wander up Temple St for the night market and sampling the street food are also worthwhile.

Three Days

With another day to look around, you could wander around Central and Sheung Wan, poking your head into traditional shops before lunching and gallery-hopping in Soho. Take a tram to Wan Chai for a night of Chinese opera or theatre at the Hong Kong Arts Centre and strut your stuff at a Wan Chai bar before dining late at 369 Shanghai.

One Week

If you have one week you can see many of the sights listed in the Hong Kong Island and Kowloon chapters, visit an outlying island (choose Lantau for the big Buddha, the fabulous walks and the beaches), jump aboard a bus or the Kowloon-Canton Railway (KCR) for the New Territories (Kam Tin and surrounds, the Sai Kung Peninsula or the Mai Po March area are all sure bets), take a day trip to or spend the night in Macau and head for Shenzhen on the mainland via the Mass Transit Railway (MTR) for half a day.

PLANNING
When to Go

October, November and most of December are probably the best months to visit Hong Kong. Temperatures are comfortable, skies are clear and the sun shines. January and February are cloudier and colder but dry.

March to May are not optimum months in Hong Kong. It's warmer but the humidity is high, and fog and drizzle can make getting around – and enjoying the territory's natural beauty – difficult. The sweltering heat and humidity in June, July and August can make sightseeing a sweaty proposition and it is also the rainy season. Still, there's a lot of sunshine and, after all, it's summer. September is a grand month if you like drama; the threat of a typhoon can seem to loom almost every other day.

Under normal conditions, Hong Kong hotels have a high season from March to June and September to January. During this time the rates usually go up, rooms are harder to find and the airfares to and from Hong Kong are higher. In recent years, however, the slump in the economy and the downturn in tourism has seen fierce competition in the airline and hotel industries.

Travel in and out of Hong Kong can be extremely difficult during Chinese New Year (late January/early February) – particularly to China – when more than half of the Hong Kong SAR is on the move. Flights are usually full, and the border with China becomes a living hell. On the other hand, the mass exodus leaves Hong Kong all but empty, and a growing number of shops and restaurants only close for one day during the holiday instead of the traditional four days.

If you're planning to leave Hong Kong for the UK or the USA in August, book your flight early. You will be competing for seats with tens of thousands of Hong Kong students going back to university or college.

Maps

Decent tourist maps are easy to find in Hong Kong, and they're usually free. The Hong Kong Tourism Board (HKTB) hands out copies of its *Visitors' Guide Map* at its information centres at the airport, the Star Ferry terminal in Tsim Sha Tsui and The Centre in Central. It is published four times a year, covers the northern coast of Hong Kong Island from Kennedy Town to North Point and part of Kowloon Peninsula, and is crammed with useful tourist information. More detailed maps can be found in the back pages of the HKTB's free *Traveller's Guide*.

Another free map you'll find everywhere is the *AOA Street Map* but it's full of advertising and difficult to use. *The Map*, from the people who bring you *HK Magazine* (see Listings in the Entertainment section), is more user-friendly.

Lonely Planet's *Hong Kong City Map* (HK$35) has five separate maps with varying scales, a street index and an inset map of Hong Kong's rail network.

Universal Publications (UP; W www.up.com.hk) produces many maps of Hong Kong, including the 1:80,000 *Hong Kong Touring Map* (HK$22) and the 1:9000 *City Map of Hong Kong & Kowloon* (HK$25). It also publishes detailed street maps of Hong Kong Island and Kowloon (HK$22 each), with scales below 1:8000.

The *Hong Kong Official Guide Map* (HK$45) produced by the government has both overall and district maps and is available from most bookshops.

If you're looking for greater detail, topographical accuracy and good colour reproduction, it's worth investing in the *Hong Kong Guidebook* (HK$62), a street atlas to the entire territory published by UP and updated annually. Compiled in both English and Chinese, it also includes useful information such as ferry timetables, hotel listings and a separate booklet called the *Public Transport Boarding Guide*, which is the only complete listing of bus and minibus routes available.

A larger format of this is UP's *Hong Kong Driving Guide* (HK$88), with a spiral binding. It does not include the transport booklet.

Along with everything from flying charts to plans of the so-called New Towns in the New Territories, the Lands Department of the Hong Kong government produces a series of seven *Countryside Series* maps that are useful (if not obligatory) for hiking in the hills; see Maps in the New Territories and Outlying Islands chapters and The Hong Kong Trail in the Hong Kong Island chapter for details. These maps are available from two Map Publication Centres (W info.gov.hk/landsd/mapping): the North Point branch (☎ 2231 3187), 23rd floor, North Point Government Offices, 333 Java Rd; and the Yau Ma Tei branch (☎ 2780 0981), 382 Nathan Rd. Both outlets are open from 9am to 6pm on weekdays and to 1pm on Saturday.

What to Bring

The short answer is as little as possible. Keep in mind that you can and will buy things in Hong Kong, so don't burden yourself with a lot of unnecessary junk. If you arrive in summer (or even late spring), you'll wish you'd only brought your toothbrush, bathing suit and a towel – the slightest movement will bring you out in a sweat.

Even so, there are some things that you may want to bring from home. A daypack can be handy. A beltpack or bumbag is OK for maps, extra film and miscellaneous items, but don't use it for valuables, as it's an easy target for pickpockets.

Plastic sandals or thongs (flip-flops) are useful for shower rooms and the beach. Nylon running or sports shoes are best as they are comfortable, washable and light.

If you plan to stay at hostels and Chungking Mansions–style guesthouses (see Places to Stay in the Kowloon chapter), pack a towel and a plastic soap container, or buy these when you arrive. Bedclothes and padlocks are usually provided, though you might want to take along your own sheet bag and lock.

Other items you might need include a torch (flashlight), an adaptor plug for electrical appliances (such as a cup or coil immersion heater to make your own tea or instant coffee), sunglasses, sun block, a few clothes pegs and premoistened towelettes or a large cotton handkerchief that you can soak in fountains and use to cool off while touring in the warmer months.

Business or name cards, though hardly mandatory, are a good idea and will give you 'face'. See Identity under Society & Conduct in the Facts about Hong Kong chapter.

RESPONSIBLE TOURISM

If you take the general advice offered in the Dos & Don'ts section under Society & Conduct in the Facts about Hong Kong chapter, you'll be all right. But there are a couple of things to consider that are specific to Hong Kong.

Hong Kong is a very crowded city even before the peak season brings in yet more millions. Be patient as you try to make your way down Nathan Rd in Tsim Sha Tsui or Queen's Rd Central. Everyone is just as keen to move along as you are.

Almost 7 million people create a lot of trash (see Ecology & Environment in the

People caught littering face hefty fines.

Facts about Hong Kong chapter). Please put your litter in the bin; these are found everywhere in Hong Kong. And if you hike or picnic in the countryside, take your trash back with you. Be particularly careful in 'fragile' areas such as the Mai Po Marsh in the New Territories. People who litter or spit in the street now face on-the-spot fines of HK$600.

If you'd like to know more about the problems caused by tourism worldwide, contact Tourism Concern (☎ 020-7753 3330, 𝐖 www.tourismconcern.org.uk), Stapleton House, 277–281 Holloway Rd, London N7 8HN, England.

TOURIST OFFICES
Local Tourist Offices
If awards were handed out for the most efficient, knowledgeable and helpful tourist information service in the world, the enterprising Hong Kong Tourism Board (HKTB; ☎ 2807 6453, fax 2806 0303, 𝐞 info@hktourismboard.com), formerly the Hong Kong Tourist Association (HKTA), would win the top prize hands down. Staff are welcoming and have reams of information. Most of their literature is free, though they also sell a few useful publications and books as well as postcards, T-shirts and other souvenirs.

Before you depart, check its visitors Web site (𝐖 www.discoverhongkong.com), which will answer any question you could possibly have. If you still can't find what you're looking for, check HKTB's database, which can be accessed from the visitors Web site or found directly at 𝐖 www.hktouristinfo.com.

The multilingual HKTB Visitor Hotline (☎ 2508 1234), operating from 8am to 6pm daily, is like a personal guide. Lost in the New Territories? Looking for a Chiu Chow restaurant in Sheung Wan? Want to know if the Tsim Sha Tsui shop where you're buying your camera is reliable and a member of the HKTB? Just phone the hotline and ask.

The following HKTB Visitor Information & Service Centres can be found on Hong Kong Island, in Kowloon and at Hong Kong International Airport:

Hong Kong Island Ground floor, The Centre, 99 Queen's Rd Central. Open from 8am to 6pm daily. Tourist literature and access to the HKTB Web site and database via iCyberlink screen available 24 hours.

Hong Kong International Airport Chek Lap Kok. HKTB centres are located in Halls A and B on the arrival level and the transfer area T2. They are open from 7am to 11pm daily. Tourist literature and access to the HKTB Web site and database via iCyberlink screen are available 24 hours.

Kowloon Star Ferry Concourse, Tsim Sha Tsui. Open from 8am to 6pm daily.

You can also take advantage of HKTB's Infofax service (fax 90060 77 1128 or 852 90060 77 1128 from abroad), which provides detailed information on HKTB member hotels, restaurants and shops as well as sights, sports, tours and so on. Simply punch in the number and push the start or send button. You'll immediately receive a list of topics and the appropriate fax numbers to call to receive data on everything from visas and immigration to key sights and travel to mainland China and Macau. From overseas you'll just pay the standard long-distance rate. If calling from within Hong Kong, the phone company charges HK$2 per minute from 8am to 9pm, and HK$1 at other times.

Tourist Offices Abroad

You'll find HKTB offices at the following overseas locations:

Australia (☎ 02-9283 3083, fax 9283 3383, Ⓔ sydwwo@hktourismboard.com) Level 4, Hong Kong House, 80 Druitt St, Sydney, NSW 2000

Canada (☎ 416-366 2389, fax 366 1098, Ⓔ yyzwwo@hktourismboard.com) 3rd floor, 9 Temperance St, Toronto, Ontario M5H 1Y6

China
Beijing: (☎ 10-6518 6018, fax 6518 6020, Ⓔ bejwwo@hktourismboard.com) Rooms 902–903, Office Tower 1, Henderson Centre, 18 Jianguomennei Dajie, Dongcheng District, Beijing 100005
Shanghai: (☎ 021-6385 1242, fax 6385 1490, Ⓔ shawwo@hktourismboard.com) Room 808, Shui On Plaza, 333 Huai Hai Zhong Rd, Shanghai 200021

France (☎ 01 42 65 66 64, fax 01 42 65 66 00, Ⓔ parwwo@hktourismboard.com) 1st floor, 37 Rue de Caumartin, 75009 Paris

Germany (☎ 069-959 1290, fax 597 8050, Ⓔ fraww48o@hktourismboard.com) Humboldt Strasse 94, D-60318 Frankfurt

Italy (☎ 011-669 0238, fax 668 0785, Ⓔ itawwo@hktourismboard.com) c/o Adam and Partner srl, Corso Marconi 33, 10125 Turin

Japan
Tokyo: (☎ 03-5219 8288, fax 5219 8292, Ⓔ tyowwo@hktourismboard.com) 2nd floor, Kokusai Building, 3-1-1 Marunouchi, Chiyoda-ku, Tokyo 100-0005
Osaka: (☎ 06-6229 9240, fax 6229 9648, Ⓔ osawwo@hktourismboard.com) 8th floor, Osaka Saitama Building, 3-15-13 Awaji-machi, Chuo-ku, Osaka 541-0047

New Zealand (☎ 09-307 2580, fax 307 2581, Ⓔ aukwwo@hktourismboard.com) 2nd floor, 99 Queen St, Auckland 1001

Singapore (☎ 336 5800, fax 336 5811, Ⓔ sin wwo @hktourismboard.com) 9 Temasek Blvd, #34-03 Suntec Tower Two, Singapore 038989

South Korea (☎ 02-778 4401, fax 778 4404, Ⓔ korwwo@hktourismboard.com) c/o Glocom Korea, Suite 1105, Pakinam Building, 188-3 Eulchiro 1-Ka, Chung-Gu, Seoul

Spain (☎ 93-414 1794, fax 201 8657, Ⓔ bcnwwo@hktourismboard.com) c/o Sergat España, Pau Casals 4, 08021 Barcelona

Taiwan (☎ 02-2581 6061, fax 2581 6062, Ⓔ tpewwo@hktourismboard.com) 9th floor, 18 Chang An East Rd, Section 1, Taipei

UK (☎ 020-7533 7100, fax 7533 7111, Ⓔ lonwwo@hktourismboard.com) 6 Grafton St, London W1S 4EQ

USA
New York: (☎ 212-421 3382, fax 421 8428, Ⓔ nycwwo@hktourismboard.com) 115 East 54th St, 2nd floor, New York, NY 10022-4512
Los Angeles: (☎ 310-208 0233, fax 208 2398, Ⓔ laxwwo@hktourismboard.com) Suite 2050, 10940 Wiltshire Blvd, Los Angeles, CA 90024-3915
Chicago: (☎ 312-329 1828, fax 329 1858, Ⓔ chiwwo@hktourismboard.com) 401 North

Michigan Ave, Suite 1640, Chicago, IL 60611
San Francisco: (☎ 415-781 4587,
ⓔ sfowwo@hktourismboard.com) 130 Montgomery St, San Francisco, CA 94104

VISAS & DOCUMENTS
Passport
A passport is essential for visiting Hong Kong, and if yours is within a few months of expiration get a new one immediately. If you'll be staying for some time in Hong Kong, it's wise to register with your consulate. This makes the replacement process much simpler if you lose your passport or it is stolen.

Hong Kong residents are required to carry an officially issued identification card at all times. Visitors *must* carry their passports with them as the immigration authorities do frequent spot checks to catch illegal workers and those who overstay their visas and this is the only form of ID acceptable to the Hong Kong police.

Visas
The vast majority of travellers, including citizens of the European Union (EU), Australia, New Zealand, the USA and Canada, are allowed to enter the Hong Kong SAR without a visa and stay three months. Holders of British or EU United Kingdom passports can stay up to six months without a visa, but British Dependent Territories and British Overseas citizens not holding a visa only have three months. Holders of Japanese, South African and the majority of South American passports do not require visas for a visit of one month or less.

If you do require a visa, you must apply beforehand at the nearest Chinese consulate or embassy (see the Chinese Embassies & Consulates section later). Visitors have to show that they have adequate funds for their stay (a credit card should do the trick) and that they hold an onward or return ticket. Ordinary visas cost HK$135, transit visas HK$70.

Visitors are not permitted to take up employment, establish any business or enrol as students. If you want to work or study, you must apply for an employment or student visa beforehand. It is very hard to change your visa status after you have arrived in Hong Kong. Anyone wishing to stay longer than the visa-free period must apply for a visa before travelling to Hong Kong. For details on applying for a work permit, see the Work section later in this chapter.

Visa Extensions In general, visa extensions (HK$135) are not readily granted unless there are special or extenuating circumstances such as cancelled flights, illness, registration in a legitimate course of study, legal employment, marriage to a local etc.

For information contact the Hong Kong Immigration Department (☎ 2824 6111, ⓦ www.info.gov.hk/immd), 2nd floor, Immigration Tower, 7 Gloucester Rd, Wan Chai.

Hong Kong Identity Card
Anyone who stays in Hong Kong for longer than three months must hold a Hong Kong Identity Card, and this rule is very strictly enforced. Inquire at the Immigration Department's ID-issuing office (☎ 2598 0888), 24th floor, Immigration Tower, 7 Gloucester Rd, Wan Chai. Be sure to take your passport with you.

Travel Insurance
You should seriously consider taking out travel insurance. This not only covers you for medical expenses and luggage theft or loss but also for cancellation or delays in your travel arrangements. Cover depends on your insurance and type of airline ticket, so ask both your insurer and your ticket-issuing agency (often one and the same) to explain where you stand. Ticket loss is also covered by travel insurance.

Paying for your airline ticket with a credit card often provides limited travel accident insurance, and you may be able to reclaim the payment if the operator doesn't deliver. In the UK, for instance, institutions issuing credit cards are required by law to reimburse consumers if a company goes into liquidation and the amount in contention is more than UK£100. Ask your credit card company what it's prepared to cover.

Driving Licence & Permits

Hong Kong allows most foreigners over the age of 18 to drive for up to 12 months with their valid local licenses. It's still a good idea to carry an International Driving Permit (IDP) as well. This should be obtainable from your local automobile association for a reasonable fee (eg, HK$90 in Hong Kong).

Anyone driving in the territory for more than a year will need a Hong Kong licence valid for 10 years (HK$900). Apply to the Transport Department Licensing Division (☎ 2804 2600, Ⓦ www.info.gov.hk/td), 41st floor, Immigration Tower, 7 Gloucester Rd, Wan Chai. There is another licence-issuing office on the 3rd floor of the United Centre, 95 Queensway, Admiralty.

Hostel Cards

A Hostelling International (HI) card or equivalent is of relatively limited use in Hong Kong. If you arrive without a card, you can buy one from the Hong Kong Youth Hostels Association (HKYHA; ☎ 2788 1638, Ⓔ hkyha@datainternet.com, Ⓦ www.yha.org.hk), Room 225–226, Block 19, Shek Kip Mei Estate, Kowloon, for HK$110/50 (Hong Kong residents over/under 18) or HK$180 (nonresidents). You are allowed to stay at any of Hong Kong's HKYHA hostels without a membership card, but you will have to buy a 'Welcome Stamp' (HK$30) for each night of your stay. Once you've stayed six nights, you are issued a card.

For information on Hong Kong's seven hostels, most of which are in the New Territories, see the Accommodation section later in this chapter.

Student & Youth Cards

The International Student Identity Card (ISIC), a plastic ID-style card with your photograph, provides discounts on some forms of transport and cheaper admission to museums and other sights. If you're aged under 26 but not a student, you can apply for a International Youth Travel Card (IYTC) card issued by the Federation of International Youth Travel Organisations (FIYTO), which gives much the same discounts and benefits. Hong Kong Student

Travel (☎ 2730 3269, Ⓦ www.hkst.com.hk), Room 835A, Star House, 3 Salisbury Rd, Tsim Sha Tsui, can issue you an ISIC for HK$100 in a week or HK$150 in a day. Make sure you bring your student ID from home or other credentials along with you.

Seniors Cards

Many attractions in Hong Kong offer reduced-price admission for people over 65. Any passport or ID with a photo should be sufficient proof.

Hong Kong Museums Pass

Passes allowing multiple entries to six of Hong Kong's museums (Hong Kong Museum of Coastal Defence on Hong Kong Island; Hong Kong Science Museum, Hong Kong Museum of History, Hong Kong Museum of Art and the Hong Kong Space Museum in Kowloon; and Hong Kong Heritage Museum in the New Territories) and valid for a week/month are available for HK$30/50 from any HKTB outlet.

Hong Kong VIP Cards

This card, available free at HKTB information offices, offers discounts of 10% to 50% on certain organised tours and free souvenirs at selected shops.

Copies

All important documents (passport data page and visa page, credit cards, travel insurance policy, air/bus/train tickets, driving licence etc) should be photocopied before you leave home. Leave one copy with someone at home and keep another with you, separate from the originals.

EMBASSIES & CONSULATES
Chinese Embassies & Consulates

If you need a visa to visit Hong Kong, you must apply to a Chinese embassy or consulate beforehand.

Key Chinese embassies and consulates around the world include the following:

Australia (☎ 02-6273 4780, fax 6273 4878)
15 Coronation Drive, Yarralumla, Canberra ACT 2600
Consulates: Melbourne, Perth, Sydney

Canada (☎ 613-789 3434, fax 789 1414) 515 St Patrick St, Ottawa, Ontario K1N 5H3
Consulates: Calgary, Toronto, Vancouver
France (☎ 01 47 36 02 58, fax 01 47 36 34 46) 9 Avenue Victor Cresson, 92130 Issy les Moulineaux
Consulates: Marseilles, Strasbourg
Ireland (☎ 01-269 1707) 40 Ailesbury Rd, Dublin 4
Italy (☎ 06-8535 0118, fax 841 3467) Via Bruxelles, 6500198 Roma
Consulates: Florence, Milan
Japan (☎ 03-3403 3064, fax 3403 3345) 3-4-33 Moto-Azabu, Minato-ku, Tokyo 106
Consulates: Fukuoka, Nagasaki, Osaka, Sapporo
Malaysia (☎ 03-242 8585, fax 241 4552) 229 Jalanampang, 59450 Kuala Lumpur
Consulate: Kuching
Netherlands (☎ 070-350 8479, fax 354 2389) Adriaan Goekooplaan 7, 2517 JX, The Hague
New Zealand (☎ 04-472 1384, fax 472 1998) 2-6 Glenmore St, Wellington
Consulate: Auckland
Singapore (☎ 735 3867, fax 735 9639) #11-01/03, Tanglin Shopping Centre, 19 Tanglin Rd
South Korea (☎ 771 3726, fax 319 5103) 83 Myong-dong 2-ga, Chunggu, Seoul
Consulate: Busan
South Africa (☎ 012-342 9366, fax 342 4154) 972 Pretorius St, Arcadia, 0002 Pretoria
Consulates: Capetown, Durban
Thailand (02-247 7553, fax 247 2214) 57 Ratchadaphisek Rd, Huay Kwang, Bangkok 10310
Consulates: Chiang Mai, Songkhla
UK (☎ 020-7299 4049, fax 020-7636 9756) 31 Portland Place, London, W1N 3AH
Consulates: Edinburgh, Manchester
USA (☎ 202-338 6688, fax 588 9760) 2201 Wisconsin Ave NW, Washington, DC 20007
Consulates: Chicago, Houston, Los Angeles, New York, San Francisco

Consulates in Hong Kong

Because Hong Kong is not a nation but a region of China, other countries have consulates, not embassies, here.

There's a complete list of consulates in the *Yellow Pages* as well as in the back pages of the *Hong Kong Guidebook* atlas and street directory. Some smaller countries are represented by honorary consuls, normally local businesspeople employed in commercial firms, so it's advisable to phone beforehand to find out if the consul is available.

Travellers with queries about visas to Macau and other issues should contact the Hong Kong branch of the Macau Government Tourist Office (☎ 2857 2287), Room 336, Shun Tak Centre, 200 Connaught Rd, Sheung Wan.

Australia (☎ 2827 8881) 23rd & 24th floors, Harbour Centre, 25 Harbour Rd, Wan Chai
Canada (☎ 2810 4321) 11th–14th floors, Tower I, Exchange Square, 8 Connaught Place, Central
China (☎ 2585 1700) 5th floor, Lower Block, China Resources Building, 26 Harbour Rd, Wan Chai
France (☎ 2529 4316) 26th floor, Tower II, Admiralty Centre, 18 Harcourt Rd, Admiralty
Germany (☎ 2105 8788) 21st floor, United Centre, 95 Queensway, Admiralty
Indonesia (☎ 2890 4421) 127–129 Leighton Rd, Causeway Bay
Japan (☎ 2522 1184) 46th floor, Tower I, Exchange Square, 8 Connaught Place, Central
Laos (☎ 2544 1186) Room 1002, Arion Commercial Centre, 2–12 Queen's Rd West, Sheung Wan
Malaysia (☎ 2527 0921) 24th floor, Malaysia Building, 50 Gloucester Rd, Wan Chai
Myanmar (☎ 2827 7929) Room 2436, Sung Hung Kai Centre, 30 Harbour Rd, Wan Chai
Netherlands (☎ 2522 5127) Room 5702, Cheung Kong Centre, 2 Queen's Rd Central
New Zealand (☎ 2877 4488) Room 6508, Central Plaza, 18 Harbour Rd, Wan Chai
Philippines (☎ 2823 8518) Room 602, United Centre, 95 Queensway, Admiralty
Russian Federation (☎ 2877 7188) Room 2932, Sun Hung Kai Centre, 30 Harbour Rd, Wan Chai
Singapore (☎ 2527 2212) Room 901–902, Tower I, Admiralty Centre, 18 Harcourt Rd, Admiralty
South Africa (☎ 2577 3279) Room 2706, Great Eagle Centre, 23 Harbour Rd, Wan Chai
South Korea (☎ 2529 4141) 5th floor, Far East Finance Centre, 16 Harcourt Rd, Admiralty
Taiwan (☎ 2525 8316) Chung Hwa Travel Service, 4th floor, Lippo Tower I, 89 Queensway, Admiralty
Thailand (☎ 2521 6481) 8th floor, Fairmont House, 8 Cotton Tree Drive, Central
UK (☎ 2901 3000) 1 Supreme Court Rd, Admiralty
USA (☎ 2523 9011) 26 Garden Rd, Central
Vietnam (☎ 2591 4517) 15th floor, Great Smart Tower, 230 Wan Chai Rd, Wan Chai

Your Own Embassy

It's important to realise what your own embassy – the embassy of the country of which you are a citizen – can and can't do to help you if you get into trouble. Generally, it won't be much help in emergencies if the trouble you're in is your own fault. Remember that you are bound by the laws of the country you are in. Your embassy will not be sympathetic if you end up in jail after committing a crime locally, even if such actions are legal in your own country.

In genuine emergencies you might get some assistance, but only if other channels have been exhausted. For example, if you need to get home urgently, a free ticket home is exceedingly unlikely – the embassy would expect you to have insurance. If you have all your money and documents stolen, it might assist with getting a new passport, but a loan for onward travel is out of the question.

CUSTOMS

Even though Hong Kong is a duty-free port, there are items on which duty is still charged. Import taxes on cigarettes and alcohol, in particular, are high: 90% on spirits and 40% on beer alone.

The duty-free allowance for visitors coming into Hong Kong (including from Macau and the mainland) is 200 cigarettes (or 50 cigars or 250g tobacco) and 1L of alcohol. Apart from these limits there are few other import taxes, so you can bring in reasonable quantities of almost anything.

Firecrackers and fireworks are banned in Hong Kong but not in Macau and mainland China, and people crossing the border are sometimes thoroughly searched for these. Customs officers are on high alert for drug smugglers. If you're arriving from Thailand or Vietnam, be prepared for a rigorous examination of your luggage.

MONEY
Currency

The local currency is the Hong Kong dollar (HK$), which is divided into 100 cents. Bills are issued in denominations of HK$20 (grey), HK$50 (blue), HK$100 (red; a 'red one'), HK$500 (brown) and HK$1000 (yellow; a 'gold one'). You'll occasionally still come across HK$10 notes (green), but these are now being phased out. There are little copper coins worth HK$0.10, HK$0.20 and HK$0.50 and silver-coloured HK$1, HK$2, HK$5 and HK$10 coins.

Hong Kong notes are issues by three banks: HSBC (formerly the Hongkong and Shanghai Bank), the Standard Chartered Bank and the Bank of China. This shouldn't make any difference to travellers, however, as each denomination is the same colour.

Exchange Rates

The Hong Kong dollar has been pegged to the US dollar at a rate of about US$1 to HK$7.80 since 1983. Thus it moves in line with the US dollar against other foreign currencies. The 'peg', as it's called, often comes under attack by analysts, as it limits Hong Kong's fiscal policy options, but it looks like remaining in place for some time to come.

Exchange rates are as follows:

country	unit		HK$
Australia	A$1	=	HK$4.17
Canada	C$1	=	HK$5.04
China	Y1	=	HK$0.94
European Union	€1	=	HK$7.11
Japan	¥100	=	HK$6.52
Macau	M$1	=	HK$0.97
New Zealand	NZ$1	=	HK$3.43
Singapore	S$1	=	HK$4.45
Switzerland	Sfr1	=	HK$4.70
Taiwan	NT$1	=	HK$0.23
Thailand	B1	=	HK$0.17
UK	UK£1	=	HK$11.33
USA	US$1	=	HK$7.80

Exchanging Money

One of the main reasons why Hong Kong has become the financial centre of Asia is because it is unregulated. It has no currency exchange or import/export controls; locals and foreigners can take or send in or out as much money as they please.

Cash Nothing beats cash for convenience – or risk. It's still a good idea, however, to travel with at least some cash, if only to tide you over until you get to an exchange facility.

Banks generally offer the best rates, though three of the biggest ones – HSBC, Standard Chartered and the Hang Seng Bank – levy a HK$50 commission for each transaction on non-account holders. If you're changing the equivalent of several hundred US dollars or more, the exchange rate improves, which makes up for the fee. Hong Kong is littered with branches of these banks, so you should have no trouble finding one.

Travellers Cheques These offer protection from theft but are becoming less common with the preponderance of ATMs. Most banks will cash travellers cheques, and all charge a fee, often irrespective of whether you are an account holder or not. HSBC charges 0.375% of the total amount, Standard Chartered adds on a HK$50 commission and Hang Seng charges HK$60.

Lost or Stolen Travellers Cheques Thomas Cook (☎ 2853 9888) and American Express (☎ 800 962 403) can often arrange replacement cheques within 24 hours.

ATMS Plastic cards make the perfect travelling companions: they're ideal for major purchases, let you withdraw cash from selected banks and ATMs, they don't snore and they never want the window seat.

Hong Kong ATMs are usually linked up to international money systems like Cirrus, Maestro, GlobalAccess or Plus.

Credit Cards The most widely accepted credit cards in Hong Kong are American Express (AmEx), Visa, Diners Club, JCB and MasterCard, pretty much in that order. When signing credit card receipts, make sure you always write a 'HK' in front of the dollar sign if there isn't one already printed there.

If you plan to use a credit card make sure you have a high enough credit limit to cover major expenses like car hire or airline tickets. Alternatively, leave your card

in credit when you start your travels. And don't just carry one card, go for two: an American Express or Diners Club card with a MasterCard or Visa card. Better still, combine cards and travellers cheques so you have something to fall back on if an ATM swallows your card or the bank won't accept it.

Some shops in Hong Kong may try to add a surcharge to offset the commission charged by credit companies, which can range from 2.5% to 7%. In theory, this is prohibited by the credit companies, but to get around this many shops will offer a 5% discount if you pay cash. It's your choice.

Lost or Stolen Credit Cards If a card is lost or stolen you must inform both the police (see the Emergencies section later in this chapter) and the issuing company as soon as possible; otherwise, you may have to pay for the purchases that the unspeakable scoundrel has made using your card. Here are some 24-hour numbers for cancelling your cards:

AmEx	☎ 2811 6162, 2277 1010
Diners Club	☎ 2860 1888
JCB	☎ 2366 7211
MasterCard	☎ 800-966 677
Visa	☎ 800-900 782

The last number may be able to help you or at least point you in the right direction should you lose your Visa card but, in general, you must deal with the issuing bank in the case of an emergency. Round-the-clock emergency numbers include: Chase Manhattan Bank (☎ 2890 8188); Citibank (☎ 2860 0333); HSBC (☎ 2748 4848); and Standard Chartered Bank (☎ 2886 4111).

International Transfers International telegraphic transfers are fast and efficient. If you instruct your bank back home to send you a draft, be sure you specify the bank and the branch to which you want your money directed, or ask your home bank to tell you where a suitable one is located. The whole procedure will be easier if you've authorised someone back home to access your account.

Money sent by telegraphic transfer should reach you within a week; by mail, allow at least two weeks. When it arrives, it will most likely be converted into local currency – you can take it as is or buy travellers cheques. The charge for this service is usually HK$100 to HK$150.

All of the major banks in Hong Kong provide this service. HSBC's international transfer desk (☎ 2748 3322) is on the 3rd floor of the main branch at 1 Queen's Rd Central. A specialist in telegraphic transfers is Western Union (☎ 2528 5631), Shop 2038, 2nd floor, United Centre, 95 Queensway, Admiralty.

Black Market No foreign currency black market exists in Hong Kong. If anyone on the street does approach you to change money, assume it's a scam. For information about buying renminbi, the Chinese currency, see the Information sections of the China Excursion – Shenzhen and China Excursion – Zhuhai chapters.

Moneychangers Avoid the exchange counters at the airport; they offer some of the worst rates in Hong Kong. The rates offered at hotels are only marginally better than those at the airport.

Licensed moneychangers such as Chequepoint are abundant in tourist areas such as Tsim Sha Tsui. While they are convenient (they are open on Sunday, holidays and late into the evenings) and take no commission per se, the exchange rates offered are equivalent to a 5% commission. These rates are clearly posted, though if you're changing several hundred US dollars or more you might be able to bargain for a better rate. Before the actual exchange is made, the moneychanger is required by law to give you a form to sign that clearly shows the amount due to you, the exchange rate and any service charges.

The half-dozen moneychangers operating on the ground floor of Chungking Mansions on Nathan Rd in Tsim Sha Tsui usually offer good rates. One excellent moneychanger is Wing Hoi Money Exchange (☎ 2723 5948), Ground floor, Shop 9B, Mirador Arcade, 58 Nathan Rd, Tsim Sha Tsui. It'll change just about any currency for you as well as travellers cheques.

Personal Cheques Personal cheques are still widely used in Hong Kong – a group of diners will often write separate cheques to pay for their share of a meal.

If you plan to stay a while in Hong Kong – or even travel around Asia and return – you might open a bank account here. There is no need to be a resident, and current and savings accounts can be opened in Hong Kong dollars or almost any other major currency.

Security
Hong Kong has its share of pickpockets, who operate in crowded areas such as the Star Ferry piers and the Peak Tram. Whichever way you decide to carry your funds and documents, it makes sense to keep most of them out of easy reach of thieves in a money-belt or something similar. You should be sure to keep something like US$50 apart from the rest of your cash in the event of an emergency.

Costs
Sad to say but Hong Kong has become a pricey destination. At the same time, Hong Kong has lost its edge when it comes to picking up bargains – it takes a lot of searching to find a shop with quality goods at low prices.

You can do Hong Kong on a budget, however. It's possible to survive in Hong Kong for HK$250 a day, but it will require a good deal of self-discipline. Accommodation is the biggest expense, but you can get it down to less than HK$100 a night by staying in grotty guesthouses or even as low as HK$35 a night if you elect to stay in Hong Kong's far-flung hostels. Remember, though, that what you save in accommodation costs will go toward transport.

The true Spartan could, theoretically, spend the night in a dorm, have three fast-food or simple Chinese meals a day, travel on the tram and ferry, and only spend about HK$150 a day. Food is actually quite reasonable if you choose your restaurants carefully.

One of the easiest ways to deplete your wallet is to frequent Hong Kong's bars. Prices for beer and cocktails are on a par with those in Tokyo and more expensive than London. A beer usually costs HK$30 to HK$50, and cocktails are slightly more. One way to avoid these prices is to drink at happy hour, which virtually every bar in the territory has between 4pm and 8pm or even later. Happy-hour prices are usually half the normal ones or you get two drinks for the price of one. 'Self-caterers' will find the beer and spirits in the two largest supermarket chains, Wellcome and Park 'N' Shop, good value.

Tipping & Bargaining

Hong Kong is not a particularly tip-conscious place and there is no obligation to tip, say, taxi drivers; just round the fare up. It's almost mandatory to tip hotel staff at least HK$10, and if you make use of the porters at the airport, about HK$2 a suitcase is expected. The porters putting your bags on a push cart at Hong Kong or Kowloon Airport Express station do not expect a gratuity, however. It's all part of the service.

Most hotels and many restaurants add a 10% service charge to the bill. Check for hidden extras before you tip; some mid-range hotels charge HK$3 to HK$5 for each local call when they are actually free throughout the territory and some restaurants consistently get the bill wrong.

Bargaining, on the other hand is *de rigueur* in Hong Kong, except in department stores and clothing chain shops. Some visitors operate on the theory that you can get the goods for half the price originally quoted. Many Hong Kong residents believe that if you can bargain something down that low, then you shouldn't buy from that shop anyway. If the business is that crooked – and many are, particularly in the Tsim Sha Tsui tourist ghetto – it will probably find other ways to cheat you – like selling electronics with missing components or no warranty.

Price tags should be displayed on all goods. If you can't find a price tag you've undoubtedly entered one of those business

establishments with 'flexible' (read rip-off) prices. For more information see the boxed text Tally, Ho Tai Tai! in the China Excursion – Shenzhen chapter.

Taxes & Refunds

There is no sales tax in Hong Kong. The only tax visitors are likely to encounter is the 5% government tax on hotel rates.

POST & COMMUNICATIONS
Post

Hong Kong's postal system, now called Hong Kong Post, is generally excellent; local letters are often delivered the same day they are sent and there's still one delivery on Saturday. The staff at post offices generally speak good English, and mail boxes are clearly marked in English.

Postal Rates Letters sent locally cost HK$1.30/2.10 for up to 30/50g.

For airmail, Hong Kong Post divides the world into two zones. Zone 1 is most of Asia including India but not Japan and Zone 2 is the rest of the world (eg, Americas, Australasia, Europe). The rates for letters and postcards are HK$2.50 for Zone 1 and HK$3.10 for Zone 2 for the first 20g. Up to 30g costs HK$4.60/5.40 for Zone 1/2 and it's HK$1.20/1.30 for each additional 10g. Aerograms are HK$2.30 for both zones. Allow at least three days for delivery of letters, postcards and aerograms to the UK and about five to the USA.

The rates for surface mail are HK$2.30/2.60 for the first 20g in Zone 1/2. Rates for the first 50g are HK$4/4.50 in Zone 1/2. Letters/postcards weighing the same amounts and destined for China, Macau or Taiwan cost HK$1.60/2.70. Small parcels (about HK$60 for 2kg) shipped by surface take six to 10 weeks to reach the USA or UK.

There are coin-operated vending machines outside most post offices, and many 7-Eleven convenience stores have packs of 10 stamps with face values of HK$1.30 (local) and HK$3.10 (Zone 2). The Post Shop attached to the GPO in Central sells all sorts of stationery as well as cardboard boxes of various sizes (open 8am to 6pm Monday to Saturday).

Sending Mail On Hong Kong Island, the General Post Office (GPO; ☎ 2921 2222) is west of the Star Ferry. In Kowloon, the main post office is on the ground floor of Hermes House, 10 Middle Rd, Tsim Sha Tsui. Both are open 8am to 6pm Monday to Saturday and till 2pm on Sunday.

Speedpost Letters and small parcels sent via Hong Kong Post's Speedpost (☎ 2921 2288) should reach almost any destination within four days and are automatically registered. Speedpost rates vary enormously according to destination; every post office has a schedule of fees and a timetable.

Courier Services Private companies offering courier delivery service include DHL (☎ 2765 8111), Federal Express (☎ 2730 3333) and TNT (☎ 2331 2663). All three companies have numerous pick-up points and many MTR stations have DHL branches, including the ones at Central (☎ 2877 2848) next to exit F and at Admiralty (☎ 2529 5778) next to exit E.

Receiving Mail If a letter is addressed c/o Poste Restante, GPO Hong Kong, it will go to the GPO on Hong Kong Island. If you want your letters to go to Kowloon, have them addressed c/o Poste Restante, 10 Middle Rd, Tsim Sha Tsui, Kowloon. Mail is held for two months.

Telephone

Local Calls & Rates All calls made from a private phone in Hong Kong are local calls and therefore free. From public pay phones they cost HK$1 for five minutes. The pay phones accept HK$1, HK$2 and HK$5 coins. Hotels charge between HK$3 and HK$5 for local calls.

International Calls & Rates The country code for Hong Kong is ☎ 852. All landline numbers in the territory have eight digits (except ☎ 800 toll-free numbers) and there are no area codes.

To call someone outside Hong Kong dial ☎ 001, then the country code, area code (you usually drop the initial zero if there is one) and the number. To call Melbourne, where the area code is ☎ 03, in Australia (country code ☎ 61), you would dial ☎ 001-61-3-1234 5678. If you're using someone else's phone and you want to know the cost of the call, dial ☎ 003 instead of ☎ 001 and the operator will call back to report the cost.

Remember that phone rates are cheaper in Hong Kong from 9pm to 8am on weekdays and throughout the weekend. If the phone you're using has the facility, dial ☎ 0060 first then the number at any time. Rates will be cheaper.

International direct dial calls to almost anywhere in the world can be made from most public telephones in Hong Kong, but you'll need a phonecard. These are available as stored-value cards (HK$70 and HK$100) and as Hello Smartcards (five denominations from HK$50 to HK$500). The latter allow you to call from any phone – public or private – on your penny by punching in a PIN code. You can buy them at any PCCW-HKT branch (see the following paragraph) as well as 7-Eleven and Circle K convenience stores, Mannings pharmacies and Wellcome supermarkets.

Hongkong Telecom no longer has a monopoly on phone services; companies now providing services are Hutchison Telecom (☎ 1220), New T&T (☎ 121 121), New World Telecom (☎ 1238) and Hongkong Telecom's latest avatar, PCCW-HKT (☎ 1000, mobile enquires ☎ 1010, international hotline ☎ 10060).

PCCW-HKT (W www.hkt.com), whose alphabet soup-like anagram stands for Pacific Century Cyber Works-Hongkong Telecom, has retail outlets called i.Shops (☎ 2888 0008) throughout the territory, where you can buy phonecards, mobile phones and accessories and make international calls. The most convenient Hong Kong Island branch is on the ground floor of 161–163 Des Voeux Rd Central (open 9am to 7pm daily) and in Kowloon next to the main post office on the ground floor of

Hermes House, 10 Middle Rd, Tsim Sha Tsui (open 10am to 10pm daily). The call centre of the latter is in the basement and opens from 7am to midnight daily.

Another option is to make use of the 'country direct' service, which connects you directly to a local operator in the country dialled. You can then make a reverse-charge or credit-card call with a telephone credit card valid in that country. A few places, including Hong Kong International Airport, some hotels and shopping centres, have home direct phones where you simply press a button labelled USA, UK, Canada etc to be put through to your home operator. If using a pay phone you'll need a coin or phonecard for the initial connection.

Australia	☎ 800 0061
Canada	☎ 800 1100
New Zealand	☎ 800 0064
UK	☎ 800 0044
USA (AT&T)	☎ 800 1111
USA (MCI)	☎ 800 1121
USA (Sprint Express)	☎ 800 1877

Mobile Phones Hong Kong has the world's highest per-capita usage of mobile telephones and pagers and they work *everywhere*, including road tunnels and the MTR underground railway. Any GSM-compatible phone can be used in Hong Kong.

PCCW-HKT i.Shops rent and sell mobile phones, SIM chips and phone accessories. Handsets can be rented for HK$250 a week, rechargeable SIM chips cost HK$200, network rental is HK$200 a week and local calls cost HK$2.20 a minute. The SIM chips and phones are IDD compatible, but there's an extra charge if you need a roaming service to take to Macau or China. A roaming chip costs HK$300. SIM chips are also available at 7-Eleven and Circle K convenience stores, Wellcome supermarkets and Mannings pharmacies.

If you're in Hong Kong for more than two weeks it may become cheaper to buy a phone and network package. But you should shop around: Hong Kong's mobile phone service providers all work on a knife's edge.

Useful Numbers The following are some important telephone numbers and codes. See also Emergencies later in this chapter. Both the telephone directory and the *Yellow Pages* are available online. See Digital resources for their addresses.

International Dialling Code	☎ 001
International Fax Dialling Code	☎ 002
Local Directory Inquiries (English)	☎ 1081
International Directory Inquiries	☎ 10013
International Operator	☎ 10010
International Credit Card Calls	☎ 10011
Reverse-Charge/Collect Calls	☎ 10010
Time & Weather	☎ 18501
Dial-a-Weather Service	☎ 187 8966

eKno Communication Service

Lonely Planet's eKno global communication service provides low-cost international calls – for local calls you're usually better off with a local phonecard. eKno also offers messaging services, email, travel information and an online travel vault, where you can store important documents. You can join online at ⓦ www.ekno.lonelyplanet.com, where you will find the local-access numbers for the 24-hour customer-service centre.

Fax

Per-page fax rates at i.Shops and call centres range from HK$10 (Hong Kong) and HK$30 (rest of Asia) to HK$35 (USA) and HK$45 (Europe). You can receive faxes for about HK$10 a page. Most hotels and even some hostels allow guests to send and receive faxes. The surcharge for sending is usually 10%. If dialling your own fax for an overseas transmission, use the international fax code (☎ 002).

Email & Internet Access

The Internet is very popular in Hong Kong. Most businesses are likely to have a Web site and just about anyone you're likely to do business with can be contacted by email.

Internet Service Providers ISPs often used in Hong Kong include PCCW-HKT's Netvigator (☎ 1833 833, ⓔ premserv@netvigator .com), HKNet (☎ 2110 2288, ⓔ info@ hknet.com) and PSI Net (☎ 2331 8123).

America Online's customer service number is ☎ 2892 2627.

Internet Cafes Many hotels and guest-houses have Internet access. There are also plenty of cybercafes throughout the territory; Pacific Coffee Company outlets, for example, often have terminals. In most places logging on is free if you buy a drink or snack. See Email & Internet Access under Information in the Hong Kong Island and Kowloon chapters for details. Most public libraries in Hong Kong have free Internet access. See the Libraries section in this chapter.

DIGITAL RESOURCES

Lonely Planet's Web site (W www.lonely planet.com) links to Hong Kong sites via SubWWWay and covers travel news at Scoop. Other useful sites include:

bc Magazine (entertainment)
    W www.bcmagazine.net
HKTB Databank
    W www.hktouristinfo.org
Hong Kong Calling (tourism)
    W www.hongkongcalling.com
Hong Kong Information Services Department
    W www.info.gov.hk
Hong Kong Tourism Board (HKTB)
    W www.discoverhongkong.com
South China Morning Post
    W www.scmp.com.hk
Telephone Directories
    W www.hkt.com/directory
Totally Hong Kong (entertainment, lifestyle)
    W www.totallyhk.com

CitySync *Hong Kong* is Lonely Planet's digital city guide for Palm OS hand-held devices. With CitySync you can quickly search, sort and bookmark hundreds of Hong Kong's restaurants, hotels, attractions, clubs and more – all pinpointed on scrollable street maps. Purchase or demo City-Sync *Hong Kong* at W www.citysync.com.

BOOKS

There's no shortage of books dealing with things Hong Kong, but the mark up on them in local bookshops can be high. See what you can pick up at home before you travel.

For a selection of the best outlets, see Bookshops in the Information section of the Hong Kong Island and Kowloon chapters.

Most books are published in different editions by different publishers in different countries. Fortunately, bookshops and libraries search by title or author, so are best placed to advise you on the availability of the following titles.

Lonely Planet

Lonely Planet's *China* has a chapter dealing with the Hong Kong SAR. *Hong Kong Condensed* is a pocket guide for those on shorter visits. The *Cantonese phrasebook* is a complete guide to *gwóng dùng wá*. *World Food: Hong Kong* will take you on a culinary tour of the territory.

Guidebooks

Anyone who wants a complete assessment of the territory's best restaurants in all price categories should pick up a copy of the annual *HK Magazine Restaurant Guide*, which covers some 500 eateries, including some in Macau and Shenzhen. It appears free as an insert in the magazine in February and costs HK$50 subsequently. To order your own copy call *HK Magazine's* editorial office (☎ 2850 5065, fax 2543 1880, e asiacity@asia-city.com.hk).

Hong Kong's Best Restaurants, with 150 rather tame reviews of top-end restaurants, is published annually by Hong Kong Tatler Magazine. *bc Magazine: The Guide* has more critical reviews of some 350 Hong Kong restaurants in all price categories.

A welcome new addition to Hong Kong's bookshelf is *Ruins of War: A Guide to Hong Kong's Battlefields and Wartime Sites* by Ko Tim Keung and Jason Wordie.

Anyone anticipating a move to Hong Kong might pick up a copy of Fiona Campbell's *Setting up in Hong Kong*, which will help you do just that.

Admittedly somewhat out of date, the reprinted *Hong Kong Guide, 1893* from Oxford University Press is entertaining reading.

Walking & Nature Guides *Hong Kong's Country Parks* by Stella Thrower is an excellent introduction to walking in the countryside. Updated annually, *Hong Kong Pathfinder* by Martin Williams features some two dozen day walks in Hong Kong's hinterland. *Exploring Hong Kong's Countryside: A Visitor's Companion* by Edward Stokes is well written and illustrated and the maps are good. *Magic Walks*, good for easy hiking in the New Territories and outlying islands, is written by Kaarlo Schepel, the patriarch of Hong Kong walkers.

A walking guide with a twist is *Discovering Hong Kong's Cultural Heritage* by Patricia Lim, with 12 walks through traditional areas of the New Territories. Two lovely pictorials dealing with the countryside are *Hong Kong's Wild Places: An Environmental Exploration* by Edward Stokes and *The MacLehose Trail* by Tim Nutt, Chris Bale and Tao Ho.

The *Coastal Guides* series, published by the Friends of the Earth, include guidemaps (HK$55 each) to Sai Kung as well as Lamma, Lantau and Hong Kong Island.

The Urban Council, now disbanded, no longer publishes its 'fill-in-the-blank' nature identification guides, with titles ranging from *Hong Kong Insects* and *Hong Kong Mosquitoes* to *Hong Kong Shrubs* and *Hong Kong Poisonous Plants*, but you may find some old stock at the Government Publications Office in Admiralty (see Bookshops under Information in the Hong Kong Island chapter for details).

The Birds of Hong Kong and South China by Clive Viney, Karen Phillips and Lam Chiu Ying is the definitive guide with which to identify the territory's feathered creatures.

Travel

Formasia's *Old Hong Kong*, a large pictorial of old photographs, comes in three volumes: Volume I covers the period from 1860 to 1900; Volume II from 1901 to 1945; and Volume III from 1950 to 1997.

An Eye on Hong Kong is a portfolio of contemporary photographs by Keith Mac-Gregor. If you like your views from on high, pick up a copy of *Over Hong Kong* by David Dodwell and Kaysan Bartlett.

History & Politics

A History of Hong Kong by GB Endacott, first published in 1958, is a classic that covers everything you'd ever want to know about Hong Kong's past. It's pretty dull going, though. If you like pictures with your history, *The Hong Kong Story* by Caroline Courtauld and May Holdsworth and *The Illustrated History of Hong Kong* by Nigel Cameron are good choices.

One of the best histories of the territory is *Hong Kong: Epilogue to an Empire* by Jan Morris, which moves effortlessly between past and present as it explains what made Hong Kong so unique among the colonies of the British empire.

Hong Kong Illustrated: Views & News 1840–1890, compiled by John Warner, is a large sketchbook dealing with the territory's early history. Maurice Collis' *Foreign Mud* tells the sordid story of the Opium Wars that Britain fought with China. *The Taipans: Hong Kong's Merchant Princes* by Colin N Crisswell deals with the European traders and 'factors' who profited from those wars.

The Last Governor by Jonathan Dimbleby is a well-written account of Chris Patten's tenure as governor of Hong Kong immediately before the 1997 handover. Stephen Vines' excellent *Hong Kong: China's New Colony* examines the territory after its change of landlords.

The government yearbook, entitled *Hong Kong 2000, Hong Kong 2001* etc, and published by the Hong Kong Information Services Department, is a goldmine of information about the government, politics, economy, history, arts and just about any other topic relevant to Hong Kong. It usually appears in June or July of the following year.

General

Culture Shock! Hong Kong: A Guide to Customs and Etiquette by Betty Wei and Elizabeth Li is an excellent introduction to Hong Kong culture and modus operandi. Oxford University Press's Images of Asia series includes several thin volumes on Hong Kong topics. Among them are *Temples of the Empress of Heaven*, *Chinese New Year* and *The Cheongsam*.

Hong Kong: Somewhere between Heaven and Earth, edited by Barbara-Sue White, is an anthology of writings on Hong Kong, both old and new. *Hong Kong Collage* is a collection of contemporary stories and other writings edited by Martha PY Cheung.

Arguably the most famous (if hardly the best) novel set in Hong Kong is *The World of Suzie Wong* by Richard Mason, the unlikely story of a Wan Chai prostitute with a heart of gold published in 1957.

The only real English-language novelist that Hong Kong has produced (to date) was the late Austin Coates. His charming *Myself a Mandarin* was based on his work as a special magistrate dealing in traditional Chinese law in the New Territories of the 1950s. *The Road* is his riveting tale of the government's attempt to build a highway across Great Island (which sounds suspiciously like Lantau), and the effect it has on the government, the builders and the islanders.

An Insular Possession by Timothy Mo is a novel set in pre-colonial Hong Kong. *Tai-Pan* by James Clavell, almost as thick as the *Yellow Pages*, is a rather unrealistic tale of Western traders in Hong Kong's early days, but it's an easy read. The sequel to *Tai-Pan*, also set in Hong Kong, is another epic called *Noble House* about a fictitious *hong*, or major trading house. A favourite and a rocking good read is the Robert Elegant novel *Dynasty*, which describes the life and times of a young Englishwoman who marries into a family not unlike the powerful Ho Tungs.

Spy-thriller writer John Le Carré's *The Honourable Schoolboy* is a story of espionage and intrigue set in the Hong Kong of the early 1970s. *Triad* by Derek Lambert is a violent fictionalised account of the Chinese underworld of the territory.

The private lives of Hong Kong Chinese families are captured in *Chinese Walls* by Sussy Chako and *The Monkey King* by Timothy Mo. *Kowloon Tong* by Paul Theroux is an incredibly annoying novel about an expatriate family's insecurities on the eve of the handover.

Three books dealing with the outlying islands and written by long-term (or one-time) residents are worth having a flip through.

Getting to Lamma by Jane Alexander is a fictional adventure that ends up on Lamma Island. A crime novel with a delightful title (if little else) is *The Cheung Chau Dog Fanciers' Society* by Alan B Pierce. *Hong Kong Belongers* by Simon Barnes is the tortuous and mostly unbelievable story of a young expat journalist who lives on a fictitious island much like Lamma.

FILMS

Hong Kong, which actively promotes itself as a location for films and publishes, through the Film Services Office (FSO; ☎ 2594 5758, Ⓦ www.fso-tela.gov.hk), a chunky and useful *Guide to Filming in Hong Kong* each year, has been the setting of many foreign-made films (memorable or otherwise), including: *Love is a Many-Splendored Thing* (1955), starring William Holden and Jennifer Jones as his Eurasian doctor paramour, with great shots on and from Victoria Peak; *The World of Suzie Wong* (1960), with Holden again and Nancy Kwan as the pouting Wan Chai bar girl; *Lord Jim* (1965), parts of which were also shot at Angkor Wat, starring Peter O'Toole; *Enter the Dragon* (1973), Bruce Lee's first foreign-made kung fu vehicle; *The Man with the Golden Gun* (1974), with Roger Moore as James Bond and filmed partly at Tsim Sha Tsui's Bottoms Up nightclub (see Entertainment in the Kowloon chapter); *Year of the Dragon* (1985), with Micky Rourke; and *Tai-Pan* (1986), the less-than-successful film version of James Clavell's doorstop novel (don't miss the bogus typhoon footage).

More recent foreign films shot partly or in full here include *Double Impact* (1991), *Mortal Kombat* (1995) and *Rush Hour* (1998).

NEWSPAPERS & MAGAZINES

Some 60 daily newspapers and more than 700 periodicals are published in the well-read territory of Hong Kong. Naturally, the vast majority of the publications are in Cantonese, with the two largest-selling dailies being the *Oriental Daily News* and the government's gadfly, the *Apple Daily*.

There are two local English-language newspapers (both HK$7): The daily *South*

China Morning Post (W www.scmp.com), which generally tows the government line and is known as the 'Pro China Morning Post', has the larger circulation and is read by more Hong Kong Chinese than expatriates. Its classified advertisement sales make it the world's most profitable newspaper. The tabloid *Hong Kong iMail* (W www .hk-imail.com.hk), which has replaced the defunct *Hong Kong Standard* and is published Monday to Saturday, is generally more rigorous in its local reporting. The Beijing mouthpiece *China Daily* prints a Hong Kong edition.

Asian editions of *USA Today* and the *International Herald Tribune*, as well as the *Asian Wall Street Journal,* are printed in Hong Kong.

Hong Kong also has its share of English-language news magazines, including the *Far Eastern Economic Review, Asiaweek* and a slew of Asian-focused business magazines. *Time, Newsweek* and the *Economist* are all available in the current edition. *Hong Kong Tatler* and *Home Journal* are for those interested in local lifestyle articles.

RADIO & TV
Radio Television Hong Kong (RTHK) is a government-funded but editorially independent broadcasting system.

Radio
The most popular English-language radio stations are RTHK Radio 3 (567 & 1584 kHz AM, 97.9 & 106.8 MHz FM); RTHK Radio 4 (classical music; 97.6 to 98.9 MHz FM); RTHK Radio 6 (BBC World Service relay; 675 kHz AM); Commercial Radio (864 kHz AM); Metro Plus (1044 kHz AM); HMV (864 kHz AM); Hit Radio (99.7 MHz FM); FM Select (104 MHz FM); and Quote AM (alternative and dance music; 864 kHz AM). The *South China Morning Post* publishes a daily guide to radio programs.

TV
Hong Kong's terrestrial TV stations are run by two companies, Television Broadcasts (TVB) and Asia Television (ATV). Each company operates one Cantonese-language channel and one English one (TVB Pearl and ATV World). The program schedule is listed daily in the *South China Morning Post* and in a weekly Sunday supplement. There's also the *Entertainment Weekly* (HK$18).

There are also two cable channels (Cable TV and iTV) and four satellite stations.

VIDEO SYSTEMS
Like most of Europe and Australasia, Hong Kong uses the PAL system, which is incompatible with the American and Japanese NTSC system and the French SECAM system.

PHOTOGRAPHY & VIDEO
Film & Equipment
Almost everything you could possibly need in the way of photographic accessories is available in Hong Kong. Stanley St on Hong Kong Island is the place to look for reputable camera stores.

Photo developing is very cheap; to develop a roll of 36 exposures and have them printed costs HK$40 to HK$50 for size 3R and HK$50 to HK$60 for size 4R. Any photo shop will take four passport-size photos for about HK$30.

Photographing People
Hong Kong Chinese people are used to camera-clicking tourists and won't normally throw a fit if you take their photo. Many older Chinese people, however, strongly object to having their picture taken, so be considerate.

Airport Security
You will have to put your camera and film through the X-ray machine at Hong Kong International Airport. The machines are film-safe for most kinds of film. Professional photographers using ultra-sensitive film (eg, ASA 1000) do need to worry about this, especially if the film is repeatedly exposed. One way to combat the problem is to put the film(s) in a protective lead-lined bag, though it's probably safer and easier to have the film hand-inspected if possible.

TIME

Hong Kong Standard Time is eight hours ahead of GMT/UTC. Hong Kong does not have daylight-saving time. When it's noon in Hong Kong it's 11pm the day before in New York; 8pm the day before in Los Angeles; 4am in London; noon in Singapore, Manila and Perth; and 2pm in Melbourne and Sydney.

ELECTRICITY
Voltages & Cycles

The standard is 220V, 50 Hz (cycles per second) AC. Electrical shops in Hong Kong sell pocket-sized transformers that step down the electricity to the 110V used in the USA and Canada, however, most mini-transformers are only rated for 50W. This is sufficient for an electric razor or laptop computer but not for those electric heater coils that some travellers carry to make tea and coffee. It's easier just to buy another one.

Plugs & Sockets

Hong Kong's plug and socket system can be a bit confusing for the uninitiated. The vast majority of electric outlets are designed to accommodate the British three square pins but some take three round prongs and others just two pins. Not surprisingly, inexpensive plug adaptors are widely available in Hong Kong, even in supermarkets.

WEIGHTS & MEASURES

Although the international metric system is in official use in Hong Kong, traditional Chinese weights and measures are still common. At local markets, meat, fish and produce are sold by the *leung*, equivalent to 37.8g, and the *gan* (catty), which is about 600g. There are 16 leung to the gan. Gold and silver is sold by the *tael*, which is exactly the same as a leung.

LAUNDRY

Laundries are easy to find everywhere in Hong Kong – hey, this is China – though they're never self-service. Most hotels, guesthouses and even hostels have a laundry service. Prices at laundries are normally around HK$28 for the first 3kg, and then HK$7 for each additional kilogram.

Drycleaners are easy to spot and some laundries offer the service as well. Drycleaning a shirt costs around HK$15, a skirt HK$30 and trousers HK$35 to HK$40. One of the better chains is Martinizing, with a branch (☎ 2525 3089) at 7 Glenealy in Central. The Valet Shop in the basement of the Furama Hotel (☎ 2525 5111), 1 Connaught Rd Central, is also reliable.

TOILETS

Hong Kong has never had as many public toilets as other world-class cities but that seems to be changing, with some new ones being built and old ones reopened. They are always free.

There are public toilets in the Central Market on Hong Kong Island; in the small sitting-out area linking Lan Kwai Fong and Wellington St; past the turnstiles of the Star Ferry; and most parks. The ferries to the outlying islands are all equipped with toilets. If desperate, pop into a big hotel. Staff generally won't stop you.

Equip yourself with tissues; public toilets in Hong Kong are inevitably out of toilet paper.

LEFT LUGGAGE

There are left-luggage lockers in major KCR train stations, including the terminus at Hung Hom, and the Macau and China ferry piers on Hong Kong Island and in Tsim Sha Tsui. The Hong Kong Airport Express station has a left-luggage office open from 6am to 1am daily, and there are counters on levels 5, 6, 7 and 8 at the airport on Chek Lap Kok.

Generally the machines do not use keys but spit a numbered chit or ticket when you deposit your money and close the door. You have to punch in this number when you retrieve your bag(s) so keep it somewhere safe or write the number down elsewhere. Some lockers have a maximum storage time of three days, so read the instructions carefully.

If you're going to visit Macau or the mainland and will be returning to Hong Kong, most hotels and even some budget hostels have left-luggage rooms and will let you leave your gear behind, even if you've already checked out and won't be staying on your return. There is usually a charge for this service; be sure to inquire first to avoid any unpleasant surprises when you come back to pick up the bag.

HEALTH

In general, health conditions in Hong Kong are good. The government insists that Hong Kong's tap water is perfectly safe to drink and does not need to be boiled. However, most local Chinese boil it anyway, more out of habit than necessity. Bottled water is widely available.

The most serious health crisis to rock Hong Kong in decades was the outbreak of avian flu not long after the handover in 1997, which killed six people and led to the slaughtering of the territory's entire chicken population. It reappeared in May 2001 but no deaths were reported. For information, see the boxed text below.

Immunisations & Precautions

There are no specific vaccination requirements for Hong Kong.

Pack or buy plenty of sun block in summer, especially if travelling by ferry or going on boating trips: sunlight reflected on water can burn you more quickly and intensively.

Mosquito repellent is mandatory in the countryside, particularly during the rainy season.

Take the usual precautions when it comes to sex; condoms are available in convenience stores, pharmacies and supermarkets.

Medical Services

Medical care is generally of a high standard in Hong Kong, though public hospital staff are grossly underpaid and facilities stretched. Attendance at out-patient clinics is on a first-come, first-served basis and costs HK$195 per visit. Private hospital treatment is expensive, but not exorbitant as in the USA and you'll have less of a wait for treatment.

For general hospital inquiries call ☎ 2300 6555. The Hong Kong Medical Association (HKMA) has a MediLink hotline (☎ 90000 223 322) with recorded information on medical access during holiday periods.

One for the Birds

The killer avian flu that caught Hong Kong unaware in the salad days of the SAR in mid-1997 was a perfect Darwinian example of a virus' ability to mutate. Previously the bane solely of chickens and certain other feathered creatures, this rather nasty influenza known as H5N1 managed to cross the species gulf and by August of that year, 16 people were infected and another six had died. Containment at source was the strategy used to wipe the virus from the territory, and some 1.4 million chickens were put down at the end of the year. The public image of surgical slaughter was sadly compromised by the sight of dogs and cats dragging dead chickens from mounds of plastic bags, however.

Lessons had been learned, though, and when the influenza struck again in May 2001, killing more than 1000 chickens in seven markets, the government immediately ordered the slaughter of 1.2 million chickens and other poultry and banned the import of live birds from the mainland. The quick response seemed to do the trick, and there were no cases of it having been transmitted to humans.

The good news is that the virus is a very rare disease, is not an epidemic and cannot (as yet) be transmitted from human to human. Avian flu can only be contracted over very small distances and can be effectively destroyed by cooking poultry at temperatures of over 72°C. Those most at risk are employees of the chicken rearing and slaughter industries that deal with live poultry, so eating a chicken burger at McDonald's was never a high-risk activity. Even so, many Hong Kong people gave chicken meat a wide berth until the official all clear in early March 1998.

Public and private hospitals with 24- hour accident and emergency departments include:

Hong Kong Island
Hong Kong Central (private; ☎ 2522 3141) 1B Lower Albert Rd, Central
Matilda & War Memorial (private; ☎ 2849 0700, 24-hour help line ☎ 2849 0123) 41 Mt Kellett Rd, The Peak
Queen Mary (☎ 2855 3838) 102 Pok Fu Lam Rd, Pok Fu Lam

Kowloon
Baptist (private; ☎ 2339 8888) 222 Waterloo Rd, Kowloon Tong
Princess Margaret (☎ 2990 1111) Lai King Hill Rd, Lai Chi Kok
Queen Elizabeth (☎ 2958 8888) 30 Gascoigne Rd, Yau Ma Tei

New Territories
Prince of Wales (☎ 2632 2211) 30–32 Ngan Shing St, Sha Tin

Dental Services
Private dental clinics can be found throughout Hong Kong; some hospitals also offer emergency dental services. To find a dentist nearby, ask your hotel or call the Dental Council (☎ 2873 5862).

Pharmacies
Mannings and Watson's are the two main pharmacy chains in Hong Kong, with branches in every shopping centre and dozens of high street shops. Most are open until 10pm. The hospitals listed previously have dispensing chemists on duty 24 hours.

Traditional Medicine
Traditional Chinese medicine is extremely popular in Hong Kong, both as a preventative and a cure. Eu Yan Sang (☎ 2544 3870), 152–156 Queen's Rd Central, is probably the most famous practice in town and the doctors speak good English. The store is also an interesting place to browse as many of the healing ingredients are displayed and explained.

HIV/AIDS Organisations
Numerous government and volunteer groups provide services for people with HIV or AIDS, including:

AIDS Concern Helpline (☎ 2898 4422)
HIV Information & Drop-In Centre (☎ 2523 0531) St John's Cathedral, 4–8 Garden Rd, Central (enter from Battery Path)
Hong Kong AIDS Foundation (☎ 2513 0513, inquiries ☎ 2560 8528, ⓔ hkaf@asiaonline.net) 5th floor, Shau Kei Wan Jockey Club Clinics, 8 Chai Wan Rd, Shau Kei Wan
Hong Kong Department of Health AIDS Unit (24-hour hotline ☎ 2780 2211)

WOMEN TRAVELLERS
Attitudes Towards Women
Respect for women is deeply ingrained in Chinese culture. Despite the Confucianist principle of the superiority of men, women in Chinese society often call the shots and wield a tremendous amount of influence at home, in business and in politics. In general, there is a strong sense of balance between men and women in Hong Kong.

Safety Precautions
Hong Kong is a safe city for women although common-sense caution should be observed, especially at night. Few women – visitors or residents – complain of bad treatment, intimidation or aggression. Having said that, some Chinese men regard Western women as 'easy' and have made passes at foreigners even in public places. 'Boob bashing' – being elbowed by a male passerby in the chest area – was once widespread in Hong Kong but seems to have died out.

If you are sexually assaulted call the Hong Kong Rape Hotline (☎ 2572 2222).

Women's Organisations
Among the most important and/or active women's organisations are:

Hong Kong Council of Women (☎ 2386 6255) 4 Jordan Rd, Yau Ma Tei, Kowloon
Hong Kong Federation of Women (☎ 2833 6518, fax 2833 6909) Flat B, 10th floor, Jonsim Place, 228 Queen's Rd East, Wan Chai
International Women's League (☎ 2782 2207, fax 2782 2839) 2nd floor, 28 Ferry St, Jordan, Kowloon

[continued on page 74]

Chinese Food

Title Page: The presentation of food is an art in Hong Kong, with even a simple dim sum snack getting the design treatment.
(Photograph by Oliver Strewe)

Clockwise from top left: Traditional way of cooking and serving dim sum; winter melon soup; three bowls of noodles with vegetables and meat; water spinach with chili; yin yang sweet soup

I f the pursuit of wealth is the engine that drives Hong Kong, its fuel is food. Noodles are slurped, succulent seafood savoured, dishes at banquets praised for their presentation, freshness and texture as well as taste, and many chefs enjoy celebrity status. Food – and the business of eating it – is taken *very* seriously in Hong Kong.

Chinese food – be it Cantonese, Chiu Chow, northern Chinese, Shanghainese or Sichuan – is not the only cuisine. The territory also has some of the world's top international eateries, ranging from trendy Italian to basic Thai. But 'Hong Kong food' really means Chinese food – in all its incarnations.

Depending on the district, it can be especially hard to find a good-quality, inexpensive restaurant that has a menu in English. If you don't read or speak Cantonese, the problem can be lessened by eating *dim sum*. The dishes are usually wheeled around on trolleys, so it's just a matter of pointing at what catches your eye. You can even point at what your neighbour is eating – people won't be offended.

Chinese are fond of giving dishes fanciful names. You'll almost certainly need help with things like 'Buddha jumped over the fence', 'ants climbing trees' and 'coral and jade'. Be warned – dishes prefaced with 'white flower' may contain tripe.

The best source for exploring the culinary world of Hong Kong is the annual *HK Magazine Restaurant Guide* (HK$50), which reviews 500 eateries. For other food guides, see Books in the Hong Kong Facts for the Visitor chapter.

Table Etiquette

The Chinese don't expect foreigners to understand all of their dining customs. But there are a few things that are useful to know.

Chinese meals are social and very noisy events. Typically, a group of people sit at a round table and order dishes from which everyone partakes; ordering a dish just for yourself would be unthinkable. It's not unusual for one person at the table to order on everyone's behalf.

If you are attending a formal affair or eating at someone's home, it's best to wait for some signal from the host before digging in. You will most likely be invited to take the first taste. Often your host will serve it to you, placing a piece of meat, chicken or fish in your bowl. If a whole fish is served, you might be offered the head, the cheeks of which are considered to be the tastiest part. It's alright to decline; someone else will gladly devour the delicacy.

The Chinese think nothing of sticking their chopsticks into a communal dish. Nicer restaurants will provide separate serving chopsticks or even spoons; use them if they do so.

Never, ever, flip a fish over to reach the flesh on the bottom. The next fishing boat you pass will capsize. Just use your chopsticks to break off pieces through the bones.

Everyone gets an individual bowl of rice or a small soup bowl. It's quite acceptable to hold the bowl close to your lips and shovel the contents

All illustrations in this Section by Enjarn Lin

into your mouth with chopsticks. An alternative is to hold a spoon in one hand and use the chopsticks to push the food onto the spoon. Then use the spoon as you normally would.

If the food contains bones, just put them out on the tablecloth or into a separate bowl. Restaurants are prepared – the staff change the tablecloth after each customer leaves.

Chinese make use of toothpicks after a meal and even between courses. Cover your mouth with one hand while using the toothpick with the other.

Beer, soft drinks or even brandy *may* be served with the meal; tea most definitely will. When your waiter or host pours your tea, thank them by tapping your middle and index fingers lightly on the table. When your teapot needs a refill, signal this by taking the lid off the pot.

Toasts in Hong Kong are usually limited to *'yam seng'* (roughly, 'down the hatch'). Raising your tea or water glass in a toast is not very respectful so unless you have deep-rooted convictions against alcohol, it's best to drink at least a mouthful.

Rice

Rice is an inseparable part of virtually every Chinese meal. The Chinese don't ask: 'Have you had your dinner/lunch yet?', but: 'Have you eaten rice yet?' Rice comes in lots of different preparations – as a porridge called *juk* ('congee' in English) served with savouries at breakfast, or fried with tiny shrimps, pork or vegetables and eaten at lunch or as a snack. But plain steamed white rice – fragrant yet neutral – is what you should order at dinner.

Main Dishes

The Cantonese love fresh, simply prepared seafood and fish. Pork, chicken, duck and beef are also relished and served braised, steamed, or fried. It's not unusual for dishes to be served with tiny saucers filled with various sauces, with soy sauce *(see yau)*, hot mustard *(baat gai)* and chilli sauce *(laat jiu jeung)* the most common ones.

The small bottles on the table usually contain soy sauce and vinegar. The vinegar may be a dark colour, easily confused with soy sauce, so taste some before pouring. Sauces aren't dumped on food – instead the food is dipped into a separate dish. Staff will usually let you know which sauce goes with which dish.

Regional Variations

China can be divided into many geographical areas, and each area has a distinct style of cooking. Northern China, for example, is suited to growing wheat, so noodles, dumplings and other gluten-based preparations are common. In the south, where the climate is warm and wet, rice is the staple. The Sichuan area, where spices grow well, is famous for its fiery hot dishes. Coastal areas, needless to say, excel at seafood preparations.

Tradition and culture play a part as well. The Cantonese, adventurous when it comes to food, are known for their willingness to eat virtually anything. Consequently, animals with physical and/or sexual prowess (real or imagined) are widely sought after; the Chinese are firm believers in the adage: 'You are what you eat'.

A difference between Chinese food in Hong Kong and on the mainland is that local dishes tend to be more refined, influenced by international tastes and made with higher-quality ingredients. To some, this means less flavourful food.

Cantonese Cuisine
Originating in Guangdong province, Cantonese food is by far the most popular cuisine in Hong Kong. The flavours are more subtle than other Chinese cooking styles, and the sauces are rarely strong.

The Cantonese are almost religious about the importance of fresh ingredients. It is common to see tanks in seafood restaurants full of finned and shelled creatures.

The increase in foreign travel by local people means there's more experimentation these days. Macadamia nuts find their way into scallop dishes, XO brandy is the base for a sauce served with beef and you're just as likely to find sautéed cod slices with pine seeds and fresh fruit on a menu as you are traditional steamed grouper.

Seasonal foods still play a big role in what's on offer: hotpots of pork innards in winter, dried scallops with sea moss at Chinese New Year and 'winter' melon soup in August.

Expensive dishes – some of which are truly tasty, others that appeal more for their 'face' value – include abalone, shark's fin and bird's nest. Pigeon is a Cantonese speciality, served in various ways but most commonly roasted.

A unique Cantonese taste sensation is 1000-year-old eggs (also known as 100-year-old eggs), which are actually just a month or two old. They are duck eggs soaked in a lime solution, which turns the egg white-green and the yolk a greenish-black. These are usually served as a starter or condiment. Another speciality is salted duck eggs. The eggs are soaked in a saline solution to crystallise the yolk and impart a lovely flavour to the interior. Salted duck eggs make a tasty, though filling, breakfast.

Favourite Cantonese dishes include:

houhyau choisam	蠔油菜心	choisum, a green Chinese vegetable (rape) with oyster sauce
chìngcháu gailán	清炒芥蘭	stir-fried Chinese broccoli

haaihyuhk pah dāumiu	蟹肉扒豆苗	sautéed pea shoots with crab meat
chìngjìng sēkbànyue	清蒸石斑魚	steamed grouper (or garoupa) with soy sauce
geungchung guhkhaaih	薑蔥焗蟹	baked crab with ginger and spring onions
baakcheukha	白灼蝦	poached fresh prawns served with dipping sauces
sījìu yauyu	豉椒鱿魚	stir-fried cuttlefish with black bean and chilli sauce
sàilanfàdaijí	清炒芥蘭	stir-fried broccoli with scallops
jìuyim paigwat	椒鹽排骨	deep-fried spareribs served with coarse salt and pepper
houhyau ngauyuk	蠔油牛肉	stir-fried sliced beef with oyster sauce
sàng sìu gap	紅燒鴿	roast pigeon
sìnning jìnyüengài	西檸煎軟雞	lemon chicken
haaiyuhk sukmei gang	蟹肉粟米羹	crab and sweet corn soup
she gang	蛇羹	snake soup

Dim Sum A uniquely Cantonese 'meal', dim sum is eaten as breakfast, brunch or lunch. The term literally means 'to touch the heart', but 'snack' is more accurate. The act of eating dim sum is usually referred to as *yum cha*, or 'to drink tea', as tea is always served in copious amounts. The HKTB distributes a useful pamphlet called *Hong Kong Snacks Guide*, with recommended places to try dim sum.

Dim sum restaurants are normally brightly lit and very large and noisy. Eating dim sum is a social occasion and something best done in a group. The delicacies are normally steamed in small bamboo baskets. Typically, each basket contains three or four identical pieces; you pay by the number of baskets you order. You don't need a menu. Just stop the waiter and take a basket from the cart being wheeled  around. It will be marked down on a bill left on the table. Each pushcart has a different selection, so take your time and order as they come – it's said that there are about 1000 dim sum dishes.

Popular dim sum dishes are:

chà sìu bàu	叉燒包	steamed barbecued pork buns
hà gáu	蝦餃	steamed shrimp dumplings
sìu mai	燒買	steamed pork and shrimp dumplings
chéung fán	腸粉	steamed rice-flour rolls with shrimp, beef or pork
chìng cháu sichoi	清炒時菜	fried green vegetable of the day
chùn gúen	春卷	fried spring rolls

fán gwó	粉果	steamed dumplings with shrimp and bamboo shoots
fūng jáu	鳳爪	fried chicken's feet
gòn sìu yìmīn	乾燒伊麵	dry-fried noodles
ho yīp fān	荷葉飯	rice wrapped in lotus leaf
pai gwàt	排骨	braised spare ribs (usually bite-sized with black beans)
sàn jùk ngau yōk	山竹牛肉	steamed minced beef balls
fu pei gun	腐皮卷	crispy beancurd rolls

Noodles & Congee Both are hallmarks of Hong Kong's indigenous fast food. The telltale sign of these local specialities is a restaurant window fogged from the steam of bubbling vats. You'll also see *chà sìu* (roast pork) and *chà sìu ngap* (roast duck) hanging from hooks in windows, the fat dripping into pans below.

Congee (rice porridge) is usually eaten at breakfast, but can also make a filling lunch. Stay clear of the pig's intestines and order shredded chicken. Noodles come in a variety of colours, textures and ways of being cooked.

Typical dishes at noodle shops include:

chà sìu fan	叉燒飯	barbecued pork with rice
hainan gai	海南雞飯	Hainan chicken (steamed chicken served with chicken-flavoured rice)
singjau chaaumih	星洲炒飯	Singapore noodles (rice noodles stir-fried with curry powder)
yangchow chaaufan	揚州炒飯	fried rice
gai juk	雞粥	chicken congee
yupin juk	魚片粥	congee with sliced fish
wonton min	雲吞麵	wonton noodle soup
sin hawonton	鮮蝦雲吞	wonton made with prawns
yudan	魚蛋	fish balls

Chiu Chow Cuisine Chiu Chow (Chaozhou in Mandarin) food comes from the region around Shantou (Swatow) in north-east Guangdong province. Sauces can be on the sweet side and often use orange, tangerine or sweet bean as flavouring agents. Chiu Chow specialities include shark's fin and bird's nest soups and deep-fried prawn and crabmeat balls served with a honey sauce. Duck and goose, cooked in an aromatic sauce that is used again and again and known as *lo sui*, or 'old water', are also popular. Chiu Chow chefs are known for their skill in carving raw vegetables into wonderful floral designs.

Chiu Chow dishes to try include:

dāi yuechi tòng	魚翅湯	shark's fin soup
tong jìng hai	凍蒸蟹	cold steamed crab

tim suen hung xiu ha (hai) kau	甜酸紅燒蝦	prawn (crab) balls with sweet, sticky dipping sauce
seklau gai	石榴雞	steamed egg-white pouches filled with minced chicken
bàkgù sàilanfà	北菰西蘭花	stewed broccoli with black mushrooms
chui jau lou sui ngoh	潮州鹵水鴨	goose
chìngjìu ngauyōksì	青椒牛肉	fried shredded beef with green pepper
chin jui gai	川椒雞	diced chicken fried in a light sauce
fòngyue gailán	鳳魚芥蘭	fried kale with dried fish
jang hèungngap	炸香鴨	deep-fried spiced duck
bìngfà gòngyin	冰花宮燕	cold sweet bird's nest soup (dessert)

Northern Chinese Cuisine Cuisine from Beijing and the north-central provinces hails from the wheat basket in the cold north of China. Steamed bread, dumplings and noodles figure more prominently than rice. Lamb, seldom seen in the south, appears on menus thanks to the region's nomadic and Muslim populations.

The most famous speciality of northern Chinese cuisine is Peking duck, served with pancakes, plum sauce and shreds of spring onion. Another northern favourite is Mongolian hotpot, which is an assortment of meats or fish and vegetables cooked in a burner on the table. Hotpot is usually eaten during winter.

Beggar's chicken, another popular dish, was supposedly created by a pauper who stole a chook but had no pot to cook it in. Instead, he plucked it, covered it with clay and put it on the fire. Nowadays, the bird is stuffed with mushrooms, pickled Chinese cabbage, herbs and onions, then wrapped in lotus leaves, sealed in clay and baked all day in hot ashes.

Favourite dishes from the north are:

bàkgìng tinngap	北京填鴨	Peking duck
foogwai gài	富貴雞	beggar's chicken
bàkgìng fùngcháu làimīn	北京拉麵	noodles fried with shredded pork and bean sprouts
chòngyau béng	蔥油餅	pan-fried spring onion cakes
bàkgùpa jùnbākchoi	北菰扒津白菜	Tianjin cabbage and black mushrooms
gòncháu ngauyōksì	乾炒牛肉絲	dried shredded beef with chilli sauce
san yeung yug	涮羊肉	Mongolian hotpot
sànsìn tòng	三鮮湯	clear soup with chicken, prawn and abalone
congbao yangyok	蔥爆羊肉	sliced lamb with onions on a sizzling platter

Shanghainese Cuisine The cuisine of the Shanghai area contains more oil and is generally richer and somewhat sweeter than other Chinese cuisines. Seafood, preserved vegetables, pickles and salted meats are widely used, and there are lots of dumplings on the menu. Another speciality are the dishes of cold meats served with various sauces. There are a large number of Shanghai restaurants in Hong Kong.

The following are a few dishes to get you started:

fótúi síuchoi	火腿紹菜	Shanghai cabbage with ham
nghèung ngauyōk	五香牛肉	cold spiced beef
sungsúe wongyue	松鼠黃魚	sweet-and-sour yellow croaker fish
chung pei hai	重皮蟹	hairy crabs (an autumn dish)
hongsìu ju sau	紅燒豬手	richly simmered pigs knuckle
ja jígài	炸子雞	deep-fried chicken
jui gà	醉雞	'drunken chicken' (chicken marinated in cold rice wine)
sēunghói chòcháu	上海炒伊麵	fried Shanghai-style (thick) noodles with pork and cabbage
sinyōk siulong bàu	鮮肉小龍包	steamed minced pork dumplings
lungjín hajen	龍井蝦仁	shrimps with 'dragon-well' tea leaves

Sichuan Cuisine China's west-central provinces of Sichuan and Hunan are known for their fiery food, though in reality the heat is nothing compared with, say, Thai food. Chillies are widely used, along with aniseed, coriander, fennel seed, garlic and peppercorns. Dishes are simmered to give the chilli peppers time to work into the food. Not all dishes (eg, camphor smoked duck) are hot. These provinces are a long distance from the coast, so pork, chicken and beef – and not seafood – are the staples.

Some favourites include:

sùenlā tòng	酸辣湯	hot-and-sour soup with shredded meat (and sometimes congealed pig's blood)
dan dan mīn	擔擔麵	noodles in savoury sauce
chuipei wongyuepin	脆皮黃魚片	fried fish in sweet-and-sour sauce
Sichuan minghà	四川明蝦	Sichuan chilli prawns
chìngjìu ngauyōksì	青椒牛肉絲	sautéed shredded beef and green pepper
huiguo rou	回鍋肉	slices of braised pork with chillies
gòngbau gàidìng	宮保雞丁	sautéed diced chicken and peanuts in sweet chilli sauce

jèungcha háu ngap	樟茶烤鴨	Duck smoked with camphor wood
mapo dāufōo	麻婆豆腐	stewed beancurd with minced pork and chilli
ma ngei seung xu	螞蟻上樹	'ants climbing trees' (bean-thread noodles braised with minced pork)
yuehèung kéijí	魚香茄子	sautéed eggplant in a savoury, spicy sauce
gònbìn seigwai dāu	乾煸四季豆	pan-fried spicy string beans

Vegetarian Food

This has undergone a renaissance in recent years; vegetarian food is consumed by the health-conscious and by Buddhists everywhere. Large monasteries often have vegetarian canteens, though you can also find many restaurants in Kowloon and on Hong Kong Island.

The Chinese are masters at adding variety to vegetarian cooking and creating 'mock meat' dishes. Chinese vegetarian food is based on soybean curd (tofu) to which chefs do some miraculous things. Not only is it made to taste like any food you could  possibly think of, it's also made to look like it as well. A dish that is sculptured to look like spare-ribs or a chicken can be made from layered pieces of dried bean curd, or fashioned from mashed taro root.

Chinese vegetarian dishes include:

bòlo cháufān	菠蘿炒飯	fried rice with diced pineapple
chìngdūn bàkgù tòng	清炖北菇湯	black mushroom soup
chùn gúen	冰花宫燕	vegetarian spring rolls
gàmgù súnjìm	北菰筍尖	braised bamboo shoots and black mushrooms
jàilöumēi	齋鹵味	mock chicken, barbecued pork or roast duck
lohon choi	羅漢齋	stewed mixed vegetables
lohonjài yìmīn	羅漢齋伊麵	fried noodles with stewed vegetables
yehchoi gúen	椰菜卷	cabbage rolls

Dessert

Western-style dessert is not a big-ticket item in Chinese restaurants. Locals will traditionally end a meal with sweet soups – sometimes made of red bean or almonds – or fresh fruit.

At dim sum you may find egg custard tarts (best when served warm), steamed buns with sweet red-bean paste, coconut snowballs (sweet rice-flour balls dressed with coconut slices) and various other sweets made with sesame seeds.

Fruit

Along with peaches, pears and apples from North America and Europe, Hong Kong imports an enormous variety of fruits from Australia, South Africa and South-East Asia. Many of these are excellent, though some tropical varieties spoil rapidly after being picked. You'll also find that prices are several times higher than in the Philippines, Thailand or Vietnam.

Special fruits to look out for include:

carambola – This is also known as star fruit, which is exactly what it looks like when sliced.

durian – A large fruit shaped like a rugby ball that has tough spikes and looks impenetrable. After breaking it open with a big knife and peeling off the skin, you'll encounter the next obstacle, a powerful odour that many can't abide. The creamy fruit is actually delicious – it tastes of garlic custard with alcohol sprinkled on top – and is even used to make ice cream in South-East Asia. The durian season runs from April to June. They spoil easily and cost a bundle.

jackfruit – This large segmented fruit is fine stuff when ripe, but tastes a bit like American chewing gum.

longan – The name means 'dragon eyes' in Chinese. The skin is brown, and the clear fruit crunchy, but otherwise the taste is similar to that of a lychee. Its season is from around June through early August.

lychee – A red, pulpy fruit with white flesh. It has a single seed; the smaller the seed the better the fruit. The lychee is one of the main agricultural exports of southern China, especially Guangdong province, where there are lychee tours in season (April to June).

mango – The variety found in Hong Kong are the yellow-skinned fruits from the Philippines.

pomelo – The pomelo is similar to a large grapefruit but drier.

Hami melon – A large oval melon with the skin of a cantaloupe, this sugary fruit comes from China's Xinjiang province and is very popular – and expensive.

Right: A selection of dim sum. The act of eating dim sum is usually referred to as yum cha.

HONG KONG TOURIST ASSOCIATION

[continued from page 64]

GAY & LESBIAN TRAVELLERS

In July 1991 the enactment of the Crimes (Amendment) Ordinance removed criminal penalties for homosexual acts between consenting adults over the age of 18. Since then, gay groups have been lobbying for legislation to address the issue of discrimination on the grounds of sexual orientation.

The gay scene in Hong Kong has undergone quite a revolution over a few short years. A cluster of bars and clubs has opened in Central and in Tsim Sha Tsui, and there are gay-oriented saunas scattered throughout the territory. See the Entertainment section in the Hong Kong Island and Kowloon chapters for venue details. Despite these changes, however, Hong Kong Chinese remain a fairly conservative society, and it can still be risky for gays and lesbians to come out to family members or their employers.

Horizons (☎ 2815 9268) is a phone-line counselling service staffed by volunteers

---

Herbs & Needles: Chinese Medicine Unmasked

Chinese herbal medicine is holistic, meaning it seeks to treat the whole body rather than focusing on a particular organ or disease. It seems to work best for the relief of unpleasant symptoms (stomach ache, sore throat etc), common colds, flu and for some serious long-term conditions that resist Western medicines, such as migraine headaches, asthma and chronic backache. A well-known Chinese cure-all, the ganoderma mushroom, appears to have an effect on certain chronic intestinal diseases, but for most acute life-threatening conditions, such as heart problems or appendicitis, it is still wise to see a Western doctor.

When taking herbal medicine, be wary of the tendency of some manufacturers to claim that a product contains potent and expensive ingredients; some herbal formulas may list the horn of the endangered rhinoceros. Widely acclaimed as a cure for fever, sweating and hot flushes, rhino horn is so rare it's practically impossible to buy and any formula listing it may, at best, contain water buffalo horn. In any case, who on God's green earth would want to contribute to the slaughter of an endangered species?

There are generally few side-effects when taking Chinese medicine. Compared with a drug like penicillin, which can bring about serious allergic reactions, herbal medicines are fairly safe. Nevertheless, herbs are still medicines; there's no need to gobble them like vitamins if you're feeling fine.

In Chinese medicine, a broad-spectrum remedy such as snake gall bladder may be good for treating colds, wind and poor circulation, but there are many different types of these ailments. The best way to treat anything with herbal medicine is to see a Chinese herbalist and get a specific prescription. The pills on sale in herbal medicine shops are generally broad-spectrum, while a prescription remedy will usually require that you take home bags full of specific herbs and cook them into a thick broth.

When you visit Chinese doctors, you might be surprised by what they discover about your body. For example, the doctor will almost certainly take your pulse and may tell you that you have a 'slippery' or 'thready' pulse. Chinese doctors have identified more than 30 different kinds of pulses. A pulse can be 'empty', 'leisurely', 'bowstring' or even 'regularly irregular'. The doctor may then examine your tongue and pronounce that you have 'wet heat', as evidenced by a slippery pulse and a red, greasy tongue.

Many Chinese medicines are powders that come in vials. Typically, you take one or two vials a day. Some of these powders are relatively neutral-tasting while others are very bitter and difficult to swallow. If you can't tolerate the taste, you may want to buy some empty gelatine capsules and fill them with the powder.

The Chinese notion of health food differs somewhat from that of the West. While the Western variety emphasises low-fat, high-fibre and a lack of chemical additives, the Chinese version puts its main emphasis on the use of traditional ingredients and herbs.

who provide information and advice to local and visiting gay men, lesbians and bi-sexuals.

Lesbians should contact Queer Sisters (☎ 2314 4348, ⓦ www.qs.org.hk), GPO Box 9313.

DISABLED TRAVELLERS

Disabled people have to cope with substantial obstacles in Hong Kong, including the stairs at the MTR and KCR stations as well as pedestrian overpasses, narrow and crowded footpaths and steep hills. People whose sight or hearing is impaired must be extremely cautious of Hong Kong's crazy drivers.

On the other hand, some buses are now accessible by wheelchair, taxis are never hard to find and most buildings have lifts. Wheelchairs can negotiate the lower decks of most of the ferries.

In some (but not all) upmarket hotels there are specially designed rooms for disabled people. Those that provide such

---

Herbs & Needles: Chinese Medicine Unmasked

It is a widely held belief in China that overwork and sex wears down the body and that such 'exercise' will result in a short life. To counter the wear and tear, some Chinese practice jinbu (the consumption of tonic food and herbs). This can include, for example, drinking raw snake's blood or bear's bile, or eating deer antlers, all of which are claimed to improve vision, strength and sexual potency.

Like herbal medicine, Chinese acupuncture tends to be more helpful for treating long term conditions (such as chronic headaches) than sudden emergencies (eg, acute appendicitis). But there are occasions when acupuncture can be used for more serious conditions. For example, surgical operations have been performed using acupuncture as the only anaesthetic. In this case, a small electric current is passed through the needles, which are usually inserted in the head.

The exact mechanism by which acupuncture works is not fully understood. The Chinese talk of energy channels or meridians, which connect the needle insertion point to the particular organ, gland or joint being treated. The acupuncture point is sometimes quite far from the area of the body being treated.

Having needles stuck into you might not sound pleasant, but if done properly it doesn't hurt. Knowing just where to insert the needle is crucial. Acupuncturists have identified more than 2000 insertion points, but only about 150 are commonly used.

While the procedure is relatively painless, one should not forget that AIDS and hepatitis can be spread easily by contaminated needles. In Hong Kong disposable acupuncture needles are routinely used, but this is not always the case in the mainland. If you're going to experiment with acupuncture in Shenzhen or Zhuhai, find out first if the doctor has throw-away needles.

Massage is another traditional healing technique loosely related to acupuncture. The Chinese variety is somewhat different from the popular techniques practised by people in the West. One traditional Chinese method employs cups placed on the patient's skin. A burning piece of alcohol-soaked cotton is briefly put inside the cup to drive out the air before it is applied. As the cup cools, a partial vacuum is produced, leaving a nasty looking but harmless 'welt' on the skin. The mark goes away after a few days.

Moxibustion is a variation on the theme. Various types of herbs, rolled into what looks like a ball of fluffy cotton, are held near the skin and ignited. This method can be spiced up by igniting the herbs on a slice of ginger. The idea is to apply the maximum amount of heat possible without burning the patient. This heat treatment is supposed to be good for diseases such as arthritis and earache.

There's a plethora of books on the subject, including *Chinese Medicine* by Ted J Kaptchuk and *The Streetwise Guide to Chinese Herbal Medicine* by Wong Kang Ying and Martha Dahlen. If you want a more advanced text, Daniel Reid's *A handbook of Chinese Healing Herbs* is good. *The Ancient Healing Art of Chinese Herbalism* by Anna Selby is richly illustrated.

rooms are indicated in the Places to Stay section in the Kowloon and Hong Kong Island chapters.

Hong Kong International Airport at Chek Lap Kok has been designed with facilities for passengers with disabilities and publishes a useful brochure entitled *Hong Kong International Airport: Special Needs*, which is available from the Hong Kong Airport Authority (☎ 2824 7111, fax 2824 0717). Ramps make moving between levels simple, and lifts are equipped with audible indicators. Electric carts are also available in the terminal; built-in features include disabled toilets, telephones and drinking fountains. For the blind or partially blind, a tactile guide path has been incorporated into the departures kerb and from the Airport Express platform to information counters and help phones.

For further information about facilities and services for the disabled in Hong Kong, contact the Joint Council for the Physically and Mentally Disabled (☎ 2864 2931, fax 2864 2962).

SENIOR TRAVELLERS
Most forms of transport in Hong Kong offer discounts (usually half-price) to people aged 65 and over, and seniors over 60 get discounts at many museums and on organised tours. If you would like further information, contact the Hong Kong Society for the Aged (☎ 2511 2235), Room 1601–3, Tung Sun Commercial Centre, 194 Lockhart Rd, Wan Chai. Helping Hand (☎ 2522 4494) is another organisation that deals with issues relating to the elderly.

TRAVEL WITH CHILDREN
Although Hong Kong's crowds, traffic and pollution might be off-putting to some parents, Hong Kong is a great travel destination for kids. Food and sanitation is of a high enough standard that you needn't fear for their health, and the territory is jam-packed with things to entertain the young 'uns. What's more, Hong Kong people love children.

A number of hotels give special concessions for families with children (reduced

rates or free extra bed etc). Most public transport and museums offer half-price fares and admissions to children under the age of 12.

Most hotels in Hong Kong will be able to recommend a babysitter if you've got daytime appointments or want a night out *sans* child. Otherwise call Rent-A-Mum (☎ 2523 4868, e rentamum@hknet. com), at 12A Amber Lodge, 21–25 Hollywood Rd, Central, a reputable agency that supplies qualified English-speaking sitters for HK$$95 per hour.

Lonely Planet's *Travel with Children* has useful tips, including advice on travel health.

USEFUL ORGANISATIONS
Here is a list of some useful organisations, including some good contacts for doing business in Hong Kong:

American Chamber of Commerce (☎ 2526 0165, fax 2537 1682, e amcham@amcham .org.hk) 19th floor, Bank of America Tower, 12 Harcourt Rd, Central. This is the most active overseas chamber of commerce in Hong Kong.

The Chinese General Chamber of Commerce (☎ 2525 6385, w www.cgcc.org.hk) 7th floor, Chinese General Chamber of Commerce Building, 24–25 Connaught Rd Central. Authorised to issue Certificates of Hong Kong origin for trade purposes.

The Chinese Manufacturers' Association of Hong Kong (☎ 2545 6166) 3rd floor, CMA Building, 64–66 Connaught Rd Central. Operates testing laboratories for product certification and can also issue Certificates of Hong Kong origin.

Community Advice Bureau (☎ 2815 5444, fax 2815 5977, e cab@cab.org.hk) Volunteer expats answer questions for new Hong Kong residents. Open from 9.30am to 4.30pm on weekdays. Since it's volunteer work, you shouldn't bother the staff with trivia.

Employers' Federation of Hong Kong (☎ 2528 0536) Suite 2004, Sino Plaza, 255–257 Gloucester Rd, Causeway Bay

Hong Kong Consumer Council (HKCC; hotline ☎ 2929 2222, 2921 6228) Ground floor, Harbour Building, 38 Pier Rd, Central. Can help with complaints about dishonest shopkeepers and the like.

Hong Kong General Chamber of Commerce (☎ 2529 9229) 22nd floor, United Centre, 95

Queensway, Admiralty. Offers a host of services for foreign executives and firms such as translation, serviced offices, secretarial help and printing.

Hong Kong Industrial Technology Centre Corporation (☎ 2788 5400) HKPC Building, 78 Tat Chee Ave, Yau Yat Tsuen, Kowloon

Hong Kong Information Services Department (☎ 2842 8777, ⓦ www.info.gov.hk) The HKISD can answer specific questions or direct you to the appropriate government department to handle your inquiry. It is best to try the HKTB Visitor Hotline (☎ 2508 1234) first, however.

Hong Kong Natural History Society (☎ 2993 3330, fax 2993 7709, ⓔ dingle@hkstar.com) This society organises countryside hikes in winter and boat trips to the remoter islands in summer. Membership for the society costs HK$100/150 per person/couple.

Hong Kong Trade Department (☎ 2392 2922) Trade Department Tower, 700 Nathan Rd, Mong Kok. A source for trade information, statistics, government regulations and product certification. Offers information and assistance to overseas investors at its One Stop Unit (☎ 2737 2434), 14th floor, Ocean Centre, 5 Canton Rd, Tsim Sha Tsui.

Hong Kong Trade Development Council (HKTDC; ☎ 2584 4333, ⓦ www.tdctrade.com) 38th floor, Office Tower, Convention Plaza, 1 Harbour Rd, Wan Chai North. Co sponsors or takes part in trade fairs, publishes a wealth of material on Hong Kong markets and runs the TDC Information Centre (☎ 2248 4000) at the nearby Hong Kong Convention and Exhibition Centre (see the following Libraries section). Its fax service (☎ 2584 4188) offers a list of more than 100,000 Hong Kong manufacturers, business and services.

Labour Department (☎ 2852 3509) 12th floor, Harbour Building, 38 Pier Rd, Central. Contact this department for labour-relations problems and queries.

Royal Asiatic Society (☎ 2813 7500, ⓦ www.royalasiaticsociety.org.hk) Organises lectures, hikes and field trips, operates a lending library and puts out publications of its own.

LIBRARIES

Hong Kong has a fairly extensive public library system; you will find a list on the Internet at ⓦ www.lcsd.gov.hk. The most useful for travellers is the main library (☎ 2921 2555) in the High Block of City Hall, opposite Queen's Pier in Central.

With a passport and a deposit of HK$130, foreign visitors can get a temporary library card, which allows them to borrow books from the library. The library is open from 10am to 7pm Monday to Thursday, till 9pm on Friday, and till 5pm at the weekend (closed on public holidays).

The TDC Information Centre (☎ 2248 4000) located in the New Wing, Hong Kong Convention and Exhibition Centre (HKCEC), 1 Expo Drive, Wan Chai North, run by the government Hong Kong Trade Development Council, is well stocked with relevant books and CD ROMS. It's open from 9am to 6pm weekdays and to 1pm on Saturday.

For more information on the library, which is located at the British Council in Central, see the Cultural Centres section later in this chapter.

UNIVERSITIES

Hong Kong now has eight universities. The University of Hong Kong (☎ 2859 2305, ⓦ www.hku.hk), established in 1911, is the oldest and most difficult to get into. Its campus is on the western side of Hong Kong Island in Pok Fu Lam. The Chinese University of Hong Kong (☎ 2609 8898, ⓦ www.cuhk.edu.hk), established in 1963 and most applicants' second choice, is situated on a beautiful campus at Ma Liu Shui north of Sha Tin in the New Territories. The Hong Kong University of Science & Technology (☎ 2358 6302, ⓦ www.ust.hk) admitted its first students in 1991, and is situated at Tai Po Tsai in Clearwater Bay in the New Territories.

The aforementioned three have been ranked among the top 10 universities – first, sixth and seventh places respectively – in Asia by *Asiaweek* magazine.

The City University of Hong Kong (☎ 2788 9191, ⓦ www.citu.edu.hk), on Tat Chee Ave in Kowloon Tong, was known as the City Polytechnic of Hong Kong when set up in 1984. It is not to be confused with the Hong Kong Polytechnic University (☎ 2766 5100, ⓦ www.polyu.edu.hk) in the Hung Hom district of Kowloon, which was set up in 1972.

Hong Kong's three other universities are:

Hong Kong Baptist University (1956; ☎ 2339 7400, W www.hkbu.edu.hk) Located in Kowloon Tong.
Hong Kong Institute of Education (1994; ☎ 2948 8888, W www.ied.edu.hk) A teachers' college with campuses at Ting Kok in the north-east New territories and in Yau Ma Tei in Kowloon.
Lingnan University (1967; ☎ 2616 3017, W www.ln.edu.hk) Found in Tuen Mun in the New Territories.

CULTURAL CENTRES

Some of the major cultural centres in Hong Kong include:

Alliance Française (☎ 2527 7825) 2nd floor, 123 Hennessy Rd, Wan Chai. Also has a library and offers a wide range of cultural activities.
British Council (☎ 2913 5125) 3 Supreme Court Rd, Admiralty. Provides English-language classes, sponsors cultural programs and has a library, which can be used for free and has Internet access. You have to be a member of the library to borrow books, CDs and videos.
Dante Alighieri (☎ 2573 0343) 7th floor, 133 Wan Chai Rd, Wan Chai. Offers courses in language and other subjects.
Goethe Institute (☎ 2802 0088) 14th floor, Hong Kong Arts Centre, 2 Harbour Rd, Wan Chai.

DANGERS & ANNOYANCES
Crime

Despite Hong Kong's obvious prosperity and relative low unemployment rate, there are plenty of people who live on the margin of society, and the crime rate appears to be on the rise after dropping dramatically just after the handover.

It's more likely that you will be the victim of theft committed by one of your fellow travellers than by a local person. There have been a disturbing number of reports of foreigners having had their property stolen by their room mates in hostels and guesthouses.

Hong Kong does have its share of local pickpockets and thieves. If you set a bag down, keep an eye on it. This applies to restaurants and pubs, particularly in touristed areas, as well. If your bag doesn't

accompany you to the toilet, don't expect to find it when you return.

Hong Kong has a serious drug problem. There are estimated to be more than 40,000 drug addicts in Hong Kong, 85% of whom are hooked on heroin, which they smoke rather than inject. Some addicts finance their habit by working in the sex industry; others resort to pickpocketing, burglary and robbery.

It is safe to walk around just about anywhere in Hong Kong at night, though it's best to stick to well-lit areas. Tourist districts like Tsim Sha Tsui are heavily patrolled by the police.

Smuggling

Professional smugglers often target Westerners to carry goods into countries like Vietnam and India where those goods are prohibited or the import taxes are high. The theory is that customs agents are less likely to stop and search foreigners. These small-time smuggling expeditions, or 'milk runs', either earn the Westerner a fee or a free air ticket to another destination.

Smuggling is a lot more risky than that. A traveller staying at Chungking Mansions was solicited to smuggle 7kg of gold into Nepal for a fee of US$2000. He got caught and was given four years in prison. Another traveller was stopped at Seoul airport wearing three mink coats under his jacket. He was fined and given two months in jail before being booted out of the country. There are also cases of travellers being used as 'mules' to carry drugs hidden inside electronic goods.

Rudeness

There have been many complaints that Hong Kong people are rude, pushy, humourless and impatient. The hostility has not died out altogether, but it has toned down.

If you do encounter some irritability, try to remember that you are in one of the most densely populated places on the planet. Crowds, the frenetic pace, traffic, pollution and the heat and humidity in summer all add up to create some pretty frayed tempers. You are visiting, have all the time in the world and will (probably) leave. People here will remain, doing their jobs, raising their families, dreaming their dreams and making their plans in cramped, high-rise blocks. Please try to have a little patience.

Other Annoyances

Like every place in the world, Hong Kong has its own way of doing things, its own idiosyncrasies, some of which can be pretty irritating.

Cantonese is a language that lends itself to high decibels. Disposable foam (not wax) earplugs are the best solution.

Air-conditioning is cranked up full throttle in many restaurants in Hong Kong (5°C seems to be the preferred temperature), and some places actually stock woollen shawls for customers' use. Getting into a taxi on a warm August afternoon is like entering a refrigerator on wheels.

Among some people's greatest annoyances are the legions of sub-continental touts on Nathan Rd in Tsim Sha Tsui who will try to sell or rent you everything from a cheap and nasty 'copy watch' to a boy, a girl or a German Shepherd with which you can 'take your pleasure'. Many travellers have found that the only way to really shake off these people is to shout *very* loudly at them.

EMERGENCIES

In the event of an emergency phone ☎ 999 for the fire services, police or an ambulance.

The St John's Ambulance Service can be reached on ☎ 2576 6555 on Hong Kong Island, ☎ 2713 5555 in Kowloon and ☎ 2639 2555 in the New Territories.

If you are robbed, you can obtain a loss report for insurance purposes at the Central Police Station, 10 Hollywood Rd, Central. Have a look around while the officer in charge laboriously types up your report; it's one of the most interesting colonial buildings in Hong Kong.

Other important numbers include:

MediLink (Hong Kong Medical Association hot line)	☎ 90000 223 322
Bushfire Control Centre	☎ 2720 0777
Tropical Cyclone Warning Inquiries	☎ 2926 1473

LEGAL MATTERS

Most foreigners who get into legal trouble in Hong Kong are involved in drugs. *All* forms of narcotics are highly illegal in Hong Kong. It makes no difference whether it's heroin, opium, 'ice', Ecstasy or marijuana – the law makes no distinction. If police or customs officials find dope or even smoking equipment in your possession, you can expect to be arrested immediately. Police sometimes spot-check the bars in the Lan Kwai Fong nightlife area in Central.

Drink driving has long been overlooked in Hong Kong, but the police are beginning to crack down. Patrol cars are being equipped with breathalysers, and stiffer penalties are being imposed.

If you run into legal trouble, the Legal Aid Department (24-hour hotline ☎ 2537 7677) provides both residents and visitors with representation, subject to a means and merits test.

BUSINESS HOURS

Office hours are from 9am to either 5.30pm or 6pm on weekdays, and from 9am to noon or 1pm on Saturday. The lunch hour is from 1pm to 2pm. Banks are open from 9am to 4.30pm or 5pm weekdays and 9am to 12.30pm on Saturday.

Many Hong Kong companies still run on a 5½-day working week, but this concept is beginning to fall out of favour, with staff required to work one or maybe two Saturdays a month.

Shops and stores that cater to the tourist trade keep longer hours, but almost nothing opens before 9am. For specifics, see When to Shop in the Shopping section later in this chapter.

Restaurants generally open from 11.30am to 2.30pm for lunch and 6pm to 11pm for dinner. Of course, there are many exceptions to this rule. Some pubs keep the kitchen open until 1am, and Chinese corner noodle shops often run from early in the morning until the wee hours. Bars generally open at noon or 6pm and close anywhere between 2am to 6am. Happy hours at bars are generally from 4pm to 8pm, but you will find some that are much more flexible.

PUBLIC HOLIDAYS & SPECIAL EVENTS
Public Holidays

Western and Chinese culture combine to create an interesting mix – and number! – of public holidays in Hong Kong. Determining the exact date of some of them is tricky as there are traditionally two calendars in use in Hong Kong: the Gregorian solar (or Western) calendar and the Chinese lunar one.

The following are public holidays in Hong Kong:

New Year's Day 1 January
Chinese New Year Late January/early February (three-day festival)
Easter Late March/early April
Ching Ming Early April
Buddha's Birthday April/May
Labour Day 1 May
Dragon Boat Festival June
Hong Kong SAR Establishment Day 1 July
Mid-Autumn Festival September/October
China National Day 1 & 2 October
Cheung Yeung Mid/late October
Christmas & Boxing Day 25 & 26 December

Traditional Festivals

Many of the Chinese festivals, both public holidays and privately observed affairs, go back hundreds, even thousands, of years, and the true origins of some are often lost in the mists of time. The reasons for each festival vary and you will generally find that there are a couple of explanations.

Kitchen God Festival (mid-January) Rarely observed festival honouring the Kitchen (or Stove) God, who is associated with family unity, decides the longevity of each family member and reports to the Emperor of Heaven.

Chinese New Year (late January/early February) Hong Kong's most important holiday period and decidedly not the time to visit. See the boxed text Kung Hei Fat Choi!

Lantern Festival (mid to late February) Colourful lantern festival called Yuen Siu, the 15th day of the first moon.

Ching Ming (early April) A family celebration when Chinese people visit and clean the graves of ancestors. Food and wine is left for the spirits, and incense and paper money is burned. The festival is thought to have its origins during the Han dynasty, about 2000 years ago.

Tin Hau Festival (late April/early May) In honour of Tin Hau, the patroness of fisherfolk and one of the territory's most popular goddesses. The best place to see the festival is at the Tai Miu temple in Joss House Bay. It's not on any normal ferry route, but at festival time the ferry company puts on excursion trips that get very crowded.

Cheung Chau Bun Festival (late April/early May) An unusual festival observed uniquely on Cheung Chau. See the boxed text Going for the Buns under Cheung Chau in the Outlying Islands chapter.

Birthday of Lord Buddha (May) A public holiday in Hong Kong since 1999, it is also called the Bathing of Lord Buddha. Buddha's statue is taken from monasteries and temples and ceremoniously bathed in scented water. The best place to observe this event is Po Lin Monastery on Lantau, at the Ten Thousand Buddhas Monastery in Sha Tin or the Miu Fat Monastery at Lam Tei near Tuen Mun in the New Territories.

Dragon Boat Festival (June) Double Fifth (Tuen Ng), the fifth day of the fifth moon, commemorates the death of Qu Yuan, a poet-statesman of the 3rd century BC who hurled himself into the Mi Lo River in Hunan province to protest against a corrupt government. Traditional rice dumplings are eaten in memory of the event and dragon-boat races are held in Hong Kong, Kowloon and the outlying islands. Races are held at Shau Kei Wan, Aberdeen, Yau Ma Tei, Tai Po as well as on Lantau and Cheung Chau but the most famous are those at Stanley.

Birthday of Lu Pan (mid to late July) A master architect, magician, engineer, inventor and designer, Lu Pan (born 507 BC, according to legend) is worshipped by anyone connected with the building trade.

Maidens' Festival (mid-August) A minor holiday, also known as Seven Sisters Day, reserved for girls and young lovers and held on the seventh day of the seventh moon.

Hungry Ghosts Festival (late August/early September) Celebrated on the first day of the seventh moon, when the gates of hell are opened and 'hungry ghosts' (restless spirits) are freed for two weeks to walk the earth. On the 14th day of the seventh moon, paper 'hell' money and votives in the shape of cars, houses and clothing are burned for the ghosts, and food is offered. Many people will not swim, travel, get married, move house or indulge in other 'risky' activities during this time.

Mid-Autumn Festival (September/October) Held on the 15th night of the eighth moon, this is among Hong Kong's most colourful festivals and the favourite of most Westerners. It marks an uprising against the Mongols in the 14th century when plans for a revolution were passed around in little round cakes. Moon cakes are still eaten and there are many delicious varieties.

Birthday of Confucius (September/October) Celebrated on the seventh day of the eighth moon, it is marked by religious services at the Confucian Temple in Causeway Bay.

Cheung Yeung (mid/late October) On the ninth day of the ninth month, based on a story from the Eastern Han dynasty (in the first two centuries AD). An old soothsayer advised a man to take his family to a high place to escape a plague. On returning to his village the man found every living thing destroyed. Many people still head for the hills on this day. Cheung Yeung is also a time to visit the graves of ancestors.

Kung Hei Fat Choi!

The Lunar New Year is the most important and anticipated holiday on the Chinese calendar. Expect a lot of colourful decorations but not much public merry-making; for the most part, this is a festival for the family and more akin to Christmas than our New Year. There is a fantastic fireworks display over Victoria Harbour on the evening of the second day, however, and one of the largest horse races is held at Sha Tin on day three. Flower markets at Victoria Park in Causeway Bay and at Sha Tin, Tai Po and Yuen Long in the New Territories are lively and colourful affairs.

Chinese New Year, which is also called Spring Festival, begins on the first new moon after the sun enters Aquarius (somewhere between 21 January and 19 February) and ends, at least officially, 15 days later. But in Hong Kong it is celebrated for four days and is a three-day public holiday only.

The build-up to the holiday – the end of the month known as the 'Bitter Moon' since it's the coldest part of the year in Hong Kong – is very busy as family members clean house, get haircuts and cook, all of which are activities prohibited during the holiday. Debts and feuds are settled and all employees – Chinese and foreigners alike – get a one-month New Year bonus.

You'll see many symbols placed in shop windows, on restaurant tables and illuminated in neon on the skyscrapers of Central. They may look odd to you, but they all have special meaning for people here. Chinese use a lot of indirect speak and 'punning' (for lack of a better term) is very important in the use of symbols. A picture of a boy holding a goldfish (gamyu) and a lotus (he) is wishing you 'abundant gold and harmony' since that's what the words can also mean when a different tone is used to say them. Symbols of bats (the winged variety) are everywhere; its name in Chinese (fu) also means 'good luck'. The peach and plum blossoms decorating restaurants and public spaces symbolise both the arrival of spring and 'immortality'; the golden fruit of the kumquat tree is associated with good fortune. The red and gold banners you'll see in doorways are wishing all and sundry 'prosperity', 'peace' or just 'spring'.

This punning also carries over into food eaten during the Lunar New Year holidays. Dried seaweed (choi) and oysters (houshi) is a popular dish as the names of the key ingredients can also mean 'prosperity' and 'good business'. Lots of fish, chicken (gai), which also means 'luck', and prawns (ha, or 'laughter') is served as are noodles for 'longevity'.

Not surprisingly in this Mammon-worshipping territory, much of the symbolism and well wishing has to do with wealth and prosperity. Indeed, 'kung hei fat choi', the most common New Year greeting in southern China, literally means 'respectful wishes, get rich'. Mandarin speakers in the mainland wish one another 'gonghe xinxi', which changes the 'get rich' to a more demure 'blessings for the new year'.

The laisee (hongbao in Mandarin) packet is very important among Cantonese people. It's a small red and gold envelope in which bills in pairs or sums of eight (bat, which also means 'prosper') are enclosed. If someone wishes you 'kung hei fat choi', and you are younger than they or unmarried, you can respond 'laisee dai lou' (give me laisee) and you should receive a packet. But be aware that it works both ways, and you may find yourself handing out more laisee than you bargained for.

The first day of Chinese New Year will fall on 12 February in 2002, 1 February in 2003, 22 January in 2004, 9 February in 2005 and 29 January in 2006.

Special Events

Hong Kong hosts hundreds of cultural, business and sporting events each year. Exact dates vary from year to year, so if you want to time your visit to coincide with a particular event, it would be wise to check HKTB's Web site (W www.discoverhongkong.com). The following is just a brief summary of important annual events:

City Festival The Fringe Club sponsors three weeks of performances in late January/early February by an eclectic mix of up-and-coming local and overseas artists and performers.

Hong Kong Marathon Organised by the Hong Kong Amateur Athletic Association, this major event is held in Sha Tin, usually in February.

Hong Kong Arts Festival The territory's most important cultural event is a month-long extravaganza of music, performing arts and exhibitions by hundreds of local and international artists; held in February/March.

Invitational Seven-a-Side Rugby Tournament The 'Rugby Sevens', Hong Kong's premier sporting event, is held over three days in March and attracts teams from all over the world.

Hong Kong International Film Festival This festival in April brings in hundreds of films from around the world and is used to showcase new, local and regional productions.

International Dragon Boat Races This event is usually held in late June or early July, a week after the local dragon boat races.

Hong Kong Fashion Week The main parades and events during this mid-July extravaganza are held at the Hong Kong Convention and Exhibition Centre, but look out for well-dressed shindigs in shopping centres around town.

Children's Arts Carnival This unusual festival in August promotes performances by children's groups.

Asian Regatta This October event is organised by the Hong Kong Yachting Association.

Chinese Arts Festival This new festival held in October/November features performing groups from both home and abroad.

Festival of Asian Arts This is one of Asia's major cultural events, bringing in musicians, dancers, opera singers and other performance groups from all over the region; held every other year in October/November.

Hong Kong Open Golf Championships Hong Kong's premier golfing event is held annually in November.

European Film Festival This event is held at the Hong Kong Arts Centre in November.

Hong Kong International Cantonese Opera Festival This December festival showcases both local and foreign troupes.

ACTIVITIES

Hong Kong offers countless ways to keep fit and have fun. From tennis courts and go-karts to long-distance hiking trails and public swimming pools, you'll hardly be stumped for something to do during your visit.

One excellent all-round option is the South China Athletic Association (SCAA; ☎ 2577 6932, fax 2890 9304), 88 Caroline Hill Rd, Causeway Bay. The SCAA has facilities for badminton, billiards, bowling, tennis, squash, table tennis, gymnastics, fencing, yoga, judo, karate, golf and dancing. Short-term membership for visitors is only HK$50 a month. Another good place to know about is the nearby Hong Kong Amateur Athletic Association (☎ 2504 8215, fax 2577 5322), Room 2015, Sports House, 1 Stadium Path, So Kon Po, Causeway Bay, which houses all sorts of sports clubs.

Badminton & Table Tennis

It's widely acknowledged that the Chinese are the best table-tennis players in the world, and Hong Kong Chinese are crazy for badminton. For information on these two sports, phone the Hong Kong Table Tennis Association (☎ 2575 5330) and the Badminton Association (☎ 2504 8318), Room 2005, Sports House, 1 Stadium Path, So Kon Po, Causeway Bay, for details.

Bowling

Some of the best facilities are at the SCAA (see earlier).

In Kowloon and the New Territories, bowling alleys tend to be located in the backwaters. One of the most accessible is the AMF Bowling Centre (☎ 2732 2255) at City One Shatin, Ngan Shing St, Sha Tin.

Cricket

Hong Kong has two very exclusive cricket clubs: the Hong Kong Cricket Club (☎ 2574 6266), Wong Nai Chung Gap Rd, above Deep Water Bay on Hong Kong Island, and the Kowloon Cricket Club (☎ 2367 4141), Jordan Path, Jordan.

For information contact the Hong Kong Cricket Association (☎ 2504 8102, fax 2577 8486, ✉ hkca@hkabc.net), Room 1019, Sports House, 1 Stadium Path, Happy Valley.

Cycling

There are bicycle paths in the New Territories, mostly around Tolo Harbour. The paths run from Sha Tin to Tai Po and continue up to Tai Mei Tuk. You can rent bicycles in these three places, but the paths get very crowded on the weekends. Bicycle rentals are also available at Shek O on Hong Kong Island and on Lantau Island.

Although the Hong Kong Cycling Association (☎ 2573 3861), Room 1015, Sports House, 1 Stadium Path, So Kon Po, Causeway Bay, mainly organises races, you can call them for information. To find out about areas for mountain biking or for equipment, ask the helpful staff at the Flying Ball Bicycle Co (☎ 2381 3661), 201 Tung Choi St, Mong Kok.

Fishing

While there are almost no restrictions on deep-sea fishing, it's a different story at freshwater reservoirs, where the season runs from September to March and there are limits on the quantity and size of fish taken. A licence from the Water Supplies Department (☎ 2824 5000), 1st floor, Immigration Tower, 7 Gloucester Rd, Wan Chai, costs HK$24 and is valid for three years.

Fitness Centres

Getting fit is big business in Hong Kong, with the largest slices of the pie shared out between a few big names. TLC Fitness Chain has branches in Admiralty (☎ 2866 9968), Causeway Bay (☎ 2576 7668) and Jordan (☎ 2730 5038). California Fitness Centre has branches in Central (☎ 2522 5229), 1 Wellington St, and Wan Chai (☎ 2877 7070), as well as in Causeway Bay (☎ 2577 0004) and Tsim Sha Tsui (☎ 2366 8666). New York Fitness (☎ 2543 2280), 32 Hollywood Rd, Central, offers aerobics,

personal training, physiotherapy, massage and beauty therapy. Weekly membership costs HK$500.

Go-Karting

Go-karting is now possible at the popular Karting Mall (☎ 2718 8199) on the site of the old Kai Tak airport in Kowloon.

The big event of the year for karting enthusiasts is the Hong Kong Kart Grand Prix, held in late November or early December. For more details contact the Hong Kong Kart Club (☎ 2504 8293, fax 2577 8885), Room 1015, Sports House, 1 Stadium Path, So Kon Po, Causeway Bay.

Golf

Golf is the fastest-growing sport in Hong Kong. Most courses are private but open to the public. Greens fees for visitors vary but range from HK$450 for two rounds at the nine-hole Deep Water Bay Golf Club (☎ 2812 7070), Island Rd, Deep Water Bay, on Hong Kong Island to HK$1400 at the 18-hole Fanling Golf Course (☎ 2670 1211), Fan Kam Rd, Fanling, New Territories. The Discovery Bay Golf Club (☎ 2987 7273) is perched high on a hill, offering impressive views, as is the Shek O Country Club (☎ 2809 4458), Big Wave Bay Rd, on the south-eastern edge of Hong Kong Island. The Clearwater Bay Golf and Country Club (☎ 2719 1595) is on the tip of the Clearwater Bay Peninsula in the New Territories. One of the most dramatic links – to play in Hong Kong – for the scenery if not the par – is the Jockey Club Kau Sai Chau Public Golf Course (☎ 2791 3380) on an island of that name in the bay off Sai Kung town. Be sure to bring your passport and handicap card.

Hiking

Hiking in Hong Kong has become so popular in recent years that many trails are crowded on weekends; try to schedule your walks mid-week. The territory's four main trails are: the MacLehose Trail (100km; New Territories), Wilson Trail (78km; Hong Kong Island and New Territories), the Lantau Trail (70km) and the Hong Kong

Trail (50km). See the relevant chapters in this book for details.

Good maps will save you a lot of time, energy and trouble. The Map Publication Centres (see the Maps section under Planning at the beginning of this chapter) has a series of excellent topographical maps as does Universal Publications. Both the Country & Marine Parks Authority (☎ 2420 0529) and the HKTB (☎ 2508 1234) produce useful leaflets detailing good hikes, including the latter's *Hong Kong Walks*, with both urban strolls and countryside hikes. For walking and nature guides, see the Books section earlier in this chapter.

When trekking in Hong Kong some basic equipment is necessary. Most important is a full water bottle. Other useful items include food, a rain suit, sun hat, toilet paper, maps and compass. Boots are not necessary; the best footwear is a good pair of running shoes.

Hikers should remember that the high humidity during spring and summer can be enervating. October to mid-March are the best months for strenuous treks. At high elevations, such as parts of the Lantau and MacLehose Trails, it can get very cold so it's essential to bring warm clothes.

Track conditions vary widely – not all are concrete paths. Snakes are rarely encountered but can be avoided by keeping to the trails and not walking through dense undergrowth.

Mosquitoes are a nuisance in the spring and summer, so a good mosquito repellent is essential. Mosquito coils (incense) are also effective when you're resting, but should not be used inside a tent or any other enclosed area.

Both the YMCA (☎ 2369 2211) and the YWCA (☎ 2524 8424) regularly arrange walks around such areas as Silvermine to Pui O, Shek O to Chai Wan and other popular routes. Climbers should contact the Hong Kong Mountaineering Union (☎ 2747 7003, fax 2770 7115), which offers courses in leisure, rock and sport climbing.

Serious walkers might consider joining in the annual Trailwalker event, a gruelling race across the MacLehose Trail in the New

Territories in November. For more information, call the Trailwalker Charitable Trust (☎ 2520 2525).

Horseback Riding

The Hong Kong Riding Union (☎ 2488 6886, mobile ☎ 9025 8866), based in Kowloon Tong, organises rides in the New Territories. On Hong Kong Island, lessons are available at the Pok Fu Lam Riding School (☎ 2550 1359) for HK$350 per hour.

Kayaking & Canoeing

The Cheung Chau Windsurfing Centre (☎ 2981 8316, 2981 5063) at Tung Wan Beach in Cheung Chau rents single/double kayaks for HK$50/80 per hour.

The Hong Kong Canoe Union (☎ 2504, 8185, fax 2838 9037), Sports House, 1 Stadium Path, So Kon Po, Causeway Bay, can help you find other canoeing enthusiasts. Canoeing facilities are available through the Tai Mei Tuk Water Sports Centre (☎ 2665 3591) at Tai Mei Tuk in the New Territories. You can also inquire at the Wong Shek Water Sports Centre (☎ 2328 2370), Wong Shek pier, Sai Kung, New Territories.

Martial Arts

Chinese kung fu *(gongfu)* is the basis for many Asian martial arts. There are several organisations offering training in various schools of Chinese martial arts *(wushu)* as well as other Asian disciplines. Popular Chinese martial arts include tai chi *(taijiquan)* and wing chun, Bruce Lee's original style and native to Hong Kong.

The HKTB (☎ 2508 1234) offers free tai chi lessons from 8.15am to 9.15am on Tuesday, Friday and Saturday in the Garden Plaza of Hong Kong Park, next to the Admiralty MTR station.

Otherwise check the classified pages of the English newspapers and magazines for contact numbers. You could also go to the parks in the early morning in search of someone who will teach you. Among those listed below, the Hong Kong Tai Chi Association charges HK$500 a month for weekly classes, and the Hong Kong Wushu Union only has classes for children.

Hong Kong Chinese Martial Arts Association (☎ 2504 8164) 9th floor, 687A Nathan Rd, Kowloon
Hong Kong Tai Chi Association (☎ 2395 4884) 11th floor, 60 Argyle St, Kowloon
Hong Kong Wushu Union (☎ 2504 8226) Room 1018, Sports House, 1 Stadium Path, So Kon Po, Causeway Bay
Viewpoint Club (☎ 2385 5908) 3rd floor, Front Portion, 105 Argyle St, Mong Kok
Wing Tsun Martial Arts Association (☎ 2385 7115) 8th floor, A block, 440–442 Nathan Rd, Kowloon
YMCA (☎ 2369 2211) 41 Salisbury Rd, Tsim Sha Tsui

Kung Fu Supplies in Wan Chai has everything you need to get started in Chinese martial arts. See Sporting Goods under Shopping in the Hong Kong Island chapter.

Orienteering
The Outward Bound School (☎ 2792 4333, 2792 0055), Tai Mong Tsai, New Territories, organises orienteering courses, camping and barbecues and teaches wilderness survival. It's geared towards helping young adults build character and self-esteem, though it is not limited to teenagers. For information contact the Orienteering Club at ☎ 7684 2842.

Running
Good places to run on Hong Kong Island include Harlech and Lugard roads on the Peak, Bowen Rd above Wan Chai, the track in Victoria Park and the racecourse at Happy Valley (as long as there aren't any horse races on!). In Kowloon, a popular place to run is the Promenade that runs along the waterfront in Tsim Sha Tsui East.

For easy runs followed by beer and good company, contact Hash House Harriers, GPO Box 1057, Hong Kong, a lively organisation with branches worldwide. You can get in touch with the Ladies' Hash House Harriers at W www.ladieshash.com. The inappropriately named Ladies Road Runners Club (☎ 2904 9247, 2537 4593), PO Box 20613, Hennessy Rd Post Office, Wan Chai, allows men to join in the fun.

Every 7am to 8.30am on Sunday from April to December, the Adventist Hospital (☎ 2574 6211 ext 777), Wong Nai Chung Gap Rd, Happy Valley, organises a running clinic.

Sauna & Massage
This is a great way to relax following any activity, whether it's been a strenuous hike through the hills or a frantic day of dodging fellow shoppers in Causeway Bay. The places below are all reputable establishments.

Crystal Spa (☎ 2722 6600) Basement 2, Harbour Crystal Centre, 100 Granville Rd, Tsim Sha Tsui. Sauna for men/women costs HK$300/120 or HK$550/280 with massage.
Hong Kong Sauna (☎ 2572 8325) 388 Jaffe Rd, Wan Chai. This funky place is one of the oldest saunas in town. It only takes men and a one-hour sauna and massage will cost you HK$148.
New Paradise Health Club (☎ 2574 8807) 414 Lockhart Rd, Wan Chai. Services include sauna, steam room, spa bath and massage for both men and women. Sauna and massage costs HK$198.
Sunny Paradise Sauna (☎ 2831 0123) 339–347 Lockhart Rd. This place is for men only and sauna/massage starts at HK$340/240.

Scuba Diving
Diving in Hong Kong is not as rewarding as it once was due to pollution, but some areas in the far north-east are still worthwhile.

Bunn's Diving Equipment (☎ 2893 7899), 2nd floor, Yee Wo Mansions, 38–40 Yee Wo St, Causeway Bay, organises dives in Sai Kung on Sunday (9am to 4.30pm) for HK$380. Mandarin Divers (☎ 2554 7110), Ground floor, Unit 2, Aberdeen Marina Tower, 8 Shum Wan Rd, Aberdeen, has a whole range of diving activities on offer, and courses at all levels. Another outfit that offers diving courses is Pro Dive Education Centre (☎ 2890 4889, W www.divehk.com), 2nd floor, 127 Lockhart Rd, Wan Chai.

Skating
The Hong Kong Amateur Roller Skating Association (☎ 2504 8203, fax 2577 5671) can provide information on venues around the territory.

One of the best ice-skating rinks in Hong Kong is in Cityplaza Two (☎ 2885 4697),

1st floor, Cityplaza Shopping Centre, 18 Tai Koo Shing Rd, Quarry Bay. In Kowloon, there's a fabulous new rink at the upper ground floor of the Festival Walk shopping mall, Tat Chee Ave, Kowloon Tong called the Glacier (☎ 2265 5830). It's open 10.30am to 10pm weekdays, 8.30am to 10pm Saturday and 1pm to 5.30pm Sunday. It costs HK$50 on weekdays, and HK$60 on weekends for one of three sessions. The Sky Rink at the Dragon Centre (☎ 2307 9264), at the corner of Yen Chow St and Cheung Sha Wan Rd, Sham Shui Po, isn't half as nice. It's open from 8.30am to 1pm (HK$35) and 1pm to 10pm (HK$40) on weekdays and 8.30am to 10pm (HK$50) at the weekend.

Soccer

There are over 130 soccer fields in Hong Kong; contact the Leisure and Cultural Services Department (☎ 2603 4567, W www .lcsd.gov.hk) to locate the soccer field nearest to you.

Some easily accessible fields include:

Hong Kong Island
Blake Garden Po Hing Fong, Sai Ying Pun
King George V Park Hospital Rd, Sai Ying Pun
Southern Playground Hennessy Rd, Wan Chai
Victoria Park Causeway Bay

Kowloon
Kowloon Park Tsim Sha Tsui
Kowloon Tsai Park La Salle Rd, Shek Kip Mei
MacPherson Playground Sai Yee St, Mong Kok
Morse Park Fung Mo St, Wong Tai Sin

Squash

Hong Kong has upwards of 600 public squash courts. The most modern facilities are at the Hong Kong Squash Centre (☎ 2521 5072), bordering Hong Kong Park on Cotton Tree in Central. It costs under HK$30 per half-hour, and you should book in advance. There are also squash courts in Queen Elizabeth Stadium (☎ 2591 1331), 18 Oi Kwan Rd, Wan Chai.

Other venues include Kowloon Tsai Park (☎ 2336 7878), La Salle Rd, Shek Kip Mei

in Kowloon, and the Sports Institute (☎ 2681 6188), 25 Yuen Wo Rd, Sha Tin.

Swimming

The most accessible beaches are on the southern side of Hong Kong Island, but the best ones are on the outlying islands and in the New Territories. For a list of beaches deemed safe enough for swimming, check the Environmental Protection Department's Web site (W www.info.gov.hk/epd/beach).

From April to October some three dozen gazetted beaches in Hong Kong are staffed by lifeguards and the shark nets are inspected daily. From the first day of the official swimming season until the last, expect the beaches to be chock-a-block on weekends and holidays. When the swimming season is officially declared over, the beaches become deserted no matter how hot the weather.

At most of the beaches you will find toilets, showers, changing rooms, refreshment stalls and sometimes restaurants.

Hong Kong also has about a dozen public swimming pools. There are excellent pools in Kowloon Park (Tsim Sha Tsui) and Victoria Park (Causeway Bay). Most of these are closed between November and March, but heated indoor pools, such as the one at the South China Athletic Association (☎ 2890 7736), 88 Caroline Hill Rd, Causeway Bay, and the Morrison Hill Swimming Pool (☎ 2575 3028), 7 Oi Kwan Rd, Wan Chai, are open all year.

Tennis

The Hong Kong Tennis Centre (☎ 2574 9122), Wong Nai Chung Gap Rd, is on the spectacular pass in the hills between Happy Valley and Deep Water Bay on Hong Kong Island. It's open from 7am until 11pm daily, but it's only easy to get a court during working hours. It costs HK$42/57 per hour during the day/evening.

There are 14 courts, open from 7am to 10pm daily, in Victoria Park (☎ 2570 6186). The Bowen Road Sports Ground (☎ 2528 2983) in the Mid-Levels has four courts (open from 7am until 5pm daily) that cost HK$42 per hour. The South China

Athletic Association (☎ 2577 6932) also operates tennis courts at King's Park in Yau Ma Tei.

Water-skiing

The areas for water-skiing are on the southern side of Hong Kong Island: Deep Water Bay, Repulse Bay, Stanley and Tai Tam. Contact the Hong Kong Waterski Association (☎ 2504 8168) for more information.

Windsurfing

Windsurfing is extremely popular in Hong Kong; the territory's only Olympic gold medal (Atlanta, 1996) so far is in this sport. The best months for windsurfing are September to December when a steady northeast monsoon blows. Windsurfing during a typhoon is not recommended! Boards and other equipment are available for rent in Stanley on Hong Kong Island, at the Windsurfing Centre (☎ 2792 5605) in Sha Ha just past Sai Kung in the New Territories and at the Cheung Chau Windsurfing Centre (see Cheung Chau in the Outlying Island chapter for details). The Windsurfing Association of Hong Kong (☎ 2504 8255), Room 1001, Sports House, 1 Stadium Path, So Kon Po, Causeway Bay, has courses for people under 18.

Yachting & Sailing

Even if you're not a member, you can check with any of the following clubs to see if races are being held and whether an afternoon's sail aboard one of them is possible: Aberdeen Boat Club (☎ 2552 8182), Aberdeen Marina Club (☎ 2555 8321) and Royal Hong Kong Yacht Club (☎ 2832 2817) in Causeway Bay on Hong Kong Island and Hebe Haven Yacht Club (☎ 2719 9682) in the New Territories.

A major sailing event in Hong Kong is the Hong Kong–Manila yacht race, which takes place every two years. Phone the Hong Kong Yachting Association (☎ 2504 8158) or the Royal Hong Kong Yacht Club (☎ 2832 2817) for details.

You can rent smaller sailboats and Hobiecats at St Stephen's Beach in Stanley. Hobies rent for around HK$200 per hour.

If there is a group of you, you should consider hiring a junk for the day or evening. Included in the price is usually eight hours of vessel hire, plus a captain and deckhand. Charterboats (☎ 2555 8377) in Aberdeen hire out 35-person junks for HK$2500 on weekdays and HK$3000 to HK$3500 at the weekend.

COURSES

The Community Advice Bureau (see Useful Organisations earlier in this chapter) is a fabulous source of information on courses of all kinds in Hong Kong. The YMCA (☎ 2369 2211) and the YWCA (☎ 2524 8424) both offer a broad range of cultural classes and three-month courses on everything from basic Cantonese and mah jong to watercolour painting and tai chi.

For the visual arts, check with the Hong Kong Museum of Art (☎ 2721 0116), the Hong Kong Visual Arts Centre (☎ 2521 3008) or the Hong Kong Arts Centre (☎ 2582 0200). The Fringe Club (☎ 2521 7251), 2 Lower Albert Rd, in Central offers any number of courses and workshops.

Language

The Chinese University of Hong Kong (☎ 2609 8898, W www.cuhk.edu.hk), Ma Liu Shui, New Territories, offers regular courses in Cantonese and Mandarin. Classes can be arranged through the New Asia Yale Centre in the China Language Institute. There are three terms a year – one 10-week summer term and two regular 15-week terms. Other good places to check out are the School of Professional and Continuing Education at Hong Kong University (☎ 2547 2225) and the British Council (☎ 2913 5555).

A number of private language schools cater to individuals or companies. These informal schools offer more flexibility and even dispatch teachers to companies to teach the whole staff. Considering all the native Chinese speakers in town, tuition is not cheap, often running at around HK$300 plus per hour for one-on-one instruction. Language schools to consider include the following:

Chinese Language Institute of Hong Kong
(☎ 2523 8455) 17th floor, Yue Shing Commercial Building, 15 Queen Victoria St, Central
Chinese Language Society of Hong Kong
(☎ 2529 1638) 18th floor, Kam Chung Commercial Building, 19–20 Hennessy Rd Wan Chai
Venture (☎ 2507 4985) Flat 1A, 1st floor, 163 Hennessy Rd, Wan Chai

Dance

The Jean M Wong School of Ballet (☎ 2886 3992) has a half-dozen centres around the territory that offer courses in Chinese ethnic minority dance as well as Balinese dance, ballet, jazz dance and other Western styles. Prices are reasonable at HK$150 per hour.

Salsa, Latin, ballroom, rock and roll, and disco classes are offered at Island Dance (☎ 2987 0592, fax 2987 1571), 18–20 Lyndhurst Terrace, Central.

Cooking

The Towngas Cooking Centre (☎ 2576 1535) in Causeway Bay has classes in a vast range of Chinese cooking styles. You can learn three simple Chinese dishes in two hours on Wednesday mornings for HK$85 at the Home Management Centre (☎ 2510 2828) in North Point.

Pottery

The Pottery Workshop (☎ 2525 7949) at the Fringe Club, 2 Lower Albert Rd, Central (enter from Wyndham St), has classes on throwing and firing pots but they're expensive at HK$1700 for three hours of instruction over a week.

WORK

Travellers on tourist visas in Hong Kong are not supposed to accept employment. It is possible to obtain under-the-table work, but there are stiff penalties for employers who are caught hiring foreigners illegally. Still, many foreigners end up teaching or doing some other kind of work to earn extra money.

For professional jobs, registering with Hong Kong personnel agencies or headhunters is important. Drake Executive (☎ 2848 9288) is a popular employment agency that often advertises. You can always check the classified advertisments in the English-language local newspapers. The Thursday and Saturday editions of the *South China Morning Post* or the Friday edition of *iMail* are particularly helpful. *Recruit*, a free job seekers' tabloid, is available after 5pm on Monday, Wednesday and Friday in all MTR stations. *HK Magazine* also has a jobs section.

Work Permits

To work legally you need to have a work permit. The Hong Kong authorities require proof that you have been offered employment, usually in the form of a contract. The prospective employer is obligated to show that the work you plan to do cannot be performed by a local person. If you're planning on working or studying in Hong Kong, it could be helpful to have copies of transcripts, diplomas, letters of reference and other professional qualifications in hand.

In general, visitors must leave Hong Kong (Macau does not qualify) in order to obtain a work permit, returning only when it is ready. Exceptions are made, however, especially if the company explains that it urgently needs to fill a position. Work visas are generally granted for between one and three years. Extensions should be applied for a month before the visa expires.

From overseas, applications for work visas can be made at any Chinese embassy or consulate. For more information in Hong Kong, contact Immigration Department (☎ 2824 6111, Ⓦ www.info.gov.hk/immd), 2nd floor, Immigration Tower, 7 Gloucester Rd, Wan Chai.

Income Tax

The personal income tax system has a maximum marginal rate of 15%, and you don't pay any tax for your first year (though it's retrieved in your second year). The first HK$100,000 earned is tax-free. Many employers offer medical schemes and other incentives, such as a month's bonus at Chinese New Year.

Language Tutoring

Many of the professional Hong Kong Chinese who made the permanent move away from the territory took with them their excellent English-language skills. This, coupled with an increasing emphasis on the use of Mandarin, has led to a decline in the level of spoken English.

This decline has created job opportunities for foreigners trained as racecourse commentators, financial editors, magazine editors, TV and radio presenters, tour guides and, of course, English language teachers. Those with English-language teaching degrees (eg, TEFL) will find a bountiful market for their skills.

If you don't have the qualifications, you can still contact schools about teaching conversation classes. Alternatively you could advertise yourself as a one-on-one teacher of conversational English; expect to earn at least HK$250 an hour (many Hong Kong Chinese have their company pay for extracurricular English lessons). A good idea is to advertise yourself locally (eg, on Wellcome and Park 'N' Shop supermarket notice boards).

Translating If you're fluent in one or more foreign languages, you might get work as a translator. You can find dozens of companies listed in the *Yellow Pages* under 'Translators and Interpreters'. Some of these include Multilingual Translation Services (☎ 2581 9099), Polyglot Translations (☎ 2851 9099) and Language Line (☎ 2511 2677).

Bar & Restaurant Work

Good places to start looking for work in the catering industry are bars and Western restaurants in Lan Kwai Fong, Soho, Wan Chai, Tsim Sha Tsui and Yung Shue Wan on Lamma Island. Besides finding catering work, you may meet people in Western-style bars and restaurants with tips on English-teaching opportunities, modelling jobs, secretarial work and so on. Be warned that no bar or restaurant will hire you if you don't have a Hong Kong ID card and work permit.

Other Work

Occasionally Westerners can find work standing around as extras in Hong Kong films, work which demands long hours for little pay. If you have martial arts skills, a great sense of humour, appalling acting ability and a love of adventure, you too could be the next evil Western star in Hong Kong's frenetic cinema industry.

Modelling is another possibility for both men and women. Modelling agencies are listed in the *Yellow Pages*, but contacts are vital and the agencies are of limited help. Stunning looks and an impressive portfolio are more than a plus – they're a necessity.

ACCOMMODATION

There are three basic types of accommodation in Hong Kong: cramped guesthouses; adequate but uninspiring mid-range hotels; and luxury hotels, some of which are considered among the world's finest. Within each category there is a good deal of choice, and you should be able to find a comfortable place to stay.

The prices, even for budget accommodation, are higher than most other Asian cities but cheaper than those in Europe and the USA. It's worth bearing in mind that in recent years many guesthouses and hotels have dropped their prices and that mid-range and even some top-end hotels are offering 'winter packages' to attract customers.

The HKTB deals with some 80 hotels in Hong Kong; details, including prices and photos, can be found on their Web site.

Reservations

Making an advance reservation for accommodation is not essential, but can save a lot of time and money. If you fly into Hong Kong without having booked, the Hong Kong Hotels Association (HKHA; ☎ 2383 8380, fax 2362 2383, e hrc@hkha.org) has reservation centres at the airport and can get you a mid-range or top-end hotel room sometimes 50% cheaper than if you were to walk in yourself.

Booking through a travel agent can also garner substantial discounts, sometimes as much as 40% off the walk-in price. If you're in Hong Kong and want to book either a mid-range or luxury hotel, call Phoenix Services Agency (☎ 2722 7378) or Traveller Services (☎ 2375 2277), both of which are in Tsim Sha Tsui and listed under Travel Agencies in the Hong Kong Getting There & Away chapter. They can often get you a 20% to 30% discount.

Camping

The Country & Marine Parks Authority (☎ 2420 0529) maintains a total of 33 no-frills camp sites in the New Territories and outlying islands. These are clearly labelled on the *Countryside Series* maps. They are all free. Camping is prohibited on the 36 public beaches patrolled by lifeguards, but is generally OK on remote beaches.

You can camp at the hostels managed by the Hong Kong Youth Hostels Association (HKYHA) with the exception of the Jockey Club Mount Davis hostel on Hong Kong Island and Bradbury Lodge at Tau Mei Tuk in the New Territories. The fee, which allows you to use the hostel's toilet and washroom facilities, is HK$16 for HKYHA or Hostelling International (HI) members, HK$25 for nonmembers.

The availability of fuel is limited in camp sites so the most useful kind of stove is the type that uses disposable gas canisters, available at hardware and department stores throughout Hong Kong. A few hi-tech camp stoves can use diesel fuel, which is readily available. Kerosene is very difficult to find and ditto for 'white gas'. Local people use bags of charcoal for cooking on picnics and when camping.

Hostels

The Hong Kong Youth Hostels Association sells HKYHA and HI cards (see Hostel Card under Visas & Documents for details) and is the place to buy hostel paraphernalia (guidebooks, patches etc). The office is inconveniently located in a hideous housing estate near Shek Kip Mei MTR station. It is possible to buy membership cards at the hostels, but be sure to take along a visa-sized photo and some identification.

All of the hostels have separate toilets and showers for men and women and cooking facilities, including free gas, refrigerators and utensils. They provide blankets, pillows and sheet bag, though you may prefer to take your own.

Prices for a bed in a dormitory range from HK$30 to HK$75 a night, depending on the hostel and whether you are a junior (under 18 years of age) or senior member. Bradbury Lodge has family rooms for two/four people at HK$220/260 a room and rooms at Jockey Club Mount Davis hostel can accommodate two/three/four/six people for HK$150/225/300/450. If you're not an HKYHA or HI member, you can still stay at the hostels, but you'll be charged HK$30 more per night. After six nights, you automatically become a member.

Only Bradbury Lodge and Jockey Club Mount Davis hostels are open daily. They allow check-in from 7am to between 5.30pm and 7pm on weekdays, and to 1pm on Saturday. The rest of the hostels open on Saturday night and the eve of public holidays only. All hostels are shut between 11pm and 7am so forget about any late-night partying. Normally, travellers are not permitted to stay more than three days, but this can be extended if the hostel has space.

If making a booking more than three days in advance, ring or email the HKYHA head office. International computerised bookings are also possible. To reserve a bed less than three days before your anticipated stay, call the hostel directly. The phone numbers of the individual hostels are listed in the Places to Stay sections of the relevant chapters.

Remember that theft is a problem in any dormitory-style accommodation. The problem usually comes from your fellow travellers, not the management of the hostels. Most hostels have lockers available – be sure to use them.

Guesthouses

Dominating the lower end of the market are guesthouses, usually a block of tiny rooms squeezed into a converted apartment or two. Often there are several guesthouses operating out of the same building. Your options are greater if there are two of you. Find a double room in a clean guesthouse for HK$150 to HK$200 and your accommodation costs fall to a more bearable level.

Depending on the season and location, try to negotiate a better deal as a lot of places will be eager to fill empty rooms. Some guesthouses are swish, with doubles for up to HK$400.

Most guesthouses will at least have a public pay phone if there isn't one in your room. More and more are now offering Internet access as well.

Hotels

Most of what could be called budget places to stay in the city are guesthouses. Furthermore, there seem to be fewer and fewer hotels in the mid-range category.

Hong Kong's mid-range hotels can be as expensive as the top-end places in other cities. High demand and soaring property values keep accommodation costs high. Prices start anywhere from HK$700 to somewhere around HK$2000 for a double room. Singles are sometimes priced a bit lower. The average price you're likely to encounter is around HK$1000, though there is little to distinguish one room from another.

At the very least, rooms will have a separate bathroom with, shower, bath and toilet, air-conditioning, telephone and TV. Some hotels also supply in-house cable TV systems, minibars, toiletries and other small amenities. Many have business centres, email facilities and Internet access.

Be warned that most mid-range hotels charge from HK$3 to HK$5 for local calls unless you are a long-term resident (one month or more).

For those who can afford HK$2000 or more for a room, a stay in one of Hong Kong's luxury hotels is one of life's great experiences, with top-notch accommodation and service that is as smooth as silk. Of course, you should be selective – there are plenty of average hotels that charge top-end rates too. A few, such as the Peninsula, Island Shangri-La and Mandarin Oriental, offer comfort, amenities and service that

compete with or surpass that of the world's finest five-star hotels. All of these hotels have an elegant range of suites, for those who want both space and comfort.

As well as offering the finest in terms of comfort, many of these excellent hotels are home to some of the best restaurants and bars in Hong Kong. If shopping is on your itinerary, Hong Kong's best hotels have all the big names in fashion and style under one roof in elegant shopping malls.

Hotels in Hong Kong add 10% service and 5% government tax to your bill, something you won't be troubled with when staying at a guesthouse.

Rental Accommodation

It is worth looking at the flats advertised almost daily in the property pages of the English press, starting at around HK$4000 a month and usually in the Kowloon area. These are whole floors in apartment blocks that have been converted by landlords into makeshift studios (28 to 40 sq metres) that have a bathroom, TV, air-conditioning and a phone. You sometimes get to use a common kitchen.

Most Hong Kong Chinese prefer to live in tall, modern, lift-equipped high-rises and shun the old, smaller *tong lau*, or 'Tang buildings', which are usually five to seven storeys tall and often don't have lifts. The tong lau are much cheaper than the high-rises and sometimes have more character, though they are generally not as clean. There are no management fees, usually just a monthly cleaning fee which is only HK$100 to HK$200.

In the upmarket housing estates with central locations, fine sea views and security guards, rents start at around HK$10,000 a month for a studio flat and move up to around HK$20,000 for two bedrooms. Monthly management fees are extra. On Hong Kong Island, you can find these estates on the Peak, the Mid-Levels, Pok Fu Lam (especially Baguio Villa and Mt Davis), Happy Valley (Stubbs Rd), South Horizons in Ap Lei Chau, Deep Water Bay, Repulse Bay, Stanley and Shek O. In the New Territories, check out Tai Po (Hon Lok

Yuen), Yuen Long (Fairview Park), Clearwater Bay and Sai Kung. In the outlying islands, only Discovery Bay on Lantau Island falls into this category.

A one-bedroom apartment in the Mid-Levels will cost anywhere from HK$15,000 to HK$50,000 a month. That same apartment will go for somewhat less in Tsim Sha Tsui or Wan Chai. The districts on eastern Hong Kong Island, western Hong Kong Island (eg, Kennedy Town) and north-eastern or north-western Kowloon, are more affordable – you may find a one-bedroom apartment (roughly 60 sq metres) for HK$8000 a month. The most expensive place is the Peak, where rents can easily top HK$100,000 a month.

Apartments are measured in square feet in Hong Kong and the measurement is taken from the outside wall surface *in*; it sometimes even includes the lift lobby. That's the reason why the apartment you were interested in looked so much smaller than you thought it would.

The cheapest apartments are in the unsightly public housing estates that tend to be concentrated in Kowloon; more than half of all Hong Kong residents live in these places. A much better option is to find an apartment on one of the outlying islands, Lantau or Lamma, perhaps.

Apartments are generally rented with little or no furniture, but used furnishings can sometimes be bought from departing foreigners. Check the notice boards at pubs or around expatriate housing areas. Also check the classified advertisements of the weekend English-language papers and *HK Magazine*.

If you are stuck for accommodation, 'leave flats' are worth investigating. Employees on contract are rewarded every couple of years with long holidays and usually rent their apartments out while they're away. The usual duration is three months, during which time you are responsible for the rent and the wages of the *amah* (servant). These are listed in a separate section of the classifieds in the English-language papers.

Estate agents usually take a fee equivalent to one month's rent. Other up-front expenses include a deposit, usually equal to two months' rent, and, of course, the first month's rent in advance.

Those staying in Hong Kong for between one and three months may be interested in serviced apartments, high-priced flats rented out for a short term that have become more and more common, particularly in and around Central. Some of these are listed under Places to Stay in the relevant chapters.

FOOD

Hong Kong does not live by *dim sum*, *cha siu fan* (barbecued pork with rice) and *chau min* (fried noodles) alone, but Chinese food in its various incarnations is clearly what the territory does best (see the special section Chinese Food in this chapter). Still, the surfeit of other cuisines available at the territory's restaurants – from Russian and Argentinean to Korean and Indonesian – will have you spoiled for choice and begging for more.

Hong Kong Chinese have always been ready and more than willing to try something different or unusual in their own cuisine – braised, steamed or stir-fried whatever as long as it had 'its back to the sky', or perhaps something sweet in a long, hard pod. Over the years they've been less adventurous with 'foreign' (including other Asian) cuisines. With people travelling much more frequently these days, that has all changed, and there are few places on earth with a more cosmopolitan cuisine.

Unfortunately, eating well in Hong Kong is not as cheap as it once was. Plush, spacious surroundings and exotic cuisines are expensive, mainly because a high proportion of the price of a restaurant meal goes into paying for the space occupied by the customer's bottom. That said, it's still relatively easy to eat on a budget in Hong Kong. Almost every residential and commercial neighbourhood has cheap noodle shops, and 'takeaway lunchboxes' of fried rice or noodles should cost no more than HK$20. At lunch time also keep your eyes peeled for pavement signs advertising set lunches, usually at Hong Kong–style Western restaurants, where as little as HK$35 will get you soup, a main course, dessert and tea or coffee.

The best hunting grounds for budget eateries are the little back streets off Hollywood Rd in Central, Sheung Wan, Wan Chai, Causeway Bay and Tsim Sha Tsui. Most of these areas have the steady flow of commuters or residents needed to support a large number of noodle shops, fast-food joints and so on. They all have plenty of mid-range restaurants serving various Asian cuisines as well, and this is where Hong Kong truly comes into its own.

The HKTB distributes a useful quarterly called *Hong Kong District Food Guide* with suggested restaurants throughout the territory. For more comprehensive listings, see the Books section earlier in this chapter.

Asian Food

Hong Kong's glut of Thai eateries fields the diner with a lot of choice, but there's some very good ones and as many bad ones. Vietnamese, Indonesian/Malaysian and Filipino are other South-East Asian favourites (in that order); the best places to look are Causeway Bay and Tsim Sha Tsui.

Korean barbecues restaurants, where you cook *à table* and share up to a dozen small dishes of crisp vegetables and spicy *kimchi* (hot pickled cabbage), can be found everywhere, but especially in Sheung Wan. They're particularly good fun and very popular. Some Korean restaurants have a set-price, all-you-can-eat barbecue.

Japanese restaurants are never cheap unless you go for the places where the sushi is served on a conveyer belt. A Japanese meal can cost up to double what you'd spend at a comparable Chinese restaurant.

One option you shouldn't overlook is Hong Kong's Indian restaurants. Chungking Mansions has a vast array of Indian 'messes' (simple, usually unlicensed restaurants) serving basic but authentic Indian and Pakistani cuisine. See Places to Eat in the Kowloon chapter for details.

Vegetarian Food

Western vegetarian food is reasonably hard to come by in Hong Kong if you want anything more exotic than a salad, but there are quite a few Asian vegetarian options. See the special section Chinese Food for the home-grown variety.

Indian vegetarian cuisine is considerably spicier than its Chinese counterpart. Some Indian restaurants are exclusively vegetarian, but most offer a combined menu. Even if you're not vegetarian, it's worth trying tasty meatless dishes such as vegetable *biryani*.

There are quite a few vegetarian Indian restaurants in Chungking Mansions and elsewhere in Kowloon as well as on Hong Kong Island; see Places to Eat in those chapters for details.

Fast Food

Travellers often find themselves eating a lot more fast food in Hong Kong than they thought they would. Cost is one reason – a Big Mac here is cheaper than virtually anywhere else in the world. Fast food is also easier to order than dishes in many hole-in-the-wall Chinese restaurants.

Hong Kong counts hundreds of the usual international chain food outlets such as McDonald's, KFC, Hardee's and so on.

Hong Kong also has several home-grown fast-food chains that serve Western as well as Chinese food. The four biggest ones are Cafe de Coral, Maxim's, Dai Pai Dong and Fairwood. Breakfast at any of these can be *congee* (rice porridge with savoury condiments) as easily as ham and eggs. For lunch and dinner there's a range of different dishes, from pepper steak to home-style bean curd preparations. Most chains also have afternoon 'tea' or snack menus – a chicken leg, hot dog or fried radish cake with tea or coffee.

Among the easiest (if not the best) places to buy sandwiches, soups, filled baked potatoes and baked goods in Hong Kong are Oliver's Super Sandwiches and Delifrance outlets; you'll find them everywhere, from Central to Tuen Mun. Genroku Sushi is a Japanese fast-food chain where raw fish on rice balls is served on a conveyer belt. For locations of these outlets see Places to Eat in the relevant chapters.

Self-Catering

Wellcome and Park 'N' Shop, the two major supermarket chains, have branches all over Hong Kong. 7-Eleven convenience stores are ubiquitous and open 24 hours; Circle K outlets also abound.

Delicatessens are blossoming in Hong Kong. Gastronomes can head to a number of quality outlets, including Oliver's Food Stores, which are positively pungent with the aroma of herbs, spices, cheeses, dried sausages, patés and fine wines. Seibu department store in the Pacific Place mall in Admiralty has one of the best food halls in town, with dozens of imported cheeses, meats, snacks and luxury foods.

DRINKS
Nonalcoholic Drinks

Tea In Chinese restaurants tea is either offered free of charge or costs a couple of dollars for a large pot that can be refilled indefinitely. There are three main types of tea: green or unfermented tea; *bolei,* which is fermented tea and is also known as black tea; and *oolong*, which is semi-fermented tea. In addition, there are many different types of tea, including jasmine *(heung ping)*, which is a blend of tea and flower petals. Chinese tea is *never* served with milk or sugar.

On the other hand, Chinese add lots of things to Western tea. Milk tea *(nai cha)* uses an extremely strong brew so the flavour can punch through the heavy dose of condensed milk. Lemon tea *(ningmeng cha)* is also strong, and is often served with several whole slices of fresh lemon. The memory of one popular Hong Kong beverage that still brings on the dry heaves is *yuan yang*, a concoction that is half-tea, half-coffee.

Coffee The last few years have seen a miniature explosion of cafes in Hong Kong. In general they are expensive but serve a wide range of coffees. Local people enjoy chilled coffee *(dong gafei)*, a soft drink really, which can also be bought everywhere in cans. They come in various degrees of strength and consistency.

Juices Corner sundry shops and stalls in Hong Kong sell a whole range of made-on-the-spot fruit juices that cost about HK$6, but avoid the ones where the liquidisers (blenders) are already full and just spun around a couple of times for each customer. Orange, melon and sugarcane juices are the best; the bark of the latter is stripped with a machete and the pith pulverised in a grinder.

Soft Drinks Fleecy is *not* a term we use to describe the rip-off merchants who run the electronics shops in Tsim Sha Tsui. It is, in fact, the name of a sweet cold drink popular in Hong Kong. Fleecy always contains some sort of lumpy mixture, usually red or green mung beans, pineapple or some other fruit, and black grass jelly. Condensed milk or ice cream is usually part of the mixture. You can sample these drinks almost anywhere, including Chinese fast-food joints.

In any convenience store or supermarket you'll find a whole range of soft drinks, both local and imported. Another rather off Hong Kong favourite is boiled cola with lemon and ginger added. This is a speciality of the Dai Pai Dong chain.

Alcoholic Drinks

Beer Lager is by far and away the most popular alcoholic beverage in Hong Kong, and there's a wide choice of the amber nectar in supermarkets, convenience stores and bars. Hong Kong has two major breweries: Carlsberg (Denmark) and San Miguel (Philippines). These are the most widely available brands, along with those the breweries produce under licence, including Lowenbrau and Kirin.

Imported beers are popular, and most bars have a selection, mostly in bottles but sometimes on tap. There are good English draught bitters and ales as well as Guinness, though the taste suffers a bit in transit. Tsingtao, China's slightly fruity export beer, is sold everywhere.

Drinking beer in Hong Kong's bars is ridiculously expensive unless you target happy hour. See Pubs & Bars under Entertainment for details.

Wine Though the Chinese tend to refer to all home-grown alcohol as 'wine' in English, the majority are spirits distilled from grains like rice, sorghum or millet. Most are potent, colourless and extremely volatile. They are available in supermarkets, restaurants and a few bars.

The best known, and most expensive, Chinese 'wine' is *mao tai*, distilled from millet. Another delicacy is *goh leung* (*gao liang* in Mandarin), which is made from sorghum. The easiest on the palate is probably *siu hing jau*, more commonly known by its name in Mandarin, *shao xing jiu*.

In recent years, affluent Hong Kong Chinese have developed a taste for Western wine, especially the red variety, and speciality wine shops have sprung up around the territory. The choice is usually quite odd, with only plonk and top-shelf vintages on offer.

Brandy & Spirits Among Hong Kong's wealthier drinkers, cognac is the tipple of choice. Indeed, the territory accounts for more than 10% of the worldwide market and has the world's highest per capita consumption. Hong Kong residents generally drink it neat, but rarely sip; sometimes you'll even see a group of enthusiastic diners shouting *Gon bui!* (*Gan bei!* in Mandarin), literally 'empty glass', and downing it like shots of whisky or tequila. Supermarkets, department stores, restaurants and bars usually have a decent selection of other spirits and wines. Certain spirits can also be bought cheaply at supermarkets – no-name brands are excellent value.

ENTERTAINMENT
When you want to be wowed, Hong Kong is a capable entertainer. Most weeks, half a dozen local arts companies perform anything from Cantonese opera to an English-language version of a Chekhov play. Locally cultivated drama and dance is among the most enjoyable in Asia, and the schedule of foreign performances is also often impressive; recent imports have included French equestrian opera, a franchise of *Riverdance* and a John Lill 'piano fest'.

The Hong Kong government subsidises the cost of international acts, so ticket prices can be very reasonable. Expect to pay around HK$50 for a seat up the back for a local performance and up to HK$300 for a top-class international act.

Listings
To find out what's on in Hong Kong, pick up a copy of *HK Magazine*, a comprehensive entertainment listings magazine that also has lively articles on current trends in the city, reviews of restaurants and bars, and a classified ad pullout section called *black + white*. It's free, appears on Friday and can be picked up at restaurants, bars, shops and hotels throughout the territory.

Also worth checking out is *bc Magazine* (W www.bcmagazine.net), a monthly guide to Hong Kong's entertainment and partying scene. One of the most useful features in this highly visual and glossy publication is the complete listing of bars and clubs. It is also free and can usually be found alongside *HK Magazine* racks.

The *South China Morning Post* has daily arts and entertainment reviews and listings and a Friday liftout called *24/7*; most of its contents is available online (W www.total lyhk.com). The HKTB has several free information publications, including the monthly *Official Hong Kong Guide* and a weekly *What's On* leaflet.

Bookings
You can book tickets for films, concerts and a great variety of cultural events over the phone or Internet via Cityline (☎ 2317 6666, W www.cityline.com.hk). You pay by credit card and collect the ticket at the cinema, theatre or other venue usually by inserting your card into a special machine dispensing the tickets.

Bookings for most cultural events can also be made by telephoning URBTIX (☎ 2734 9009) from 10am to 8pm. Tickets can either be reserved with a passport's number and picked up within three days or paid for in advance by credit card. There are URBTIX windows at the City Hall in Central, the Hong Kong Arts Centre in Wan

Chai and the Hong Kong Cultural Centre in Tsim Sha Tsui.

Ticket City (☎ 2805 2804, W www.ticketcity-asia.com) books seats for some concerts and shows.

For films in most cinemas, you can buy tickets in advance through Cityline. Tickets for Broadway cinemas can be booked on ☎ 2388 3188.

Pubs & Bars

Watering holes in Hong Kong run the gamut from relatively authentic British-style pubs with meat pies, darts and warm beer to piss-elegant, neon-lit, 'here's looking at me' minimalist lounges.

Depending on where you go, beers cost at least HK$35 to HK$40 a pint, which is likely to be more expensive than the shirt on your back if you bought it in Hong Kong. Overall, Lan Kwai Fong on Hong Kong Island is the best – and most expensive – area for pubs, but there are also plenty in Wan Chai and in Tsim Sha Tsui.

Happy Hour During certain hours of the day, most pubs, bars and even certain discos and nightclubs give substantial discounts on drinks (usually half-price) or offer two for every one purchased. Happy hour is usually in the late afternoon or early evening – 4pm to 8pm, say – but the times vary widely from place to place. Depending on the season, the day of the week and the location, some pubs' happy hours run from midday till as late as 9.30pm and start again after midnight.

Discos & Clubs

Hong Kong has an active club scene, and many bars have started offering dance and theme nights. Most of the club nights take place on Friday and Saturday, but there are some mid-week venues. Cover charges range from HK$100 to HK$500+ when a foreign DJ with a name is mixing or there's an internationally recognised band on stage. On some nights, you may get in free (or for a cheaper cover) if you are among the first 50 or so through the door or dressed in 70s gear (or whatever) on theme nights.

Hong Kong's most talked about dance parties are one-off raves, held in venues as diverse as the airport hotel and the ferry pier at Kwun Tong. Raves are advertised in *HK Magazine* and *bc Magazine* as well as on the Internet (W www.hkrave.com). Raves usually kick off around 11pm, push through to 7am and cost HK$200 to HK$400.

For non-ravers, there are plenty of mainstream discos in Wan Chai and Tsim Sha Tsui where you can dance till you drop or the sun rises, whichever comes first. See the Entertainment sections in the Hong Kong Island and Kowloon chapters for details.

Nightclubs Hostess clubs come in two varieties in Hong Kong: the sleaze-pits mostly found on Peking Rd in Tsim Sha Tsui and Lockhart Rd in Wan Chai and the more 'respectable' establishments in Tsim Sha Tsui East. The difference is that the former blatantly try to cheat customers, while the latter don't need to – they're up front about their astronomical prices. The respectable hostess clubs offer live music, featuring Filipino bands and topless dance shows. An evening out in any of these places could easily cost HK$1000 or more.

Be wary of places where an aggressive tout, often female, stands at the entrance, and tries to persuade you to go inside. It's likely that there will be signs on the front door announcing 'Drinks Only HK$40' and naughty pictures to stimulate, er, your interest. Inside, a cocktail waitress, wearing nothing but her knickers, will serve you a drink. She will probably be friendly and chat for a few minutes. It will be one of the most expensive conversations of your life for the bill you're presented with will be in excess of HK$500.

When (or if) you protest, staff will undoubtedly point to the tiny sign posted on the wall behind a vase which informs you of the HK$400 service charge for talking to the waitress. If you balk at paying the fee or can't, don't be surprised if two gorillas suddenly happen to be standing by your elbows, who will frog-march you to the nearest ATM. You've just met your first Hong Kong Triad members.

Pop, Rock & Jazz

Canto-pop is the name for the local pop music (see Popular Music in the Music section of the Facts about Hong Kong chapter). If you give it a chance, you'll discover some worthwhile tunes (or ones that you won't be able to get out of your head for your entire stay).

There are usually a few decent rock bands (both local and imported) playing around town, and numerous bars have house band that play dance tunes. Hotel bars and clubs have Filipino bands who can play 'Hotel California' in their sleep (and yours).

A few venues, most notably the Jazz Club, bring in well-known jazz and blues musicians from time to time.

For details see the Entertainment sections in the Hong Kong Island and Kowloon chapters.

Concert Venues Hong Kong has at last arrived on the big-name concert circuit, and a growing number of internationally celebrated bands and solo acts, including Sting, Primal Scream, Oasis and Prodigy, perform in Hong Kong.

Big concerts are usually held either at the HITEC Rotunda (☎ 2620 2222), Trademart Drive, Kowloon Bay, or in the New Wing of the Hong Kong Convention and Exhibition Centre (☎ 2582 7887), 1 Expo Drive, Wan Chai. These are not huge venues, so the ticket prices are quite high.

Another venue is the 12,500-seat Hong Kong Coliseum (☎ 2355 7234), 9 Cheong Wan Rd, located behind the KCR station in Hung Hom. The sound is abysmal here, however.

Queen Elizabeth Stadium (☎ 2591 1347), 18 Oi Kwan Rd, Wan Chai, is OK for sporting events, but it's a lousy place to see a concert. You'd get better acoustics in an empty aircraft hanger.

Smaller acts are sometimes booked into the Ko Shan Theatre (☎ 2740 9222), Ko Shan Rd, Hung Hom. The sound at this venue isn't great either, but the back portion of the seating area is open-air, and most of the seats offer a good view of the stage.

Classical Music

In Hong Kong there are classical music concerts performed every week by one of the local orchestras (see Classical Music in the Facts about Hong Kong chapter for details) or a foreign ensemble. Many performances are held at the Hong Kong Cultural Centre (☎ 2734 2010) on Salisbury Rd in Tsim Sha Tsui just east of the Star Ferry terminal, which is home to the Hong Kong Philharmonic and the Hong Kong Chinese Orchestra. It is worth stopping by there to pick up a monthly schedule.

On Hong Kong Island the most important venues are: the Academy for the Performing Arts (☎ 2584 8554), 1 Gloucester Rd, Wan Chai; the Hong Kong Arts Centre (☎ 2582 0200), 2 Harbour Rd, Wan Chai; and City Hall Theatre (☎ 2921 2840), Edinburgh Place, next to the Star Ferry terminal in Central.

The New Territories also has three important cultural centres: Sha Tin Town Hall (☎ 2694 2536), 1 Yuen Ho Rd, Sha Tin; Tuen Mun Town Hall (☎ 2450 1105), 3 Tuen Hi Rd, Tuen Mun; and Tsuen Wan Town Hall (☎ 2414 0144), Yuen Tun Circuit, Tsuen Wan.

Cinemas

Hong Kong has more than 60 cinemas with some 172 screens. Most show local films (with English subtitles) or Hollywood blockbusters dubbed into Cantonese, but a few – Cine-Art House in Wan Chai, UA Pacific Place in Admiralty, Broadway Cinematheque in Yau Ma Tei – screen more interesting current release and studio films. See Cinemas under Entertainment in the Hong Kong Island and Kowloon chapters for more details.

Cinemas usually screen five sessions (12.30pm, 2.30pm, 5.30pm, 7.30pm and 9.30pm, with extra 4pm and 11.30pm screenings at the weekend). You must select a seat when you buy a ticket, which costs between HK$40 and HK$70, depending on the location and the policy of the cinema. Tickets are usually half-price on Tuesday and the last screening of the day at weekends (usually 11.30pm) is HK$40.

Almost all Hong Kong films showing in Hong Kong have Chinese and English subtitles. You can confirm that the film has English subtitles by checking its Censorship License in the cinema.

The publications *HK Magazine* and the *South China Morning Post* have listings for film screenings.

Theatre

Local theatre groups mostly perform at the Hong Kong Arts Centre, the Academy for Performing Arts or the Hong Kong Cultural Centre (see Classical Music earlier in this section). Performances are mostly in Cantonese, though summaries in English are usually available.

Smaller theatre companies occasionally present plays in English at the Fringe Club (☎ 2521 7251, W www.hkfringeclub.com), 2 Lower Albert Rd, Central.

SPECTATOR SPORTS

Sporting events are well covered in the sports section of Hong Kong's English-language newspapers. Many of the annual sporting events don't fall on the same day or even month every year, so contact the HKTB for further information.

Cricket

The Hong Kong International Cricket Sixes is held in late September/early October. This two-day event at Hong Kong Stadium sees teams from Australia, England, India, New Zealand, Pakistan and the Caribbean battle it out in a speedy version of the game.

Horse Racing

Without a doubt, horse racing is Hong Kong's biggest spectator sport, probably because it's the only form of legalised gambling in the territory and, boy, do Hong Kong Chinese people like to wager a bet! There are about 65 meetings a year at two racecourses: one in Happy Valley on Hong Kong Island and the other at Sha Tin in the New Territories (see the relevant chapters for more details).

The racing season lasts from late September to June. Normally, races at Sha Tin are held on Saturday from 11am while at Happy Valley, races are on Wednesday evening from about 7pm. But this schedule isn't etched in stone and sometimes extra races are held on Sunday and public holidays.

You'll need your passport to attend a race if you want to get a tourist ticket available to people who have been in the territory for less than 21 days. If you qualify, you'll be admitted despite the crowds and can also walk around next to the finish area.

If you want to attend the races, a seat in the public stands at Happy Valley costs HK$10. A visitor's badge to sit in the members' box costs HK$50. These badges can be purchased at the gate on the day of the race, or up to two days in advance at any branch of the Hong Kong Jockey Club (HKJC).

Betting is organised by the HKJC, and many combinations are available, including the quinella (picking the first and second place-getters in a race), double quinella (picking the first and second from two races), the treble (picking the winner from three specific races) and the six-up (picking the first or second from all six of the day's races). The HKJC (information hotline ☎ 1817, ☎ 2966 1333, W www.hkjockey club.com) maintains off-track betting centres around the territory including those at 39–41 Hankow Rd in Tsim Sha Tsui, 64 Connaught Rd in Central and 134–145 Gloucester Rd in Wan Chai.

Rugby

The Seven-A-Side Invitational Rugby Tournament, popularly known as the Rugby Sevens or just 'the Sevens', sees teams from all over the world come together in Hong Kong in late March/early April for three days of lightning fast (15-minute) matches at Hong Kong Stadium (☎ 2895 7895). Even non-rugby fans scramble to get tickets (adults/children HK$750/250) for the Sevens is a giant, international, three-day party.

For details on the tournament and buying tickets, contact the Hong Kong Rugby Football Union (☎ 2504 8311, W www.hk sevens.com.hk), Room 2001, Sports House, 1 Stadium Path, So Kon Po, Causeway Bay.

Soccer

Hong Kong has a lively amateur soccer league. Games are played on the fields inside the Happy Valley racecourse and at Mong Kok Stadium, Boundary St, Mong Kok. The sports section of the English-language papers carries information on when and where matches are held. Alternatively you can contact the Hong Kong Football Association (☎ 2712 9122), 55 Fat Kwong St, Ho Man Tin, Kowloon.

Tennis

Several international tennis tournaments are held each year in Victoria Park in Causeway Bay. The largest is the Salem Open in April; the Marlboro Championship is usually held in October. Check the local English-language newspapers for information on times and ticket availability.

SHOPPING

Shopping in Hong Kong is not just about buying stuff: it's a social activity, a form of recreation, a way of life for many. Though it isn't the bargain basement it once was, Honkers still wins for variety and for its passionate embrace of competitive consumerism. Any international brand worth its logo sets up shop here, and there are a slew of local brands worth your parting with a few 'red ones' as well. Clothing, shoes, jewellery, luggage and, to a degree, electronic goods are the city's strong suits – all of them can be made to order.

There are no sales taxes so the marked price is the price you'll pay. Credit cards are widely accepted, except in markets. It's rare for traders to accept travellers cheques or foreign currency as payment. Sales assistants in department or chain stores rarely have any leeway to give discounts, but you can try bargaining in owner-operated stores and certainly in markets.

The HKTB produces a handy little booklet called *A Guide to Quality Merchandise*, which lists shops that are HKTB members.

When to Shop

In the Central and Western districts, shop hours are generally 10am to 6pm and in Causeway Bay and Wan Chai from 10am to 9.30pm or 10pm. In Tsim Sha Tsui, Mong Kok and Yau Ma Tei, they are from 10am to 9pm. Many places close for major holidays – sometimes for up to a week – especially Chinese New Year.

Winter sales are during the first three weeks in January and the summer ones in late June/July.

How to Shop

How you shop is important in Hong Kong. The territory is *not* a nest of thieves just waiting to rip you off as some guidebooks seem to suggest, but there are a lot of pitfalls just waiting for the uninitiated to trip into.

Whatever you're in the market for, always check prices in a few shops, take your time and return to a shop several times if necessary. Don't buy anything expensive in a hurry and always get a manufacturer's guarantee or warranty that is valid worldwide. When comparing camera prices, for example, make sure you're comparing not only the same camera body but also the comparable lenses and any other accessories.

If you have any trouble with a dodgy merchant, call the HKTB (☎ 2807 6453) if he or she is a member of that association (the HKTB logo will be displayed on the front door or in some other prominent place). Otherwise, contact the Hong Kong Consumer Council (☎ 2929 2222).

If you are determined to take legal action against a shopkeeper, the Small Claims Tribunal (☎ 2825 4667) is the place to contact for cases involving less than HK$15,000. The Community Advice Bureau (☎ 2815 5444) can help you find a lawyer.

Duty Free The only imported goods on which there is duty in Hong Kong are alcohol, tobacco, perfumes, cosmetics, cars and some petroleum products. In general, almost anything – cameras, electronics, jewellery and so on – will be cheaper when you buy it outside duty-free shops.

Warranties & Guarantees Every guarantee should carry a complete description of the item (including model and serial numbers), as well as the date of purchase, the name and address of the shop it was purchased from, and the shop's official stamp.

Many imported items come with a warranty registration with the words 'Guarantee only valid in Hong Kong'. If it's a well-known brand, you can often return this card to the importer in Hong Kong to get a warranty card for your home country.

A common practice is to sell grey-market equipment (ie, imported by somebody other than the official local agent). Such equipment may have no guarantee at all, or the guarantee might only be valid in the country of manufacture (which will probably be either China or Japan).

Refunds & Exchanges Most shops are loathe to give refunds, but they can usually be persuaded to exchange untampered purchases: make sure you get a detailed receipt which enumerates the goods as well as the payment.

There is really no reason to put a deposit on anything unless it is an article of clothing being made for you or you've ordered a new pair of glasses. Some shops might ask for a deposit if you're ordering an unusual item that's not normally stocked, but this isn't a common practice.

Rip-Offs While most shops are honest, there are plenty that are not. The longer you shop in Hong Kong, the more likely it is that you'll run into a shopkeeper who is crooked.

The most common way for shopkeepers to cheat tourists is to simply overcharge. In the tourist shopping district of Tsim Sha Tsui, you'll rarely find price tags on anything. Checking prices in several shops therefore becomes essential. But Hong Kong merchants weren't born yesterday; they know tourists comparison-shop. So staff will often quote a reasonable or even low price on a big-ticket item, only to get the money back by overcharging on small items or accessories.

Spotting overcharging is the easy part. Sneakier tricks involve merchants removing vital components that should have been

included free (like the connecting cords for the speakers on a stereo system) and demanding more money when you return to the shop to get them. You should be especially wary if staff want to take the goods into the back room to 'box it up'. Another tactic is to replace some of the good components with cheap or defective ones. Only later will you discover that the 'Nikon' lens turns out to be a cheap copy.

Watch out for counterfeit-brand goods. Fake labels on clothes are the most obvious example, but there are fake Rolex watches, fake Gucci leather bags, even fake electronics goods. Pirated music tapes, CDs and DVDs are a positive steal (in more ways than one) for as little as HK$30 but are of poor quality and rapidly deteriorate.

Hong Kong's customs agents have been cracking down on the fake electronics and cameras, and the problem has been pretty much solved. However, counterfeit brand-name watches remain very common and are constantly being flogged by the irritating touts patrolling Nathan Rd. If you discover that you've been sold a fake brand-name watch by a shopkeeper when you thought you were buying the genuine article, call the police. This is definitely illegal.

Shipping Goods Goods can be sent home by post, and some shops will package and post the goods for you, especially if it's a large item. Also, find out whether you will have to clear the goods at the country of destination. If the goods are fragile, it is sensible to buy 'all risks' insurance. Make sure you keep all the receipts.

Smaller items can be shipped from the post office. United Parcel Service (UPS; ☎ 2735 3535) also offers services from Hong Kong to some 40 countries. It ships by air and accepts parcels weighing up to 30kg. DHL (☎ 2765 8111) is another option.

Where to Shop
Shopping Areas The main shopping districts are Tsim Sha Tsui, Central and Causeway Bay.

Tsim Sha Tsui is a curious mixture of tackiness and sophistication. Nathan Rd is the main tourist strip, a huge avenue with side streets full of camera, watch and electronics shops and leather and silk emporia. Although this is the part of town where you're most likely to get ripped off, Tsim Sha Tsui is also home to a large number of above-board designer and signature shops. Some of these are found in Nathan Rd, but the bulk are in Harbour City, a labyrinth of a shopping complex that stretches nearly 1km from the Star Ferry terminal north along Canton Rd. Tsim Sha Tsui East has a string of mostly upmarket shopping malls, the biggest being the Tsim Sha Tsui Centre at 66 Mody Rd.

Central has a mix of mid-range to top-end shopping centres and street-front retail; it's popular with locals and tourists alike. This is a good place to look for cameras, books, antiques and designer threads.

Causeway Bay has perhaps the largest weekend crowds and the broadest spectrum in terms of price. It is a crush of department stores and smaller outlets selling designer and street fashion, electronics, sporting goods and household items. In this area you'll also stumble upon lively street markets. Jardine's Bazaar and the area behind it are home to stalls and shops peddling cheap clothing, luggage and footwear.

Other shopping districts include Sheung Wan and Wan Chai on Hong Kong Island and Mong Kok in Kowloon.

Wan Chai is another good spot for medium- and low-priced clothing, sporting goods and footwear, but the area caters mainly for locals. The district has little glamour, but it's well worth sifting through for bargains.

For antiques and curios, head for Hollywood Rd in Sheung Wan, where there is a long string of shops selling Chinese and Asian items. Some of the really good spots have genuine finds, but be careful about what you buy.

Mong Kok caters mostly to local shoppers, and it offers good prices on clothing, sporting goods, camping gear, footwear and daily necessities. There's nothing very exotic, but for everyday items it's a popular spot, and it's fun to see how local people shop and what they are buying.

Markets For budget shopping, there's no better place to start than at one of Hong Kong's street markets.

Hong Kong's biggest market is the night market held on Temple St, which basically runs parallel to (and west of) Nathan Rd in Yau Ma Tei. If it's cheap (and in many cases shoddy) it'll be available: clothes, fake designer goods, watches, leather goods, pens, alarm clocks, radios, knives, cheap jewellery, pirated CDs, tapes and DVDs, illegal porn, potions, lotions and hundreds of other downmarket items. Alongside the market are numerous noodle and seafood restaurants and stalls where you can grab a bite in between purchases.

The Tung Choi St market, two blocks east of the Mong Kok MTR station, mainly sells cheap clothes. People start setting up their stalls as early as noon, but it's better to arrive between 6pm and 10pm, when there's a lot more on offer. Another bustling market is on Apliu St (open noon to 9pm) in Sham Shui Po, one block west of Sham Shui Po MTR station.

If you're looking strictly for clothing, try Jardine's Bazaar in Causeway Bay. A bit more upmarket and fun is the Stanley market, located in the village of Stanley on southern Hong Kong Island.

At any of these markets, it's good to check out the shops on the sides of the street, which are hidden behind all the street stalls. This is often where you'll find the real bargains, if there are any, and the staff are generally less pushy.

For more information see Shopping in the Hong Kong Island and Kowloon chapters.

Factory Outlets Another place to hunt down bargains is one of Hong Kong's factory outlets. Most of these deal in ready-to-wear garments, but there are a few that also sell carpets, shoes, leather goods, jewellery and imitation antiques. Often prices aren't that much less than in retail shops, and it's important to check purchases carefully, as refunds are rarely given and many articles are factory seconds and imperfect.

If you decide to shop in these outlets, pick up a copy of *The Smart Shopper in*

Hong Kong by Carolyn Radin, which is available in most bookshops. The HKTB also has useful handouts entitled *Factory Outlets for Locally Made Fashion* and *Factory Outlets for Jewellery*.

Shopping Centres Hong Kong is a mall-rat's heaven but don't feel compelled to visit more than a couple; the same brands turn up over and over again. The following is a brief rundown of what distinguishes the major shopping centres:

Cityplaza (☎ 2568 8665) 111 King's Rd, Tai Koo Shing, Quarry Bay. The largest shopping centre in eastern Hong Kong and directly linked up to the MTR. Being farther from the main business district, it charges retailers lower rents, which can translate into lower prices for shoppers.
Festival Walk (☎ 2520 8025) 80–88 Tat Chee Ave, Kowloon Tong. A sparkling new shopping centre with Hong Kong's largest cinema and ice-skating rink. There's a good middle-rung selection of shops, excellent disabled access and toilets on every level.
Harbour City (☎ 2118 8668) Canton Rd, Tsim Sha Tsui. An enormous place, with 700 shops in 4 zones. Every major brand is represented.
International Finance Centre (IFC) Mall (☎ 2147 3538) 1 Harbour View St, Central. A bright new centre with high-fashion boutiques, the great Eating Plus cafe-restaurant (see Places to Eat in the Hong Kong Island chapter) and the Airport Express terminus downstairs. Toilets are in short supply.
The Landmark (☎ 2842 8149) 1 Pedder St, Central. Lots of high fashion and good eating in this pleasant, open space.
Pacific Place (☎ 2801 4197) 88 Queensway, Admiralty. Piped jazz, free telephones and the classiest range in town.
Prince's Building (☎ 2921 2194, 2921 2199) 10 Chater Rd, Central. Prince's Building. Poky and disorienting but worth a look for its speciality fashion, toy and kitchenware shops.
Times Square (☎ 2118 8888) 1 Matheson St, Causeway Bay. A dozen floors of retail organised by type. There's food on the 11th, 12th and 13th floors, including some monster *dim sum* spots.

What to Buy

The following is intended as a guide to what sorts of goods are available in Hong Kong shops, department stores and malls. For specific outlets and their address, see Shopping in the Hong Kong Island and Kowloon chapters.

Antiques & Curios Hong Kong has a rich and colourful array of Asian antiques and curios, but serious collectors will restrict themselves to the reputable antique shops and auction houses. This is an area where the buyer can easily be fooled. Hong Kong imports many forgeries and expert reproductions from China and South-East Asia. Just remember that most of the really good pieces are in private collections and are often sold either through Christie's or Sotheby's, especially at their auctions in spring (March to May) and autumn (September to November).

Christie's (☎ 2521 5396) 28th floor, Alexandra House, 16–20 Chater Rd, Central
Sotheby's (☎ 2524 8121) 5th floor, Standard Chartered Bank Building, 4–4A Des Voeux Rd Central

Most of Hong Kong's antique shops are bunched along Hollywood Rd in Sheung Wan. The shops at the western end tend to be cheaper in price and carry more dubious 'antiques'. Some of them stock a range of old books and magazines, Chinese propaganda posters, badges from the Cultural Revolution and so on.

For Chinese handicrafts and other goods (hand-carved wood pieces, ceramics, paintings, cloisonné, silk garments) the main places to go are the large China-run department shops scattered throughout the territory. One of the biggest and best chains is Chinese Arts & Crafts. A bit more pedestrian is the Yue Hwa Chinese Products Emporium, but it is a great place to pick up little gifts for friends. Even more down-market are the CRC department stores.

Hong Kong is also an excellent place to buy fine art. For information on specific shops, consult the Shopping sections in the Kowloon and Hong Kong Island chapters as well as the Contemporary Art special section.

Cameras & Video Cameras When shopping for a camera, keep in mind that you should never buy one that doesn't have a price tag. This will basically preclude 99% of the shops in Tsim Sha Tsui. The best place to look for cameras is Stanley St in Central. Tsim Sha Tsui has a couple of shops on Kimberley Rd dealing in used cameras.

In and around the Tsim Sha Tsui rip-off zone, practically every video store has a demonstration TV set up in the rear of the store. You can expect a demonstration in which only the most expensive 'digital' video camera produces a crisp image. What you won't be told is that the TV is rigged so that it will only work properly with the overpriced digital model. You also won't be told that the 'digital' model is not digital at all, but an ordinary camera for which you get to pay double.

If you want to buy a camcorder, you must decide which standard you want, PAL, NTSC or SECAM (see Video Systems earlier in this chapter). A wrong choice would be a costly mistake, so pay careful attention to the labels.

Carpets While not really that cheap in Hong Kong, there is a good selection of silk and wool (new and antique) carpets. Imported carpets from Afghanistan, China, India, Iran, Pakistan, Tibet and Turkey are widely available. The best carpets have a larger number of knots per square inch (over 550) and are richer in detail and colour than cheaper carpets. Silk carpets are generally hung on the wall rather than used on the floor. Older carpets are dyed with natural vegetable dye. The bulk of Hong Kong's carpet and rug shops are clustered around Wyndham St in Central. There are also a few places in Ocean Terminal, part of the Harbour City shopping centre in Tsim Sha Tsui.

Clothing & Shoes For bargain threads, one of the best known places is Granville Rd in Tsim Sha Tsui. The eastern end is not much more than a row of downmarket shops with bins and racks of discount clothing, including a fair amount of factory rejects.

On Hong Kong Island, Jardine's Bazaar in Causeway Bay has low-cost garments, though it may take some hunting to find anything decent. There are several sample

shops and places to pick up cheap jeans in Lee Garden Rd and Li Yuen St in Central.

The street markets at Temple St (Yau Ma Tei), Tung Choi St (Mong Kok) and Apliu St (Sham Shui Po) have the cheapest clothes; see the previous Markets section.

For mid-priced items, Causeway Bay and Tsim Sha Tsui, particularly east of Nathan Rd, are good hunting grounds. Take the time to pop into one of the dozens of Baleno, Giordano, U2 or Esprit clothing stores branches. These specialise in well made and affordable mainstream fashion items.

The eastern end of Lockhart Rd in Causeway Bay is a good place to look for footwear. Check around though, as some places have considerably better prices than others on the same product. It's also worth taking a stroll down Johnston Rd in Wan Chai, which has lots of mid-priced and budget clothing outlets.

Although many people still frequent Hong Kong's tailors, getting a suit or dress made is no longer a great bargain. For a quality piece of work you'll probably pay close to what you would in New York or London. An exception might be some of the Indian tailors on the streets of Tsim Sha Tsui. Remember that you usually get what you pay for; the material is often good but the work may be shoddy. Remember that most tailors will require a 50% nonrefundable deposit and the more fittings you have, the better the result.

Computers Hong Kong is a popular place to buy personal computers and laptops. While prices are competitive, it is also important to pay careful attention to what you buy and where you buy it from. Computers are prone to breakdowns, so finding a shop with a good reputation for honesty is vital.

You may have your own ideas about what kind of computer you want to buy, but if you're just visiting Hong Kong you would be wise to choose a brand-name portable computer with an international warranty, such as Hewlett-Packard, Compac or Acer.

Be careful: you may be hit with a steep import tax when you return to your home country. Save your receipt; the older the machine, the less you're likely to pay in import duty. The rules in many countries say that the machine is tax-exempt if over one year old, and some shops in Hong Kong will even write you a back-dated receipt on request.

Electronics Sham Shui Po is a good neighbourhood to search for electronic items. You can even buy (and sell) second-hand goods. If you take any of the west exits from the MTR at Sham Shui Po station, you'll find yourself on Apliu St, one of the best places in Hong Kong to search for the numerous plug adaptors you'll need if you plan to use your purchase in Hong Kong, Macau and/or the mainland.

Mong Kok is another very good neighbourhood to look for electronic gadgetry. Starting at Argyle St and heading south, explore all the side streets running parallel to Nathan Rd, such as Canton Rd, Tung Choi, Sai Yeung Choi, Portland, Shanghai and Reclamation Sts.

There are also quite a few electronics shops in Causeway Bay, their windows stuffed full of camcorders, CD players and other goodies. Locals generally avoid these places – apparently many of these shops are under the same ownership, ensuring that the prices are high throughout the area.

It's best to avoid the electronics shops in Tsim Sha Tsui, many of which are skilled at fleecing foreign shoppers.

Ivory The only carved ivory products being sold legally in Hong Kong are those that were manufactured before a 1989 ban came into effect or are made of marine ivory (eg, walrus tusks). Ivory retailers need to have all sorts of documentation proving where and when the goods were made. Many countries, including the USA, now ban the importation of ivory altogether, no matter how or when it was manufactured.

Jade The Chinese attribute various magical qualities to jade, including the power to prevent ageing and accidents. The circular disc with a central hole worn around many necks in Hong Kong represents heaven in Chinese mythology.

If you're interested in looking at and possibly purchasing jade, head for the Jade Market in Yau Ma Tei, about a 10-minute walk from Yau Ma Tei MTR station. Unless you're fairly knowledgeable about jade, though, it's probably wise to limit yourself to modest purchases.

Fake jade does indeed exist; the deep green colour associated with some jade pieces can be achieved with a dye pot, as can the white, red, lavender and brown of other pieces. Green soapstone and plastic is also passed off as jade too.

Jewellery Jewellery exporting is big business in Hong Kong. This is because gemstones are imported, cut, polished, set and re-exported using cheap Chinese labour. In theory, this should make Hong Kong a cheap place to purchase jewellery. In reality, retail prices are only marginally lower than elsewhere. Your only real weapon in getting a decent price is the intense competition in Hong Kong.

Opals are said to be the best value in Hong Kong because this is where opals are cut. Diamonds are generally not a good deal, because the world trade is mostly controlled by a cartel. Hong Kong does not have a diamond-cutting industry and must import from Belgium, India, Israel and the USA.

A couple of reputable jewellery shop chains, including King Fook and Tse Sui Luen, will issue a certificate that not only states exactly what you are buying but guarantees that the shop will buy it back at a fair market price. It's worthwhile buying from one of these places; if you later become dissatisfied with your purchase, you can at least get most of your money back on a trade-in.

If you've bought something and want to find out its value, you can have it appraised. There is a charge for this service, and some stones (such as diamonds) may have to be removed from their setting for testing. You can contact the Gemmological Association of Hong Kong (☎ 2366 6006) for the current list of approved appraisers. One company that does appraisals is Valuation Services (☎ 2869 4350, ⓔ ed@gemvaluation.com), GPO Box 11996, Hong Kong.

Leather Goods & Luggage Most of what gets sent to the Hong Kong market from China is export quality, but check carefully because there is still a lot of rubbish on sale. All the big brand names like Gucci and Louis Vuitton are on display in Hong Kong department stores, and you'll find some local vendors in the luggage business, including the excellent Mandarina Duck.

Music Hong Kong is pretty much on the ball when it comes to tunes. HMV (inquiries ☎ 2832 9886) has four large outlets, including one in the Central Building, 1–3 Pedder St, Central, which is open from 9am to 10pm daily. CDs sell for around HK$130. HMV also does a large range of video CDs, DVDs and music and film zines. Don't expect to find tapes anywhere though – it's CDs only.

You can also buy CDs at the street markets on Temple St in Yau Ma Tei and Tung Choi St in Mong Kok, but these are usually pirated and the sound quality is poor.

Hong Kong is not a great place for Chinese musical instruments. There are a few shops along Wan Chai Rd between Johnston and Morrison Hill roads in Wan Chai, but what is on offer is generally not good value for money. You'd do better taking the train up to Shenzhen and looking there.

Watches Shops selling watches are ubiquitous in Hong Kong and you can find everything from a Rolex to Russian army timepieces and diving watches. As always, you should avoid the shops that do not have price tags on the merchandise. The big department stores and City Chain are fine but compare prices.

Getting There & Away

AIR

The Airport

The days of daredevil landings at Hong Kong's Kai Tak International Airport in east Kowloon ended in July 1998 when the territory's new award-winning airport opened on an island off the northern coast of Lantau. Despite the mixed feelings surrounding the demise of Kai Tak, the breathtaking descents over Kowloon – passengers could actually see into housing estate flats – were never worth the overall inefficiency that was the old airport's hallmark.

Kai Tak's single runway stretching into Kowloon Bay was one of the world's busiest, with aircraft movements often separated by only a few minutes during the day and all scheduled flights banned after midnight. There were long lines at immigration and customs and facilities were limited due to lack of space. Kai Tak's only real benefit was its central location.

Hong Kong International Airport (☎ 2181 0000, Ⓦ www.hkairport.com) at Chek Lap Kok is the result of a HK$160 billion airport core program that saw an island literally flattened and extended through land reclamation. The airport is connected to the mainland by several spans, including the 2.2km-long Tsing Ma Bridge, one of the world's largest suspension bridges and capable of supporting both road and rail transport. New motorways to and from the airport were constructed, including the 12.5km North Lantau Highway, and a massive harbour reclamation project made way for the six-lane Western Harbour Crossing, connecting the western part of Hong Kong Island with Kowloon for the first time. The Airport Railway Tunnel, carrying the 34km-long Airport Express high-speed train from Hong Kong Island to Kowloon and Chek Lap Kok, was laid on the seabed of Victoria Harbour to the east of the crossing.

The new airport's two runways and expanded facilities have cut back on the time departing passengers spend checking in and waiting as well as the time arriving passengers need to clear immigration and customs and claim their baggage. At maximum capacity, the airport will be able to handle 40 aircraft movements an hour, representing some 87 million passengers a year.

Warning

The information in this chapter is particularly vulnerable to change: Prices for international travel are volatile, routes are introduced and cancelled, schedules change, special deals come and go, and rules and visa requirements are amended. Airlines and governments seem to take a perverse pleasure in making price structures and regulations as complicated as possible. You should check directly with the airline or a travel agent to make sure you understand how a fare (and ticket you may buy) works. In addition, the travel industry is highly competitive and there are many lurks and perks.

The upshot of this is that you should get opinions, quotes and advice from as many airlines and travel agents as possible before you part with your hard-earned cash. The details given in this chapter should be regarded as pointers and are not a substitute for your own careful, up-to-date research.

The futuristic passenger terminal, designed by the award-winning British architect Sir Norman Foster, consists of eight levels, with check-in on level 7, departures on level 6 and arrivals on level 5. Retail outlets – including banks and moneychangers – total 140, there are 20 cafes, restaurants and bars and almost 300 check-in counters.

The Hong Kong Tourism Board (HKTB; ☎ 2508 1234) maintains information and services centres on all three passenger levels. Staff are usually on duty from 7am to 11pm daily. See Local Tourist Offices in the Hong Kong Facts for the Visitor chapter for details.

On the same levels you'll find counters run by the Hong Kong Hotels Association

(HKHA; ☎ 2383 8380). If you're looking for mid-range or top-end hotel accommodation and you haven't booked in advance, the HKHA can often get you a room at a half to two-thirds the price you would pay if you went directly to the reception desk in a hotel. Be aware that the hotels association does not handle hostels, guesthouses or other budget accommodation. For more information, see Accommodation in the Hong Kong Facts for the Visitor chapter.

It's wise to change as little money as possible with the moneychangers at the airport as the rates there are not optimum. There are several ATMs in the arrivals hall that support most major global networks and dispense Hong Kong dollars.

If you are booked on a scheduled flight on most airlines (but *not* a charter flight) and are taking the Airport Express to Chek Lap Kok, you can check in your bags and receive your boarding pass on the day of your flight at the in-town check-in counters at either of the Hong Kong and Kowloon Airport Express stations. You are required, however, to check yourself in at least 90 minutes before your flight. The counters are open from 5.35am to 12.30am daily.

Airlines

More than 60 international airlines operate services between Hong Kong International Airport and some 120 cities around the world. Hong Kong is the main gateway to China and much of East and South-East Asia. Consequently, the international air service is excellent, and competition keeps the fares relatively low compared with other countries in the region.

The following is a list of the major airlines represented in Hong Kong. Where applicable, reservation and/or reconfirmation telephone numbers (res) are followed by flight information numbers (info). Please note that the China National Aviation Corporation (CNAC) contact numbers are also good for Air China (CA), China Eastern Airlines (MU), China Northern Airlines (CJ), China Northwest Airlines (WH), China Southern Airlines (CZ) and China Southwest Airlines (SZ).

You can check flight schedules on the Hong Kong & Macau Airline Timetable Web site (Ⓦ www.hktimetable.com).

Aeroflot (SU; ☎ res 2537 2611, info 2769 6031) Room 1606, Tower Two, Lippo Centre, 89 Queensway, Admiralty

Air Canada (AC; ☎ res 2867 8111 info 2122 8124) Room 1608-12, Tower I, New World Tower, 18 Queen's Rd Central

Air France (AF; ☎ res 2524 8145, info 2501 9590) Room 2502-10, Jardine House, 1 Connaught Place, Central

Air India (AI; ☎ res 2522 1176, info 2116 8730) Room 3008-9, The Center, 99 Queen's Rd Central

Air New Zealand (NZ; ☎ res 2524 9041, info 2842 3642) 17th floor, Li Po Chun Chambers, 189 Des Voeux Rd Central

Alitalia (AZ; ☎ res 2543 6998, info 2769 6046) Room 806, Vicwood Plaza, 199 Des Voeux Rd Central

All Nippon Airways (NH; ☎ res 2810 7100, info 2810 7332) Suite 501, One International Finance Centre, 1 Harbour View St, Central

American Airlines (AA; ☎ res 2826 9269, info 2826 9102) 10th floor, Peninsula Office Tower, 18 Middle Rd, Tsim Sha Tsui

Angel Air (☎ 2375 9883) Room 14, Miramar Tower, 1 23 Kimberley Rd, Tsim Sha Tsui

Ansett Australia (AN; ☎ res 2527 7883, info 2842 3642) 17th floor, Li Po Chun Chambers, 189 Des Voeux Rd Central

Asiana Airlines (OZ; ☎ res 2523 8585, info 2769 7782) Room 3407, Gloucester Tower, 11 Pedder St, Central

British Airways (BA; ☎ res 2822 9000 info 2822 9060) 24th floor, Jardine House, 1 Connaught Place, Central

Cathay Pacific Airways (CX; ☎ res 2747 1577, info 2747 1234) 10th floor, Peninsula Office Tower, 18 Middle Rd, Tsim Sha Tsui

China Airlines (CI; ☎ res 2868 2299, info 2769 8391) 3rd floor, St George's Building, 2 Ice House St, Central

China National Aviation Corporation (CNAC; ☎ 2973 3666, info 2973 3733) Ground floor, CNAC Building, 10 Queen's Rd Central; (☎ 2922 1028) 2nd floor, CNT House, 120 Johnston Rd, Wan Chai

Continental Airlines (CO; ☎ res 3198 5777, info 2180 2180) Room 5801, The Center, 99 Queen's Rd Central

Czech Airlines (OK; ☎ 2868 3231) Room 24, New Henry house, 10 Ice House St, Central

Delta Air Lines (DL; ☎ res 2526 5875) Room 2503A, Caroline Centre, 28 Yun Ping Rd, Causeway Bay

Air Travel Glossary

Alliances Many of the world's leading airlines are now intimately involved with each other, sharing everything from reservations systems and check-in to aircraft and frequent-flyer schemes. Opponents say that alliances restrict competition. Whatever the arguments, there is no doubt that big alliances are the way of the future.

Courier Fares Businesses often need to send urgent documents or freight securely and quickly. Courier companies hire people to accompany the package through customs and, in return, offer a discount ticket which is sometimes a bargain. However, you may have to surrender all your baggage allowance and take only carry-on luggage.

Fares Airlines traditionally offer 1st class (coded F), business class (coded J) and economy class (coded Y) tickets. These days there are so many promotional and discounted fares available that few passengers pay full fare.

Lost Tickets If you lose your airline ticket, an airline will usually treat it like a travellers cheque and, after inquiries, issue you with another one. Legally, however, an airline is entitled to treat it like cash and if you lose it then it's gone forever. Take very good care of your tickets.

Onward Tickets An entry requirement for many countries is that you have a ticket out of the country. If you're unsure of your next move, the easiest solution is to buy the cheapest onward ticket to a neighbouring country or a ticket from a reliable airline which can later be refunded if you do not use it.

Open-Jaw Tickets These are return tickets where you fly out to one place but return from another. If available, this can save you backtracking to your arrival point.

Overbooking Since every flight has some passengers who fail to show up, airlines often book more passengers than they have seats. Usually excess passengers make up for the no-shows, but occasionally somebody gets 'bumped' onto the next available flight. Guess who it is most likely to be? The passengers who check in late. If you do get 'bumped', you are normally offered some form of compensation.

Reconfirmation Some airlines require you to reconfirm your flight at least 72 hours prior to departure. Check your travel documents to see if this is the case.

Restrictions Discounted tickets often have various restrictions on them – such as needing to be paid for in advance and incurring a penalty to be altered or cancelled. Others are restrictions on the minimum and maximum period you must be away.

Round-the-World Tickets RTW tickets give you a limited period (usually a year) in which to circumnavigate the globe. You can go anywhere the carrying airlines go, as long as you don't backtrack. The number of stopovers or total number of separate flights is decided before you set off and they usually cost a bit more than a basic return flight.

Ticketless Travel Airlines are gradually waking up to the realisation that paper tickets are unnecessary encumbrances. On simple one-way or return trips, reservations details can be held on computer and the passenger merely shows ID to claim their seat.

Transferred Tickets Airline tickets cannot be transferred from one person to another. Travellers sometimes try to sell the return half of their ticket, but officials can ask you to prove that you are the person named on the ticket. On an international flight, tickets are compared with passports.

Dragonair (KA; ☎ res 2868 6777, info 3193 3888) Room 4609-11, Cosco Tower, 183 Queen's Rd Central

Emirates Airlines (EK; ☎ res 2526 7171, info 2216 1088) 11th floor, Henley Building, 5 Queen's Rd Central

EVA Airways (BR; ☎ res 2810 9251, info 2769 8218) Room 701-3, Wheelock House, 20 Pedder St, Central

Garuda Indonesia (GA; ☎ res 2840 0000, info 2769 6689) 7th floor, Henley building, 5 Queen's Rd Central

Gulf Air (GF; ☎ 2882 2892, info 2769 8337) Room 2508, Caroline Centre, 28 Yun Ping Rd, Causeway Bay

Japan Airlines (JL; ☎ res 2523 0081, info 2769 6525) Room 2001, Gloucester Tower, 11 Pedder St, Central

KLM Royal Dutch Airlines (KL; ☎ res 2808 2111, info 2116 8730) Room 2201-3, World Trade Centre, 280 Gloucester Rd, Causeway Bay

Korean Air (☎ res 2368 6221, info 2769 7511) Shop G12 15, Tsim Sha Tsui Centre, 66 Mody Rd, Tsim Sha Tsui East

LOT Polish Airlines (LO; ☎ 2869 0668) Room 1701, Silver Fortune Plaza, 1 Wellington St, Central

Lufthansa Airlines (LH; ☎ res 2868 2313, info 2769 6560) Room 1109-10, Wing Shan Tower, 173 Des Voeux Rd Central

Malaysia Airlines (MH; ☎ res 2521 8181, info 2769 6038) 23rd floor, Central Tower, 28 Queen's Rd Central

Northwest Airlines (NW; ☎ res 2810 4288, info 2752 7347) Room 2908, Alexandra House, 16-20 Chater Rd, Central

Philippine Airlines (PR; ☎ res 2301 9300, info 2769 6253) Room 305, East Ocean Centre, 98 Granville Rd, Tsim Sha Tsui East

Qantas Airways (☎ res 2822 9000, info 2822 9060) 24th floor, Jardine House, 1 Connaught Place, Central

SAS Scandinavian Airlines (SK; ☎ res 2865 1370, info 2180 2180) suite 1401, Harcourt House, 39 Gloucester Rd, Wan Chai

Singapore Airlines (SQ; ☎ res 2520 2233, info 2769 6387) 17th floor, United Centre, 95 Queensway, Admiralty

South African Airways (SA; ☎ 2877 3277) 8th floor, Tower II, Admiralty Centre, 18 Harcourt Rd, Central

Swissair (SR; ☎ res 3002 1330, info 2769 6031) 8th floor, Tower II, Admiralty Centre, 18 Harcourt Rd, Central

Thai Airways International (TG; ☎ res 2876 6888, info 2769 6038) 24th floor, United Centre, 95 Queensway, Admiralty

Trans World Airlines (TW; ☎ 2851 1411) mezzanine floor, Sun House, 90 Connaught Rd Central

United Airlines (UA; ☎ res 2810 4888, info 2801 8617) 29th floor, Gloucester Tower, 11 Pedder St, Central

Vietnam Airlines (☎ 2810 6880) suite 3012, One International Finance Centre, 1 Harbour View St, Central

Virgin Atlantic Airways (VS; ☎ res 2532 6060, info 2180 2180) 27th floor, Kinwick Centre, 32 Hollywood Rd, Central

Buying Tickets

You will have to choose between buying a ticket direct to Hong Kong, then making other travel arrangements when you arrive, and buying a ticket allowing various stopovers in Asia. The latter could fly you from Sydney to London, with stopovers in Denpasar, Jakarta, Hong Kong, Bangkok, Calcutta, Delhi and Istanbul, for example.

Your plane ticket will probably be the single most expensive outlay in your travel budget, but you can reduce the cost by finding cut-rate fares. Stiff competition has resulted in widespread discounting, which is very good news for travellers, but you still have to shop around carefully. Talk to recent travellers, look at the ads in newspapers and magazines and watch for special offers.

Most important of all, remain flexible. The cheapest fares usually apply to a few seats per flight only, for example, so be prepared to switch dates to get the best rates. Mid-week travel, with a weekend overnight, is often cheaper.

When you're looking for bargain airfares, it's prudent to go to a travel agent rather than directly to the airline. Airlines *do* have promotional fares and special offers, but generally they only sell fares at the official listed price.

One exception is booking on the Internet. Many airlines offer some excellent fares via the Web. Also, many travel agents around the world have Web sites, which can make the Internet a quick and easy way to compare prices. However, if you're putting together a complicated itinerary, it might be best to deal face-to-face with a travel agent. They'll be able to advise you about inconvenient stopovers, arrival and departure times, and the various types of tickets available.

Call the airline first to gauge the price of the cheapest tickets and use that as your starting point when talking to travel agents. If you want the cheapest flight, tell the agent that, and then make sure you understand the restrictions on the ticket. Fares will vary according to your point of departure, the time of year, how direct the flight is and flexibility. With the cheapest tickets, you sometimes have to pay the travel agent first and then collect the ticket at the airport.

Most airlines divide the year into a 'high' or 'peak' (ie, expensive) season, a 'shoulder' (less expensive) season and a 'low' or 'off' (cheap) season. In the northern hemisphere, the high season is roughly June to September and the low season November to February. Holidays (Christmas and Chinese New Year) are treated as high season even though they are in the low season. In the southern hemisphere, the seasons are reversed.

If you purchase a discounted ticket and later want to make changes to your route or get a refund, you'll need to contact the original travel agent. Airlines only issue refunds to the purchaser of a ticket – usually the travel agent who bought the ticket on your behalf. Many travellers change their routes halfway through their trip, so think carefully before you buy a ticket that is not easily changed or refunded. Don't bother buying half-used tickets from other travellers, no matter how low the price. You won't be able to board the flight unless the name on the ticket matches that on your passport.

One thing to avoid is using a ticket back to front. Say you want to fly from Japan, where tickets are relatively expensive, to Hong Kong, where tickets are much cheaper, and back. It is possible to pay by cheque or credit card, have a friend or travel agent in Hong Kong mail you the ticket and use it in reverse. Problem is, the airline's computer records will show that the ticket was issued in Hong Kong rather than in Japan, and the airline can refuse to honour it. With the increase in the use of printed voucher tickets in recent years, however, people are doing this again, but the practice remains risky.

Ticket Types Normal economy-class tickets are *not* economical fares. Essentially they are full-fare tickets, but ones that give you maximum flexibility and are valid for 12 months. They are also fully refundable, as are unused sectors of a multiple ticket.

Advance purchase excursion (APEX) tickets are sold at a discount, but will lock you into a tight schedule. APEX tickets must be bought at least 14 days in advance, do not usually permit stopovers, and may have minimum and maximum stays along with fixed departure and return dates. Unless you must return on a certain date, it's best to purchase APEX tickets on a one-way basis only.

Group (or package) tickets are well worth considering and you do actually have to travel with the group once you arrive. However, once the departure date is booked, it may be impossible to change it – you can only depart with the group, even if you never meet another one of its 'members'. There could be other restrictions – you might have to complete the trip in 60 days, for example, or fly only during the low season or on weekdays.

Round-the-world (RTW) tickets, valid for between 90 days and a year, are put together by two or more airlines and allow you to make a circuit of the world using a combination of routes. An RTW ticket makes it possible to combine a visit to Hong Kong with a beach holiday in Thailand as well as stopovers in Europe and the USA. The departure date from your home country usually determines the fare (ie, high- or low-season rates). The flight dates (but not the overall routeing) are changeable en route, and most packages require you to keep moving in the same direction.

In the UK, prices start at an absolute minimum of UK£700, though UK£1200 is probably a more realistic figure. In Australia, count on paying at least A$2500. US prices for tickets with stops in Europe and South-East Asia might start as low as US$1200 but US$2000 is a more realistic figure. In Hong Kong, count on paying from HK$18,500.

A good travel agent can put together RTW fares at much lower prices than the joint airline deals. Remember, though, that these 'tailor-made' RTW tickets will usually make use of discounted (and therefore relatively inflexible) fares.

Some airlines offer full-time students and those under 26 discounts of up to 25% on tickets. But these discounts are generally only available on normal economy-class fares. You wouldn't get one, for instance, on an APEX or RTW ticket as these are already discounted.

Another option is a courier flight, where an air-freight company uses your checked luggage allowance to send its parcels. The drawbacks are that your stay abroad may be limited to one or two weeks, your luggage is usually restricted to carry-on, and there is unlikely to be more than one courier ticket available for any given flight. These arrangements usually have to be made a month or more in advance and are only available on certain routes. Courier flights are occasionally advertised in newspapers, or you can check the telephone book for air-freight companies.

Travel Agencies If you're buying a ticket in Hong Kong, you might find that the cheapest flights being advertised are by obscure agencies whose names have yet to reach the telephone directory. Many such firms are honest and solvent, but there are a few rogues who will take your money and run, only to reopen elsewhere a month or two later under a new name. Paying by credit card may offer some protection, as many card issuers provide refunds if you can prove you didn't get what you paid for.

A more common ruse to get you to part with your money is the request for a nonrefundable deposit on an air ticket. You pay a deposit for the booking, but when you go to pick up the tickets the staff claim that the flight is no longer available and will offer you a seat on another flight at a much higher price than you'd agreed upon.

It is best not to put down a deposit at all, but rather to pay for the ticket in full and get a receipt, which should clearly show that there is no balance due and that the full amount is refundable if the ticket you requested is not issued. Tickets are normally issued the day after the booking is made, but you must pick up the really cheap tickets (ie, group or package tickets) yourself at the airport from the 'tour leader' (who you will never see again once you've got the ticket).

If you think you have been ripped off, the HKTB can apply some pressure – and apparently has a fund to handle cases of outright fraud – but only if the agency is a member of the HKTB, which most of the budget ones are not.

One of the best places in Hong Kong to buy tickets (especially RTW ones) is Phoenix Services Agency (☎ 2722 7378, fax 2369 8884, ⓔ phoenix1@netvigator.com), room A, 7th floor, Milton Mansion, 96 Nathan Rd, Tsim Sha Tsui. The staff are friendly, patient and work very hard to get you the best possible price. Another dependable agency on Kowloon side that gets good reviews is Traveller Services (☎ 2375 2066, fax 2375 2050, ⓔ travelhk@asiaonline.net), room 1012, Silvercord Tower 1, 30 Canton Rd, Tsim Sha Tsui.

Many travellers use Sincerity Travel, operated by Hong Kong Student Travel (☎ 2730 3269, ⓦ www.hkst.com.hk), room 835A, Star House, 3 Salisbury Rd, Tsim Sha Tsui. This business doesn't offer the bargain fares it used to but it's still worth a try. If you hold an International Student Identity Card (ISIC), you can get a discount. They have seven other branches in Hong Kong, including one in Central (☎ 2868 6933), room 1107, Lane Crawford House, 70 Queen's Rd Central.

On Hong Kong Island, a long-established and highly dependable outfit is Concorde Travel (☎ 2526 3391, fax 2845 0485, ⓔ info@concorde-travel.com), 1st & 7th floors, Galuxe Building, 8–10 On Lan St, Central. Two others that have a loyal clientele are Aero International (☎ 2543 3800), 6th floor, Cheung's Building, 1–3 Wing Lok St, Sheung Wan, and Natori Travel (☎ 2810 1681, fax 2576 0311), room 1502, Melbourne Plaza, 33 Queen's Rd Central.

Travellers with Special Needs

If you have special needs of any sort – you're travelling in a wheelchair, taking a baby, on a special diet – let the airline staff know as soon as possible so that they can make the necessary arrangements.

Travellers with special dietary preferences or requirements (eg, vegetarian, kosher, salt-free) can request appropriate meals with advance notice. If you are travelling in a wheelchair, most international airports can provide an escort from check-in desk to plane where needed, and ramps, lifts, toilets and phones are generally available.

In general, children under two travel for 10% of the standard fare or, on some carriers, for free as long as they don't occupy a seat. Reputable international airlines usually provide nappies (diapers), tissues, talcum and all the other paraphernalia needed to keep babies clean, dry and at least half-happy. Children aged between two and 12 can usually occupy a seat for 50% of the full fare and 67% of a discounted one. They are allowed the standard baggage allowance.

Departure Tax

Airport departure tax at Chek Lap Kok is HK$80; children under 12 do not pay the tax. It is usually included in the price of the ticket. Travellers making the run to Macau by helicopter (see the Air section of the Macau Getting There & Away chapter for details) must also pay the departure tax.

The USA

The flight options across the Pacific corridor are bewildering. The *New York Times*, *LA Times*, *Chicago Tribune* and *San Francisco Chronicle* all have weekly travel sections in which you'll find any number of budget travel agents' ads. Council Travel (☎ 1-800-226 8624, ⓦ www.counciltravel.com) and STA Travel (☎ 1-800-781 4040, ⓦ www.statravel.com) have offices in major cities nationwide.

San Francisco-based Ticket Planet (☎ 1-800-799 8888, ⓦ www.ticketplanet.com) is an online agency with an excellent reputation and lots of RTW offerings. You might also try Priceline (ⓦ www.priceline.com), a 'name your price' service on the Web. Just enter your destination, dates of travel and the price you're willing to pay for

a ticket. If one of the participating carriers has an empty seat for which it would rather get something instead of nothing, they'll email you back within an hour.

The cheapest fares are offered by bucket shops. San Francisco is the bucket shop capital of the USA, though some good deals can be found in Los Angeles, New York and other cities. Such agencies can be found in the *Yellow Pages* or advertise in the major daily newspapers. If you're on the West Coast, a more direct way is to wander around San Francisco's Chinatown – especially in the Clay St and Waverly Place area. Many of the bucket shops are staffed by recent arrivals from Hong Kong and Taiwan who speak little English. Inquiries are best made in person.

Another very cheap option is a courier flight; one-way fares are sometimes available. You can find out more about courier flights and fares from the Colorado-based Air Courier Association (☎ 1-800-282 1202, ⓦ www.aircourier.org); the International Association of Air Travel Couriers (IAATC; ☎ 561-582 8320, ⓦ www.courier.org); and Now Voyager Travel (☎ 212-431 1616, ⓦ www.nowvoyagertravel.com). Most charge an annual membership fee.

If you're heading to Hong Kong during the low season, carriers like Asiana Airlines, Korean Air, China Airlines and Philippine Airlines can get you there from the West Coast for around US$700. Most of these flights make a stop in the carrier's home country, eg, Asiana Airlines and Korean Air take you through Seoul, China Airlines through Taipei, Philippine Airlines through Manila. This is not always such a bad thing, as it's usually easy to arrange a stopover for little or no extra charge.

Fares from other parts of the USA depend on whether you are flying from a major domestic airport. Flying from large cities like Atlanta, Chicago or Denver shouldn't cost too much more than from New York. If you're coming from somewhere off the major air routes, be prepared to pay more.

From Hong Kong, Philippine Airlines has a return fare to Los Angeles for as low as HK$3500; China Airlines and Asiana charge HK$4000. If you don't want to stop over, you should expect to pay anything from HK$4500 to HK$7000. Direct flights to the East Coast (on United or Northwest, for example) range from HK$6000 to HK$10,000, depending on the season.

Canada
Travel CUTS (☎ 604-659 2887 in Vancouver, ☎ 416-614 2887 in Toronto, W www .travelcuts.com) has offices in all major Canadian cities. You might also scan the travel agents' ads in the *Globe & Mail*, *Toronto Star* and *Vancouver Province*. From Vancouver return flights to Hong Kong are available from about C$900; add C$300 or C$400 for those from Toronto or Montreal.

If you're heading to Canada from Hong Kong, a direct return flight to Toronto will cost HK$7000 to HK$8500 though you'll do better on Korean Air (HK$5000 to HK$6000) if you don't mind stopping in Seoul. A return ticket to Vancouver will cost between HK$4000 and HK$6000 on Korea Air and EVA Airways.

Australia
STA Travel (☎ 131 776 Australia-wide, W www.statravel.com.au) and Flight Centre (☎ 131 600 Australia-wide, W www .flightcentre.com.au) are major dealers in cheap airfares and have branches in cities throughout Australia. The weekend travel sections in the *Sydney Morning Herald* and Melbourne's *The Age* have many ads offering cheap fares to Europe.

Fares to Hong Kong are relatively expensive, and the cheapest tickets easily available are APEX ones. The published return fares on Qantas Airways and Cathay Pacific Airways are usually around A$1400, but are often discounted. Low-season fares on Ansett start at around A$980. You can also usually get free stopovers in either Singapore, Bangkok or Kuala Lumpur if you fly with Singapore Airlines, Thai Airways International or Malaysia Airlines.

In Hong Kong tickets to Melbourne and Sydney will cost between HK$4000 and HK$6000, leaping to HK$8000 during holidays such as Christmas and the Chinese

New Year. Domestic-flight add-ons are available for HK$700 per sector.

New Zealand
In Auckland, STA Travel (☎ 09-309 0458), 10 High St, and Flight Centre (☎ 09-309 6171), National Bank Towers, corner of Queen and Darby sts, are popular travel agents. Both have branches throughout the country. Ads for other agencies can be found in the travel section of the *New Zealand Herald*.

The cheapest fares to Europe are routed through Asia. With Thai International (via Bangkok) and Malaysia Airlines (via Kuala Lumpur), return fares from Auckland to Hong Kong can range from NZ$1800 in the low season to NZ$2300 in the high season (ie, May to August and around Christmas). A 90-day return ticket on Singapore Airlines from Hong Kong to Auckland costs about HK$6600. You should be able to fly to Auckland and back on Malaysia Airlines for HK$5000.

The UK
If you're looking for a cheap way to Asia, London is Europe's major centre for discounted fares. In general, airfare discounting in the UK is a long-running business – agents advertise fares openly in the travel sections of the weekend newspapers as well as in the entertainment listings magazine *Time Out* and the freebie *TNT Magazine*.

Reliable travel agencies in the UK include STA Travel (☎ 0870-160 0599 , W www .statravel.co.uk), which has a central office at 85 Shaftsbury Ave, London W1, with other branches in London and Manchester. USIT Campus (☎ 0870-240 1010, W www.usitcampus.co.uk), 52 Grosvenor Gardens, London SW1, has some 50 branches throughout the UK. Both of these agencies sell tickets to all travellers, but cater especially to young people and students. Charter flights can work out a cheaper alternative to scheduled flights, especially if you do not qualify for the under-26 and student discounts.

Trailfinders (☎ 020-7938 3939, W www .trailfinders.com), 215 Kensington High St,

London W8, is another recommended travel agency, which also has branches in Manchester, Glasgow and other cities. Flightbookers (☎ 020-7757 2444, W www .ebookers.com), 177–178 Tottenham Court Rd, London W1, is another good place to check fares.

You might also nose around Chinatown in London's Soho. Significant bargains are usually offered as the Chinese community are regular fliers to Hong Kong. Some of these outlets only deal with Chinese customers, but Reliance Tours (☎ 020-7439 2651), 12 Little Newport St, London WC2, is a good bet, as is Samtung Travel (☎ 020-7437 6888), 12 Newport Place, London WC2. Even before the price-slashing started, you could pick up return tickets in Chinatown for around UK£450.

It all depends on the season and your flexibility, but you should be able to fly to Hong Kong and back for between UK£500 and UK£700, with some fares from agents in Chinatown undercutting even those.

Good deals from London or Manchester can often be found with British Airways, Gulf Air, Malaysia Airlines, KLM Royal Dutch Airlines, Singapore Airlines and Thai Airways International. Some of these airlines do not charge extra if passengers want to make a stop along the way; some even encourage this by offering stopover packages. Just remember that in general, the cheaper the airfare the more inconvenient the route. Gulf Air and Singapore Airlines offer the best value for money in terms of comfort and attention to passenger's needs (even though flights go via Dubai and Singapore, respectively).

From Hong Kong, Singapore Airlines has a return fare to London of HK$3500 on its morning flight (via Singapore), though this usually costs more like HK$6000 to HK$7000. At the time of writing, Virgin Atlantic and British Airways were offering 30-day return tickets for HK$4500, but prices are generally HK$5600/8000 in the low/high season. One-way flights are generally half the price of return tickets. On Malaysia Airlines, Gulf Air or Emirates Airlines, count on HK$4800 to HK$7000.

Continental Europe

Though London is the travel discount capital of Europe, there are several other cities in the region where you'll find a wide range of good deals, particularly Amsterdam, Athens and even Paris. From most cities in continental Europe, general return fares to Hong Kong are from US$500 to US$800, depending on the gateway and the season.

Many travel agencies have ties with STA Travel, where cheap tickets can be purchased and STA-issued tickets can be altered free the first time around (usually for a US$25 fee subsequently). Outlets in major cities include:

International Student & Youth Travel Service (ISYTS; ☎ 01-322 1267, fax 323 3767) 11 Nikis St, Upper Floor, Syntagma Square, Athens.
NBBS Reizen (☎ 020-624 09 89) Rokin 66, Amsterdam
Passaggi (☎ 06-474 0923, fax 482 7436) Stazione Termini FS, Galleria di Tesla, Rome
STA Travel (☎ 030-311 0950, fax 313 0948) Goethe Strasse 73, 10625 Berlin
Voyages Wasteels (☎ 08 36 68 22 06 in France, ☎ 01 43 62 30 00 outside the country, fax 01 43 25 46 25) 11 rue Dupuytren, 75006 Paris

Belgium, Switzerland and the Netherlands are also good places for buying discount air tickets. In Antwerp, WATS Reizen (☎ 03-226 16 26), De Keyserlei 44, has been recommended. In Zurich, try SSSR Voyages (☎ 01-297 11 11), Leonhardstrasse 10. In Amsterdam, a good agency to try is Malibu Travel (☎ 020 626 32 30), Prinsengracht 230.

Paris has several agencies worth trying, including: Forum Voyages (☎ 08 03 83 38 03), with a branch at 11 Ave de l'Opéra (1er); Nouvelles Frontières (☎ 08 25 00 08 25), with an outlet at 13 Ave de l'Opéra (1er); and Voyageurs du Monde (☎ 01 42 86 16 00), 55 Rue Sainte Anne (2e). The last specialises in travel to Asia and is highly recommended.

China

There are few bargain airfares to and from China as the government regulates the prices. Depending on the season, seats can be difficult to book due to the enormous volume of business travellers and Asian tourists, so plan far ahead. Some one-year normal return fares are: Beijing HK$4600; Chengdu HK$4500; Guangzhou HK$1020; Kunming HK$3200; and Shanghai HK$3300. One-way fares are exactly half the return price.

You should be able to do better than that, however. To Beijing, China Southern Airlines has a fixed return ticket for as low as HK$2300. An open ticket valid for 30 days on the same airline is HK$3500 and a 90-day one on Dragonair costs HK$3900. Group and charter flights are available to Chengdu, gateway to Tibet, for HK$2600 and HK$3500 respectively.

If you plan to fly to a destination in China from Hong Kong, you might save a small amount of money by heading for Shenzhen and boarding the aircraft at Huangtian Airport there. See Getting There & Away in the China Excursion – Shenzhen chapter.

Macau

For information on helicopter shuttle services between Hong Kong and Macau run by East Asia Airlines (☎ 2108 4838, 2859 3255) see Hong Kong in the Air section of the Macau Getting There & Away chapter.

North-East Asia

Japan is not a good place to buy cheap air tickets. In Tokyo, try STA Travel (☎ 03-5485 8380), Star Plaza Aoyama Building, 1-10-3 Shibuya. The cheapest fares start at around ¥550,000 for a round trip on United Airlines or Northwest Airlines. Japan Airlines and All Nippon Airways usually charge ¥560,000 to ¥575,000. Prices out of Hong Kong to Japan are usually around HK$6500, though Northwest and United have a 17-day excursion for HK$3600.

In Seoul one reliable discount travel agency is Joy Travel Service (☎ 02-776 9871, fax 756 5342), 10th floor, 24-2 Mukyo-dong, Chung-gu (directly behind City Hall). You might also try the discount shops on the 5th floor of the YMCA building, Chongno 2-ga, which is next to the Chonggak metro station). Asiana Airlines usually has the cheapest flights between Hong Kong and Seoul at around HK$2800 for a 14-day return. Cathay Pacific Airways' 17-day return is HK$3600.

Upwards of 15 flights a day link Taiwan and Hong Kong, with many of the seats taken by Taiwanese businessmen shuttling to and from China. Return fares on the Hong Kong to Taipei or Kaohsiung runs are HK$1700 in the low season and HK$2200 in the high season. A reliable agency in Taiwan is Jenny Su Travel (☎ 02-2594 7733, fax 2592 0068), 10th floor, 27 Chungshan N Rd, Section 3, Taipei. Otherwise, look for discount travel agencies that advertise in the local English-language newspapers, the *China Post* or *China News*.

South-East Asia

The Hong Kong to Thailand route offers some of the best deals in Asia. Cheap tickets abound, with return flights to Bangkok costing HK$1600 on Angel Air and HK$1800 on Gulf Air and Emirates Airlines. On Cathay Pacific, expect to pay from HK$2300 to HK$3500. In Bangkok, STA Travel (☎ 02-236 0262), 33 Surawong Rd, is a good and reliable place to start ticket shopping. For even cheaper fares try the travel agents on Khao San Rd.

In Singapore, STA Travel (☎ 737 7188), Orchard Parade Hotel, 1 Tanglin Rd, offers competitive discount fares to Asian and other destinations. Other agents advertise in the *Straits Times* classified columns. A Hong Kong-Singapore flight can cost anything from HK$2100 for a 30-day return on Garuda Indonesia to a minimum HK$3000 for the same thing on Cathay Pacific. Qantas sometimes has cheaper fares at around HK$2550 on offer.

To and from Indonesia, Garuda Indonesia has direct flights from Jakarta to Hong Kong, and from Denpasar to Hong Kong via Jakarta. There are numerous agencies selling discount tickets around Kuta Beach in Bali; several are on the main strip, Jalan Legian. In Jakarta, there are a few on Jalan Jaksa. A direct ticket to Jakarta on Cathay Pacific will cost HK$4500 to HK$5000, but if you don't mind – or want – a stopover, choose any of the following: Garuda via Singapore (HK$2800), Thai International via Bangkok (HK$3500); Singapore Airlines via Singapore (HK$3500).

Some sample return fares from Hong Kong to other South-East Asian destinations include: Kuala Lumpur HK$2000; Kathmandu HK$3600; Manila HK$1600; Pnomh Penh HK$2750; and Yangon (Rangoon) HK$2750. A five-day group ticket to Hanoi or Ho Chi Minh City (Saigon) costs about HK$1900.

Other Regions

There are numerous flights between Hong Kong and Russia (Moscow, HK$4950 return), the Middle East (Dubai, HK$4500 return), Africa (Johannesburg, HK$6000 return) and South America (Rio de Janeiro, HK$9500).

LAND
China

The only way in and out of Hong Kong by land is through mainland China. The options for surface travel to and from China have increased dramatically since the handover, with buses and trains departing throughout the day to destinations as close as Shenzhen and as far as Beijing. Travellers should be aware that, although the Hong Kong SAR is now an integral part of China, visas are still required to cross the border with the mainland.

China Visas Everyone except Hong Kong Chinese residents of the territory must have a visa to enter China. Holders of most – but not all – passports can get a visa on the spot for HK$100 at the Lo Wu border crossing, the last stop on the Kowloon-Canton Railway (KCR; see Visas under Information in the Shenzhen and Zhuhai chapters for the important details). This particular visa limits you to a maximum stay of five days within the confines of the Shenzhen Special Economic Zone *only* and the queues at most times are mammoth, requiring a wait of one to two hours. Even if you plan to visit just Shenzhen, it is *highly* recommended that you shell out the extra money and get a proper China visa. Who knows? You might like the mainland so much you'll want to carry on. There has been talk of issuing a visa good for all of the Pearl River delta, but

at present this is valid for groups of five people or more.

Visas can be arranged by China Travel Service (CTS; ☎ 2851 1788, W www.ctshk .com), the PRC's government-owned travel agency, and most travel agents, including those listed under Buying Tickets in the Air section of this chapter. Agents will charge HK$180 to HK$200 for a single-entry visa, HK$250 for one allowing two entries. If you want to do it yourself, go to the Visa Office of the People's Republic of China (☎ 2827 9569), 5th floor, Lower Block, 26 Harbour Rd, Wan Chai (open 9am to noon and 2pm to 5pm on weekdays). Visas processed in three days cost HK$180, and HK$380 in a single day. You must supply two photos, which can be taken at photo books in the MTR and at the visa office for about HK$30. Any photo-processing shop can oblige as well. Four photos cost HK$32.

Most CTS offices in Hong Kong, including the branches in Tsim Sha Tsui and Mong Kok, are open from 9am to 5pm daily. Locations include:

Hong Kong Island
Causeway Bay (☎ 2808 1131) Room 609, 2-20 Paterson St
Central (Head Office; ☎ 2853 3888, fax 2541 9777) Ground floor, CTS House, 78-83 Connaught Rd Central
Wan Chai (☎ 2832 3888) Ground floor, Southern Centre, 138 Hennessy Rd

Kowloon
Mong Kok (☎ 2789 5970) 2nd floor, Tak Po Building, 62-72 Sai Yee St
Tsim Sha Tsui (☎ 2315 7188) 1st floor, Alpha House, 27-33 Nathan Rd

Bus The good news is that you can reach virtually any major destination in Guangdong province, including Guangzhou, from Hong Kong by bus. The bad news is that very few of these call on Shenzhen proper. With KCR services so fast, efficient and cheap, just about everyone takes the train. It's a different story if you're heading for Shenzhen's Huangtian Airport, however.

Buses depart from eight major locations: one on Hong Kong Island, and the rest in Kowloon and the New Territories.

Admiralty Hong Kong's Citybus (☎ 2736 3888, 2873 0818 for a recording, W www .citybus.com.hk) runs five buses a day to Shenzhen airport from the bus station at Admiralty on Queensway. The first leaves at 8.10am, the last at 1.40pm. Tickets cost HK$100 (children and seniors HK$80). Buses to Guangzhou (adults/children and seniors HK$110/90) depart from the same station between 7.30am and 9.30am.

Citybus coaches call at China Hong Kong City in Tsim Sha Tsui and City One Shatin in Sha Tin before crossing the border with the mainland.

Tsim Sha Tsui You can board buses to Shenzhen airport, 35km south-west of Shenzhen town, and Guangzhou at the station below China Hong Kong City on Canton Rd in Tsim Sha Tsui. Buses depart for the airport five times between 8.30am and 2pm and about three times between 8am and 10am for Guangzhou. See the previous Admiralty listing for details.

The Eternal East bus company (☎ 2723 2923, 2751 1512, fax 2317 1586) has services to points throughout southern China, including Guangzhou (HK$100/180 one-way/return), Foshan (HK$150/280), Changshan (HK$320/580 and Xiamen (HK$350/680). Buses leave from outside their office in the Hankow Centre, 5-15 Hankow Rd, Tsim Sha Tsui. Some excellent packages also include two days/one night to Guangzhou (HK$680), Foshan (HK$880), Shantou (HK$1380) and Xiamen (HK$1300). Prices include return bus transportation and accommodation for two people.

Buses to points in southern China, including Guangzhou and Xiamen, also leave from the Cross-Border Bus Station (☎ 2317 7900) on Scout Path just off Austin Rd, Tsim Sha Tsui, between 7am and 6.30pm.

Hung Hom The transport division of CTS (☎ 2764 9803, W www.ctshk.com) runs between six and 10 buses a day to Guangzhou (HK$100) and other destinations in southern China from a series of stops on Cheong Wan Rd behind (south of) the KCR station at Hung Hom and just in front of the Hong Kong Coliseum. The first bus leaves at 7.30am, the last at 5.40pm.

Mong Kok CTS also runs hourly buses to Guangzhou and the rest of southern China from stops along Nelson St, opposite the CTS Mong Kok branch at 62-72 Sai Yee St.

Sha Tin Buses headed for Shenzhen airport depart City One Shatin on Tak Wing St in Sha Tin five times between 9am and 2.30pm. They leave for Guangzhou between 8am and 10am.

Hong Kong International Airport Buses run by CTS, Eternal East, Global Express (☎ 2375 0099) and Airport Chinalink (☎ 9747 1202) link Hong Kong airport at Chek Lap Kok with many points in southern China, including Guangzhou, Dongguan and Foshan. Eternal East and Airport Chinalink run up to 16 buses a day from the airport to major hotels in downtown Shenzhen, with the first departing at 10am and the last at 8.30pm. Tickets are available in the arrivals hall and buses leave from the airport tour coach station. The fare is HK$150/100 for adults/children and seniors.

Train Reaching Shenzhen is a breeze. Just board the KCR train at Hung Hom (HK$66/33 in 1st/2nd class) or any KCR station along the way (Kowloon Tong, Sha Tin, Tai Po Market etc) and ride it to Lo Wu; China is a couple of hundred metres away. For more details on KCR services, see Train under Public Transport in the Hong Kong Getting Around chapter.

The most comfortable way to reach Guangzhou by surface is via Kowloon-Guangzhou express train via Dongguan, which covers the 182km route in approximately two hours.

High-speed trains leave Hung Hom station for Guangzhou East train station seven times a day at 8.25am, 9.25am, 11.05am, 12.10pm, 1.25pm, 2.30pm and 4.45pm. They leave Guangzhou at 8.30am, 9.50am, 11am, 11.36am, 2.28pm, 3.50pm and 5.20pm. One-way tickets cost HK$230/180 in 1st/2nd class for adults and HK$115/90 for children under nine. You are allowed only one piece of luggage weighing up to 20kg. Additional bags cost HK$90 each.

There are also direct rail links between Hung Hom and Shanghai and Hung Hom and Beijing. Trains to Beijing West train station (via Guangzhou East, Changsha, Wuchang and Hankou) leave on alternate days, take 28 hours and cost HK$574/934/1191 for a hard/soft/deluxe soft sleeper. Prices for children are HK$366/604/788. The trains to Shanghai (via Guangzhou East and Hangzhou East) also leave on alternate days and take 28 hours. One-way fares are HK$508/825/1039 for a hard/soft/deluxe soft sleeper, with the equivalent prices for children HK$320/527/680.

There is one daily departure to Zhaoqing (adults/children HK$235/117) via Guangzhou East and Foshan at 2.30pm.

Immigration formalities at Hung Hom are completed before boarding; you won't get on the train without a visa (see China Visas under Land earlier in this chapter). Passengers are requested to arrive at the station 45 minutes before the train departs. To get to the Hung Hom station from Tsim Sha Tsui by public transport, take bus No 5C from the Star Ferry terminal or the No 8 green minibus from Hankow Rd.

Tickets can be booked up to 60 days in advance at CTS or the KCR station in Hung Hom. If tickets are booked on the phone (☎ 2947 7888), passengers must collect them at least one hour before the train departs. Tickets can also be bought at Kowloon Tong and Sha Tin KCR stations and at the Mong Kok MTR station.

A word of advice – if you haven't booked in advance, you could try to buy a ticket at the KCR ticket window or at the CTS counter in Hung Hom station. However, the queues are miles long at the former and the latter block-books tickets and will probably refuse to sell you one. Instead, make your way to the counter just before the entrance to the platforms. Tickets are always available there.

A cheaper but less convenient option is to take the KCR train to Lo Wu, cross through immigration into Shenzhen and catch a local train to Guangzhou. There are around

20 trains to and from Guangzhou daily, and the ride takes between 2½ to three hours. Ticket prices are Y41 (hard seat) and Y65 (soft seat). There is also an express train that takes 1½ hours and costs Y70.

If you're planning to do a lot of train travel in China from Hong Kong, CTS can book onward train connections from Guangzhou as well as between other major destinations (eg, Shanghai to Beijing). This is worth looking into, as buying a ticket in Guangzhou for, say, Beijing or Chengdu, can be a nightmare of long lines, pickpockets and frustration.

Europe

You *can* reach Hong Kong by rail from Europe, though most travellers following this route also tour China. Don't take this rail journey just to save money – a direct flight from Europe to Hong Kong works out to be about the same price or even less. Do the overland trip for the adventure and to take a good, long look at Russia, Mongolia and China.

The Trans-Siberian Railway is a term used generically for the Trans-Mongolian (7865km from Moscow via Ulaan Baatar to Beijing) and the Trans-Manchurian (9001km from Moscow via Harbin to Beijing) as well as the Trans-Siberian proper (9289km from Moscow to Vladivostok); they use the same tracks across Siberia, but have different routes east of Lake Baikal. The Turkestan-Siberian (or Trans-Kazakhstan) runs between Moscow and Ürümqi in north-west China.

From Beijing there are trains to Kowloon every other day (see Train under the previous China section). The minimum time needed for the whole journey (one way) is roughly 10 days.

In Hong Kong, tickets for the Beijing to Moscow journey can be booked at Moonsky Star (☎ 2723 1376, fax 2723 6653, W www.monkeyshrine.com), 4th floor, flat 6, E block, Chungking Mansions, 36-44 Nathan Rd, Tsim Sha Tsui. The staff are knowledgeable, helpful and can organise visas and tailor your ticket to include stops en route. The all-inclusive price from Hong Kong is about US$600.

Moonsky also has an office in Beijing (☎ 010-6591 6519, fax 6591 6517, e Monkey China@compuserve.com). Arranging trips through China and Russia can be very difficult and time-consuming; allow three to four weeks if booking in Hong Kong and at least two weeks in Beijing. Also, it can be difficult to book this trip during the summer high season. Low season shouldn't be a problem, but plan as far ahead as possible.

If you're travelling from Europe, one recommended agency is the Russia Experience (☎ 020-8566 8846, fax 8566 8843, w www.trans-siberian.co.uk), Research House, Fraser Rd, Perival, Middlesex UB6 7AQ, England. See also the Russian National Tourist Office's site (w www.interknowledge.com/Russia) for information.

Lonely Planet's *Russia, Ukraine & Belarus* has a chapter on trans-Siberian travel. There will be a new Lonely Planet guide, *Trans-Siberian Railway,* available in June, 2002. *The Big Red Train Ride* by Eric Newby should be your first choice as reading material to take along for the ride.

SEA
Departure Tax
When leaving Hong Kong by sea for China or Macau, there is a departure tax of HK$19, but it's an 'invisible' tax as it's almost always included in the price of the ticket.

China
Regularly scheduled ferries link Hong Kong with many coastal towns and cities on the Pearl River delta, with one major exception – Shenzhen. You can, however, reach Shenzhen's Huangtian Airport and Shekou by boat, as well as Guangzhou, Zhuhai and other ports not normally of interest to travellers.

High-speed ferries (☎ 2921 6688, w www.turbojet.com.hk) leave the China ferry terminal on Canton Rd in Tsim Sha Tsui for Fuyong ferry terminal (Shenzhen airport) eight times a day between 7.30am and 7pm. There are as many return sailings from Fuyong starting at 9am, but the last two (at 7.30pm and 8.45pm) terminate at the Macau ferry terminal in Central, not in

Kowloon. Fares from Kowloon start at HK$189, from the airport at HK$171.

Ferries also depart from the China ferry terminal for Guangzhou at 7.30am and 2pm, with return sailings at 10.30am and 4.30pm. The economy-class fare from Kowloon is HK$198, from Guangzhou HK$189.

Some 13 Jetcats run by Shekou Passenger Ferry Lines (☎ 2526 5305, 2736 1387) link Hong Kong with Shekou, a port about 20km west of Shenzhen town, easily accessible by bus or taxi to the centre and a lively nightlife area in its own right, from 7.45am to 9pm daily. Eight of these leave from the China ferry terminal in Tsim Sha Tsui, while the rest go from the Macau ferry terminal in Central. Return sailings from Shekou are from 7.45am to 9.30pm. Ticket prices start at HK$90, and the trip takes one hour.

Zhuhai, the Special Economic Zone north of Macau, can also be reached from Hong Kong a dozen times a day from 7.45am to 9.30pm on ferries operated by the Chu Kong Passenger Transportation Co (☎ 2858 3876). Seven of the ferries depart from the China ferry terminal in Kowloon, while the rest go from the Macau ferry terminal on Hong Kong Island. The dozen return sailings from Zhuhai start at 8am and finish at 9.30pm. Fares start at HK$177 and the trip takes 70 minutes.

Chu Kong also has ferries to a number of other ports in southern Guangdong province, including Zhongshan and Dongguan (four to six sailings a day). Ferries run by a company called Expert Fortune (☎ 2375 0688, 2517 3494) link the China ferry terminal in Tsim Sha Tsui with Nansha.

Macau
For details on the myriad choices available for getting to and from Macau by sea, see the Getting There & Away chapter in the Macau section.

ORGANISED TOURS
It's so easy to organise a tour yourself once you've arrived in Hong Kong that it hardly pays to do so beforehand. See Organised Tours in the Hong Kong Getting Around chapter for details.

Getting Around

TO/FROM THE AIRPORT

Hong Kong International Airport (☎ 2181 0000, Ⓦ www.hkairport.com) at Chek Lap Kok on the north coast of Lantau Island is much farther away from the town centre than Kai Tak, Hong Kong's former airport, and getting into town can be costly. The Airport Express line of the Mass Transit Railway (MTR) is the most popular transport choice, although a gaggle of much cheaper buses connect the airport with Kowloon, the New Territories and Hong Kong Island.

Airport Express

Airport Express trains (☎ 2881 8888, Ⓦ www.mtr.com.hk) depart from Hong Kong station in Central every 10 minutes from 5.50am to 12.48am daily, calling at Kowloon station in Jordan and at Tsing Yi Island before reaching Airport station. The last train leaves the airport for all three stations at 12.48am. Running at speeds of up to 135km/h, trains make the journey from Central/Kowloon/Tsing Yi in only 23/20/12 minutes respectively.

One-way adult fares from Central/Kowloon/Tsing Yi are HK$90/80/50, with children and seniors paying half-price. Return fares, valid for a month, are HK$160/140/90. A same-day return is equivalent to a one-way fare.

Airport Express has two shuttle buses on Hong Kong Island (H1 and H2) and six in Kowloon (K1 to K6), with free transfer for passengers between Hong Kong and Kowloon stations and major hotels. They run from some time after 6am to 11pm. Schedules and routes are available at Airport Express and MTR stations and on the MTR/Airport Express Web site.

Bus

Most major areas of Hong Kong Island, Kowloon and the New Territories are connected with the airport by bus, of which there is an enormous choice. The various buses are run by different companies; see

Bus under Public Transport later in this chapter for details.

The most useful for travellers are the 'airbuses' A11, A12 and the A21, which go to or near the major hotel and guesthouse areas on Hong Kong Island and in Kowloon. These buses are air-conditioned, have plenty of room for luggage, and announcements are made in English and Chinese notifying passengers of hotels at each stop. But they are also the most expensive; there are cheaper options such as taking local bus E11 to Hong Kong Island or shuttle bus S1 to Tung Chung and then the MTR to Kowloon or Central.

The following lists give the bus numbers, the service provider, routes, fares and frequencies for the airport buses most frequently used by visitors. Bus drivers in Hong Kong cannot give change, but it is available at the ground transportation centre at the airport as are Octopus cards (see Travel & Tourist Passes under Public Transport later in this chapter for details). Normal returns are double the one-way fare though there is a discount for those returning within the same day. Unless stated otherwise, children and seniors pay half the fare.

From the airport the following buses go to Hong Kong Island:

A11 (Citybus) Sheung Wan, Central, Admiralty, Wan Chai, Causeway Bay, Tin Hau MTR station; HK$40/60 one way/same-day return; every 15 to 20 minutes from 6am to midnight

E11 (Citybus) Sheung Wan, Central, Admiralty, Wan Chai, Causeway Bay; HK$21; every 15 to 20 minutes from 5.20am to midnight

N11 (Citybus) Sheung Wan, Central, Admiralty, Wan Chai, Causeway Bay; HK$31; every 20 minutes from 12.15am to 4.45am

A12 (Citybus) Sheung Wan, Central, Admiralty, Wan Chai, Causeway Bay, Tin Hau, Fortress Hill, North Point, Quarry Bay, Sai Wan Ho, Shau Kei Wan, Chai Wan, Siu Sai Wan; HK$45/67.50 one way/same-day return; every 15 minutes from 6am to midnight

If you're heading for areas in Kowloon choose:

A21 (Citybus) Mong Kok, Yau Ma Tei, Jordan, Tsim Sha Tsui, Kowloon-Canton Railway (KCR) station at Hung Hom; HK$33/49.50 one way/same-day return; every 10 minutes from 6am to midnight

N21 (Citybus) Tsing Yi Rd West, Mei Foo Sun Chuen, Lai Chi Kok, Cheung Sha Wan, Sham Shui Po, Prince Edward, Mong Kok KCR Station; HK$23; every 20 minutes from 12.15am to 5.30am

The following buses connect the airport with points in the New Territories and Outlying Islands. Some of them terminate at MTR stations, from where you can reach destinations in Kowloon and on Hong Kong Island at a lower cost than the more direct buses.

A31 (Long Win) Tsing Yi, Kwai Chung, Tsuen Wan MTR; HK$17; every 15 to 20 minutes from 6am to midnight. The MTR fares from Tsuen Wan to Tsim Sha Tsui/Central are HK$9/13

N31 (Long Win) Tung Chung, Tsing Yi, Tsuen Wan MTR; HK$20; every 20 to 30 minutes from 12.20am to 5am

A35 (New Lantao) Tong Fuk Village, Mui Wo, HK$14 (HK$23 on Sunday and public holidays); every 30 to 40 minutes from 6.30am to 12.05am

N35 (New Lantao) Tong Fuk Village, Mui Wo, HK$20 (HK$30 on Sunday and public holidays); every hour from 12.30am to 5am

S1 (Citybus) Tung Chung MTR; HK$3.50; every six to 10 minutes from 5.30am to midnight. The MTR fares from Tung Chung to Tsim Sha Tsui/Central are HK$17/23

DB02R (Discovery Bay Transportation) Discovery Bay; HK$28; every 30 minutes from 5am to 12.30am

S55P (Citybus) Chek Lap Kok Ferry Pier; HK$3; every 30 minutes from 6.18am to 9.03pm. This is the bus to take if you're going to or coming from Tuen Mun by high-speed ferry (see the following Boat section)

You can also reach Shenzhen and other points in southern China directly from the airport. For details see the Hong Kong Getting There & Away chapter and the Getting There & Away section in the China Excursion – Shenzhen chapter.

Taxi

Taking a taxi to or from the airport at Chek Lap Kok is an expensive affair; on top of the fare shown on the meter, passengers are required to pay a HK$30 toll for using the Lantau Link in both directions (making a total of HK$60).

A taxi to the Star Ferry in Tsim Sha Tsui and the Kwun Tong MTR in Kowloon costs roughly HK$285 and HK$340 respectively. On Hong Kong Island a taxi should cost HK$350/370/380/430 to Central/Wan Chai/Causeway Bay/Aberdeen. To Tsuen Wan and Sha Tin in the New Territories it costs HK$235 and HK$325 though the fare is somewhat cheaper if you manage to get a New Territories taxi. A taxi to the Tung Chung MTR station should cost about HK$40.

There are limousine service counters in the arrivals hall and at the ground transportation centre, including Dah Chong Hong (☎ 2262 1888) and Intercontinental Hire Cars (☎ 2336 6111). Expect to pay from HK$360 to destinations in urban Kowloon and around HK$390 to Hong Kong Island.

Boat

High-speed ferries run by Airport Ferry Services (☎ 2987 7351) link the airport with Tuen Mun in the New Territories. They depart from Tuen Mun every 20 to 40 minutes between 6am and 10.40pm; the first ferry from Chek Lap Kok pier leaves at 6.15am and the last at 11pm. The one-way fare is HK$15/10 for adults/children and seniors. The trip takes between nine and 12 minutes. To reach the pier from the airport, catch bus S55P.

PUBLIC TRANSPORT

When it comes to public transport, nobody does it better than Hong Kong. Buses, ferries, trains and trams are plentiful, cheap, fast and efficient; you'll rarely wait more than a few minutes for the conveyance of your choice. What's more, armed with a stored-value Octopus card (see the following Travel & Tourist Passes section) you need never fumble for a coin or a note again.

Hong Kong is a small and crowded place and certain forms of public transport, especially the MTR, can get very crowded during rush hour on weekdays and Saturday morning; the Outlying Islands ferries are chock-a-block with holidaymakers on Sunday. Save your sanity and try to avoid these times if you can.

Travel & Tourist Passes

The Octopus 'smart card', originally designed for the MTR, is now valid on most forms of public transport in Hong Kong and will even allow you to make purchases at some branches of 7-11 and Circle K. All you do is touch (or rather 'zap') fare-deducting processors installed at stations, ferry piers, on minibuses etc with the Octopus card and the fare is deducted, showing you how much credit you still have left.

The Octopus card comes in two basic denominations: HK$150 for adults and HK$70 for children and seniors. Both denominations include a refundable deposit of HK$50. If you want to add more money to your card, just go to one of the add-value machines or the ticket offices located at every station. The maximum amount you can add is HK$1000, and the card has a maximum negative value of HK$35, which is recovered the next time you reload (thus the HK$50 deposit). Octopus fares are between 5% and 10% cheaper than ordinary fares on the MTR, KCR and Light Rail Transit (LRT) systems.

You can purchase Octopus cards at ticket offices or customer service centres in MTR, KCR and LRT stations as well as at Outlying Islands ferry piers on both sides. If you have any queries, call the Octopus hotline on ☎ 2266 2266.

The much-advertised Airport Express Tourist Octopus card is not really worth the microchip embedded into it. It costs HK$200 (including HK$50 deposit) and allows one single trip on the Airport Express, three days' unlimited travel on the MTR and HK$20 usable value on other forms of transport. In the end you can get your deposit back (plus any part of the HK$20 'usable value' still on the card) or keep the card, emblazoned with that lovely word 'tourist', as a souvenir.

Bus

Hong Kong's extensive bus system offers a bewildering number of routes that will take you just about anywhere in the territory. Most visitors use the buses to explore the south side of Hong Kong Island and the New Territories. The north side of Hong Kong Island and most of Kowloon are well-served by the MTR.

Although buses pick up and discharge passengers at stops everywhere along the way, on Hong Kong Island the most important bus stations are below Exchange Square in Central and at Admiralty. From these stations you can catch buses to Aberdeen, Repulse Bay, Stanley and other destinations on the south side of Hong Kong Island. In Kowloon, the bus station at the Star Ferry in Tsim Sha Tsui is the most important, with buses to Hung Hom station (or Kowloon station for the KCR) and points in eastern and western Kowloon. Almost all so-called New Towns in the New Territories are important transport hubs, though Sha Tin is particularly so, with buses travelling as far afield as Sai Kung, Tung Chung and Tuen Mun.

There are no good bus maps and because buses are run by a number of different private operators, there is no longer a comprehensive directory to the whole territory. Your best option is Universal Publications' *Hong Kong Guidebook* (see Maps under Planning in the Hong Kong Facts for the Visitor chapter), which includes a pull-out *Public Transport Boarding Guide* in Chinese (mostly) and English. The Hong Kong Tourism Board (HKTB) has useful leaflets on the major bus routes on Hong Kong Island, Kowloon, the New Territories and Lantau Island, which can be downloaded from their Web site (see Local Tourist Offices in the Hong Kong Facts for the Visitor chapter) and the major bus companies (see the following list) detail all their routeings on their Web sites.

Most buses run from about 5.30am or 6am until midnight or 12.30am, but there are a handful of useful night bus services in addition to the ones linking the airport with various parts of the territory. The N121, which operates every 15 minutes from 12.45am to 5am, runs from the Macau ferry pier on Hong Kong Island and through the Cross-Harbour Tunnel to Chatham Rd South in Tsim Sha Tsui East before continuing on to eastern Kowloon and Ngau Tau Kok. Bus No 122 runs from North Point on Hong Kong Island, through the Cross-Harbour Tunnel to Chatham Rd South, the northern part of Nathan Rd and on to Mei Foo Sun Chuen, in the north-west part of Kowloon. You can catch these two buses near the tunnel entrances on either side of the harbour.

Other useful night buses that cross the harbour include: the N111, which runs from Victoria Park in Causeway Bay on Hong Kong Island to Choi Hung in eastern Kowloon; the N112, which runs from Victoria Park in Causeway Bay to the Prince Edward MTR station in Kowloon; the N118, which runs from Siu Sai Wan in the north-eastern part of Hong Kong Island to Sham Shui Po in north-west Kowloon; and the N170, which runs from Sha Tin in the New Territories to Wah Fu, a large estate near Aberdeen in south-west Hong Kong Island.

Bus fares range from HK$1.20 to HK$45, depending on the destination and how many sections you ride the bus. Night buses cost from HK$12.80 to HK$23. Payment is made into a fare box upon entry so, unless you're carrying an ever-so-convenient Octopus card (see the previous Travel & Tourist Passes section), have plenty of coins handy as the driver does not give change.

Hong Kong's buses are run by a half-dozen private operators, carrying some 3.9 million passengers a day. Though it's much of a muchness of who's driving you from A to B or even C, you may want to check the routeings on their Web sites.

Citybus (☎ 2736 3888, 2873 0818 for a recording, **W** www.citybus.com.hk); 960 yellow buses; 108 bus routes mostly on Hong Kong Island with some cross-harbour and airport buses

Discovery Bay Transportation Services (☎ 2987 0208); has two routes that serve Tung Chung on northern Lantau and also the airport

KCRC Bus Service (☎ 2468 7799, **W** www .kcrc.com); a total of 21 bus routes to feed the KCR East Rail and Light Rail Transit (LRT) systems

Kowloon Motor Bus (KMB) Co (☎ 2745 4466, **W** www.kmb.com.hk); 4065 red and cream buses; 385 bus routes in Kowloon and the New Territories with some cross-harbour buses

Long Win Bus Co (☎ 2261 2791, **W** www .kmb.com.hk); 159 buses; KMB subsidiary operating 15 routes to north Lantau and the airport

New Lantao Bus Co (☎ 2984 9848, **W** www .kcm.com.hk/); 90 single-deck buses; KMB subsidiary operating 18 routes on Lantau Island

New World First Bus Services (☎ 2136 8888, **W** www.nwfb.com.hk); 730 green, white and orange buses; 93 Hong Kong Island and cross-harbour routes

Public Light Buses This is an official term and no-one ever uses it in conversation. 'Public light buses' are vans with no more than 16 seats. They come in two varieties. Minibuses are cream-coloured with a red roof or stripe, which pick up and discharge passengers wherever they are hailed. Maxicabs, cream-coloured with a green roof or stripe, operate on fixed routes. Thus minibuses are more like cabs and maxicabs are more like buses. Just try not to think about it…

There are 4350 public light buses running in the territory, divided equally between minibuses and maxicabs.

Minibuses Red minibuses can be handy for short distances, such as from Central to Wan Chai or Causeway Bay, and you can be assured of a seat – passengers are not allowed to stand by law. The destination is displayed on the front in large Chinese characters, usually with a smaller English translation below. They'll stop for you most anywhere, but not in restricted zones or at busy bus stops.

The problem for non-Chinese-speakers is not getting on but getting off the minibus. There are no buttons or bells, so you must call out your stop. Moreover, minibus drivers rarely speak English. If you call out, 'stop here please', there is a pretty good chance the driver will do so, but otherwise try the Cantonese version *yáhùh lòhk* (have to get down), which sounds like 'yow lok' or simply *nì doh* (here), pronounced like 'lido'.

Minibus fares range from HK$2 to HK$20. The price to the final destination is displayed on a card propped up in the windscreen, but this is also often only in Chinese. Fares are equal to or higher than those on the bus, but drivers often increase their fares on rainy days, at night and over holiday periods. You usually hand the driver the fare when you get off and change is given. You can use your Octopus card on some minibuses.

If you're in Central on Hong Kong Island, the best place to catch minibuses to Wan Chai and other points east is on the ground level of Exchange Square. If heading west towards Kennedy Town, walk up to Stanley St, near Lan Kwai Fong. There are a few minibuses that cross the harbour late at night, running between Wan Chai and Mong Kok. On Hong Kong Island, minibuses can be found on Hennessy and Fleming roads. In Kowloon you may have to trudge up Nathan Rd as far as Mong Kok or over to the Hung Hom station before you'll find one. Minibuses to the New Territories can be found at the Jordan and Choi Hong MTR stations in Kowloon.

Maxicabs More commonly known as 'green minibuses', maxicabs operate on some 295 routes, more than half of which are in the New Territories, and serve at designated stops. Fares range from HK$2 to HK$22.50, according to distance. You must put the exact fare in the cash box as you descend; no change is given. In Tsim Sha Tsui the No 1 green minibus (HK$3.20) runs from the Star Ferry terminal to Tsim Sha Tsui East every five minutes or so between 8.15am and 10.15pm. On Hong Kong Island, another No 1 green minibus leaves from Edinburgh Place east of the City Hall and Star Ferry terminal for the Peak every five to 12 minutes from 7.10am to 12.25am.

Mass Transit Railway (MTR)

The Mass Transit Railway (Map 16; ☎ 2881 8888, Ⓦ www.mtrcorp.com/train), Hong Kong's underground rail system, is a phenomenon of modern urban public transport. Sleek, pristine clean and always on time, it is also rather soulless.

Though it costs a bit more than other forms of public transport, the MTR is the quickest way to get to most destinations in the urban areas. Trains run every two to four minutes from around 6am to sometime between 12.30am and 1am daily.

The MTR travels on just over 77km of track and is made up of five lines, including the Airport Express covered in the earlier To/From the Airport section. The Island line extends along the northern coast of Hong Kong Island from Sheung Wan in the west to Chai Wan in the east. The Tsuen Wan line runs from Central station and travels alongside the Island line as far as Admiralty, where it crosses the harbour and runs through central Kowloon, terminating at Tsuen Wan in the New Territories. The Kwun Tong line, which begins at Yau Ma Tei, shares that and two subsequent stations with the Tsuen Wan line when it branches off and heads for eastern Kowloon before crossing the eastern harbour and ending at Quarry Bay. The Tung Chung line shares the same rail lines as the Airport Express, but stops at two additional stations in Kowloon along the way. It terminates at Tung Chung New Town on Lantau Island, a place of no particular interest to travellers but one that offers cheaper transport options to and from the airport. The MTR connects with the Kowloon-Canton Railway (KCR) at Kowloon Tong station *only*.

For short hauls, the MTR is not great value. If you want to cross the harbour from Tsim Sha Tsui to Central, for example, at HK$9 the MTR is more than four times the price of the Star Ferry with none of the views and is only marginally faster. If your destination is farther away – North Point, say, or Kwun Tong – the MTR is considerably faster than a bus or minibus and about the same price. If possible, it's best to avoid the rush hours: 7.30am to 9.30am and 5pm to 7pm, including Saturday morning. Some 2.4 million people use the MTR every day, most of them at those times.

Travelling by the MTR is child's play; everything – from the ticket-vending machines to the turnstiles – is automated. The system uses the stored-valued Octopus cards (see the earlier Travel & Tourist Passes section), really the only way to go, and single-journey tickets with a magnetic coding strip on the back. When you pass through the turnstile, the card is encoded with the station identification and time. At the other end, the exit turnstile sucks in the ticket, reads where you came from, the time you bought it and how much you paid. If everything is in order, it will let you through. If you underpaid (by mistake or otherwise), you can make up the difference at an MTR service counter; there are no fines since no-one gets out without paying. Once you've passed through the turnstile with your new ticket, you have 90 minutes to complete the journey before it becomes invalid.

Ticket prices range from between HK$4 and HK$26; children and seniors pay between HK$3 and HK$13, depending on the destination. Ticket machines take HK$10, HK$5, HK$2 and HK$1 notes and HK$0.50 coins, and give change; a few in each station also accept HK$20 notes. The machines have a touch-sensitive screen with highlighted destinations. You can also buy tickets from MTR service counters and get change from the Hang Seng bank branches located in most stations.

Smoking, eating and drinking are not permitted in MTR stations or on the trains, and violators are subject to heavy fines. You are not allowed to carry large objects or bicycles aboard trains either, though backpacks and suitcases are fine.

There are no toilets in any of the MTR stations. Like the 90-minute limit on a ticket's validity, the reasoning behind that is to get bodies into stations, bums on seats or hands on straps, and bodies out onto the street again as quickly as possible.

About the only problem you may have in using the system is determining the appropriate exit for your destination. Exit signs use an alphanumerical system and there can be as many as 10 to choose from. We give the correct exit for sights and destinations wherever possible throughout this book, but you may find yourself studying the exit table from time to time and scratching your head.

Should you leave something behind on the MTR, contact the lost property office (☎ 2861 0020) at Admiralty station between 7.30am and 10.30pm daily.

Train

The MTR underground system notwithstanding, Hong Kong has two 'real' train systems that are crucial for travellers heading for China and/or getting around the New Territories.

Kowloon-Canton Railway (KCR) The KCR (Map 15; ☎ 2602 7799, 2468 7799, W www.kcrc.com) is a single-line, 34km-long commuter railway running from southern Kowloon to the border with mainland China at Lo Wu and carrying some 740,000 passengers a day. The tracks are the same as those used by the express trains to cities in Guangdong province as well as to Shanghai and Beijing, but the trains are different, looking more like subway carriages.

Strictly speaking this is the KCR East Rail, with extensions to Tsim Sha Tsui East, Ma On Shan on the Sai Kung Peninsula and Lok Ma Chau on the border with the mainland scheduled to open in 2004. The new KCR West Rail, a separate 30.5km-long line due to open in 2003, will link Hung Hom station with Tuen Mun via Yuen Long in the New Territories.

The KCR is a quick way to get up to the New Territories, and the ride offers some nice vistas, particularly around the University and Tai Po Market stations. The southernmost station on the line at Hung Hom (which is actually called the Kowloon KCR station, but everyone calls it Hung Hom) can be reached most easily from Tsim Sha Tsui by taking the No 8 green minibus (HK$4.30) from Middle Rd. Bus K16 runs along the same route (Monday to Saturday only). You can transfer from the MTR to the KCR at Kowloon Tong station *only*.

Trains run every five to 10 minutes, except during rush hour, when they depart every three minutes. The first train leaves

Hung Hom at 5.30am and the last departs from Lo Wu at 12.20am less than an hour after the border between Hong Kong and Shenzhen is closed.

KCR fares are cheap, with a half-hour ride to Sheung Shui costing just HK$9 (1st class costs double), although the 40-minute trip to the border at Lo Wu costs HK$33. Children and seniors pay reduced fares of between HK$1.50 and HK$16.50.

Light Rail Transit (LRT) The LRT (Map 15; ☎ 2468 7788, Ⓦ www.kcrc.com), which first began operations in 1988, but has been extended several times since then, is rather like a modern, air-conditioned version of the trams in Hong Kong, but it's much faster, reaching speeds of up to 70km/h. It runs along a track parallel to the road and stops at designated stations. The LRT is owned and run by the KCR and carries some 370,000 passengers a day.

At present, only those travellers visiting the temples of the western New Territories will make much use of the LRT as it essentially just links the New Town of Tuen Mun with Yuen Long. But that will all change in 2003 when it is integrated with the new KCR West Rail (see the previous section) and, by extension, the MTR.

There are eight LRT lines connecting various small suburbs with Tuen Mun to the south and Yuen Long to the north-east. The system operates from 5.30am to 12.30am Monday to Saturday, and from 6am to midnight on Sunday and public holidays. Trains run every five to 13 minutes, depending on the time of day. Fares on the LRT are HK$4 to HK$5.80, depending on the number of zones (from No 1 to No 5) travelled; children and seniors pay from HK$2 to HK$2.90. If you don't have an Octopus card, you can buy single-journey tickets from vending machines on the platforms.

The system of fare collection is unique for Hong Kong: there are no gates or turnstiles and customers are trusted to validate their ticket or Octopus card when they board. That trust is enforced by occasional spot checks, however, and the fine is 50 times the maximum adult fare, or HK$290 at present.

Trams
Hong Kong's trams, operated by Hongkong Tramways Ltd (☎ 2548 7102, Ⓦ www.info .gov.hk/td/eng/transport/tram/html) are tall and narrow double-decker streetcars, the only all double-deck wooden-sided tram fleet in the world. They roll (and rock and rattle) along the northern side of Hong Kong Island on 16km of track, carrying 280,000 passengers daily. The electric tram line first began operating in 1904 on what was then the shoreline of Hong Kong Island. This helps to understand why roads curve and dogleg in ways that don't seem quite right.

Trams operate between 6am and about 1am and run every two to 10 minutes, but they often arrive bunched together. Be prepared to elbow your way through the crowd to alight, particularly on the lower deck.

Hong Kong's trams are not fast but they're cheap and fun; in fact, apart from the Star Ferry (see that section under Boat later in this chapter) no form of transport is nearer and dearer to the hearts of Hong Kongers. For a flat fare of HK$2 (children and seniors HK$1) dropped into a box

Only double-decker trams in the world

JOHN HAY

beside the driver as you descend, you can go as far as you like, whether it's one block or to the end of the line.

A special tourist ticket that allows unlimited rides on the trams as well as the Star Ferry for four days is available for HK$30 (children/seniors HK$9/14). It's not much of a deal though; you'd have to make 15 trips over that period just to break even.

Tram routes often overlap. Some start at Kennedy Town and run to Shau Kei Wan, while others run only part of the way; one turns south and heads for Happy Valley. The longest run, from Shau Kei Wan to Kennedy Town (with a change at Western Market), takes about 1½ hours. The six routes from west to east are as follows:

Kennedy Town – Western Market
Kennedy Town – Happy Valley
Kennedy Town – Causeway Bay
Whitty Street (Sai Ying Pun) – North Point
Western Market (Sheung Wan) – Shau Kei Wan
Happy Valley – Shau Kei Wan

Try to get a seat at the front window on the upper deck for a first-class view while rattling through the crowded streets. Tall passengers will find it uncomfortable standing up as the ceiling is low, but there is more space at the rear of the tram on both decks.

Peak Tram The Peak Tram is not a tram at all, but a cable-hauled funicular railway that has been climbing some 373m along a steep gradient to the highest point on Hong Kong Island since 1888. While a few residents on the Peak and in the Mid-Levels actually use it as a form of transport – there are four intermediate stops before you reach the top – the Peak Tram is really intended to transport visitors and locals to the attractions, shops and restaurants in the Peak Tower and Galleria. For schedules, frequencies and fares, see Getting There & Away under The Peak in the Hong Kong Island chapter.

Boat

Although certain ferry services have been axed in recent years (eg, Central to Jordan Rd in Kowloon and to Tuen Mun and Tsuen Wan in the New Territories), Hong Kong still relies very much on boats to get across the harbour and reach the Outlying Islands.

Hong Kong's cross-harbour ferries are faster and cheaper than buses and the MTR. They're also great fun and afford stunning harbour views. Since the advent of the Lantau Link, ferries are not the only way to reach Lantau, but for the other Outlying Islands, they remain the only game in town.

Smoking is prohibited on all ferries, and the fine is a hefty HK$5000. The cross-harbour ferries ban the transport of bicycles, which means the only way to get a bicycle across the harbour is in the boot (trunk) of a taxi. You can take bicycles on the ordinary ferries to the Outlying Islands, however.

Star Ferry You haven't been to Hong Kong until you've taken a ride on a Star Ferry (☎ 2366 2576, 2367 7065, ⓦ www.starferry .com.hk), that wonderful fleet of boats first launched in 1888 with names like *Morning Star*, *Night Star Celestial Star*, *Twinkling Star* and so on (see the boxed text Borne on a Star). Try to take the trip on a clear night from Kowloon side to Central. It's not half as dramatic in the other direction.

The Star Ferry operates on four routes, but by far the most popular one is the run between Tsim Sha Tsui and Central. The trip takes about seven minutes and departures are frequent. Fares are a mere HK$1.70/2.20 on the lower/upper deck for adults and HK$1.20/1.30 for children. Seniors ride for free. The coin-operated turnstiles do not give change, but you can get this from the ticket window – unless, of course, you're carrying an Octopus card.

For details on the special four-day tourist pass valid on the trams and the Star Ferry, see the previous Trams section.

The four ferry routes are:

Central (Star Ferry pier) – Tsim Sha Tsui; every four to 10 minutes from 6.30am to 11.30pm daily; HK$2.20/1.70 upper/lower deck (children HK$1.20/1.30, seniors free)
Central (Star Ferry pier) – Hung Hom; every 15 to 20 minutes from 7.20am to 7.20pm weekdays, every 20 minutes from 7am to 7pm weekends; HK$5.30 (children HK$2.70, seniors free)

Wan Chai – Tsim Sha Tsui; every eight to 20 minutes from 7.30am to 11pm Monday to Saturday; every 12 to 20 minutes from 7.30am to 10.50pm Sunday; HK$2.20 (children HK$1.30, seniors free)

Wan Chai – Hung Hom; every 15 to 20 minutes from 7.08am to 7pm weekdays, every 20 to 22 minutes from 7.08am to 7.10pm weekends; HK$5.30 (children HK$2.70, seniors free)

Other Cross-Harbour Ferries Three other ferry companies operate cross-harbour routes, including Discovery Bay Transportation Service from Central to Tsim Sha Tsui East and New World First Ferry from North Point to Hung Hom and Kowloon City (see the Outlying Islands chapter for contact numbers). The Fortune Ferry Co has services (☎ 2994 8155) linking North Point and Kwun Tong.

Central (Queen's pier) – Tsim Sha Tsui East; every 20 minutes from 7.40am (from 8am on Sunday) to 8.20pm daily; HK$4.50 (children & seniors HK$2.30)

North Point – Hung Hom; every 20 minutes from 7.20am to 7.20pm daily; HK$4.50 (children & seniors HK$2.30)

North Point – Kowloon City; every 20 minutes from 7.10am to 7.30pm daily; HK$4.50 (children & seniors HK$2.30)

North Point – Kwun Tong; every 15 to 30 minutes from 7.15am to 7.45pm Monday to Saturday, every 30 minutes from 7am to 7.30pm Sunday; HK$5 (children & seniors HK$2.50)

Outlying Islands Ferries Two companies – New World First Ferry Services and the Hong Kong & Kowloon Ferry Co – run the lion's share of regularly scheduled ferries to Cheung Chau, Lamma, Lantau and Peng Chau from the Outlying Islands ferry terminal in Central, a short distance to the northwest of the Star Ferry pier. You can reach Lamma throughout the week from Aberdeen, and on weekends boats also make the run between Tsim Sha Tsui and Cheung Chau as well as Lantau. Discovery Bay can be reached by ferry throughout the day and night from the Star Ferry pier in Central.

For details on schedules, frequencies and fares for ferries serving these and other destinations, see the introductory Getting There & Away section in the Outlying Islands chapter as well as the individual Getting There & Away sections for each of the islands.

Other Boats Sea and harbour transport is not limited to ferries in Hong Kong. You'll encounter several other types of boats as you travel farther afield.

A *kaido* (or *kaito*) is a small to medium-sized 'ferry' that can make short runs on the open sea. Only a few kaido routes operate on regular schedules (eg, the ones from Peng Chau to the Trappist Haven Monastery and Discovery Bay and from Aberdeen to Sok Kwu Wan on Lamma); most simply adjust

---

Borne on a Star

There are few modes of transport anywhere that can claim they sparked a riot, but Hong Kong's Star Ferry can. In 1966, when Communist China was locked in the grip of the sham they now call the Cultural Revolution, agitators used the ferry company's fare increase of HK$0.05 as pretext for fomenting violent demonstrations. The disturbances continued for almost a year.

Mention of the Star Ferry service between Pedder's Wharf (now reclaimed land) and Tsim Sha Tsui first appeared in a December 1888 newspaper article. At that time, boats sailed 'every 40 minutes to one hour during all hours of the day' except on Monday and Friday, when they were seconded for coal delivery. Service has continued ever since, with the only major suspension occurring during WWII. The Star Ferry was something of a war hero; during the Japanese invasion boats were used to evacuate refugees and Allied troops from the Kowloon Peninsula.

Until the Cross-Harbour Tunnel opened in 1978 and the first line of the MTR two years later, the Star Ferry was the only way to cross the harbour. At rush hour long queues of commuters would back up as far as the General Post Office on the Hong Kong side and Star House in Kowloon.

supply to demand. Kaidos run most frequently on weekends and public holidays.

A *sampan* is a motorised launch that can only accommodate a few people. Sampans are generally too small to be considered seaworthy, but they can safely zip you around typhoon shelters like that in Aberdeen and Cheung Chau Harbours.

Bigger than a sampan but smaller than a kaido, is a *walla walla*, water taxis operating in Victoria Harbour, that are a dying breed. Most of the customers are sailors stationed on ships anchored in the harbour. You can sometimes find them to transport you across the harbour after the MTR and regular ferries stop running. On Hong Kong Island look for them at Queen's pier on the east side of the Star Ferry. On Kowloon side, walla wallas can sometimes be found at Tsim Sha Tsui, south-east of the Star Ferry.

CAR & MOTORCYCLE

For a neophyte to consider driving in Hong Kong would be sheer madness. Traffic is heavy, the roads can get hopelessly clogged and the new system of highways and bridges is complicated in the extreme. And if driving the car doesn't destroy your holiday sense of spontaneity, parking the damn thing will. If you are determined to see Hong Kong under your own steam, do yourself a favour and rent a car with a driver.

It's not possible to rent a motorcycle in Hong Kong, but if you're staying for a while you can buy one. The best place to look for a motorcycle, new or used, is on Caroline Hill Rd in Causeway Bay on Hong Kong Island, where there is a string of shops.

Hitching

Hitching is never entirely safe in any country in the world, and we don't recommend it. Travellers who decide to hitch should realise that they are taking a small but potentially serious risk. People who choose to hitch are safer if they travel in pairs and let someone know where they are planning to go.

Road Rules

Vehicles drive on the left-hand side of the road in Hong Kong, as in the UK, Australia and Macau, but *not* in China. Seat belts must be worn by the driver and *all* passengers, in both the front and back seats. Police are strict and give out traffic tickets at the drop of a hat.

For more details see Driving Licence & Permits under Visas & Documents in the Hong Kong Facts for the Visitor chapter.

Rental

Unless you're planning a whirlwind excursion to the New Territories, there's not much need to rent a car in Hong Kong. Even then, you may do better with public transport.

Car rental firms accept International Driver's Permits or driver's licences from your home country. Drivers must usually be at least 25 years of age. Daily rates for small cars start at HK$580/720. There are weekend and weekly deals available. For example, Avis (☎ 2890 6988, fax 2895 3686), Bright Star Mansion, 93 Leighton Rd, Causeway Bay, will rent you a Honda Civic for the weekend (from 2pm on Friday to 10.30am Monday) for HK$1200; the same car costs HK$580/2400 for a day/week. Rates include unlimited kilometres.

If you're looking for a car with a driver, contact Ace Drayage (☎ 2893 0541, fax 2834 1769), 16 Min Fat St, Happy Valley, which charges HK$160 per hour (minimum three hours). Avis' chauffeur-driven cars are much more expensive: HK$300 with a minimum of four hours.

TAXI

Hong Kong taxis are a bargain when compared with other major world cities and, with more than 18,000 cruising the streets, they're usually easy to flag down.

When a taxi is available, there should be a red 'For Hire' sign illuminated on the meter and visible through the windscreen. At night the 'Taxi' sign on the roof will be lit up as well. Taxis will not stop at bus stops or in restricted zones where a yellow line is painted next to the kerb. A relatively new law requires that everyone in a vehicle, including taxis, wears a seat belt. Both driver and passenger(s) are fined if stopped by the police, and most drivers will gently remind you to buckle up before proceeding.

'Urban taxis' – those in Kowloon and on Hong Kong Island – are red with silver roofs. New Territories taxis are green with white tops, and Lantau Island taxis are blue.

Hong Kong and Kowloon taxis tend to avoid each others' turf as the drivers' street geography on the other side of the harbour can be pretty shaky. Hong Kong and Kowloon taxis maintain separate ranks at places like the Hung Hom station and the Star Ferry and will usually refuse to take you to 'the other side'. In any case, if you're travelling from Hong Kong Island to Kowloon (or vice-versa), choose the correct cab as you'll save on the tunnel toll (see the following information). New Territories taxis are not permitted to pick up or put down passengers in Kowloon or on Hong Kong Island.

The flag fall for taxis in Hong Kong and Kowloon is HK$15 for the first 2km and HK$1.40 for every additional 200m. In the New Territories it's HK$12.50 for the first 2km and HK$1.20 for each additional 200m. On Lantau the equivalent charges are HK$12 and HK$1.20. There is a luggage fee of HK$5 per bag but, depending on the size, not all drivers insist on this payment. It costs an extra HK$5 to book a taxi by telephone. Try to carry smaller bills and coins; most drivers are hesitant to make change for anything over HK$100. You can tip up to 10%, but most Hong Kong people just leave the little brown coins and a dollar or two.

Passengers must pay the toll if a taxi goes through any of Hong Kong's harbour or mountain tunnels or uses the Lantau Link to Tung Chung or the airport. Though the Cross-Harbour Tunnel costs only HK$10, you'll be required to pay HK$20 if, say, you take a Hong Kong taxi from Hong Kong Island to Kowloon. If you manage to find a Kowloon taxi returning 'home', you'll pay only HK$10. (It works the other way round as well, of course). Similarly if you cross the harbour via the Western Harbour Tunnel you must pay the HK$35 toll plus HK$15 for the return unless you can find a cab heading for its base. There's no way of avoiding the whopping great toll of HK$30 in *both* directions when a taxi uses the Lantau Link, however.

There is no double charge for the other tunnels: Eastern Harbour Crossing HK$15; Aberdeen HK$5; Lion Rock HK$8; Shing Mun HK$5; Tate's Cairn HK$10; Tseung Kwan HK$3; Discovery Bay HK$50.

It's not as hard as it used to be, but you may have some trouble hailing a cab during rush hour, when it rains or during the driver shift-change period (around 4pm). Taxis are also in higher demand after midnight. There are no extra late-night charges and no extra passenger charges, though some taxis are insured to carry four passengers and some five. You can tell by glancing at the licence plate.

Some taxi drivers carry a card that lists some 50 destinations in Cantonese, English and Japanese. Even if the card doesn't list your specific destination, it will certainly have some place nearby. It's never a bad idea to have your destination written down in Chinese, however.

Though most Hong Kong taxi drivers are scrupulously honest, if you feel you've been ripped off, take down the taxi or driver's licence number (usually displayed on the sun visor in front) and call the police (☎ 2527 7177) or Transport Department hotline (☎ 2804 2600) to lodge a complaint. Be sure to have all the relevant details: when, where and how much. Also contact the police if you leave something behind in a taxi; most drivers turn in lost property.

BICYCLE

Cycling in urbanised Kowloon or Hong Kong Island would be suicidal, but in the quiet areas of the islands (including southern Hong Kong Island) or the New Territories, a bike can be a lovely way to get around. It's not really a form of transport, though – the hilly terrain will slow you down – but more recreational. Be advised that bicycle rental shops and kiosks tend to run out of bikes early on weekends if the weather is good. See the Activities sections in the relevant chapters for details.

WALKING

Although much of Hong Kong is best seen on foot, walking around isn't necessarily easy or relaxing, especially in the business districts. Poorly designed pedestrian crossings, the crushing crowds and buses hurtling along just centimetres from the footpath can make a stroll anything but enjoyable. The complexity of pedestrian flyovers around Central, Admiralty and Wan Chai can drive visitors insane, but there's often no other way to get to the other side. Pedestrians-only areas are virtually nonexistent, and builders and craftspeople in areas like Wan Chai and Mong Kok frequently use the pavement as their own private workshops. Watch your step and persevere – you will be rewarded with the sights, sounds and smells that make up the world of Hong Kong.

Rural Hong Kong is a whole different matter, with the New Territories, the Outlying Islands and even Hong Kong Island itself offering some outstanding walks and hikes. The MacLehose Trail runs over the hills and mountains and down into the deep valleys of the New Territories for 100km. The 70km-long Lantau Trail takes in some of the most majestic views of peaks and sea anywhere in the world. The 50km-long Hong Kong Trail spans the length of Hong Kong Island and takes you up and out of the city and into the hills. The less adventurous might want to stick to the 3.5km circuit around Victoria Peak or head out to Lamma or Cheung Chau for less demanding walks.

The HKTB's *Hong Kong Walks* has a sampling of strolls and hikes in Hong Kong, Kowloon, two of the Outlying Islands and the New Territories.

Central Escalator

One of Hong Kong's long-standing problems has been that while many middle-class residents live in the Mid-Levels, the lower portion of the Peak, they work in the skyscraper jungle down below. The roads are narrow and the distance is more vertical than horizontal, making the walk home a strenuous climb, especially in the humid summer months. The result has been a rush-hour nightmare of bumper-to-bumper taxis, minibuses and private cars.

Then someone came up with what is officially called the Central-Mid-Levels Escalator and Walkway System but known simply as the 'Central Escalator' – one of Hong Kong's more, well, unusual forms of transport. Basically, it consists of three moving walkways and 20 elevated escalators that can be reversed; they run down in the morning (until 10am) and up the rest of the day and evening. It's 800m long at present and runs from the Central Market on Des Voeux Rd, along Cochrane and Shelley sts in Soho and up to Conduit Rd in the Mid-Levels. It is the longest escalator in the world.

When the government announced plans to build the system in the late 1980s, many thought it was playing an April Fool's joke, particularly because one of the English-language television stations had done just that several years before with an announcement that all west-bound pedestrian traffic in Central would have to walk on the left side and everyone going east would have to walk on the right side. It finally opened in 1993, having run some 500% over budget, but no one is complaining and certainly not laughing about it now. To judge from the rush-hour crowds using it every day, the Central Escalator has been a smashing success.

ORGANISED TOURS

Tourism is one of Hong Kong's main money-spinners, so it's not surprising that there is a mind-boggling number of tours available to just about anywhere in the territory. If you only have a short time in Hong Kong or don't want to deal with public transport, an organised tour may be just what you're looking for. Some tours are standard excursions covering major sights on Hong Kong Island such as Victoria Peak, while other tours take you on harbour cruises, out to the islands or through the New Territories.

The People to People program organised by the HKTB is not a tour as such but is unique in that it allows you to visit temples, art galleries, teahouses, even a tai chi class, meet and speak with the owners or organisers and even participate. It's an excellent way to learn first-hand about Hong Kong culture. Contact the HKTB (see Local Tourist Offices in the Hong Kong Facts for the Visitor chapter) for this season's schedule.

For tours to Macau, Zhuhai and Shenzhen, see the Getting There & Away chapter in the Macau section of this book, and the Getting There & Away sections in the China Excursion – Shenzhen and China Excursion – Zhuhai chapters.

Air

If you hanker after seeing Hong Kong from on high – whatever the expense – consider chartering a helicopter. Heliservices (☎ 2523 6407, fax 2525 4342, W www .heliservices.com.hk) has chartered Squirrels available for HK$2500 for each 15-minute period while Heli Hong Kong (☎ 2108 4838, fax 2858 3100, W www .helihongkong.com) charges HK$4750 for 30 minutes in a Bell JetRanger. Count on about HK$7500 for a 45-minute copter flight, over and back from, say, Lantau.

Bus

For first-time visitors to Hong Kong trying to get their bearings, Splendid Tours & Travel (☎ 2316 2151, fax 2312 2031) has some interesting 'orientation' tours of Hong Kong Island and Kowloon and the New Territories. They last four to five hours and cost HK$280 (children HK$190).

Some of the most popular surface tours of the New Territories are offered by the HKTB. The ever popular six-hour Land Between Tour takes in the Yuen Yuen Institute temple complex in Tsuen Wan, Tai Mo Shan lookout, the fishing village of Sam Mun Tsai as well as several other sights and includes lunch (HK$385/335 for adults/ children and seniors). The slightly shorter Heritage Tour, which does not include lunch, takes in such New Territories historical sights as Man Mo Temple in Tai Po and the walled village of Lo Wai (HK$305/265 for adults/concession). Call the HKTB tour operations department (☎ 2807 6390) between 9am and 5pm daily. These tours can also be booked through other travel agents and tour operators, including Gray Line (☎ 2368 7111).

The HKTB also offers two versions of its Come Horseracing Tour during the racing season (September to June): the Classic Tour, including admission to the Visitors' Box of the Hong Kong Jockey Club Members' Enclosures and lunch (HK$490), and the more plebeian Race Tour (HK$120).

Boat

Many agents, including Gray Line and Splendid Tours & Travel, have tours of Victoria and Aberdeen Harbours, but the company specialising in these is Watertours (☎ 2926 3868, W www.watertourshk.com), Shop 5C, G/F, Star House, 3 Salisbury Rd, Tsim Sha Tsui. Some 10 different tours of the harbour and the islands as well as dinner and cocktail cruises are available. Prices range from HK$220 (children HK$130) for the Morning Harbour & Noon Day Gun Firing Cruise to HK$610 (children HK$510) for the Highlight of the Night Cruise. If you want to take in the enormity of the Tsing Ma Bridge, Watertours' Afternoon Western Shoreline Cruise (adults/children HK$220/130) will take you there.

Walking

The HKTB has recorded walking tours highlighting the architecture and cultural heritage of Central on Hong Kong Island, Tsim Sha Tsui and Hung Hom in Kowloon and Tai Po in the New Territories. The tours last about four hours and can be rented from HKTB visitor centres in Central and Kowloon between 8am and 1pm daily. They cost HK$50 plus HK$500 deposit for the audio system and headset, which must be returned by 5pm the same day.

Three long-time expatriate residents of Hong Kong offer five different guided nature walks in south-western Hong Kong Island (Dragon's Back), Kowloon (Lion Rock), the New Territories (Tai Mo Shan, Sai Kung) and Lantau Island. They last between 3½ and five hours and cost from HK$275 to HK$320. Any of the following people can be contacted for details: Kaarlo Schepel (☎ 2577 6319, fax 2890 7542, e sharflat@netvigator.com); Dr Martin Williams (☎ 2981 3523, fax 2981 5593, e martinw@hkstar.com); and Paul Etherington (☎ 2486 2112, mobile ☎ 9300 5197, e pesc@netvigator.com).

Hong Kong Island

Though Hong Kong Island makes up only about 7% of the territory's total land area, its importance as the historical, political and economic centre of Hong Kong far outweighs its size. It was here that the original settlement, Victoria, was founded.

Most of the major businesses, government offices, a good many top-end hotels and restaurants, nightlife areas and exclusive residential neighbourhoods are on Hong Kong Island. It is where you'll find the ex-governor's mansion, the stock exchange, the legislature, the territory's premier shopping districts, the original horse-racing track and a host of other places that define Hong Kong's character. Not surprisingly, a good deal of Hong Kong's sights are also on the island. Virtually everything of importance in Hong Kong starts, finishes or is taking place on Hong Kong Island.

The commercial heart of Hong Kong pumps away on the northern side of the island, where banks and businesses and a jungle of high-rise apartment blocks and hotels claim a good part of its 80 sq km. Since the handover in 1997, there have been a few visible changes – the occasional red and yellow flag of the People's Republic of China fluttering in the breeze, the former name of the Prince of Wales Building partially obscured, snatches of Mandarin being spoken by visitors from the mainland. But generally the island remains as it was before: a metropolis of a few preserved monuments overwhelmed by a dazzling modernity.

Looking across from Tsim Sha Tsui on Kowloon side will impress you with how unbelievably built up and crowded the northern side of Hong Kong Island is. About the only bits of visible greenery are the steep hills rising up from behind the skyscrapers. And along with moving up (in every sense of the word) Hong Kong continues to move out. Reclamation along the harbour edge continues to add the odd metre every so often, and buildings once on the waterfront are now several hundred metres back.

Highlights

- A stroll down Hollywood Rd in Central, picking, paying and (hopefully) not getting ripped off in the antique and curio shops
- An afternoon at Stanley Market and lunch in Murray House, Hong Kong's oldest colonial building
- A visit to Shek O, Hong Kong Island's last remaining village, and a swim in Big Wave Bay
- Dinner at Central's M at the Fringe restaurant and a night of bopping in nearby Lan Kwai Fong
- A hair-raising ride up the Peak Tram to the Island's highest point
- An early morning walk through the aviaries in the Hong Kong Zoological & Botanical Gardens
- Wan Chai – anywhere – in the wee hours but especially one of the big Filipino clubs
- A visit to the world's kitchiest theme park – Tiger Balm Gardens

The southern side of Hong Kong Island is of a totally different character to the north. The coast is dotted with fine beaches, where the water is actually clean enough to swim in. The best beaches are at Big Wave Bay, Deep Water Bay, Shek O, Stanley and Repulse Bay. Expensive villas perch on the hillsides overlooking the coast, and the impression is sometimes more of the Riviera than an overcrowded Asian territory.

INFORMATION
Tourist Offices

The main office of the Hong Kong Tourism Board **(Map 4)** (HKTB; ☎ 2508 1234) is on the ground floor of The Center, 99 Queen's Rd Central and is open from 8am to 6pm daily.

Email & Internet Access

There are many places – cybercafes, coffee shops and even some restaurants – where you can check your emails and surf the Web on Hong Kong Island.

Avanti Network Cybercafe (☎ 3101 6363, Ⓦ *www.avanti-net.com, The Broadway, 54-62 Lockhart Rd, Wan Chai)* **Map 6** This cybercafe is run by young people who know their stuff and will get you out of any tight corner. HK$30 buys you an hour on-line, a drink and a snack.

Cash On-Line Cyber Cafe (☎ 2972 2068, Ⓦ *www.cashon-line.com, Shop 9-12, Excelsior Plaza, 24-26 East Point Rd, Causeway Bay)* **Map 6** Open 8.30am-10pm daily. This is probably the most professional cybercafe on Hong Kong Island and charges HK$30 for the first half-hour plus drink and HK$10 for every subsequent 30 minutes. There's a branch in Tsim Sha Tsui too.

Cyber Cafe (☎ 2582 8888 ext 2506, *Atrium, Hong Kong Convention & Exhibition Centre, 1 Expo Drive, Wan Chai)* **Map 6** Open 7.30am-6.30pm daily. You can use either of a couple of terminals for the price of a beverage.

Jah (☎ 2581 1025, 20-26 Peel St, Central) **Map 5** Open noon-2am. This ultra-trendy minimalist cafe-bar has two terminals that customers can use.

Kublai's Cyber Diner (☎ 2529 9117, 3rd floor, One Capital Place, 18 Luard Rd, Wan Chai)* **Map 6** Open noon-11pm daily. This Mongolian restaurant gone international coffee shop charges an outrageous HK$48 for 30 minutes online (including a drink). Enter the shop from Jaffe Rd.

Pacific Coffee Company (☎ 2868 5100, *Shop 1022, International Finance Centre, 1 Harbour View St, Central)* **Map 4** Open 7am-10pm Mon-Sat, 8.30am-9pm Sun. You can access the Internet for free at this place and many other branches of the coffee shop chain.

Spaghetti House (☎ 2147 5543, *International Finance Centre, Shop 2004, 1 Harbour View St, Central)* **Map 4** Some branches of this cheap and cheerful pasta and pizza chain offer free though limited Internet access, including this one.

Bookshops

Hong Kong Island has the territory's widest selection of bookshops.

Angelo de Carpi (☎ 2857 7148, 18 Wo On Lane, Lan Kwai Fong, Central)* **Map 5** This is nominally a gay and lesbian bookshop but much more of a boyzone than a lipstick lesbian lounge. Blokes should find this cellar-like space a comfortable hang-out.

Bookazine (☎ 2521 1649, Pacific House, 20 Queen's Rd Central)* **Map 4** Bookazine stocks excellent titles of local interest. It has nine other outlets on Hong Kong Island, including a Wan Chai branch (☎ 2527 2092, Shop 8 & 9, 3rd floor, Hopewell Centre, 183 Queen's Rd East).

Cosmos Books (☎ 2866 1677, 30 Johnston Rd, Wan Chai)* **Map 6** This independently owned chain with a branch in Tsim Sha Tsui has a good selection of Chinese-related books in the basement. Upstairs there are English-language books (nonfiction is quite strong) plus one of the city's best stationery departments.

Government Publications Office (☎ 2537 1910, Queensway Government Offices, 66 Queensway, Admiralty)* **Map 4** Open 9am-6pm Mon-Fri, 9am-1pm Sat. All publications produced by the Hong Kong government are available from this outlet.

Hong Kong Book Centre (☎ 2522 7064, Basement, On Lok Yuen Bldg, 25 Des Voeux Rd Central)* **Map 4** This place has a vast selection of books and magazines. There's another pleasantly cluttered Hong Kong Book Centre branch (☎ 2523 8847) in the basement of The Landmark.

Kelly & Walsh (☎ 2522 5743, Shop 304, Pacific Place, 88 Queensway, Admiralty)* **Map 4** This store has a good selection of art, design and culinary books and the staff know the stock. The children's books are shelved in a handy kids' reading lounge.

JPC Bookshop (☎ 2868 6844, 9 Queen Victoria St, Central)* **Map 4** This excellent bookshop has a good range of books about China and tapes for studying the language. It's especially strong in maps. There are seven other branches in the territory including one in Wan Chai (☎ 2838 2081, 158 Hennessy Rd).

POV 2 (☎ *2865 5116, Shop A, 1st floor, Hong Kong Mansion, 137-147 Lockhart Rd, Wan Chai)* **Map 6** This bookshop deals essentially with two themes: cinema and gay and lesbian studies.

Professional Bookshop (☎ *2526 5387, Shop 104A, Alexandra House, 16-20 Chater Rd, Central)* **Map 4** The Professional carries an excellent selection of business, legal and other professional titles.

Tai Yip Art Book Centre (☎ *2524 5963, 72 Wellington St, Central)* **Map 5** Tai Yip has a terrific selection of books about anything Chinese and artsy: calligraphy, jade, bronze, costumes, architecture, symbolism. This is a good place to look deeper if you're planning on buying art in Hong Kong; it's also a good place for picking up beautiful gift cards. There's a branch in Hong Kong City Hall (☎ *2523 0496, Low Block, Edinburgh Place, Central)* and the Hong Kong Museum of Art in Tsim Sha Tsui.

Times Bookshop (☎ *2525 8797, Shop B, Hong Kong Club Bldg, 3 Jackson Rd, Central)* **Map 4** Times Bookshops have some five outlets dotted around Hong Kong, including a Causeway Bay branch (☎ *2504 2383, Shop P315-316, 3rd floor, World Trade Centre, 280 Gloucester Rd)* **(Map 6)**. These branches offer an average range of books and stationery.

GETTING AROUND

One of the best ways to see the north side is to jump on one of the green double-deck trams that trundle between Kennedy Town in the west and Shau Kei Wan in the east. Try to board during mid-morning or mid-afternoon when there's a better chance of grabbing a front seat on the upper deck. The trams are slow, and while this may not be ideal for rushed commuters, if you want to sit back and get a feel for Hong Kong city life, this is the way to do it. For HK$2, it's also one of the best bargains.

To get to the southern part of Hong Kong Island, the bus is the way to go.

CENTRAL

Most visitors to Hong Kong pass through Central at some stage, be it for sightseeing,

taking care of errands such as changing money or buying plane tickets, or en route to the bars and restaurants of Lan Kwai Fong and Soho. In fact, many business travellers spend all their time in this district, where most of Hong Kong's larger international companies have their offices. Not surprisingly, Central has some impressive architectural treasures (see the special section Contemporary Architecture in this chapter) that can be quite magnificent, especially at night. An eclectic assortment of historical civic buildings and churches as well as parks, gardens and other green 'lungs' round out the picture.

A good place from which to start exploring Central is the **Star Ferry terminal (Map 4)**, from where the floating green workhorses transport passengers to and from Tsim Sha Tsui and other points. A short distance to the south-west is **Jardine House (Map 4)** *(Connaught Rd Central)*, a 40-storey silver monolith punctured with porthole-like windows and formerly known as the Connaught Centre. Hong Kong Chinese like giving things (and people) nicknames and the centre has been dubbed the 'House of 1000 Arseholes'. To the east of Jardine House is a small plaza with the sculpture *Double Oval* by Henry Moore.

West of the Connaught Centre is **Exchange Square (Map 4)**, a complex of three elevated office towers and home to the Hong Kong Stock Exchange. Access is via a network of overhead pedestrian walkways that stretches west to Sheung Wan and has links to many of the buildings on the other side of Connaught Rd. The ground level of the complex is given over to the Exchange Square bus and minibus station. The stock exchange is located at the main entrance to Towers I and II. Guided tours of the stock exchange are possible but are generally intended for people involved in the financial field and must be requested in writing five days in advance (fax 2868 4084).

Outside Exchange Square Towers I and II is a seating area surrounding a fountain, which is an excellent place to relax, especially in the early evening. The statue in front of the Forum shopping mall is of a tai chi *taijiquan* posture known as 'snake creeps down', although the sculpture is simply called 'Taiji'. It's by the Taiwanese sculptor, Zhu Ming. There are also some amusing bronzes of water buffaloes both standing and lying down.

Taking the pedestrian walkway over Connaught Rd will bring you into the heart of Central. Most of the buildings are office blocks, but visitors with an eye towards shopping can check Prince's Building and The Landmark, both of which cater to more well-heeled consumers. **The Center (Map 4)**, which does some amazing chameleon-like colour changes by night, is where HKTB's main office is located (see the Information section earlier in this chapter).

The Cenotaph (Map 4)

Due south of the Star Ferry pier is a pedestrian underpass that surfaces alongside the Cenotaph (Greek for 'empty tomb'), a

memorial to Hong Kong residents killed during the two world wars. It is similar to the one on Whitehall in London. To the west is the esteemed Mandarin Oriental Hotel, open to all who have the dosh, and to the east the even more prestigious **Hong Kong Club**, which was still not accepting Chinese members until well after WWII. The original club building, a magnificent colonial four-storey structure, was torn down in 1981, despite public outcry and replaced with the modern monstrosity you see now.

Statue Square (Map 4)

Statue Square is across from the Cenotaph on the south side of Chater Rd. Statue Square is notable for its collection of fountains and covered sitting-out areas; it is best known in Hong Kong as the meeting place of choice for thousands of Filipino migrant workers on the weekend, especially Sunday, when it becomes a cacophony of Manilans,

---

· Maid in Hong Kong

Almost every household in Hong Kong has an *amah*, either a live-in maid who cooks, cleans, minds the children and/or feeds the dog or someone who comes in once or twice a week. In the old days amahs were invariably Chinese spinsters who wore starched white tunics and black trousers, put their hair in a long plait and had a mouthful of gold fillings. Their employers became their families. Today, however, those amahs are virtually extinct, and the work is now done by foreigners – young women (and increasingly men) from the Philippines, Indonesia, Thailand and Nepal on two-year renewable visas.

Filipinos are by far the largest group, accounting for almost a third of the territory's 203,000 foreign domestic workers. On Sunday, Filipino maids take over the pavements and public squares of Central. They come in their thousands to share food, gossip, play cards, read the Bible and do one another's hair. You can't miss them around Statue Square, Exchange Square and the plaza below the Hongkong and Shanghai Bank building.

Reader Liz Storrar writes of her impressions of a Sunday spent with amahs in Central: 'I had read of these gatherings in *Hong Kong* by Jan Morris, but was unprepared for the scale and for the emotional impact. I had planned to spend my last day sunning myself on a beach but instead was infected by the joy these women had in each others' company and stayed amongst them for some hours. They chatted ceaselessly, the noise of the chatter giving a strangely fascinating, almost musical, loud hum to the area. There were so many of them, yet the experience was so peaceful, so energising. They were like birds released from cages for a time.'

In many ways, that's exactly what they are like. For young Filipinos, a contract to work in Hong Kong is a dream come true, an escape from the dust and poverty of the provincial Philippines, even if the minimum monthly salary is a paltry HK$3850. But it doesn't come without a heavy price. According to a report released by the government-sponsored Asian Migrant Centre in early 2001, almost a quarter of foreign domestic helpers in Hong Kong suffer abuse from their employers, as many as 3000 of the sexual variety.

Vizayans and Ilocans (see the boxed text Maid in Hong Kong).

The square derives its name from the numerous effigies of British royalty once on display here; in fact, the Chinese characters for it mean 'Empress Statue Square'. The statues were spirited away by the Japanese during the occupation of Hong Kong during WWII. Though all were found intact in Japan after the war, in deference to anti-colonialist sentiment at the time, only Queen (and Empress) Victoria was brought back to Hong Kong – not to Central but to Victoria Park in Causeway Bay. The sole survivor in the square is a bronze likeness of Sir Thomas Jackson, a particularly successful former chief manager of the Hongkong and Shanghai Bank.

Fittingly, Sir Thomas is gazing at the stunning headquarters of what is now the **HSBC** (formerly the Hongkong and Shanghai Bank), designed by British architect Norman Foster in 1985. The two bronze **imperial lions** guarding the bank's main entrance are known as Stephen and Stitt after two bank employees who worked here in the 1930s. The Japanese used the lions as target practice during the occupation and you can still see bullet holes in the one to the right.

To the east of the Hong Kong Bank building is the old **Bank of China** (BOC) building, which now houses another mainland bank (Sin Hua Bank) and an exclusive club; the BOC has moved to new headquarters in the awesome **Bank of China** building (IM Pei, 1990) to the south-east.

Legislative Council Building The colonnaded and domed neoclassical building on the east side of the square is the **Old Supreme Court**, which was built in 1912 of granite quarried in eastern Kowloon and now serves as the seat of the Legislative Council. In front of the building is a blindfolded statue of the Greek god Themes, who represents justice. This is a good place to watch Hong Kong's grassroots political movements in action; protests are routinely staged outside the east entrance of the Legislative Council building on Jackson Rd.

Across Jackson Rd to the east is **Chater Garden**, where many Hong Kong Chinese practise their tai chi early in the early morning. If you were to continue east, you'd soon reach Admiralty and the Wan Chai district.

Li Yuen St East & West

These two narrow alleyways linking Des Voeux Rd with Queen's Rd Central are simply called 'the lanes' by Hong Kong residents and were traditionally the place to go for fabric and piece goods. Most of those vendors have now moved to Western Market (see Clothing & Textiles in the Shopping section).

Central Market (Map 4)

It should be easy to locate Central Market, a short distance to the west on Queen's Rd Central; if the wind is blowing in the right direction, you'll smell it before you see it. It's a four-storey affair and more a zoo than a market, with everything from chickens and quail to eels and crabs, alive or freshly slaughtered. If you want to see even more exotic produce for sale and how and why Hong Kong Chinese housewives choose what they do for their families' lunch and dinner, head uphill to the **Graham St Market**.

Central Market marks the start of the 800m-long **Central Escalator**, which transports pedestrians through Central and Soho and as far as Conduit Rd in the Mid-Levels.

Lan Kwai Fong & Soho (Map 5)

South of Queen's Rd Central and up the hill is Lan Kwai Fong, a narrow, L-shaped pedestrian street that is Hong Kong Island's chief party neighbourhood (see the Entertainment section) and popular with expats and Hong Kong Chinese alike. The bars are nothing to get excited about, but it's a fun place to do a little pub-crawling. Lan Kwai Fong has a number of good places to eat but you'll find even more to the west in the 'restaurant mall' district of Soho (from 'South Of HOllywood Rd). At lunch time on weekdays the area becomes a 'black mountain' (what the Chinese call a 'crowd') of office workers trying to squeeze a decent meal into a short break.

St John's Cathedral (Map 4)

Built in 1847, St John's Cathedral *(4-8 Garden Rd; admission free; open 7am-6pm daily)*, entered from Battery Path, is one of the few colonial structures left in Central. Criticised for blighting the colony's landscape when it was first erected, this Anglican church is now lost in the forest of skyscrapers that make up Central. Services have been held continuously since the church opened, except in 1944 when the Japanese Imperial Army used it as a social club. The cathedral suffered heavy damage and after the war the front doors were remade using timber salvaged from HMS *Tamar*, a British warship that used to guard the entrance to Victoria Harbour, and the beautiful stained-glass East Window replaced. You walk on sacred ground in more ways than you know at St John's; it is the only piece of freehold land in Hong Kong.

Behind the cathedral and to the northwest is the **former French Mission Building**, a charming structure built for the Russian consul in Hong Kong in the mid-19th century but extensively rebuilt in 1917. It served as the headquarters of the provisional colonial government after WWII and is now home to the **Court of Final Appeal**, the highest judicial body in Hong Kong.

Both the cathedral and the French Mission Building are on Battery Path, a tree-lined walk that takes you back to Queen's Rd Central.

Hong Kong Park (Map 4)

Hong Kong Park *(Cotton Tree Drive; admission free; park open 6.30am-11pm daily, conservatory & aviary open 9am-5pm daily)* is one of the most unusual parks in the world, deliberately designed to look anything but natural and emphasising artificial creations such as its fountain plaza, conservatory, artificial waterfall, indoor games hall, playground, tai chi garden, viewing tower, museum and arts centre. For all its artifice, the park is beautiful in its own weird way and, with a wall of skyscrapers on one side and mountains on the other, makes for some dramatic and interesting photographs.

Perhaps the best feature of the park is the **aviary**. Home to more than 800 birds representing some 30 different species, it's a huge and very natural-feeling place. Visitors walk along a wooden bridge suspended some 10m above the ground and on eye level with the tree branches, where most of the birds are to be found.

Hong Kong Park is an easy walk from either Central or Admiralty, or you can take bus No 3B, 12M, 23, 23B, 40 or 103; alight at the first stop on Cotton Tree Drive.

Flagstaff House Museum of Teaware

At the park's northern tip is the Flagstaff House Museum of Teaware *(☎ 2869 0690, 10 Cotton Tree Drive; admission free; open 10am-5pm Tues-Sun)*, built in 1846 as the home of the commander of the British forces and the oldest colonial building still standing in its original spot in Hong Kong. The museum, a branch of the Hong Kong Museum of Art, houses a collection of antique Chinese teaware – bowls, teaspoons, brewing trays, sniffing cups (used particularly for enjoying the fragrance of oolong tea from Taiwan) and, of course, teapots made of porcelain or purple clay from Yixing. The **KS Lo Gallery** on the first floor contains a collection of rare Chinese ceramics and seals.

Hong Kong Visual Arts Centre Housed in the former **Victoria Barracks**, the Hong Kong Visual Arts Centre *(☎ 2521 3008, 7A Kennedy Rd; admission free; open 10am-9pm Wed-Mon)* supports local sculptors, printmakers and potters and stages temporary exhibitions.

Hong Kong Zoological & Botanical Gardens (Maps 4 & 7)

First established in 1864, these excellent gardens *(☎ 2530 0154, Albany Rd; admission free; gardens open 6am-10pm daily, zoo & aviaries open 6am-7pm daily, greenhouses open 9am-4.30pm daily)* are a pleasant collection of fountains, sculptures, greenhouses, a playground, a zoo and some fabulous aviaries. There are hundreds of species of birds, exotic trees, plants and shrubs on display. The zoo is surprisingly comprehensive and is also one of the world's leading centres for the captive breeding of endangered species.

The gardens are divided by Albany Rd, with the plants and aviaries in the area to the east close to Garden Rd, and most of the animals to the west. The animal displays seem to be mostly primates like lemurs, gibbons, macaques and orang-utans; other residents include a lone jaguar and radiated tortoises.

The Zoological & Botanical Gardens are at the top (ie, southern) end of Garden Rd. It's an easy walk from Central, but you can also take bus No 3B, 12 or 12M from the stop in front of the Connaught Centre on Connaught Rd Central. The bus takes you along Upper Albert and Caine roads on the northern boundary of the gardens. Get off in front of the Caritas Centre at 2 Caine Rd and follow the path across the street and up the hill to the gardens.

Ex-Government House (Map 4)

Parts of the erstwhile residence of the colonial governor of Hong Kong (information ☎ 2530 2003, Upper Albert Rd), opposite the northern end of the Zoological & Botanical Gardens, date back to 1856. Other features were added by the Japanese during the occupation of Hong Kong in WWII.

The current chief executive, Tung Chee Hwa, refused to occupy Government House after assuming power, claiming the fung shui wasn't satisfactory. But everyone knows it was because he wanted to de-emphasise the position of Hong Kong SAR chief executive and Hong Kong governor.

Ex-Government House is closed to the public except for one Sunday in March when azaleas in the mansion gardens are in bloom.

Lower Albert Rd & Ice House St

Below Upper Albert Rd is, appropriately enough, Lower Albert Rd, where the massive **SAR Government Headquarters** (18 Lower Albert Rd) is located. The attractive off-white stucco and red brick structure at the top of the road is the **Dairy Farm Building (Map 5)** (2 Lower Albert Rd), built for the Dairy Farm Ice and Cold Storage Company in 1898 and renovated in 1913. Today

it houses the **Fringe Club**, the excellent **M at the Fringe** restaurant and the illustrious **Foreign Correspondents' Club of Hong Kong** (☎ 2521 1511). Towering above the Dairy Farm Building on the opposite side of the road is the **Bishop's House (Map 5)**, official residence of the Anglican bishop of Victoria for 130 years.

From the Dairy Farm Building, Ice House St (no prizes for guessing where the name came from) doglegs into Queen's Rd Central. Just before it turns south, a wide flight of stone steps leads down to **Duddell St**. The **wrought-iron gas lamps** at the top and bottom of the steps were placed here between 1875 and 1889 and are listed monuments.

SHEUNG WAN (MAP 4)

West of Central is Sheung Wan and beyond that the contiguous district of Sai Ying Pun, which is often called Western by English speakers. While this area once had something of a feel of old Shanghai about it, much of that has disappeared under the jackhammers, and old 'ladder streets' (steep inclined streets with steps) once lined with stalls and street vendors have been cleared away to make room for more buildings or the Mass Transit Railway (MTR).

Nevertheless, traditional shops and business still abound and the area is worth exploring. **Man Wa Lane**, for example, a block east of Sheung Wan MTR station, is a good location if you want to buy a name chop, a stone seal that has a name carved in Chinese on the base. Chops are sometimes made of jade or wood. When dipped in ink, the chop can be used as a stamp.

From Queen's Rd Central, walk or take the Central Escalator south to **Hollywood Rd**. At its eastern end, this street is lined with upmarket antique and carpet shops and the wonderful **Central Police Station** (10 Hollywood Road), built in 1864 and not open to the public (if you really want to get inside we're sure it can be arranged). Once you head west from, say, Aberdeen St, the scenario changes: you'll soon be passing traditional wreath and coffin makers as well as several funeral shops with hell money and paper votives in the shape of cars, telephones and VCRs to help the dearly departed enjoy themselves and get around on the other side. The 'antique' (really curio) shops also get a whole lot more, well, junky and are more interesting for that.

To the south of Hollywood Rd and running parallel to it just past the Man Mo Temple is Upper Lascar Row, known to Hong Kong people as Cat St. This narrow street used to be famous for its arts and crafts and 'diamonds to rust' piles of curios and junk, but many dealers have not gone, either going out of business or moving to the nearby **Cat Street Galleries** (*Casey Bldg, 38 Lok Ku Rd; open noon-10pm*), which is entered from Upper Lascar Row. But even the galleries now appear to have enjoyed better days, with five floors of arts and crafts, antiques and souvenirs reduced to just two.

A short distance to the west, next to **Hollywood Rd Park** and before Hollywood Rd debouches into Queen's Rd West is **Possession St**. This is thought to be where commodore Gordon Bremmer and a contingent of British marines planted the Union flag on 26 January 1841 and claimed Hong Kong Island for the crown. If you've wondered why Queen's Rd runs in such a serpentine fashion as it heads eastward, now you know: it once formed the shoreline of Hong Kong Island's northern coast.

Man Mo Temple

Man Mo Temple (*Cnr Hollywood Rd & Ladder St; admission free; open 8am-6pm daily*) is one of the oldest and most famous in Hong Kong. Literally 'civil and military', Man Mo is dedicated to two deities. The civil deity is a Chinese statesman of the 3rd century BC and the military one Kwan Tai (or Kuanti), a Han Dynasty soldier born in the 2nd century AD and now worshipped as the red-cheeked God of War. Kwan Tai's popularity in Hong Kong probably has more to do with his additional status as the patron god of restaurants, pawn shops, the police force and secret societies such as the Triads.

Outside the entrance are four gilt plaques on poles that are carried at procession time. Two plaques describe the gods being worshipped; the others request silence and respect within the temple grounds and warn menstruating women to keep out of the main hall. Inside the temple are two antique chairs shaped like houses, which are used to carry the two gods at festival time.

The area around the temple was used for location shots in the 1960 film *The World of Suzie Wong*, based on the novel by Richard Mason. The building to the right of the temple appears as Suzie's hotel, although the real hotel Luk Kwok (called Nam Kok in the film and now rebuilt) is in Wan Chai.

HONG KONG UNIVERSITY (MAP 3)

West of Sheung Wan takes you through the Sai Ying Pun and Shek Tong Tsui districts to Kennedy Town, a residential district at the end of the tram line. The chief attraction of this area is Hong Kong University, founded in 1911, and its museum.

To get to this area take bus No 3B from in front of the Connaught Centre on Connaught Rd Central or bus No 23, 40, 40M or 43 from Admiralty and get off at the main entrance on Bonham Rd, opposite St Paul's College.

Fung Ping Shan Museum

The Fung Ping Shan Museum (☎ 2975 5600, *University of Hong Kong, 94 Bonham Rd; admission free; open 9.30am-6pm Mon-Sat, 1.30pm-5.30pm Sun*) houses collections of ceramics and bronzes, plus a lesser number of paintings and carvings. The bronzes are in three groups: Shang and Zhou dynasty ritual vessels; decorative mirrors from the Warring States period to the Tang, Song, Ming and Qing dynasties; and Nestorian crosses from the Yuan dynasty. (The Nestorians were a Christian sect that arose in Syria, and at some stage arrived in China, probably during the Tang dynasty.) The museum's collection of Yuan dynasty bronzes is the largest in the world. The museum is closed public holidays.

The ceramics collection includes Han dynasty tomb pottery and recent works from the Chinese pottery centres of Jingdezhen and Shiwan in China.

MID-LEVELS (MAP 4)

As a solidly residential area the Mid-Levels has little to offer tourists in the way of sights. The renovated Moorish Romantic-style **Ohel Leah Synagogue** *(70 Robinson Rd)*, built between 1878 and 1902 when that style was all the rage in Europe, is worth a look (though you won't get in unless you want to attend a Sabbath service). It is named after Lea Gubbay Sassoon, matriarch of a wealthy (and philanthropic) Sephardic Jewish family who can trace its roots back to the beginning of the colony.

Hong Kong Museum of Medical Sciences

This small museum *(☎ 2549 5123, 2 Caine Lane; open 10am-5pm Tues-Sat, 1-5pm Sun)* of medical implements and accoutrements such as an old dentistry chair, an autopsy table, herbal medicine vials and chests, is less interesting for its exhibits than for its architecture. It is housed in what was once the Old Pathological Institute, a breezy Edwardian-style brick and tiled structure built in 1904.

The museum is entered at the intersection of Caine Rd and Ladder St. You can get to the museum on bus No 26 from The Landmark. Get off at the Man Mo Temple and walk up Ladder St. Alternatively, minibus No 8 or 22 from the Star Ferry will drop you off at the corner of Caine Rd and Ladder St. The museum is just below you. A donation is requested.

THE PEAK (MAP 7)

On your first really clear day in Hong Kong, make tracks for the Peak, the highest point on the island. Not only is the view one of the most spectacular cityscapes in the world, it's also a good way to put Hong Kong and its layout into perspective. Repeat the trip up on a clear night, as the views of the illuminated city below are superb.

The Peak has been *the* place to live in Hong Kong ever since the British moved in. The taipans (company bosses) built summer houses here to escape the heat and humidity (it's usually about 5°C cooler up here than lower down). The Peak is still the most

fashionable place to live, as reflected by the astronomical property prices and bumper-to-bumper luxury cars.

There are two main buildings on the Peak: the seven-level **Peak Tower**, the huge titanium anvil rising above the Peak Tram terminus and containing theme entertainment venues, shops and restaurants, and the adjacent **Peak Galleria**, an overblown, overpriced four-floor shopping mall with some 60 shops and restaurants.

The Peak, and particularly the Peak Tower with all its attractions, is a good place to bring the kids. The **Peak Explorer** *(☎ 2849 0668, Level 4, Peak Tower, 128 Peak Rd; adult/child HK$75/32; open 9am-10pm daily)* is a motion simulator that takes you into space. **Ripley's Believe It or Not Odditorium** *(☎ 2849 0818, Level 3, Peak Tower, 128 Peak Rd, adult/child & senior HK$65/46; open 9am-10pm daily)* is similar to the branches of this chain seen around the world, with some 450 exhibits of the weird and not so wonderful (mannequins of women weighing tonnes, stuffed five-legged calves and skulls with crowbars embedded in them). A combination ticket for both attractions costs adult/child HK$80/62, or HK$110/69 including a return trip on the Peak Tram.

There's also an outpost of **Madame Tussaud's** *(☎ 3128 8288, Ⓦ www.madame-tussauds.com, Level 2, Peak Tower, 128 Peak Rd; adult/concession HK$75/50; open noon-8pm daily)*. The kid-friendly **Mövenpick Marché** restaurant (see the Peak section under Places to Eat later in this chapter), with roaming clowns and other live entertainment, is on levels 6 and 7 and there is a **viewing terrace** with coin-operated binoculars on level 5.

Both the Peak Tower and Galleria are designed to withstand winds of up to 270km/h, theoretically more than the maximum velocity of a No 10 typhoon. You can reach the **Peak Galleria viewing deck**, which is larger than the one in the Peak Tower, by taking the escalator to the 3rd level. Inside the mall you'll find a number of expensive restaurants and retail shops, from art galleries to duty free.

Victoria Peak

When people refer to the Peak, they generally mean the plateau at an elevation of 396m with the Peak Tower and Galleria and the surrounding residential area. Victoria Peak (552m), about 500m to the west of the Peak Tram terminus up steep Mt Austin Rd, is actually the summit. The **old governor's mountain lodge** is near the top. It was burned to the ground by the Japanese during WWII, but the **gardens** remain and are open to the public.

You can walk around Victoria Peak without expending too much energy. Harlech Rd on the south side and Lugard Rd on the north slope form a 3.5km loop around the summit; the tree-shaded sitting-out area where they meet is a pleasant place to rest. The walk takes about an hour and is illuminated at night. If you feel like a longer walk, you can continue for another 2km along Peak Rd to Pok Fu Lam Reservoir Rd, which leaves Peak Rd near the car park exit. This goes past the reservoir to the main Pok Fu Lam Rd, where you can get the No 7 bus to Aberdeen or back to Central.

Getting There & Away

Half the fun of going up to the Peak is riding the **Peak Tram** (☎ *2522 0922; one-way/ return adult HK$20/30, child HK$6/9, senior HK$7/14*), a funicular that goes from Central to the Peak Tower, running every 10 minutes from 7am to midnight daily, making between one and four stops along the way in about 10 minutes. It's such a steep ride that the floor is angled to help standing passengers stay upright. Running for more than a century, the tram has never had an accident.

In 1885 everyone thought Phineas Kyrie and William Kerfoot Hughes were mad when they announced their intention to build a tramway to the top, but it opened three years later, silencing the scoffers and wiping out the sedan-chair trade in one go. Since then, what was originally called the High Level Tramway has been stopped only by WWII and the violent rainstorms of 1966, which washed half the track down the hillside.

The tram station is behind the St John's Building at 33 Garden Rd, at the south-west corner of Hong Kong Park and about 650m south-west of the Star Ferry terminal. Avoid going on Sunday and public holidays when there are usually long queues. If you have an Octopus card (see Travel & Tourist Passes under Public Transport in the Hong Kong Getting Around chapter) you can beat the lines and go straight onto the tram.

Between 10am and 11.45pm, the brown-coloured, open deck bus No 15C (HK$3) ferries passengers between the Star Ferry and the Peak Tram station.

Of course there are also other ways to reach the Peak. Bus No 15 from Exchange Square, bus No 15B from Wan Chai and Causeway Bay and green minibus No 1 from Edinburgh Place near the Star Ferry terminal will all take you directly to the top.

HONG KONG TRAIL (MAP 3)

Hong Kong Island has a surprising number of walking trails. For those who like a challenge, it is possible to tramp the length of Hong Kong Island on the rugged 50km-long Hong Kong Trail. Starting from the Peak Tram station on the Peak, the trail follows Lugard Rd to the west and drops down the hill to Pok Fu Lam Reservoir near Aberdeen, before turning east and zigzagging across the ridges. The trail traverses four country parks: **Pok Fu Lam Country Park** south of Victoria Peak; **Aberdeen Country Park** east of the Peak; **Tai Tam Country Park** on the eastern side of the island; and **Shek O Country Park** in the south-east. Tai Tam is the largest and most beautiful of the four, with its dense emerald woods and trickling streams. The Hong Kong Trail skirts the northern side of **Tai Tam Reservoir**, the largest body of water on the island.

It's possible to hike the entire trail in one day, but it's quite a slog; most walkers pick a manageable section to suit. There are no designated camping sites along the trail.

If you want to do this hike, purchase the *Hong Kong Trail* map (HK$30) published by the Country & Marine Parks Authority, available from the Government Publications Office, 66 Queensway, Admiralty. *Exploring Hong Kong's Countryside* by Edward Stokes is a useful book.

Apart from gaining section No 1 of the trail on the Peak, you can reach section No 6 (Tai Tam) on bus No 6 or 61 from Exchange Square and section No 7 (Tai Tam Bay and Shek O) on bus No 14.

WAN CHAI (MAP 6)

East of Central is one of Hong Kong's most famous districts, Wan Chai (or 'Little Bay' in Cantonese). If you choose to believe some of the tourist brochures, Wan Chai is still inseparably linked with the name of Suzie Wong – not bad considering that the book dates back to 1957 and the movie to 1960. Although Wan Chai had a reputation during the Vietnam War as a seedy red-light district, today it is mainly a centre for shopping, drinking and business. If you want to see how far Wan Chai has come since Suzie Wong did (again and again), check the fortress-like **Hong Kong Convention and Exhibition Centre** (☎ 2582 8888, 1 Expo Drive), which is due north of the Wan Chai MTR station. For more information see the special section Contemporary Architecture in this chapter.

Two of Hong Kong's most important cultural venues – the **Academy for the Performing Arts** (☎ 2584 8554, 1 Gloucester Rd) and the **Hong Kong Arts Centre** (☎ 2582 0200, 2 Harbour Rd) stand side by side to the south-west of the convention centre. The latter contains the **Pao Sui Loong Galleries** (☎ 2582 0256, 2582 0200, 4th & 5th floors, Hong Kong Arts Centre, 2 Harbour Rd; admission free; open 10am-8pm daily during exhibitions), with local and international exhibitions focusing on contemporary art.

This is all 'new' Wan Chai. To the south and south-east and sandwiched between Johnston Rd and Queen's Rd East are row after row of narrow streets harbouring all sorts of interesting traditional shops, markets and mini-factories where you can see the 'real' Hong Kong at work: watchmakers, blacksmiths, shoemakers, printers, sign-makers and so on.

In an alley on the south side of Queen's Rd East is **Tai Wong Temple** (127 Queen's Rd East), also known as Hung Sing Temple, where fortune-tellers used to do a brisk trade. It is still active, if somewhat subdued.

A couple of blocks to the east of the temple is the **Hopewell Centre** (183 Queen's Rd East), a 40-storey cylinder and the flagship building of the Hong Kong property and construction magnate Gordon Wu. The centre's tacky revolving restaurant is accessed by two bubble-shaped external elevators. Though it's a short trip, the elevator ride is a great way to get an aerial view of Wan Chai. A short distance to the east is the **Old Wan Chai Post Office** (Cnr Queen's Rd East & Wan Chai Gap Rd), built in 1913 and now a resources centre operated by the Environmental Protection Department (☎ 2835 1918). If you were to follow Wan Chai Gap Rd uphill, you'd eventually reach the Peak.

Wan Chai Market (264 Queen's Rd East) was built in the geometric Bauhaus style in 1937. It has yet to be listed and may be torn down for yet another block of flats.

CAUSEWAY BAY & SURROUNDS (MAP 6)

Causeway Bay or Tung Lo Wan (Copper Gong Bay) in Cantonese was the site of a British settlement in the 1840s and was once an area of godowns (a Hong Kong word for warehouses) and a well-protected harbour for fisherfolk and boatpeople.

The new Causeway Bay, one of Hong Kong's top shopping and nightlife areas, was built up from swampland and the bottom of the harbour. Jardine Matheson, one of Hong Kong's largest hongs (major trading houses or companies), set up shop here, which explains why some of the streets in the district bear its name: Jardine's Bazaar, Jardine's Crescent and Yee Wo St (the name for Jardine Matheson in Cantonese).

Causeway Bay is primarily for shopping and, to a lesser degree, dining out. The biggest and best shopping mall is in **Times Square** (☎ 2118 8888 1 Matheson St), an enormous retail/office/restaurant with a dozen floors of retail organised by type. It stands in sharp contrast with the decrepit 1950s low-rise tenements surrounding it.

Typhoon Shelter

Not so long ago the waterfront used to be a mass of junks and sampans huddling in the

Causeway Bay Typhoon Shelter for protection, but these days it's nearly all yachts. The land jutting out to the west is **Kellett Island**, which has been a misnomer ever since a causeway connected it to the mainland in 1956, and further land reclamation turned it into a peninsula. It is home to the **Royal Hong Kong Yacht Club** (☎ 2239 0363, *Hung Hing Rd)*, which retains its 'Royal' moniker in English only. The Cross-Harbour Tunnel linking Causeway Bay and Hung Hom surfaces here.

Noonday Gun

Noel Coward made the so-called Noonday Gun *(281 Gloucester Rd,)* famous with his satirical song *Mad Dogs and Englishmen* (1924) about colonials who braved the fierce heat of the sun at midday while the local people sensibly remained indoors: 'In Hong Kong they strike a gong/And fire off a noonday gun/To reprimand each inmate/Who's in late'.

Built in 1901 by Hotchkiss in Portsmouth, this recoil-mounted three-pounder is one of the few vestiges of the colonial past in Causeway Bay and its best known landmark. It stands in a small garden opposite the Excelsior Hotel on Gloucester Rd and is fired at noon every day.

Exactly how this tradition got started remains a mystery. Some people say that Jardine Matheson fired the gun without permission to bid farewell to a departing managing director or to welcome one of their incoming ships. The authorities were so enraged by the company's insolence that, as punishment, Jardine's was ordered to fire the gun every day.

The Noonday Gun is accessible via a tunnel through the basement car park in the World Trade Centre, just west of the Excelsior Hotel. From the taxi rank in front of the hotel, look west for the door marked 'Stairway No 2, Position 6'.

Victoria Park

One of the biggest patches of greenery on the northern side of Hong Kong Island, Victoria Park is a popular escape. The best time to stroll around is in the morning during the week when it becomes a forest of people practising the slow-motion choreography of tai chi. In the evening it becomes the domain of Hong Kong's young lovers, most of whom live in cramped flats with their very extended families.

Between April and October you can take a dip in **Victoria Park swimming pool** (☎ 2770 8347; *adult/child & senior HK$19/ 9; open 6.30am-9pm).* The park becomes a **flower market** a few days before the Chinese New Year. It's also worth a visit during the Mid-Autumn (Moon) Festival when people turn out en masse carrying lanterns.

Victoria Park is the site of the annual **Tiananmen Square massacre vigil** held on the evening of 4 June, which attracts thousands of people. It is a very moving occasion, accompanied by songs and speeches, while everyone sits on the ground with candles of remembrance.

The po-faced **statue of Queen Victoria**, which once graced Statue Square in Central, is in the park.

Tin Hau Temple

Due east of Victoria Park, Hong Kong Island's most famous Tin Hau Temple *(101 Tin Hau Temple Rd)* is tiny and dwarfed by surrounding high-rises. Before reclamation, this temple dedicated to the patroness of seafarers stood on the waterfront. This has been a site of worship for 300 years, though the current structure is only about 200 years old. The temple bell dates from 1747. The central shrine contains an effigy of Tin Hau with a blackened face. To the right of the main shrine is an ossuary with funereal plaques.

The temple is a five-minute walk from the Tin Hau MTR station.

Tiger Balm Gardens

The mind-blowing Tiger Balm Gardens (☎ 2890 5365, *Tai Hang Rd; admission free; open 9.30am-4pm)* in the Tai Hang district south-east of Causeway Bay, comprise three hectares of grotesque, luridly painted Buddhist statuary in various degrees of decay.

[continued on page 150]

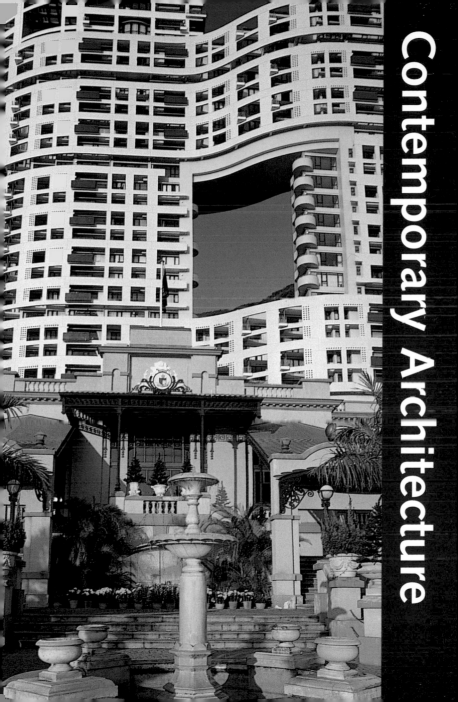

Contemporary Architecture

JOHN HAY

RICHARD I'ANSON

JOHN HAY

Title Page: A distinctive apartment block in Repulse Bay, Hong Kong. The hole is a concession to the laws of feng shui or geomancy. (Photograph by Jon Davison)

Top left: Former KCR Clock Tower at night near the Hong Kong Cultural Centre, Tsim Sha Tsui, Kowloon.

Top Right: Completed in 1992, Central Plaza is Hong Kong's tallest building.

Bottom: The Hong Kong Convention & Exhibition Centre was the site of the 1997 handover ceremony.

While it may not be Manhattan, Hong Kong has an increasingly attractive skyline (it was *always* dramatic) that is further enhanced by the surrounding water and mountains, the *sine qua non* of traditional Chinese painting.

Hong Kong's verticality was born out of necessity – the scarcity of land and the sloping terrain has always put property at a premium in this densely populated city. While reclaiming land has been a solution since 1851, going up offers a viable, less costly alternative.

Some buildings, such as Central Plaza, seize height at all costs; others are smaller but revel in elaborate detail (the Hongkong and Shanghai Bank building). A privileged few are even able to make the audacious choice to go horizontal (the Hong Kong Convention & Exhibition Centre).

It's not unfair to say that truly inspired modern architecture only reached Hong Kong when Sir Norman Foster's award-winning Hongkong and Shanghai Bank building opened in Central in 1986. For the first time the territory was seeing what modern architecture can and should be: Innovative, functional and startlingly beautiful.

Hong Kong has more than its fair share of booby-prize winners, but before anyone gets too judgmental about the territory's New Towns and their less-than-inspired housing estates, they should spare a thought for the thousands of refugees and illegal immigrants that were swamping the territory every day following the end of WWII, during the Cultural Revolution and in the late 1970s and early 80s. The government had to move them from squatter settlements and shoehorn them into housing blocks quickly; aesthetics took a backseat to four walls and a roof.

Along with the buildings listed in this section, other modern structures worth noting include:

Exchange Square (8 Connaught Place, Central), a 52-storey multi-towered complex built on an elevated podium above the fray of Central

International Finance Centre (1 Harbour View St, Central), a tapering pearl-coloured colossus atop the IFC Mall and Hong Kong station, terminus of the Airport Express and Tung Chung MTR lines

Academy for the Performing Arts (1 Gloucester Rd, Wan Chai), with its striking triangular atrium and an exterior Meccano-like frame that is a work of art in itself

Entertainment Building (30 Queen's Rd Central), neoclassical-inspired and clad in warm beige granite

Kadoorie Biological Sciences Building (University of Hong Kong, 94 Bonham Rd, Pok Fu Lam), a high-tech building, with its cylindrical external staircases

Lee Theatre Plaza (99 Percival St, Causeway Bay), which was built on the site of the old Lee Theatre and retains, in modern form, a wonderful large staircase

Those wanting to learn more about Hong Kong's contemporary architecture should pick up a copy of the illustrated *Skylines Hong Kong* by Peter Moss or the more serious *Hong Kong: A Guide to Recent Architecture* by Juanita Cheung and Andrew Yeoh.

Bank of China Tower

The 70-storey Bank of China Tower *(1 Garden Rd, Central)*, Hong Kong's second-tallest structure after Central Plaza, became something of a symbol of Hong Kong immediately after it was completed in 1990. Impressive and daring as it is, the building is very much a brash and hard-edged synopsis of the 1980s. In purely physical terms, it dominates not just its immediate environment but the entire Hong Kong skyline. For face reasons, the Bank of China Tower did its very best to dwarf its neighbour but one, the Hong Kong and Shanghai Bank, the symbol of the exiting power.

The asymmetry of the building is puzzling at first glance, but is really a simple geometric exercise. Rising from the ground like a cube, it is successively reduced, quarter by quarter, until the south-facing side is left to rise upward. The staggered truncation of each triangular column creates a prismatic effect.

Although it was designed by Chinese-born American architect I M Pei, the building is clearly Western in inspiration: 'I didn't design a pagoda', he told journalists. Chinese elements are incorporated but muted. The segments of the building rising upwards are claimed to be analogous to bamboo sections, and the two-tonne granite base suggests Beijing's ancient city gates.

Many local Hong Kong Chinese see the building as a huge violation of the principles of fung shui. For example, the bank's four triangular prisms are negative symbols in the fung shui handbook; being the opposite to circles, these contradict what circles suggest – money, perfection and prosperity. Furthermore, the huge crosses on the sides of the building suggest negativity and its shape has been likened to a praying mantis (a threatening symbol), complete with radio masts as antennae.

The Bank of China Building is stymied by its location, stranded in a web of flyovers and not easily accessible to pedestrians. If you can negotiate your way there, take the express lift to the public viewing gallery on the 47th floor for a panoramic view of Hong Kong.

KELLI HAMBLET

Central Plaza At just under 374m, Central Plaza *(18 Harbour Rd, Wan Chai)*, completed in 1992, is Hong Kong's tallest building. The glass skin of the tower has three different colours – gold, silver and ter-racotta – and the overall impression is rather garish. Altogether the construction is very Hong Kong: upwardly mobile, crisp and in your face. The Sky Lobby on the 46th floor offers a breathtaking panoramic sweep over Victoria Harbour and Kowloon.

The tower is triangular in design with indented corners. Sitting atop the building is a 64m mast standing on a tripod. The base of the building is notable for its landscaped garden and public plaza. Though somewhat isolated by major roadways, the building is successfully connected to other buildings by numerous overhead public walkways (including ones from the Hong Kong Convention & Exhibition Centre and the Wan Chai MTR station).

Central Plaza is the second highest reinforced concrete structure in the world. Less well known is that it is also the world's biggest clock. There's method to the madness of those four lines of light shining through the glass pyramid at the top of the building between 6pm and midnight. The bottom level indicates the hour: red is 6pm; white 7pm; purple 8pm; yellow 9 pm; pink 10pm; green 11pm When all four lights are the same colour, it's right on the hour. When the top light is different from the bottom ones, it's 15 minutes past the hour. If the top two and bottom two are different, it's half-past the hour. If the top three match, it's 45 minutes past the hour.

Hong Kong Convention & Exhibition Centre Extension

The ambitious extension to the Hong Kong Convention & Exhibition Centre *(1 Expo Drive, Wan Chai)*, variously compared to a bird's wing, a banana leaf and a lotus petal, was built on an arrowhead-shaped re-claimed island and connected to the existing complex by a covered walkway. With its dramatic backdrop of cutting-edge buildings and its location on the harbour, the extension was designed as Hong Kong's landmark and ready in time to be the setting for the official handover ceremony on 30 June 1997.

Low and horizontal – two unusual qualities in Hong Kong – the structure has an uplifting design that gives the impression that the building is preparing for flight, and its curves add anticipated move-ment to an otherwise static shoreline. Perhaps the best aspect is from the outside – the promenade surrounding the wing offers wonderful views over to Central to the west and Tsim Sha Tsui to the north.

Hong Kong Cultural Centre

There's never been a building as controversial in Hong Kong as the Cultural Centre – it has been com-pared to everything from a cheesily tiled loo to a petrol station. Despite all that it has become a dynamic focus for the arts in Hong Kong and a challenge to the notion that the territory is devoid of culture.

Occupying the most prime piece of Tsim Sha Tsui waterfront, the Cultural Centre is asymmetrically weighted and wave-like. The pronounced shape lifts upwards at the sides in a celebratory gesture, facing the reserved traditionalism of the old KCR clock tower opposite. Leading away from the Cultural Centre is a wonderful promenade that looks out over Victoria Harbour to the magnificent architectural spectacle of Hong Kong's Central district.

Lippo Centre Designed by American architect Paul Marvin Rudolph (a former student of Walter Gropius of Bauhaus fame), the Lippo Centre *(89 Queensway, Admiralty)* epitomises the rather brash naivety of the 1980s (rapidly becoming nostalgia territory) in steel and reflective glass. One glance at the structure's lumpy protrusions and hulking outline and you know you're in shoulder-pad land.

The centre's two towers are of different heights: one is 36 floors and the other 40 floors. The protrusions hanging from the sides of the building are clumped in three groups and consist of 'sky-rooms'. The overall design is challenging and commands attention, but sadly the building, full of vigour and enthusiasm when it opened in 1988, is looking a bit tarnished and weather-beaten now.

Hong Kong International Airport Passenger Terminal
Most travellers when they arrive won't have to go far to enjoy modern Hong Kong architecture for they'll be right inside one of the best recent examples – Hong Kong International Airport at Chek Lap Kok. Designed by the Mott Consortium, which included Sir Norman Foster's design firm, the terminal, which opened in 1998, is the largest single airport building in the world, with an overall length of 1.27km and a floor area of 500,000 sq metres.

From the air the terminal looks like a massive bird or aeroplane. The planning is open and wide, with a welcoming interior for those in transit. The airport's boarding gates are on a Y-shaped concourse leading from the central base.

The vaulted roof is a lightweight steel membrane and covers an area of 18 hectares, spanning the entire building in a complex geometry of linked vaults. Roof supports had to be designed to withstand vast structural forces – up to 300 tonnes in some places. At the side, the roof hangs over the terminal's glass perimeter – a circumference of 5km. The glass walls of the building are clear to a height of at least 4m, allowing unrestricted views out to the aircraft and surrounding sea.

Hongkong & Shanghai Bank Building The Hongkong and Shanghai Bank *(1 Queen's Rd Central)* is a masterpiece of precision, sophistication and innovation. And why not? It was the world's most expensive building (it cost about US$1 billion to build) when it opened in 1986 and was much more expensive than the nearby (and much taller) Bank of China Tower.

Hong Kong people call the glass and aluminium structure the 'Robot Building', and it's easy to see why: the gears, chains, motors and other moving parts of the escalators and lifts are all visible. The stairwells are only walled in with glass, affording dizzying views to workers inside the building. Structurally, the building is equally radical, built on a 'coat-hanger' frame.

The framework of the building is a staggering achievement. Observable from outside the building are five huge trusses from which the floor levels hang. Supporting the trusses are eight groups of four-column steel clusters clad in aluminium. By using this technique, the architect eliminated the need for a central core. The resulting atrium gives the building a sense of space and light. If you stand in the atrium and look up, you can see how the whole structure hangs, rather than ascends. The building is flexible – the flooring, for example, is constructed from movable panelling.

The building reveals architect Sir Norman Foster's desire to create areas of public and private space and to break the mould of previous bank architecture. The ground floor is public space, which people can traverse without entering the building, from there, escalators rise to the main banking hall. The building is inviting to enter – not guarded or off-limits. This sensation is encouraged by the imaginative use of natural light. Hung on the south side of the building are 480 computer-controlled mirrors that reflect natural light into the atrium, a 'sun scoop' in architectural parlance.

It's worth taking the escalator to the 1st floor to gaze at the cathedral-like atrium and the natural light filtering through; there's a reception desk there where you can pick up an information booklet on the building.

The Centre The 73-storey, star-shaped Centre *(99 Queen's Rd Central)*, which most travellers will end up visiting at some stage (the main branch of the Hong Kong Tourism Board is on the ground floor), has quickly become a landmark in the western part of Central. The steel and glass tower, very vaguely reminiscent of New York's Empire State Building, rises from a landscaped plaza that allows pedestrian flow. But what really sets the Centre apart is the awesome and almost hypnotic light show at night that sends colour lights cascading down the building's protruding 'spines'. Be on the lookout at 9pm, 10pm and 11pm; the 175 programs controlling the display pitch it to almost hallucinogenic levels.

KELLI HAMBLET

[continued from page 144]

Officially known as the Aw Boon Haw Gardens, they were built in 1935 for HK$16 million by Aw Boon Haw, a Burmese businessman who had made his fortune from the Tiger Balm cure-everything medication.

Keep an eye open for the seven-storey pagoda, which sadly cannot be climbed, a hillside of visibly frightened blue plaster seals, and the worrying Ten Judges of Hell Court, a wall of plaster reliefs depicting what's going to happen to those – us? – who misbehave when the chips are down. Traitors will have their hearts cut out, corrupt officials will be hammered to death, prostitutes (female *and* male depicted) will be deep-fried and – this was the early 20th century – the treacherous will be run over by a car.

The gardens are a bit of a trudge up Tai Hang Rd via Tung Lo Wan Rd. The easiest way to reach them is on bus No 11 from Exchange Square, Admiralty or Yee Wo St in Causeway Bay.

HAPPY VALLEY

Happy Valley, or Pau Ma Dei (horse running place) in Cantonese, a popular residential area for expats since the early days of British settlement, has some interesting **cemeteries** to the west and south-west of Wong Nai Chong Rd. These are divided into Protestant, Roman Catholic, Muslim, Parsi and Hindu sections and date back to the founding of Hong Kong as a colony.

The district's most important drawing card is what is in the centre of circular Wong Nai Chong Rd. You can reach Happy Valley by tram or bus No 75, 90 or 97 from Exchange Square. It's about a 15-minute walk from Times Square in Causeway Bay.

Happy Valley Racecourse

Apart from mahjong and the Mark Six Lottery, racing is the only form of legalised gambling in Hong Kong, and *very* popular. The SAR has the highest per capita betting on horse races in the world with an annual turnover of HK$80 billion-plus.

The first horse races were held in 1846 at Happy Valley and became an annual event.

Now there are some 65 meetings a year split between Happy Valley and the newer, larger track at Sha Tin in the New Territories (see that chapter for details). The racing season is September to June with most race meetings in Happy Valley taking place on Wednesday evening.

If you've been in Hong Kong for less than 21 days you can get a tourist ticket to attend the races (see Horse Racing under Spectator Sports in the Hong Kong Facts for the Visitor chapter for details).

Hong Kong Racing Museum Racing buffs can wallow in the history of the place at the Hong Kong Racing Museum (☎ 2966 8065, 2nd floor, Happy Valley Stand, Happy Valley Racecourse, Wong Nai Chung Rd; admission free; open 10am-5pm Tues-Sun, 10am-12.30pm racing days). The most important event in the history of the Happy Valley racetrack (individual winnings notwithstanding) was the huge fire in 1918 that killed hundreds of people. Many of the victims were buried in the cemeteries surrounding the track.

QUARRY BAY

The main attraction in Quarry Bay is one of Hong Kong's finest shopping malls, the **Cityplaza Shopping Centre (Map 3)** (☎ 2568 8665, 111 King's Rd, Tai Koo Shing), which is directly linked up to the MTR. Although not normally considered a tourist attraction, it has much to be recommended as shopping is much more pleasant once you get out of the tourist zones and prices are often lower.

SAI WAN HO

The new Hong Kong Film Archive (Map 3) (☎ 2739 2139, W www.lcsd.gov.hk, 50 Lei King Rd; admission free) preserves, catalogues, studies and documents Hong Kong films and related material (magazines, posters, records, scripts, etc). A 110-seat **cinema** (☎ 2734 9009; admission HK$20-30) shows Hong Kong and other films here during festivals and themed 'weeks'.

To reach the film archive take the MTR to Sai Wan Ho and follow exit A. Lei King Rd is two blocks to the north-west.

SHAU KEI WAN
Hong Kong Museum of Coastal Defence (Map 3)

The Hong Kong Museum of Coastal Defence (☎ 2569 1500, 175 Tung Hei Rd; adult/child & senior $10/5 Fri-Tues, free Wed; open 10am-5pm Fri-Wed) doesn't exactly sound like a crowd-pleaser but this excellent new museum is as much about peace as it is war. Part of the fun is just to enjoy the museum's location. It has been built into the Lei Yue Mun Fort (1887), which took quite a beating during WWII and has sweeping views down to the Lei Yue Mun Channel and south-eastern Kowloon.

Exhibitions in the old Redoubt, which you reach by escalator from the street level, cover Hong Kong's coastal defence over six centuries: from the Ming and Qing dynasties (1368 1911) and through the colonial years and Japanese invasion to the resumption of Chinese sovereignty. There's a historical trail through the casemates, tunnels and observation posts almost down to the coast.

To reach the museum take the MTR to Shau Kei Wan station and follow exit B2. From here follow the museum signs on Tung Hei Rd (part of the busy Eastern Ireland Corridor) for about 15 minutes. There is a free shuttle bus from the Heng Fa Chuen MTR station at the weekend and on public holidays. Bus No 85 between Shau Kei Wan and Chai Wan also stops nearby.

CHAI WAN

Out at the eastern end of Hong Kong Island is Chai Wan, a district of nondescript office buildings, warehouses and workers' flats. However, there is one small museum that is worth trekking out here to see.

Law Uk Folk Museum (Map 3)

The Law Uk Folk Museum (☎ 2896 7006, 14 Kut Shing St; admission free; open 10am-1pm & 2pm-6pm Tues-Sat, 1pm-6pm Sun & public holidays) is housed in two restored Hakka village houses that have been standing here for more than two centuries. The quiet courtyard and surrounding bamboo groves are peaceful and evocative, but the displays within are rather shabby.

In the main building there is an extensive collection of rod puppets and miniature theatre sets along with a video (Cantonese only) at 11am, noon, 3pm, 4pm and 5pm.

The farmhouses in the courtyard have been kitted out with simple but charming furniture, household items and farming implements.

To reach the museum take the MTR to Chai Wan (exit E). Kut Shing St is a five-minute walk to the west.

SHEK O

Shek O, on the south-east coast and the last real village on Hong Kong, has one of the best beaches on the island. And because it is not as accessible as beaches on the southern coast of the island, it's less crowded.

The village has **miniature golf**, and **paragliding** and **abseiling** from the **Dragon's Back**, the 280m-high ridge to the west of the village.

Shek O is small so it's easy to get your bearings; the beach is about a five-minute walk from the bus stop. En route you'll pass a couple of good restaurants (see Places to Eat later in this chapter). If you take the road leading off to the left you'll enter a maze of small homes, which gradually grow in size and luxury as you head out along the peninsula to the east of the beach. This is the **Shek O Headlands**, home to some of Hong Kong's wealthiest families.

Walking is possible around Shek O beach, though the terrain is steep and the underbrush quite thick in spots. Or take advantage of the bicycle rental shops (HK$20 a day) and pedal up to **Big Wave Bay**, another fine beach 2km to the north of Shek O. To get there follow the road out of town, past the **Shek O Country Club** (☎ 2809 4458, Big Wave Bay Rd), turn east at the roundabout and keep going until the road ends.

To reach Shek O, take the MTR to Shau Kei Wan and board bus No 9 there. On Sunday and public holidays bus No 390 goes direct to Shek O from Exchange Square.

STANLEY (MAP 9)

Stanley is on the south-east side of Hong Kong Island, about 15km as the crow flies from Central. Some 2000 people lived here when the British took control of the territory in 1841, making it one of the largest settlements on the island at the time. A prison was built near the village in 1937 – just in time to be used by the Japanese to intern expatriates. Now it's used as a maximum security prison.

Hong Kong's contingent of British troops was housed in Stanley Fort at the southern end of the peninsula until 1995. It has now been taken over by the PLA.

There's a **beach** to the north-east (that never gets as crowded as the one at Repulse Bay) where you can rent windsurfers. But the village's main attraction is the dominating **Stanley Market** *(open 10am-6.30pm daily)*, a covered mart filled with bric-a-brac, cheap clothing and junk that fills the alleys and the lanes to the south-west of Stanley Village Rd. It's best to go during the week; at the weekend the market is bursting at the seams (and hems and collars) with both tourists and locals alike. The most important dragon boat races are held at Stanley during the festival of that name in June.

The most interesting building in the village itself is the **Old Stanley Police Station** *(88 Stanley Village Rd)*, a two-storey structure built in 1859, which now houses government offices.

On a peninsula across the bay from Stanley Main St, the waterfront promenade lined with bars and restaurants, stands the phoenix-like **Murray House**, a three-storey colonnaded affair built in 1848 that took colonial pride of place in Central (where the Bank of China now stands) until 1982. It was re-erected here in 2000 after, well, a slight glitch (see the boxed text Don't Know Much about History).

At the western end of Stanley Main St and through a modern plaza is a **Tin Hau Temple**, built in 1767 and said to be the oldest building in Hong Kong. It has undergone a complete renovation since then however, and is now a concrete pile (though the interior is traditional).

Behind the Tin Hau Temple is a huge residential estate but if you follow the path

Don't Know Much about History

Hong Kong does not have a stellar track record when it comes to preserving old buildings. Though things have improved over the past decade or so, traditionally if a structure sat on a 'valuable' piece of land (ie, virtually every square centimetre of the built-up areas) or got in the way of progress (ie, money) it was given a kiss on the derrière by the wrecker's ball and brought down, living on in old photographs and the memories of a dwindling population.

It came as no surprise when the government announced in 1982 that Murray House, Hong Kong's oldest colonial building, was going to have to make room for the new Bank of China; bigger and better old buildings nearby had met similar fates. But because Murray House had a Grade 1 classification, they couldn't just smash it to pieces as they had the old Hong Kong Club and the Central Post Office. Instead, the building would be dismantled and its 4500 pieces numbered and stored for 'safekeeping' and erection elsewhere. Time passed and when heritage societies demanded to know its whereabouts, the government admitted it had misplaced some of the pieces.

Scene and time change…It's the mid 1990s and – hurrah! hurrah! – the government has found the missing bits stored in crates in Tai Tam. Problem was that the pillars and blocks had been wrapped in plastic sheeting and the numbers written or etched into their sides had spontaneously erased due to moisture building up on the soft limestone. It took workers 3½ years to put this colossal puzzle back together again and, when they'd finished, they had six extra columns that they didn't know what to do with.

As you approach Murray House, which now contains displays on its history and two chain restaurants (see Places to Eat later in this chapter), you'll see these idle columns standing rather forlornly off to the left. Note, too, some of the numbers still visible on the building blocks to the right of the entrance.

that passes by the temple and continue up the hill, you'll reach the **Kwun Yam Temple**. Above the temple is a pavilion housing a massive **statue of the Goddess of Mercy** looking out to sea. The pavilion was built in 1977 after a woman and her daughter claimed that they saw the statue move and a bright light shine from its forehead.

From the village you can walk south along Wong Ma Kok Rd to **St Stephen's Beach**, which has a cafe, showers and changing rooms, and sailboats and windsurfing boards for hire in summer.

Turn east (or right) when you get to a small road leading down to a jetty. At the end of the road, turn south and walk past the boathouse to the beach. Bus 73A will take you close to the intersection with the small road. Opposite the bus stop is a **cemetery** for military personnel and their families. The oldest graves date back to 1843.

Getting There & Away

To get to Stanley from Central take bus No 6, 6A, 6X or express bus No 260 from the Exchange Square bus station. Bus No 6 climbs over the hills separating the north and south sides of the island. It's a scenic, winding ride; make sure you sit on the upper deck on the right-hand side for some impressive (and heart-stopping) views. Bus No 260, which goes via the Aberdeen Tunnel, is quicker and perhaps better suited for those prone to motion sickness.

From Tang Lung St in Causeway Bay you can take the No 40 green minibus, which runs from 6.30am to 4.30am (adults HK$9-11, children HK$4.50-5.50, depending what time you board).

If you're coming from Shau Kei Wan, an exciting ride on bus No 14 takes you to Stanley via the Tai Tam Tuk reservoir. Bus Nos 73 and 973 connect Stanley with Repulse Bay and Aberdeen.

WILSON TRAIL (MAP 3)

This 78km-long trail traverses Hong Kong Island and is a bit unusual in that its southern section (10.7km) is on the island while its northern part (67.3km) is in the New Territories. The trail was named after Sir David Wilson, Hong Kong governor from 1987–92.

The trail begins about 1km to the north of Stanley; if you jump on bus No 6, 6A, 6X or 260 you will pass the beginning of the trail, which leads north from Stanley Gap Rd. Coming from Central, you want to alight about 2km from Repulse Bay. The first steeply rising section of the trail is all concrete steps. You soon reach the summit of **Stanley Mound** (385m), topped by a pavilion. The summit is also known as the Twins (or Ma Kong Shan in Cantonese). On a clear day you'll have an excellent view of Stanley, Repulse Bay and as far as Lamma Island. The trail continues north over Violet Hill, intersects the Hong Kong Trail, passes **Mt Butler**, drops down into the urban chaos and terminates at the Quarry Bay MTR station. Take the train across to Lam Tim and pick up the trail outside the station.

For details on the northern section of this trail, see the New Territories chapter.

REPULSE BAY

Repulse Bay's long **beach** with tawny sand is the most popular one on Hong Kong Island. Packed at the weekend and even during the week in summer, it's a good place if you like people watching. Middle Bay and South Bay, about 10 and 30 minutes to the south respectively, have beaches that are usually much less crowded. Repulse Bay Beach, with showers and changing rooms and shade trees at the road side, is an attractive place but the water is pretty murky.

Toward the eastern end of Repulse Bay beach is an unusual **Kwun Yam Temple**. The area is full of statues and mosaics of the Goddess of Mercy and inside is a cafe and the headquarters of the Hong Kong Life-Saving Society. The sprawling temple houses an amazing assembly of figures, deities and figures. In front of the temple is **Longevity Bridge**; crossing it is supposed to add three days to your life.

Repulse Bay is home to some of Hong Kong's richest residents, and the hills around the beach are strewn with luxury apartment blocks. The hill to the north-west of the beach was once topped with a mock

Gothic castle (for real – it was called Eu-cliff), but it has since been knocked down and replaced with hideous apartment buildings with castle-like windows.

The Repulse Bay *(109 Repulse Bay Rd)*, which replaced the wonderful old colonial Repulse Bay Hotel, bulldozed in the early 1980s, is a popular forum for faux-antique shops and restaurants.

Getting There & Away

Bus Nos 6, 6A, 61, 260 and 262 (Monday to Saturday only) from Central's Exchange Square bus station all pass by Repulse Bay. Minibuses leave every 15 minutes or so from a stop just to the left as you exit from the Star Ferry in Central. To get to Repulse Bay from Aberdeen take bus No 6, 6A, 73, 260 or 973.

DEEP WATER BAY

This is a quiet little bay with a **beach** flanked by a dose of shade trees located a few kilometres north-west of Repulse Bay. There are a few nice places to eat and have a drink and there is a barbecue pit at the east end of the beach. If you want a dip in the water, this spot is usually less crowded than Repulse Bay. Overlooking the beach is the **Deep Water Bay Golf Club** *(☎ 2812 7070, Island Rd)*. Deep Water Bay Beach is a centre for **wake boarding**. For information ring ☎ 2523 1924 or ☎ 2516 1222.

To get here from Central, take bus No 6A, 260 or 262 (Monday to Saturday only) from the Exchange Square bus station. Bus Nos 73 and 973 connect Deep Water Bay with Aberdeen to the west and Repulse Bay and Stanley to the east.

ABERDEEN & SURROUNDS (MAP 8)

For many years Aberdeen or, in Cantonese, Heung Gong Tsai (Little Fragrant Harbour) was one of Hong Kong's top tourist attractions because of the large number of people (estimated at over 6000) who lived and worked on the junks moored in the harbour here. Over the years the number of boats has dwindled as more and more of the 'boat people' have moved into high-rises or abandoned fishing as a profession.

Sampan tours can easily be arranged along **Aberdeen Promenade**, which runs south and parallel to Aberdeen Praya Rd. You can have your choice of private operators, which generally mill around the eastern end of the promenade, or licensed operators registered with the HKTB, such as the *Aberdeen Sampan Co (☎ 2873 0310)*. The private sampans usually charge HK$60 per person for a 30-minute ride (about HK$100 to Lamma), though you should easily be able to bargain this down if there are several of you. You can get a free 10-minute tour by hopping on one of the boats out to the two floating restaurants (see Places to Eat later in this chapter) and then riding back. These leave every five minutes or so.

On the southern side of the harbour is the island of **Ap Lei Chau** (Duck's Tongue Island). It used to be a centre for building junks, but now it's covered with housing estates, including a huge one called **South Horizons**. There's not much to see there, but Ap Lei Chau is famous for its factory outlets and a walk across the bridge to the island affords good views of the harbour and some nocturnal shots of the floating restaurant fully illuminated. From Aberdeen Promenade you can get a boat across to Ap Lei Chau for HK$1.80/1 adults/children under 12.

If you've got time to spare, a short walk through Aberdeen will bring you to a **Tin Hau Temple** *(Cnr Aberdeen Main & Aberdeen Reservoir Rds)*, which was undergoing a total renovation the last time we visited. Built in 1851, it's a sleepy spot but remains an active house of worship. Close to the harbour is the **Hung Hsing shrine** *(Cnr Aberdeen Main Rd & Old Main St)*, a ramshackle collection of altars and smoking incense pots.

If you're feeling vigorous, the entrance to **Aberdeen Country Park** and **Pok Fu Lam Country Park** is about a 15-minute walk north along Aberdeen Reservoir Rd. From there you can walk up to Victoria Peak and catch the Peak Tram or a bus or minibus down to Central.

Getting There & Away

A tunnel linking Aberdeen with the northern side of Hong Kong Island provides rapid access to and from Central. From the bus station below Exchange Square, take bus No 7 or 70 or the express 70M from Admiralty. Bus No 7 goes via Hong Kong University and Pok Fu Lam while Nos 70 and 70M go via the tunnel. Bus Nos 73 and 973 from Aberdeen will take you along the southern coast to Ocean Park, Repulse Bay and Stanley.

Ocean Park (Map 3)

Ocean Park (☎ 2552 0291, Ocean Park Rd; adult/child $150/75; open 10am-6pm daily) to the south-east of the Aberdeen town centre is a fully fledged amusement park, complete with roller coaster and other stomach-turning rides. It is also something of a marine park, with a wave cove that houses seals, sea lions and penguins, daily dolphin and killer-whale shows and an aquarium. The **Atoll Reef** is particularly impressive, with around 4000 fish on display. The walk-through **Shark Aquarium** has hundreds of different sharks on view and scores of rays. Bird-watchers are also catered for, with aviaries and a flamingo pond.

The park is in two sections. The entrance is on the lowland side and linked to the main section on the headlands above by a scenic (and rather frightening for some) cable-car ride. The park's main section affords a beautiful view of the South China Sea and at the rear entrance is the **Middle Kingdom**, a sort of Chinese cultural village with temples, pagodas, traditional street scenes and staff dressed in period garments. There are also arts and crafts demonstrations, live theatre and Cantonese opera.

Getting There & Away The most convenient way to get to Ocean Park is via a special Citybus van that leaves from the bus station next to Admiralty MTR station every 15 to 20 minutes from 9.10am and costs HK$12/6 for adults/children. Citybus sells a package ticket that includes transportation and admission to Ocean Park for HK$174/87 adults/children. There is also a special Ocean Park Citybus that leaves the Star Ferry terminal and costs the same as the one from Admiralty. It leaves every 15 to 20 minutes from 10am to 3.30pm; the last

bus back to the Star Ferry terminal departs at 4.30pm (6.30pm on Sunday).

A slightly cheaper but more time-consuming way get to Ocean Park is to catch bus No 70 from the Exchange Square in Central and get off at the first stop after the tunnel. From there it's a 10-minute walk to the park. The No 6 green minibus (HK$7.50) from Central's Star Ferry terminal takes you directly to Ocean Park, but does not run on Sunday and public holidays. Bus No 629 from Admiralty also goes here. Bus Nos 73 and 973 link Ocean Park with Aberdeen to the west and Repulse Bay and Stanley to the east.

PLACES TO STAY – BUDGET

At the budget end of the spectrum, things aren't wildly exciting on Hong Kong Island though there are a few good-value options available in the Causeway Bay area. Depending on the season, guesthouses are often struggling to fill beds and rooms; most will offer discounts to anyone staying longer than a couple of nights.

Hostels

Hong Kong Island has one hostel run by the Hong Kong Youth Hostels Association (HKYHA)

Jockey Club Mount Davis Hostel (☎ 2817 5715, fax 2788 3105, Mt Davis Path, Kennedy Town) **Map 3** Juniors/seniors from HK$40/65, 2-/3-/4-/6-person family room HK$250/260/300/450. On the top of Mt Davis in the north-west part of Hong Kong Island, off Victoria Rd, is a very clean and quiet 104-bed hostel with great views of Victoria Harbour. Problem is, it's so far away from everything. There are cooking facilities, a TV and recreation room and secure lockers. Call ahead to make sure there's a bed before you make the trek out there. The hostel is open daily throughout the year. Check-in time is from 7am to 11pm. You can check out at 1pm on Sunday and holidays; otherwise you must vacate the room by 10am.

There are several ways to reach Jockey Club Mount Davis Hostel, depending on where you're coming from. The easiest way is to catch the hostel shuttle bus from the

Shun Tak Centre, 200 Connaught Rd, in Sheung Wan from where the ferries to Macau sail, but there are only four departures a day: at 9.30am, 7pm, 9pm and 10.30pm. Alternatively, you can catch bus No 47A from Admiralty or minibus No 54 from the outlying islands ferry terminal and alight at Felix Villas, at the junction of Victoria Rd and Mt Davis Path. From there, walk back 100m. Look for the YHA sign and follow Mt Davis Path (*not* to be confused with Mt Davis Rd). There is a shortcut to the hostel which is signposted halfway up the hill. The walk takes 30 to 40 minutes.

A taxi from Central should cost about HK$30.

Guesthouses (Map 6)

Just about all of the guesthouses on Hong Kong Island are located in Causeway Bay. Quite a few are on or around Paterson St.

Alisan Guest House (☎ 2838 0762, fax 2838 4351, e alisangh@hkstar.com, Flat A, 5th floor, Hoito Court, 275 Gloucester Rd, Causeway Bay) Singles/doubles/triples HK$280/320/380. This excellent and spotlessly clean place has 30 rooms with air-conditioning, showers and toilets. The multilingual owners are always willing to please.

Jetvan Travellers' House (☎ 2890 8133, fax 2510 7601, e shuikuk@ctimail3.com, Flat A, 4th floor, Fairview Mansion, 51 Paterson St, Causeway Bay) Singles/doubles with bath HK$300/350 per night, HK$1250/2300 per week. This rather cramped but upbeat place is run by a group of young Hong Kong Chinese.

Kai Woo Hung Wan Guesthouse (☎ 2890 5813, fax 2890 5725, Flat A1, 11th floor, 27 Paterson St) Singles/doubles HK$350/380. The rooms at this place are OK, but you'll have a hard time communicating with the owners.

Noble Hostel (☎ 2576 6148, fax 2577 0847, Flat A3, 17th floor, 27 Paterson St, Causeway Bay) Singles/doubles with shared bath HK$250/300, with private bath HK$300/360. This is certainly one of the best-value guesthouses on the island. Every room is squeaky clean and is equipped with

a private phone and air-conditioning. The hostel continues to expand and has now spread into three different buildings.

Wang Fat Hostel (☎ 2895 1015, mobile ☎ 9353 0514, fax 2576 7509, e wangfath@netvigator.com, Flat A2, 3rd floor, Paterson Bldg, 47 Paterson St, Causeway Bay) Singles/doubles with shared bath HK$180/200, with private bath HK$220/250. This excellent 50-room series of hostels is just about the best deal in the territory. It's quiet and clean and each room has a private phone, TV and fridges. There's also free Internet access. The affable owner speaks good English and Japanese and can organise most anything for you.

West of this area is the Central Building at 531 Jaffe Rd, which can also be entered from 12 Cannon St. It has been cleaned up in recent years and offers reasonably priced and clean accommodation. Most of these guesthouses rent rooms by the hour as well so be prepared for a little background noise – day or night.

Lung Poon Villa (☎ 2838 9868, fax 2838 2434, flat L, 2nd floor, Central Bldg, 531 Jaffe Rd, Causeway Bay) Rooms from HK$250. This is a relatively clean place with a friendly owner.

Lung Tin Guest House (☎ 2832 9133, flat F & G, 2nd floor, Central Bldg, 531 Jaffe Rd, Causeway Bay) Rooms HK$250. Rooms in this pleasant place have shower, TV and telephone.

Leighton Rd to the south-east of the Causeway Bay MTR station is another area to look.

Causeway Bay Guest House (☎ 2895 2013, fax 2895 2355, Flat B, 1st floor, Lai Yee Bldg, 44A-D, Leighton Rd) Singles/doubles/triples HK$250/350/400. On the south side of Causeway Bay and wedged between a pub and a church, this seven-room guesthouse, entered from Leighton Lane, gets booked up quickly so phone ahead. All rooms are quite clean and have attached bathrooms.

Emerald House (☎ 2577 2368, 1st floor, 44 Leighton Rd, Causeway Bay) Doubles HK$450. This guesthouse features clean but small double rooms with private bath.

Turn right as you go through the passage and go up to the 1st floor.

Phoenix Apartments (70 Lee Garden Rd) These apartments are nearby with a plethora of sleazier guesthouses. Most of these are 'love hotels'; prices tend to be more expensive at the weekend and during the day. Make sure to confirm the checkout time before paying as it can be early.

Dragon Inn (☎ 2576 3849, Flat G, 2nd floor, Phoenix Apartments, 70 Lee Garden Rd, Causeway Bay) Weekday doubles HK$380. This place has English-speaking staff.

Wah Lai Villa (☎ 2576 2768, Flat A&B, 4th floor, Phoenix Apartments, 70 Lee Garden Rd, Causeway Bay) Rooms from HK$300. Wah Lai has a sleazy, slight tarnished feel but is a cheap option.

Yee Woo Guest House (☎ 2890 2112, Flat J, 6th floor, Phoenix Apartments, 70 Lee Garden Rd, Causeway Bay) Doubles HK$250. This is more of a guesthouse than a love hotel and is recommended.

Hotels

Hong Kong Island really only has one budget hotel.

YWCA Building (☎ 2915 2345, fax 2915 5677, e ywbldg@ywca.org.hk, 38C Bonham Rd, Mid-Levels) **Map 4** Singles/doubles from HK$350/660, monthly packages HK$4700-5900. This place is not in the most convenient of locations, but it's open to all and very cheap.

PLACES TO STAY – MID-RANGE

Mid-range prices vary considerably, with doubles costing anywhere from HK$700 to HK$1800. Sometimes there is not a great deal to distinguish mid-range from top-end hotels, except perhaps a certain ambience and sense of style.

Remember that if you are flying into Hong Kong, the Hong Kong Hotels Association (HKHA; ☎ 2383 8380) has a reservation centre at the airport and can get you a mid-range or top-end hotel room sometimes 50% cheaper than if you were to walk in yourself. See Accommodation in the Hong Kong Facts for the Visitor chapter for more details.

Bishop Lei International House (☎ 2868 0828, fax 2868 1551, 4 Robinson Rd, Mid-Levels) **Map 4** Singles/doubles from HK$1080/1280, suites from HK$3800, monthly packages from HK$11,400. This 205-room hotel is not sitting in the lap of luxury and a bit away from the action, but it's close to the Zoological & Botanical Gardens and has its own swimming pool and gym.

Charterhouse (☎ 2833 5566, fax 2833 5888, 209-219 Wan Chai Rd, Wan Chai) **Map 6** Singles HK$950-1600, doubles HK$1500-1700, suites from HK$2000. This property near the Morrison Hill sports area is a fantastic deal. You're almost getting top-end accommodation for mid-range rates.

Empire (☎ 2866 9111, fax 2861 3121, 33 Hennessy Rd, Wan Chai) **Map 6** Rooms HK$1400-2000, suites from HK$2200, weekly/monthly packages from HK$3800/13,800. With its sunny staff, pleasant rooms and small swimming pool on the 21st floor terrace, the Empire is a good option and an easy hop from the Convention Centre. Enter the hotel from Fenwick St.

Garden View International House (☎ 2877 3737, fax 2845 6263, e gar_view@ywca.org.hk, 1 MacDonnell Rd, Central) **Map 4** Rooms HK$1000-1200, suites HK$1800-2000, monthly packages from HK$14,000. Hovering on the border of Central and the Mid-Levels, the YWCA-run Garden View (130 rooms) overlooks the Zoological & Botanical Gardens. It's the only place in the area that falls outside the luxury category. Accommodation here is plain but comfortable (there's good air-conditioning) and there's an outdoor swimming pool.

Grand Plaza (☎ 2886 0011, fax 2886 1738, e grandplazahotel@grandhotel.com.hk, 2 Kornhill Rd, Quarry Bay) Rooms HK$850-1850, suites from HK$2100, monthly packages from HK$14,800. This 248-room place is in the far-flung reaches of Quarry Bay, but it's cheap.

Harbour View International House (☎ 2802 0111, fax 2802 9063, e hvihymca@netvigator.com, 4 Harbour Rd, Wan Chai) **Map 6** Rooms HK$1150-1650, monthly packages from HK$9900. Right next door to the Hong Kong Arts Centre and a mere stroll to the Convention Centre and Wan Chai ferry terminal, this YMCA-run, 320-room hotel is excellent value, with simply furnished but adequate rooms, most of which look over Victoria Harbour.

New Cathay (☎ *2577 8211, fax 2576 9365, 17 Tung Lo Wan Rd, Causeway Bay)* **Map 6** Singles from HK$740, doubles from HK$1050, suites from HK$2000. This 225-room cheesy but cheap hotel faces the Victoria Park side of Causeway Bay and is just down the road from the Tiger Balm Gardens, should you want to get closer to nirvana.

Newton (☎ *2807 2333, fax 2807 1221, 218 Electric Rd, North Point)* Rooms HK$900-1600, suites from HK$2600. This 363-room hotel on the corner of Oil St is a real find. Sure it's in less-than-sexy North Point, but you can easily walk to Causeway Bay through Victoria Park and it's *Hong Kong Old Restaurant* (see North Point under Places to Eat later in this chapter) has some of the best Shanghainese food in town.

South Pacific (☎ *2572 3838, fax 2893 7773, 23 Morrison Hill Rd, Wan Chai)* **Map 6** Rooms HK$1000-2000, suites from HK$2800. This flash, 293-room hotel has a rather odd location south of Wan Chai, but you'll be closer to the traditional back streets of the district and to open green spaces around Queen Elizabeth Stadium.

The Wesley (☎ *2866 6688, fax 2866 6633, 22 Hennessy Rd, Wan Chai; enter from Anton St)* **Map 4** Rooms HK$700-1800, monthly packages from HK$7800. This central, 22-storey property with 250 rooms is one of the best deals on the island, but there are very few facilities and the service is cavalier at best.

Wharney (☎ *2861 1000, fax 2865 6023,* e *wharney@wlink.net, 57-33 Lockhart Rd, Wan Chai)* **Map 6** Singles HK$1000-1600, doubles HK$1200-1800, suites from HK$2400, weekly/monthly packages from HK$3010/10,500. Noteworthy for its rooftop swimming pool and outdoor whirlpool, the 320-room Wharney is a mid-range option in the heart of Wan Chai.

PLACES TO STAY – TOP END

Prices for Hong Kong's top-end hotels are high – as you might expect – but in most cases, the money you spend usually brings a level of comfort and service unmatched elsewhere.

Double rooms in this category start at about HK$1600 and go up (and up) from there. Rates reflect the astronomical cost of Hong Kong real estate, especially in the areas with the best views.

Century Hong Kong (☎ *2598 8888, fax 2598 8866, 238 Jaffe Rd, Wan Chai)* **Map 6** Singles HK$1500-1800, doubles HK$1600-2000, suites from HK$3200. The slightly tacky Century Hong Kong has an enviable location in the heart of Wan Chai and all the mod-cons you could possibly want.

Conrad International (☎ *2521 3838, fax 2521 3888, Pacific Place, 88 Queensway, Admiralty)* **Map 4** Rooms HK$2850-3350, suites from HK$5700. A member of the Hilton Hotels group, the Conrad is elegant without being stuffy. It gets enthusiastic reviews for its attention to business travellers' needs and the foyer bar/lounge is a gossipy, corporate hang-out.

Excelsior (☎ *2894 8888, fax 2895 6459, 281 Gloucester Rd, Causeway Bay)* **Map 6** Rooms HK$1900-2500, suites from HK$3800. This 866-room hotel, part of the Mandarin Oriental Group and a Causeway Bay landmark, offers some decent outlets, fabulous harbour views and convenient shopping.

Furama (☎ *2525 5111, fax 2845 9339,* e *hotel@furama.com.hk, 1 Connaught Rd Central)* **Map 4** Rooms HK$2000-2300, suites from HK$2800. This 470-room shoebox is hardly Hong Kong's favourite hotel but it has some wonderful outlets, including the *La Ronda* revolving restaurant on the top floor with its pile-it-up buffet at lunch and dinner.

Grand Hyatt (☎ *2588 1234, fax 2802 0677, 1 Harbour Rd, Wan Chai)* **Map 6** Singles HK$3200-4000, doubles HK$3450-4250, suites from HK$3800. The towering 570-room Hyatt is slightly more relaxed than the rest of the deluxe deck here. Its gourmet Chinese restaurant is celebrated and with good reason.

Island Shangri-La (☎ *2877 3838, fax 2521 8742, Pacific Place, Supreme Court*

Rd, Admiralty) **Map 4** Rooms HK$2400-3550, suites from HK$5800. The 56-storey Shangri-La's sterile exterior conceals its swish sophistication. The hotel has a wonderful atrium and bubble lifts link the 39th and 56th floors. Take a quick ride up; you'll catch a glance of the hotel's signature 60m-high painting, a mountainous Chinese landscape said to be the largest in the world.

JW Marriott (☎ 2810 8366, fax 2845 0737, Pacific Place, 88 Queensway, Admiralty) **Map 4** Rooms HK$3000-3300, suites from HK$6000. Though business travellers make up a large proportion of the Marriott's clientele (that would explain the seasonal changes in room rates), this 600-room hotel is also popular with shopaholics who can feed their addiction in the adjoining Pacific Place shopping mall. The city-view (cheaper) rooms actually have views of the hills and not just the next building's air-con infrastructure.

Luk Kwok (☎ 2866 2166, fax 2866 2622, e *lukkwok@lukkwokhotel.com, 72 Gloucester Rd, Wan Chai)* **Map 6** Singles HK$1460-1760, doubles HK$1600-1900, suites from HK$3200. The original Luk Kwok, which featured as the Nam Kok brothel in *The World of Suzie Wong* (see Books in the Hong Kong Facts for the Visitor chapter), has long since been demolished and it's now a 196-room hotel housed in a not-unattractive modern tower block. There aren't that many frills or outlets here, but the staff are keen and helpful.

Mandarin Oriental (☎ 2522 0111, fax 2810 6190, 5 Connaught Rd Central) **Map 4** Rooms HK$2950-4200, suites from HK$5500. The Mandarin has much old-world charm. Styling is subdued, and in some rooms maybe even a bit outdated, but the service, food and atmosphere are stellar. If you're on business and want to give or get good face, splash out and stay here. You'll be a winner every time. *The Café (ground floor)* with Asian dishes from HK$120 to HK$145, sandwiches HK$120 to HK$135, and pasta HK$125 to HK$155, is quite simply the best hotel coffee shop in town.

Park Lane (☎ 2293 8888, fax 2576 7853, 310 Gloucester Rd, Causeway Bay) **Map 6** Rooms HK$2000-3300, suites from HK$5000. With restful views of Victoria Park to the east and the shopper's paradise of Causeway Bay to the west, the Park Lane is the perfect hotel for those who want to be both in and out of the action.

Regal Hongkong (☎ 2890 6633, fax 2881 0777, 88 Yee Wo St, Causeway Bay) **Map 6** Rooms HK$2100-3000, suites from HK$5500. Though double-glazing keeps the traffic of busy Yee Wo St at bay, this Sino-baroque palace dripping with gilt may be a bit too central and, well, shiny for some. The rooftop Roman-style pool – all mosaics and columns supporting nothing – is over the top in the nicest sort of way.

Renaissance Harbour View (☎ 2802 8888, fax 2802 8833, 1 Harbour Rd, Wan Chai) **Map 6** Rooms HK$2100-2500, suites from HK$3600. This spectacular, 860-room hotel adjoins the Hong Kong Convention and Exhibition Centre, ensuring steady suit-and-tie custom. Deal-cutters are catered to with a well-equipped business centre and discrete restaurants. Leisure travellers will appreciate informed concierges and, perhaps, the flashy nightclub *Club ing* on the 4th floor. The Harbour View has the largest outdoor pool of any hotel in town (naturally it looks over the harbour), and also has kiddies' pools.

Ritz-Carlton (☎ 2877 6666, fax 2877 6778, 3 Connaught Rd Central) **Map 4** Rooms HK$3200-3800, suites from HK$4200. This is a truly beautiful hotel, with plush guestrooms that manage to be cosy and incredibly distinguished at the same time. Views from harbour-side rooms are – surprise, surprise – breathtaking, but the best view in the hotel might be from the pool. Lay back and soak up the skyline.

PLACES TO STAY – LONG-TERM RENTALS
Hotels
If you're planning to stay in Hong Kong longer than a month, many hotels (eg, the Wesley and Wharney in Wan Chai and the Bishop Lei in the Mid-Levels) offer extraordinarily good value long-term packages starting at under HK$8000 a month, depending on the season and length of stay.

Serviced Flats (Map 4)

A number of agencies, including Asiaxpat (W *www.asiaxpat.com*) will help you find a serviced flat, but they usually cater to the very top end of the market, with studios measuring a mere 38 sq metres in Happy Valley starting at HK$16,000 a month.

Hanlun Habitats (☎ *2533 7200, fax 9028 5838, 22 Mosque St, Mid-Levels*) This agency has two properties with serviced and furnished flats that are within striking distance of each other in the Mid-Levels and easily accessible to Central and Soho. *Daisy Court* (☎ *2533 7200, fax 2810 1870, 22 Mosque St*) has one-bedroom flats measuring about 50 sq metres for HK$15,750 to HK$20,070 a month, depending on the floor and the view, while *Lily Court* (☎ *2822 9500, fax 2521 9529, 28 Robinson Rd*) has two-bedroom flats of about 65 sq metres for between HK$23,500 and HK$31,590 a month.

The Bauhinia (☎ *2156 3000, fax 2156 3004, 119-120 Connaught Rd Central*) This very central outfit, entered from Man Wa Lane, has more than 100 furnished and serviced flats for between HK$15,000 and HK$21,000 for a 50 sq metre one-bedroom and HK$23,000 and HK$28,000 for a two-bedroom flat of between 85 and 90 sq metres.

PLACES TO EAT

Catering facilities on Hong Kong Island run the gamut from internationally renowned restaurants in five-star hotels and Asian fusion enjoyed at pavement cafes to an embarrassment of ethnic cuisines – from Indian and Mexican to Chiu Chow and Vietnamese – served in tiny little holes-in-the-wall upstairs, downstairs or in some obscure chamber.

Central, Soho & Mid-Levels

Though there are many exceptions to the rule, Central and its trendy (and rather fast) kid sister Soho to the south-west are not the places to find authentic ethnic cuisine, but Westernised versions of same along with some cutting-edge international and fusion food.

Chinese The over-refined and designed *China Lan Kwai Fong* (Map 5) (☎ *2536 0968, 17-22 Lan Kwai Fong, Central*) has dishes from HK$100, and two-/four-/six-person set dinners for HK$380/680/1150. In the heart of the Fong, it becomes accessible to those other than brokers or solicitors on Sunday when a dim sum buffet costs HK$128.

Dai Pai Dong (☎ *2851 6389, 128 Queen's Rd Central*) **Map 4** Breakfast HK$22-30. Noodles & rice dishes from HK$48. This chain of cheap Chinese eateries takes its name from the Cantonese for 'food stalls', which were ubiquitous in Hong Kong until the health department – in its infinite wisdom – decided they were a threat to humanity. Not a bad choice for something fast and inexpensive. There's also a Causeway Bay branch (☎ *2882 3239, 67 Lee Garden Rd*).

Hunan Garden (☎ *2868 2880, 3rd floor, The Forum, Exchange Square, Connaught Rd Central*) **Map 4** Meals about HK$250. Elegant and expensive, this upmarket place specialises in spicy Hunanese food, which is often hotter that the Sichuan variety. The fried chicken with chilli is excellent and the seafood dishes (unusual in Hunan cuisine) are recommended.

Island Restaurant (☎ *2525 5111, 4th floor, Furama Hotel, 1 Connaught Rd Central*) **Map 4** Meals from HK$250. Island serves classy (and pricey) Cantonese food. Try the delicious deep-fried squid stuffed with mashed shrimp or the sliced pigeon with bamboo shoots.

Jasmine (☎ *2524 5098, Shop 5, Basement, Jardine House, Connaught Rd Central*) **Map 4** Meals HK$150. This cleaned-up version of the standard Cantonese eatery is relatively inexpensive for its location and the food is good.

Jim Chai Kee (☎ *2850 6471, 98 Wellington St, Central*) **Map 5** Noodles from HK$10. This local shoebox is where to head if you want a quick and cheap fix of rice or soup noodles (a major hangover cure).

Lin Heung Tea House (☎ *2544 4556, 160-164 Wellington St, Central*) **Map 4** Meals from HK$120. This old-style Cantonese restaurant packed with older men reading newspapers, extended families and office groups has so-so dim sum offered from trolleys, but it's particularly recommended for a bite late at night.

Nathan Rd, Tsim Sha Tsui

A neon extravaganza, Kowloon

Breathtaking view from Victoria Peak of high-rises by the harbour

Souvenir dolls in peasant costumes for sale at Stanley Market.

Cantonese opera performance

Soya beans fermenting at a soy sauce factory.

Delivery! Graham St Market, Hong Kong Island

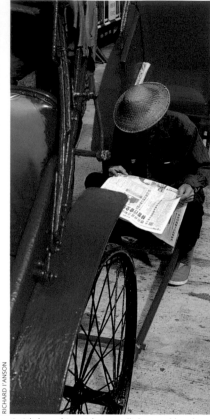
A rickshaw driver takes a well-deserved break.

Incense is important in many Chinese religions; here, burning coils of incense are hanging in a temple.

Luk Yu Tea House (☎ 2523 5464, 24-26 Stanley St, Central) **Map 5** Meals about HK$150. This old-style teahouse is a museum piece in more ways than one. Dim sum is served 7am to 6pm daily.

Mak's Noodle (☎ 2854 3810, 77 Wellington St, Central) **Map 4** Meals under HK$100. Readers have written in praising this nearby noodle shop but go for lunch or eat early; it's shut tight by 8pm.

Ning Po Residents Association (☎ 2523 0648, 4th floor, Yip Fung Bldg, 2-18 D'Aguilar St, Central) **Map 5** Cold dishes HK$60-90, mains HK$75-160. The Ning Po offers tasty and well-prepared Shanghainese food and is very popular with expats and locals alike.

Super Star Seafood Restaurant (☎ 2525 9238, Basement, Wilson House, 19-27 Wyndham St, Central) **Map 5** Meals from HK$250. Though a branch of yet another chain, the Super Star has some of the best Cantonese fish dishes in Central.

Tai Woo (☎ 2526 2920, 15B Wellington St, Central) **Map 5** Dim sum HK$20-23 per serving, 11am-4.30pm daily. This very authentic Cantonese eatery may look like a 'closed shop' but persevere with the help of the special section Chinese Food in the Hong Kong Facts for the Visitor chapter and you'll be amply rewarded.

Yung Kee Restaurant (☎ 2522 1624, 32-40 Wellington St, Central) **Map 5** Meals HK$200-250. This long-standing institution is probably the most famous Cantonese restaurant in Central. The roast goose here has been the talk of the town since 1942, and its dim sum is excellent. Dim sum is served 2pm to 5pm daily.

American An almost carbon copy of a 1950s chrome and glass American version, *Al's Diner* (**Map 5**) (☎ 2521 8714, Shop F, 27 D'Aguilar St, Central) has the usual burgers fit for a giant (from HK$70), plates of fries and ribs.

The Bayou (☎ 2526 2118, 9-13 Shelley St, Soho) **Map 5** Mains HK$132-168, set lunch HK$100. This popular spot in the Soho neighbourhood serves authentic New Orleans-style Cajun and Creole food. Try the Cajun barbecued ribs or the voodoo pasta.

Tony Roma's Famous for Ribs (☎ 2521 0292, 1st floor, California Tower, 30-32 D'Aguilar St, Central) **Map 5** Pasta HK$118-148, mains HK$172-198. The name says it all. A fat slab of ribs starts at HK$172.

Asian Fusion A jewel of a restaurant in a jewel of a hotel is *Vong* (**Map 4**) (☎ 2825 4028, 25th floor, Mandarin Oriental Hotel, 5 Connaught Rd Central) with meals from HK$400. It serves a successful blend of Vietnamese and French food and the views alone make it all worthwhile.

Australian & British Surprisingly, there are few genuine Australian restaurants in Hong Kong though British pubs serving the usual grub are everywhere.

Bull and Bear (☎ 2525 7436, Ground floor, Hutchison House, 10 Harcourt Rd, Central) **Map 4** Set lunch HK$88. Sticking to what the Brits do best, the Bull and Bear serves uninspired but comforting – to some – pub grub (bangers and mash, mushy peas, meat pies).

Elgin Tastes (☎ 2810 5183, 38 Elgin St, Soho) **Map 5** Entrees HK$85-105, mains HK$170-195, set lunch HK$100. While this place describes itself as 'Nouveau Australian', it's hard to see how it differs from any other fusion/international place. Maybe that's the point. Food is inventive though expensive, the decor pleasant in an '80s kind of way.

Soho Soho (☎ 2147 2618, 9 Old Bailey St, Soho) **Map 5** Meals from HK$150-200. New British food has taken off in post-colonial Hong Kong with chuppies and Brits on expense accounts. It's creative (crumpet with smoked salmon), comforting (roasted cod with new potatoes) and meaty (chump of lamb with a pepper crust).

French The small, elegant French bistro *2 Sardines* (**Map 5**) (☎ 2973 6618, 43 Elgin St, Soho) deserves the crowds it draws in. It offers starters from HK$56 to HK$86 and mains HK$156 to HK$280. The eponymous fish dish comes grilled with a zesty sauce; the calf's liver is worth trying too.

Bistrot de Paris *(☎ 2869 1132, 4-6 On Lan St, Central)* **Map 4** Set dinners HK$250. Le Bistrot offers an unpretentious French dining experience and is deservedly popular. Set dinners are available if you'd prefer to get cosy in a booth rather than spend time hovering over the menu.

Café des Artistes *(☎ 2526 3880, Upper ground floor, California Tower, 30-32 D'Aguilar St, Central)* **Map 5** Meals from HK$300. This place serves surprisingly good Provençale food and the views of Lan Kwai Fong passers-by are mesmerising.

Le Rendez-Vous *(☎ 2905 1808, 5 Staunton St, Soho)* **Map 5** Savoury galettes and sweet crepes from HK$7-43. This tiny, nautically themed crepe house also does baguettes (HK$12-40) and salads (HK$33). The crepes come filled with classic combos like mushroom and cheese along with more adventurous spicy inventions. There's a full bar too with happy hour from 6pm to 8pm.

German & Austrian A place with solid German fare is ***Bit Point*** **(Map 5)** *(☎ 2523 7436, 31 D'Aguilar St, Central)* with meals from HK$150. It's essentially a bar, where beer drinking is taken seriously, and the cigarette smoke can get pretty thick at times. Happy hour is from 4pm to 9pm.

Mozart Stub'n *(☎ 2522 1763, 8 Glenealy, Central)* **Map 4** Meals about HK$300. This classy, almost fastidious Austrian (do *not* say German) establishment has excellent food and wines and a delightful atmosphere.

Schnurrbart *(☎ 2523 4700, 29 D'Aguilar St, Central)* **Map 5** Bar snacks HK$65, mains HK$95-135. 'Moustache' serves up hearty *Bierstube* fare like the best of the wurst and German meatloaf along with lots and lots of suds.

Indian The old ***Ashoka*** **(Map 5)** *(☎ 2524 9623, 57-59 Wyndham St, Central),* with mains for HK$50 to HK$70, still charges top rupee for ordinary fare, but it's convenient to the pubs of Lan Kwai Fong and still draws in the crowds.

Greenlands India Club *(☎ 2522 6098, 1st floor, Yu Wing Bldg, 64-66 Wellington St, Central)* **Map 5** Lunch-time buffet HK$68. Greenlands' low prices and high-quality food ensure that it is always packed.

Gunga Din's Club *(☎ 2523 1439, Lower ground floor, 57-59 Wyndham St, Central)* **Map 5** Dishes HK$60-95. Everyone's favourite curry house is supposed to be for members only but anyone can eat here. Substantial if not sublime tiffin.

India Curry House *(☎ 2523 2203, 3rd floor, 10 Wing Wah Lane, Central)* **Map 5** Set lunches HK$43-49. This cheap little eatery, long a hang-out, has good value and a very obliging staff.

India Today *(☎ 2801 5959, 1st floor, 26-30 Elgin St, Soho)* **Map 5** Mains HK$75-95. This upstairs eatery named after a popular Indian news weekly serves some of the best curries in Central.

Koh-i-Noor *(☎ 2877 9706, 1st floor, California Entertainment Bldg, 34-36 D'Aguilar St, Central)* **Map 5** Kebabs from HK$68, curries from HK$60. This pricier sister-restaurant of the one in Tsim Sha Tsui serves equally fine northern Indian cuisine.

Tandoor Indian Restaurant *(☎ 2845 2299, 3rd floor, On Hing Bldg, 1-9 On Hing Terrace, Central)* **Map 4** Meals about HK$200. Another local favourite, the Tandoor has an open kitchen so you can see how it's all being done.

International The food at *Alibi* **(Map 5)** *(☎ 2167 8989, 73 Wyndham St, Central)* is good rather than excellent though the buffet lunch (HK$130) pulls in the crowds. It has starters from HK$75 to HK$152 and mains HK$160 to HK$230. The decor is imaginative and this is the place to spot Hong Kong's most beautiful people – in every sense.

Après *(☎ 2524 7722, Upper basement, 79 Wyndham St, Central)* **Map 5** Set lunch HK$95. This cool watering hole is also a cafe with good-value meals in an outdoors-is-indoors setting.

Aqua *(☎ 2545 9889, 49 Hollywood Rd, Central)* **Map 5** Set lunches HK$100-170. This ultra chichi and minimalist place on the corner of Lyndhurst Terrace is one of the latest places to open on Hollywood Rd.

Eating Plus (☎ 2868 0599, Shop 1009, International Finance Centre, 1 Harbour View St, Central) **Map 4** Main noodle dishes HK$58-68, side dishes HK$25-28, set meal with juice HK$98. Style comes cheap at this very vogue eatery and bar near the outlying islands ferry and Airport Express terminals. Lunch and dinner, taken at communal tables, extend to soups, noodles (a successful mix of East and West) and rice dishes, including risotto.

Le Jardin (☎ 2526 2717, 1st floor, Winner Bldg, 10 Wing Wah Lane, Central) **Map 5** Set lunches HK$35-45. This cheap and cheerful eatery above D'Aguilar St featuring an open veranda seating area has loads of atmosphere. It's a popular drinking spot at night open till 2am.

Jimmy's Kitchen (☎ 2526 5293, Basement, South China Bldg, 1-3 Wyndham St, Central) **Map 4** Meals from HK$250. High on nostalgia and one of the oldest names in the game, Jimmy's, a Hong Kong feature for nearly seven decades, rests on its laurels. The char-grilled king prawns, baked onion soup, black pepper steak and a whole medley of desserts (including its famous baked Alaska) all compete for the diners' attention. There's a branch in Tsim Sha Tsui.

Landau (☎ 2827 7901, Ground floor, on Hing Bldg, 1-9 On Hing Terrace, Central) **Map 4** Meals from HK$350. In the same stable as Jimmy's but at a gold (as opposed to green) expense account credit card level, this colonial throwback serves solid international fare.

M at the Fringe (☎ 2877 4000, 1st floor, Fringe Club, 2 Lower Albert Rd, Lan Kwai Fong) **Map 5** 2-/3-course lunch HK$148/168. This palace of creative gastronomy is simply the best restaurant in Hong Kong. When Melbournian Michelle Garnaut opened the place in 1988, she single-handedly brought Hong Kong into a new stratosphere of food and dining experience. The menu changes constantly (except for her signature lamb dish) and everything is superbly designed, created and cooked. Save and go – but book well in advance.

Italian A bevy of Italian places have arrived on the scene in recent years. Most aren't bad, but there are only a few that really justify the prices you have to shell out for the authentic tastes of Italia.

Fat Angelo's (☎ 2973 6808, 49A-C Elgin St, Soho) **Map 5** Salads HK$30, pasta HK$65-135, mains HK$125-170. Fat Angelo's is probably the most successful restaurant to have opened in Soho. The key to its success? Huge portions at relatively low prices.

Club Pasta e Pizza (☎ 2545 1675, Basement, 11 Lyndhurst Terrace, Central) **Map 5** Pasta HK$75-88, small/large pizza from HK$48/75, set lunch HK$68. This independent, simple eatery gets consistently good reviews.

Spaghetti House (☎ 2523 1372, Basement, 10 Stanley St, Central) **Map 5** Pasta HK$48-62, small/large pizza from HK$72/99. You wouldn't want to take a date to this or any branch of the cheap and cheerful chain, but it's OK for a pizza or bowl of pasta.

Va Bene (☎ 2845 5577, 58-62 D'Aguilar St, Central) **Map 5** Meals about HK$300, set lunch HK$138. This smart restaurant bears a striking resemblance to a neighbourhood trattoria. It's a good choice for a special date or an extravagant celebration. Book ahead; dress smart.

Japanese Eating Japanese food in Central can leave you all but bankrupt if you don't choose carefully, but there are a few affordable options.

Beppu Menkan (☎ 2536 0816, 5-11 Stanley St, Central) **Map 5** Noodles HK$31-59, rice dishes HK$45-47. This is a fast-food Japanese option in the middle of Central specialising in beef noodles.

Kiyotaki Japanese Restaurant (☎ 2877 1803, 24 Staunton St, Soho) **Map 5** Sushi/sashimi course HK$150/120, tempura course HK$110. This restaurant is one of the few truly budget options for Japanese food in Soho.

Tokio Joe (☎ 2525 1889, 16 Lan Kwai Fong, Central) **Map 5** Sushi HK$25-65, set lunch HK$120-165. This place serves watered-down Japanese cuisine to the uninitiated and is not overwhelmingly expensive.

Yorohachi (☎ *2524 1251, 6 Lan Kwai Fong, Central*) **Map 5** Set lunch HK$95-135. Yorohachi in the heart of Lan Kwai Fong offers an excellent-value teppanyaki grill and takeaway lunch boxes.

Yoshinoya Noodles (☎ *2520 0953, Ground floor, China Hong Kong Tower, 8-12 Hennessy Rd, Wan Chai*) **Map 4** Soup noodles HK$21-33. This fast-food Japanese place near the Wesley Hotel in Wan Chai has another seven outlets around the territory.

Jewish & Kosher If it's Ashkenazic and Sephardic glatt kosher food you want, then *Shalom Grill* (Map 4) (☎ *2851 6300, 2nd floor, Fortune House, 61 Connaught Rd Central*) serves it up. Starters are from HK$25 to HK$40, mains HK$55 to HK$70. Don't expect cordon bleu, but if you're in the mood for felafel or gefilte fish or you simply answer to a higher authority on matters culinary, this is the place.

Korean A fairly authentic and central Korean eatery where you should book in advance is *Secret Garden* (Map 4) (☎ *2801 7990, Shop 5, Bank of America Tower, 12 Harcourt Rd, Central*) with soups from HK$100 to HK$160, rice and noodle dishes HK$100 to HK$140.

Malaysian They're not exactly Penang or Malacca standard but the Malaysian curries at *Coco Curry House* (Map 5) (☎ *2523 6911, 8 Wing Wah Lane, Central*) are tasty and filling. Noodles and rice dishes are HK$40 to HK$65, curries HK$58 to HK$70.

Mexican A fair few places in Hong Kong claim to serve Mexican food, a cuisine as diametrically opposed to Chinese as you can imagine, but with very few exceptions, they should be given a wide berth.

Caramba! (☎ *2530 9963, 26-30 Elgin St, Soho*) **Map 5** Combination plates HK$118-148. With a blinding selection of tequilas, this 'Mexican cantina' provides a cosy and intimate venue for a fix of *fajitas*, enchiladas and *chimichangas*.

Middle Eastern You won't get bombs a la carte and takeaway Semtex at *Beirut* (Map 5) (☎ *2804 6611, 33 D'Aguilar St, Central*) but authentic Lebanese dishes like *kibbeh* food. Meze is HK$45 to HK$65, and mains from HK$80.

Habibi (☎ *2544 9298, 112-114 Wellington St, Central*) **Map 4** Meze HK$45-60, mains HK$90-170. If you hanker for Egyptian food and the Cairo of the 1930s, go the extra distance and visit Habibi.

Nepalese A little over the top in decor and price is *Kath+Man+Du* (Map 5) (☎ *2869 1298, 11 Old Bailey St, Soho*), but it's a great choice if you want to try 'nouvelle Nepalese' (not an oxymoron). Meals range from HK$150 to HK$250.

Nepal (☎ *2869 6212, 14 Staunton St, Soho*) **Map 5** Mains HK$78-128, set dinner HK$178. Nepalese flavours and treats are in abundance here. Waiters rush across the road with overflowing plates to Nepal's sister-restaurant *Sherpa* (Map 5) (☎ *2973 6886, 11 Staunton St, Soho*), which shares the same menu.

Portuguese & Macanese If you don't make it to Macau (shame on you), you might consider *Casa Lisboa* (Map 5) (☎ *2869 9631, 21 Elgin St, Soho*), an attractive little place, with mains ranging from HK$142 to HK$148.

Russian The food at Russian restaurant *Troika* (Map 5) (☎ *2801 7839, 26-30 Elgin St, Soho*) is eminently forgettable, but the decor (a tsar's wet dream is the only possible description) is worth a visit as are the charming, affable Nepalese staff. Meals range from HK$300. Ukrainian borscht is HK$76, beef stroganoff HK$178 and a selection of three types of caviar is HK$380.

Spanish & South American In the heart of Soho is cosy *La Comida* (Map 5) (☎ *2530 3118, 22 Staunton St, Soho*) with authentic *cuchina española*. Tapas are HK$48 to HK$62, paella for two from HK$98.

Cubana (☎ *2869 1218, 47B Elgin St, Soho*) **Map 5** Meals from HK$200. This two-storey Cuban place has a good selection of tapas and serious cocktail pitchers. There's live Cuban music and salsa dancing Thursday and Sunday.

Rico's (☎ 2840 0937, 44 Robinson Rd, Mid-Levels) **Map 4** Tapas HK$42-90, mains HK$130-200. In the same stable and just up the road from Phuket's (see the following Thai section), Rico's has tapas and expensive Spanish main dishes in a pleasant Mediterranean atmosphere.

Thai Ever since Hong Kong Chinese people decided that spicy, smoky Sichuan cuisine was oh so passé and fiery Thai was trendy, there's been a glut of Thai eateries in this area.

Good Luck Thai (☎ 2877 2971, 13 Wing Wah Lane, Central) **Map 5** Curries HK$37-55. After sinking a few beers in Lan Kwai Fong, fight your way over to this chaotic and fun eatery for a cheap fix of Thai food.

Heartbeat Thai Restaurant by Supatra (☎ 2522 5073, Allied Capital Resources Bldg, 32-38 Ice House St, Central) **Map 5** Soups HK$48-69, curries HK$128-158. This restaurant is the creation of Supatra, grande dame of upmarket Thai food in Hong Kong. It's super trendy, but all of the food is done perfectly.

Phuket's Seafood Grill Club (☎ 2868 9672, Lower ground floor, Shop D, 30-32 Robinson Rd, Mid-Levels) **Map 4** Soups & Thai salads HK$48-65, curries HK$65-78. This Mid-Levels restaurant, entered from Mosque Junction, is a cosy spot, with a mural of a Thai beach to enhance the mood for an escape to Thailand's most popular island destination. The food (mainly seafood) is not authentic but it's a convenient choice if you're staying in the Mid-Levels.

Thai Lemongrass (☎ 2905 1688, 3rd floor, California Tower, 30-32 D'Aguilar St, Central) **Map 5** Set lunch/dinner HK$200/300. This quiet, discreet and very smart place serves up such treats as pomelo salad, spicy green Papaya salad and mussels in red curry.

Vegetarian The *Fringe Club* (Map 5) (☎ 2521 7251, 2 Lower Albert Rd, Lan Kwai Fong) does a vegetarian lunch buffet from noon to 2pm Monday to Saturday, which costs from HK$65 to HK$75.

Vietnamese Cheap but tasty meals for those on a rock-bottom budget are available at *Bon Appetit* (Map 5) (☎ 2525 3553, 14B Wing Wah Lane, Central), a Vietnamese restaurant with snacks from HK$18 to HK$26, filled baguettes HK$26 to HK$29, and noodles HK$20 to HK$30.

Indochine 1929 (☎ 2869 7399, 2nd floor, California Tower, 30-32 D'Aguilar St, Central) **Map 5** Salads HK$58-96, mains HK$118-200. It's not cheap, but the mood at this place of colonial Vietnam will certainly bewitch you. The work of the talented designer Lilian Tang, the old photographs, lighting and memorabilia are just an appetiser of what's to come – excellently prepared and well-presented Vietnamese food.

Pearl Vietnamese Restaurant (☎ 2522 4223, 7 Wo On Lane, Central) **Map 5** Dishes HK$22-32. This tiny place is an inexpensive option for noodles or rice when frequenting the bars of the Fong.

Cafes The civilised *China Tee Club* (Map 4) (☎ 2521 0233, 1st floor, Pedder Bldg, 12 Pedder St, Central) is perfect for a cuppa after finishing your shopping at Shanghai Tang's below (or Blanc de Chine above, for that matter). Meals are from HK$150.

Delifrance (☎ 2810 5941, 1st floor, Pacific House, 20 Queen's Rd Central) **Map 4** Sandwiches from HK$25. Delifrance is the place to come if you're craving croissants, doughnuts and pastries. They also serve coffee and tea.

Le Fauchon (☎ 2537 2938, Shop 3-5, Ground floor, The Forum, Exchange Square, Connaught Rd Central) **Map 4** Breakfast HK$38-74, sandwiches HK$38-95, pasta HK$70-85. This branch of the Parisian gourmet shop does proper meals as well as their usual exquisite pastries, cakes and sandwiches. You can eat in or take away. There's also an Admiralty branch (☎ 2918 1101, Shop 405, Pacific Place, 88 Queensway).

T W Cafe (☎ *2544 2237, Shop 2, Capitol Plaza, 2-10 Lyndhurst St, Central)* **Map 5** Afternoon tea HK$34. T W Cafe is a tiny place that has more than 20 types of coffee on offer, as well as a smattering of light snacks.

Uncle Willie's Deli (☎ *2522 7524, 36 Wyndham St, Central)* **Map 5** Soups HK$45, sandwiches HK$65, tarts HK$18. This is a relaxing but smart deli, which serves the best breakfasts and sandwiches in town.

Fast Food *Beyrouth Cafe Central* (☎ *2854 1872, Shop A, Lyndhurst Bldg, 39 Lyndhurst Terrace, Central)* **Map 5** Dishes HK$37-45, sandwiches HK$30-35. There is cheap, but not especially authentic, Lebanese food available at the small Beyrouth Cafe Central till late.

Chop Chop Cafe (☎ *2526 1122, Winner Bldg, 17 Wing Wah Lane, Central)* **Map 5** Set meals with drink HK$35-45. The Chop Chop is a small, cheap eatery where you can fill up on baked potatoes, casseroles and other speedy cuisine.

Hong Kong Baguette (☎ *2868 3716, 18 Lan Kwai Fong, Central)* **Map 5** Sandwiches HK$35-60, small/medium/large pizzas from HK$50/70/88. This is a great venue for sandwiches and snacks. It's open till late.

Midnight Express (☎ *2525 5010, 3 Lan Kwai Fong, Central)* **Map 5** Meals from HK$35-55. Open 10am-4am daily. As the name implies, this does late-night fast food. The fare is a motley mix of Greek, Indian, Mexican and Italian.

Oliver's Super Sandwiches (☎ *2525 8087, Shop 10, 1st floor, The Forum, Exchange Square, Connaught Rd Central)* **Map 4** Soups HK$12-16, salads HK$20-32, sandwiches HK$26-35. This chain offers reasonable quality cooked breakfasts, sandwiches, salads and cakes. You'll find other Central branches in the Prince's Building (☎ *2523 0006, Shop 233-237, 10 Chater Rd)*, Citibank Plaza (☎ *2526, 2685, Shop 2, Lower ground floor, 3 Garden Rd)* and The Landmark (☎ *2877 6631, Shop B43, Basement, 1 Pedder St, Central)*.

Self-Catering There are three floors of meat, vegetables, fish and poultry at *Central Market* **(Map 4)** *(Queen's Rd Central)* between Jubilee and Queen Victoria Sts with daily prices posted on a large notice board. If you really want to rub elbows with the proletariat, this is the place to do it.

Graham St Market (Graham St, Central) The stalls and shops lining Graham St south and up the hill from Queen's Rd Central to Hollywood Rd are positively groaning with high-quality vegetables, fruit, meat and seafood.

Euromart (☎ *2537 1108, 36A Staunton St, Soho)* **Map 5** This is a European-style convenience store full of cheeses, wines, hams and coffees.

Oliver's (☎ *2869 5119, Shop 201-205 Prince's Bldg, 10 Chater Rd, Central)* **Map 4** This old standby delicatessen stocks a wide range of cheeses, sausages, pâtés and fine wines.

Sweet Secrets (☎ *2545 8886, Shop D Lower ground floor, 27 Hollywood Rd Central)* **Map 5** This bakery and sweets shop, entered from Cochrane St, sells some of the finest cakes, tarts, pastries and chocolates in Central.

Shueng Wan

West of Central, the Sheung Wan district stands out for two different cuisines: Chinese (in particular, Chiu Chow) and Korean.

Chinese A cavernous place near the Western Market, *Golden Dragon Restaurant* **(Map 4)** (☎ *2541 3233, 1st floor, 7 On Tai St)* is a good choice for dim sum, which is available from 7am to 5pm daily. Meals are about HK$150.

Golden Snow Garden Restaurant (☎ *2815 8128, Ground floor, 7 On Tai St,* **Map 4** Meals from HK$120. Cheaper than its upstairs neighbour, this place specialises in the flavours of Shanghai, Sichuan and the north. Dim sum is served 11am to 3pm daily.

Ho Choi Seafood Restaurant (☎ *2850 6722, 287-291 Des Voeux Rd)* **Map 4** Dim sum HK$42-78. This place, entered from Cleverly St, is popular for dim sum and

Cantonese seafood. The menu is in Chinese only so get your pointing finger ready.

Leung Hing Seafood Restaurant (☎ 2850 6666, 32 Bonham Strand West) **Map 4** Meals from HK$150. The staple ingredients of Chiu Chow cuisine – shellfish, goose and duck – are extensively employed and delectably prepared at this local place.

Korean Sheung Wan has always been a 'Little Korean' and is the best place on the island to look for *bulgogi* (Korean barbecue) and *kimchi* (spicy fermented cabbage).

Korea Garden (☎ 2542 2339, 1st floor, Blissful Bldg, 247 Des Voeux Rd Central) **Map 4** Meals about HK$100. The slightly toned down Korean food here attracts young Hong Kong Chinese.

Lee Fa Yuen Korea House Restaurant (☎ 2544 0007, Honwell Commercial Centre, 119-21 Connaught Rd Central) **Map 4** Meals about HK$150. The Korea House, entered from Man Wa Lane, is acknowledged as having some of the most authentic Korean barbecue, kimchi and appetisers in Hong Kong and is always filled with Korean expats – the ultimate stamp of approval.

The Peak (Map 7)

You'd hardly venture all the way up Victoria Peak for a meal; food here takes its place in the queue behind the views. But there are a few choices.

Mövenpick Marché (☎ 2849 2000, Levels 6 & 7, Peak Tower, 128 Peak Rd) Dishes HK$48-68. More a Singaporean concept than a Hong Kong one, the Marché consists of different stalls preparing Asian food from which you can order anything from noodles to teppanyaki.

Peak Lookout Hong Kong (121 Peak Rd) Formerly known as the Peak Café, at the time of writing the new Peak Lookout Hong Kong was set to reopen in late 2001. The new renovations are aimed at creating a 1920s feel. International food will be available when the restaurant reopens. The views from here are to the south of the island – the harbour. In the long term, the new owner hopes to build a viewing platform looking out over the South China Sea.

Park 'N' Shop (level 2, Peak Galleria, 118 Peak Rd) This is a convenient branch of the supermarket chain if you want to stock up on snacks and drinks before embarking on a walk.

Wan Chai & Admiralty

Wan Chai (and to a lesser extent Admiralty) is a happy hunting ground for ethnic restaurants. Name your cuisine and MTR, bus or tram it down to the Wanch. You're bound to find it here.

Chinese The low-key **369 Shanghai Restaurant** (Map 6) (☎ 2527 2343, 30-32 O'Brien Rd, Wan Chai) serves Shanghainese food that's nothing like five-star, but does the dumpling job fairly well. Soups range from HK$38 to HK$58, cold dishes HK$32 to HK$50. The place is family-run and there are some good comfy booths at the front window.

American Restaurant (☎ 2527 7277, 20 Lockhart Rd, Wan Chai) **Map 6** Meals about HK$150. The friendly American, which chose it's name to pull Yank sailors cruising the Wanch through its doors for sustenance, has been serving decent northern Chinese cuisine for over 50 years. Most of its customers are regulars. As you'd hope, the Peking duck and the beggar's chicken (order in advance) are very good.

Beijing Shui Jiao Wong (☎ 2527 0289, 118 Jaffe Rd, Wan Chai) **Map 6** Dishes HK$22-33. You won't find better (or cheaper) northern-style dumplings (HK$23-29), *guo tie* (HK$31-33) and soup noodles (HK$22-27) anywhere in Hong Kong.

Carriana Chiu Chow Restaurant (☎ 2511 1282, 151 Gloucester Rd, Wan Chai) **Map 6** Meals from HK$150. For Chiu Chow food, the Carriana, entered from Tonnochy Rd, still rates right up there after all these years. Try the cold dishes (sliced goose with vinegar, crab claws), pork with tofu or the Chiu Chow chicken.

Dynasty (☎ 2802 8888, Renaissance Harbour View Hotel, 1 Harbour Rd, Wan Chai) **Map 6** Meals from HK$200. This hotel restaurant serves some of the most innovative dim sum in town.

East Ocean Seafood Restaurant (☎ 2827 8887, 3rd floor, Harbour Centre, 25 Harbour Rd, Wan Chai) **Map 6** Meals from HK$200. Though the East Ocean may not be among the top 10 restaurants in the world, as the incomparable food critic Patricia Wells once said it was (opening a half-dozen branches may have compromised quality just a wee bit), it still serves some of the best and inventive Cantonese seafood dishes in town.

Liu Yuan Restaurant (☎ 2845 1199, 2nd floor, CRE Bldg, 297-307 Hennessy Rd, Wan Chai) **Map 6** Meals from HK$250. This superb and quite stylish Shanghai restaurant is well worth spending the extra money on. The crab claws cooked with duck egg and the tiny prawns steamed with tea leaves are superb.

Lung Moon Restaurant (☎ 2572 9888, 130-136 Johnston Rd, Wan Chai) **Map 6** Meals about HK$120. The dining experience at this very basic Cantonese place has not changed a great deal since the 1950s, and the prices, while not quite still at 1950s levels, are still reasonable.

One Harbour Road (☎ 2588 1234, 7th & 8th floors, Grand Hyatt Hotel, 1 Harbour Rd, Wan Chai) **Map 6** Meals about HK$300. This is probably the classiest hotel Chinese restaurant in town. In addition to the beautiful design and fab harbour view, six pages of gourmet dishes await your perusal.

Steam & Stew Inn (☎ 2529 3913, 21-23 Tai Wong St East, Wan Chai) **Map 6** Meals from HK$100. The Inn serves 'home-style' Cantonese food, most of which is steamed, stewed or boiled. The food is good and free of monosodium glutamate (MSG).

Tim's Kitchen (☎ 2527 2982, Shop C, 118 Jaffe Rd, Wan Chai) **Map 6** Dishes HK$10-60. When as many Hong Kong Chinese queue up outside a restaurant at lunch time as they do at Tim's every day, you can be sure that the food is both inexpensive and of excellent quality.

Victoria City (☎ 2827 9938, 3rd floor, Sun Hung Kai Centre, 30 Harbour Rd, Wan Chai) **Map 6** Meals from HK$200. Dim sum 11am-2.30pm daily. Many in Hong Kong consider the dim sum served here to be the best in the territory.

Yè Shanghai (☎ 2918 9833, Shop 332, Pacific Place, 88 Queensway, Admiralty) **Map 4** Cold dishes HK$48-60, mains HK$78-200. This groovy place takes street-level Shanghainese cuisine and gives it a tweak here and there. The drunken pigeon is a wine-soaked winner and the steamed dumplings are perfectly plump.

Yin King Lau Restaurant (☎ 2520 0106, 113 Lockhart Rd, Wan Chai) **Map 6** Meals from HK$150. This restaurant is just OK and will leave the real Sichuan food enthusiast yearning for more authentic cuisine. Still, for the uninitiated it's a start.

American The fare at *Dan Ryan's Chicago Grill* (Map 4) (☎ 2845 4600, Shop 114, Pacific Place, 88 Queensway, Admiralty), a re-creation of a Chicago lounge restaurant, always satisfies, be it the oyster stew or ribs (half/full rack HK$132/198), sandwiches (HK$55-112) or salads (HK$98-130). There's a big-screen video showing sports shows. There's a branch in Tsim Sha Tsui.

British There's really no other contender to *Harry Ramsden's* (Map 6) (☎ 2832 9626, 213 Queen's Rd East, Wan Chai) for fish and chips in Hong Kong. It's cheery and relatively cheap, and the food consistently good; the service is a bit slow and sloppy, but the fish is excellent. HK$98 gets you a fine haddock, chips, beans and a soft drink in the restaurant; it's HK$59 in the take-away section.

Filipino The friendly *Cinta* (Map 6) (☎ 2527 1199, Shing Yip Bldg, 10 Fenwick St, Wan Chai) restaurant and lounge has a South-East Asian menu longer than the Bible that covers all bases from *murtabak* and *gado-gado* to *bami*, but with a strong emphasis on Pinoy dishes. Meals are about HK$120.

Cinta-J (☎ 2529 6622, Shop G4, Malaysia Bldg, 69 Jaffe Rd, Wan Chai) **Map 6** Meals about HK$120. This sister-restaurant of Cinta offers similar fare but metamorphoses into a cocktail lounge in the evening and stays open till 5am.

French With its head in the clouds, *Petrus* **(Map 4)** (☎ *2820 8590, 2877 3838, 56th floor, Island Shangri-La Hotel, Pacific Place, 88 Queensway, Admiralty)* is one of the finest restaurants in Hong Kong. The five-/six-course set dinner is HK$700/850.

Greek If it's a good time you crave, then *Bacchus* **(Map 4)** (☎ *2529 9032, Basement, China Hong Kong Tower, 8-12 Hennessy Rd, Wan Chai)* is the place. Meals are from HK$250. The food is deliciously different and the service friendly and upbeat. On some nights there is live entertainment.

Indian A favourite of expats who love authentic Indian food, *Jo Jo Mess Club* **(Map 6)** (☎ *2527 3776, 1st floor, 86 Johnston Rd, Wan Chai)*, entered from Lee Tung St, has dropped a bit in quality in recent years, so we're told. Meals are about HK$100. There's a lunch buffet (HK$75) on Wednesday and Friday, including a half-pint of beer.

Shaffi's Malik (☎ *2572 7474, 185 Wan Chai Rd, Wan Chai)* **Map 6** Starters HK$18-22, kebabs HK$48-57, curries HK$44-50. This place boasts that it is 'probably the oldest Indian restaurant in town serving the best Indian cuisine'. Neither claim is true but it's cheap – and here.

Viceroy (☎ *2827 7777, 2nd floor, Sun Hung Kai Centre, 30 Harbour Rd, Wan Chai)* **Map 6** Meals from HK$200. Viceroy has been an institution in Hong Kong for almost two decades: an upmarket Indian restaurant with traditional music and a fun place to party later on (see Comedy under Entertainment later in this chapter).

Indonesian A Wan Chai fixture since Suzy Wong was dragging the streets, *Shinta Indonesian Restaurant* **(Map 4)** (☎ *2143 6370, Shop B, Ground floor, 4-6 Hennessy Rd or 6 Queen's Rd East, Wan Chai)* is a Sino-Indonesian eatery that is dimly lit and laid-back and serves passable, rather diluted Indonesian fare. Rijsttafel is HK$88, set lunch HK$55.

International The main (some might say only) reason to come to *Cat Street Bar &*

Restaurant **(Map 6)** (☎ *2865 1008, 1st floor, Capital Place, 18 Luard Rd, Wan Chai)* is for the cheap lunches available, though there is salsa every Tuesday evening. Set lunches are from HK$45 to HK$55.

China Town (☎ *2861 3588, 78-82 Jaffe Rd, Wan Chai)* **Map 6** Asian and Western snacks HK$30-65, mains HK$65-95. From the people who brought you Mad Dogs and Joe Bananas is this stylish pseudo-Shanghainese bar as seen by a set designer. But is it a restaurant or a bar? Most people are still out to lunch on that one.

Louis' Steak House (☎ *2529 8933, 1st floor, Malaysia Bldg, 50 Gloucester Rd, Wan Chai)* **Map 6** Steaks HK$180-230. This is the sort of place that Hong Kong Chinese used to frequent when they wanted fancy Western cuisine. Sort of '50s but Louis' still has its charms.

The Open Kitchen (☎ *2827 2923, 6th floor, Hong Kong Arts Centre, 2 Harbour Rd, Wan Chai)* **Map 6** Set lunch/dinner from HK$50/75. This well-lit, smart restaurant with great views of the harbour serves a mix of Indian, Malaysian, Japanese and Italian dishes. If you're taking in a play or a concert at the Arts Centre, this is an excellent spot to have a meal before or afterward.

Simply Healthy (☎ *2137 9797, 138 Lockhart Rd, Wan Chai)* **Map 6** Soups HK$10-17, set breakfast/lunch/tea HK$18/30/17. This fabulous outlet run by a catering firm promotes diets that are low in fats, sugar and salt, high in fibre and devoid of MSG.

Italian The food at old standby *La Bella Donna* **(Map 6)** (☎ *2802 9907, 1st floor, Shui On Centre, 6-8 Harbour Rd, Wan Chai)* is hardly spectacular but is an inexpensive option for *cucina italiana*. Starters range from HK$45 to HK$75, pasta HK$70 to HK$105, pizzas HK$68 to HK$80, and mains HK$95 to HK$185.

Cine Città (☎ *2529 0199, Starcrest Bldg, 9 Star St, Wan Chai)* **Map 4** Starters HK$55-78, pasta HK$108-118. This very flash restaurant with an Italian film theme is in an area of south-west Wan Chai that might just become the new Lan Kwai Fong restaurant and nightlife district.

Grappa's (☎ *2868 0086, Shop 132, Pacific Place, 88 Queensway, Admiralty*) **Map 4** Meals from HK$250. This is a top-notch venue for antipasto, fettuccini and other Italian dishes though not everyone likes dining in a mall.

Pepperoni's Pizza & Cafe (☎ *2861 2660, 54 Jaffe Rd, Wan Chai*) **Map 6** Small pizzas HK$55-65, salads HK$45-55. This branch of the celebrated pizzeria in Sai Kung is an inexpensive option for pizza and pasta in the Wanch.

Rigoletto's (☎ *2527 7144, 14 Fenwick St, Wan Chai*) **Map 6** Meals from HK$250. This trattoria makes an effort but has become very localised and toned down.

Japanese A huge place done up in traditional Japanese decor is *Shabu Shabu* (**Map 6**) (☎ *2893 8806, Ground floor, Kwan Chart Tower, 6 Tonnochy Rd, Wan Chai*), which offers a warm welcome and relatively reasonable prices. Sushi and sashimi is HK$30 to HK$40, tempura HK$65 to HK$180, and hotpot meals HK$70 to HK$90.

Suikenkan (☎ *2573 1308, Shop D, Kingstown Mansion, 313-323 Jaffe Rd, Wan Chai*) **Map 6** Meals from HK$250. This bar and restaurant has a nifty samurai theme and an early evening happy hour that sees many drinkers turn into diners after the third or fourth *banzai* (bottoms up).

Mexican With its warm mustard-coloured decor and brass bar, *Coyote Bar & Grill* (**Map 6**) (☎ *2861 2221, 114-120 Lockhart Rd, Wan Chai*) describes itself as 'Mexican with attitude'. *Si, señor, claro*. Combination platters are HK$101 to HK$121, fajitas HK$132 to HK$142.

Pan-Asian For stunning views over Victoria Harbour and Central, fabulous decor and smooth design, try *Port Cafe* (**Map 6**) (☎ *2582 7731, level 3, Phase 2, Hong Kong Convention & Exhibition Centre, 1 Expo Drive, Wan Chai*) in the colossal convention centre. Meals are about HK$250 to HK$350. While not cheap, it is a stylish, sophisticated addition to the Hong Kong dining scene.

Portuguese Less-than-inspired Chinese-Portuguese (*not* Macanese) food and a low-key pub are the main features at *Portucale* (**Map 6**) (☎ *2527 9266, 2520 0016, Shop A 33 Lockhart Rd, Wan Chai*) which has meals from about HK$150 to HK$200.

Thai The first Westernised (ie, toned-down) Thai restaurant to hit the scene two decades ago, *Chili Club* (**Map 6**) (☎ *2527 2872, 1st floor, 88 Lockhart Rd, Wan Chai*) has slipped a few notches with all the competition, but it's still a popular destination on the Hong Kong spice route. Soups are HK$38 to HK$75, mains HK$40 to HK$180.

Patong Thai Restaurant (☎ *2861 1006, 12-22 Queen's Rd East, Wan Chai*) **Map 4** Starters HK$48-70, curries HK$70-90, set menu for two HK$190. This rather stylish Thai restaurant is pricey but just the ticket if you feel like going upmarket.

Tan Ta Wan Restaurant (☎ *2865 1665, Shop 9, Rialto Bldg, 2 Landale St, Wan Chai*) **Map 4** Starters from HK$40, curries HK$40-50, seafood dishes HK$100-145. Bunch of Thai amahs can't bare the ersatz Thai food they get in Hong Kong. Open a restaurant. Result – the most authentic Thai food in Hong Kong outside of Kowloon City.

Vegetarian The strictly Buddhist *Healthy Mess Vegetarian Restaurant* (**Map 6**) (☎ *2527 3918, 51-53 Hennessy Rd, Wan Chai*) sports the Buddhist swastika on its business card and is very popular with Chinese noncarnivores. Dim sum is HK$2.50 to HK$5, dishes HK$48 to HK$60. This place serves tasty, filling food and is warmly recommended.

Vegetarian Court (☎ *2510 0483, 1st floor, CRE Bldg, 297-307 Hennessy Rd, Wan Chai*) **Map 6** Dishes from HK$40. Not just another little vegetarian place in Wan Chai, the Court is Shanghainese as well, promising bigger, fuller flavours.

Vegetarian Garden (☎ *2893 8355, 128 Johnston Rd, Wan Chai*) **Map 6** Meals about HK$100. One of a number of Buddhist vegetarian restaurants in town, this place has takeaway dim sum on the ground floor and a restaurant downstairs.

Vietnamese A sterilised version of a Vietnamese restaurant, *Saigon* **(Map 6)** (☎ 2598 7222, 2nd floor, Sun Hung Kai Centre, 30 Harbour Rd, Wan Chai) has cheap set lunches and shares the same space with its sister-restaurant *Milano* (☎ 2598 1222), allowing you to devise your own pho-caccia. Meals are about HK$200.

Saigon Beach (☎ 2527 3383, 66 Lockhart Rd, Wan Chai) **Map 6** Noodles & rice HK$26-33, mains HK$58-62. This popular little hole-in-the-wall may not impress at first sight, but the affable service and food is well worth sharing a table with strangers, which you undoubtedly will have to do.

Cafes A branch of popular bakery and patisserie *Delifrance* **(Map 4)** (☎ 2520 0959, Shop A1-A3, Queensway Plaza, 91-93 Queensway, Admiralty) can be found near the Admiralty MTR station. Sandwiches start at HK$30.

Fast Food Wan Chai has the usual range of international chain fast-food joints as well as a few more appetising home-grown places.

Oliver's Super Sandwiches (☎ 2598 1112, Shop B, Ground floor, ☎ 2510 0483, 1st & 2nd floor, CRE Bldg, 297-307 Hennessy Rd, Wan Chai) **Map 6** Sandwiches HK$26-35, soups HK$12-16, salads HK$20-32. This is a convenient branch of the popular sandwichery.

Self-Catering The *Seibu Department Store* **(Map 4)** (☎ 2971 3888, Level L1 & L2, Pacific Place, 88 Queensway, Admiralty) has the largest stock of imported foods (Western and Asian, with an emphasis on Japanese) in Hong Kong, supplying a range of imported cheeses, breads and chocolates. It's open 11am to 8pm daily.

Causeway Bay

Causeway Bay is a strange amalgam of restaurants and cuisines but, apart from a selection of rather slick and overpriced European places on Fashion Walk (or Houston St) north-east of the Causeway MTR station, this is the place for Chinese and other Asian (particularly South-East Asian) food.

Chinese 'Gizzard soup' and 'stomach tidbit' are two of the less alluring menu items at *Chuen Cheung Kui* **(Map 6)** (☎ 2577 3833, 108-120 Percival St) but the pulled chicken, a Hakka classic, is the dish to insist upon. Meals are about HK$150 to HK$200.

Fook Hing Hotpot Seafood Restaurant (☎ 2891 3886, 4th floor, Elizabeth House, 250 Gloucester Rd, Wan Chai) **Map 6** Meals from HK$150. Seafood cooked *à table* in various flavoured broths is a winter and cold weather treat and this is just about the best place to try it on the island. Enter the restaurant from Percival St.

Global Forever Green Taiwanese Restaurant (☎ 2890 3448, 93-95A Leighton Rd) **Map 6** Meals from HK$150. Entered from Sun Wui Rd, this is the best place in town for Taiwanese food. Try traditional specialities such as the oyster omelette, fried tofu and *sanbeiji* (three-cup chicken). Noodle dishes are good value, but other prices are fairly high.

Hangzhou Restaurant (☎ 2894 9705, 9 Lan Fong Rd) **Map 6** Meals about HK$120. This place serves authentic Hangzhou food, a less salty and oily variant of Shanghainese cuisine.

Heichinrou (☎ 2506 2333, Shop 1003, Food Forum, Times Square, 1 Matheson St) **Map 6** Meals from HK$150. This Chinese restaurant is arguably the most elegant of the dozen or so that make up the Food Forum and has excellent dim sum.

Irene's (☎ 2882 2070, 4 Sun Wui Rd) **Map 6** Starters from HK$28-60, mains from HK$100. This wonderful place serves New Chinese cuisine amid space-age decor.

King Heung Restaurant (☎ 2577 1035, 59-65 Paterson St) **Map 6** Cold dishes HK$65-80, main dishes from HK$80. This is an excellent and quite stylish northern Chinese restaurant.

Nanking Kitchen (☎ 2577 2696, Shop A, Florida Mansion, 9-11 Cleveland St) **Map 6** Dishes HK$18-20. The mainland city of Nanjing's only real claim to fame (beyond that infamous treaty – see the History section in the Facts about Hong Kong chapter) is noodles fried with beef, a meat not eaten very frequently by the Chinese.

Red Pepper (☎ 2577 3811, 7 Lan Fong Rd) **Map 6** Meals from HK\$150-250. This long-established restaurant is among the best – though more expensive – options for Sichuan food. The sliced pork in chilli sauce and the Sichuan noodles are particularly recommended.

Sze Chuen Lau (☎ 2891 9027, 466 Lockhart Rd) **Map 6** Meals from HK\$200. This Sichuan (Sze Chuan is how they used to spell it) restaurant has been around forever and is not the most authentic place in town, but the orange beef, smoked duck and chilli prawns will please.

Tai Woo Seafood Restaurant (☎ 2893 0822, 27 Percival St) **Map 6** Meals from HK\$150. Tai Woo is as well know for its vegetarian dishes (try the bean curd with vegetarian crab roe) as it is its seafood. Better still, it's open till 3am.

Yunnan Kitchen (☎ 2506 3309, Shop 1205, Food Forum, Times Square, 1 Matheson St) **Map 6** Meals about HK\$150, buffet lunch HK\$78. This place does a pretty good job of capturing the taste of Yunnan cuisine, a slightly milder version of Sichuan. Specialities include Yunnan ham, fried Dali vermicelli and fresh prawns stuffed in bamboo.

American A technicolour good-time eatery in the heart of the Fashion Walk boutique and restaurant area, ***Paper Moon*** (Map 6) (☎ 2881 5070, Shop B Greenfield Mansion, 8 Kingston St) serves up massive portions of supposedly American food. Pasta is HK\$72 to HK\$78, burgers HK\$52 to HK\$58, and steaks HK\$88 to HK\$98. It's well-intentioned, but often misses the mark. Great place for the kids and there's usually live music in the evening.

International The super groover hang-out ***Dining Area*** (Map 6) (☎ 2915 0260, 17 Lan Fong St) has beautifully presented Euro-Canto food. There's freaky stuff going down in the kitchen. It's the kind of place where you might get wasabi in your focaccia and artichokes with your fried noodles. Never mind – it all tastes fine and everyone looks like a star.

Tai Ping Koon (☎ 2576 9161, 6 Pak Sha Rd) **Map 6** Starters from HK\$40, mains HK\$118-180. This place has been around since 1860 and is such a period piece that we're hesitant to even include it. Tai Ping Koon offers an incredible mix of Western and Chinese flavours. Try the borscht (HK\$41) and the smoked pomfret (HK\$118) or roast pigeon (HK\$188).

Italian The Italian-American *La Festa* **(Map 6)** (☎ 2838 9318, Shop D & E, Block A, Lockhart House, 440 Jaffe Rd) takes its cue from Fat Angelo's and piles it on high. Large/small pizza is from HK\$78/108, mains HK\$118 to HK\$248.

Japanese Causeway Bay has a lot of Japanese restaurants because of all the Japanese department stores (and tourists) that used to be based here before the Land of the Rising Sun essentially went bankrupt. Still, the district remains one of the best areas in Hong Kong for Japanese food – both faux and genuine.

Ichiban (☎ 2591 0683, 15 Morrison Hill Rd) **Map 6** Noodles HK\$38-40. For a down-to-earth atmosphere, try Ichiban. It has the atmosphere of an *izakaya* (a Japanese-style pub) and seems to tolerate enthusiastic bouts of sake drinking.

Isshin (☎ 2506 2220, Shop 1304, Food Forum, Times Square, 1 Matheson St) **Map 6** Meals about HK\$300. Isshin is not cheap but does rate among the best of Hong Kong's Japanese restaurants.

Tomokazu (☎ 2833 6339, Shop B, Lockhart House, 441 Lockhart Rd) **Map 6** Set lunches HK\$50-120. For Japanese food, this place is a bargain.

Korean The *Arirang* (Map 6) (☎ 2506 3298, Shop 1102, Food Forum, Times Square, 1 Matheson St) is a branch of the upmarket Korean restaurant chain with two more outlets in Tsim Sha Tsui. Meals are from HK\$250.

Korea Restaurant (☎ 2577 9893, 58 Leighton Rd) **Map 6** Barbecue HK\$65-80, set courses HK\$75-90. This is a good place for an authentic Korean barbecue but the surrounds are a little, well, frayed and gloomy. Still, it's a cheap place to eat.

Sorabol Korean Restaurant (☎ 2881 6823, 17th floor, Lee Theatre Bldg, 99 Percival St) **Map 6** Meals about HK$150. This is the Korean's Korean restaurant, with helpful staff to boot.

Malaysian & Indonesian The *Banana Leaf Curry House* (**Map 6**) (☎ 2573 8187, 440 Jaffe Rd) is a branch of a chain and dishes up Malaysian/Singaporean food served on a banana leaf; your hands are the cutlery if you choose to go authentic. Meals are from HK$100. There are some five other outlets, including one across the Harbour in Tsim Sha Tsui.

Indonesian Restaurant (☎ 2577 9981, 28 Leighton Rd) **Map 6** Mains HK$48-138. This Indonesian restaurant serves pretty authentic *rendang* (HK$65) gado-gado (HK$48) and the like.

Indonesia Padang Restaurant (☎ 2576 1828, 85 Percival St) **Map 6** Meals from HK$100. This is another popular option for Indonesian food in Causeway Bay.

Mexican Although *La Placita* (**Map 6**) (☎ 2506 3308, Shop 1301, Food Forum, Times Square, 1 Matheson St) does average Mexican food, what sets it apart is its celebrated salsa nights held every Sunday from 6.30pm (entry HK$100, HK$80 after 8.30pm, including one drink). Meals are from HK$180.

Russian The smallish *Queen's Cafe* (**Map 6**) (☎ 2576 2658, Eton Tower, 8 Hysan Ave) has been around since 1952 (though obviously not at the bottom of the same modern high-rise), which accounts for its subdued yet assured atmosphere. The borsch and meat set meals – White Russian dishes that filtered through China and have an old-fashioned taste to them – are pretty good.

Thai It might not be the best Thai in town, but *Golden Elephant Thai Restaurant* (**Map 6**) (☎ 2506 1333, Shop 1101, Food Forum, Times Square, 1 Matheson St) is almost certainly the highest. Set lunches are

HK$49 to HK$64. There's a branch in Tsim Sha Tsui.

Vegetarian Long-established *Kung Tak Lam* (**Map 6**) (☎ 2890 3127, Lok Sing Centre, 31 Yee Wo St) is more modern-feeling than most vegetarian eateries and is usually packed out. Meals are around HK$100. All the vegetables are grown organically and all dishes are free of MSG.

Vegi Food Kitchen (☎ 2890 6660, Ground floor, Highland Mansions, 8 Cleveland St) **Map 6** Soups HK$50-58, mains HK$50-95. This place is pretty serious about its vegetarianism – there's a sign here warning you not to bring meat or alcohol onto the premises – and creates some of the most memorable mock meat dishes in Hong Kong.

Vietnamese The *Perfume River Vietnamese Restaurant* (**Map 6**) (☎ 2576 2240, 89 Percival St) has been a reliable spot for Vietnamese food such as *pho*, a hotpot of noodles, meat or shellfish and fragrant herbs, and fried spring rolls wrapped in lettuce leaves, for as long as we can remember. Meals are from HK$120.

Yin Ping Vietnamese Restaurant (☎ 2832 9038, 24 Cannon St) **Map 6** Rice dishes HK$29-78, hotpot dishes HK$50-52, set lunches HK$33-46. This little place is the 'anchor' Vietnamese restaurant on a street with more than a few. If it's full, try sister-restaurant *Green Cottage* (☎ 2832 2863, 32 Cannon St) a few doors down.

Cafes While hot meals are available at *Delifrance* (**Map 6**) (☎ 2506 3462, The Marketplace, Shop B208, Basement, Times Square, 1 Matheson St) for lunch and dinner, the emphasis at this branch of the chain is croissants, pastry, soup, sandwiches and coffee. Sandwiches are from HK$25, set lunches HK$29 to HK$45.

Saint's Alp Teahouse (☎ 2147 0389, 476 Lockhart Rd) **Map 6** Meals from HK$50. This branch of the chain of cheap but clean Taiwanese-style cafes is a good pit stop for lunch or a snack while shopping in Causeway Bay.

Happy Valley

Adventist Vegetarian Cafeteria (☎ 2574 6211, 7th floor, Hong Kong Adventist Hospital, 40 Stubbs Rd) Soups from HK$6, mains from HK$16. Open 6am-7.30am, noon-1.30pm & 5pm-7.30pm. This is one of the greatest bargains in Hong Kong and anyone can eat here.

Amigo (☎ 2577 2202, Amigo Mansion, 79A Wong Nei Chung Rd) Meals about HK$300. This old-style international restaurant, where the waiters still wear black tie and white gloves, is a place full of memories.

North Point

Hong Kong Old Restaurant (☎ 2807 2333, Basement, Newton Hotel, 218 Electric Rd, North Point) Meals from HK$200. Those in the know say that this hotel restaurant serves the best Shanghainese food in Hong Kong.

June (☎ 2234 6691, 56 Electric Rd) Noodle dishes HK$50-70, sushi/sashimi plates HK$250/300, set lunches HK$60-100. By all accounts this place, at Yacht St, serves the most authentic affordable Japanese food on Hong Kong Island.

Quarry Bay

The Continental (☎ 2563 2209, 2 Hoi Wan St) Meals from HK$250. This is an excellent Modern Australian in far-flung Quarry Bay and worth the trip out here for its carrot soup and rigatoni pasta. From the MTR station at Quarry Bay, take the Tong Chong St and Devon House exit. Hoi Wan St runs north toward the end of Tong Chung St.

Shek O

Black Sheep (☎ 2809 2021, 452 Shek O Village) Meals from HK$250. This extremely popular Croatian-run restaurant with an international menu and two nearby locations is indeed a black sheep – altogether different from anything else you'll find in these parts.

Shek O Chinese & Thai Seafood Restaurant (☎ 2809 4426, 303 Shek O Village) Meals from HK$120. This hybrid is hardly authentic in either category, but the portions are generous, the staff convivial, the Tsingtao beers keep a-comin'.

Stanley (Map 9)

The Boathouse (☎ 2813 4467, 86-88 Stanley Main St) Pasta starters HK$88-99, mains HK$88-125. This powder-blue eatery facing the water is one of the most attractive restaurants in Stanley. A table on the roof garden is something to covet. Salads, bruschetta and Mediterranean-inspired mains make up the bulk of the Boathouse's fleet.

Chilli N Spice (☎ 2899 0147, Shop 101, Murray House, Stanley Plaza) Noodle dishes HK$35-42, mains HK$60-130. A branch of the ever-growing pan-Asian chain has found its way into Hong Kong's oldest (and now reconstructed) colonial building. Expect no surprises, but the venue and views are great.

The Curry Pot (☎ 2899 0811, 6th floor, 90B Stanley Main St) Mains HK$75-148. It's a rather odd place to eat Indian food, but the surrounds are terribly upmarket and the views to die for.

El Cid (☎ 2899 0858, Shop 102, Murray House, Stanley Plaza) Tapas HK$30-65. El Cid does justice to Spanish classics such as paella and has an excellent assortment of tapas.

Lucy's (☎ 2813 9055, 64 Stanley Main St) Starters HK$60-80, mains HK$140-175. This easy-going, cool oasis within the hustle and bustle of the market doesn't overwhelm with choice, but with quality food.

Pepperoni's (☎ 2813 8605, 64 Stanley Main St) Small pizzas HK$55-65, salads HK$45-55. This branch of a pizzeria chain is right in the heart of the market area. While not as famous (or frequented) as its cousin in Sai Kung, this place has decent pizzas.

Stanley's French Restaurant (☎ 2813 8873, 2813 8615, 1st & 2nd floors, Oriental Bldg, 90B Stanley Main St) Mains HK$160-170. This place, with its seaside setting, attentive staff and, above all, finely prepared dishes, will more than justify the trip out to Stanley. Don't expect French food though; that's just the name.

Stanley's Italian Restaurant (☎ 2813 7313, 92B Stanley Main St) Meals from HK$250. Next door you get pizza, pasta, osso bucco and a ground-level view of the sea.

Stanley's Oriental Restaurant (☎ 2813 9988, *Ground & 4th floors, Oriental Bldg, 90B Stanley Main St*) Meals about HK$180. Chinese, Thai and a variety of other pan-Asian dishes are available in the same building as Stanley's French but on upper and lower floors.

Wellcome Supermarket (*80 Stanley Village Rd*) This branch of the supermarket chain is convenient for beach supplies, food and drink.

Repulse Bay

The Verandah (☎ 2812 2722, *1st floor, The Repulse Bay, 109 Repulse Bay Rd*) Starters HK$142-192, mains HK$250-280. This pricey restaurant, in the building that replaced the splendid colonial Repulse Bay hotel in 1989, is well respected for its attention to detail, which seems to be on service, decor and (draw a notch or two) food in that order. It has stunning views of Repulse Bay. There's afternoon tea (HK$128) from 3pm to 5.30pm.

The Palm Court Cafe (☎ 2812 2903, *Shop 6110, The Repulse Bay, 109 Repulse Bay Rd*) Sandwiches HK$26-32. This little cousin of the Verandah in the courtyard below is a good place to buy makings for a picnic on the beach.

Wellcome Supermarket (*Shop 6123, The Repulse Bay, 109 Repulse Bay Rd*) Open 8am-10pm daily. This large supermarket can supply you with all your picnic needs.

Aberdeen (Map 8)

Aberdeen Ruby Chinese Restaurant (☎ 2518 8398, *Shop 2, 1st floor, Aberdeen Centre, Nam Ning St*) Meals from HK$100. This cavernous restaurant is *the* place for dim sum in Aberdeen, judging from the hordes of hopefuls waiting for tables.

Lo Yu Vietnam Restaurant (☎ 2814 8460, *Shop C, Ground floor, Kong Kai Bldg, 184-188 Aberdeen Main St*) Dishes HK$30-55. A lot of Vietnamese boat people who made their way to Hong Kong in the late 1970s never made it past the original 'Fragrant Harbour', which is Aberdeen's name in Cantonese. Expect authentic and very cheap dishes.

Floating Restaurants There are two floating restaurants moored in Aberdeen Harbour specialising in seafood. The food gets bad press and these outfits are not really recommended except as a spectacle and a fun night out. There's free transport for diners from the pier on Aberdeen Promenade; see the Aberdeen section for details.

Jumbo Floating Restaurant (☎ 2553 9111, 2873 7111, *Shum Wan Pier Drive, Wong Chuk Hang*) Meals HK$150-250, dim sum HK$30-80 7.30am-5pm daily. This is the better of the two floating restaurants.

Tai Pak Floating Restaurant (☎ 2553 9111, 2873 7111, *Shum Wan Pier Drive, Wong Chuk Hang*) Meals HK$150-250. This recently renovated palace on the surf has no dim sum but plenty of seafood.

ENTERTAINMENT

For information about evenings out of a more highbrow calibre – classical music concerts, theatre, opera and the like as well as where to find out about them – see Entertainment in the Hong Kong Facts for the Visitor chapter.

Central, Soho, Mid-Levels & Sheung Wan

Much of Central's nightlife revolves around Lan Kwai Fong, a narrow alleyway that doglegs south and then west from D'Aguilar St. In the not-so-distant past it was an area of squalid tenements and rubbish, but it has since been scrubbed, face-lifted and closed to traffic.

In recent years 'the Fong' has been given a run for its money (of which it takes in loads) by the upstart Soho area, but that's more of a restaurant scene and Lan Kwai Fong still rules among late-night revellers and club goers.

Lan Kwai Fong's clientele tends to be young, hip and well-to-do, with designer mobile phones stuck to their ears, trendy gear on their backs and flash jewellery on their digits. Be warned that it is an extremely expensive area in which to party, with a beer costing anywhere up from HK$50 except during the cheesy two- or three-hour happy hours available at most places, when the prices 'drop' to HK$30 or so.

Lan Kwai Fong made world news on New Year's Eve in 1992 when disaster occurred. The street was so mobbed with drunken revellers that when would-be partygoers tried to push southward from D'Aguilar St, people began to fall over and some 21 people were crushed or trampled to death, with many others injured. Since then, the authorities have instituted 'crowd control', with limits to the customers allowed inside each establishment, and sidewalk cafes banned.

Pubs & Bars A sparkly white chill-out bar with a gleaming, trendy mostly Chinese crowd is *Antidote* (Map 5) (☎ 2526 6559, 15-19 Hollywood Rd, Central) Entered from Ezra's Lane off Cochrane St, Antidote is lazy during the week, loud and dancy on weekends. Snacks are available.

Captain's Bar (☎ 2522 0111, Ground floor, Mandarin Oriental Hotel, 5 Connaught Rd Central) **Map 4** This is a clubby, suited place which serves ice-cold draught beer in chilled silver mugs. This is a good place to talk business, at least until the covers band strikes up at 9pm. It's a bit of a pulling zone for women and men of a certain age.

Club 64 (☎ 2523 2801, 12 Wing Wah Lane, Central) **Map 5** This bucks the trend toward pretentious bars in the Lan Kwai Fong area. It's a laid-back sort of place with a conscience *and* a memory: it recalls 4 June 1989, the date of the Tiananmen Square massacre in Beijing. It's still one of the best bars in town for nonposeurs, angry young people and those who want simple, unfussy fun. From 2.30pm to 9pm, Club 64 also has one of Hong Kong's better happy hours, with pints of draught beer for HK$24 and bottles for HK$21.

Club 1911 (☎ 2810 6681, 27 Staunton St, Soho) **Map 5** This is a refined place with Art Nouveau details and some colonial nostalgia. Happy hour is from 5pm to 9pm.

La Dolce Vita (☎ 2186 1888, Cosmos Bldg, 9-11 Lan Kwai Fong, Central) **Map 5** Let's hope this place with the heart-shaped bar is not as 'sweet' as 'life' gets, otherwise we're all going to have to get a new one. It's where the gorgeous young things go to watch each other and preen themselves. Go there to check the latest in Hong Kong fashions but not to drink outside happy hour (from 3pm to 7pm) or you'll blow the airfare.

Club Feather Boa (☎ 2857 2586, 38 Staunton St, Soho, Central) **Map 5** The scenario at this plush lounge hidden behind gold drapes: 'trashy princess meets debauched gentleman for a cocktail but ends up drinking bottled beer from a chunky stemmed glass'. Part lounge, part bordello – part those curtains.

Dublin Jack (☎ 2543 0081, 37-43 Cochrane St, Central) **Map 5** This Irish pub is almost the real thing and a very popular after-hours watering hole for expats. Happy hour is from noon to 8pm.

Globe (☎ 2543 1941, 39 Hollywood Rd, Central) **Map 5** This unpretentious and tiny place gets packed out by expats after work. Happy hour is staggered: 5pm to 7pm, 9pm to 10pm and midnight to 1am.

Godown (☎ 2523 8893, Lower ground floor, Citibank Plaza, 3 Garden Rd, Central) **Map 4** What used to be the daggiest bar in Central is now an all-day bar and restaurant in sparkly new premises.

Mad Dogs (☎ 2810 1000, Century Square, 1 D'Aguilar St, Central) **Map 5** The first truly authentic British pub to hit Hong Kong is still going strong almost two decades on but in yet another location. There's a cheap lunch buffet (HK$80), a carvery at Sunday lunch (HK$95) and live music three or four nights a week. Happy hour is from opening till 10pm.

Milk Bar (☎ 2869 0922, Commercial Bldg, 17-22 Lan Kwai Kong, Central) **Map 5** This boozer with a terrace and a long bar is a low-key option in the heart of the Fong.

Oscar's (☎ 2804 6561, Ground floor, 2 Lan Kwai Fong, Central) **Map 5** This high-fashion watering hole (and restaurant) is where you can play 'spot the model'.

Petticoat Lane (☎ 2973 0642, 2 Tun Wo Lane, Central) **Map 5** This salon is small, subdued and much more suited to chatting than bopping.

Phi-B (☎ 2869 4469, Basement, Harilela House, 79 Wyndham St, Central; enter from Pottinger St) **Map 5** You can either kick off the night or bring the pace down at this trendy orange and turquoise bar. When the DJ pumps it up, the crowd spills onto the front steps for stargazing and air-gulping. Happy hour is from 5pm to 9pm.

Post 97 (☎ 2186 1817, 1st floor, Cosmos Bldg, 9-11 Lan Kwai Fong, Central) **Map 5** Open 9.30am-1am Sun-Thur, 9.30am-3am Fri & Sat. During the daytime this comfortable spot above the Fong is essentially a restaurant (breakfast HK$49, buffet lunch/dinner HK$125/200) and coffee shop. At night it turns into a popular bar and gets packed very quickly.

Visage Free (☎ 2546 9780, Amber Lodge, 21-25 Hollywood Rd, Central) **Map 5** Entered from Cochrane St, this is a cheerful almost-Soho bar, which defies its dungeon setting. It's less trendy than most bars around here, maintaining a low key feel.

Yelt's Inn (☎ 2524 7790, 42 D'Aguilar St, Central) **Map 5** Rather passé, no? Who was Yeltsin? This Russian-themed place has a bubbly party atmosphere and extremely loud music, but vodka seems to have followed Boris into the wilderness.

Wine Bars If you've had enough of headache-inducing San Mig beer and stale popcorn, there are some fine wine bars that offer a bit more comfort.

Uncle Eric's Vintage Wine Bar (☎ 2586 1421, 19 On Lan St, Central) **Map 4** This is a minute but intimate spot for a quiet chat and a glass of wine.

Staunton's Wine Bar & Cafe (☎ 2973 6611, 10-12 Staunton St, Soho) **Map 5** Staunton's is swish, cool and on the ball with decent wines, a central escalator-watching scene and a lovely terrace upstairs. Happy hour is from 6pm to 9pm.

The Wine Room (☎ 2525 5111, Furama Hotel, 1 Connaught Rd Central) **Map 4** This place has made a name for itself with its quality wines though the selection is rather small.

Discos & Clubs As in any world-class city, the club scene in Hong Kong changes with the speed of summer lightning so it would be in your interest to flip through any of the publications under Listings in the Entertainment section of the Hong Kong Facts for the Visitor chapter.

bl.ush (☎ 2522 6428, Shop D & E, Felicity Bldg, 54-58 Hollywood Rd, Central) **Map 5** This hot new club is in spitting distance from Lan Kwai Fong and Soho.

C Club (☎ 2530 3695, Basement, California Tower, 30-32 D'Aguilar St, Central) This is a new chilled place managed by young 'uns that promises to still be hotter than most on the Fong.

California (☎ 2521 1345, Ground floor, California Tower, 30-32 D'Aguilar St, Central) This place is selective and pretentious, but still packs in the crowds when the dining tables are cleared off the dance floor. Although there's no cover charge, you'll be stung viciously on the beer. No shorts.

CE Top (☎ 2544 3584, 2544 3584, 3rd & 9th floors, 37-43 Cochrane St, Central) **Map 5** This rooftop club, entered from Gage St, is a stayer in Hong Kong's flighty club scene. Different nights on different levels feature a mix of house, trance, garage, soul and drum 'n' bass. Club Elements on Friday night (3rd floor) gets into hard house and breakbeats from 5am. Some nights have a strong gay leaning.

Club 1997 (☎ 2186 1819, Ground floor, Cosmos Bldg, 9-11 Lan Kwai Fong, Central) **Map 5** Entry HK$50-150. This shmoozery has a selectively enforced 'members only' policy to turn away the badly dressed; make an effort, mate. Arrive before 11pm and you'll pay just HK$97 to get in (if you can, that is).

Drop (☎ 2543 8856, On Lok Mansion, 39-43, Hollywood Rd, Central) **Map 5** Swanky, late-night venue of the 'too trendy for nerds' set.

The Green Parrot (☎ 2537 8083, Basement, 40 D'Aguilar St, Central) **Map 5** This loud and boisterous basement pub becomes a dancing venue for teenyboppers after 9pm from Monday to Saturday.

Insomnia (☎ 2525 0957, Lower ground floor, Ho Lee Commercial Bldg, 38-44 D'Aguilar St, Central) **Map 5** Open 8am-6am Mon-Sat, 2pm-5am Sun. This is the place to come if (and when) you can't sleep.

They do food, too, such as all-day breakfast (HK$75), fish and chips (HK$80) and sandwiches and burgers (HK$50-55).

Queen's Bar & Disco (☎ *2522 7773, 1st floor, Theatre Lane, Central*) **Map 4** Bar by day and pulsating Canto-disco by night. The generous happy hour goes from 5pm to 11pm.

Red Rock (☎ *2868 3884, Lower ground floor, 57-59 Wyndham St, Central*) **Map 5** Open 11.30pm-2am Mon-Thur, 11.30pm-5am Fri & Sat. This attractive establishment backing onto the walkway above Lan Kwai Fong is a very successful chameleon: a decent restaurant at lunch and dinner (mains HK$88-238) and popular dance venue by night (and morning).

Gay & Lesbian Venues Along with the mostly gay and lesbian clubs and bars listed here, *CE Top* **(Map 5)** (☎ *2544 3584, 3rd & 9th floors, 37-43 Cochrane St, Central*), entered from Gage St, has a strong gay following on certain nights while *Club 1997* **(Map 5)** (☎ *2186 1819, Ground floor, Cosmos Bldg, 9-11 Lan Kwai Fong, Central*) has a gay happy hour from 6pm to 10pm, with half-price drinks and shows.

Home (☎ *2545 0023, 2nd floor, 23 Hollywood Rd, Central*) **Map 5** Entry $100 Sat & Sun. Open 7pm-3am Mon-Fri, 10pm-6am Sat. A meet 'n' greet for the beautiful people early on, this place turns into a bump 'n' grind later in the evening.

Propaganda (☎ *2868 1316, Ground floor, 1 Hollywood Rd, Central*) **Map 5** Entry free Mon-Wed, HK$80 after 10.30pm Thur, HK$70/140 before/after 10.30pm Fri, HK$150/230 before/after 10.30pm Sat. Open 9pm-2.30am Mon-Thur, 9pm-4am Fri & Sat. This unbelievably expensive place, with attitude in size XXXL is where everyone gay ends up at some point on a weekend night. It's entered from Ezra's Lane, which runs between Pottinger and Cochrane Sts. There's a large dance floor, a long undulating bar and plenty of mirrors so punters can talent-spot themselves.

Rice Bar (☎ *2851 4800, 33 Jervois St, Sheung Wan*) **Map 4** Open noon-2am. This small and vibey bar, on the corner of Mercer St, with a lounge area is a more mature (not necessarily in age) place than the Hollywood Rd area bars. There's a bit of dancing as it gets later.

Works (☎ *2868 6102, 1st floor, 30-32 Wyndham St, Central*) **Map 5** Open 7pm-2am Tues-Sun. This club is the midway point on a night out for most and sees some heavy cruising.

Zip (☎ *2523 3595, 2 Glenealy Rd, Central*) **Map 4** Open 6pm-2am. This is where most boyz out on the town start the evening before moving on to Works and Propaganda. It's a small place and can get very crowded at the weekend.

Rock & Pop A tiny place which manages to squeeze entire bands onto its minuscule upstairs stage at the weekend is *F-Stop* **(Map 5)** (☎ *2868 9607, 14 Lan Kwai Fong, Central*), open 4pm to 2am Sunday to Thursday, 4pm to 4am Friday and Saturday. You'll know the place from its huge neon guitar above the entrance outside.

GIG (☎ *2521 2203, Ground floor, Commercial Bldg, 17-22 Lan Kwai Fong, Central*) **Map 5** This new kid on the block below Milk Bar looks like going somewhere. Happy hour is from 5pm to 9pm weekdays.

Nokia Gallery (☎ *2521 7251, Fringe Club, 2 Lower Albert Rd, Lan Kwai Fong*) **Map 5** Up on the border of the Lan Kwai Fong quadrant, this avant-garde pub/club is the venue for a whole medley of trendy sounds from rock and pop to jazz and world music. There's live music from 10.30pm on Friday and Saturday nights.

Jazz & Blues More of a supper club (starters HK$50-95, mains HK$105-170, set lunch HK$88) with jazz rather than a serious jazz club with supper is *Brown* **(Map 4)** (☎ *2971 0012, 30-32 Robinson Rd, Mid-Levels*). Jazz is performed from 10pm Wednesday to Sunday, with jam sessions 10pm Sunday. Entry is HK$100.

The Jazz & Blues Club (☎ *2845 8477, 2nd floor, California Entertainment Bldg, 34-36 D'Aguilar St, Central*) **Map 5** Local acts HK$60-100, overseas bands HK$300.

This venue has long been *the* oasis where true jazz aficionados have supped, and many jazz greats have graced its small stage. The club also books blues, rock, folk and other musical acts, both local and foreign. Members pay half-price entry.

Folk A rowdy watering hole where some of the patrons occasionally get up on stage to demonstrate their talent (or lack of it) is *Hardy's Folk Club* (**Map 5**) (☎ 2522 4448, *35 D'Aguilar St*). There are folk acts scheduled occasionally. Its sister-pub, *Hardy's II* (**Map 5**) (☎ 2524 0042, *Upper ground floor, Wilson House, 19-27 Wyndham St, Central*) is more of a boozer with canned music.

Cinemas One of the only movie houses in Central geared towards English language films is *Queen's Theatre* (**Map 4**) (☎ 2522 7036, *Luk Hoi Tung Bldg, 31 Queen's Rd Central*) The Queen, entered from Theatre Lane, is a great old barn of a place and a very atmospheric spot to catch a film.

Theatre Two theatres at Hong Kong's trendiest louche spot are *Star Alliance Theatre* and *Lycos Asia Theatre* (**Map 5**) (☎ 2521 7251, *Ground & 1st floors, Fringe Club, 2 Lower Albert Rd, Lan Kwai Fong*) They host eclectic local and international performances (HK$50-200) in both Cantonese and English.

Wan Chai & Admiralty

Wan Chai has been sleaze territory ever since it was first port of call for American sailors and GIs on R&R from the battlefields of Vietnam. Much of the western part of the district has cleaned up its act in recent years, but hostess bars still line Lockhart Rd and there's lots of zippy club action and late-night cover band venues.

Pubs & Bars Most of the best bars and pubs line the western ends of Jaffe and Lockhart roads. As in Lan Kwai Fong, on weekend nights this area is crawling with partygoers.

Champagne Bar (☎ 2588 1234, *Grand Hyatt Hotel, 1 Harbour Rd, Wan Chai*

North) **Map 6** The Art Deco surrounds, the baby grand and that vintage glass of bubbly (that could cost up to HK$400) here are sure to impress.

Delaney's (☎ 2804 2880, *2nd floor, One Capital Place, 18 Luard Rd*) **Map 6** Delaney's is an incongruously located – yet immensely popular – Irish pub. The food is good too; the kitchen goes through 400kg of potatoes a week.

Devil's Advocate (☎ 2865 7271, *48-50 Lockhart Rd*) **Map 6** This pleasant newcomer has been luring away trade from other pubs in the area, with its front wall giving onto the pavement and charming Filipino staff.

Horse & Groom (☎ 2519 7001, *161 Lockhart Rd*) **Map 6** What used to be called the 'House of Doom' and a favourite watering hole of hacks and has-beens has gone local and is as much a popular lunch venue as a drinking spot. Happy hour is from 6pm till 10pm.

Horse & Carriage (☎ 2529 6917, *Hing Bong Mansion, 113-121 Lockhart Rd*) **Map 6** The same can be said for the Groom's sister-pub just down the road, where a set lunch is a mere HK$38.

LA Café (☎ 2526 6863, *Shop 2, Lippo Centre, 89 Queensway, Admiralty*) **Map 4** Entry HK$50, The LA Cafe has a large and loyal following of late-night revellers. Happy hour is from 3pm to 9pm. On weekends, Club Lollipop takes over the dance floor with '70s and '80s hits from 9pm to 2am.

Old China Hand (☎ 2865 4378, *104 Lockhart Rd*) **Map 6** This place has a generous happy hour from noon till 10am, Internet access and set lunches for HK$69.

Royal Arms (☎ 2529 9911, *1st floor, Henan Commercial Bldg, 90 Jaffe Rd*) **Map 6** This pub certainly doesn't feel English, but it's good enough for a relatively cheap beer and a plate of greasy chips.

Discos & Clubs Hong Kong's main club galaxy revolves around Wan Chai. With a well-established reputation for all-night marathon dancing with liquid and chemical assistance, this is where the late-night crowd settles in for the wee hours.

Big Apple (☎ 2529 3461, 20 Luard Rd, Wan Chai) **Map 6** Entry HK$120 Mon-Thur, HK$150 Fri & Sat (including one drink). The Big Apple is frequently nominated as one of Hong Kong's raunchiest night spots. It's a hang-out for a young immigrant crowd hell bent on having a good time.

Carnegie's (☎ 2866 6289, 55 Lockhart Rd) **Map 6** Entry HK$50 Fri & Sat. This place keeps a lot of rock memorabilia, which makes it all seem a bit Hard Rock Cafe-ish. From 9pm on Friday and Saturday, however, the place fills up with revellers. Bands are booked to play on Wednesday, Friday, Saturday and Sunday. There's free vodka from 10pm to 11pm on Tuesday and champagne for women from 9pm till late on Wednesday.

Club ing (☎ 2824 0523, 4th floor, Renaissance Harbour View Hotel, 1 Harbour Rd, Wan Chai) **Map 6** Entry HK$160 (including one drink). There is free entry and drinks for women on Thursday. Entered from the Renaissance Harbour View Hotel, this newly fitted out club is popular with a young Cantonese crowd. Dress smartly (no sandals, sneakers, tank tops).

Dusk till Dawn (☎ 2528, 76-84 Jaffe Rd) **Map 6** There's live music nightly from 10pm at this extremely popular dance club, with an emphasis on beats and vibes so irresistible that you'll get your booty shaking for sureeee.

JJ's (☎ 2588 1234 ext 7323, Grand Hyatt Hotel, 1 Harbour Rd, Wan Chai) **Map 6** Open 5.30pm-2am Mon-Thur, 5.30pm-3am Fri, 6pm-4am Sat. Entry HK$100 Mon-Thur, HK$200 Fri & Sat. Not as suity as you might think, JJ's is the disco for Hong Kong's divine dahlings, with DJs spinning funky house from 10pm nightly except Sunday. Dress up – no shorts, no sandals, no jogging clothes.

Joe Bananas (☎ 2529 1811, 23 Luard Rd) **Map 6** Entry HK$100 after midnight Sun-Thur, after 9pm Fri & Sat. Signs advertise wet T-shirt and 'Full Monty' competitions – that's the tone. If you go with friends, you can have some unreconstructed fun; unaccompanied females should expect

a good sampler of really bad pick-up lines. The bar has a daily happy hour from 11.30am to 10pm, two-for-one cocktails on Tuesday and free drinks for women after 6pm on Wednesday.

Neptune Disco II (☎ 2865 2238, 98-10 Jaffe Rd, Wan Chai) **Map 6** Entry HK$150 men (including one drink), HK$50 women. Open until around 7am. This place lacks the seedy character of its erstwhile progenitor but is still the place people frequent to dance. So if you're not bopping, you shouldn't be here. The place hops at the Sunday afternoon tea dance.

New Makati (☎ 2527 8188, 1st floor, 100 Lockhart Rd) **Map 6** Entry HK$100/50 men/women (including one drink). Open till 5am daily. It has to be said: you can't go lower than this sleazy pick-up joint, complete with dimly lit booths and Filipino amahs who just wanna have fun.

Tango Martini (☎ 2147 3203, 2nd floor, Empire Land Commercial Centre, 81-85 Lockhart Rd, Wan Chai) **Map 6** This groovy animal-print place is puuurfect for a late-nighter in Wan Chai.

Nightclubs If your idea of a good time is paying handfuls of 'gold ones' (HK$1000 notes) to a topless waitress for a brainless conversation, you should either a) have *your* head examined, or b) visit one of the many hostess bars in Wan Chai.

New Tonnochy Nightclub (☎ 2511 1383, 1-5 Tonnochy Rd) **Map 6** This is the classiest, trashiest of the lot, dripping with Sino-baroque furnishings and features.

Rock & Folk A venue that derives its name from what everyone calls this district is *The Wanch* (☎ 2861 1621, 54 Jaffe Rd). It has live music (mostly rock and folk) seven nights a week from 9pm (10pm on Friday and Saturday), with the occasional solo guitarist thrown in. Jam night is at 10pm on the first Wednesday of each month. The Wanch has particularly good happy hours, which run from 11am to 6pm and 7pm to 10pm. And what happens between 6pm and 7pm? It's 'madness hour', when drinks are cheaper still.

Cinemas Certain cultural organisations show foreign films from time to time, including the *Alliance Française* (Map 6) (☎ 2527 7825, 2nd floor, 123 Hennessy Rd, Wan Chai) and the *Goethe Institut* (Map 6) (☎ 2802 0088), 14th floor, Hong Kong Arts Centre, 2 Harbour Rd, Wan Chai).

For both studio and mainstream films, this area can boast two of the best and most comfortable cinemas in the territory.

Cine-Art House (☎ 2827 4820, Sun Hung Kai Centre, 30 Harbour Rd, Wan Chai) Map 6 The Cine-Art is an alternative cinema specialising in English-language flicks.

Lim Por Yen Theatre (☎ 2582 0232, bookings ☎ 2582 0200, Hong Kong Arts Centre, 2 Harbour Rd, Wan Chai) Map 6 This theatre is the place for classics, revivals, alternative screenings and travelling film festivals. The annual European Film Festival is usually held in November.

UA Pacific Place (☎ 2869 0322, L1, Pacific Place, 88 Queensway, Admiralty) Map 4 This is Hong Kong's plushest cinema and has the best sound system.

Comedy This cabaret venue *Charlie Luciano's* (Map 6) (☎ 2529 6888, 1st floor, 18 Fenwick St, Wan Chai) has a penchant for comedy, both home-grown and imported. Entry is HK$120 to HK$150, and shows start around 10.30pm. If you don't want dinner and a show, you can stand at the bar and giggle from there. The artists are usually English, American or Canadian; the laughs are pretty mainstream.

Punchline Comedy Club (☎ 2317 6666, 2827 7777, 2nd floor, Sun Hung Kai Centre, 30 Harbour Rd, Wan Chai) Map 6 Entry $200-300. The Viceroy, a 'hot venue' with 'cool cuisine' – which is Indian, so go figure – hosts this alternative comedy club.

Causeway Bay

Compared with Wan Chai and the Lan Kwai Fong area of Central, Causeway Bay is relatively tame after dark. Like Soho, it's more a place to have a meal than party. Still, there are a few pubs and bars that do a thriving business.

Pubs & Bars Seeping blue lights and white chairs that turn a bar into an instant zone is *Area* (Map 6) (☎ 2575 6300, 21 Sharp St East) Not large, but smooth and snappy with inventive drinks, slow electronica and a zipless crowd sipping cocktails and chewing their words.

King's Arms (☎ 2895 6557, Ground floor, Sunning Plaza, 9-11 Sunning Rd) Map 6 Outside tables far enough away from the rat race make this place attractive.

Royal's Pub (☎ 2832 7879, 21 Cannon St) Map 6 In case you missed the Tudor-style pubs in Wan Chai, this punctuation-challenged and gloomy place will oblige. It's mainly the domain of Hong Kong Chinese these days, but foreigners are made to feel more than welcome.

Oscar's (☎ 2861 1511, Shop P309-311, level 3, World Trade Centre, 280 Gloucester Rd) Map 6 This branch of the trendy Lan Kwai Fong drinkery packs out with suits looking at models and models glaring at thinner models after work on weekdays.

Brecht's Circle (☎ 2576 4785, 123 Leighton Rd) Map 6 Open till 2am Sun-Thur, 4am Fri & Sat. Brecht's is very small and fairly unusual. It's an arty kind of place given more to intimate, cerebral conversation than serious raging.

Cyrano's (☎ 2820 8591, 56th floor, Island Shangri-La Hotel) Map 4 Open 6pm-2am. If you need to get high before you drink, take the lift up to this bar. The bartenders are skilled; good views and live jazz (from 9pm) are a feature here.

Dickens Bar (☎ 2837 6782, Basement, Excelsior Hotel, 281 Gloucester Rd) Map 6 This evergreen place has for a long time been a popular place with expats and Hong Kong Chinese. There's a great buffet lunch for HK$98 and lots of big-screen sports.

Shakespeare Pub (☎ 2833 0029, 30 Cannon St) Map 6 Same old, same old, this is another one of those mock-Tudor pubs that smell of old fat and stale beer and attract young Hong Kong Chinese who like to play drinking games.

Discos & Clubs You won't find anything like the club scene in Causeway Bay that you will in Wan Chai or the Lan Kwai Fong area, but there are a few places to consider.

Mine (☎ 2267 8822, Shop J, Lockhart House, 441 Lockhart Rd, Causeway Bay) **Map 6** Entry HK$50-180. This cavernous place on the ground floor and in the basement just over the 'border' (Canal Rd) from Wan Chai will do for most. It's popular with local over-21s, who make full use of its seven karaoke rooms.

Stix (☎ 2839 3397, 310 Gloucester Rd) **Map 6** This hell-for-leather themed place is flavour of the month at the moment. It serves American-style diner food too.

Cinemas Causeway Bay is packed with cinemas but, with few exceptions, most of them show bogus Hollywood blockbusters and Hong Kong and mainland films.

JP Cinema (☎ 2881 5005, JP Plaza, 22-36 Paterson St) **Map 6** Be prepared for huge crowds at the weekend at this place, at the corner of Great George St.

UA Times Square (☎ 2506 2822, Ground floor, Times Square, 1 Matheson St) **Map 6** This comfortable cineplex is just above the Causeway Bay MTR station.

Happy Valley
Pink Mao Mao (☎ 2961 3350, 1 Wang Tak St) This place, which probably has more to do with the Pink Panther (*mao* is 'cat' in Chinese) than a gay Zedong, has live music and attracts a rather young chuppie/expat mix.

North Point
Sunbeam Theatre (☎ 2563 2959, Kiu Fai Bldg, 423 King's Rd) Entry HK$$50-300. Cantonese opera can be seen here throughout the year, not the easiest type of event to attend in Hong Kong these days. Performances generally run for about a week, and are usually held in the evening (sometimes there are matinees). The theatre is right above the North Point MTR station, on the north side of King's Rd, near the intersection with Shu Kuk St.

Quarry Bay
East End Brewery (☎ 2811 1907, 23-27 Tong Chong St) This place out in Quarry Bay is a beer-lovers' must. You can choose from almost 30 beers and lagers from around the world, including a couple of local microbrews.

Chai Wan
Pink (☎ 2147 7737, 2607 8688, Ground floor, 8 Commercial Tower, 8 Sun Yip St) You may think it beyond or even beneath you to travel all the way to Chai Wan for a club, but the über crowd doesn't. This place packs and raves.

Stanley (Map 9)
Stanley boasts a fair few pubs that get going in the late afternoon and continue until the wee hours.

Beaches (☎ 2813 7313, 92B Stanley Main St) This place spills out onto the sidewalk.

Lord Stanley's Bar & Bistro (☎ 2813 9130, 92A Stanley Main St) Lord Stanley's offers loud music, big TV sports and decent food by the waterfront and is always packed.

Smugglers' Inn (☎ 2813 8852, 90A Main St) Snacks HK$20-40. This good-value place is arguably the most popular of the three drinking venues.

SHOPPING
Central and Causeway Bay are the main shopping districts on Hong Kong Island, with Wan Chai lagging pretty far behind.

The most glitzy of Hong Kong's shopping malls is Pacific Place, 88 Queensway, opposite the Admiralty MTR station. The Landmark in Central has designer boutiques, shops selling crystal and so on. The World Trade Centre and Times Square in Causeway Bay are places where you'll find everything under one roof. Many local people shop at Cityplaza and the adjacent Kornhill Plaza in Quarry Bay, near Tai Koo MTR station. Prices are slightly lower in areas not frequented by tourists.

Antiques & Curios
Hollywood Rd is a prime location if you are interested in shopping for antiques. As you proceed westward the shops drop notch

after notch in quality and price. It's easy to get lost in some of these dusty emporiums, but be cautious – tread carefully through this minefield of fakes and forgeries.

Arch Angel Antiques (☎ 2851 6828, 53-55 Hollywood Rd, Central) **Map 5** This place, founded on the auspicious day of 8 August 1988 (8/8/88; see Superstitions under Society & Conduct in the Facts about Hong Kong chapter), has a good selection of affordable antiques and curios.

Chine Gallery (☎ 2543 0023, 42A Hollywood Rd, Central) **Map 5** The carefully restored furniture – the lacquered cabinets are lovely – at this shop come from all over China and hand-knotted rugs are sourced from remote regions like Xinjiang, Ningxia, Gansu and Inner Mongolia.

Honeychurch Antiques (☎ 2543 2433, 29 Hollywood Rd, Central) **Map 5** This fine shop, run by a British couple for nigh on four decades, specialises in antique Chinese furniture, jewellery and old English silver.

Karin Weber Antiques (☎ 2544 5004, 32A Staunton St, Soho) **Map 5** Karin Weber has an enjoyable mix of Chinese country antiques and contemporary Asian artworks.

Mountain Folkcraft (☎ 2523 2817, 12 Wo On Lane, Central) **Map 5** This is one of the nicest shops in Central for folk craft, with bolts of batik and sarongs, clothing, wood carvings and lacquerware made by ethnic minorities in China and other Asian countries.

Wattis Fine Art (☎ 2524 5302, 2nd floor, 20 Hollywood Rd, Central) **Map 5** No-one owns more antique maps or has a better collection of them for sale than Jonathan Wattis entered from Old Bailey St.

Tibetan Gallery (☎ 2530 4863, 55 Wyndham St, Central) **Map 5** This shop has an impressive selection of Tibetan religious art and artefacts.

Zitan (☎ 2523 7584, Yu Yuet Lai Bldg, 43-55 Wyndham St, Central) **Map 5** If you're hunting for quality items, try this shop, which has a superb range of antique Chinese furniture.

Sotheby's (☎ 2524 8121, 5th floor, Standard Chartered Bank Bldg, 4-4A Des Voeux Rd Central) & *Christie's* (☎ 2521 5396, 28th floor, Alexandra House, 16-20 Chater Rd, Central) **Map 4** If you're in Hong Kong in April or November, take the opportunity to attend one of the big antique dealer auctions. The pre-auction previews are usually held at the Furama Hotel by Sotheby's and in the JW Marriott Hotel by Christie's. Both auction houses have regular sales in ceramics, jade, modern and jadeite jewellery, stamps, snuff bottles, works of art, traditional and contemporary Chinese paintings and calligraphic works.

Cameras & Photo Equipment

Stanley St, in Central, is one of the best spots in Hong Kong for buying photographic equipment, and competition is keen. Everything carries price tags, though some low-level bargaining might be possible.

Everbest Photo Supplies (☎ 2522 1985, 28B Stanley St, Central) **Map 5** This extremely reliable shop is where many of Hong Kong's pros go.

Photo Scientific (☎ 2525 0550, 6 Stanley St, Central) **Map 5** This is the favourite of Hong Kong's resident professional photographers. You might find equipment elsewhere for less, but Photo Scientific has a rock-solid reputation with labelled prices, no bargaining, no arguing and no cheating.

There are several places in Central that do very high-quality photo-processing.

Color Six (☎ 2526 0123, 18A Stanley St, Central) **Map 5** This has the best photoprocessing in town. Colour slides can be professionally processed in just three hours, and many special types of film unavailable elsewhere in Hong Kong are on sale here. Naturally prices aren't the lowest in town (developing costs are from HK$1.20 per exposure plus HK$14 per roll), but the quality is excellent.

Robert Lam Color (☎ 2869 8622, 43 Wellington St, Central) **Map 5** This photoprocessor for the pros charges about the same as Color Six, but offers nowhere near the same quality of service.

Carpets & Rugs

The bulk of Hong Kong Island's carpet and rug shops are clustered on Wyndham St in

Central, although there are some large retailers locted in Wan Chai and in Kowloon as well.

Al-Shahzadi Persian Carpet Gallery (☎ 2834 8396, 265 Queen's Rd East, Wan Chai) **Map 6** This shop has quality carpets from Afghanistan, Iran and Russia, but nothing Chinese.

Mir Oriental Carpets (☎ 2521 5641, 52 Wyndham St, Central) **Map 5** This is the largest stockist of fine rugs in Hong Kong, with thousands of carpets from around the world flying in and out of the shop.

Cigars

For some people (men and women alike), cigar smoking is an unparalleled delight.

Cigar Express Central (☎ 2110 9201, Upper ground floor, Cheung Fai Bldg, 45-47 Cochrane St, Central) **Map 5** This branch of a Hong Kong chain with five outlets sells everything from a HK$10 Piedra stogie to a hand-rolled Cuban Cohiba Pyramid for HK$320 a pop.

Clothing & Textiles

Jardine's Bazaar in Causeway Bay has low-cost garments, though it may take some hunting to find anything decent. There are several sample shops and places to pick up cheap jeans in Lee Garden Rd and in Li Yuen St, which runs between Queen's and Des Voeux roads in Central.

The eastern end of Lockhart Rd in Causeway Bay is a good place to look for footwear. It's also worth taking a stroll down Johnston Rd in Wan Chai, which has lots of mid-priced and budget clothing outlets.

One well-known upmarket area for clothes shopping is Fashion Walk (or Houston St) in Causeway Bay, with more than 30 boutiques and two dozen restaurants within a block of the intersection of Paterson and Kingston Sts.

Blanc de Chine (☎ 2524 7875, room 201, 2nd floor, Pedder Bldg, 12 Pedder St, Central) **Map 4** This sumptuous store specialises in traditional men's Chinese jackets, off the rack or made to measure. There's also a lovely selection of silk dresses for women.

Carpet Centre (☎ 2850 4993, Shop A, Lower ground floor, 29 Hollywood Rd, Central) **Map 5** No, you're not being asked to don a dhurry. What this place has is pashmina shawls, ranging in price from HK$350 to HK$880. It's entered from Cochrane St.

Fortune Tailor (☎ 2877 1677, 76 Queen's Rd Central) **Map 5** This tailor is very reasonably priced (three suits for HK$2000, five pairs of trousers for HK$1000) and central.

Garex Ison (☎ 2537 3326, 26 Wyndham St, Central) **Map 5** This local designer works with textures and layers to come up with stylish women's suits, tops and bottoms.

Miu Miu (☎ 2523 7833, Shop B24, The Landmark, 1 Pedder St, Central) **Map 4** Super-cute and creative threads for neo-adults are available here. The shoes are exceptionally stylish.

Shanghai Tang (☎ 2525 7333, Ground floor, Pedder Bldg, 12 Pedder St, Central) **Map 4** Started by flamboyant Hong Kong businessman David Tang, Shanghai Tang has sparked something of a fashion wave in Hong Kong with its updated versions of traditional yet almost neon-coloured Chinese garments. It also has accessories and delightful gift items.

Western Market (☎ 2815 3586, 323 Des Voeux Rd & New Market St, Sheung Wan) **Map 4** Open 10am-7pm daily. All the old textile vendors were driven out of the alleys linking Queen's and Des Voeux roads in Central in the early 1990s and moved to this renovated old market built in 1906. You'll find Chinese knick-knacks and chotchkies on the ground floor, piece goods on the 1st floor and a decent Chinese restaurant on the 2nd floor.

Computers

Most people buy computers in Kowloon, where there is a much greater choice and prices are lower. But Hong Kong Island does have one reasonable computer arcade – the 10th to 12th floors of Windsor House in Causeway Bay (open 11am to 9pm daily).

Computer Consultants (☎ 2576 3756, Shop 1150-1151, Windsor House, 311 Gloucester Rd, Causeway Bay) **Map 6** The computer your humble author is working on at this moment was bought at CC.

Department Stores
Hong Kong's department stores are not cheap, so if you're looking for bargains look elsewhere.

Lane Crawford (☎ 2524 7875, 70 Queen's Rd Central) **Map 5** This is Hong Kong's original Western-style department store with branches in Admiralty *(☎ 2118 3388, L1 & L2, Pacific Place, 88 Queensway)* and Causeway Bay *(☎ 2118 3638, Ground & 1st floors, Times Square, 1 Matheson St).*

Hong Kong Chinese department stores in Central include *Wing On* **(Map 4)** *(☎ 2852 1888, 211 Des Voeux Rd)* and *Sincere* **(Map 4)** *(☎ 2544 2688, 173 Des Voeux Rd).*

The few remaining Japanese department stores are concentrated around Causeway Bay. They include *Sogo* **(Map 6)** *(☎ 2833 8338, 555 Hennessy Rd),* with a huge supermarket open 10am to 11.30pm daily, and *Mitsukoshi* **(Map 6)** *(☎ 2576 5222, 500 Hennessy Rd).*

In Admiralty there's *Seibu* **(Map 4)** *(☎ 2971 3888, L1 & L2, Pacific Place, 88 Queensway).*

Chinese Emporiums These emporiums owned and run by mainland interests are a different kettle of fish, concentrating on Chinese arts and crafts, cheap clothing and the daily necessities.

Chinese Arts & Crafts (☎ 2523 3933, Shop 230, Pacific Place, 88 Queensway, Admiralty) **Map 4** Mainland-owned CAC is probably the best place to buy quality bric-a-brac and other Chinese chotchkies. Next to the China Resources Building there's also a huge Wan Chai branch **(Map 6)** *(☎ 2827 6667, Lower Block, Hong Kong Exhibition Centre, 26 Harbour Rd).*

CRC Department Store (☎ 2524 1051, Chiao Shang Bldg, 92 Queen's Rd Central) **Map 4** This huge Chinese emporium is cheaper than Chinese Arts & Crafts and can

supply you, along with Chinese souvenirs and other miscellany, with plastic buckets, padded jackets and herbal tonics. There's also a Causeway Bay branch **(Map 6)** *(☎ 2577 0222, 488 Hennessy Rd).*

Yue Hwa Chinese Products Emporium (☎ 2522 2333, 39 Queen's Rd Central) **Map 4** This is some people's favourite Chinese emporium.

Eyeglasses
Both frames and lenses can be cheaper (in some case, much cheaper) than what you pay at home.

Ocean Optical (☎ 2868 5670, Shop 9, Ground floor, Standard Chartered Bank Bldg, 4-4A Des Voeux Rd Central) **Map 4** We know of no better optician in Hong Kong.

Fine Art & Galleries
Galerie du Monde (☎ 2525 0529, Shop 328, Pacific Place, 88 Queensway, Admiralty) **Map 4** This long-established upmarket gallery shows mostly figurative work from relatively established mainland Chinese painters.

Galerie Martini (☎ 2526 9566, 99F Wellington St, Central) **Map 4** This small upstairs art nook shows international contemporary art. The exhibitions swing between introducing relatively established Western artists to Hong Kong and giving exposure to local artists on the rise.

Hanart T Z Gallery (☎ 2526 9019, 2nd floor, Henley Bldg, 5 Queen's Rd Central) **Map 4** Hanart is *la crème de la crème* of art galleries in Hong Kong and was instrumental in establishing the reputation of many of the painters and sculptors discussed in the special section Contemporary Art in the Facts about Hong Kong chapter.

Plum Blossoms (☎ 2521 2189, 17th floor, Coda Plaza, 51 Garden Rd, Central) **Map 4** The shop where Rudolf Nureyev used to buy his baubles is one of the most exquisite and well established in Hong Kong.

Schoeni Art Gallery (☎ 2542 3143, 27 Hollywood Rd, Central) **Map 5** This Swiss-owned gallery, which has been a feature on Hollywood Rd for over 20 years, specialises in modern mainland Chinese art as well as

Chinese antique furniture and South-East Asian ceramics. There's a nearby branch gallery (☎ 2869 8802, 21-31 Old Bailey St, Soho) with an even larger collection of modern fine art.

Flowers

Anglo-Chinese Florist (☎ 2845 4212, 23-25 D'Aguilar St, Central) **Map 5** Open 8am-11pm daily. If you've been invited to someone's home and wish to bring flowers as is *de rigueur* here, stop by Anglo-Chinese. Nobody does them better.

Food & Drink

Lock Cha Tea Shop (☎ 2805 1360, 290A Queen's Rd Central, Sheung Wan) **Map 4** This favourite shop, entered from Ladder St, sells Chinese teas of infinite variety as well as tea sets, wooden tea boxes and well-presented gift packs of various cuppas.

Minamoto Kitchoan (☎ 2577 5702, Shop B, Winway Bldg, 50 Wellington St, Central) **Map 5** This Japanese sweets shop goes to unbelievable bother to make sweets so intricate that eating them seems crude or cruel or both. Do it anyway and bite into a *tousenka*, a big pink peach the stone of which has been replaced by a baby green peach.

Red or White (☎ 2789 3136, 45-47/4B Cochrane St, Central) **Map 5** This hole-in-the-wall shop has an excellent (though pricey) wine selection with authoritative advice available from the French owner.

Watson's Wine Cellar (☎ 2147 3641, 36 Queen's Rd Central) **Map 4** You won't get a lot of advice at this wine emporium, entered from D'Aguilar St, but the choice is enormous. There are half a dozen outlets around the territory including a Causeway Bay branch (☎ 2895 6975, Basement, Windsor House, 311 Gloucester Rd).

Jewellery & Objets d'Art

Two major jewellery store chains, King Fook and Tse Sui Luen, guarantee to buy back any jewellery at the current wholesale price if you want or need to return it. Of course, be sure you get a certificate and bear in mind that you need to be in Hong Kong to take advantage of the plan.

King Fook (☎ 2822 8573, 30-32 Des Voeux Rd Central) **Map 4** King Fook tends to be more modern than Tse Sui Luen, with a large range of watches and upmarket fountain pens as well as jewellery.

Tse Sui Luen (☎ 2921 8800, Commercial House, 35 Queen's Rd Central) **Map 4** This is the most sparkling of Tse Sui Luen's dozen or so outlets, and is worth visiting for its sheer opulence or garishness or however you see it.

Liuligongfang (☎ 2973 0820, Shop 20-22, Central Bldg, 1-3 Pedder St, Central) **Map 4** Exquisite coloured glass objects, both practical (vases, candlestick holders, jewellery etc) and ornamental (figurines, crystal Buddhas, breathtaking sculptures) from a renowned Taiwanese glass sculptress are available here.

Magic Water Gallery (☎ 2506 3836, Shop 833, Times Square, 1 Matheson St, Causeway Bay) **Map 6** This wonderful shop selling what can only be described as water sculptures should open as a museum. Go in and they'll have to drag you out.

Music

HMV (☎ 2739 0268, 1st floor, Central Bldg, 1 Pedder St, Central) **Map 4** Open 10am-10pm daily. This Aladdin's cave not only has Hong Kong's largest choice of CDs, DVDs and cassettes, but a great range of music zines. There's also a Causeway Bay branch (☎ 2504 366, 1st floor, Windsor House, 311 Gloucester Rd).

Hong Kong Records (☎ 2845 7088, Shop 252, Pacific Place, 88 Queensway, Admiralty) **Map 4** This local outfit has a good selection of Cantonese and international sounds, including Chinese traditional music, jazz, classical and composer music.

Tower Records (☎ 2506 0811, Shop 731-732, Times Square, 1 Matheson St, Causeway Bay) **Map 6** This rather small branch of the American music retail giant should be your third choice when looking for CDs, DVDs, records and cassettes.

Pharmaceuticals

New Wing Hing Dispensary (☎ 2523 0980, 85 Queen's Rd Central) **Map 4** If you're looking for personal, informed service, eschew the McDonald's-style chains of drug stores like Watson's and Mannings and head for New Hing Wing, entered from Queen Victoria St.

Sporting Goods

Bunn's Diving Equipment *(☎ 2893 7899, 2nd floor, Yee Wo Mansions, 38-40 Yee Wo St, Causeway Bay)* **Map 6** Masks, snorkels, fins, regulators, tanks – Bunn's has them all in as many colours, shapes and sizes as you care to name.

Cobra International *(☎ 2544 2328, Shop 102, Vicwood Plaza, 199 Des Voeux Rd Central)* **Map 4** This a great shop, with hiking gear and accessories on offer.

Discovery Camping & Outdoor Equipment *(☎ 2891 0587, 1st floor, Fu Tat Commercial Bldg, 137 Wan Chai Rd, Wan Chai)* **Map 6** This small place has a good range of tents, sleeping bags and other camping gear.

Kung Fu Supplies *(☎ 2891 1912, flat 6A, 188-192 Johnston Rd, Wan Chai)* **Map 6** If you need to stock up on martial arts accessories or just want to thumb through a decent collection of books on the subject, visit this place.

Po Kee Fishing Tackle *(☎ 2544 1035, 6 Hillier St, Central)* **Map 4** These guys have got the market cornered – hook, line and sinker – on fishing supplies.

Quicksilver *(☎ 2836 6073, 1st & 2nd floors, 10 Pak Sha Rd, Causeway Bay)* **Map 6** This is the place to come for surfwear.

Sunmark Camping Equipment *(☎ 2893 8553, 1st floor, 124 Wan Chai Rd, Wan Chai)* **Map 6** Head here for hiking and camping gear and waterproof clothing of all sorts.

Wind 'n' Surf *(☎ 2366 9293, Shop A1, Lower ground floor, Wilson House, 19-27 Wyndham St, Central)* **Map 5** This is a choice spot for windsurfing equipment and supplies.

Zone-3 *(☎ 2723 6816, Flat E, 1st floor, Hoi Top Bldg, 19 Cannon St, Causeway Bay)* **Map 6** This is the place for extreme sports gear and apparel.

Kowloon

The name 'Kowloon' is thought to have originated when the last emperor of the Song dynasty passed through the area during his flight from the Mongols in the late 13th century. He is said to have counted eight peaks on the peninsula and commented that there must therefore be eight dragons there. Of course there are, he was assured by his retainers, and they emerge at dawn to frolic in the harbour. But the young emperor was reminded that since he himself was present, there were now nine dragons. Kowloon is thus derived from the Cantonese words *gáu*, meaning 'nine', and *long*, the word for 'dragon'.

Kowloon proper, the area ceded 'in perpetuity' to Britain by the Convention of Peking (1860), extends north from the waterfront as far as Boundary St in Mong Kok. It covers just over 11 sq km, but land reclamation and encroachment into the New Territories over the past 150-odd years has quadrupled its size.

Kowloon's most important district, Tsim Sha Tsui, has none of the slickness or sophistication of Hong Kong Island's Central, except within the confines of its top-end hotels. The territory's historical and financial 'capital' lies on Hong Kong Island; Kowloon is the hinterland, a riot of commerce and tourism set against a gritty backdrop of crumbling tenement blocks.

In general, Kowloon is unexciting architecturally. Height restrictions for buildings, due to the proximity of the old Kai Tak Airport in south-eastern Kowloon, gave it a much lower skyline than that of northern Hong Kong Island. However, there are a few impressive exceptions, both old and new. Love it or hate it, the Hong Kong Cultural Centre is a bold stab at turning Hong Kong into something more than a city obsessed with wealth. The Peninsula Hotel is housed in one of Hong Kong's greatest colonial buildings and, at night, the promenade running east and north-east along Victoria Harbour from the Star Ferry terminal

Highlights

- An organ recital – or any musical performance – in the concert hall of the Hong Kong Cultural Centre
- Afternoon tea in the lobby of the oh-so-swish Peninsula Hotel
- An evening stroll along the Tsim Sha Tsui East Promenade, from the Star Ferry terminal to the Hong Kong Coliseum
- A walk down memory lane at the Hong Kong Museum of History
- A cheap and authentic curry lunch at one of the Indian or Pakistani messes in that rabbit warren called Chungking Mansions
- A day of shopping on and off Nathan Rd, in Tsim Sha Tsui's Harbour City complex or the Festival Walk mall in Kowloon Tong
- An evening of nosh, bargains and maybe even Cantonese opera at the Temple St night market in Yau Ma Tei
- An early morning visit to the Yuen Po St Bird Garden in Mong Kok

offers a technicolour backdrop of Central and Wan Chai – the subject of countless postcards and snapshots. And there are some green spaces. Kowloon Park offers a haven for those tired of trudging up and down Nathan Rd. What's more, Kowloon (and in particular Tsim Sha Tsui) has the lion's share of Hong Kong's most important museums. A mere stroll from the Star Ferry terminal will take you to treasure-troves devoted to Hong Kong art and to space exploration; museums exploring the world of science and Hong Kong history are a short distance away.

INFORMATION
Tourist Offices

The Kowloon branch of the Hong Kong Tourism Board **(Map 12)** (HKTB; ☎ 2508

1234) is at the Star Ferry concourse in Tsim Sha Tsui and open from 8am to 6pm daily.

Email & Internet Access (Map 12)

There are a few places to check your emails in Kowloon.

Cash On-Line Cyber Cafe (☎ 2366 0030, Shop 1B, Haiphong Mansion, 99-101 Nathan Rd, Tsim Sha Tsui) Open 8.30am-10pm daily. HK$30 for the first half-hour plus drink and HK$10 for each additional 30 minutes. This is a very professionally run cybercafe and highly recommended. There's another branch in Causeway Bay.

i-Cable Station (☎ 3101 0318, Shops 205 & 205A, 2nd floor, Ocean Terminal, Zone C, Harbour City, Canton Rd, Tsim Sha Tsui) This place has a wall-full of broadbanded PCs available for free use, and good coffee on site.

Shadowman Cyber Cafe (☎ 2366 5262, 7 Lock Rd, Tsim Sha Tsui) Open 8.30am-midnight daily. The first 20 minutes is free with any purchase, HK$10 for every 15 minutes after that. This is an excellent place to surf the Web and have lunch (sandwiches HK$25 to HK$48, mains from HK$55).

Bookshops

Cosmos Books (☎ 2367 8699, 96 Nathan Rd, Tsim Sha Tsui) **Map 12** Go to the Cosmos for English-language nonfiction about China and things Chinese (not novels). The shop is entered from Granville Rd.

Page One (☎ 2778 2808, Lower ground 1, Festival Walk, 80-88 Tat Chee Ave, Kowloon Tong) This is the territory's largest general-interest bookshop and has its own popular cafe.

Park Bookstore (☎ 2787 7988, 1st floor, Rex House, 648 Nathan Rd, Mong Kok) **Map 11** Mostly Chinese gay literature, videos and video CDs for men. Once you've found the narrow building entrance, walk to the back and up the stairs.

Swindon Books (☎ 2366 8001, 13-15 Lock Rd, Tsim Sha Tsui) **Map 12** This is one of the best bookshops in Hong Kong. There are three other branches, including a nearby *outlet* (☎ 2730 6877, Shops 246 & 249, Ocean Terminal, Zone C, Harbour City, Canton Rd, Tsim Sha Tsui).

Tai Yip Book Company (☎ 2732 2088, 1st floor, Hong Kong Museum of Art, 10 Salisbury Rd, Tsim Sha Tsui) **Map 12** This place has an excellent and extensive range of art books and cards.

Times Bookshop (☎ 2367 4340, Basement, Golden Crown Court, 66-70 Nathan Rd, Tsim Sha Tsui) **Map 12** This bookshop, with an average range of books and paper supplies, has another Tsim Sha Tsui branch (☎ 2992 0942, Shop B21, Sun Arcade, 28 Canton Rd).

Getting Around

Although Kowloon boasts the highest number of buses and MTR stations in the territory, most districts are best seen on foot. Buses and minibuses travel frequently up and down Nathan Rd, but there is no convenient tram to jump on and off. Most of the areas of interest (and the ones with the highest concentration of hotels, restaurants, bars and other amenities) are spaced far apart.

Museum Shuttle The HKTB runs a Museum Shuttle departing from the Kowloon Hotel (corner of Nathan and Middle roads) and stopping at the Hong Kong Science Museum and the Hong Kong Museum of History before carrying on to the Hong Kong Heritage Museum in Tai Wai (near Sha Tin in the New Territories). It then returns to Tsim Sha Tsui, calling at the Hong Kong Museum of Art and the Hong Kong Space Museum before terminating at the Kowloon Hotel. There are 11 departures every Wednesday, Friday and Sunday, with the first at 10am and the last at 5.30pm. A one-month pass, allowing unlimited use of the bus and entry to the five museums, costs HK$80 and can be purchased at any HKTB outlet.

For information about the Hong Kong Museums Pass, see Visas & Documents in the Hong Kong Facts for the Visitor chapter.

TSIM SHA TSUI (MAP 12)

The hotel and shopping district of Tsim Sha Tsui ('Tsimsy' to locals) lies at the very tip of the Kowloon Peninsula to the south of

Austin Rd. Almost a square kilometre of shops, restaurants, pubs, topless bars, fast-food joints and camera and electronics shops are clustered on either side of Nathan Rd. This is what most travellers see as they first step off the bus from the airport.

Former KCR Clock Tower

Immediately south-east of the Star Ferry terminal is this 45m-high clock tower, once part of the southern terminus of the Kowloon-Canton Railway (KCR), built in 1915. Operations moved to the modern train station at Hung Hom to the north-east in late 1975. The station was demolished in 1978, though you can see a scale model of what it looked like if you visit the Hong Kong Railway Museum in Tai Po in the New Territories (see that chapter for details). A new station is being built nearby that will allow travel to Hung Hom and the existing KCR East Rail as well as the new KCR West Rail, which will terminate in Tuen Mun.

Ocean Terminal

To the north of the clock tower is **Star House** *(3 Salisbury Rd)*, a frayed-looking retail and office complex. At its western end is the entrance to Ocean Terminal, the long building jutting into the harbour. It is part of the massive **Harbour City** shopping mall that stretches for half a kilometre north along Canton Rd.

Ocean Terminal is filled with top-end shops selling antiques and curios, carpets, designer clothing, jewellery and the like, while the adjoining **Ocean Centre** largely caters to everyday shoppers. Ocean Terminal is not the place for cheap souvenir hunting, but it's an interesting place for a stroll.

Hong Kong Cultural Centre

The odd building clad in pink ceramic tiles behind the clock tower and opposite Star House is the Hong Kong Cultural Centre *(☎ 2734 2009, 10 Salisbury Rd; open 9am-11pm Mon-Sat, 1pm-11pm Sun & public holidays)*, one of Hong Kong's most distinctive – if not loved – landmarks (see the special section Contemporary Architecture).

Though its design remains controversial, the centre is a world-class venue, with a 2000-seat concert hall that seats 1750, a studio theatre for 320, rehearsal studios, an arts library and an impressive main lobby. The concert hall even has a Rieger Orgelbau pipe organ (with 8000 pipes and 93 stops), the largest in South-East Asia. Upwards of 900 annual performances attract more than 800,000 people to the venue. On the centre's south side is the start of the viewing platform from where you can admire Victoria Harbour and the skyline of Central and gain access to the Tsim Sha Tsui East Promenade (see Tsim Sha Tsui East later in this chapter). Forty-minute afternoon tours are conducted (adult/concession HK$10/5).

Hong Kong Museum of Art

Part of the cultural centre complex, the Hong Kong Museum of Art *(☎ 7221 0116, 10 Salisbury Rd; adult/child & senior HK$10/5 Fri-Tues, free Wed; open 10am-6pm Fri-Wed)* has seven galleries over six floors exhibiting Chinese antiquities, Chinese fine art, historical pictures, contemporary Hong Kong art and temporary international exhibitions. The seventh gallery houses the Xubaizhi collection of painting and calligraphy. **Salisbury Gardens**, leading to the entrance, is lined with sculptures by contemporary Hong Kong sculptors.

The exhibits are tastefully displayed, and there are audio guides for HK$10. Take a seat in the hallway and enjoy the harbour views or the bookshop sells a wide range of art books, prints and cards.

Hong Kong Space Museum

Adjoining the cultural centre is the Hong Kong Space Museum *(☎ 2721 0226, 10 Salisbury Rd; adult/concession HK$10/5 Thur-Mon, free Wed; open 1pm-9pm Mon, Wed-Fri, 10am-9pm Sat, Sun & public holidays)*, another peculiar-looking building, this time shaped like a golf ball.

The museum is divided into three parts: the **Hall of Space Science**, the **Hall of Astronomy** and the ever-popular **Space Theatre**, one of the largest planetariums in the world. Exhibits include a lump of moon rock, models of a rocket ship and NASA's 1962 Mercury space capsule.

The Space Theatre screens 'sky shows' and **IMAX films** (daily except Monday) lasting about 40 minutes; they are mostly in Cantonese, but translations by headphones are available. The first show is at 1.30pm weekdays (12.20pm Saturday, 11.10am Sunday), the last at 8.30pm. Tickets cost HK$32/16 adults/concession, or HK$24/12 in the front stalls. Advance bookings can be made up to one hour before show time by phone.

The Peninsula Hotel

More than a Hong Kong landmark, the Peninsula (☎ 2920 2888, Cnr Salisbury & Nathan Rds), the throne-like building opposite the space museum, is one of the world's great hotels. Before WWII it was one of several prestigious hotels like Raffles in Singapore, the Peace in Shanghai and the Strand in Rangoon (now Yangon).

Land reclamation has robbed the hotel of its top waterfront location since it first opened its doors in 1928 and the 20-storey twin tower extension behind it is no architectural masterpiece, but the breathtaking interior is worth a visit. Take afternoon tea (from HK$165; 2pm to 7pm daily), one of Hong Kong's greatest pastimes – dress neatly and be prepared to line up for a table. You can listen to the string quartet, and salivate at tiny cut sandwiches and dainty cakes. For more details on the Peninsula, see Places to Stay – Top-End later in this chapter.

Nathan Rd

Kowloon's main thoroughfare was named after Sir Matthew Nathan, governor of Hong Kong from 1904 to 1907. As Kowloon was very sparsely populated at the time and such a wide road thought unnecessarily extravagant, it was dubbed 'Nathan's Folly'.

Now the southern end of Nathan Rd is known as the **Golden Mile**, reflecting both the price of property in this high-rent area and the retailers' success. Though lacking any tourist sights per se, the lower end of this boulevard is a sight in itself. Ramshackle blocks stacked with seedy guesthouses

awkwardly rub shoulders with top-end hotels; touts sell fake Rolexes and tailors ply their trade on street corners. Those staying at Chungking Mansions, Mirador Mansion or Golden Crown Court (see Places to Stay – Budget later in this chapter) will have this frenetic scene at their very doorstep.

Kowloon Mosque & Islamic Centre

North of the intersection of Nathan and Haiphong roads, the Kowloon Mosque and Islamic Centre (☎ 2724 0095, 105 Nathan Rd) is the largest Islamic house of worship in Hong Kong. The present building, with its dome and carved marble, was completed in 1984. It occupies the site of a mosque built in 1896 for Muslim Indian troops.

Muslims are welcome to attend services, but non-Muslims should ask if it's OK to look inside. Permission is usually given, but make sure you are dressed modestly and have removed your shoes or sandals.

Kowloon Park

Once the site of a barracks, Kowloon Park is an oasis of greenery and a refreshing escape from the hustle and bustle of Tsim Sha Tsui. Pathways and walls criss-cross the grass, birds hop around in cages, and towers and ancient banyan trees dot the landscape. **Sculpture Walk**, featuring works by local sculptors, is an interesting addition, and the excellent **Kowloon Park Swimming Complex** (☎ 2724 3577; adult/child & senior HK$19/9; open 6.30am-9pm Apr-Oct) comes complete with waterfalls. Visit on a weekday; on weekends there are so many bathers it's tough to find the water.

Hong Kong Observatory

What was until the handover called the Royal Observatory (☎ 2926 8200, 134A Nathan Rd) is housed in a two-storey colonial structure just east of the Kowloon Park Swimming Complex. It was built in 1883 and declared a historic monument exactly a century later. It continues to monitor Hong Kong's weather and sends up those frightening signals when a typhoon is heading for the territory (see the boxed text Typhoon!).

Typhoon!

A typhoon is a violent tropical cyclone, a massive whirlpool of air currents often tens of kilometres high and hundreds of kilometres wide. Feeding off moisture, tropical cyclones can only survive over warm oceans – once typhoons hit land, they quickly die out. The 'eye' of the cyclone is generally tens of kilometres wide and basically a column of descending air, which is much calmer than the surrounding vortex.

Cyclones can last for as long as a few weeks, but not all will mature into typhoons. Only about half the cyclones in the South China Sea ever reach typhoon ferocity. The gradation of tropical cyclones ascends as follows: tropical depression (up to 62km/h); tropical storm (63km/h to 87km/h); severe tropical storm (88km/h to 117km/h); and typhoon (118km/h or more).

Hong Kong is a small target, so the chances of a direct hit (when winds of typhoon intensity pass within 100km of the city) is actually small. There is a numbering system to warn of typhoons. No 1 (its visual symbol being the letter 't') means that a tropical cyclone is within 800km of the territory. No 3 (an upside-down 't') – there is no No 2 – warns that winds of up to 62km are blowing in Victoria Harbour, there is a risk of Hong Kong being hit and people should take precautions such as securing flower pots on balconies and terraces. The system then jumps to No 8 (a triangle), which means that there are sustained winds of between 63km/h and 117km/h. People are instructed to stay indoors, to fix adhesive tape to exposed windows to reduce the damage caused by broken glass, businesses shut down and ferries stop running. No 9 (a double triangle) warns that gale or storm force winds are increasing and No 10 (a cross) is the most severe, with winds reaching upward from 118km/h and gusts exceeding 220km/h.

Only 13 typhoons have reached No 10 since the end of WWII, despite the average 16 that appear in the vicinity each year. The most famous ones in recent years included: Typhoon Wanda (1962), the most ferocious of all, delivering hourly mean wind speeds of 133km/h and peak gusts of 259km/h; Typhoon Ellen (1983), which killed 22 people and injured over 300 (insurance claims totalled over HK$300 million); and Typhoon York (1999), which had the No 10 signal up the longest of any other typhoon – 11 hours.

Everyone who has lived in Hong Kong long enough has a typhoon story – 'I got up to go to the toilet and the air-conditioner had blown onto the bed'; 'I touched the window and the pane of glass was buckling like a taut skin'; 'Stop signs were being snapped like swizzle sticks along Canine Rd' – and as many have attended 'typhoon parties', impromptu gatherings held when people are stranded.

Rain, which can fall so heavily in Hong Kong that it sounds like a drum roll as it hits the pavement, can cause deadly landslips. Hong Kong also now has a 'heavy rain warning system' that is colour-coded (in ascending degrees of severity) amber, red and black.

TSIM SHA TSUI EAST (MAP 12)

This large chunk of land east of Chatham Rd South, built entirely on reclaimed land, is a cluster of shopping malls, hotels, theatres, restaurants and nightclubs. There are none of the old, crumbling buildings of 'real' Tsim Sha Tsui – and like most reclaimed areas, it has that soulless, cheesy, artificial feel that will take decades to remove.

Tsim Sha Tsui East Promenade

Along with the Peak, this amazing waterfront walkway offers some of the best views in Hong Kong. Lovely during the day, at

Standing Buddha, Ten Thousand Buddhas Monastery, Sha Tin

RICHARD I'ANSON

LEE FOSTER

JOHN HAY

The sweet smell of incense…

Man Ho Temple is on Hollywood Rd in Central, Hong Kong Island.

RICHARD I'ANSON

Crowds of people make offerings in the grounds of the Wong Tai Sin temple complex in Kowloon.

OLIVER STREWE

The harbour view from Kowloon's Regent Hotel.

MARK DAFFEY

MARK DAFFEY

Unhappy punter returning from Happy Valley?

Woman practising Tai Chi with a fan, Aberdeen

RICHARD I'ANSON

Aberdeen's high-rise apartments, complete with washing, attest to Hong Kong's dense population.

night the view of Central lit up in neon is mesmerising. Best of all you can turn your back on the landfill of Tsim Sha Tsui East. You'll find yourself accompanied by lovers, joggers, musicians, photographers with tripods, and people fishing right off the walkway. The promenade becomes a 'black mountain' of people during the Chinese New Year fireworks displays in late January/early February and again in June during the Dragon Boat Festival.

Hong Kong Science Museum

The Science Museum (☎ 2732 3232, 2 Science Museum Rd; adult/concession HK$25/ 12.50 Tues & Thur-Sun, free Wed; open 1pm-9pm Tues-Fri, 10am-9pm Sat, Sun & public holidays) is a multilevel complex with more than 500 displays on computers, energy, physics, robotics, telecommunications and health. Two-thirds of the exhibits are 'hands on', which helps to keep younger visitors interested.

Hong Kong Museum of History

The Hong Kong Museum of History (☎ 2724 9042, 100 Chatham Rd South; adult/ concession $10/5 Tues & Thur-Sun, free Wed; open 10am-6pm Tues-Sat, 1pm-6pm Sun) has over 500 exhibits focusing on the territory's archaeology, natural history, ethnography and local history.

The museum takes visitors on a fascinating walk through the area's past. There are replicas of village dwellings, traditional Chinese costumes and beds, and a re-creation of an entire 19th-century street block from 1881, including an old Chinese medicine shop.

The large collection of 19th and early 20th-century photographs is very atmospheric, as are the models of Hong Kong's trams, but a favourite is the mishmash of toys and collectibles from the 1960s and '70s when 'Made in Hong Kong' meant 'Christmas stocking trash'.

HUNG HOM (MAP 12)

Among Hung Hom's features, other than the massive train station, are the adjacent 12,500-seat **Hong Kong Coliseum** (☎ 2355 7234, 9 Cheong Wan Rd), which hosts concerts and

sporting events; the **Hong Kong Polytechnic University** (☎ 2766 5100, Hong Chong Rd), opposite the station; and one of the strangest shopping venues in the territory, the **Whampoa** (☎ 2128 7428, 18 Tak Fung St), a full-scale concrete model of a luxury cruiser liner.

YAU MA TEI (MAP 11)

Immediately to the north of Tsim Sha Tsui is the Yau Ma Tei district, pronounced 'yow ma day' and meaning 'place of sesame plants'. The Jade Market, a Tin Hau Temple and the Temple St night market are just a short walk from Yau Ma Tei MTR station.

There are many interesting **walks** to take along the streets running east to west between Kansu St and Jordan Rd (Map 12): **Nanking St** (mahjong shops); **Saigon St** (herbalist shops, old-style tailors, pawnshops); and **Ning Po St** (paper goods like kites, and paper votives, such as houses, mobile phones and 'hell money', to burn for the dead). The HKTB's free Hong Kong Walks brochure contains walks in Yau Ma Tei and Mong Kok.

Jade Market (Map 12)

The Jade Market (Kansu St; open 10am-4pm), near the Gascoigne Rd overpass just west of Nathan Rd, has stalls selling all varieties and grades of jade from inside a large covered market. Unless you really know your nephrite from your jadeite it's probably not wise to buy any expensive pieces here. Vendors apparently use a 'members-only' sign language to communicate prices between one another; outsiders are likely to get fleeced.

You can reach the market easily on foot from either the Jordan or Yau Ma Tei MTR stations. Bus No 9 from the Star Ferry bus station will drop you off at the Kowloon Central Post Office (405 Nathan Rd), which is just around the corner.

Tin Hau Temple

A couple of blocks north of the Jade Market is this decent-sized temple (open 8am-6pm) dedicated to Tin Hau, the Goddess of Seafarers. The temple complex also houses an altar dedicated to Shing Wong, the God of the City, and to To Tei, the Earth God.

To the east of the main temple is a long row of fortune-tellers.

Temple St Night Market (Maps 11 & 12)

Temple St is the liveliest night market in Hong Kong, and *the* place to go for cheap clothes, food, watches, pirate CDs, fake labels, footwear, cookware and everyday items.

Any marked prices should be considered mere suggestions – this is definitely a place to bargain and bargain hard.

For street food, head to the section of Temple St north of the temple. You can get anything from a simple bowl of noodles to a full meal. There are also a few seafood and hotpot restaurants in the area.

Hawkers set up at 6pm and are gone by midnight. The market is at its best from about 7pm to 10pm, when it's clogged with stalls and people. You might even get lucky and catch a performance of Cantonese opera.

The easiest way to get to the market is to walk along Man Ming Lane to Temple St from the Yau Ma Tei MTR station (exit C).

MONG KOK (MAP 11)

Mong Kok is one of Hong Kong's most congested working-class residential areas, as well as one of its busiest shopping districts. You'd never guess the meaning of its name in Cantonese: 'Prosperous Point'.

This is where locals come to buy everyday items such as jeans, tennis shoes, kitchen supplies, computer accessories and so on. Take a look at Fife St, which has an amazing collection of stalls selling old records, books, ceramics, machinery and music scores. Mong Kok is also a good place to buy backpacks, hiking boots and sporting goods (see that section under Shopping later in this chapter).

Two blocks east of the Mong Kok MTR station (exit D3) is the Tung Choi St market (*open 1pm-11pm daily*), which runs from Argyle St in the north to Dundas St in the south.

The streets west of Nathan Rd reveal Hong Kong's seamier side, for this is where you'll find some of the city's seediest brothels. Mostly run by Triads, these places are often veritable prisons for young women. The Hong Kong Police routinely raid these places, but a look at the rows of pastel-coloured neon strip lights on so many blocks is an indication that it's 'business as usual' despite the change in landlords. This is not a part of town where you'd want to spend a lot of time after midnight.

Yuen Po St Bird Garden & Flower Market

This market (*open 7am-8pm daily*) is a wonderful place to visit, if only to marvel at how the Hong Kong Chinese (especially men) fuss and fawn over their feathered friends. The Chinese have long favoured birds as pets; you often see local men walking around airing their birds and feeding them tasty creepy-crawlies with chopsticks.

They especially like songbirds, and a bird's prowess in singing will determine its value. Some birds are also considered harbingers of good fortune, which is why you'll see some men carrying birds to the racetrack. Bats are especially lucky, but you don't see many of those at the races.

There are hundreds of birds for sale here, along with elaborate cages carved from teak and bamboo. The market is officially open till 8pm, but most everyone's gone by 6pm. Adjacent to the bird garden is the flower market on Flower Market Rd, which keeps the same hours.

To get to the bird garden and flower market, take the MTR to Prince Edward station, come out of exit B2 and walk east along Prince Edward Rd West for about 10 minutes.

NEW KOWLOON (MAP 10)

The southernmost 31 sq km of the New Territories is officially called New Kowloon and encompasses such districts (from west to east) as Sham Shui Po, Kowloon Tong, Wong Tai Sin and Diamond Hill. Since Boundary St just above Mong Kok technically marks the division between Kowloon and the New Territories, these places – strictly speaking – belong to the latter. But they look and feel and consider themselves to be part of Kowloon and are thus considered

Triads

Hong Kong's Triads, which run the territory's drug, prostitution and gambling rackets, were not always the gangster operations they are today. They were originally founded as patriotic and secret societies that opposed the corrupt and brutal Qing (Manchu) dynasty and aided the revolution that brought down that moribund dynasty in 1911. The fact that these organisations had adopted Kwan Tai (Kuanti), the God of War, and the upholder of righteousness, integrity and loyalty, as their patron leant them further respectability.

Unfortunately, the Triads descended into crime and illicit activities during the civil war on the mainland, and came in droves to Hong Kong after the Communists came to power in 1949. Today they are the Chinese equivalent of the Mafia. Sporting such names as 14K, Bamboo Union, Water Room and Peace Victory Brotherhood, the Triads have been increasingly successful at recruiting disaffected teenagers in Hong Kong's high-rise housing estates.

The Triad armoury is a hellish array of weapons ranging from meat choppers (cleavers) and machetes to pistols and petrol bombs. If people default on a loan, Triad members encourage repayment by attacking them in the middle of the street with large knives.

Membership in a Triad is illegal in Hong Kong; indeed, it's an offence even to claim to be a member. Yet the Triads seem to be growing and have been trying to use wealth to muscle into legitimate businesses. Many fear that the growing influence of the Triads could drive out established businesses and hurt Hong Kong's economy in the long term.

It was the Communists who smashed the Triad-controlled drug racket in Shanghai after the 1949 revolution. The Triads have long memories and, before the handover, many Hong Kong-based hoods moved their operations to ethnic Chinese communities in countries like Australia, Canada and the USA. Thailand got more than its share, and even the Philippines received some of this 'overseas investment' – Triad-arranged kidnappings of wealthy Chinese families living there became something of a growth industry. However, since 1997 many Triad have moved back into Hong Kong and have even expanded their operations into the mainland, establishing links with corrupt government cadres and high-ranking soldiers in the People's Liberation Army.

It's unlikely that many foreign travellers will encounter Triad members directly during their stay in Hong Kong. The Triad-controlled brothels of Mong Kok and Sham Shui Po shun foreign clientele and it would be mad to get mixed up with drugs on the streets of Kowloon or Wan Chai. You may have the misfortune of meeting one or two of these unsavoury characters if you frequent hostess clubs (a good reason to avoid these places). Do what is expected of you; gorillas don't take 'no' for an answer and never have a sense of humour.

---

so. 'New Kowloon' is an official designation, and never used by Hong Kong people.

Sham Shui Po

Sham Shui Po is a residential area of high rises on the Tsuen Wan line of the MTR. It is famous for its computer emporiums and its market, and can boast an important archaeological find – the Lei Cheng Uk Han Tomb.

From the Sham Shui Po MTR station follow exit A2 and you'll soon fall right into **Apliu St market**, which features everything from clothing to CDs, at rock bottom prices. The market spills over into Pei Ho St.

Sham Shui Po is also the place for computers and components; see the Shopping section later in this chapter.

For somewhere to eat, head for the **Dragon Centre** (☎ 2307 9264, *Cnr Yen Chow St & Cheung Sha Wan Rd)*, a working-class mall. Take exit C1 from the MTR if going there directly. It doesn't look like a shopping centre at first glance, but an external escalator will take you from street level beside the bus depot up to the first shopping floor.

At nine levels, the Dragon Centre towers above the surrounding apartment blocks. There's an excellent *food hall* on level 8

(HK$35 buys a meal of soup, egg, pork and rice). It's packed with family groups on weekends and it can be hard to find a seat during lunch time. On the same level, there's also the **Sky Rink ice-skating rink** (☎ 2307 9264).

The attractive **police station** *(37A Yen Chow St)* south of the Dragon Centre was built in 1925.

Lei Cheng Uk Han Tomb Museum The Lei Cheng Uk Han Tomb Museum *(☎ 2386 2863, 41 Tonkin St; admission free; open 10am-1pm & 2pm-6pm Fri-Sat & Mon-Wed, 1pm-6pm Sun & public holidays)* is built around a late Han Dynasty (AD 25–220) burial vault.

The tomb was discovered in 1955 when the hillside was being levelled for an estate, and it is one of Hong Kong's earliest surviving historical monuments. Believe it or not, it was once on the coast. The tomb consists of four barrel-vaulted brick chambers in the form of a cross and set around a domed central chamber. It's encased in a concrete shell for protection and you can only peek through a plastic window; it's a bit of a journey for an anticlimactic peek through Perspex.

The museum also contains some 58 pottery and bonze items taken from the tomb, including a sweet little clay house and a granary. The delightful **Lei Cheng Uk Han Garden** is next to the museum at the corner of Tonkin St and Po On Rd.

To reach the tomb, take bus No 2 from the Star Ferry, which stops in front of the museum on Tonkin St. The nearest MTR station is Cheung Sha Wan (exit A3), a 10-minute walk to the south-west.

Kowloon Tong

This is a posh residential area north-east of Mong Kok with colleges, universities – both the **Hong Kong Baptist University** (☎ 2339 7400), Hong Kong's most generously endowed, and the **City University of Hong Kong** (☎ 2788 9191) are in the neighbourhood – and bridal shops and salons with names like Cité du Louvre, where brides-to-be can buy their finery, have their photos done and even do the deed itself.

Kowloon Tong, which is on the Kwun Tong MTR line, and the only station where you can transfer to the KCR, can claim the territory's most luxurious shopping mall – **Festival Walk** *(☎ 2520 8025, 80-88 Tat Chee Ave)* – and in typical Hong Kong fashion, it can boast a fair few superlatives itself. Festival Walk has the largest cinema, bookshop and ice-skating rink in the territory (see the Entertainment, Information and Activities sections, respectively, in this chapter).

Kowloon City

This rather low-rent neighbourhood just west of the old Kai Tak Airport has two drawing cards: a wonderful park that was once the infamous Kowloon Walled City and a string of authentic and excellent-value Thai restaurants (see Places to Eat). The airport, which sits on a prime chunk of land, is now abandoned and awaits development. It supports the popular **Karting Mall go-kart track** *(☎ 2718 8199; open 10am-2am daily)* for the moment.

Kowloon Walled City Park The walls that enclose this beautiful park *(admission free; open 6.30am-11pm daily)* were once the perimeter of a notorious village that technically remained part of China throughout British rule, as it was never included in the 1898 lease of the New Territories. The enclave was known for its vice, prostitution, gambling, illegal dentists and sheer poverty. In 1984 the Hong Kong government acquired the area, rehoused the residents elsewhere and built pavilions and ponds filled with turtles and goldfish, and planted exquisite trees and shrubs, including a long hedge coaxed into the form of a dragon. The park opened in 1996. Close to the Carpenter Rd entrance of the park is the renovated **Yamen building**, once an almshouse. It contains displays on the history of the walled city with a scale model of the village in the mid-19th century.

To reach Kowloon Walled City Park take bus No 1 from the Star Ferry bus station and alight at Tung Tau Tsuen Rd opposite the park. The closest MTR station is Lok Fu (exit B), a 20-minute walk along Junction Rd to the north.

Wong Tai Sin

The district of Wong Tai Sin to the north of Kowloon City is known for two things: its enormous and faceless housing estate and one of the most active temples in the territory.

Wong Tai Sin Temple This large Taoist temple complex *(Lung Cheung Rd; admission free; open 7am-6pm),* adjacent to the Wong Tai Sin housing estate, was built in 1973 and is dedicated to the god of that name (see the boxed text The Gods & Goddesses of South China in the Facts about Hong Kong chapter). The image of the god in the main temple was brought to Hong Kong from China in 1915 and initially installed in a temple in Wan Chai, where it remained until being moved to the present site in 1921.

Like most Chinese temples, this one is an explosion of colourful pillars, roofs, lattice work, flowers and shrubs. If you come in the early evening Friday evening is the busiest time – you can watch hordes of businessmen and secretaries praying and divining the future with *chim,* bamboo sticks that must be shaken out of a box on to the ground and then read (they're available free to the left of the main temple).

Behind the main temple and to the right are the **Good Wish Gardens**, replete with colourful pavilions (the hexagonal **Unicorn Hall** with carved doors and windows is the most beautiful), zigzag bridges and artificial ponds. A donation of HK$2 is requested to visit the gardens.

Just below the main temple and to the left as you enter the complex is an arcade filled with dozens of booths operated by fortune tellers, some of whom speak English.

The busiest times at the temple are around the Chinese New Year, Wong Tai Sin's birthday and at weekends. There is no admission fee for visiting this or any other temple in Hong Kong, but a donation of HK$1 or HK$2 is requested at the main entrance (it all goes to the Tung Wah Group of Hospitals). Getting to the temple is easy: ride the MTR to Wong Tai Sin station, take exit B2 and then follow the signs or crowds or both.

Diamond Hill

The residential district of Diamond Hill, which spreads out below the peak of that name and is due east of Wong Tai Sin, contains Hong Kong's newest and (some would say) most beautiful house of worship.

Chi Lin Nunnery This large Buddhist complex *(☎ 2354 1882, 5 Chi Lin Drive; admission free; open 9am-4pm Thur-Tues)* was built in the Tang dynasty style, completely of wood, and opened in 1998. It is a serene place with lotus ponds and immaculate bonsai. The design is intended to demonstrate the harmony of humans with nature and is pretty convincing – until you look up at the looming neighbourhood highrises.

You enter the complex through the **Sam Mun**, a series of three gates representing the Buddhist precepts of compassion, wisdom and 'skillful means'. The first courtyard, with lotus ponds, gives way to the **Hall of Celestial Kings**, with a large statue of the seated Buddha surrounded by the deities of the four cardinal points. Behind that is the **main hall** containing a statue of the Sakyamuni Buddha flanked by two seated bodhisattvas and two standing disciples. The wooden **Pagoda of the Ten Thousand Buddhas** beckons from a knoll to the north-east. The **Lotus Pond Garden** *(open 6.30am-7pm daily),* next to the main entrance, is a delight.

To reach the nunnery from the Diamond Hill MTR station, take exit C2 and walk east along Fung Tak for five minutes.

Lei Yue Mun (Map 3)

To the south-east of the old Kai Tak Airport is a residential neighbourhood called Kwun Tong, and a bit farther south-east is the rapidly modernising fishing village of Lei Yue Mun. *Lei yue* means 'carp' and *mun* is 'gate'; the 'carp gate' refers to the channel separating south-east Kowloon from Hong Kong Island. Across the water on the island, and looming on the hillside is the 19th-century **Lei Yue Mun Fort**, which now contains the Hong Kong Museum of Coastal Defence (see the Shau Kei Wan section of the Hong Kong Island chapter).

The 'village' of Lei Yue Mun is one of Hong Kong's prime seafood venues. It's a colourful and lively place to dine by the water at night. You can get here on bus No 14C from the Kwun Tong MTR station. Take it all the way to the end of the line, which is the area of Yau Tong, then walk south along Lei Yue Mun Praya Rd.

PLACES TO STAY

Kowloon is home to an incredible cross section of society, from the wealthy residential areas of Kowloon Tong and Ho Man Tin to the tenements of Mong Kok and Kowloon City. Travellers on a budget will be bowled over by the volume of guesthouses stacked vertically in the crumbling blocks of Nathan Rd, including the infamous Chungking Mansions, as well as Mirador Mansion and Golden Crown Court.

Those with a bit (or a lot) more cash will also be impressed. Hong Kong's poshest hotel, the Peninsula, is just across the road from Chungking Mansions and a huge range of other guesthouse and hotels catering to all budgets can be found between these two extremes.

If you are flying into Hong Kong, the Hong Kong Hotels Association (HKHA; ☎ 2383 8380, fax 2362 2383, e hrc@hkha .org) has a reservation centre at the airport and can get you a mid-range or top-end hotel room sometimes 50% cheaper than if you were to walk in yourself.

PLACES TO STAY – BUDGET

For definition purposes, budget in Hong Kong is any place where you can get a double room for under HK$500. The cheapest doubles usually start at about HK$150, but with the correct season on your side you should be able to haggle the price down.

Chungking Mansions (Map 12)

There is probably no other place in the world like Chungking Mansions (*36-44 Nathan Rd, Tsim Sha Tsui; open 7.30am-midnight*), *the* budget accommodation ghetto of Hong Kong. This huge, ramshackle high-rise dump in the heart of Tsim Sha Tsui, accessed via Chungking Arcade,

is almost a city in itself. Virtually all needs can be catered for here – from finding a bed to a place to eat, to shopping and getting your hair cut.

You may be put off by the undercurrent of sleaze and the peculiar odours – a potent mixture of cooking fat, incense and shit – but don't seek sanctuary in the lifts; they're like steel coffins on cables. Perhaps the best introduction to Chungking is Wong Kar Wai's cult film *Chung-king Express* (1994), which captures all the sleaze in a haunting series of stories.

For years there had been talk about tearing down this eyesore and fire trap. A crackdown on fire-safety violations finally came at the end of 1993, and many guesthouses were forced to shut down. Others survived by upgrading: smoke alarms, sprinklers and walls made of fireproof material. In 2000 the lifts themselves were given a face-lift, though they still move like molasses in January.

The character of Chungking has changed. Many of the guesthouses now serve as long-term boarding houses for workers from developing countries in the Subcontinent and Africa, and matchbox rooms are often occupied by two, three or even four people. Backpackers have started migrating to guesthouses in other buildings, but Chungking is still the cheapest place to stay in Hong Kong.

Adding to the excitement are the occasional midnight raids by Hong Kong's boys and girls in blue. For the most part the police are looking for illegal immigrants; have your passport or a photocopy, a receipt for it from the travel agency and/or some other

All types stay at the Chungking Mansions.

picture ID card. One thing travellers should really guard against is drugs; a few grams of hashish in your backpack could leave you with a lot of explaining to do.

The entrance to Chungking Mansions is via Chungking Arcade, a parade of shops that faces Nathan Rd. You will find lifts labelled A to E. There are only two cramped and overworked lifts for each 17-storey block, and long queues form at 'rush hour'. Otherwise there's always the less-than-salubrious stairs.

Despite the dilapidated appearance, most of the little guesthouses are OK – generally clean and often quite comfortable, though rooms are the size of cupboards. Standards do, however, vary; your best bet is to opt for the hotels that have a high percentage of foreign travellers.

Bargaining for a bed or room is always possible, though you won't get very far in the height of the season. You can often negotiate a cheaper price if you stay more than, say, a week, but never try that on the first night – stay one night and find out how you like it before handing over more rent. Once you pay, there are *no* refunds. Always be sure to get a receipt, and paying for a room in advance so that you can have it on a certain day is not advised.

Rooms will typically come with air-conditioning and TV, although the phones are often communal and located in the lobby. Local telephone calls are free from residential phones in Hong Kong, so be suspicious if staff charge you. Many guesthouses can get you a Chinese visa quickly, and some have laundry service. Also, be prepared for varying levels of English fluency among guesthouse concierges.

The guesthouses here have been listed by block and in descending order from the top floor down. Many of the guesthouse owners and managers engage in all sorts of other 'beezness' and often lock their establishment during the days.

Chungking Mansions is also a cheap place to eat (see the Indian food listings under Places to Eat later in this chapter). The ground floor is filled with shops selling everything imaginable, though the

mezzanine floor has better deals. You can pick up all sorts of electrical goodies, such as alarm clocks and radios, made on the mainland and dirt cheap.

Guesthouses – A Block This block has the densest concentration of guesthouses and frequent long queues to get into the lifts; you may find yourself using the stairs more than you expected.

Travellers Hostel (☎ 2368 7710, fax 2368 2505, Flat A1, 16th floor) Dorm beds HK$65, double rooms without/with bath HK$120/130; singles without shower HK$90. This popular dormitory is a landmark in this building and cooking facilities are available. An Englishman who sells used paperbacks and very old Lonely Planet titles from his room has lived here for some two decades.

Kyoto Guesthouse (☎ 2721 3574, mobile ☎ 9077 8297, Flat A8, 15th floor) Doubles without/with shower from HK$100/150, singles without shower HK$90. Mrs Kam runs a basic but comfortable place.

Park Guesthouse (☎ 2368 1689, fax 2367 7889, Flat A1, 15th floor) Singles with shared/private bath HK$120/150, doubles HK$150/200. This guesthouse is clean, air-conditioned and friendly.

Hawaii Guesthouse (☎ 2366 6127, Flat A7, 14th floor) Singles/doubles HK$100/120. This place is run by Mama, who seems to keep the house and everyone in it (mostly African transient workers) in order.

Rhine Guesthouse (☎ 2367 1991, fax 2316 2428, mobile ☎ 9703 7019, Flat A1, 13th floor) Doubles without/with bath HK$150/180. This friendly place run by kind Mrs Cheung has a *branch* (☎ 2721 6863, Flat A8, 11th floor) in the same block.

Peking Guesthouse (☎ 2723 8320, fax 2366 6706, mobile ☎ 9464 3684, Flats A1 & A2, 12th floor) Singles/doubles/triples with bath HK$150/180/300. Peking has friendly management and the place is spotless.

Double Seven Guesthouse (☎ 2367 1406, Flat A7, 7th floor) Singles from HK$150. This is a pretty basic place.

First Guesthouse (☎ 2739 5986, fax 2368 5601, Flat A1, 7th floor) Singles/doubles with bath HK$120/150. These people also own the New York Guesthouse located in B Block.

Welcome Guesthouse (☎ 2721 7793, fax 2311 5558, ⓔ guesthousehk@hotmail.com, Flat A5, 7th floor) Singles without shower HK$100, singles/doubles with shower HK$150/220. The name of this place says it all; it's very welcoming. What's more, it has a laundry service.

Chungking House (☎ 2366 5362, fax 2721 3570, 4th & 5th floors) Singles/doubles with bath HK$260/360. This large place covering two floors is pretty swish (and expensive) by Chungking standards.

Guesthouses – B Block This block is the nastiest and has almost as many guesthouses as A Block, so you may still queue for the lifts. The stairwells support a large amount of wildlife, including a rare species of aggressive flying cockroach. Be grateful for the stray cats as they keep the rats in check.

Tom's Guesthouse (☎ 2367 9258, fax 2366 6706, Flat B7, 16th floor) Singles without/with bath HK$100/150, doubles without bath HK$/120, doubles with bath HK$180-250. Tom's, a clean, friendly and popular place, has large branches in *Block A* (☎ 2722 4956, Flat A5, 8th floor) and *Block C* (☎ 2722 6035, Flat C1, 16th floor), so you'll always find a room here.

Hong Kong Guesthouse (☎ 2367 2632, fax 2369 3821, Flat B1 & B2, 11th floor) Singles/doubles HK$150/220. This place, a bit of a sty but friendly, is under the same management as the Travellers Hostel in Block A and has similar facilities.

Kowloon Guesthouse (☎ 2369 9802, fax 2739 6635, Flat B5 & B7, 10th floor) Singles HK$130-140, doubles HK$200-250. This is one of the larger places in this block and is very popular with Africans.

New York Guesthouse (☎ 2721 8953, fax 2368 5601, Flat B3, 7th floor) Singles without shower HK$110, doubles with shared bath HK$160-180. This place, clean but not especially welcoming, is owned by the same people who run First Guesthouse in Block A.

Kamal Guesthouse (☎ 2739 3301, fax 2724 1506, ⓔ hsinds@netvigator.com, Flat B6, 6th floor) Singles without shower HK$100, doubles with shower HK$160-200. The 'super high-class rooms' that Kamal touts are hardly that, but acceptable at the price.

Dragon Inn (☎ 2368 2007, fax 2724 2841, ⓔ dragoninn@asiaonline.net, Flat B3 & B5, 3rd floor) Singles/doubles/triples without bath HK$150/200/270, with bath HK$200/240/300. This clean place doubles as the Dragon International Travel Agency, with cheap air tickets and other services available in-house.

Guesthouses – C Block C Block is cleaner, the lifts less crowded and the stairwells and hallways tidier; the block's residents' association is obviously doing its job.

Garden Guesthouse (☎ 2368 0981, mobile ☎ 9264 9668, Flat C5, 16th floor) Singles with shower HK$150. This is a clean place favoured by backpackers. They have a branch (☎ 2366 0169, Flat C5, 7th floor) in the same block.

Osaka Guesthouse & *New Grand Guesthouse* (☎ 2311 1702, mobile ☎ 9336 5358, Flat C3 & C5, 13th floor) Singles HK$120-150, doubles HK$170-200. These are owned by the same guy. All rooms have private bath, air con and TV.

New Chungking Guesthouse (☎ 2368 0981, Flat C1, 7th floor) Singles HK$120-140, doubles HK$180-200. This place is very clean and pleasant.

Maharaja Guesthouse & *Ranjeet Guesthouse* (☎ 2368 9943, fax 2366 5331, Flats C1 & C6, 4th floor) Singles HK$100, doubles HK$200-250. These are recently redecorated with TV and telephones, and are owned by the same affable guy.

Guesthouses – D Block This block is clean and relatively uncrowded; the new marble 'lobby' in front of the lift is quite impressive.

New Shanghai Guesthouse (☎ 2311 2515, Flat D2, 16th floor) Singles/doubles with shower HK$150/260. This is an old-style guesthouse run by an elderly woman. It's clean and there's a laundry service.

New China Town Guesthouse (☎ *2723 2014, mobile* ☎ *9185 2216, fax 2367 3333, Flat D8, 10th floor*) Singles HK$120-150, doubles HK$200-250. This guesthouse is owned by an affable Indian. There's a branch *(Flat E2, 10th floor)* in E Block.

Fortuna Guesthouse (☎ *2366 4524, Flat D1, 8th floor)* Singles/doubles HK$160/ 180. This place is quite clean, but you'll have difficulty communicating with the elderly owner.

Royal Inn & *Royal Plaza Inn* (☎ *2367 1424, fax 2369 7680, Flat D1, 5th floor)* Singles with shared/attached bath HK$150/ 180, doubles with bath HK$200-280. These places have a sign that says 'deluxe rooms'. They aren't really, but the Indian staff speak good English.

Guesthouses – E Block This area is a backwater and relatively clean and quiet. The guesthouses are thinning out here and there are light to moderate queues for the lifts.

Mandarin Guesthouse (☎ *2366 0073, mobile* ☎ *9484 4382, fax 2722 1293, Flat E5, 13th floor)* Singles/doubles with shower HK$150/200. The fact that this place is under-subscribed, makes it attractive.

Yan Yan Guest House (☎ *2366 8930, 2721 0840, Flat E1, 8th floor)* Singles HK$130-150, doubles HK$150-180. This is one of the last Chinese-owned guesthouses in E Block. The very swish *New Yan Yan Guesthouse (mobile* ☎ *9489 3891, Flat E5, 12th floor)* is under the same management and in the same block.

Mirador Mansion (Map 12)

Mirador Mansion *(58 Nathan Rd, Tsim Sha Tsui)*, above an arcade of that name between Mody and Carnarvon roads, is a scaled-down version of Chungking Mansions, but considerably cleaner and roomier. Much of the backpacker clientele has moved here in recent years, with the result that there can be heavy queues for the lifts during peak hours.

First-Class Guesthouse (☎ *2724 0595, fax 2724 0843, Flat D1, 16th floor)* Singles/ doubles HK$150/180. While its name

might be a little ambitious, the FC is clean and bright and the staff friendly. All rooms have attached bath.

Man Hing Lung (☎ *2722 0678, fax 2311 6669,* ℮ *mhlhotel@hkstar.com, Flat F2, 14th floor)* Singles HK$120-180, doubles HK$200-250. This is a decent place with clean rooms, a good atmosphere and Internet access. If you need a roommate, the very friendly management will put you in with another traveller.

Kowloon Hotel & *New Garden Hostel* (☎ *2311 2523, fax 2368 5241, Flats D1, E1 & F1, 13th floor)* Dorm beds HK$60-70, singles with shared bath HK$100, singles with bath HK$150, twin bedroom HK$200, doubles HK$350-400. This is a vast place with more than 65 rooms. The twin bedrooms have a phone and fridge, and a great view over to Central. The doubles are on the 10th floor. There have been some complaints about the large number of beds in the dorm rooms.

London Hostel (☎ *2369 1201, fax 2739 0187, Flat F2, 13th floor)* Rooms with shared/private bath HK$150/250. This place is owned by the same people who run the popular Ajit Guesthouse one floor down.

Ajit Guesthouse (☎ *2369 1201, fax 2739 0187, Flat F3, 12th floor)* Rooms with shared/private bath HK$150/250. This place, with clean rooms, is deservedly popular with travellers.

Cosmic Guesthouse (☎ *2739 4952, fax 2311 5260, Flat A2, 12th floor)* Dorm beds HK$60, singles with shower HK$160, doubles HK$200, big doubles HK$220. This is a very clean, recently refurbished, quiet guesthouse with a polite owner. There's a branch (☎ *2366 8588, Flat F3, 6th floor)* in the same building.

Hung Kiu Guesthouse (☎ *2312 1505, mobile* ☎ *9370 2325, fax 2311 4258, Flat C3, 8th floor)* Singles with shower HK$180, doubles HK$280. This is relatively new and clean, but you'll need an interpreter to get *any* point across.

Lucky Guesthouse (☎ *2367 3522, mobile* ☎ *9366 6235, fax 2367 3325, Flat A11, 7th floor)* Singles/doubles/triples with bath

HK$150/250/350. This place is clean and tidy and the owner speaks excellent English.

Mini Hotel (☎ 2367 2551, fax 2367 2114, e mini_hotel@hotmail.com, Flat F2, 7th floor) Dorm beds HK$80, singles/doubles HK$160/200. This is actually more a guesthouse than a hotel, but what's in a name?

Charles Inn (☎ 2301 3078, fax 2301 3678, Flat F2, 6th floor) Singles/doubles HK$250/250. This is a clean and tidy place.

Man Lee Tak Guesthouse (☎ 2739 2717, fax 2368 1233, Flat A1, 6th floor) Singles HK$150-170, doubles HK$200-250. This place is a decent option.

Mei Lam Guesthouse (☎ 2721 5278, mobile ☎ 9095 1379, fax 2723 6168, e meilam guesthouse@biz.netvigator.com, Flat D1, 5th floor) Singles/doubles from HK$180/250. The rooms at this place are fine and all have baths and TVs, but the owner speaks almost no English.

Garden Hostel (☎ 2311 1183, fax 2721 2085, Flat F4, 3rd floor) Dorm beds HK$60, singles/doubles with shower HK$150/180. This is a decent place; it has a patio and the staff speak good English. They claim that it's 'recommended by Lonely Planet' but we've received complaints from several female readers about the owner's behaviour. Be advised.

Lily Garden Guesthouse (☎ 2724 2612, fax 2312 7681, Flat A9, 3rd floor) Dorm beds HK$60, singles with shower HK$180, doubles HK$200-220, triples HK$300-400. Lily Garden has small but clean rooms. It's an efficient but not especially friendly place. This is part of a group of guesthouses under the same management that includes the *New Osaka Guesthouse* (☎ 2724 2612, Flat F2, 5th floor) in the same block.

Golden Crown Court (Map 12)

Golden Crown Court (66-70 Nathan Rd, Tsim Sha Tsui), opposite the south-east corner of Kowloon Park, has undergone a transformation in recent years and now offers a host of clean, smart guesthouses that are more expensive than those at Chungking or Mirador Mansions. The following are a couple of the better options:

Golden Crown Guesthouse (☎ 2369 1782, fax 2739 5084, Flats B2 & H, 5th floor) Dorm beds HK$80, singles without/with shower HK$250/350. This clean place has a friendly owner.

Fuji Hotel (☎ 2367 2883, fax 2367 2880, 4th floor) Rooms HK$320; 10% discount for stays more than seven days. This new place is pretty posh and reasonable value for the money.

Cumberland House (Map 12)

Cumberland House (227 Nathan Rd, Yau Ma Tei), just above the Jordan MTR station, has a couple of seriously sleazy guesthouses that you should investigate only if you're desperate.

New Lucky House (Map 12)

New Lucky House (300 Nathan Rd, Yau Ma Tei) is in a slightly better neighbourhood than most of the other guesthouses. There are eight places to choose from in various price ranges. From the top to the bottom floor, the rundown is as follows:

Ocean Guesthouse (☎ 2385 0125, fax 2782 6441, 11th floor) Singles/doubles HK$200/250. All eight rooms in this rather comfy place have TVs, telephones and baths.

Nathan House (☎ 2384 0143, 10th floor) Singles/doubles HK$150/200. This tidy place is run by a woman who is something of a comedian.

Overseas Guesthouse (☎ 2384 5079, 9th floor) Singles/doubles with shared bath HK$180/200. This place is clean and friendly.

Tung Wo Guest House (☎ 2385 6152, fax 2780 7906, Flat D, 9th floor, New Lucky House, 300 Nathan Rd) Singles/doubles HK$140/160. This little four-room place is cheap but not so nice.

Hakka's Guest House (☎ 2770 1470, fax 2771 3656, Flat L, 3rd floor) Singles & doubles HK$250, triples HK$300. This is one of the nicest guesthouses in New Lucky House, but communication with staff is almost impossible.

Hitton Guest House (☎ 2770 4880, fax 2770 1363, Flat G, 3rd floor) Rooms HK$180. The owners here are charming.

Other Budget Accommodation

Not all budget accommodation in Kowloon is bunched together in one building.

Anne Black Guesthouse (☎ 2713 9211, fax 2761 1269, e annblack@ywca.org.hk, 5 Man Fuk Rd, Yau Ma Tei) Singles HK$330-385, doubles from HK$429. This guesthouse, which welcomes men and women, is located near Pui Ching and Waterloo roads in Mong Kok, uphill from and behind a Caltex petrol station.

Caritas Bianchi Lodge (☎ 2388 1111, fax 2770 6669, e cblresv@bianchi-lodge .com, 4 Cliff Rd, Yau Ma Tei) **Map 11** Singles/doubles/triples HK$360/410/510. Though it's just off Nathan Rd (and a goalie's throw from Yau Ma Tei MTR station) the rear rooms are very quiet and some have views onto King's Park.

Caritas Lodge (☎ 2339 3777, fax 2338 2864, e reservation@caritas-lodge.com, 134 Boundary St, Mong Kok) **Map 11** Singles/doubles/twins HK$385/440/660. This place is not as nice as the Caritas Bianchi Lodge, but it's close to the bird market and the New Territories is (officially) just across the road.

Dadol Hotel (☎ 2369 8882, 1st floor, Champagne Court, 16-20 Kimberley Rd, Tsim Sha Tsui) **Map 12** Rooms from HK$420. This 41-room hotel in a rundown shopping arcade is central but faded.

Rent-a-Room Hong Kong (☎ 2366 3011, mobile ☎ 9023 8022, fax 2366 3588, W www.rentaroomhk.com, Flat A, 2nd floor, Night Garden, 7-8 Tak Hing St, Yau Ma Tei) **Map 12** Singles HK$300, doubles HK$350-400, triples HK$450. This fabulous place run by Thomas Tang is going to change the face of budget accommodation in Hong Kong. He's got 40 positively immaculate rooms in various flats just over the 'border' from Tsim Sha Tsui on a leafy street and around the corner from the Jordan MTR station. Each has shower, TV, telephone (no charge for local calls) and there's free use of a washing machine. Larger rooms have a fridge.

Salisbury (☎ 2268 7000, fax 2739 9315, W www.ymcahk.org.hk, 41 Salisbury Rd, Tsim Sha Tsui) **Map 12** Dorm beds HK$199. This YMCA-run place has dorm beds (four beds per room) on the 9th floor. They're more than three times what you'd pay at Chungking or Mirador but the 'Y' is pretty plush. There are restrictions however: check-in is at 2pm and check-out at 11am; no-one can stay more than seven consecutive nights and walk-in guests aren't accepted if they've been in Hong Kong for more than 10 days.

Star Guesthouse (☎ 2723 8951, fax 2311 2275, Flat B, 6th floor, 21 Cameron Rd, Tsim Sha Tsui); *Lee Garden Guesthouse* (☎ 2367 2284, e charliechan@iname.com, 8th floor, D Block, 36 Cameron Rd) **Map 12** Small single with shared bath HK$200, doubles with bath HK$250, triples HK$400. These two excellent guesthouses are owned and run by the charismatic Charlie Chan, who can arrange most things for you. Long-term stayers get good discounts.

YMCA International House (☎ 2771 9111, fax 2388 5926, W www.ymcaintl househk.com, 23 Waterloo Rd, Yau Ma Tei) **Map 11** Dorm beds HK$220. This place isn't a budget option, but there is dormitory accommodation.

PLACES TO STAY – MID-RANGE

A double room at a mid-range hotel costs between HK$500 and HK$1800 per night. Once you go beyond that level you're in the super luxurious category. Some medium-priced hotels are as expensive as top-end choices, but lack the overall quality of the more elegant hotels. A good mid-range hotel is about HK$1000.

Some mid-range hotels offer cable TV and mini refrigerators. Many have business centres and email facilities; some have modern or unusual amenities. Be advised that some mid-range hotels charge up to HK$5 for a local call; guesthouses and top-end hotels usually don't. Often this is not clearly stated, so ask beforehand.

BP International House (☎ 2376 1111, fax 2376 1333, W www.megahotels.com.hk, 8 Austin Rd, Tsim Sha Tsui) **Map 12** Singles HK$990-1450, doubles HK$1100-1500, suites from HK$2950. This huge, 538-room hotel overlooks Kowloon Park from its north-west corner and is relatively convenient to most places of interest in Tsim Sha Tsui. The rooms are dowdy but comfortable; some of the more expensive rooms have good harbour views. There are bunk rooms available. Haggle before you book; prices are often reduced by half depending on the season and day of the week.

Booth Lodge (☎ *2771 9266, fax 2385 1140, 11 Wing Sing Lane, Yau Ma Tei)* **Map 11** Rooms HK$620-1200. This spotlessly clean place on a quiet street is run by the Salvation Army and an excellent choice.

Concourse Hong Kong Hotel (☎ *2397 6683, fax 2381 3768,* W *www.hotel concourse.com.hk, 22 Lai Chi Kok Rd, Mong Kok)* **Map 11** Doubles HK$800-1460, suites HK$2060. This hotel is run by China Travel Service. It's popular with tourists from mainland China, so don't expect service with a smile. The place scrambles at the edge of stylishness, but ends up excelling at adequacy. The neighbourhood is loud but you're very close to the Prince Edward MTR if you need an escape hatch.

Dorsett Seaview Hotel (☎ *2782 0882, fax 2781 8800,* W *www.pearlsea.com.hk, 268 Shanghai St, Yau Ma Tei)* Singles HK$880-1280, doubles HK$1280-1580, suites from HK$2400. What was until recently the Pearl Seaview does big trade in group tours from China. The rooms in this tall, thin building are fine and the Temple St and Jade Markets and Nathan Rd retail are within easy reach. The Tin Hau Temple is practically outside the front door.

Eaton Hotel (☎ *2782 1818, fax 2782 5563,* W *www.eaton-hotel.com, 380 Nathan Rd, Yau Ma Tei)* **Map 12** Rooms HK$1380-2680. This hotel in the huge New Astor Plaza complex, entered from Pak Hoi St, has a grand lobby and a number of fine outlets, including the relaxing Planter's Bar.

Empire Kowloon (☎ *2862 6588, fax 2865 5300,* W *www.asiastandard.com, 62 Kimberley Rd, Tsim Sha Tsui)* Rooms HK$1400-2000, suites from HK$2200. This brand-new sister hotel of the Empire in Wan Chai on Hong Kong Island is a designer hotel boasting a central location and a truly magnificent indoor swimming pool and spa.

Goodrich Hotel (☎ *2332 2020, fax 2332 3138,* e *goodrichhotel.vom.hk, 92-94 Woo Sung St, Yau Ma Tei)* **Map 12** Singles HK$580, doubles HK$680-880. The inviting, air-conditioned lobby is let down by the stuffy, slightly shabby rooms. It's right near the Temple St market and Jordan MTR and, unfortunately, also near a rubbish collection point. The quoted rates seem pretty liquid – try negotiating.

Grand Tower Hotel (☎ *2789 0011, fax 2789 0945,* W *www.grandhotel.com.hk, 627-641 Nathan Rd, Mong Kok)* **Map 11** Rooms HK$750-1700, suites from HK$2400. This place is an excellent deal for the price and within easy walking distance of the Mong Kok MTR station.

Guangdong International Hotel (☎ *2739 3311, fax 2721 1137,* W *www.gdihml.com .hk/gdhk, 18 Prat Ave, Tsim Sha Tsui)* **Map 12** Rooms HK$850-1300, suites from HK$2200. This mainland-owned pile of grey polished granite has 245 rooms towering over the heart of Tsim Sha Tsui.

Imperial Hotel (☎ *2366 2201, fax 2311 2360,* W *www.imperialhotel.com.hk, 30-34 Nathan Rd, Tsim Sha Tsui)* **Map 12** Singles HK$950-1700, doubles HK$1100-2000. The unrenovated rooms with faded pink bathrooms are prim, proper and squeaky clean. The hotel is so well located that the noise of Nathan Rd leaks right into the street-facing rooms – light sleepers should request a back room.

Kimberley Hotel (☎ *2723 3888, fax 2723 1318,* W *www.kimberley.com.hk, 28 Kimberley Rd, Tsim Sha Tsui)* **Map 12** Singles HK$1100-1750, doubles HK$1200-1850, suites HK$2150. The 546-room Kimberley isn't even slightly glam, but it's one of the better mid-range hotels in Tsim Sha Tsui, with assured staff and good rooms and facilities, including golf nets and a fabulous hot and cold spa bath. The lobby is on the 2nd floor.

Kowloon Hotel (☎ *2929 2888, fax 2739 9811,* e *khh@peninsula.com, 19-21 Nathan Rd, Tsim Sha Tsui)* **Map 12** Singles HK$1300-2550, doubles HK$1400-2650, suites from HK$3600. Part of the Peninsula stable, the 736-room Kowloon Hotel has a second-string feel, with its comically ostentatious lobby. Nevertheless, the hotel is popular for its unflappable service, decent rooms and the wonderful Wan Loong Court dim sum restaurant in the basement (see Chinese under Places to Eat later in this chapter).

Majestic Hotel (☎ *2781 1333, fax 2781 1773, 📧 info@majestichotel.com.hk, 348 Nathan Rd, Yau Ma Tei)* **Map 12** Rooms HK$950-1850, suites from HK$3000. This 387-room hotel housed in a 15-storey glass tower, entered from Saigon St, is close to the Jordan MTR station.

Metropole Hotel (☎ *2761 1711, fax 2761 0769, 🌐 www.metropole.com.hk, 75 Waterloo Rd, Yau Ma Tei)* **Map 11** Rooms HK$850-1580, suites from HK$3200. This 487-room baroque palace is a bit out of the way, but has some excellent outlets and facilities, including a huge outdoor swimming pool. Check the 50m-wide mural *Magnificent China* rising above the podium.

Miramar Hotel (☎ *2368 1111, fax 2369 1788, 🌐 www.miramarhk.com, 118-130 Nathan Rd, Tsim Sha Tsui)* **Map 12** Rooms HK$1100-1800, suites from HK$3800. This landmark (and very central hotel) has recently been renovated and reclad. The two-bedroom Imperial Chinese Suite is just to die for and a 'snip' at HK$15,000 a night.

Nathan Hotel (☎ *2388 5141, fax 2770 4262, 📧 nathanhk@hkstar.com, 378 Nathan Rd, Yau Ma Tei)* **Map 12** Singles HK$500-950, doubles HK$600-1300, triples HK$780-1450. The Nathan Hotel, which is entered from Pak Hoi St, is surprisingly quiet and pleasant; even the cheapest rooms are spacious, clean and serene. It's in a good location, right near the Jordan MTR station and the Temple St night market.

New Astor Hotel (☎ *2366 7261, fax 2722 7122, 🌐 www.newastorcom.hk, 11 Carnarvon Rd, Tsim Sha Tsui)* **Map 12** Doubles HK$880-$1180, suites from HK$2800. If you want to walk out of your hotel and get a face full of Hong Kong, this could be the place. It's close to Nathan Rd and right in the epicentre of the shopping mayhem of Carnarvon and Granville roads. The rooms

are a bit frayed, but reasonably priced and adequately appointed.

New Kings Hotel (☎ *2780 1281, fax 2782 1833, 473 Nathan Rd, Yau Ma Tei)* **Map 11** Singles HK$550-600, doubles HK$650-750. This place may look off the track, but it's hard by the Yau Ma Tei MTR station. The New Kings is a long-established place and the Temple St market is nearby.

Newton Hotel (☎ *2787 2338, fax 2789 0688, 🌐 www.newtonkln.com, 66 Boundary St, Mong Kok)* Rooms HK$750-1020. If you don't mind being in a noisy neighbourhood, the Prince Edward MTR is an easy five-minute walk away and you're close to the Mong Kok market, clothes stalls and noodle houses. The hotel itself is reasonable for the price – no surprises. There's also a Newtown Hotel of a similar standard in North Point on Hong Kong Island.

Park Hotel (☎ *2366 1371, fax 2739 7259, 📧 park2@chevalier.net, 61-65 Chatham Rd South, Tsim Sha Tsui)* **Map 12** Singles HK$900-1500, doubles HK$1000-1600, suites from HK$2200. The Park is busy and congenial with slightly dated rooms of good size. Family suites are available. The cavalcade of Kowloon museums is just over the road; the hustle of Granville Rd is a block away.

Ramada Hotel Kowloon (☎ *2311 1100, fax 2311 6000, 📧 hotel@ramada-kowloon .com.hk, 73-75 Chatham Rd South, Tsim Sha Tsui)* **Map 12** Rooms HK$1300-2050, suites from HK$2800. This Ramada has definitely seen better days (decades?), but the location, within striking distance of Kowloon's most important sights, and shopping and restaurant districts, is good.

Pruton Prudential Hotel (☎ *2311 8222, fax 2311 4760, 🌐 www.guangzhou.net/pru tonhk, 222 Nathan Rd, Yau Ma Tei)* **Map 12** Rooms HK$1000-2000, suites from HK$2700. This 434-room, 17-storey glass-tower hotel is very much in the centre of the action and counts some 100 boutiques in the massive shopping mall below it.

Royal Pacific Hotel & Towers (☎ *2736 1188, fax 2736 1212, 🌐 www.royalpacific .com.hk, China Hong Kong City, 33 Canton Rd, Tsim Sha Tsui)* **Map 12** Rooms

HK$1080-2100, suites from HK$2200. Choose between cheaper rooms in the hotel section or flashier rooms in the harbour-facing tower. The location is good: there's a walkway to Kowloon Park, leading onto Nathan Rd and the MTR station. At the back, the hotel is connected to the ferry terminal from where boats sail for Macau and China. It's also a mere skip to the shopping overkill of Harbour City.

Royal Plaza Hotel (☎ 2928 8822, fax 2606 0088, W www.royalplaza.com.hk, 193 Prince Edward Rd West, Mong Kok) **Map 11** Rooms HK$1000-1680, suites from HK$2800. The plushness is a bit overdone, but the Plaza is comfortable and central; it sits atop the KCR. The heated no-steam bathroom mirrors are a stroke of genius and the large outdoor pool is a lounge lizard's nirvana. The Mong Kok KCR station is accessible through the adjoining Grand Century Place shopping centre, making this a handy spot if you've business in the New Territories or China.

Salisbury (☎ 2268 7000, fax 2739 9315, W www.ymcahk.org.hk, 41 Salisbury Rd, Tsim Sha Tsui) **Map 12** Dorm beds HK$199, singles from HK$620, doubles HK$665-825, suites from HK$1080. If you can manage to book a room at the YMCA-run Salisbury, you'll be rewarded with professional service and excellent exercise facilities. The 303 rooms are comfortable but somewhat worn so keep your eyes on the harbour view. The four-bed dormitory rooms (see the listing in the previous Budget section) are a bonus, as are the family rooms.

Shamrock Hotel (☎ 2735 2271, fax 2736 7354, W www.yp.com.hk/shamrock, 223 Nathan Rd, Yau Ma Tei) **Map 12** Rooms HK$650-1200. The Shamrock has recently undergone a massive face-lift and is beginning to look like many of the faceless towers lining Nathan Rd and in Tsim Sha Tsui East. You should be able to get a much better deal than just the rack rate here.

Stanford Hillview Hotel (☎ 2722 7822, fax 2723 3718, W www.stamfordhillview .com, 13-17 Observatory Rd, Tsim Sha Tsui) **Map 12** Rooms HK$880-1580, suites from HK$2380. A decent place, entered

from Knutsford Terrace; near the food, fun and all-night dancing of Knutsford Terrace, but set back from the Nathan Rd in a quiet, leafy little corner of Tsim Sha Tsui. The rooms are forgettable but OK.

Stanford Hotel (☎ 2781 1881, fax 2388 3733, W www.stanfordhongkong.com, 118 Soy St, Mong Kok) **Map 11** Singles HK$780-1480, doubles HK$830-1480. This 200-room hotel is equidistant between the Mong Kok MTR and KCR stations and a hop, skip and a jump to the bird market.

Windsor Hotel (☎ 2739 5665, fax 2311 5101, W www.windsorhotel.com.hk, 39-43A Kimberley Rd, Tsim Sha Tsui) **Map 12** Rooms HK$950-1400, suites from HK$2400. This 166-room hotel is ideally situated for anyone intending to do a lot of shopping in Tsimsy.

YMCA International House (☎ 2771 9111, fax 2388 5926, W www.ymcaintl househk.com, 23 Waterloo Rd, Yau Ma Tei) **Map 11** Dorm beds HK$220, singles HK$560-850, doubles HK$680-850, suites from HK$1100. Though a bit out of the way, this 427-room hotel with all the mod-cons is a steal for what it offers; so you must book well in advance. This place is open to men and women.

PLACES TO STAY – TOP END

When you mention the words 'hotel' and 'Hong Kong', many people think of the Peninsula, which opened in 1928 and is the matriarch of the territory's luxury hotels. Across from the Pen is the Regent, with a much more modern feel to it and fabulous views. These are Kowloon's two 'face' hotels.

Tsim Sha Tsui East, an area of reclaimed land to the north-east that has yet to come of age, is weighted down with top-end hotels. It's not very convenient for public transport, but most of the hotels here run shuttle buses to Tsim Sha Tsui proper and/or Central. You'll find many more top-end hotels lining Nathan Rd as it travels north from the harbour.

You can get discounts of up to 30% at many hotels by booking your room through a local travel agency or the Hong Kong Hotels Association (see Accommodation in the

Hong Kong Facts for the Visitor chapter for details).

Grand Stanford Inter-Continental (☎ 2721 5161, fax 2732 2233, Ⓦ www .grandstanford.com, 70 Mody Rd, Tsim Sha Tsui East) Singles HK$2100-2900, doubles HK$2200-3000, suites from HK$3900. This 579-room palace offers excellent discounts, depending on the season and the day of the week. Part of its harbour view is marred by the unsightly Hung Hom Bypass.

Harbour Plaza (☎ 2621 3188, fax 2621 3311, Ⓦ www.harbour-plaza.com, 20 Tak Fung St, Hung Hom) Singles HK$2200-3250, doubles HK$2350-3400. This massive 417-room hotel on the waterfront in less-than-desirable Hung Hom is owned by property magnate Li Ka-shing and is where mainland honchos like Premier Jiang Zemin stay when they visit Hong Kong.

Holiday Inn Golden Mile (☎ 2369 3111, fax 2369 8016, Ⓦ www.goldenmile.com, 50 Nathan Rd, Tsim Sha Tsui) **Map 12** Singles HK$1000-1500, doubles HK$1050-1600, suites from H$3500. The business-like Golden Mile isn't a bad place to base yourself. The rooms are Holiday Inn-reliable and you've got the brilliant Avenue (see International under Places to Eat later in this chapter) restaurant on the 1st floor, the schmoozy Hari's bar (see Rock & Folk under Entertainment later in this chapter) on the mezzanine level and Deli Corner for all your picnic needs in the basement.

Hyatt Regency (☎ 2311 1234, fax 2739 8701, Ⓔ general@hyattregency.com.hk, 67 Nathan Rd, Tsim Sha Tsui) **Map 12** Rooms HK$1250-2500, suites from HK$4400. The Hyatt, on the 'wrong' side of Nathan Rd and sitting atop a sad little shopping arcade, is lower priced than most of its neighbours and a relaxed kind of hotel. Its Chinese Restaurant (see Places to Eat later) is justly revered and there's one of the cheesiest bars in Hong Kong – the Chin Chin, with a shaken-not-stirred 1960s vibe.

Kowloon Shangri-La (☎ 2721 2111, fax 2723 8686, Ⓦ www.shangri-la.com, 64 Mody Rd, Tsim Sha Tsui East) **Map 12** Singles HK$2300-3350, doubles HK$2500-3550,

suites from HK$4200. This 725-room extravaganza is not nearly as swish as its sister hotel in 'new' Wan Chai, but the views and its eight restaurants, including the superb French Margaux, are stunning.

Marco Polo Hong Kong, Gateway & Prince hotels (☎ 2113 0088, fax 2113 0011, Ⓦ www.marcopolohotels.com, Harbour City, 3 Canton Rd, Tsim Sha Tsui) **Map 12** Singles HK$2300-3530, doubles HK$2400-3630, suites from HK$3960. The Marco Polo Hong Kong is the linchpin in the Marco Polo Hotel group's Canton Rd trio, which includes the Marco Polo Gateway and the Marco Polo Prince – both of which are in the Harbour City complex on Canton Rd to the north. The Marco Polo Hong Kong Hotel is slightly closer to the Star Ferry and a bit higher priced; it's got an outdoor pool and plenty of shopping in the attached mall. The Marco Polo Gateway is a flash hotel with good business facilities, while the Prince, at the northern end of Harbour City, is the slick younger sister, with smart and newly renovated rooms. If you stayed in one of these hotels, you could do all your shopping, eating and entertaining in Harbour City and never go outdoors.

New World Renaissance Hotel (☎ 2369 4111, fax 2369 9387, Ⓦ www.renaissance hotels.com/hkgnw, 22 Salisbury Rd, Tsim Sha Tsui) **Map 12** Rooms HK$1700-2000, suites from HK$3300. This recently renovated Kowloon stalwart is popular with European group tours. Rooms with harbour views speak for themselves; in-facing rooms are a little disappointing. There's an outdoor pool set in a huge but somewhat unkempt garden with a spectacular view.

Hotel Nikko (☎ 2739 1111, fax 2311 3122, Ⓦ www.hotelnikko.com.hk, 72 Mody Rd, Tsim Sha Tsui East) **Map 12** Rooms HK$2360-3560, suites from HK$5850. Another almost faceless TST East hotel, this time with 444 guestrooms and loads of Japanese tourists. It's not a very efficiently run place, but the harbour views are stunning.

Peninsula Hotel (☎ 2920 2888, fax 2722 4170, Ⓦ www.peninsula.com, Cnr Salisbury & Nathan Rds, Tsim Sha Tsui) **Map 12** Rooms HK$3000-4900, suites from

HK$5600. Lording it over the southern tip of Kowloon, Hong Kong's finest hotel evokes colonial elegance and actually resembles a huge throne. Classic European-style rooms boast faxes, VCRs, CD players and marble bathrooms. Many rooms in the Pen's 20-storey addition offer spectacular harbour views; in the original building, you'll have to make do with interior sumptuousness. Some of the outlets, such as the French restaurant Gaddi's (see Places to Eat) and The Bar (see Jazz & Blues under Entertainment), are the best eating and drinking spots of their class in the territory.

Regal Kowloon Hotel (☎ 2722 1818, fax 2369 6950, W www.regal-hotels.com, 71 Mody Rd, Tsim Sha Tsui East) **Map 12** Rooms HK$1100-2700, suites from HK$5000. This place is a bargain by Tsim Sha Tsui East standards, but the blush-pink decor that seems to sneak into every room and outlet may grate.

The Regent (☎ 2721 1211, fax 2739 4546, www.regenthotels.com, 18 Salisbury Rd, Tsim Sha Tsui) **Map 12** Rooms HK$3100-4500, suites from HK$5500. The 514-room Regent is to rock stars what the Pen is to royalty. The hotel with the best position in the territory tilts at modernity while bowing to colonial traditions, such as a fleet of Rolls Royces, uniformed doormen and incessant brass polishing. The emphasis on service ensures a lot of return custom. The restaurants (eg, the superb Lai Ching Heen; see Chinese under Places to Eat) are excellent and the foyer bar has the best view in Hong Kong. Even if you don't stay here, drop by for a drink. Things may change soon, though; the UK brewery Bass has bought the hotel and plans to rebrand it as an Inter-Continental.

Royal Garden (☎ 2721 5215, fax 2369 9976, W www.theroyalgardenhotel.com .hk, 69 Mody Rd, Tsim Sha Tsui East) **Map 12** Singles HK$2100-2600, doubles HK$2250-2750, suites from HK$3700. This often-overlooked, 442-room hotel has an impressive garden atrium, a stunning rooftop pool that is covered in winter and Sabatini, one of the best Italian restaurants in Hong Kong (see Places to Eat).

Sheraton Hong Kong Hotel & Towers (☎ 2369 1111, fax 2739 8707, W www.sher aton.com/hongkong, 20 Nathan Rd, Tsim Sha Tsui) **Map 12** Singles HK$2200-3300, doubles HK$2400-3600, suites from HK$3300 (hotel) and HK$4300 (towers). This very American hostelry at the start of Nathan Rd is as central as you'll find. Choose between rooms in the hotel or in the towers; the towers offer superior harbour views (and higher prices).

PLACES TO EAT
Kowloon doesn't have quite the same range of restaurants as Hong Kong Island does, but you will still find quite an assortment of ethnic eateries in Tsim Sha Tsui. What's more, prices are usually a little lower than those on the island.

Chinese
The choice of Chinese food from all the major regions is enormous in Kowloon.

Canton Court (☎ 2739 3311 ext 176, 1st floor, Guangdong International Hotel, 18 Prat Ave, Tsim Sha Tsui) **Map 12** Meals from HK$200. This place serves excellent dim sum from 7am-3pm daily.

Chinese Restaurant (☎ 2311 1234, 2nd floor, Hyatt Regency Hong Kong, 67 Nathan Rd, Tsim Sha Tsui) **Map 12** Meals from HK$350. This restaurant has acquired a good reputation for its original Cantonese food. The seafood is great and the high ceilings and traditional booth seating – based on Chinese teahouses of the 1920s – make for an unusual dining experience.

Chong Fat Chiu Chow Restaurant (☎ 2383 3114, 2383 1296, 60-62 South Wall Rd, Kowloon City) **Map 10** Meals from HK$150. While this place is not easy to get to and communications will be limited, it has some of the best and freshest Chiu Chow seafood in the land. Don't miss the crab dishes, *sek lau gai* (chicken wrapped in little sacks made of egg white) and the goose.

Dai Pai Dong (☎ 2317 7728, 70 Canton Rd, Tsim Sha Tsui) **Map 12** Breakfast HK$22-30, noodles & rice dishes from HK$48. This modern version of the outdoor food stall serves breakfast (bacon and eggs,

Cream-and-red minibuses stop when hailed.

The Star Ferry crosses Victoria Harbour.

Double-decker trams on Hong Kong Island.

Taxis are always available, except in a typhoon!

The available choices are wide and varied in Hong Kong, both at markets and outside temples.

Hong Kong Fire Services insignia

Calligraphy at the Wong Tai Sin temple complex

Traditional lanterns on a Kowloon temple.

porridge, instant noodles), lunch and dinner (noodles), but it's best to come at afternoon tea for such oddities as *yuan yang* (half-tea, half-coffee), boiled cola with lemon and ginger and toast smeared with condensed milk.

Delicious Food Chow Noodle Restaurant (☎ 2367 0824, 22 Prat Ave, Tsim Sha Tsui) **Map 12** Meals about HK$50. This simple restaurant is worth trying for a cheap lunch, though the decor is a bit basic.

Dynasty (☎ 2369 4111 ext 6361, Level 4, New World Renaissance Hotel, 22 Salisbury Rd, Tsim Sha Tsui) **Map 12** Meals from HK$250. The traditional rosewood furniture and ambience of this hotel restaurant make for an authentic Cantonese dining experience. Specialities include steamed sliced pork with preserved shrimp paste and fresh salmon with rice noodle strips.

Eastern Palace Chiu Chow Restaurant (☎ 2730 6011, Shop 307-308, Marco Polo Hong Kong Hotel Shopping Arcade, Zone D, Harbour City, 3 Canton Rd, Tsim Sha Tsui) **Map 12** Meals about HK$200. Dim sum is served from 11.30am to 3pm daily.

Extremely Good Restaurant (☎ 2394 8414, 148-150 Sai Yeung Choi St South, Mong Kok) **Map 11** Dishes HK$20-36. This busy noodle shop is known for its wonton soups and shredded pork noodles with spicy bean sauce. This is an eat-and-go sort of place – don't come here if you feel like slurping slowly and lingering.

Fook Lam Moon (☎ 2366 0286, 1st floor, 53-59 Kimberley Rd, Tsim Sha Tsui) **Map 12** Meals from HK$250. One of Hong Kong's top Cantonese restaurants, the Fook Lam Moon takes care of its clients from the minute you walk out of the lifts, with cheongsam-clad hostesses waiting to escort you to your table. Sample the pan-fried lobster balls, a house speciality.

Great Shanghai Restaurant (☎ 2366 8158, 1st floor, 26-36 Prat Ave) **Map 12** Meals from HK$150-200. This restaurant may be a bit touristy, but that makes it easier to negotiate for non-Chinese speakers. The stir-fried freshwater shrimps are a speciality.

Happy Garden Noodle & Congee Kitchen (☎ 2377 2604, 68-80 Canton Rd, Tsim Sha Tsui) **Map 12** Noodles HK$20-35,

soup noodles HK$30-38, congee HK$13-30. This is a budget option, where you can fill up on great soup noodles and congee for very little.

Harbour View Seafood (☎ 2722 5888, 3rd floor, West Wing, Tsim Sha Tsui Centre, 66 Mody Rd, Tsim Sha Tsui East) **Map 12** Meals from HK$200. This place has stunning harbour views and good dim sum, served 11am to 5pm daily.

Hing Kee (☎ 2384 3647, 19 Temple St, Yau Mat Tei) **Map 11** Meals HK$20-50. There's only one dish served at this semi-outdoor stall – rice cooked over charcoal in an earthenware pot and topped with either beef or chicken. It's a traditional winter dish, but there are enough rice fans to keep the stall in business all year. Yau Mat Tei is entered from Hi Lung Lane.

Islam Food (☎ 2382 2822, 1 Lung Kong Rd, Kowloon City) **Map 10** Meals from HK$100. If you fancy trying *hui* (Chinese Muslim) food (eg, minced beef with pickled cabbage stuffed into sesame rolls) head for this place in Kowloon City.

Jade Garden Restaurant (☎ 2730 6888, 4th floor, Star House, 3 Salisbury Rd, Tsim Sha Tsui) **Map 12** Meals HK$150-250, dim sum HK$16-36. People turn their noses up at the Maxim's chain of 'Garden' restaurants, but they're not half bad, service is excellent and the food reliable, if somewhat predictable. This branch is just opposite the Tsim Sha Tsui Star Ferry terminal. It's particularly well known for its dim sum.

Lai Ching Heen (☎ 2721 1211, Ground floor, Regent Hotel, 18 Salisbury Rd, Tsim Sha Tsui) **Map 12** Meals from HK$400. On the harbour side of the Regent Hotel, the Lai Ching Heen has repeatedly won awards for its refined Cantonese cuisine. The menu changes with each lunar month, and if the selections get confusing there's always a waiter hovering nearby to act as a guide.

North Sea Fishing Village (☎ 2723 6843, Basement, Auto Plaza, 65 Mody Square, Tsim Sha Tsui East) **Map 12** Meals from HK$150. If you can ignore the cheesy nautical decor, this place is celebrated for its inexpensive fish dishes. It also has good dim sum.

Peking Restaurant (☎ 2730 1315, 1st floor, 227 Nathan Rd, Tsim Sha Tsui) **Map 12** Meals HK$120. This no-frills restaurant keeps Peking duck fans merrily chomping away. If duck doesn't do it for you, try the Peking-style crab dishes and pastries.

Royal Garden Chinese Restaurant (☎ 2721 5215, Royal Garden Hotel, 69 Mody Rd, Tsim Sha Tsui East) **Map 12** Meals from HK$200. This is one of the best places in Hong Kong for dim sum.

Snake King (☎ 2383 6297, 11 Lung Kong Rd, Kowloon City) **Map 10** Soups HK$30-120. Should you visit Hong Kong in winter and are anxious to indulge in a taste of one of these slithering 'narrow fellows', the Snake King can oblige.

Snow Garden Shanghai Restaurant (☎ 2736 4341, 10th floor, 219 Nathan Rd) **Map 12** Meals HK$150-250. This is another popular venue for Shanghai food; come here for drunken pigeon, braised sea cucumber and sautéed freshwater shrimps, or just try the *siu long bao* (traditional Shanghai meat-filled steamed buns).

Spring Deer (☎ 2366 4012, 1st floor, 42 Mody Rd, Tsim Sha Tsui) **Map 12** Whole Peking duck HK$280. This is probably Hong Kong's most famous (not best, mind) Peking restaurant and serves some of the crispiest Peking duck in town. While not exactly budget dining, it won't break the bank either. This place is extremely popular, so book several days in advance.

Spring Moon (☎ 2315 3160, 2920 2888, 1st floor, Peninsula Hotel, Salisbury Rd, Tsim Sha Tsui) **Map 12** Meals from HK$400. This restaurant in the Peninsula Hotel is grand and impressive – and the food ain't half bad either.

Tai Fung Lau Peking Restaurant (☎ 2366 2494, Windsor Mansion, 29-31 Chatham Rd, Tsim Sha Tsui) **Map 12** Half/whole Peking duck HK$130/240. If you can't get into the Spring Deer, try this place, which serves some fine northern specialities.

Wan Loong Court (☎ 2734 3722, Basement, Kowloon Hotel, 19-21 Nathan Rd, Tsim Sha Tsui) **Map 12** Meals HK$150-250. There's wonderful Cantonese food here with modern touches; the dim sum takes some beating. Standout dumplings include steamed beef with tangerine peel, and groupa with lemongrass and minced squid. The house-special dessert is *tai chi* cake, a chestnut paste and poppy seed pastry.

Wu Kong Shanghai (☎ 2366 7244, Basement, Alpha House, 27-33 Nathan Rd, Tsim Sha Tsui) **Map 12** Cold dishes HK$64-110, meat mains HK$56-80, seafood mains HK$100-160. This place and its signature dishes, cold pigeon in wine sauce and crispy fried eels, are excellent. The beggar's chicken (HK$340) is also excellent. Dim sum is served all day.

American (Map 12)

Buddy's Famous Seafood (☎ 2199 7998, 31 Ashley Rd, Tsim Sha Tsui) Starters HK$40-85, mains HK$110-190. From the same stable as Fat Angelo's is this American (almost New England-style) seafood restaurant that delivers real clam chowder and steamed clams.

Café Rouge (☎ 2383 8188, 16 Nam Kok Rd, Kowloon City) **Map 10** Set lunches HK$42-45, set dinners HK$85-105. This mostly American-style restaurant with a French name is a welcome oasis in *very* ethnic Kowloon City.

Dan Ryan's Chicago Grill (☎ 2735 6111, Shop 200, Ocean Terminal, Zone C, Harbour City, Canton Rd, Tsim Sha Tsui) Sandwiches HK$75-112, salads HK$98-130, mains HK$95-135, half/full rack ribs HK$132/198. The theme here is 'Chicago', including a model elevated rail system overhead and Chicago weather and news bulletins broadcast in the loos. It is *the* place for burgers and ribs in Hong Kong.

Hard Rock Cafe (☎ 2375 1323, Ground & 1st floors, Silvercord Shopping Centre, 30 Canton Rd, Tsim Sha Tsui) Burgers & set lunches from HK$88. Why you'd come here is beyond us, but here it is should you need onion rings, chicken strips and/or a 'Hard Rock Cafe Kowloon' T-shirt.

Planet Hollywood (☎ 2377 7888, Marco Polo Hong Kong Hotel Shopping Arcade, Zone D, Harbour City, 3 Canton Rd, Tsim Sha Tsui) Sandwiches & burgers HK$78-98.

Join the long queues of diners eager to sample the standard American fare.

Ruby Tuesday *(☎ 2376 3122, Shop 283, Ocean Terminal, Zone C, Harbour City, Canton Rd, Tsim Sha Tsui)* Mains HK$118-188, salad bar HK$72. This place boasts 'awesome food' and a 'serious salad bar'; it's just, like, gotta be American. Huge portions.

Asian Fusion
Felix *(☎ 2366 6251, 28th floor, Peninsula Hotel, Salisbury Rd, Tsim Sha Tsui)* **Map 12** Meals from HK$400. The food here is East meets West, but most people come here to gawk at the decor: high ceilings, vast windows, hulking copper-clad columns surrounding Art Deco-style table settings.

Filipino
Mabuhay *(☎ 2367 3762, 11 Minden Ave, Tsim Sha Tsui)* **Map 12** Mains HK$40-65. This dark and dank place serves authentic Filipino food, which is not to everyone's taste (lots of garlic, lots of tamarind and little of anything else). Still, the staff are friendly and the *sinigang* (HK$50-75), described as 'our own tom yum gung, sir,' by the waiter, is good.

French (Map 12)
Gaddi's *(☎ 2366 6251, Peninsula Hotel, Salisbury Rd, Tsim Sha Tsui)* Meals from HK$600. Legendary for decades, Gaddi's still holds onto its reputation as *the* French restaurant in Hong Kong. It has boasted virtually the same menu (and some of the same staff, apparently) for more than 30 years. The atmosphere is a bit stilted, making it hard to relax, but the food will probably keep you excited.

Au Trou Normand *(☎ 2366 8754, 1st floor, Taurus Building, 63 Carnarvon Rd, Tsim Sha Tsui)* Meals from HK$250. The 'Norman hole', which takes its name from the custom in Normandy of drinking a glass of Calvados (apple brandy) in the middle of the meal to 'dig a hole' and allow room for more courses, is a much cheaper place to try the local version of *la cuisine française*. It's a comfortable, easy-going place and highly recommended.

German & Austrian (Map 12)
Biergarten *(☎ 2721 2302, 5 Hanoi Rd, Tsim Sha Tsui)* Set lunch HK$65. Head for the 'beer garden' for pork knuckle, sauerkraut and the selection of excellent beers on tap.

Schnurrbart *(☎ 2366 2986, 9-11 Prat Ave, Tsim Sha Tsui)* Bar snacks HK$65, mains HK$95-135. This is the Kowloon branch of the German eatery.

Weinstube *(☎ 2376 1800, 1st floor, Honeytex Building, 22 Ashley Rd, Tsim Sha Tsui)* Meals HK$150-250. *Pfannengebratener fleischkäse* (pan-fried meatloaf) and other hearty German mains await at this place, which has been going strong for over 20 years.

Indian (Map 12)
There are countless Indian residents in Kowloon. For meatless Indian meals, see the Vegetarian entry later.

Gaylord *(☎ 2376 1001, 1st floor, Ashley Centre, 23-25 Ashley Rd, Tsim Sha Tsui)* Meat mains HK$78-88, vegetarian dishes HK$52-58. The first Indian restaurant to open in Hong Kong, the Gaylord has been going strong since 1972. Dim lighting, booth seating and live Indian music set the scene for enjoying the excellent *rogan josh* (HK$69), dhal and other favourite Indian dishes.

Jhankar *(☎ 2332 3563, 2nd floor, Double Set Commercial Centre, 37A B Jordan Rd, Yau Ma Tei)* Set lunch/dinner HK$45/68. This inexpensive restaurant specialises in south Indian cuisine but also, and rather incongruously, does some Thai dishes. Enter Yau Ma Tei from Temple St.

Koh-i-Noor *(☎ 2368 3065, 1st floor, Shop 3-4, 1st floor, Peninsula Mansion, 14-16 Mody Rd, Tsim Sha Tsui)* Lunch buffet HK$45 Mon-Fri, set menu for two HK$188. One of a chain of restaurants, this branch is cheaper and less stylish than its counterpart in Central, but the food is great and the staff friendly. The speciality is north Indian food.

Surya Restaurant *(☎ 2366 9902, Basement, Lyton Building, 34-48 Mody Rd)* Mains HK$58-69. This is a cheap place to get your dosa mutton biryani, lamb *keema sali* and chicken tikka.

The greatest concentration of cheap Indian and Pakistani restaurants in Kowloon is in *Chungking Mansions (36-44 Nathan Rd, Tsim Sha Tsui)* **Map 12** Despite the grotty appearance of the building, many of these 'messes' are quite plush, though claustrophobic. The food varies in quality, but if you follow the recommendations below you should be in for a cheap and very filling meal. A good lunch or dinner will cost from about HK$50; for HK$100 you'll get a blow-out. Only one of the places is licensed, but you are usually allowed to BYO.

Delhi Club (☎ 2368 1682, Flat C3, 3rd floor, C Block) This place does very good-value Indian and Nepalese food. Try the chicken tandoori (HK$20).

Everest Club (☎ 2316 2718, Flat D6, 3rd floor, D Block) This place is pretty flash by Chungking Mansions standards and boasts a cornucopia of six 'Everest' cuisines, including Tibetan.

Islamabad Club (☎ 2721 5362, Flat C4, 4th floor, C Block) This spartan place will fill you up with Indian and Pakistani halal food.

Khyber Pass Club Mess (☎ 2721 2786, Flat E7, 7th floor, E Block) The Khyber Pass has good food served in very basic surroundings.

Swagat Restaurant (☎ 2722 5350, Flat C4, 1st floor, C Block) This place is one of the most popular in Chungking Mansions. Though the food is indeed very good, the portions huge and the decor a cut above the rest of the Chungking crowd, the main reason for its popularity might be that it's the only fully licensed mess in the entire place.

Taj Mahal Club (☎ 2722 5454, Flat B3, 3rd floor, B Block) The Taj is popular with those who like truly hot curries and like to pay little for them. Try the chicken *masala* (HK$38).

Indonesian

Java South-East Asian Restaurant (☎ 2367 1230, 38 Hankow Rd, Tsim Sha Tsui) **Map 12** Mains HK$50-70, rijstafel HK$140-170. Here you'll get rijstafel (literally, rice table) with up to 16 dishes served with a large bowl of rice. It packs out with Dutch expats, most of whom complain that the same food is a lot cheaper in Amsterdam. The *gado-gado* and *soto ayam* are also good.

International (Map 12)

Avenue (☎ 2315 1118, 1st floor, Holiday Inn Golden Mile, 50 Nathan Rd, Tsim Sha Tsui) Meals from HK$400. This wonderful Continental restaurant makes Nathan Rd its focal point.

Jimmy's Kitchen (☎ 2376 0327, 1st floor, Kowloon Centre, 29 Ashley Rd, Tsim Sha Tsui) Starters HK$60-95, mains from HK$150, set lunch/dinner HK$150-180. This place has a lengthy and generous menu that has attracted a loyal following. It's been around since 1928 and there's a branch in Central.

Italian (Map 12)

Fat Angelo's (☎ 2730 4788, 33 Ashley Rd, Tsim Sha Tsui) Salads HK$30, pasta HK$65-135, mains HK$125-170. This branch of the popular Italo-American is generous with its portions and seamless in its service.

La Taverna (☎ 2376 1945, Astoria Building, 36-38 Ashley Rd, Tsim Sha Tsui) From about HK$250. This is a popular, though not especially authentic, Italianesque eatery with very attentive service.

Valentino (☎ 2721 6449, Shop 27A, Ocean View Court, Chatham Rd South, Tsim Sha Tsui) Starters HK$98-128, pasta HK$117-128, mains HK$178-198. This long-established Italian restaurant has moved from Hanoi Rd to Chatham Rd South and gone a whole lot more upmarket (and expensive) in the process.

Sabatini (☎ 2721 5215, 3rd floor, Royal Garden Hotel, 69 Mody Rd, Tsim Sha Tsui East) Meals from HK$300. Sabatini is a direct copy of its namesake in Rome. The food and the ambience are equally memorable.

Japanese (Map 12)

Japanese food can be among the most expensive in Hong Kong, but it doesn't always have to be so.

Genki Sushi (☎ 2722 6689, Shop G7-G9, East Ocean Centre, 98 Granville Rd, Tsim Sha Tsui East) Sushi HK$9-35. This cheap and cheerful susherie, popular with young Hong Kong Chinese, doesn't have a word of English within its four walls, but you'll recognise the logo – not a cringy 'smiley face' but a frowning 'meanie face'.

Gomitori (☎ 2367 8519, *Shop LG5, Basement, Energy Plaza, 92 Granville Rd, Tsim Sha Tsui East*) Yakitori HK$150-250. This *yakitori* restaurant the size of a cupboard will grill you chicken in a variety of ways. It's always packed with Japanese expats – always a good sign.

Kyo-Zasa (☎ 2376 1888, *20 Ashley Rd, Tsim Sha Tsui*) Dishes HK$48-68. This colourful and cosy Japanese eatery is very authentic. The food is spot-on and the prices reasonable.

Kyushu-Ichiba (☎ 2314 7889, *144 Austin Rd, Tsim Sha Tsui*) Sushi HK$25-50, rice & noodle dishes HK$48-58. This inexpensive Japanese eatery is a favourite with the local young bloods of Tsim Sha Tsui.

Nadaman (☎ 2721 2111, *Basement, Kowloon Shangri-La Hotel, 64 Mody Rd, Tsim Sha Tsui East*) Meals from HK$400. We're now in big bucks territory…The authentic traditional setting at this restaurant has won it a well-deserved reputation. It is *very* expensive, though the set meals at lunch time are excellent value.

Osaka (☎ 2376 3323, *14 Ashley Rd, Tsim Sha Tsui*) Meals from HK$150. A splash of class above the hustle of Ashley Rd, this atmospheric restaurant has pinafored waitresses and a menu which extends from sushi to steaks. There are reasonably priced set lunches too.

Korean (Map 12)

Many Korean places are barbecue restaurants, where you sit around a table with a griddle in the middle, upon which you fling strips of meat or fish, and eat it with vegetables and pickles set in little bowls on your table.

Arirang (☎ 2956 3288, *Shop 2306, The Gateway, 25 Canton Rd, Tsim Sha Tsui*) Mains HK$60-160. This is a large, brightly lit restaurant that may not be the place for a romantic tête à tête, but is great for a party. It's mostly given over to barbecue.

Busan Korean Restaurant (☎ 2376 3385, *29 Ashley Rd, Tsim Sha Tsui*) Barbecue from HK$100, rice dishes HK$80. This wonderfully authentic place in the bustling hub of tourist Tsim Sha Tsui manages to stay on, despite the nearby competition.

Three-Five Korean Restaurant (☎ 2376 1545, *6 Ashley Rd, Tsim Sha Tsui*) Mains HK$88-130. This place is small but sizzlingly popular.

Malaysian & Indonesian (Map 12)

Banana Leaf Curry House (☎ 2721 4821, *3rd floor, Golden Crown Court, 68 Nathan Rd*) Meals from HK$100. This centrally located branch of a chain of Malaysian/Singaporean restaurants is convenient to the guesthouses on the southern end of Nathan Rd. There are five other branches, including one in Causeway Bay.

Satay Hut (☎ 2723 3681, *Shop 144-148, Houston Centre, 63 Mody Rd, Tsim Sha Tsui*) Meals from HK$100. This place on the 1st floor of a shopping and office complex doesn't look promising, but it serves some of the best (and most authentic) lahksa and saté in town.

Pan-Asian (Map 12)

Pep 'n' Spices (☎ 2376 0893, *Basement, 10 Peking Rd, Tsim Sha Tsui*) Lunch buffet HK$55. This friendly place serves anything that happens to be hot and spicy and Asian: from saté to *tom yum gung*. Fun for a group.

Salisbury's Dining Room (☎ 2268 7000, *4th floor, The Salisbury, 41 Salisbury Rd, Tsim Sha Tsui*) Lunch/dinner buffet HK$98/218. One of the best lunch-time bargains is the buffet at this YMCA-run hotel. The food is not exquisite, but it's good value for money, the atmosphere is cheery and it has a prime location.

A Touch of Spice (☎ 2312 1118, *10 Knutsford Terrace, Tsim Sha Tsui*) Starters HK$45-60, curries HK$75, seafood dishes HK$85-165. This is one of four trendy restaurant/bars stacked up at 10 Knutsford Terrace (the others serve Russian, Cuban and seafood). A Touch of Spice does Indonesian and Vietnamese noodles, stir-fried dishes and curries. It's pretty reasonably priced unless you go for the seafood. If you do want fish, try *Island Seafood* (☎ *2312 6663)* on the ground floor.

Spanish (Map 12)

La Tasca (☎ *2723 1072, 8 Hanoi Rd, Tsim Sha Tsui)* Mains HK\$75-95, tapas HK\$38-50. This place is famed for its tapas, but also does more substantial Spanish main courses.

El Cid (☎ *2312 1989, 14 Knutsford Terrace, Tsim Sha Tsui)* Tapas HK\$30-65. This branch of the chain does reasonable paella and has an excellent assortment of tapas and Spanish wines. Actually there are two restaurants here: one serving just tapas and another serving both tapas and main courses.

Thai (Map 10)

The district of Kowloon City, which abuts the old Kai Tak Airport to the north-east, has a high concentration of Thai residents and Thai restaurants. There are also a few Indian and Chinese restaurants. You'll eat a meal for HK\$60 and a feast for HK\$100 at all these places so it makes it worth the trip.

Friendship Thai Food (☎ *2382 8671, 38 Kai Tak Rd)* This is the most basic and authentic Thai restaurant in the area and always full of Thai domestics.

Golden Orchid Thai (☎ *2383 3076, 12 Lung Kong Rd)* Slightly more expensive than the Friendship but the food is excellent.

Cambo Thai Restaurant (☎ *2716 7318, 15 Nga Tsin Long Rd)* This place serves toned-down Thai to young Hong Kong Chinese. That it's not authentic should be apparent almost immediately; their other restaurant – at No 27 of the same street – specialises in Vietnamese (faux?) pho.

Sweet Basil Thai Cuisine (☎ *2718 1088, 31-33 Kai Tak Rd)* The Sweet Basil, a branch of a chain, serves decent Thai in very upmarket (for this neighbourhood) surrounds.

Thai Farm Restaurant (☎ *2382 0992, 21-23 Nam Kok Rd)* This place, with its wood-panelled walls and long tables, is a cut above most of the other Thai eateries – but too much attention has been given to the decor at the expense of the food.

Vegetarian

Branto Indian Pure Vegetarian Club (☎ *2366 8171, 1st floor, 9 Lock Rd, Tsim Sha Tsui)* Map 12 Meals from HK\$60. This cheap and excellent place is where to go if you want to try south Indian food. Sublime.

Higher Taste Vegetarian Dining Club (☎ *2723 0260, 6th floor, 27 Chatham Rd, Tsim Sha Tsui)* Map 12 Set lunch & dinner HK\$30 Mon-Sat, free Sun. You are invited to take off your shoes and chant 'Hare Krishna' through mouthfuls of cheap vegetarian offerings along with a colourful assortment of people.

Joyful Vegetarian (☎ *2780 2230, 530 Nathan Rd, Yau Ma Tei)* Map 11 Meals around HK\$40-60. The vegetable country-style hotpot is made with a ravishing range of fungi. There's a snack stall out the front of this Buddhist place if you need a bite on the hoof (sorry).

Kung Tak Lam (☎ *2367 7881, 1st floor, 45-47 Carnarvon Rd)* Map 12 Meals from HK\$100. Like its sister-restaurant in Causeway Bay, this MSG-free place serving Shanghai vegetarian cuisine attracts a loyal clientele who wouldn't eat anywhere else. It's won awards.

Miu Gute Cheong Vegetarian Restaurant (☎ *2771 6218, 31 Ning Po St, Yau Ma Tei)* Map 12 Meals about HK\$50. This inexpensive place is family oriented. There's a bit of spill-over bustle from Temple St, but an unruffled serenity prevails. The tofu is fresh and firm, the vegetables are the pick of the market and the tea flows freely.

Pak Bo Vegetarian Kitchen (☎ *2380 2681, Lee Tat Building, 787 Nathan Rd, Mong Kok)* Map 11 Meals about HK\$60. This place up near Boundary St isn't really worth a detour, but it's here should you be dragging the streets (and lowering your standards) in Mong Kok.

Woodlands Indian Vegetarian Restaurant (☎ *2369 3718, Shops 5 & 6, Mirror Tower, 61 Mody Rd, Tsim Sha Tsui)* Map 12 Meals about HK\$100. If you can't handle the less-than-salubrious surrounds of Chungking Mansions, this place offers inexpensive Indian meals.

Vietnamese (Map 12)

Golden Bull (☎ 2730 4866, Shop 101, 1st Floor, Ocean Centre, Zone B, Harbour City, Canton Rd, Tsim Sha Tsui) Set lunches HK$49-64. There's a queue outside this place almost every night. They're not coming for the atmosphere (noisy) or service (abrupt), but the excellent-quality, low-cost Vietnamese food. There's a branch in Causeway Bay.

Peace Garden (☎ 2721 2582, 4-4A Hillwood Rd, Tsim Sha Tsui) Meals from HK$150. Standard Vietnamese dishes upstairs on a quiet street off Nathan Rd.

Cafes (Map 12)

Café Beaubourg (☎ 2721 2939, Shop B, 58-60A Kimberley Rd, Tsim Sha Tsui) Snacks from HK$60. This narrow nook isn't even remotely like its namesake facing the Pompidou Centre in the City of Light but it offers reasonable coffee, croques-monsieur and croques-madame, and crepes both savoury and sweet.

Cafe.com (☎ 2721 6623, Shop 5, Tern Plaza, 5 Cameron Rd, enter from Cameron Lane) Espresso HK$15, sandwiches HK$12-20, salads HK$15. On offer here are 13 different coffee concoctions. There are also teas, including fruit tisanes.

Delifrance (☎ 2629 1845, Shop G101, The Gateway, 25-27 Canton Rd, Tsim Sha Tsui) Sandwiches from HK$25, set lunches HK$29-45. This is a branch of the popular bakery and patisserie chain noted for its pastries, muffins, submarine sandwiches and quiche, not to mention coffee. There's another branch (☎ 2369 2180, Ground floor, Carnarvon Plaza, 20 Carnarvon Rd, Tsim Sha Tsui) a bit farther east.

First Cup Coffee (☎ 2316 7793, 3 Lock Rd, Tsim Sha Tsui) Medium coffees HK$9-58. This hole-in-the-wall serves some excellent gourmet coffees and sweet treats. Worth going out of your way for.

Saint's Alp Teahouse (☎ 2393, 134 Sai Yeung Choi St, Mong Kok) Snacks from HK$50. There are literally dozens of these clean, cheap Taiwanese snackeries in Hong Kong – you can recognise them by the footprint in front of the name (which is written in Chinese). They're a great pit stop for frothy tea with tapioca drops and Chinese snacks like toast with condensed milk, shrimp balls, noodles and rice puddings. There's a second Mong Kok branch (☎ 2782 1438, 61A Shantung St, Mong Kok).

Fast Food (Map 12)

Hau Fook St is filled with food stalls (dishes about HK$25). It's a few blocks east of Nathan Rd in Tsim Sha Tsui and isn't included on many tourist maps. Walking north from the intersection of Carnarvon and Cameron roads, it's the first lane on your right. Most of the places don't have English menus, but you can always point.

Temple St, the area around the night market (open 8pm to 11pm; dishes from HK$20), is a traditional place for cheap eats. Market cuisine, served from a pushcart, includes fish balls or squid on skewers and there's a large choice on offer from the nearby stalls.

Oliver's Super Sandwiches (☎ 2735 0068, Shop 010, Ground floor, Ocean Centre, Zone B, Harbour City, Canton Rd, Tsim Sha Tsui) Sandwiches HK$26-35, soups HK$12-16, salads HK$20-32. This is a great place for breakfast – inexpensive bacon, eggs and toast. The sandwiches are equally good. The restaurant packs out during lunch hour, but is blissfully uncrowded at other times. There's another Tsim Sha Tsui branch (☎ 2367 0881, Shop LG1-1A, Tung Ying Building, 100 Nathan Rd), which is entered from Granville Rd.

Self-Catering (Map 12)

Delicatessen Corner (☎ 2315 1020, Basement, Holiday Inn Golden Mile, 50 Nathan Rd, Tsim Sha Tsui) This is an excellent (but pricey) place to shop for a picnic or just to pause for a pastry and coffee while thumbing through the morning papers – there's a cafe attached.

Oliver's (☎ 2730 9233, Shops 007 & 013, Ground floor, Ocean Centre, Zone B, Harbour City, Canton Rd, Tsim Sha Tsui) You'll find all sorts of exotic comestibles as well as wine and liqueurs at this popular delicatessen.

Wellcome (28 Hankow Rd, Tsim Sha Tsui) This branch of the supermarket chain is much better stocked and maintained than the other Tsim Sha Tsui branch (74-78 Nathan Rd).

Park 'N' Shop (Ground floor, Silvercord Shopping Centre, 30 Canton Rd, Tsim Sha Tsui).

ENTERTAINMENT

For the most part, Kowloon's entertainment scene plays second fiddle to the after-dark hot spots of Hong Kong Island. Still the district is littered with bars and pubs. It's just a bit tackier, less imaginative and more rundown.

For information about classical music concerts, theatre, opera and the like, see Entertainment in the Hong Kong Facts for the Visitor chapter.

You can book tickets for films, concerts and a great variety of cultural events over the phone via the Cityline, URBTIX and Ticket City agencies. Again, see Entertainment in the Hong Kong Facts for the Visitor chapter for details.

Pubs & Bars (Map 12)

There are three basic clusters of bars in Tsim Sha Tsui: along Ashley Rd; within the triangle formed by Hanoi, Prat and Chatham roads; and up along Knutsford Terrace. Tsim Sha Tsui East is the domain of swanky hostess bars and nightclubs.

Amoeba Bar (☎ 2376 0389, Ground floor, 1st floor, Honeytex Building, 22 Ashley Rd, Tsim Sha Tsui) This stylish bar, which stays open till as late as 6am, has big-screen entertainment in the basement from around 9pm. It draws a mainly Cantonese crowd. Happy hour runs from noon to 9pm.

Delaney's (☎ 2301 3980, Basement, Mary Building, 71-77 Peking Rd, Tsim Sha Tsui) This branch of a pub chain seems more authentically Irish than the original Delaney's in Wan Chai, with lots of dark wood, green felt and a long bar that you can really settle into. Happy hour is from 5pm to 8pm.

Jouster II (☎ 2723 0022, Shops A & B, Hart Avenue Court, 19-23 Hart Ave, Tsim Sha Tsui) This is a bizarre, multistorey place with medieval decor; check the knight in shining armour and miniature drawbridge. The crowd is mostly Chinese, and not very welcoming, and the noise can be deafening.

Kangaroo Pub (☎ 2376 0083, 1st & 2nd floors, 35 Haiphong Rd, Tsim Sha Tsui) The infamous kangaroo is the bane of Australian expats. But the 'Roo' gets pretty lively, and there are some decent Australian beers like Cooper's and VB, and tucker (mains HK$72-75, set dinner HK$100). This is where you come to watch Aussie Rules and rugby on satellite TV with the lads. Happy hour is from 4pm to 7pm.

Sky Lounge (☎ 2369 1111, 18th floor, Sheraton Hong Kong Hotel & Towers, 20 Nathan Rd, Tsim Sha Tsui) Before you can begin clucking your tongue about the departure lounge feel of this big, long bar, you've already started marvelling at the view. Don't take flight: sit down in a scoop chair, sip a drink and scoff international snacks.

Watering Hole (☎ 2312 2288, Basement, 1A Mody Rd, Tsim Sha Tsui) This pub with the imaginative name and generous happy hour, from 4pm to 10pm is a grotty, salt-of-the-earth kind of place popular with both Chinese and expats.

Discos & Clubs (Map 12)

Tsim Sha Tsui does not have a great deal to offer when it comes to dancing, but this small selection should satisfy even the most ardent bopper.

Bahama Mama's Caribbean Bar (☎ 2368 2121, 4-5 Knutsford Terrace, Tsim Sha Tsui) Entry $100 after 11pm Fri & Sat. Bahama Mama's theme is tropical, with palm trees and surfboards creating an 'island' feel. It's a friendly spot and stands apart from most of the other late-night watering holes in this part of town. On Friday and Saturday nights there's a DJ spinning and folks bopping on the bonsai-sized dance floor.

Boom Bar & Club (☎ 2172 7282, Shop D, Chevalier House, 45-51 Chatham Rd South, Tsim Sha Tsui) Entry HK$180. This new kid on the block is making a splash, especially with Groove@Boom, a techno and house disco every Wednesday and Friday from 11pm to 6am.

Chemical Suzy (☎ 2736 0087, AWT Centre, 2A-B Austin Ave, Tsim Sha Tsui) This is a cyber-groover hide-out with DJs, snacks and a mixed crowd. Thursday is Queer Night from 6pm to 4am.

Club Shanghai (☎ 2721 1211, Regent Hotel, 18 Salisbury Rd, Tsim Sha Tsui) Ballroom dance Thur HK$400. Club Shanghai is quite posh, with a 1930s Shanghai theme that goes as far as placing (empty) opium pipes on each table. An American house band pumps out dance tunes six nights a week.

Energy Karaoke (☎ 2366 3388, 8 Humphreys Ave, Tsim Sha Tsui) Oh, go on – be a sport. This newfangled karaoke club has private booths with hundreds of songs to choose from in Chinese, Korean, Japanese and English. Come with friends and unimpress them in your own padded cell.

In-V (☎ 2734 6640, 17th-19th floors, Renaissance New World Hotel, 22 Salisbury Rd, Tsim Sha Tsui) Entry HK$100. This club, called the Catwalk until recently, remains a hot spot for Hong Kong's monied young things. There are live bands on one floor, a disco on another and karaoke on a third. Mobile phones, designer watches, cigars and Cognac are the order of the day.

Rick's Café (☎ 2311 2255, 53-59 Kimberley Rd, Tsim Sha Tsui) Entry HK$120 Fri & Sat. Rick's, one of Tsim Sha Tsui's better-known venues, has cheesy 'Casablanca' decor, complete with palm trees. The dance floor is usually a writhing knot of Western men and Filipino girls.

Nightclubs (Map 12)

Most of Hong Kong's hostess-filled nightclubs are best avoided unless you want to pick up a chit a metre long and riddled with hidden extras. However, the following establishments are considered respectable (more or less).

Bottoms Up (☎ 2721 4509, Basement, 14-16 Hankow Rd, Tsim Sha Tsui) This place has a particular appeal for James Bond fans. Duty brought agent 007 there on one of his Asian sojourns (*The Man with the Golden Gun*, 1974), and the club is still milking it; it's naughty but nice.

China City (☎ 2723 1898, 4th floor, Peninsula Centre, 67 Mody Rd, Tsim Sha Tsui East) This two-storey place is popular with Chinese tycoons, judging from the cars parked outside.

Club Bboss (☎ 2369 2883, Lower ground floor, New Mandarin Plaza, 14 Science Museum Rd, Tsim Sha Tsui East) The biggest, most garish hostess bar in town. It's a ridiculous scene: floorshows, babes, and men drinking Cognac because they think it's classy.

Club Deluxe (☎ 2721 0277, Shop L3, New World Centre, 18 Salisbury Rd, Tsim Sha Tsui) This is a good place to burn money, especially in the VIP karaoke suites. The club has an indoor waterfall, among other exotic features.

Gay & Lesbian Venues (Map 12)

Apart from Chemical Suzy's one-nighter (see the earlier Discos & Clubs section), there's not much of a gay clubbing scene on this side of the puddle. There are a couple of OK pubs, though.

New Wally Matt Lounge (☎ 2721 2568, 5A Humphrey's Ave, Tsim Sha Tsui) The name comes from the old Waltzing Matilda pub, one of the daggiest gay watering holes in creation and where a French friend swears that the escargots on his plate were plucked from the walls of that dank and dark place. But new Wally Matt is an upbeat, busy pub, with Internet access. Happy hour is from 5pm to 10pm.

New Wally Malt Bar & Lounge (☎ 2367 6874, 3 Granville Circuit, Tsim Sha Tsui) This place behind the Ramada Hotel is more 21st century than its sister boozer, but less cruisy.

Rock & Folk (Map 12)

Chasers (☎ 2367 9487, Shop 2, Carlton Building, 2-3 Knutsford Terrace, Tsim Sha Tsui) This is a friendly, somewhat classy bar with a live Filipino covers band every night from 9.30pm. Before the band cranks up there's a jukebox to party along to. There's a bar menu till midnight, snacks till 4am and dancing most nights; weekends see a major sweat-fest.

Hari's (☎ 2369 3111 ext 1345, Mezzanine, Holiday Inn Golden Mile, 50 Nathan Rd, Tsim Sha Tsui) Tacky or classy? You decide, after you've had a couple of speciality martinis (there are over a dozen to challenge you, including wasabi and garlic ones). There's live music nightly: it's covers Monday to Saturday and 'folk classics' on Sunday. Happy hour runs from 5pm to 9pm Monday to Saturday, and all night Sunday.

Jazz & Blues (Map 12)
48th Street Chicago Blues (☎ 2723 7633, 2A Hart Ave, Tsim Sha Tsui) This welcome addition to the Tsim Sha Tsui music scene has live music most nights. It's expensive to drink here (beers HK$38-48, cocktails HK$55-75), but the happy hour (4pm-7pm) cuts prices almost in half.

The Bar (☎ 2315 3135, 1st floor, Peninsula Hotel, Salisbury Rd, Tsim Sha Tsui) For mellow 1940s and 50s jazz, take your smoking jacket along and sip Cognac at the Bar in the Pen. Your fellow tipplers will be serious business types, coutured couples and new money trying to look old. The music typically starts at 9.30pm.

Blue Note (☎ 2721 2111, Kowloon Shangri-La Hotel, 64 Mody Rd, Tsim Sha Tsui East) You know this place is trying hard when it names itself after the most famous jazz spot in the world. Come along for mostly imported talent on a rotating residency basis every night except Sunday.

Ned Kelly's Last Stand (☎ 2376 0562, 11A Ashley Rd, Tsim Sha Tsui) A great tradition continues with the Kelly Gang playing Dixieland jazz nightly till 2am. Food is available and there's never a cover charge.

Cinemas
AMC Festival Walk (☎ 2265 8545, Upper ground floor & levels 1 & 2, Festival Walk, 80-88 Tat Chee Ave, Kowloon Tong) **Map 10** This 11-screen complex at Hong Kong's poshest mall is the largest cinema in the territory.

Broadway Cinematheque (☎ 2782 0877, 2322 9000, Prosperous Garden, 3 Public Square St, Yau Ma Tei) **Map 11** This is an unlikely place for an alternative cinema, but it's worth coming up for new art-house releases and rerun screenings. There's the *Cinematheque Cafe Bar* (☎ 2388 4665) next door, which serves good coffee and decent pre-flick food (sandwiches HK$35-40, mains HK$62-78), and in the next space is – wait for it – the *Bruce Lee Museum* (admission free; open 1pm-10pm daily), a little display room filled with kung fu memorabilia.

Ocean Theatre (☎ 2377 2100, Marco Polo Hong Kong Hotel Shopping Arcade, Zone D, Harbour City, 3 Canton Rd, Tsim Sha Tsui) **Map 12** The Ocean screens the usual blockbusters.

Silvercord Cinema (☎ 2377 2100, Silvercord Shopping Centre, 30 Canton Rd, Tsim Sha Tsui) **Map 12** The Silvercord is Kowloon's most accessible cinema. Its two theatres screen the latest Hollywood releases.

SHOPPING
Shopping in Kowloon is a bizarre mix of the down-at-heel and the glamorous. Die-hard shoppers can spend the whole day in Harbour City, a mall with 700 shops in four zones (A to D) on Canton Rd in Tsim Sha Tsui, without ever seeing the light of day. From the boutique shopping arcade of the Peninsula to the stalls of the Temple St night market, you can find just about anything if you are prepared to look hard enough.

A word of warning, however. If you're looking to make some expensive purchases such as cameras, video recorders or stereo equipment, please remember that Tsim Sha Tsui is a rip-off. While it's quite all right to buy clothing, curios and lots of other things, you should look elsewhere when buying pricey hi-tech items.

Antiques & Curios (Map 12)
Most of the rich pickings for antiques lie south of Victoria Harbour, notably along *Hollywood Rd* and *Wyndham St*, in Central, but there are a few places of interest in Kowloon. There are a few antique shops in the Ocean Terminal (Zone C) section of the *Harbour City complex* in Tsim Sha Tsui, but getting a good price is considerably more difficult there than on Hong Kong Island because of the high rents.

Curio Alley This is a fun place to shop for chops, soapstone carvings, fans and other Chinese bric-a-brac. It's found in an alleyway linking Lock and Hankow roads, just south of Haiphong Rd, Tsim Sha Tsui.

Silk Road (Level 3, Marco Polo Hong Kong Hotel Shopping Arcade, Zone D, Harbour City, 3 Canton Rd, Tsim Sha Tsui) Antique shops are concentrated along this corridor; here you can find cloisonné, bronzes, jade, lacquer, ceramics, rosewood furniture and screens. *Artorient (Room 342)* has a fine selection of Buddhist and Tibetan artefacts.

Charlotte Horstmann & Gerald Godfrey (☎ 2735 7167, Shop 100D, Ocean Terminal, Zone C, Harbour City, Canton Rd, Tsim Sha Tsui) Well-known among dealers in Hong Kong, this tiny shop has a great selection of top-quality textiles, ceramics, jade and sculpture on display.

Eileen Kershaw (☎ 2366 4083, West Wing, Peninsula Hotel, Salisbury Rd, Tsim Sha Tsui) Eileen Kershaw has a splendid collection of porcelains and carpets.

Stone Village (☎ 2787 0218, 44 Flower Market Rd, Mong Kok) **Map 11** Creative plant pots, pottery figurines and tea sets plus a lot of beautiful bonsai that you're unfortunately unlikely to be able to take home.

Cameras & Photo Equipment (Map 12)

Tsim Sha Tsui is not the best place to buy cameras (or any type of photographic equipment for that matter), but not all dealers should be tarred with the same brush. There are some recommended places.

David Chan (☎ 2723 3886, Shop 15, Champagne Court, 16 Kimberley Rd, Tsim Sha Tsui) This dealer, one of the most reliable in Hong Kong, sells both new and antique cameras.

Onesto Photo Company (☎ 2723 4668, Shop 2, Champagne Court, 16 Kimberley Rd, Tsim Sha Tsui) This retail establishment, formerly trading as Kimberley Camera Company, is just as reliable as Mr Chan's. There are price tags on the equipment (a rare find in Tsim Sha Tsui), but there's always some latitude for bargaining.

Carpets & Rugs (Map 12)

In this game, it's worth knowing what you're buying; if you're in doubt, don't buy. There are a few places in *Ocean Terminal* that stock a decent range.

Carpet World (☎ 2730 4000, Shop 271, Ocean Terminal, Zone C, Harbour City, Canton Rd, Tsim Sha Tsui) This place has a huge selection of carpets and rugs, with an emphasis on Chinese ones.

Chinese Carpet Centre (☎ 2735 1030, Shops 166 & 168, Ocean Terminal, Zone C, Harbour City, Canton Rd, Tsim Sha Tsui) This place has a huge selection of new Chinese carpets and rugs.

Tai Ping Carpets (☎ 2369 4061, Shop G9-13, Wing On Plaza, 62 Mody Rd, Tsim Sha Tsui East) This large shop has an excellent selection of carpets and rugs and what you don't see you can order.

Clothing

The best hunting grounds for streetwear and groovy one-of-a-kinds are generally in Tsim Sha Tsui at the eastern end of *Granville Rd* and along *Austin Ave* (**Map 12**). You'll find better prices at the street markets on *Tung Choi St* in Mong Kok (**Map 11**) and in *Apliu St* in Sham Shui Po (**Map 10**), but the selection is not as good.

i.t (☎ 2736 9152, Shop 1030, Miramar Shopping Centre, 1-23 Kimberley Rd, Tsim Sha Tsui) **Map 12** This shop and ones nearby both sell the cute, trendy women's gear that surrounds you on the streets all day. There are i.t and I.T stores in all the major shopping areas (capitalisation denotes its 'grown up' range).

*K*facto.2y (☎ 2369 3161, 57 Granville Rd, Tsim Sha Tsui)* **Map 12** This orthographically challenged shop has streetwear, grindwear and footwear for skaters and grinders. This bit of Granville Rd is a top strip for easy heads-or-tails fashion and co-ordinates.

Ocean Boutique (☎ 2366 0889, 1 Minden Ave, Tsim Sha Tsui) **Map 12** Kiddies gear made in China and Korea, much of it with funny English misspellings. The jump suits promise rumpus while the formal dresses are both tragic and amusing.

Onitsuka (☎ 2368 1085, 15c Austin Ave, Tsim Sha Tsui) **Map 12** Basic black, threaded women's gear with trinkets, eyelets, studs and general naughtiness.

Pro Cam-Fis (☎ 2736 1382, Shop 148, Ocean Terminal, Zone C, Harbour City, Canton Rd, Tsim Sha Tsui) **Map 12** Open 10am-7pm. Outdoor men's gear, both lightweight and cold-weather, including kids' sizes.

Rag Brochure (☎ 2391 4660, Shop 4, Trendy Zone, Chow Tai Fook Centre, 580A Nathan Rd, Mong Kok) **Map 10** One of a crush of fashion outlets here selling new and vintage gear for guys and gals. This is where the cool dudes shop for clothes, cheap jewellery, watches and action figures.

Sam's Tailor (☎ 2367 9423, Shop K, Burlington Arcade, 92-94 Nathan Rd, Tsim Sha Tsui) **Map 12** Shirts from HK$100-150, suits from HK$1000. It's not certain that Sam's is the best tailor in Hong Kong, but it's the best known. Sam's has sewed for everyone – from royalty to rock stars.

Zoom (☎ 2781 0920, 65 Fa Yuen St, Mong Kok) **Map 12** Superfly treads rule in this teasing strip of sports shoe shops. All brands and breeds of sneakers get air. It's packed at the weekend.

Computers

Kowloon has a load of centres selling computers and related equipment but *caveat emptor* is the best phrase to bear in mind as you browse.

Golden Plaza Shopping Centre (Basement & 1st floor, 146-152 Fuk Wah St, Sham Shui Po) **Map 10** This centre has some computers and components, but has mostly switched over to suspicious-looking CDs, DVDs and videos.

Mong Kok Computer Centre (☎ 2781 1109, 8-8A Nelson St, Mong Kok) **Map 10** This centre has three floors of computer shops. In general, it's geared more towards the resident Cantonese-speaking market than foreigners, but you can generally get better deals than in Tsim Sha Tsui. Check *Winframe System* (☎ 2300 1238, Shop 106).

New Capital Computer Plaza (1st & 2nd floors, 85-95 Un Chau St, Sham Shui Po)

Map 10 This is a decent place, with a good range and helpful staff who can muster up enough English to close a sale.

Star Computer City (☎ 2736 2608, 2nd floor, Star House, 3 Salisbury Rd, Tsim Sha Tsui) **Map 12** This is the largest complex of computer shops in Tsim Sha Tsui. While it's not the cheapest place in Hong Kong, neither is it the most expensive (that honour goes to nearby Nathan Rd).

Department Stores (Map 12)

All the big Western-style department stores have outlets in Kowloon, some of them much bigger than their counterparts on Hong Kong Island. They include *Lane Crawford* (☎ 2118 3428, Levels 1 & 2, Ocean Terminal, Zone C, Harbour City, Canton Rd, Tsim Sha Tsui) and *Wing On* (☎ 2710 6288, Wing On Plaza, 62 Mody Rd, Tsim Sha Tsui East).

Chinese Emporiums

Most of the large Chinese department stores sell an eclectic range of ceramics, furniture, souvenirs and clothing.

Chinese Arts & Crafts (☎ 2735 4061, Star House, 3 Salisbury Rd, Tsim Sha Tsui) **Map 12** CAC, with quality chinoiserie and fixed prices, has a Yau Ma Tei branch (☎ 2730 0061, Nathan Hotel, 378 Nathan Rd).

CRC Department Store (☎ 2395 3191, Argyle Centre Tower 1, 65 Argyle St, Mong Kok) **Map 11** This place, with two branches on Hong Kong Island, sells an eclectic range of ceramics, furniture, souvenirs and clothing.

Yue Hwa Chinese Products Emporium (☎ 2384 0084, 301-309 Nathan Rd, Yau Ma Tei) **Map 12** This enormous store has everything the souvenir-hunting tourist could want. There is a Tsim Sha Tsui branch (☎ 2317 5333, 1 Kowloon Park Drive, enter from Peking Rd) **Map 12** and another nearby outlet (☎ 2368 9165, 54-62 Nathan Rd) **Map 12**.

Electronic Goods

Whatever you do, don't ever buy anything electrical along Nathan Rd; you could be seriously burned in more ways than one.

Sham Shui Po (Map 10) is a good neighbourhood to search for electrical and electronic goods; you can even buy and offload used appliances. If you take any of the west exits from the Sham Shui Po MTR station, you'll find yourself on Apliu St, where there are numerous such shops. This street is also a good area to buy any of the many permutations of plug adaptors you'll need if you're heading to China.

Mong Kok (Map 11) is another good district for electronic gadgetry. Starting from Argyle St and heading south, explore all the side streets running parallel to Nathan Rd, including Tung Choi, Sai Yeung Choi, Portland, Shanghai and Reclamation sts.

Eyeglasses

Cohen Optical (☎ 2369 0548, 45 Peking Rd, Tsim Sha Tsui) Map 12 The reliable and honest staff at this large shop are always ready and willing to cut you a deal.

Gems (Map 12)

Om International (☎ 2366 3421, 1st floor, Friend's House, 6 Carnarvon Rd, Tsim Sha Tsui) This place has an excellent selection of saltwater and freshwater pearls. The staff are scrupulously honest and friendly.

Opal Mine (☎ 2721 9933, Shop G & H, Burlington Arcade, 92-94 Nathan Rd, Tsim Sha Tsui) This place, more of a museum than a shop, has a truly vast selection of Australian opals that makes for fascinating viewing.

Jewellery & Objets d'Art (Map 12)

Chinese gold is almost pure; that's why many pieces have that dark, almost orange colour to them. Jewellers' display-windows are garishly piled high with gold ornaments: good luck trophies, Chinese zodiac animals and the odd gold bar (or tael).

J's Jewellery (☎ 2730 8593, Shop 231D, Ocean Terminal, Zone C, Harbour City, Canton Rd, Tsim Sha Tsui) Hardly your typical Hong Kong jeweller, J's has affordable baubles for those who like to glister without blistering. Most pieces are silver but some feature small diamonds.

King Fook (☎ 2313 2788, Shop G1, Miramar Shopping Centre, 1-23 Kimberley Rd, Tsim Sha Tsui) & *Tse Sui Luen* (☎ 2926 3210, Shop A & B, Ground floor, 190 Nathan Rd, Tsim Sha Tsui) Both these jewellery store chains guarantee to buy back any jewellery at its wholesale price. Be sure you get the certificate of purchase when you buy.

King Sing Jewellers (☎ 2735 7021, Shop 14, Ground floor, Star House, 3 Salisbury Rd, Tsim Sha Tsui) A long-standing jewellers with a wide selection of diamonds, pearls and gold items. The sales staff are pleasantly unpushy.

Ming's Jewellery (☎ 2721 6889, Room 31, Regent Hotel Shopping Arcade, 18 Salisbury Rd, Tsim Sha Tsui) Here you'll find a stunning selection of crafted pieces.

Music

You can pick up very cheap (we're asking no questions) CDs, DVDs and video cassettes at the *Temple St night market* (Map 12) and from *shops* in Mong Kok (Map 10).

HMV (☎ 2302 0122, Sands Building, 12 Peking Rd, Tsim Sha Tsui) Map 12 Open 10am midnight daily. This large branch store has an excellent and wide-ranging selection of CDs, video CDs and DVDs, racks of magazines, and a vast index of all CDs in existence, as well as informative staff.

Sporting Goods

Ahluwalia & Sons (☎ 2368 8334, 8C Hankow Rd, Tsim Sha Tsui) Map 12 Shabby but established, this store is well stocked with golf gear, tennis racquets, cricket bats, shirts and balls. It's cash only and no prices are marked, so haggle away.

Chamonix Alpine Equipment (☎ 2388 3626, On Yip Building, 395 Shanghai St, Mong Kok) Map 11 This two-floor shop has a wide range of camping, hiking and climbing equipment. The Hong Kong Mountaineering Training Centre (☎ 2384 8190) is also based here.

Golf Creation (☎ 2721 8869, Shops 12 & 15, Hong Kong Pacific Centre, 28 Hankow Rd, Tsim Sha Tsui) Map 12 This shop keeps chuppies equipped with the equipment of their favourite new game.

Flying Ball Bicycle Co (☎ 2381 3661, *201 Tung Choi St, Mong Kok*) **Map 11** Serious cyclists will find a great selection of bikes and accessories here.

Ming's Sports Co (☎ 2376 1387, *53 Hankow Rd, Tsim Sha Tsui*) **Map 12** This is an excellent place to buy diving equipment.

Mountaineer Supermarket (☎ 2397 0585, *1st floor, 395 Portland St, Mong Kok*) **Map 11** This is a great spot for climbing equipment and outfits.

Ocean Terminal (☎ 2118 8668, *Zone C, Harbour City, Canton Rd, Tsim Sha Tsui*) **Map 12** This large mall has a number of outlets where you can pick up sports equipment, clothing and footwear, including ***Gigasports*** (☎ 2992 0389, *Shop 033*) and ***Sporting Edge*** (☎ 2735 4255, *Shop 140A*).

Tang Fai Kee Military Surplus (☎ 2385 5169, *248 Reclamation St, Mong Kok*) **Map 11** For military surplus, head here.

Three Military Equipment Company (☎ 2395 5234, *83 Sai Yee St, Mong Kok*) **Map 11** Another good shop for outdoor gear.

Wise Mount Sports (☎ 2787 3011, *75 Sai Yee St, Mong Kok*) **Map 12** Specialising in outdoor equipment and clothing, this is another good choice for the enthusiast.

The New Territories

The New Territories were so named because they were leased to Britain in 1898, almost half a century after Hong Kong Island and four decades after Kowloon were ceded to the crown. For decades the area was Hong Kong's rural hinterland; however since WWII, when some 80% of the land was under cultivation, many parts of the NT (as the area is known locally) have become increasingly urbanised. In the past two decades the speed at which this development has taken place has been nothing short of breathtaking.

A trip to the New Territories remains imperative, not only to witness a society in transition, but to see up close what little there remains of traditional rural life.

Many Hong Kong residents make the New Territories their getaway for the weekend, and the eastern section, notably the Sai Kung Peninsula and the area around Clearwater Bay, has some of Hong Kong's most beautiful scenery and hiking trails. Life in these more rural parts of Hong Kong is more redolent of times past – simpler, slower, often more friendly.

The New Territories is large, comprising 72% of Hong Kong's land area. Strictly speaking, everything north of Boundary St in Kowloon up to the border with mainland China is the New Territories. The northernmost part of the New Territories, within 1km of the Chinese frontier, is a 'closed border area' that is fenced and well marked with signs. It marks the boundary of the Hong Kong Special Administrative Region (SAR) with the Special Economic Zone (SEZ) of Shenzhen.

Some 3.29 million people, up from less than half a million in 1970, call the New Territories home – 48% of the total population of Hong Kong. Most of them live in 'New Towns'. Since its inception in the 1950s, the New Towns Program has consumed more than half of the Hong Kong government's budget, with much of the funding spent on land reclamation, sewage,

Highlights

- A climb up Tai Mo Shan, Hong Kong's highest peak
- A visit (and allow lots of time!) to the incomparable Hong Kong Heritage Museum in Tai Wai near Sha Tin
- A hike along a section of the MacLehose Trail (eg, around the Shing Mun Reservoir and Arboretum)
- A sailing expedition to Tap Mun Chau, the most evocative and timeless island in the archipelago
- A day of bird-watching in the Mai Po Marsh
- A visit to Hoi Ha Wan Marine Park

roads and other infrastructure projects. About 60% of new housing units are government built.

In the past, the biggest impediment to growth in the New Territories was a lack of good transportation. This began to change dramatically some 20 years ago, with the opening of the Mass Transit Railway (MTR) Tsuen Wan line in 1982. In the same year, the Kowloon-Canton Railway (KCR) underwent a major expansion and the system was electrified and double tracked. The Light Rail Transit (LRT) system opened six years later. In 2003 it will be integrated with the KCR West Rail, a 30.5km-long line that will link southern Kowloon with Tuen Mun via Yuen Long.

A host of other infrastructure projects are scheduled or under construction in the New Territories, including a knot of expressways straddling the western New Territories to link Kowloon with Shekou, Bao'an and Humen in southern China; expressways connecting the eastern New Territories with Shenzhen; and – hardest to conceive – a mooted US$1.7 billion bridge linking the westernmost tip of the New Territories with

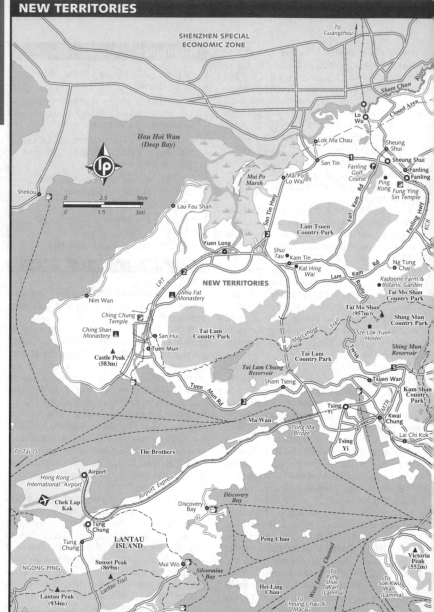

NEW TERRITORIES

SHENZHEN SPECIAL
ECONOMIC ZONE

To Guangzhou

Sham Chun River

Closed Area

Lo Wu

Lok Ma Chau

Hau Hoi Wan
(Deep Bay)

Sheung Shui

Sheung Shui

San Tin

Fanling

Fanling

Fanling Golf Course

Mai Po Lo Wai

Mai Po Marsh

Ping Kong

Fung Ying Sin Temple

Fan Kam Rd

Fanling Hwy

KCR

Shekou

Lau Fau Shan

San Tin Hwy

Lam Tsuen Country Park

Yuen Long

Shui Tau

Kam Tin

Kat Hing Wai

Ng Tung Chai

Kadoorie Farm & Botanic Garden

NEW TERRITORIES

Lam Kam Route

LRT

Miu Fat Monastery

Tai Mo Shan Country Park

Tai Mo Shan (957m)

Shing Mun Country Park

Nim Wan

Ching Chung Temple

Ching Shan Monastery

San Hui

Tuen Mun

Tai Lam Country Park

MacLehose Trail

Sze Lok Yuen Hostel

Shing Mun Reservoir

Castle Peak (583m)

Tai Lam Country Park

Twisk

Castle Peak (583m)

Tai Lam Chung Reservoir

Sham Tseng

Tai Lam Country Park

Tsuen Wan

Kam Shan Country Park

Tuen Mun Rd

MTR

Kwai Chung

To Tai O

Ma Wan

Tsing Ma Bridge

Tsing Yi

Tsing Yi

Lai Chi Kok

Hong Kong International Airport

Airport

Airport Express

The Brothers

Discovery Bay

Discovery Bay

Peng Chau

Victoria Peak (552m)

Chek Lap Kok

Tung Chung

Tung Chung

LANTAU ISLAND

Sunset Peak (869m)

Mui Wo

Silvermine Bay

West Lamma Channel

To Yung Shue Wan (Lamma)

To Sok Kwu Wan (Lamma)

NGONG PING

Lantau Trail

Lantau Peak (934m)

Hei Ling Chau

To Cheung Chau & Macau

0   2.5   5km

0   1.5   3mi

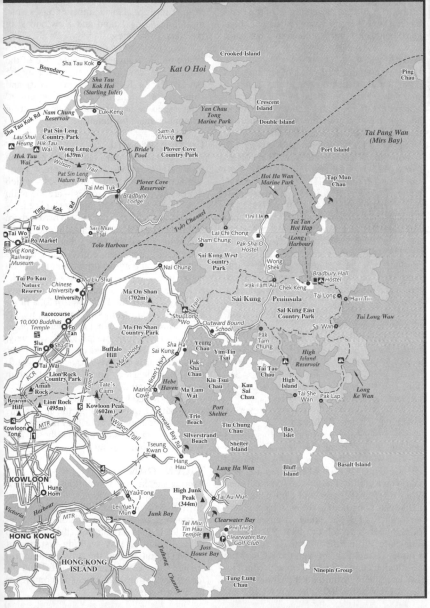

Macau or Zhuhai, using a number of islands as stepping stones. This is part of a plan to further consolidate the territories of the Pearl River Delta – Hong Kong, Macau, Zhuhai and Shenzhen – into an economic bulwark.

Maps

If you're planning to do a lot of walking in a particular area, pick up one of the *Countryside Series* maps produced by the Survey & Mapping Office of the Lands Department and available at government Map Publication Centres (see Maps under Planning in the Hong Kong Facts for the Visitor chapter).

Four maps cover the New Territories: *North-West New Territories* (HK$45), *Central New Territories* (HK$45), *Sai Kung & Clearwater Bay* (HK$50) and *North-East New Territories* (HK$45). All are 1:25,000, with larger-scale inset maps. If you're heading for either of the NT's longest trails, get a copy of the 1:25,000 *MacLehose Trail* or the 1:35,000 *Wilson Trail* (HK$30 each), produced by the Country & Marine Parks Authority and available at map centres. Universal Publications (UP) produces a 1:50,000 *Sai Kung, Clearwater Bay* (HK$18) map that contains useful information for hikers.

Travellers sticking to the built-up areas of the New Territories will find UP's *New Town Street Map* (HK$22) useful. It covers Tsuen Wan, Tuen Mun, Yuen Long, Sha Tin, Tai Po, Fanling and Sai Kung, as well as several other towns and villages.

Getting There & Away

A range of public transport options makes getting to and from the New Territories easy, at least to the New Towns and most areas of interest. The MTR (Map 16) will take you as far as Tsuen Wan (on the Tsuen Wan line) in the west and Choi Hung (on the Kwun Tong line) in the east, from where you can catch buses and minibuses to explore other parts of the New Territories. Travel to the northern New Territories is simple, fast and cheap with the KCR (Map 15), which connects Kowloon with Sha Tin, Tai Po, Sheung Shui and the Chinese border at Lo Wu. By 2003, the new KCR West Rail should be transporting passengers to the western New Territories as far as Tuen Mun. There are also a number of buses linking Hong Kong Island and Kowloon with the New Territories.

If you don't have the time or inclination to use public transport, consider one of the tours of the New Territories offered by the HKTB (Hong Kong Tourism Board) and some travel agencies. See the Organised Tours section of the Hong Kong Getting Around chapter for details.

Getting Around

Buses, run for the most part by the Kowloon Motor Bus Co (KMB; ☎ 2745 4466, W www .kmb.com.hk), and green minibuses – which run on more than 160 routes – are the main ways to get around. Catching a taxi is easy – at least to and from the New Towns; there are more than 2800 cabs cruising the streets and country roads of the NT. Ferries and *kaidos* (small, open-sea ferries) serve the remoter areas and a few large communities on the coast.

In the far west of the New Territories, the way to go is the LRT (Map 15), a modern, street-level tram system that connects Tuen Mun with Yuen Long and stops at several interesting places along the way. Once the LRT is linked up with the KCR West Rail, this will also be a way to get to and from the New Territories rather than just around them.

The HKTB has a handy information sheet with a map detailing the major bus routes in the New Territories. For more obscure or complex routes, check the KMB's Web site (details earlier).

TSUEN WAN

Among the easiest destinations in the New Territories to reach, Tsuen Wan is an industrial and residential New Town to the north-west of Kowloon. It's nothing special, but it does have a fine (though small) museum within easy walking distance of the MTR station and the hills to the north shelter some of the most colourful and interesting temple and monastic complexes in Hong Kong.

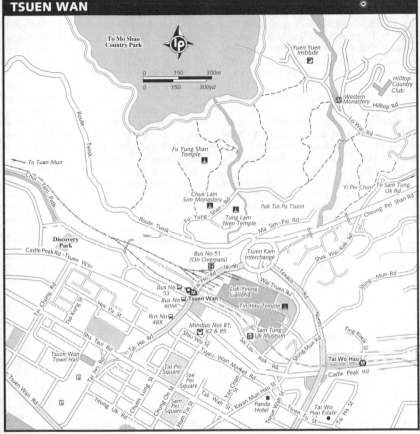

TSUEN WAN

Sam Tung Uk Museum

This imaginative and well-tended museum (☎ 2411 2001, W www.heritagemuseum.gov.hk, 2 Kwu Uk Lane; admission free; open 9am-5pm Wed-Mon) is housed in a restored 18th-century Hakka walled village, whose former residents were only resettled in 1980. Within the complex are a dozen houses containing traditional Hakka furnishings, kitchenware, wedding items and agricultural implements, most of which came from two 17th-century Hakka villages in Bao'an county in Guangdong province. There are also special exhibits on such topics as rice farming in the New Territories. Behind the restored assembly and ancestral halls is the old village school, with interactive displays on everything from the Qing-dynasty examination system to how to use an abacus.

Take exit B3 at the Tsuen Wan MTR station and walk five minutes south-east along Sai Lau Kok Rd to Kwu Uk Lane and the museum.

Places to Stay & Eat

Panda Hotel (☎ 2409 1111, fax 2409 1818, W www.pandahotel.com.hk, 3 Tsuen Wah St) Singles/doubles from HK$820/970, suites HK$1500-2800. Monthly packages from HK$9900. This 991-room hotel, the largest in the New Territories, is about 1km from the Tsuen Wan MTR station. To reach it, head south down Tai Ho Rd then turn left down Tsuen Wan Market Rd, which leads into Kwan Mun Hau St (access is from Kwan Mun Hau St).

Chianti Ristorante Italiano (☎ 2409 1111, Panda Hotel, 4th floor, 3 Tsuen Wah St) Set lunch/dinner HK$98/168. You wouldn't travel all the way to Tsuen Wan for the chianti, but Chianti Ristorante Italiano does have decent pasta dishes and the service is good.

The Luk Yeung Galleria shopping mall attached to the Tsuen Wan MTR station has a number of places to eat, including the usual *fast-food outlets*, as well as a *Park 'N' Shop* supermarket.

Getting There & Away

Tsuen Wan is the last station on the Tsuen Wan MTR line. If you're really in a hurry to get there or back, change to the new Tung Chung MTR line at Lai King, which has fewer stops.

AROUND TSUEN WAN
Chuk Lam Sim Monastery

Chuk Lam Sim Yuen (☎ 2490 3392, Fu Yung Shan Rd; open 7am-4pm daily), meaning 'bamboo forest monastery', is one of the most impressive temple complexes in Hong Kong. The temple was founded in 1927. Ascend the flight of steps to the first temple, walk to the back and enter the second. This second temple contains three of the largest golden Buddhas in the territory (though mere shadows of the big one on Lantau Island). Flanking the trio on either side is an equally impressive line-up of 12 *bodhisattvas*, or deified Buddhists. The third temple, the most active of the three, contains another large image of the Lord Gautama.

Chuk Lam Sim Yuen is north-east of the Tsuen Wan MTR station. To reach it, take minibus No 85 (HK$3.50) from Shiu Wo St, which is two blocks due south of the MTR station.

Yuen Yuen Institute & Western Monastery

The Yuen Yuen Institute *(Lo Wai Rd; open 7am-5pm daily)*, a colourful Taoist temple complex in the hills north-east of Tsuen Wan, is very much on the tourist trail but well worth a visit nonetheless. The main building is a (vague) replica of the Temple of Heaven in Beijing. On the upper ground floor are three Taoist immortals seated in a quiet hall; walk down to the lower level to watch as crowds of the faithful pray and burn offerings to the 60 incarnations of Taoist saints lining the walls.

A short distance down from the Yuen Yuen Institute, the Buddhist Western Monastery *(Lo Wai Rd; open 7am-4pm daily)* feels positively comatose compared with what's going on up the hill, but it has its charms nonetheless. The focal point of the monastery is a tall pagoda, on the 1st floor of which are five Buddhas sitting on a golden lotus. Depending on what time of day you visit, you may hear monks chanting mantras from down on the ground level.

To reach the Yuen Yuen Institute and the Western Monastery, take minibus No 81 (HK$3.60) from Shiu Wo St, two blocks due south of Tsuen Wan MTR station. Bus No 43X (HK$6) from along Tai Ho Rd, a bit farther south of the station, will drop you off on Sam Tung Uk Rd. The monastery is a short distance to the north and the institute a bit farther up the hill.

TAI MO SHAN

Hong Kong's tallest mountain is not Victoria Peak but Tai Mo Shan (New Territories map), the 'big misty mountain' that, at 957m, is nearly twice as high as that molehill (552m) on Hong Kong Island. Climbing Tai Mo Shan is not difficult, and the views from the top are impressive if the weather is clear. There are numerous hiking trails on and around it, but you'll need to bring your own food and water as none is available on the mountain itself. The *Countryside Series: Central New Territories* map is the one you want for this area (see the Maps section earlier in this chapter). One of the guided nature walks led by walking-guide author Kaarlo

Schepel takes in Tai Mo Shan, if you don't want to go it alone (see Organised Tours in the Hong Kong Getting Around chapter).

The area around **Ng Tung Chai Waterfall** is scenic and worth a detour. It is near the village of Ng Tung Chai, which is a few kilometres to the north of Tai Mo Shan and just south of Lam Kam Rd. There is actually a series of falls and streams here, reached by taking the path leading to Ng Tung Chai and the Lam Kam Rd from the radio station on the summit of Tai Mo Shan.

South-west of Ng Tung Chai is the **Kadoorie Farm & Botanic Garden** (☎ 2488 1317, W www.kfbg.org.hk, Lam Kam Rd; admission free; open 9.30am-5pm daily), a conservation and teaching centre where farmers receive practical training in crop and livestock management. The centre is open to the public; the gardens are especially lovely, with many indigenous birds, animals, insects and plants in residence.

The **Tai Mo Shan Visitor Centre** (☎ 2498 9326; open 9am-4.30pm Wed-Mon) is at the junction of Route Twisk (the name is derived from 'Tsuen Wan Into Shek Kong') and Tai Mo Shan Rd (on the MacLehose Trail).

Places to Stay
Sze Lok Yuen Hostel (☎ 2488 8188, fax 2788 3105, W www.yha.org.hk/szelok.html, Tai Mo Shan) Beds for juniors/seniors HK$25/35, camping for members/nonmembers HK$16/25. This 92-bed hostel, usually open Saturday and on the eve of public holidays only (telephone the HKYHA in advance on ☎ 2788 1638), is in the shadow of Hong Kong's highest peak. At this elevation it can get pretty chilly at night so come prepared. There are cooking facilities, but you should buy food supplies while in Tsuen Wan as none are available at the hostel.

Getting There & Away
To reach Tai Mo Shan from the Tsuen Wan MTR station, take exit A and catch bus No 51 (HK$7.60) on Tai Ho Rd North, alighting at the junction of Route Twisk and Tai Mo Shan Rd in Tsuen Kam Au. Follow Tai Mo Rd, which forms part of stage No 9 of the MacLehose Trail, east to the summit.

On the right-hand side, about 45 minutes from the bus stop, a fork in the road leads south along a concrete path to the hostel.

You can reach the Kadoorie Farm on bus No 51 by alighting where Route Twisk meets Lam Kam Rd and walking east for a couple of kilometres to the entrance, but it's easier to take bus No 64K (HK$5.30) from the Tai Po Market KCR station and get off on Lam Kam Rd near the sign for Ng Tung Chai village.

If you walk from Tai Mo Shan to the village of Ng Tung Chai, you can catch minibus No 25K (HK$4.50) to the Tai Po Market KCR station. Alternatively, you can carry on up to Lam Kam Rd and catch bus No 64K to the same destination.

MACLEHOSE TRAIL
The 100km MacLehose Trail (New Territories map), the territory's longest hiking path, spans the New Territories from Tuen Mun in the west to Pak Tam Chung on the Sai Kung Peninsula in the east. The trail follows the ridge, goes over Tai Mo Shan and passes close to **Ma On Shan** (702m), Hong Kong's fourth-highest peak. There are breathtaking views along the entire trail.

If you want to hike anywhere here, it is essential that you buy the *MacLehose Trail* map, available from two Map Publication Centres (see Maps under Planning in the Hong Kong Facts for the Visitor chapter). The trail is divided into 10 stages, ranging in length from about 4.5km (1½ hours of walking) to 15.5km (five hours).

There are many areas from which you can access the MacLehose trail by public transportation (see the list a little later in this section) but arguably the most convenient is reached by catching bus No 51 (HK$7.60) on Tai Ho Rd North (Tsuen Wan map), just north of the Tsuen Wan MTR station, and getting off where Route Twisk meets Tai Mo Shan Rd. This is the beginning (or the end) of stage No 9 of the trail. From there you have the choice of heading east towards Tai Mo Shan and **Lead Mine Pass** (10km, four hours) or west to the **Tai Lam Chung Reservoir**, through **Tai Lam Country Park**, and eventually all the way to

Tuen Mun (22km, 7½ hours), the western end of the trail. From Tuen Mun town centre, you can catch bus No 60X (HK$8.20) to Nathan Rd in Tsim Sha Tsui.

Another, perhaps more enjoyable, way to reach the trail is to take green minibus No 82 (HK$3.60) from Shiu Wo St, due south of the Tsuen Wan MTR station. The No 82 will drop you at **Pineapple Dam**, adjacent to the Shing Mun Reservoir in **Shing Mun Country Park**; the **Shing Mun Visitor Centre** (☎ 2498 1362; open 9.30am-4.30pm Wed-Mon) is on the western edge of the reservoir. You can follow the **Pineapple Dam Nature Trail** past several picnic and barbecue areas and around the reservoir itself. Villages bordering the reservoir were moved when the project was under construction.

This is an area very rich in flora and fauna, and you're bound to see many colourful butterflies, birds and pesky macaque monkeys; it's unlikely you'll see the timid deer that live in the area. The signposted **Shing Mun Arboretum** has a wide variety of fruit trees and medicinal plants.

Running south from the Shing Mun Reservoir is stage No 6 of the MacLehose trail, which will take you by **Smugglers' Ridge** and past some pretty dramatic scenery. The trail leads west and then south alongside **Kowloon Reservoir** to Tai Po Rd (4.6km, 1½ hours). From here stage No 5 of the trail heads east past a hill called **Eagle's Nest**, through woodland and up **Beacon Hill**, named after a lookout station, positioned here under Qing-dynasty Emperor Kang Xi, that fired up a beacon when enemy ships sailed into view.

From there stage No 5 of the trail runs along a ridge to **Lion Rock**, from where there is a path leading north to **Amah Rock** (see that section later in this chapter). The MacLehose trail circumvents Lion Rock but you can clamber up the path leading to it. Be warned – it is quite a tough climb, though every bit worth the effort. The vista from the top is stunning, with views of sheer cliffs and rocky crags.

Coming down from Lion Rock, the MacLehose trail leads you to **Sha Tin Pass**, where you may spot a drinks vendor. From

there you can either head south a short distance along the road and pick up green minibus No 37A (HK$2.90) at Tsz Wan Shan estate heading for Wong Tai Sin MTR in Kowloon, or walk north along a path to Sha Tin (about 2km) and jump on the KCR. If you carry on along stage No 4 of the MacLehose Trail, it will take you into the heart of **Ma On Shan Country Park** via **Tate's Cairn** (577m) and **Buffalo Hill**.

Those of you who really want to get the heart racing can join in the annual Trailwalker event, which is a race across the MacLehose Trail. For details see Hiking under Activities in the Hong Kong Facts for the Visitor chapter.

Other places to access the MacLehose Trail include (from east to west):

Pak Tam Chung (stage No 1) Bus No 94 (HK$4.20) from Sai Kung town or bus No 96R (HK$12) from Choi Hung or Diamond Hill MTR stations in Kowloon (Sunday and holidays only).
Pak Tam Au (stage Nos 2 & 3) Same as above.
Kei Ling Rd (stage Nos 3 & 4) Bus No 299 (HK$9) from Sha Tin or from Sai Kung town.
Ma On Shan (stage No 4) Bus No 99 (HK$3.10) from Sai Kung town to Nai Chung, which will drop you off at Sai Sha Rd.
Tai Po Rd (stage No 6) Green minibus No 81 (HK$3.60) from Tsuen Wan or Bus No 81C (HK$5.30) from the Kowloon KCR station.
Tuen Mun (stage No 10) Bus Nos 53 (HK$6.70) and 60M (HK$8.20) from Tsuen Wan or bus No 60X (HK$8.20) from Nathan Rd in Tsim Sha Tsui.

WILSON TRAIL

The 78km Wilson Trail begins near Stanley on Hong Kong Island and runs north for two stages (11.5km, 4½ hours) before disappearing into the Eastern Harbour Crossing tunnel at Quarry Bay (take the MTR) and resurfacing at the Lam Tin MTR station. From there (New Territories map), the trail zigzags south to **Lei Yue Mun** before turning sharply north again into the hills. The trail then takes a westward turn, heading over the summit of **Tate's Cairn**, and passes **Lion Rock** and **Beacon Hill**. The path makes another sharp turn northward, continues through **Shing Mun Country Park**, returns to civilisation near Tai Po, then disappears into the hills again at **Pat Sin Leng Country Park** (see the Plover Cove section later in this chapter) before ending at **Nam Chung Reservoir** on the Starling Inlet, not far from **Shau Tau Kok** and Hong Kong's border with the mainland.

Parts of the Wilson Trail overlap with the MacLehose Trail, particularly in the area east of Tai Mo Shan.

For information on the Hong Kong Island stages of the Wilson Trail, see that chapter.

TUEN MUN

Tuen Mun is the largest and most important New Town in the western New Territories and will soon be linked with other centres in Kowloon and the New Territories by the new KCR West Rail (scheduled for 2003). Tuen Mun's seemingly endless rows of high-rise housing estates can be off-putting at first, but they do hide a few interesting spots.

Ching Shan Monastery

Ching – or Tsing – Shan Monastery (New Territories map), which is called Castle Peak Monastery in English, is a quiet Buddhist retreat to the west of Tuen Mun town centre. It is one of the oldest monasteries in the territory and takes its name from Castle Peak a short distance to the south, which was proclaimed a sacred mountain by imperial edict in AD 969. Inside the main temples are three Buddhas seated on lotus blossoms covered in golden medallions.

Ching Shan is easy to reach, but it's a tough, uphill climb, especially in the warmer months. From the Town Centre LRT station in Tuen Mun, take line No 506 and alight at Tsing Shan Tsuen station. Walk north along Tsing Wun Rd for a few minutes and turn left at St Peter's Church. The footpath behind the church leads into Wan Shan Rd, which you should follow uphill for about 15 minutes. On the way up you'll be rewarded with a pavilion, shady groves of conifers and views across the Pearl River estuary as far as Shekou in the Shenzhen SEZ. Alternatively you can catch a taxi from Tuen Mun, which will drop you off at the steps leading up to the monastery.

Ching Chung Temple

Ching – or Tsing – Chung Koon (green pine temple; New Territories map) is a huge Taoist complex on Tsing Chung Koon Rd north-west of Tuen Mun town centre. The main temple, Sun Young Hall, which is on the left at the far end of the complex past rows of bonsai trees and ossuaries, is dedicated to Lu Sun Young, one of the eight immortals of Taoism.

Ching Chung Koon, which can get very busy during festivals, is directly opposite the Ching Chung LRT station. To reach it from the Ching Shan Monastery or Yuen Long, take line No 615. From the Town Centre station in Tuen Mun, catch line 610 and change for line 615 at Siu Hong station.

Miu Fat Monastery

Miu Fat Monastery (New Territories map) on Castle Peak Rd in Lam Tei, due north of Tuen Mun town centre, is one of the most well-kept and attractive Buddhist complexes in the territory. This is an active monastery that preserves more of a traditional character than many smaller temples; you'll see Buddhist nuns wearing brown robes in droves.

On the ground floor there's a golden likeness of the Buddha in a glass case; on the 2nd floor are three larger statues of the Lord Gautama. The 1st floor is a *vegetarian restaurant* serving set meals (HK$75) and open to all. Alternatively Lam Tei Village, a street running alongside the complex, is lined with *eateries*.

Miu Fat Monastery is easily reached by taking LRT line No 610 or No 615 to Lam Tei station. The complex is on the opposite side of Castle Peak Rd about a five-minute walk from the station.

Bus No 63X (HK$10) from Nathan Rd in Tsim Sha Tsui also stops in front of the monastery.

Getting There & Away

Bus Nos 53 (HK$6.70) and 60M (HK$5.30) start in Tsuen Wan and follow the coast to Tuen Mun. From Nathan Rd in Tsim Sha Tsui bus No 60X (HK$8.20) or 63X (HK$10) will take you to Tuen Mun town

HONG KONG

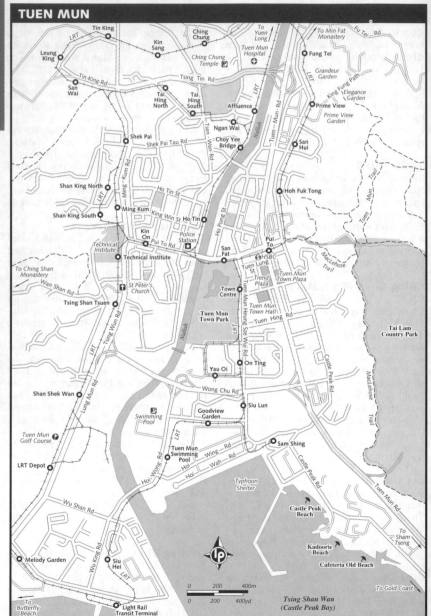

TUEN MUN

Tin King
Kin Sang
Leung King
Ching Chung
To Yuen Long
To Min Fat Monastery
Fu Tei Rd
LRT
San Wai
Tin King Rd
Ching Chung Temple
Tsing Tin Rd
Tuen Mun Hospital
Fung Tei
LRT
Grandeur Garden
King Fung Path
Elegance Garden
Tai Hing North
Tai Hing South
Affluence
Prime View
Prime View Garden
Shek Pai
Ngan Wai
Choy Yee Bridge
San Hui
Tuen Wen Rd
Shek Pai Tau Rd
Nullah
Tuen Mun Rd
Shan King North
Ho Tin St
Hoh Fuk Tong
Ming Kum Rd
Ho Pong St
Shan King South
Ming Kum
King Win St
Ho Tin
Kin On
Pui To Rd
Police Station
Pui To
HSBC
San Fat
Tuen Lung St
MacLehose Trail
Technical Institute
Technical Institute
St Peter's Church
Trend Plaza
Tuen Mun Town Plaza
To Ching Shan Monastery
Wan Shan Rd
Town Centre
Tuen Mun Town Hall
Tsing Shan Tsuen
Tuen Mun Town Park
Tuen Mun Heung See Wai Rd
Tuen Hing Rd
Tai Lam Country Park
Tsing Wun Rd
Nullah
Lung Mun Rd
LRT
Yau Oi
On Ting
Castle Peak Rd
MacLehose Trail
Shan Shek Wan
Wong Chu Rd
Siu Lun
Swimming Pool
Goodview Garden
Tuen Mun Golf Course
Wing Rd
Sam Shing
LRT Depot
Hoi Wong Rd
Tuen Mun Swimming Pool
Hoi Wah Rd
Hoi
Typhoon Shelter
Castle Peak Rd
To Sham Tseng
Castle Peak Beach
Wu Shan Rd
Tuen Mun Rd
Melody Garden
Siu Hei
Kadoorie Beach
Cafeteria Old Beach
To Gold Coast
To Butterfly Beach
Wu King Rd
LRT
Light Rail Transit Terminal
0   200   400m
0   200   400yd
Tsing Shan Wan
(Castle Peak Bay)

centre, as will No 960 (HK$18.20) from the Wan Chai Ferry pier via Admiralty and Central. Sit on the upper deck on the left side of the bus for spectacular views of the Tsing Ma Bridge linking Kowloon with Lantau Island. If you are coming from Yuen Long you can take line No 614 of the LRT.

YUEN LONG

There's nothing special at Yuen Long, but it's the last stop on the LRT line, something of a gateway to the Mai Po Marsh (see the following section) and a decent place for lunch. Dim sum is served from 7am to about 4pm daily at the *Kar Shing Restaurant* (☎ *2476 3228, Room 333-348, Yuen Long Plaza, 249-251 Castle Peak Rd)*.

MAI PO MARSH

If you're a bird-watcher, the 270-hectare Mai Po Marsh in the north-western New Territories is one of the best places in Hong Kong to meet up with some 300 species of your feathered friends. See the boxed text A Wetland for Hong Kong.

The **World Wide Fund for Nature Hong Kong** *(WWFHK; ☎ 2526 4473,* W *www.wwf .org.hk)* adjacent to the entrance of the Peak Tram at 1 Tramway Path, Central, can arrange guided visits to the marsh. Three-hour tours are HK$70, held on Saturday, Sunday and public holidays. Visitors are advised to bring binoculars and (if desired) cameras, and to wear comfortable walking shoes or boots but not bright clothing (unguided access HK$100 for permit; 9am-5pm daily).

Splendid Tours & Travel *(☎ 2316 2151, 2471 6306)* is another outfit that brings visitors to the marsh. Five-hour tours cost HK$360; held Tuesday, Thursday and Sunday, from October to April.

A Wetland for Hong Kong

Bordering Deep Bay in the north-west New Territories, Mai Po Marsh is a protected network of ponds, mudflats, reed beds and mangroves that attract some 70,000 migratory waterfowl every winter, including endangered species such as the Dalmatian pelican and black-faced spoonbill. In the centre of the 405-hectare marsh is the Mai Po Nature Reserve, jointly managed by World Wide Fund for Nature Hong Kong and the government's Agriculture, Fisheries and Conservation Department.

Despite its protected status, Mai Po's future is uncertain. The water quality in Deep Bay is among the worst in the Hong Kong

A Pied Kingfisher in flight

coastal area. The Environmental Protection Department (EPD) has found that levels of dissolved oxygen (DO) in the water have been declining since 1988; in the summer of 1996 DO levels fell to zero on one occasion. As a result, the numbers of crabs and mudskippers, on which the birds feed in winter, have declined sharply. The pollution used to come from pig manure released into Deep Bay, but a government ordinance now requires that pig slurry be treated before being flushed away. This ordinance appears to be having an effect, but a potentially larger hazard has taken its place.

Deep Bay neighbours the city of Shenzhen in mainland China, which is pumping out a rapidly increasing amount of sewage, about half of which is untreated. The only real solution to this environmental threat is for Shenzhen to build more sewage treatment facilities but, as the population of the city expands faster than its infrastructure, this will take time.

Meanwhile, increasingly wet summers in Hong Kong have flushed out and diluted many of the pollutants. The number of crabs and mudskippers has increased, but this could just reflect a temporary improvement in the region's ecology. If the lower links of the food chain are seriously imperilled, the estimated 270 species of bird that depend on Mai Po as a stopping ground during migration could disappear, taking with them mammals such as the leopard cat and otter.

Getting There & Away

Bus No 76K, which runs between Yuen Long and the Fanling and Sheung Shui KCR stations, will drop you off at Mai Po Lo Wai, a village along the main road just east of the marsh. The WWFHK car park is about a 20-minute walk from there. Alternatively, a taxi from Sheung Shui will cost about HK$60.

KAM TIN

The area around Kam Tin (New Territories map), or 'brocade field', is where the Tangs, the first of Hong Kong's mighty Five Clans, began settling in the 12th century AD and where they were eventually to build their walled villages.

Walled villages are a reminder that Hong Kong's early settlers were constantly menaced by marauding pirates, bandits and imperial soldiers. They remain one of the most popular destinations for visitors to the New Territories.

Kam Tin contains two fortified villages, Kat Hing Wai and Shui Tau. Most tourists go to Kat Hing Wai as it is just off the main road and easily accessible. Shui Tau is larger and less touristy, but don't expect to find remnants of ancient China. For details on Ping Kong, a seldom-visited walled village to the north-east, see the Fanling & Sheung Shui section.

Kat Hing Wai

This tiny village is 500 years old and was walled in some time during the early Ming dynasty (1368–1644). It's just south of Kam Tin Rd and contains one main street, off which a host of dark and narrow alleyways lead. A small temple stands at the end of the main street.

Visitors are asked to make a donation of HK$1 when they enter the village. Put the money in the coin slot by the entrance. You can take photographs of the old Hakka women in their traditional black trousers, tunics and distinctive bamboo hats with black cloth fringes, but they'll expect you to pay. Agree on a price beforehand – it's usually about HK$10.

Shui Tau

This 17th-century village, 15 minutes' walk north of Kam Tin Rd and signposted, is famous for its prow-shaped roofs decorated with dragons and fish. Tiny traditional houses huddle inside Shui Tau's walls.

The ancestral hall in the middle of the village is used as a school in the mornings, but was originally built for ancestor worship. The ancestors' names are listed on the altar in the inner hall and on the long boards down the side. The sculpted fish, on the roof of the entrance hall, symbolise luck; in Cantonese, the word for fish *(yue)* sounds similar to the word for plenty, or surplus. The large **Tin Hau Temple** on the outskirts of the village to the north was built in 1722 and contains an enormous iron bell weighing 106kg.

There's been a lot of building in recent years in and around Shui Tau, and the old sits rather uncomfortably with the new. But it remains a calm and tranquil area, and this is one of the few places in the New Territories where you're likely to see water buffalo in the cool mud of the surrounding fields.

LEE FOSTER

A Hakka woman wearing a traditional hat.

To reach Shui Tau from Kam Tin Rd, walk north and over the *nullah* (drainage channel) to Chi Ho Rd. Shui Tau is just beyond the small bridge spanning the stream.

Getting There & Away

Bus Nos 64K (HK$5.30), which links Yuen Long and the Tai Po Market KCR station, 77K (HK$5.30), between Yuen Long and the Sheung Shui and Fanling KCR stations, and 54 (HK$3.60), between Yuen Long and Shek Kong, all stop on Kam Tin Rd in Kam Tin. In Yuen Long you can board them on Castle Peak Rd. Another option is green minibus No 601 from Fung Cheung Rd in Yuen Long. Kam Tin is also accessible from Tsuen Wan on bus No 51 (HK$7.60), which goes via scenic Route Twisk.

FANLING & SHEUNG SHUI

What were two lazy country villages just a few short years ago now form one of the largest New Town conurbations in the New Territories. There's not a whole lot to see here, though the 18-hole **Fanling Golf Course** (☎ 2670 1211) on Fan Kam Rd may be a draw for some. The KCR stops in both Fanling and Sheung Shui.

Fung Ying Sin Koon

The main attraction in Fanling is Fung Ying Sin Temple on Pak Wo Rd, directly opposite the KCR station. It's another huge Taoist complex with wonderful exterior murals of Taoist immortals and the Chinese zodiac, an orchard terrace, herbal clinic and the *Vegetarian Kitchen* restaurant, with meals for about HK$60. Most important are the 10 ancestral halls behind the main temple where the ashes of the departed are deposited in what might be described as miniature tombs, complete with photographs.

Ping Kong

This sleepy walled village in the hill south of Sheung Shui is seldom visited by outsiders. Like other walled villages it is a mix of old and new, but it's a friendly place, with a lovely little temple devoted to Tin Hau in the centre. You can also go exploring around the farming area behind the village compound.

To get to Ping Kong from Sheung Shui, catch green minibus No 58K (HK$3.50) from the huge minibus station south of the Landmark North shopping mall on San Wan Rd. The mall is a short distance north-west of the Sheung Shui KCR station. Bus No 77K (HK$5.30) between Yuen Long and the Sheung Shui and Fanling KCR stations travels along Fan Kam Rd. Alight at the North District Hospital stop and walk southeast along Ping Kong Rd to the village.

A taxi from the Sheung Shui KCR station to Ping Kong will cost HK$20.

TAI PO

Tai Po, which can boast not one but two KCR stations (Tai Wo to the north-west and Tai Po Market to the south-east), is another large residential and industrial New Town and home to many of Hong Kong's high-tech industries.

Hong Kong Railway Museum

The Hong Kong Railway Museum (☎ 2653 3455, **W** *www.heritagemuseum.gov.hk, 13 Shung Tak St; admission free; open 9am-5pm Wed-Mon)* is housed in the former Tai Po Market train station (1913) and spills into the outside garden. Exhibits, including a narrow-gauge steam locomotive dating back to 1911, detail the history of the development of rail transport in the territory.

You can get to the museum most easily by alighting at the Tai Wo KCR station, walking south through the housing estate and crossing the Lam Tsuen River via the small Tai Wo Bridge leading from Po Nga Rd. The museum is a short distance to the south-east.

Tai Wo Market

This street-long outdoor wet market in Fu Shin St, a stone's throw from the Hong Kong Railway Museum, is one of the busiest and most interesting. On the same street, the **Man Mo Temple**, founded almost a century ago, is a major centre of worship for the Tai Po area.

Cycling

Bicycles can be rented in season from several stalls around Tai Po Market KCR station, but try to arrive early – they often run

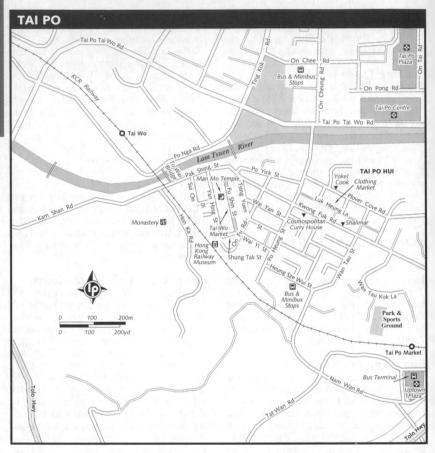

TAI PO

Tai Po Tai Wo Rd

On Chee Rd

Bus & Minibus Stops

Tai Po Plaza

On Cheung Rd

On Pong Rd

Tai Po Centre

On Tai Rd

Ting Kok Rd

KCR Railway

Tai Po Tai Wo Rd

Tai Wo

Po Nga Rd

Lam Tsuen River

Po Yick St

TAI PO HUI

Tow Wai Bridge

Pak Shing St

Man Mo Temple

Yan Hing St

Sui On St

Fu Shin St

Tseng Yuen

Wai Yan St

Yokel Cook

Clothing Market

Plover Cove Rd

Luk Heung La

Kwong Fuk Rd

Shalimar

Cosmopolitan Curry House

Kam Shan Rd

Hon Ka Rd

Monastery

Tai Wo Market

On Fu St

Wai Yi St

Po Heung St

Hong Kong Railway Museum

Shung Tak St

Heung Sze Wui St

Wan Tau St

Wan Tau Kok La

Park & Sports Ground

0   100   200m
0   100   200yd

Tai Po Market

Bus & Minibus Stops

Nam Wan Rd

Bus Terminal

Uptown Plaza

Tolo Hwy

Tat Wan Rd

Tolo Hwy

out of bikes during the busiest times. There are a number of bicycle shops lining Kwong Fuk Rd north-west of Tai Po Market KCR station.

One route not to miss is the ride to **Plover Cove Reservoir** on the north-east side of Tolo Harbour, or to the **Chinese University** in Ma Liu Shui on the south-west side of the harbour. Allow at least a half-day for either trip. There is an inland route to the university, but the coastal route has the best views. Another option is to follow Ting Kok Rd east to San Mun Tsai (see the following section).

Places to Eat

Tai Po is not the gourmet centre of the New Territories, but there are a few decent eateries to choose from to the north-west of Tai Po Market KCR station.

Cosmopolitan Curry House (☎ 2658 6915, 80 Kwong Fuk Rd) Curries HK\$58-73. The Indo-Malaysian curries at this Tai Po institution are magnificent, but be sure to book.

Shalimar (☎ 2653 7790, 127 Kwong Fuk Rd) Mains HK\$32-60, set lunch HK\$40. If you prefer your curries more Subcontinental or you can't get into the Cosmopolitan, the Shalimar is a short distance to the south-east.

Yokel Cook (☎ 2654 7981, Shop 210 Plover Cove Garden, 3 Plover Cove Rd) Mains HK$35-60. This Western-style place in a faceless shopping mall serves decent fish dishes, as well as steaks and grills. If you want something lighter they can oblige with Japanese noodles.

Getting There & Around

Tai Po is connected to Kowloon by the KCR at Tai Po Market and Tai Wo stations. You can also reach Tai Po on bus No 271 (HK$9.10) from Canton Rd in Tsim Sha Tsui, bus No 73X (HK$6.70) from Tsuen Wan or bus No 74X (HK$8.40) from the Kwun Tong MTR station.

Buses arrive and depart on On Chee Rd, north of the Lam Tsuen River, as well as Heung Sze Wui St, close to the market and railway museum. Green minibus No 501S (HK$22.50), which links Sheung Shi in northern NT and the Lam Tin MTR station in the south, stops in Tai Po.

Circular bus No 71K (HK$3) links Tai Wo and Tai Po Market KCR stations.

SAN MUN TSAI

San Mun Tsai (New Territories map) is a small fishing village on a shoe-shaped peninsula in Tolo Harbour. It's east of Tai Po, just off Ting Kok Rd en route to Tai Mei Tuk. San Mun Tsai (three gate place) is charming – a floating mix of homes belonging to the local fishing families – and gets few visitors.

To reach San Mun Tsai from Tai Po, you can either catch minibus No 20K (HK$4.40) from Tai Po Market KCR station or bus No 74K (HK$3.10) from On Chee Rd, north of the Lam Tsuen River. Both also stop on Heung Sze Wui St near the Tai Wo Market and Hong Kong Railway Museum.

PLOVER COVE

The area around the Plover Cove Reservoir (New Territories map) is good hiking and cycling country and worth a full day. It may be worthwhile getting a copy of Universal Publications' *Sai Kung, Clearwater Bay* map (see the Maps section earlier).

The reservoir was completed in 1967 and holds 230 million cubic metres of water; before then Hong Kong suffered from critical water shortages and rationing was not uncommon. Even after the reservoir opened, water sometimes had to be rationed. Taps were turned on for only eight hours a day through the dry winter of 1980–81.

The reservoir was built in an unusual way. Rather than build a dam across a river, of which Hong Kong has very few, a barrier was erected across the mouth of a great bay. The sea-water was siphoned out and fresh water – mostly piped in from the mainland – was pumped in.

Bicycles can be rented at Tai Mei Tuk, where you'll also find the **Plover Cove Country Park Visitor Centre** (☎ 2665 3413; open 9am-4.30pm Wed-Mon). Rowboats are available for hire along the picture-postcard bay.

Pat Sin Leng Nature Trail

This excellent (and easy) trail leads from the visitors centre at Tai Mei Tuk and heads north-east for **Bride's Pool**. The walk is 4km long, with an elevation gain of only 300m. The scenery is good and the two **waterfalls** at Bride's Pool are delightful, but the place gets packed on weekends. You can either return to Tai Mei Tuk via Bride's Pool Rd or, on Sunday and holidays, return to Tai Po on bus No 275R (HK$8.60). If you carry on north to Luk Keng you can catch green minibus No 56K (HK$7), which will take you to Fanling KCR station.

Pat Sin Leng Range

Those looking for a more strenuous hike can join stage No 9 of the Wilson Trail at Tai Mei Tuk and head west into the steep **Pat Sin Leng** (eight fairies) range to **Wong Leng** (639m). The trail then carries on to **Hok Tau Reservoir** and **Hok Tau Wai** (12km, four hours). You can camp at Hok Tau Wai or catch green minibus 56K (HK$7) to Fanling KCR station.

Places to Stay

There are *camp sites* managed by the Country & Marine Parks Authority at Hok Tau,

Lau Shui Heung – to the west of Hok Tau – and Sam A Chung, to the east of Bride's Pool.

Bradbury Lodge (☎ 2662 5123, fax 2788 3105, W www.yha.org.hk/bradlodg.html, 66 Ting Kok Rd, Tai Mei Tuk) Dorm beds for juniors/seniors HK$30/45, doubles/quads HK$200/260. Check-in is from 7am-10am and from 4pm (2pm on Saturday) to 11pm. Bradbury Lodge (not to be confused with Bradbury Hall in Sai Kung) is the HKYHA's flagship hostel in the New Territories. It has 96 beds and is open seven days a week year-round. Bradbury Lodge is next to the northern tip of the Plover Cove Reservoir dam wall, a few hundred metres south of Tai Mei Tuk. Camping is not permitted here.

Getting There & Away
To reach Tai Mei Tuk and the Plover Cove Reservoir from Tai Po, catch bus No 75K (HK$3.60) from the Tai Po Market KCR station or on Heung Sze Wui St near the Tai Wo Market and Hong Kong Railway Museum.

TAI PO KAU NATURE RESERVE
This forest area south of Tai Po is Hong Kong's most extensive woodlands and is home to many species of butterflies, amphibians, birds and trees. It is a superb place in which to enjoy a quiet walk, except on Sunday and holidays when crowds descend upon the place.

To get there, take bus No 74A (HK$6.70), which runs from Kwong Fuk Rd in Tai Po to Kwun Tong, and get off at Tsung Tsai Young. A trail leading into the nature reserve starts about 50m north of the bus stop. You can also take bus No 72 (HK$6) from Olympic MTR station on the Tung Chung line in Mong Kok or a taxi (about HK$25) from Tai Po Market KCR station.

CHINESE UNIVERSITY
The Chinese University of Hong Kong *(New Territories map; ☎ 2609 8898, W www .cuhk.edu.hk)*, established in 1963, is in Ma Liu Shui, south-east of Tai Po Kau and overlooking Tolo Harbour. It is situated on a beautiful campus and well worth a visit.

The university's **art museum** *(☎ 2609 7416; admission free; open Mon-Sat 10am-4.45pm, Sun 12.30pm-5.30pm)* is divided into two sections. The **West Wing Galleries** house a permanent collection of Chinese paintings, calligraphy, ceramics and other decorative arts, including 2000-year-old bronze seals and a large collection of jade flower carvings. The **East Wing Galleries** feature five to six special exhibitions each year. The museum is closed public holidays.

Places to Eat
Yucca De Lac Restaurant (☎ 2961 1630, Tai Po Rd, Ma Liu Shui) Meals about HK$150. This long-established restaurant just down from Chinese University has outside tables and restful views of Tolo Harbour. Roast pigeon is the house speciality.

Getting There & Away
You can reach Chinese University by taking the KCR to University station. A free bus outside the station travels through the campus to the administration building at the top of the hill.

Ferries from the pier on Sui Cheung St, which is due east of the university campus and a short walk north-east of University KCR station, depart for the Sai Kung Peninsula twice daily, and Tap Mun Island twice daily. For details, see the Sai Kung Peninsula and Tap Mun Chau sections later in this chapter.

SHA TIN
Lying in a narrow valley on the banks of the Shing Mun River, Sha Tin (sand field) is an enormous New Town built mostly on reclaimed land that was once a mudflat. Sha Tin retains some traditional Chinese houses, giving parts of it a historical feel absent in most of the other New Towns. Hong Kong Chinese flock to Sha Tin on the weekends to place their bets at the racecourse to the north or to shop at Sha Tin's New Town Plaza one of the biggest shopping malls in the New Territories. For visitors, the drawing cards are the Sha Tin area's temples and the best museum in Hong Kong, the Hong Kong Heritage Museum.

SHA TIN

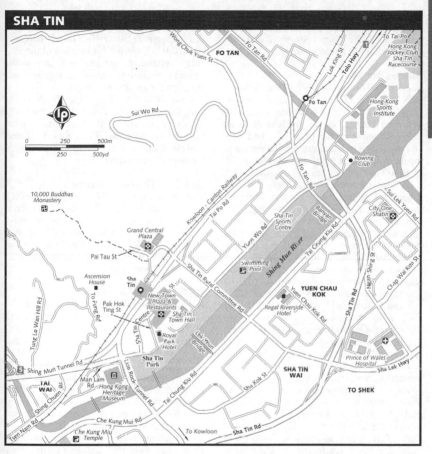

To Tai Po
Hong Kong Jockey Club Sha Tin Racecourse

Wong Chuk Yuen St

FO TAN

Fo Tan Rd

Lok King St

Tolo Hwy

Sui Wo Rd

Fo Tan

Hong Kong Sports Institute

0   250   500m
0   250   500yd

Rowing Club

10,000 Buddhas Monastery

Kowloon - Canton Railway

Tai Po Rd

Sha Tin Sports Centre

Banyan Bridge

Fo Tan Rd

City One Shatin

Sui Lek Yuen Rd

Grand Central Plaza

Yuen Wo Rd

Tai Chung Kiu Rd

Ngan Shing St

Pai Tau St

Shing Mun River

Ascension House

Sha Tin

Sha Tin Rural Committee Rd

Swimming Pool

YUEN CHAU KOK

Sha Tin Rd

Chap Wai Kon St

To Fung Rd

Pak Hok Ting St

New Town Plaza & Restaurants

St

Yuen Chau Kok Rd

Tung Lo Wan Hill Rd

Sha Tin Town Hall

Centre St

Regal Riverside Hotel

To KCR BUS

Royal Park Hotel

Lek Yeun Bridge

Prince of Wales Hospital

Sha Lek Hwy

Sha Tin Park

Shing Mun Tunnel Rd

Man Lam Rd

Hong Kong Heritage Museum

Lion Rock Tunnel Rd

Tai Chung Kiu Rd

Sha Kok St

SHA TIN WAI

TO SHEK

TAI WAI

Shing Chuen Rd

Che Kung Mui Rd

To Kowloon

Sha Tin Rd

Tsen Nam Rd

Che Kung Miu Temple

Ten Thousand Buddhas Monastery

If you're big on Buddhas, head for this monastery *(open 9am-5pm daily)*, which sits on a hillside about 500m north-west of Sha Tin KCR station. Built in the 1950s, it actually has more than 10,000 Buddhas – some 12,800 miniature statues line the walls of the main temple. Dozens of life-sized golden statues of Buddha's followers line the steep steps leading to the monastery complex. There is also a nine-storey pagoda.

From the main temple area, walk up some more steps to find a smaller temple

housing the embalmed body of the founding monk, who died in 1965. His body was encased in gold leaf and is now on display behind glass. Put a small donation in the box next to the display case to help pay for the temple's upkeep.

To reach the Ten Thousand Buddhas Monastery, take exit B at Sha Tin KCR station and walk down the ramp, passing a series of traditional village houses on the left. Do not mistake as your destination the modern Bo Fook Hill temple complex with the tacky pagoda and escalator at the end of Pai Tau St. Instead, carry on and turn left onto

Sheung Wo Che St. A series of yellow signs in English will direct you through the food stalls and to the steep path and about 400 steps leading up to the monastery.

Places to Stay

Ascension House (☎ 2691 4196, W *www .achouse.com; 33 Tao Fong Shan Rd*) Dorm beds HK$125. This 11-bed place staffed by Scandinavians is one of the best deals in Hong Kong, since the price of a bed gets you not only a free laundry service but three meals as well! To get there, take the KCR to Sha Tin Station, leave via exit B and walk down the ramp, passing a series of traditional village houses on the left. Between them is a set of steps. Go up these steps, follow the path and when you come to a roundabout, go along the uphill road to your right. After about 150m you'll come to a small staircase and a sign pointing the way to Ascension House on the right. The walk should take between 15 and 20 minutes. A taxi from the station costs around HK$20.

Regal Riverside Hotel (☎ 2649 7878, fax 2637 4748, W *www.regalhotel.com, 34-36 Tai Chung Kiu Rd*) Rooms HK$1080-1580, suites HK$2800-4800. This huge, 830-room hotel overlooks the Shing Mun River north-east of Sha Tin town centre. It boasts the decent *Boulevard Café*.

Royal Park Hotel (☎ 2601 2111, fax 2601 3666, W *www.royalpark.com.hk, 8 Pak Hok Ting St*) Rooms HK$780-1380, suites HK$2600-3780. The 448-room Royal Park is next to the New Town Plaza shopping mall. Its *Royal Park Chinese Restaurant* on the 2nd floor is considered to be one of the best in Sha Tin.

Places to Eat

The multi-level New Town Plaza shopping mall (☎ 2601 9178, 2684 9175) has more restaurants and snack bars than you can shake a chopstick at.

Banthai Thai Cuisine (☎ 2609 3686, Shop A172, 1st floor, New Town Plaza Phase 3) Meals HK$120. If you're in need of a quick fix of *tom yom gung* and *another* golden Buddha, this is the place to come. It has a loyal following.

Kaga Japanese Restaurant (☎ 2603 0545, Shop A191-193, 1st floor, New Town Plaza Phase 3) Sushi HK$14-65, tempura HK$70-92. Kaga is a bit sterile and the service somewhat abrupt, but the sushi (salmon, yellow tail tuna) and grilled eel make up for its shortcomings.

Koh-i-Noor (☎ 2601 5339, Shop A181-182, 1st floor, New Town Plaza Phase 3) Meals about HK$150. This place, with branches in Central, Tsim Sha Tsui and Taikoo Shing, is a good and stylish choice for North Indian food.

Getting There & Away

Sha Tin is on the KCR line. Alternatively you can take bus No 170 (HK$15.30) from Central or Gloucester Rd in Causeway Bay, bus No 48X from Tsuen Wan (HK$5.30), bus No 72 (HK$6) from Tai Po or bus No 263R (HK$16.80, Sunday and public holidays only) from Tuen Mun.

AROUND SHA TIN
Hong Kong Heritage Museum

Located south-west of Sha Tin town Centre in Tai Wai, Hong Kong's newest and, unequivocally, best museum (☎ 2180 8188, W *www.heritagemuseum.gov.hk; 1 Man Lam Rd, Tai Wai; adult/concession HK$10/ 5; open 10am-6pm Tues-Thur & Sat-Sun, 10am-9pm Fri*) is housed in a purpose-built structure that is reminiscent of an ancestral hall. It has both rich permanent collections and innovative temporary exhibits.

The ground floor contains a book and gift shop, the wonderful **Children's Discovery Gallery** with eight learning play zones and an orientation theatre with a 12-minute video in English and Chinese. There's also a lovely *teahouse* here with teas from HK$45 to HK$120 and snacks for HK$10.

Along with five temporary galleries, the 1st floor contains the best of the museum's permanent collections: the **New Territories Heritage Hall**, with mock-ups of traditional shops, a Hakka fishing village and history of the New Towns; the **Cantonese Opera Heritage Hall**, where you can watch old operas on video with English subtitles, 'virtually' make yourself up as a Cantonese opera

A snake handler calmly holds a King Cobra.

Fruit and vege stalls on Gresson St, Wan Chai

Preparing Chinese herbs for traditional medicine.

Chop seller and calligrapher busy at work in Man Wa Lane, Central, Hong Kong Island.

Chicken, duck and pork on display in a Wellington St shop, Central, Hong Kong Island.

Smelly but delicious durians at Temple St Night Market, Kowloon.

Tsingtao, China's export beer

Fruit juices ready to serve at a drink stall in Hong Kong.

character on computer, or just enjoy the costumes and sets; and the **Chao Shao-an Gallery**, devoted to the work of the eponymous water-colourist (1905–98) and founder of the important Lingnan School of painting.

The 2nd floor contains another thematic gallery and the **TT Tsui Gallery of Chinese Art**, an Aladdin's cave of fine ceramics, pottery, bronze, jade and lacquer ware, stone carvings, and furniture.

In the past, special thematic exhibits have dealt with Hong Kong comics, a Qing-dynasty imperial banquet and digital art. One charming exhibit showed how Hong Kong people cope with high-rise living.

Che Kung Temple

This large Taoist temple complex *(Che Kung Miu Rd, Tai Wai; open 7am-5.30pm daily)* is located diagonally opposite the Hong Kong Heritage Museum across the Shing Mun River. It's dedicated to Che Kung, a Song-dynasty general, and the main temple contains an enormous and quite powerful statue of him. The main courtyard, flanked by eight statues of Taoist immortals, is a hive of activity; fortune tellers reveal the future to the credulous in the arcade near the entrance. The temple is especially busy on the third day of the Lunar New Year, which is the good general's birthday.

Getting There & Away

To reach both the Hong Kong Heritage Museum and the temple, catch the KCR to Tai Wai station and follow the exit marked 'Che Kung Temple'. This will lead you south down Mei Tin Rd to the roundabout, where you will turn east onto Che Kung Miu Rd. The temple is about a kilometre down this road and the museum on the opposite bank of the Shing Mun River another kilometre still. Use the footbridge almost opposite the temple.

Alternatively you can take the KCR to Sha Tin station and walk south along Tai Po Rd Sha Tin to the museum. Bus No 80K (HK$3) from Sha Tin KCR station also stops near the temple or you could take a taxi (HK$15 to HK$20).

Bus No 182 (HK$15.30) from the Macau ferry pier in Central as well as Admiralty and Causeway Bay stops on Che Kung Miu Rd almost opposite the temple and near the footbridge crossing the Shing Mun River to the Hong Kong Heritage Museum.

Sha Tin Racecourse

North-east of Sha Tin town centre is Hong Kong's second racecourse *(☎ 2966 8111, Penfold Park; entry $10-50 on race days)*, which opened in 1980 and can accommodate up to 85,000 punters.

In general, races are held on Saturday afternoon, and occasionally on Sunday and public holidays. Bets are easily placed at one of the numerous computerised betting terminals run by the Hong Kong Jockey Club (HKJC). For more information, see Horse Racing under Spectator Sports in the Hong Kong Facts for the Visitor chapter.

You can pick up a list of race meetings from any HKTB information centre. If you know nothing about horseracing but would like to attend, consider joining an HKTB Come Horseracing Tour (see Organised Tours in the Hong Kong Getting Around chapter for details).

In the centre of the racetrack is eight-hectare **Penfold Park**, which is open to the public on all days except race days, Monday and the day after a public holiday. It can get packed out on weekends – an indication of just how desperate New Town residents are to find a bit of greenery among the concrete housing estates.

The KCR Racecourse station, just west of the track and park, opens on race days only. Otherwise, get off at Fo Tan Station and walk north along Lok King St, and its extension Lok Shun Path, for 20 minutes.

AMAH ROCK

It may just look like a rock, but it's an oddly shaped one and, like many local landmarks in Hong Kong, it carries a legend. It seems that for many years a fisherman's wife would stand on this spot in the hills above Lion Rock Country Park, watching for her husband to return from the sea while carrying her baby on her back. One day he didn't come back – she waited and waited. The gods apparently took pity on her and transported her to heaven on a lightning bolt, leaving her form in stone. The name of the rock in Cantonese is Mong Fu Shek, or 'gazing out for husband stone'.

As you take the KCR south from Sha Tin to Kowloon, Amah Rock is visible to the east (ie, on the left-hand side) up on the hillside after Tai Wai KCR station, but before the train enters the tunnel. Stage No 5 of the Wilson Trail (see that section earlier in this chapter) passes near Amah Rock.

SAI KUNG PENINSULA

The Sai Kung Peninsula (New Territories map) is the garden spot of the New Territories. It is also one of the last areas in Hong Kong (the outlying islands notwithstanding) reserved for outdoor activities. The hiking is excellent, there's sailing galore, and some of the best beaches in the territory.

Sai Kung Town

Sai Kung town was originally a fishing village and, although it's now more of a suburb for people working in Kowloon and on Hong Kong Island, it still has some of the feeling of a port. Fishing boats put in an occasional appearance, and down on the waterfront there's a string of seafood restaurants that draw customers from all around Hong Kong.

Sai Kung town is an excellent springboard for **hikes** into the surrounding countryside. A **kaido trip** to one (or more) of the little offshore islands and their secluded beaches is also feasible (see the boxed text Sai Kung Island Hopping).

Windsurfing equipment can be hired from the **Windsurfing Centre** (☎ 2792 5605; open 11am-5pm Mon-Fri, 10am-6pm Sat & Sun) at Sha Ha, just north of Sai Kung town. Bus No 94 (HK\$4.20), heading for the pier at Wong Shek (yellow stone), will drop you off at Sha Ha. Or you can walk there in about 15 minutes.

Places to Stay

The Sai Kung Peninsula counts about a dozen *camp sites* (managed by the Country &

Marine Parks Authority), but the closest one to Sai Kung town is at Shui Long Wo to the north on Sai Sha Rd heading for Ma On Shan.

Places to Eat

Sai Kung town is chock-a-block with eateries. Here you'll find curry, pizzas and bangers and mash just as easily as seafood.

Ali-Oli (☎ 2792 2655, 11 Sha Tsui Path) This bakery-cum-cafe has pizzas (HKK\$45), quiches (HK\$65), Cornish pasties (HK\$24) and assorted cakes and pies.

Chuen Kee Seafood Restaurant (☎ 2792 9294, 87-89 Man Nin St) Meals HK\$150-200. The granddaddy of the Sai Kung seafood restaurants, the Chuen Kee is long on quantity, with three nearby branches, but short, they say, on quality.

Duke of York (☎ 2792 8435, 42-56 Fuk Man Rd) Meals HK\$50-65. This place is more of a pub than a place to eat but OK if you're looking for blotter in the way of fish 'n' chips or basic curries. There's live music here on weekends.

Firenze (☎ 2792 0898, 60 Po Tung Rd) Starters HK\$20-55, mains HK\$90-100. This perennial Italian favourite does full meals (including a weekday dinner for two for HK\$138) as well as excellent pizzas (HK\$50 to HK\$120) and pastas (HK\$75 to HK\$80).

Hung Kee Seafood Restaurant (☎ 2792 1348, Shop 9-10, Siu Yat Building, Sai Kung Hoi Pong Square) Meals HK\$150-200. Looking right out onto the water, the Hung Kee has one of the largest selection of fish and shellfish in town.

Indian Curry Hut (☎ 2791 2929, 64 Po Tung Rd) Curries HK\$52-79, tandoori HK\$48-95. If you can't stand looking at finned creatures from the deep any longer, head for the Indian Curry House. This is also the place for vegetarians, with more than a dozen dishes on offer (HK\$46).

Italiano's (☎ 2792 9528, 20 Yi Chun St; ☎ 2792 6388, 13 Sha Tsui Path) Meals about HK\$100. This is a cheaper alternative to Firenze, with decent salads, pizzas and pasta.

Jaspa's (☎ 2792 6388, 13 Sha Tsui Path) Starters HK\$75-95, mains HK\$100-135. Jaspa's is an upmarket, casual place serving Continental food.

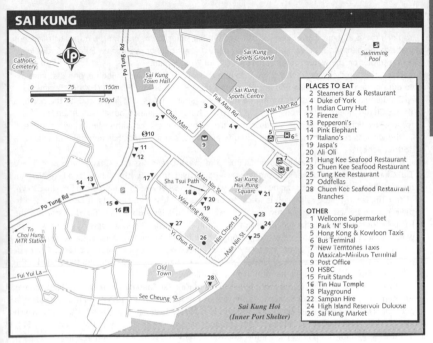

SAI KUNG

Catholic Cemetery

Sai Kung Sports Ground

Swimming Pool

Sai Kung Town Hall

Fuk Man Rd

Sai Kung Sports Centre

Wai Man Rd

Po Tung Rd

Chan Man St

Man Nin St

Sha Tsui Path

Sai Kung Hoi Pong Square

Po Tung Rd

Wan King Path

Nin Chuen St

Yi Chun St

Mac Nin St

Old Town

Fui Yui La

See Cheung St

Sai Kung Hoi
(Inner Port Shelter)

To Choi Hung, MTR Station

PLACES TO EAT
2 Steamers Bar & Restaurant
4 Duke of York
11 Indian Curry Hut
12 Firenze
13 Pepperoni's
14 Pink Elephant
17 Italiano's
19 Jaspa's
20 Ali Oli
21 Hung Kee Seafood Restaurant
23 Chuen Kee Seafood Restaurant
25 Tung Kee Restaurant
27 Oddfellas
28 Chuen Kee Seafood Restaurant Branches

OTHER
1 Wellcome Supermarket
3 Park 'N' Shop
5 Hong Kong & Kowloon Taxis
6 Bus Terminal
7 New Territories Taxis
8 Maxicab-Minibus Terminal
9 Post Office
10 HSBC
15 Fruit Stands
16 Tin Hau Temple
18 Playground
22 Sampan Hire
24 High Island Reservoir Doluose
26 Sai Kung Market

Oddfellas (☎ 2791 4123, 55-57 Yi Chun St) Starters HK$48-105, mains HK$112-210. On one side Oddfellas is a sports bar with all-day snacks and meals, including steaks and American burgers. Next door is the swish attached restaurant, if you'd prefer candlelight to TV glare.

Pepperoni's (☎ 2792 2083, Lot 1592, Po Tung Rd) Meals about HK$120. This place dishes up some fine, and the atmosphere is relaxing and fun.

Pink Elephant (☎ 2792 5296, 183 Po Tung Rd) Rice dishes & noodles HK$38-52, mains HK$48-98. An unassuming (but with dishes worth consuming) Thai restaurant.

Steamers Bar & Restaurant (☎ 2792 6991, 18-32 Chan Man St) Set lunches HK$65-70. This new, minimalist bar serves decent meals – bangers and mash (HK$50) and giant burgers (HK$65) – to a largely expatriate crowd.

Tung Kee Restaurant (☎ 2792 7453, 96-102 Man Nin St) Meals HK$150-200. This

is the pick of the crop for Cantonese seafood. It's not cheap, of course, but then the food is outstanding. Try to call first – though they have a few other branches where they'll seat you as an alternative.

For self-catering, there's a *Park 'N' Shop* (18-20 Fuk Man Rd) and a *Wellcome* (Chan Man St).

Getting There & Away

To get to Sai Kung, take the MTR to Choi Hung, take exit A1 and board bus No 92 (HK$4.20). The faster and more frequent green minibus No 1A or No 1M (HK$7.50) are accessed via exit B, as is the night minibus No 1S (12.30am to 6.10am). From Sha Tin, bus No 299 (HK$9) takes you to Sai Kung via Ma On Shan and passes some lovely bays and isolated villages on the way.

Hebe Haven

Both bus No 92 and green minibus Nos 1A and 1M from Choi Hung MTR station to

Sai Kung Island Hopping

You can make any number of easy boat trips from Sai Kung town, exploring the mosaic of islands that dot the harbour. It's a delightful way to spend a few hours or even an entire day. Kaidos leave from the pier on the waterfront, just in front of Hoi Pong Square.

The easiest (and cheapest) way to go is to jump aboard a 'scheduled' kaido (ie, one that goes according to demand and when full) bound for the small island of Yim Tin Tsai (HK$9, 15 minutes).

On the way, the boat weaves through a number of small islands. The first island, to the north, is **Yeung Chau** (sheep island). You'll be able to spot a horseshoe-shaped burial plot up on the slope; for reasons dictated by fung shui the Chinese like to position graves with decent views of the sea. To the west of Yeung Chau is **Pak Sha Chau** (white sand island), which has a popular beach on its northern shore.

Just beyond Pak Sha Chau is the northern tip of much larger **Kiu Tsui Chau** (sharp island). Kiu Tsui Chau has a couple of fine and sandy beaches: Kiu Tsui on the western shore and Hap Mun on the island's southern tip. Both can be reached by kaido (HK$8 or HK$9) directly from Sai Kung town.

Yim Tin Tsai, or 'little salt field', is so called because its original inhabitants, fisherfolk, added to their income by salt-panning. A few minutes' walk from the jetty up a small flight of steps to the left is St Joseph's Chapel, the focal point of the island. This is Yim Tin Tsai's only house of worship, which is most unusual in an area of Hong Kong where temples devoted to Tin Hau proliferate. Apparently the villagers, who all belong to the same clan, converted to Catholicism after St Peter appeared on the island to chase away pirates who had been harassing them. Beyond the chapel is the village of Yim Tin Tsai, where a handful of families still live.

Yim Tin Tsai is connected to the much larger island of **Kau Sai Chau** by a narrow spit that becomes submerged at high tide. Kau Sai Chau is the site of the Jockey Club Kau Sai Chau Golf Course, a public links that can be reached by the course's direct ferry from Sai Kung (HK$40 return), which departs daily from 6.40am to between 7pm and 9pm, depending on the day of the week. The 19th-century **Hing Shing Temple** to the south-east won a Unesco restoration award in 2000.

Beyond Kau Sai Chau is **Leung Shuen Wan** (high island) and the **High Island Reservoir**, which was built in 1978 by damming what was once a large bay with dolooses – huge cement barriers shaped like jacks. You can see one example, weighing 25 tonnes, on display on the pier in Sai Kung town. You'll also see a large sign there warning of unexploded shells still unaccounted for on some of the islands and dating back to WWII. Areas of potential danger are clearly marked.

If you want to be out on the water for a longer period or have greater flexibility as to where you go, you can hire your own boat. Finding a kaido for such a trip is no problem at all; you won't be on the pier for long before being approached by a bevy of enthusiastic kaido owners trawling for fares.

Explain to the kaido owner where you want to go, how long you want to spend there and which way you wish to return. They don't speak much English but if you point to the islands on the New Territories map in this chapter, they'll get the picture. They should understand, for example, that you want to remain on Yim Tin Tsai for about half an hour to visit the church and take in the views before returning to the boat. The usual price for this kind of trip is about HK$100 on weekdays, more at the weekend.

Sai Kung town pass the small bay of Hebe Haven (Pak Sha Wan in Cantonese, meaning 'white sand bay'; New Territories map), home of the **Hebe Haven Yacht Club** (☎ 2719 9682). You'll recognise the place easily; the fleet of yachts and other pleasure craft all but choke Marina Cove.

To swim at **Trio Beach**, opposite the marina, catch a sampan from Hebe Haven to the long, narrow peninsula called Ma Lam Wat across the bay. The beach is excellent and the sampan trip should only cost a few dollars. You can also walk to the peninsula from Sai Kung town; it's about 4km.

Ma On Shan

Ma On Shan (702m), north-west of Sai Kung town, is the fourth-highest peak in Hong Kong.

Access to the mountain is via stage No 4 of the MacLehose Trail (see that section earlier in this chapter). The trail does not actually go over the summit, but it goes very close and the spur route to the peak is obvious. Be warned – it's a steep and strenuous climb. The mountain is not to be confused with Ma On Shan New Town, with its endless rows of high-rise housing estates and shopping malls. From the peak of Ma On Shan you can walk down to the New Town and catch bus No 299 (HK$9) to Sha Tin or bus No 85C (HK$7.10) to Hung Hom.

Pak Tam Chung

This is the easternmost point on the Sai Kung Peninsula you can reach by bus. It's also the start of the MacLehose Trail.

You can get to Pak Tam Chung on bus No 94 (HK$4.20) from Sai Kung town. Sunday and holidays there is also bus No 96R (HK$12) from Diamond Hill and Choi Hung MTR stations, every 12 to 20 minutes. Along the way, the bus passes Tai Mong Tsai, where there is an **Outward Bound School** (☎ 2792 4333, 2792 0055), an international organisation that teaches wilderness survival (see Orienteering under Activities in the Hong Kong Facts for the Visitor chapter).

From Pak Tam Chung you can walk south-east to **High Island Reservoir**, which used to be a sea channel. Both ends were blocked with dams and the seawater was then siphoned out and fresh water pumped in. The reservoir opened in 1978.

While you're in Pak Tam Chung, visit the **Sai Kung Country Park Visitor Centre** (☎ 2792 7365, Tai Mong Tsai Rd; open 9am-4.30pm Wed-Mon). The centre is in the south of Pak Tam Chung, just by the road from Sai Kung. It has excellent maps, photographs and displays of the area's geology, fauna and flora.

From Pak Tam Chung, it's a leisurely 20-minute walk south along **Pak Tam Chung Nature Trail** to **Sheung Yiu Folk Museum** (☎ 2792 6365, ₩ www.heritagemuseum .gov.hk; admission free; open 9am-4pm Wed-Mon), a restored Hakka village typical of those found in the 19th century. The village was founded about 150 years ago by the Wong clan, and the museum contains farm implements, furnishings and outbuildings.

Hoi Ha, Wong Shek, Chek Keng & Tai Long

There are several rewarding hikes in this area at the northern end of the Sai Kung Peninsula, but the logistics can be a bit tricky. Be sure to take along a copy of the *Countryside Series: Sai Kung & Clearwater Bay* map or Universal Publications' *Sai Kung, Clearwater Bay*, described in the Maps section earlier.

A nice 6km walk in the area starts from the village of Hoi Ha (literally, 'under the sea'), on the coast of Hoi Ha Bay, now part of **Hoi Ha Wan Marine Park**, a protected area blocked off by concrete booms from the Tolo Channel and closed to fishing vessels. It's one of the few places in Hong Kong waters where coral still grows in abundance, and is a favourite with divers.

From Hoi Ha village, follow the trail east along the headland and then south following the coast of **Tai Tan Hoi** (long harbour) all the way to Wong Shek, from where you can catch bus No 94 (HK$4.20) to Sai Kung, or take the ferry to Ma Liu Shui, near the Chinese University.

Alternatively, there's an interesting walk through a few of northern Sai Kung Peninsula's small villages that takes in a small beach. Starting at Chek Keng, or 'red path,' to the south-east of Wong Shek, you can follow stage No 2 of the MacLehose Trail, which will take you east to the tiny village of **Tai Long** (big wave), where you can buy food and drink, then south to the waterfront village of **Ham Tin** (salty field) with a nice beach. From Ham Tin, the MacLehose trail wends southward to **Sai Wan** and around the High Island Reservoir. The return journey is about 8km.

Places to Stay

There are *camp sites* managed by the Country & Marine Parks Authority at Long Ke

Wan, a lovely bay to the south-east of High Island Reservoir, and at Yuen Ng Fan on the western fringe of the reservoir.

Bradbury Hall (☎ 2328 2458, fax 2788 3105, W www.yha.org.hk/bradhall.html, *Chek Keng*) Beds for juniors/seniors HK$25/35, camping HK$16/25 members/nonmembers. This 92-bed HKYHA hostel is right on the harbour facing Chek Keng pier. In the past it's been open at the weekend and on the eve of public holidays only, so telephone the HKYHA (☎ 2788 1638) in advance to check.

Pak Sha O Hostel (☎ 2328 2327, fax 2788 3105, W www.yha.org.hk/pakshao .html, *Ho Ha Rd*) Beds for juniors/seniors HK$25/35, camping HK$16/25 members/nonmembers. This large HKYHA hostel with 112 beds is south-west of Hoi Ha Bay and the marine park. Like Bradbury Hall, it too is not open every day. Call the HKYHA (☎ 2788 1638) for details.

Getting There & Away

Bus No 94 (HK$4.20) links Sai Kung and the pier at Wong Shek. On Sunday and public holidays there's also bus No 96R (HK$12) between Choi Hung MTR station and Wong Shek.

Boats operated by Tsui Wah Ferry Service (☎ 2527 2513) depart Ma Liu Shui for Wong Shek at 8.30am and 3pm daily, calling at Chek Keng along the way. They leave Chek Keng for Wong Shek, Tap Mun Chau and Ma Liu Shui at 10.20am and 4.40pm. Fares are HK$16 on weekdays and HK$25 at the weekend. For more details, see the following Tap Mun Chau section.

The bus from Sai Kung is another way to reach Chek Keng, but expect to do a fair bit of walking. Catch bus No 94 (HK$4.20) and alight at Pak Tam Au (it's the fourth bus stop after the entrance to Sai Kung Country Park near the top of a hill). Take the footpath at the side of the road heading east and walk for about half an hour to Chek Keng (40 minutes to Bradbury Hall hostel).

Getting to Hoi Ha is not easy, though minibus No 7 (HK$5.50) makes the run from Pak Tam Chung on Sunday and public holidays (only). Otherwise, take a taxi from there or from Sai Kung.

For the Pak Sha O Hostel, take bus No 94 from Sai Kung and get off at Ko Tong village. Walk about 100m along Pak Tam Rd and turn left onto Hoi Ha Rd. A sign about 30m ahead shows the way to Pak Sha O. Count on walking 30 to 40 minutes.

TAP MUN CHAU

Tap Mun Chau, or 'grass island', is in the north-east of the New Territories, where Tolo Harbour channel empties into Mirs Bay (Tai Pang Wan). The island is quite isolated and retains an old-world fishing village atmosphere. Indeed, many travellers say that Tap Mun is the most interesting island in all of Hong Kong. If you have the time, it's definitely worth the trip and you will be rewarded with a feeling hard to come by in Hong Kong – isolation.

The island does not have accommodation, but you may get away with pitching a tent.

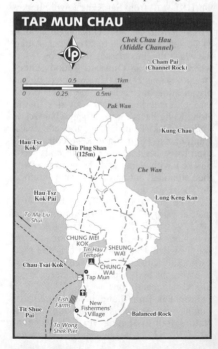

TAP MUN CHAU

As you approach Tap Mun, you'll see fishing boats bobbing abou in the small bay and, to the south, people working on fish-breeding rafts. Tap Mun is noted for its **Tin Hau Temple**, which was built during the reign of Kang Xi in the Qing dynasty and is close to where the boat docks. The Tin Hau Festival in late April/early May is very big here, although most of the celebrants come from the city. Other attractions include **Tap Mun Cave** and the beautiful **beach** on the south-east shore of the island.

Getting There & Away

From Ma Liu Shui, ferries operated by Tsui Wah Ferry Service (☎ 2527 2513) cruise through Tolo Harbour to Tap Mun and back, calling at various villages on the Sai Kung Peninsula along the way, including Chek Keng and Wong Shek.

Ferries leave Ma Liu Shui at 8.30am and 3pm daily, arriving at Tap Mun Chau at 10am and 4.20pm respectively, from where they continue on to Chek Keng and Wong Shek. They leave for Ma Liu Shui at 11.10am and 5.30pm. On Saturday, Sunday and public holidays an extra ferry leaves Ma Liu Shui at 12.30pm, arriving and departing from Tap Mun at 1.45pm. Fares are HK$16 on weekdays and HK$25 on the weekend.

An easier way to reach Tap Mun Chau, with many more departures, is by kaido from Wong Shek pier, which is the last stop on bus No 94 from Sai Kung town. The kaidos, also operated by Tsui Wah Ferry Service, run about once every two hours from 8.30am to 6.30pm on weekdays (HK$8) and hourly between the same hours at the weekend and on public holidays (HK$12). This route is particularly scenic because it cruises through the narrow Tai Tan Hoi Hap (long harbour), which is more reminiscent of a fjord in Norway than a harbour in Hong Kong.

PING CHAU

This small, crescent-shaped island, sitting in splendid isolation in Mirs Bay in the far north-east of the New Territories, is part of **Plover Cove Country Park** (☎ 2665 3413).

It's very close to the mainland and used to be one of the most popular destinations for people immigrating illegally from China by braving the sharks and the patrol boats and taking to the water. In Cantonese the island is called Tung Ping Chau, or 'east peace island', to distinguish it from Peng Chau (same pronunciation in Cantonese) near Lantau.

At one time the island supported a population of 3000, but now it is virtually deserted, its people either lured away by the promise of wealth in the urban areas or driven off the island by pirates operating from the south coast of the mainland.

The island's highest point is only about 40m, but it has unusual rock layers in its cliffs, which glitter after the rain. Ping Chau has some beautiful white sandy beaches on its east coast that are good for swimming. The longest one is **Cheung Sha Wan** to the north-east. There is a small **Tin Hau Temple** on the southern coast of the island, and some small caves dotting the cliffs. A good walking trail encircles the entire island.

Ping Chau is the site of Hong Kong's only radiation shelter, at Tai Tong just north of the pier. Ping Chau is just 12km from the mainland's Daya Bay nuclear power - station.

Places to Stay

You'll find a *camp site* managed by the Country & Marine Parks Authority at Kang Lau Shek on the extreme north-east tip of the island.

Getting There & Away

You can reach Ping Chau by ferry from Ma Liu Shui, near University KCR station, operated by Tsui Wah Ferry Service (☎ 2527 2513) – but only on weekends and public holidays. Ferries depart from Ma Liu Shui at 9am and 3.30pm on Saturday, returning at 5.15pm. The single ferry on Sunday and holidays leaves Ma Liu Shui at 9am, returning from Ping Chau at 5.15pm. Only round-trip tickets are sold (HK$80) and the trip takes 1¾ hours. The Sunday morning ferry could well be booked out; call ahead to check on availability.

CLEARWATER BAY PENINSULA

The south-eastern point of the New Territories is the Clearwater Bay Peninsula, a wonderfully untamed and rough-contoured backdrop to urban Hong Kong. It is wedged in by Junk Bay (Tseung Kwan O) to the west and Clearwater Bay (Tsing Sui Wan) to the east; Joss House Bay (Tai Miu Wan) nestles to the south. Junk Bay is now the site of enormous land reclamation and housing development, but the eastern coastline remains mostly unscarred and offers some exceptional walks, fine beaches and one of the many temples dedicated to Tin Hau on the coast of southern China.

The heart of **Clearwater Bay Country Park** is **Tai Au Mun**, from where trails head off in various directions. You can take the small road (Lung Ha Wan Rd) north to the beach of **Lung Ha Wan** (lobster bay) and return via the Tai Hang Tun-Lung Ha Wan Country Trail via **Tai Leng Tung** (291m). Tai Au Mun Rd goes south to two fine, sandy beaches: **Clearwater Bay First Beach** and, a bit farther to the south-west, **Clearwater Bay Second Beach**. In summer, try to go during the week as they both can get very crowded on the weekend.

Farther south along Tai Au Mun Rd is ancient **Tai Miu**, a temple dedicated to Tin Hau.

It is said to have been first built in the 13th century by two brothers from Fujian in thanks to the goddess for having spared their lives during a storm at sea. It is particularly busy during the Tin Hau festival in late April/early May. To the east is the **Clearwater Bay Golf and Country Club** (☎ 2719 1595). North of that is the charming village of **Poi Toi O** on the bay of that name.

From Tai Miu, hikers can take the trail up **Tin Ha Shan** (273m) and then continue on the trail to **High Junk Peak** (Tiu Yu Yung; 344m) before heading eastward back to Tai Au Mun.

Getting There & Away

To get to the Clearwater Bay Peninsula, take the MTR to Diamond Hill or Choi Hung and catch bus No 91 (HK$4.70) from either station. The bus passes Silverstrand Beach (Ngan Sin Wan) before reaching Tai Au Mun; if you wish you can get off at Silverstrand and go for a dip. If you're heading for Lung Ha Wan, get off the bus at Tai Au Mun village and start walking. Bus No 91 terminates at Clearwater Bay Second Beach. From Sai Kung, take bus No 92 (HK$4.20) to where Hiram's Hwy and Clearwater Bay Rd meet and change there to bus No 91.

Outlying Islands

The territory of Hong Kong consists of another 234 islands, apart from Hong Kong Island itself. Together these so-called outlying islands make up about 16% of the territory's total land area, but they can claim just over 1% of its population.

Hong Kong's outlying islands vary greatly in size, appearance and character. While many are little more than uninhabited rocks poking out of the South China Sea, Lantau is actually larger and higher than Hong Kong Island. Officially the islands are part of the New Territories, with the exception of Stonecutters Island, which has now become part of Kowloon through land reclamation.

Because they are so sparsely populated, the outlying islands are the territory's escape routes and its playgrounds. Among the magnets that attract local day-trippers and for eign visitors alike are relatively clean beaches, hundreds of kilometres of hiking trails, fresher air and the last remnants of traditional village life in Hong Kong. So jump aboard one of the many island ferries heading out of Hong Kong Harbour and enjoy the stunning views of mountains and water en route to a quieter, less frenetic world.

From the tranquil lanes of Cheung Chau and Peng Chau to the monasteries of Lantau and the waterfront seafood restaurants of Lamma, Hong Kong's islands offer a world of peace and quiet along with a host of sights and activities. What's more, the islands are a colourful encyclopaedia of animal and plant life – a boon for nature lovers.

Some of Hong Kong's best beaches punctuate the rocky coasts. Needless to say, the more remote stretches of sand are cleaner and quieter; go that extra distance – especially on a weekday – and you may find yourself alone on a secluded stretch of sand. It's wise to avoid visiting any of the islands on weekends, especially in summer, when it seems like half of Hong Kong is making the weary pilgrimage to these oases of calm.

Just a few decades ago, almost all of the habitable islands had villages supported by

Highlights

- A morning pilgrimage to the giant Buddha at Po Lin Monastery and a relaxing day at Cheung Sha Beach on Lantau Island
- A hike via the switchback Dog's Tooth Peak trail to Lantau Peak
- A walk from Yung Shue Wan to Sok Kwu Wan on Lamma Island, with a seafood blowout at the end, or a detour to lovely Tung O Wan
- A day of merrymaking on Cheung Chau during the Bun Festival
- A visit to the Lantau Link Visitors Centre for a mind-boggling view of Tsing Ma Bridge
- A sail to lovely Po Toi Island, with a seafood meal as the reward

the fishing industry and some market gardening. Now many of these settlements are all but deserted. Today many of the fisherfolk who stayed behind make their money not from the sea but from the rental of holiday homes and villas.

Expatriates are among the staunchest defenders of traditional island ways of life, fiercely opposing proposals to build highrises and introduce cars to the islands. Ironically, it was this influx of foreigners that helped developers justify more building projects. Developments such as Discovery Bay on Lantau's north-eastern coast, where matchbox high-rises compete for a view of the sea, could be an indication of the way the islands are heading.

Limited ferry schedules, once helped keep the outlying islands relatively unspoiled. But new ferry companies are putting faster and greater numbers of boats on their routes. High-speed ferries cut the commuting time to Discovery Bay to less than 20 minutes. The development of the North Lantau Highway, connecting Hong Kong International

Airport at Chek Lap Kok on Lantau's north coast with Kowloon and Central, has further eroded the sense of remoteness.

Only those islands accessible by public ferry are included in this chapter. Many of the more far-flung islands are popular weekend destinations for Hong Kong's flotilla of yachts and junks.

Because the tiny islands of Tap Mun Chau and Ping Chau are best reached from the New Territories, they are both covered in that chapter. The islands in this chapter are all easily accessible from Hong Kong Island, and Cheung Chau and Lantau can be reached from Kowloon at the weekend.

Maps

If you intend to do a lot of hiking and walking on the outlying islands, equip yourself with one of the excellent *Countryside Series* maps produced by the Survey & Mapping Office of the Lands Department and available at government Map Publication Centres (see Maps under Planning in the introductory Hong Kong Facts for the Visitor chapter for addresses).

Lantau Island (HK$50) is essentially a 1:25,000-scale map of Hong Kong's largest island, with several larger-scale inset maps. *Outlying Islands* (HK$45) in the same series includes large-scale maps of Cheung Chau, Lamma, Peng Chau, Ma Wan, Tung Lung Chau and Po Toi. Another useful map produced by the Country & Marine Parks Authority and available at the map centres is the 1:20,000-scale *Lantau Trail* (HK$30), with the route's dozen stages and facilities en route clearly marked. Most bookshops stock Universal Publications' 1:50,000-scale *Lantau Island, Cheung Chau* (HK$18), which is waterproof and contains useful information for hikers.

Dangers & Annoyances

Among the dangers and annoyances on the outlying islands are snakes, some of which are venomous but seldom seen, insects and other pests, such as the mammoth woodland spider and a millipede that inflicts a painful and potentially dangerous bite, and – to a lesser extent than in the past – dogs.

For the most part dogs you'll see in the villages are friendly – even cowering. If you are attacked, get a good look at the dog that bit you and then call the police. The owner may be tracked down and will have to pay your medical expenses and a fine.

If you feel the urge to plunge into the sea in some of the less accessible areas, bear in mind that Hong Kong waters are regularly patrolled by sharks.

Accommodation

Hostels, guesthouses and hotels are listed under each island. Individuals maintain booking offices for apartments and holiday villas near the ferry piers on Cheung Chau and at Mui Wo (Silvermine Bay) on Lantau. Again, see Places to Stay in those sections for details. There are some 15 camp sites along the Lantau Trail and one on Tung Lung Chau.

For those intending to stay for a while, accommodation on the outlying islands offers far better value than the equivalent in Kowloon or on Hong Kong Island. You can still rent a three-bedroom apartment with a roof terrace on Lamma for less than HK$8000 a month or a shared flat or room for as little as HK$2000 a month. Rooms and flats are advertised in the property pages of the daily English newspapers, and the advert wall just beyond the Lamma ferry pier is usually plastered with such offers.

Things to weigh in the balance, however, include transportation costs and the time spent commuting. A one-way ferry trip to Lamma, for example, costs a minimum of HK$10 from Monday to Saturday, HK$14 on Sunday, and takes a half-hour. This is offset by the island's beautiful surrounds, the lively nightlife and many restaurants, however.

Getting There & Away

The main islands are linked for the most part to Hong Kong by regular ferry services. The ferries are comfortable and cheap, mostly air-conditioned and have a basic bar that serves drinks and snacks. Smoking is prohibited on all the ferries, and offenders will be fined a maximum of HK$5000. The ferries can get very crowded on Saturday afternoon and all day Sunday, especially in summer. Depart as early as you can and return in the evening.

There are two types of ferries: large 'ordinary ferries', which, with the exception of those to Lamma, offer ordinary and deluxe classes; and smaller 'fast ferries', hovercraft that have one class only, and cut travel time by between 10 and 20 minutes, but cost between 50% and 100% more. Weekday fares apply from Monday to Saturday; prices are significantly higher on Sunday and public holidays. Unless stated otherwise, children aged four to 11 years of age, seniors over 65 years and people with disabilities pay half-fare on both types of ferries and in both classes. Return is almost always double the single fare.

The main company serving the island is New World First Ferry Services (☎ 2131 8181, fax 2131 8877, W www.nwff.com.hk), which has a customer service centre just south of pier 7 at the outlying islands ferry terminal. Its boats go to Cheung Chau, Peng Chau and Lantau and connect all three via an inter-island service. The Hong Kong & Kowloon Ferry Co (☎ 2815 6063, W www.hkkf.com.hk) serves destinations on Lamma. The timetables are subject to slight seasonal changes. They are prominently displayed at all ferry piers, but you can pick up a copy of the schedules at any HKTB information centre or download it from the HKTB Web site (W www.discoverhongkong.com).

Tickets are available from booths at the ferry piers, but you'll avoid queuing at busy times by using an Octopus card or putting the exact change into a turnstile as you enter the pier. On some of the smaller ferries the staff run out of change, so it helps to have small coins. It's rare for ticket offices to accept bills larger than HK$100.

If your time is limited, contact Watertours (☎ 2926 3868), which organises trips to some of the outlying islands. See Boat under Organised Tours in the Getting Around chapter for details. The Jubilee International Tour Centre (☎ 2530 0530, fax 2845 2469), Room 604, Far East Consortium Building, 121 Des Voeux Rd Central, is one of the many tour companies in Hong Kong that can book yachts and junks.

Getting Around

With the exception of Lantau, cars are prohibited on all of the outlying islands. On Lantau, a special 'closed-road' vehicle permit is required and is available to residents only, but there are 50 taxis serving the requirements of residents and visitors. The only traffic on the other islands are tiny cargo tractors and trailers called VVs – for 'village vehicles' – that are powered by lawn mower engines and can navigate the spindly roads. The ambulances on Lamma and Cheung Chau, for example, are only slightly wider than a refrigerator.

The islands are eminently walkable – hiking and trekking is why many people make the trip at the weekend – but bicycles can be rented on Lantau, Lamma and Cheung Chau.

CHEUNG CHAU

Cheung Chau, or 'long island' in Cantonese, is a bone-shaped island lying 10km south-west of Hong Kong Island and just off the south-eastern tip of Lantau. A one-time refuge for pirates and later an exclusive retreat for British colonials, Cheung Chau is now the most populous of all the outlying islands. Some 22,000 people, many of them commuters, are crammed onto Cheung Chau's 2.5 sq km, though very few foreigners live here nowadays.

Archaeological evidence, including a 3000-year-old rock carving uncovered just below the Warwick Hotel (see the boxed text Cheung Chau Walking Tour), shows that Cheung Chau, like Lamma and Lantau, was inhabited at least as early as the Neolithic period. The island had a thriving fishing community at the time, and the early inhabitants – Cantonese and Hakka settlers – supplemented this livelihood with smuggling and piracy.

When Canton (present-day Guangzhou) and Macau opened up to the West in the 16th century, Cheung Chau was a perfect spot from which to prey on passing ships. The infamous and powerful pirate Cheung Po Tsai is said to have had his base here in the 18th century; you can still visit the cave where he supposedly stashed his booty at the south-western tip of the island.

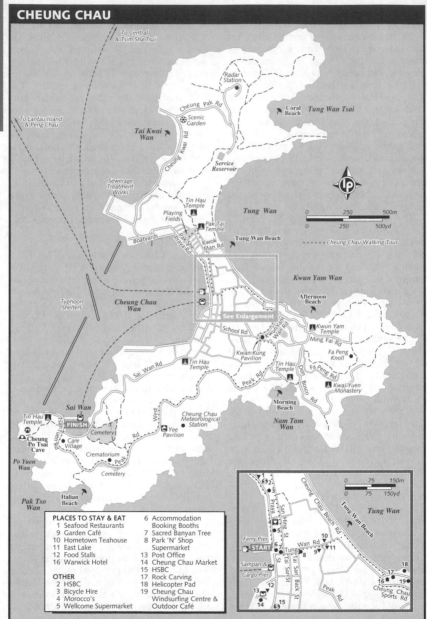

CHEUNG CHAU

PLACES TO STAY & EAT
1 Seafood Restaurants
9 Garden Café
10 Hometown Teahouse
11 East Lake
12 Food Stalls
16 Warwick Hotel

OTHER
2 HSBC
3 Bicycle Hire
4 Morocco's
5 Wellcome Supermarket

6 Accommodation
   Booking Booths
7 Sacred Banyan Tree
8 Park 'N' Shop
   Supermarket
13 Post Office
14 Cheung Chau Market
15 HSBC
17 Rock Carving
18 Helicopter Pad
19 Cheung Chau
   Windsurfing Centre &
   Outdoor Café

Fishing and aquaculture are important industries for a large number of the island's inhabitants, about 10% of whom live on junks and sampans anchored in the harbour – bring your camera for some of the best shots of traditional maritime life on the southern China coast.

Cheung Chau boasts several interesting temples, the most important being Pak Tai Temple, which hosts the annual Bun Festival, *the* red-letter day on Cheung Chau (see the boxed text Going for the Buns). The island has a few worthwhile beaches, and there are some relatively easy walks, including the one described later in this section, will take you through lush vegetation and past missionary schools, churches, retreats and cemeteries. Most can be easily done in half a day.

In recent years, Cheung Chau has become known as the 'Island of Suicides' after as many as 10 individuals asphyxiated themselves by burning barbecue charcoal in sealed rooms of holiday flats along Tung Wan Rd.

Information
HSBC (☎ 2981 1127) has two branches on Cheung Chau: at 1116 Praya St, south-east of the cargo pier and seafood stalls, and at 19A Pak She Praya Rd, north of the ferry pier. The post office is on Tai Hing Tai St south-west of the food stalls.

Cheung Chau Village
No longer really a village but a small town, the island's main built-up area lies along the narrow strip of land connecting the headlands to the north and the south. The waterfront is a bustling place and the maze of streets and alleyways that make up the village are a world of tumble-down shops selling everything from plastic buckets to hell money and historic Chinese architecture, redolent with the smell of incense and fish hung out to dry in the sun.

Cheung Chau Typhoon Shelter
Only the typhoon shelter at Aberdeen (see that section in the Hong Kong Island chapter) is larger than this one. Chartering a sampan for a half-hour costs between

Ten percent of Cheung Chau's inhabitants live on junks, which are anchored in the harbour.

HK$20 and HK$50, depending on the day, season and demand. Most sampans congregate around the cargo pier, but virtually any small boat you see in the harbour is a water taxi and can be hired. Just wave and two or three will come forward. Be sure to agree on the fare first.

Pak Tai Temple
This colourful temple is the oldest house of worship on the island and the focus of the annual Cheung Chau Bun Festival. It is dedicated to the eponymous deity Pak Tai; see the boxed text The Gods & Goddesses of South China under Religion in the Facts about Hong Kong chapter.

Legend tells us that early settlers from Guangdong province brought an image of Pak Tai, protector of fisherfolk (among other things), with them to Cheung Chau. In 1777 the statue was carried through the village and Cheung Chau was spared a plague decimating the other islands. A temple dedicated to the saviour was built six years later.

Pak Tai Temple, fronted by two fearsome stone lions, contains several items of historical interest, including a large iron sword said to have been forged in the Song dynasty (960–1279). The sword, regarded as a symbol of good luck, was recovered from the sea by a local fisherman over a century ago and presented to the god by the islanders. There is also a wooden sedan chair, made in 1894, which was used to carry Pak

Cheung Chau Walking Tour

This pleasant and not particularly strenuous walk from Cheung Chau village to Sai Wan in the south-west will take you past flotillas of junks, restaurants, noisy mahjong parlours, temples, sacred trees, beaches and some wonderful vistas of the sea. The walk will take about 2½ hours; the latter part is especially beautiful and best undertaken in good weather towards the end of the day when the temperature drops and the light conditions are best. Avoid going on the weekend if you can; everyone else will be there too.

After disembarking from the ferry, turn left and head north along Praya St, where a row of mostly seafood restaurants face the harbour. Praya St becomes Pak She Praya Rd after the turn-off for Kwok Man Rd, and from here you can look out at the many **junks and sampans** moored in the harbour. On sunny days you might see fruit, fish and seaweed being dried on rattan skips on the waterfront.

Just past Pak She Fourth Lane are playing fields; immediately to the east is colourful **Pak Tai Temple**, built in the Qing dynasty and one of the most important historical monuments on Cheung Chau. There's a **Tin Hau Temple** to the north.

Leaving the Pak Tai Temple behind you and heading south down Pak She St (*not* Pak She Praya St), you'll pass a **traditional Chinese house** (the third building on the left). Two stone lions guard the house, and behind them hang two posters of the door gods whose job it is to expel evil spirits. Pak She St is also where you'll find a number of **traditional Chinese medicine shops** and a bakery at No 46, which sells small Chinese cakes.

Farther south, and on the left at the intersection of Pak She St and Kwok Man Rd, is a small **shrine** to Tou Tei, the earth god. The islanders on Cheung Chau leave offerings to the earth god who lives in natural objects such as trees.

San Hing St, which leads off Pak She St after it crosses Kwok Man Rd, is a street of many different scents and flavours. **Herbalist shops** display wares in large glass jars and the shop at No 30 sells incense and paper hell money, which is traditionally burned at the Lunar New Year or in memory of the dead. Keep an eye open for the shop at No 80 with the bamboo hats worn by the fishing community in Cheung Chau.

Tai around the island on festival days, and two granite pillars depicting dragons.

Other Temples

Cheung Chau has several temples dedicated to **Tin Hau**, the Empress of Heaven and patroness of seafarers. One temple lies a short distance to the north-west of the Pak Tai Temple, and there is another near the waterfront at the southern end of Cheung Chau village. A third lies west of Sai Wan, or 'western bay', on the south-western tip of the island. You can walk there or catch a kaido from the cargo pier.

Tung Wan Beach

Cheung Chau's biggest and most popular (though not its prettiest) beach lies at the end of Tung Wan Rd, due east from the ferry pier. The best part of Tung Wan is the far southern end, where you'll find the Cheung Chau Windsurfing Centre. See Activities later in this section for details.

Other Beaches

The south-eastern part of Cheung Chau has the most interesting beaches. Just south of Tung Wan Beach and past the Warwick Hotel and windsurfing centre is **Kwun Yam Wan Beach**, known to English-speakers as Afternoon Beach. At the end of the beach a footpath leads uphill past the small **Kwun Yam Temple**, dedicated to the Goddess of Mercy. Continue up the footpath and look for the sign to the Fa Peng Knoll. The concrete footpath takes you past quiet, tree-shrouded villas.

From the knoll you can walk down to Don Bosco Rd (again look for the sign); it leads due south to rocky **Nam Tam Wan**, or

Cheung Chau Walking Tour

Everywhere around you will be an explosion of sound as mahjong tiles are shuffled on tables. Mahjong is not encouraged by the authorities in Hong Kong, as the only legal form of gambling at present is horse racing and the 'Mark Six' lottery.

As you turn east from San Hing St and enter Tung Wan Rd, you'll see a **sacred tree** on the right. This ancient banyan is believed to be inhabited by earth spirits, which explains the small shrine at its base. Tung Wan Rd leads up to **Tung Wan Beach** and the Warwick Hotel. Have a look at the **carving** made on a rock just below the hotel. It was discovered in 1970 and is believed to be 3000 years old. The carving consists of two identical geometric designs all but obscured by creepers.

Behind the Warwick Hotel is steep Cheung Chau Sports Rd; begin the climb and when you see a pavilion ahead, turn right onto Kwun Yum Wan Rd and past the sports ground on your left. A few minutes ahead and on the left is the **Kwan Kung Pavilion**, a temple dedicated to Kwan Tai, the God of War and Righteousness and a symbol of power and loyalty. As you walk down from the temple, turn left onto Peak Rd, which is flanked by attractive residential properties.

As you continue along Peak Rd, you'll pass the Cheung Chau Meteorological Station, which offers splendid views of the island and sea. Farther on is **Chung Lok Garden** and the **Yee Pavilion**, which is dedicated to the Chinese poet Zhang Renshi. The boulders around the temple are inscribed with eulogies from fellow poets and daubed with graffiti by local 'artists'. A bit farther south and through the trees to the left is a cemetery affording a quiet and solemn view out to sea. On the right is a crematorium.

Soon you'll come to a forked road. The path to the left leads to **Italian Beach**, the one to the right carries on to Sai Wan. If you take the latter, you'll soon walk through Care Village, a small settlement with bunker-like housing that was set up in 1968 with money from an American charity. Farther on is another sign-posted fork in the road where you can either turn left for **Cheung Po Tsai Cave** and **Tin Hau Temple** or right for the *kaido* (ferry) back to Cheung Chau village, which departs from the pier jutting into the middle of the bay. Alternatively, follow Sai Wan Rd around the bay and north back to the village (20 to 30 minutes).

Morning Beach, where swimming is possible. If you ignore Don Bosco Rd and continue walking west you'll come to the intersection of Peak and Kwun Yam Wan Rds. Kwun Yam Wan Rd and its extension, School Rd, will take you back to Cheung Chau village.

Peak Rd is the main route to the island's cemetery in the south-western part of the island; you'll pass several pavilions along the way built for coffin bearers making the hilly climb. Once at the cemetery it's worth dropping down to **Pak Tso Wan** (Italian Beach) – a sandy, isolated spot that is good for swimming. Peak Rd becomes Tsan Tuen Rd, which continues northward to Sai Wan.

Most of Cheung Chau's northern headland is uninhabited, with little more than a reservoir, radar station and a scenic garden at the end of Cheung Kwai Rd. From the highlands of Cheung Chau there are panoramic views to Lamma, Lantau and Hong Kong Islands. You can reach this area by climbing the path leading uphill next to the Pak Tai Temple. At the north-western corner of the island is **Tai Kwai Wan**, which has a protected sandy beach. On the north-eastern coast is the more isolated **Tung Wan Tsai**, or 'coral beach'.

Cheung Po Tsai Cave

This cave, on the south-western peninsula of the island, is said to have been the hiding place of the notorious pirate, Cheung Po Tsai, who had a reputation for extreme brutality. The cave's association with Cheung Po Tsai is almost certainly apocryphal as it is very small – just narrow crevices between boulders stacked on top of one another. It's a 2km walk from Cheung Chau village

HONG KONG

Going for the Buns

The annual Cheung Chau Bun Festival (Tai Chiu), held in honour of the god Pak Tai and unique to the island, takes place over eight days in late April or early May, traditionally on the sixth day of the fourth moon. It is a Taoist festival, and there are three or four days of religious observances.

The festival is renowned for its bun towers, bamboo scaffolding up to 20m high, that are covered with sacred rolls. If you visit Cheung Chau a week or so before the festival, you'll see the towers being built in the courtyard of Pak Tai Temple.

In the past, hundreds of people would scramble up the towers at the appointed hour to grab one of the buns for good luck. The higher the bun, the greater the luck, so everyone scrambled to the top. In 1978 a serious accident occurred when a tower collapsed. Now everyone must remain on *terra firma* and the buns are handed out.

Sunday, the third day of the festival, features a procession of floats, stilt walkers and people dressed as characters from Chinese legends. Most interesting are the colourfully dressed 'floating children' who are carried through the streets on long poles, cleverly wired to metal supports hidden under their clothes. The supports include footrests and a padded seat. At 24 Pak She St, just south of the Pak Tai Temple, there is a photo exhibition of these floating children.

During the celebrations several other deities are also worshipped, including Tin Hau and Hung Shing, the God of the South, both of whom are sacred to those who make their living from the sea. Homage is also paid to Tou Tei, the Earth God, and Kwun Yam, the Goddess of Mercy.

Offerings are made to the spirits of all the fish and livestock killed and consumed over the previous year. A priest reads out a decree calling on the villagers to abstain from killing any animals during the four-day festival, and no meat is consumed.

Accommodation on Cheung Chau is heavily booked throughout the festival, and even the extra ferries laid on are packed to the rafters.

---

along Sai Wan Rd or take a kaido (HK$3) from the cargo ferry pier to the pier at Sai Wan. From here the walk is less than 200m but uphill. If you really want to see everything, make sure to take a torch (flashlight).

Activities

Windsurfing has always been an extremely popular pastime on Cheung Chau. Indeed, Hong Kong's only Olympic gold medal winner to date, Lee Lai San, who took the top prize in windsurfing at the 1996 Olympics in Atlanta, grew up on Cheung Chau. The **Cheung Chau Windsurfing Centre** (☎ 2981 8316, 2981 5063, 1 Hak Pai Rd, Tung Wan Beach; open daily Apr-Dec) rents sail boards for HK$60/100/120 per hour, depending on the size, as well as single/double kayaks for HK$50/80. There are also windsurfing courses which are available for HK$550. The best months for windsurfing in Hong Kong are September, October and November.

Bicycles can be hired from the **rental kiosk** (☎ 2981 0227) at the northern end of Praya St for HK$10/30 per hour/day.

Places to Stay

Cheung Chau is not particularly well set up for overnighters. Depending on the day of the week and the season, up to a dozen different booths just opposite the ferry pier and north along Praya St rent *studios* and *apartments*. Agents include Bela Vista (☎ 2981 7299) and Kwong Yin Yi (mobile ☎ 9206 5558), but unless you have a smattering of Cantonese you might have difficulty getting what you want at a fair price. Expect to pay from HK$200 a night for a studio accommodating two people from Sunday to Friday and from HK$400 on Saturday.

Warwick Hotel (☎ 2981 0081, fax 2981 9174, Cheung Chau Sports Rd, Tung Wan Beach) Doubles with mountain/sea view HK$690/790, suites HK$1590. This six-storey, 71-room carbuncle on the butt of

Mastering chopsticks at a restaurant, Hong Kong Island.

OLIVER STREWE

Lunch at a fishing village

OLIVER STREWE

The bustling Temple St Night Market, in Kowloon, is a popular destination for an evening meal.

OLIVER STREWE

Enjoying a snack of 'coral and jade' (steamed prawns and asparagus) dumplings.

Anyone for a cuppa?

A giant's teapot at the Jabbok Tea House in the New Territories.

The art of tea-making: relaxing over tea is serious business in modern-day Hong Kong.

A herbal tea shop in Kowloon. References to tea in Chinese literature go back at least 5000 years.

Tung Wan Beach is the only game in town but does offer wonderful views across the sea to Lamma and Hong Kong Islands.

Places to Eat

South of the cargo pier at the start of Tai Hing Tai Rd are a number of *food stalls* with fish tanks where you can choose your favourite finned or shelled creatures at more or less market prices and then pay the stall holders (HK$20-40) to cook them the way you like.

Pak She Praya Rd, running north-west off Praya St, is loaded with good seafood restaurants that face the typhoon shelter and its flotilla.

Hong Kee (☎ 2981 9916, 2981 2783, 11A Pak She Praya Rd) Mains HK$25-70, fish HK$140. This is one of the top spots along this stretch and should be your first choice.

New Baccarat (☎ 2981 0606, 2981 0668, 9A Pak She Praya Rd) Meals HK$120. Head for this place next door if Hong Kee is full.

Hing Lok (☎ 2981 9773, 2A Pak She Sixth Lane) Meals HK$120-150. Hing Lok is a titch farther north than the other two restaurants mentioned, but serves excellent seafood and is within casting distance of the waterfront.

East Lake (☎ 2981 3869, 85 Tung Wan Rd) Mains HK$30-58. If you're willing to travel a bit farther afield this Cantonese restaurant is quite popular with both locals and expats, especially in the evening when tables are set up outside.

Garden Café (☎ 2981 4610, 84 Tung Wan Rd) Dishes HK$20-60. This Western-style pub and restaurant just next door is where you'll find such 'classics' as beans on toast, mushrooms on toast, chicken and mushroom pie and chips and mushy peas, but residents say standards have fallen in recent years. There's outside seating opposite.

Hometown Teahouse (☎ 2981 5038, 2981 2981, 12 Tung Wan Rd) Afternoon tea HK$30. This wonderfully relaxed place run by an amiable Japanese couple serves lunch and dinner, but the tea is what you should come for.

Wellcome (Praya St), opposite the ferry pier, and *Park 'N' Shop* (Cnr Tung Wan Rd & Tai San Back St) These two supermarkets are conveniently located near the ferry pier so you can stock up on food and drink if you are going hiking or spending the day on the beach.

Entertainment

Morocco's (☎ 2986 9767, 71 Praya Rd) The exodus of expats from Cheung Chau over the past several years has left the island all but bereft of quality drinking venues, but we'll always have Morocco's on the waterfront.

Outdoor Café (☎ 2981 5063, 1 Hak Pai Rd) This open-air, cafe-cum-pub attached to the windsurfing centre at Tung Wan Beach is known locally as Lai Kam's in honour of its owner and is a Cheung Chau institution. Come here for a sundowner and you'll remain long after dark.

Getting There & Away

To/From Central Ordinary and fast ferries for Cheung Chau depart from pier 6 at the outlying islands ferry terminal in Central approximately every half-hour between 6.15am (6.30am on Sunday) and 12.30am. There are then fast ferries at 1.30am and 4.30am until normal daytime services begin again. The last ordinary ferry back to Central from Cheung Chau leaves at 11.15pm (11.30pm on Sunday), but don't panic if you miss it: there are fast ferries at 2.20am and 5.10am seven days a week.

The trip on the ordinary ferry takes 48 minutes, and the adult one-way fare in ordinary class is HK$10.50 (HK$15.70 on Sunday and public holidays). The fares for deluxe class, which allows you to sit on the open-air deck at the stern, are HK$16.80 and HK$25 respectively. The fast ferries, which run as frequently as the ordinary ones and take just 32 minutes, cost HK$21 (HK$31 on Sunday).

To/From Tsim Sha Tsui At the weekend and on public holidays *only*, fast ferries depart from the northern side of the Tsim Sha Tsui Star Ferry pier in Kowloon. Boats leave Tsim Sha Tsui at 1.35pm and 3.35pm on Saturday and at 9.35am, 11.35am,

1.35pm and 3.35pm on Sunday and public holidays. The return ferries from Cheung Chau are at 2.15pm and 4.15pm on Saturday and 10.15am, 12.15pm, 2.15pm and 4.15pm on Sunday and public holidays. The one-way fare is HK$31 and the voyage lasts 32 minutes.

Inter-Island Services An ordinary inter-island ferry links Cheung Chau with Mui Wo (via Chi Ma Wan in most cases) on Lantau and Peng Chau throughout the day. The first ferry leaves Cheung Chau at 6am, and the last ferry is at 10.50pm; boats leave approximately every two hours. From Cheung Chau, it takes 15 minutes to reach Chi Ma Wan, a half-hour to Mui Wo and 46 minutes to Peng Chau. The flat fare is HK$8.40.

LAMMA

The territory's third-largest island after Lantau and Hong Kong, Lamma is home to fishers, farmers and commuters, and the hills above the main village, Yung Shue Wan, are strewn with small homes and apartment blocks. Known mainly for the seafood restaurants at Sok Kwu Wan, the island's 'second' village, Lamma also has some good beaches, excellent hiking and lively pubs.

Lamma is *the* island haven for expats, supported by a diverse restaurant culture and some decent bars. Low rents, the laid-back lifestyle, a strong feeling of community and appealing surrounds are all part of the attraction. Foreigners are being replaced by Chinese yuppies, or 'Chuppies', looking for the same things.

Archaeological evidence indicates that Lamma is the site of one of the earliest settlements in southern China. Archaeologists doing a routine dig at Tai Wan San Tsuen, south-east of Yung Shue Wan, unearthed objects suggesting that there was a small fishing village on the island some 5000 to 6000 years ago (see the boxed text Lamma's Hidden Secrets).

Lamma had no electricity until 1963. Plans to build an oil refinery on the island were dropped 10 years later after strong opposition from residents. Instead, Hongkong Electric constructed a huge coal-fired power

---

Lamma's Hidden Secrets

Lamma's first permanent community established itself around splendid little Sham Wan (Deep Bay) in the south of the island in approximately 4000 BC. The early settlers were a nomadic, maritime people known as the Yue, whose origins remain cloudy. Some archaeologists believe they were of Malay stock and migrated from South-East Asia. Others say they were a satellite of the Hundred Yue, a diverse group of people occupying China's south-eastern seaboard.

Sham Wan has surrendered a bounty of finds pointing to this early society, including Iron Age coins and bits of pottery. By the Bronze Age (c. 2000-900 BC), settlements had sprouted up at Sha Po Tsuen, Tai Wan San Tsuen and Lamma's 'capital', Yung Shue Wan. Tai Wan San Tsuen constitutes the most significant Bronze Age site in Hong Kong, with excavation sites revealing a number of bronze weapons worked with considerable skill.

---

station on the north-west coast; the three enormous smoke stacks are clearly visible from Hong Kong Island. The 'road' that runs across the north of the island is not a road at all, but a concrete shell covering cables that supply Hong Kong Island with its electricity.

Meanwhile, on the south-eastern side of the island, the hillsides around Sok Kwu Wan are slowly disappearing. The forested hills once visible from the bayside restaurants at Sok Kwu Wan now appear as quarries and an adjacent cement plant and there's talk of developing this area into a large housing complex. However, a tree-planting program has seen some 14,000 conifers planted in the north-western part of the island as well as in the hilly area south-east of Hung Shing Ye.

The most interesting way to see Lamma is to walk between Yung Shue Wan and Sok Kwu Wan, which takes a little over an hour, and return to Central from there. Those with extra time should carry on to Tung O Wan, an idyllic bay some 30 minutes farther south at the bottom of a steep hill, and perhaps return to Sok Kwu Wan via Mo Tat Wan.

Another excellent excursion is to arrive by ferry at Pak Kok Tsuen and follow the circular path around the northern headland before heading south for Yung Shue Wan.

Paths are generally well signposted and have been upgraded in several areas of Lamma, particularly around Sok Kwu Wan and in the southern part of the island.

If you're walking around at night, watch out for the armies of frogs and the millipedes in these parts can inflict a particularly painful sting.

Information
There's an HSBC branch (☎ 2982 0787) at 19 Main St in Yung Shue Wan. The post office is at No 3 of the same street.

Yung Shue Wan
Though it's the larger of the island's two main villages, Yung Shue Wan (Banyan Tree Bay) remains a small place – little more than one main street that follows the curve of the bay. Plastic was the big industry here, but now restaurants, bars and other tourism-related businesses are the main employers. There is a small Tin Hau Temple at the southern end of Yung Shue Wan.

Hung Shing Ye Beach
About 25 minutes' walk south-east from the Yung Shue Wan ferry pier is Hung Shing Ye Beach, the most popular one on Lamma. Arrive early in the morning or on a weekday and you'll probably find it deserted. The beach is protected by a shark net. There are also a few restaurants and drink stands nearby – open at the weekend only, except in summer – as well as the Concerto Inn, a hotel that also serves hot and cold drinks, and some mediocre Western food (see Places to Stay later in this section). The view of the power station across the bay takes some getting used to.

Continuing south from Hung Shing Ye, the path climbs steeply until it reaches a Chinese-style pavilion near the top of the hill. From this vantage point, it becomes obvious that the island is mostly hilly grassland and large boulders with relatively few trees, though more and more are being planted.

You'll pass a second pavilion offering splendid views out to sea before you reach a ridge that looks down onto Sok Kwu Wan, with its many fine restaurants and fishing boats and rafts bobbing in the bay. There's a third new pavilion a short distance to the south-west towards Lo So Shing Beach.

Lo So Shing Beach
This is the most beautiful beach on Lamma and can be reached by taking a short detour west from the main Yung Shue Wan–Sok Kwu Wan path once the second pavilion comes into view. Count on about one hour from Yung Shue Wan and 30 minutes from Sok Kwu Wan. The beach is not very big, but it has a nice cover of shade trees at the back. During the swimming season when lifeguards are on duty (ie, April to October) there is a small snack stand.

Sok Kwu Wan
Although still a small settlement, Sok Kwu Wan, or Picnic Bay, supports at least a dozen waterfront seafood restaurants that are popular with boaters. The small harbour at Sok Kwu Wan is filled with rafts from which cages are suspended and fish farmed. There's a Tin Hau Temple as you enter Sok Kwu Wan from the south. From Sok Kwu Wan you can head back to Hong Kong on the ferry or do some more walking.

Mo Tat Wan
The clean and relatively uncrowded beach at Mo Tat Wan is a mere 20-minute walk east of Sok Kwu Wan along a coastal path. Mo Tat Wan is OK for swimming, but has no lifeguards. You can also reach here by kaido from Aberdeen, which continues on to Sok Kwu Wan, but these run only on Sunday and public holidays. See To/From Aberdeen under Getting There & Away later in this section for details.

Tung O Wan
A detour to this small and secluded bay, with a long stretch of sandy beach, while walking to Sok Kwu Wan from Yung Shue Wan, is highly recommended. Just before the Tin Hau Temple at the entrance to the

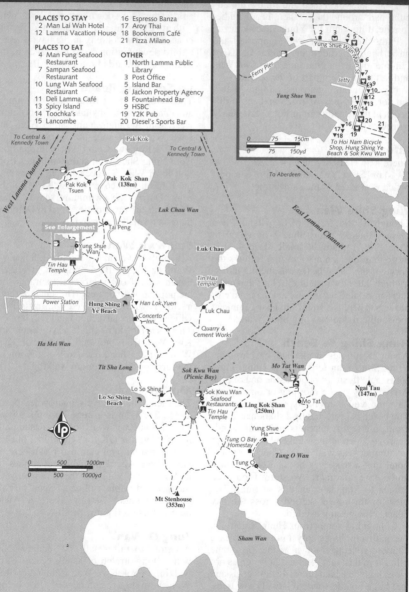

LAMMA ISLAND

PLACES TO STAY
2 Man Lai Wah Hotel
12 Lamma Vacation House

PLACES TO EAT
4 Man Fung Seafood Restaurant
7 Sampan Seafood Restaurant
10 Lung Wah Seafood Restaurant
11 Deli Lamma Café
13 Spicy Island
14 Toochka's
15 Lancombe

16 Espresso Banza
17 Aroy Thai
18 Bookworm Café
21 Pizza Milano

OTHER
1 North Lamma Public Library
3 Post Office
5 Island Bar
6 Jackon Property Agency
8 Fountainhead Bar
9 HSBC
19 Y2K Pub
20 Diesel's Sports Bar

village follow the signposted path to the right southward, up and over the hill to the tiny village of Tung O. The walk takes about 35 minutes, over a rugged landscape, and the first half is fairly strenuous. Don't do this walk at night unless it's a full moon as there are only a few street lights at the start in Sok Kwu Wan.

If coming from Mo Tat Wan, take the trail immediately to the west of the pavilion above the beach and follow the signposted path up the hill and through bamboo groves, lush fields and spectacular scenery. It takes about 25 minutes to reach the sleepy village of Yung Shue Ha (Under the Banyan Tree), perched on the fringes of the bay. All of the Chinese who live there are from the same clan and have the surname of Chow. A member of this clan, Chow Yun Fat, the bulletproof star of many John Woo films, was born and raised in Tung O, the village at the southern end of the bay.

The beach at Tung O Wan is a secluded and unspoiled stretch of sand, punctuated by chunks of driftwood and other flotsam. Travellers who fall under the bay's spell and find it difficult to leave can stay at Tung O Bay Homestay. For more information, see Places to Stay later in this section.

Sham Wan

Sham Wan is another beautiful bay to the south-west that can be reached from Tung O Wan by clambering over the hills. A trail on the left about 200m up the hill from Tung O leads south to the small and sandy beach.

Mt Stenhouse

Most of the southern part of Lamma is dominated by 353m-high Mt Stenhouse. The climb to the peak and back takes no more than two hours, but the paths are rough and not well defined.

Activities

Bicycles are available for rent for HK$15/50 per hour/day from **Hoi Nam Bicycle Shop** (☎ 2982 0128, 2982 2500, 37 Sha Po Old Village). You'll find the shop a short distance south-east of Yung Shue Wan on the main path to Sok Kwu Wan.

Places to Stay

Jackson Property Agency (☎ 2982 0606, fax 2982 0636, 15 Main St) has **studios** and **apartments** for rent on Lamma. All have TV, private bathroom, microwave and fridge; and some offer sea views. Cost is about HK$280 per night for two people from Sunday to Friday and HK$500 on Saturday.

Yung Shue Wan In the thick of the action amid all the bars and restaurants of Main St is **Lamma Vacation House** (☎ 2982 0427, 29 Main St). Rooms from HK$200 Mon-Fri, HK$400 Sat & Sun. This guesthouse is the cheapest place to stay on Lamma so don't expect the Ritz.

Man Lai Wah Hotel (☎ 2982 0220, fax 2982 0349, Po Wah Garden, 2 Main St) Rooms HK$350 Mon-Fri, HK$650 Sat & Sun. This hotel faces you as you get off the ferry. All rooms have air-conditioning and private bathroom.

Hung Shing Ye The smartest and most expensive place to stay on Lamma is **Concerto Inn** (☎ 2982 1668, 2836 3388 in Hong Kong, 28 Hung Shing Ye Beach). Standard doubles/deluxe sea-view doubles HK$408/528 Mon-Fri, HK$680/880 Sat & Sun. This beachfront hotel is away from all the action. Come here only if you really want to get away from it all.

Tung O Wan Intrepid travellers really looking to escape will head for **Tung O Bay Homestay** (☎ 2982 8461, fax 2982 8424, Tung O). Beds in eight-/four-bed rooms HK$70/90, doubles HK$270. This secluded and very basic guesthouse is on the beach. The energetic owner can throw together a cheap dinner if you give advance notice.

Places to Eat

Lamma offers a greater choice of restaurants and cuisines for all budgets than any of the other outlying islands.

Yung Shue Wan In general most people visiting Lamma head to Sok Kwu Wan for a fix of Cantonese-style seafood, but Yung Shue Wan has several decent alternatives.

Lancombe (☎ 2982 0881, 47 Main St) Meals HK$100. This popular seafood restaurant has a delightful terrace facing the sea on the 1st floor. The deep-fried squid with salt and pepper and the sweet steamed prawns are excellent.

Lung Wah Seafood Restaurant (☎ 2982 0791, 20 Main St) Meals HK$180-200. Lung Wah, just next to the HSBC, is fronted by tanks from which you can choose fish and crustaceans from the briny deep. The restaurant also does excellent dim sum from 6am to 11am (until noon at the weekend).

Man Fung Seafood Restaurant (☎ 2982 0719, 5 Main St) Meals HK$80-250. This friendly place just up from the ferry pier also has the main ingredients of its dishes on full, living display.

Sampan Seafood Restaurant (☎ 2982 2388, 16 Main St) Meals HK$75-180. Sampan remains very popular with locals – always a sure sign – both for its seafood and its pigeon dishes. It also boasts an excellent sea view.

Yung Shue Wan is hardly limited to Chinese restaurants, which is the case in Sok Kwu Wan. Among the choices are Western, vegetarian, Thai and even Indian cuisine.

Aroy Thai (☎ 2982 1150, 67 Main St) Mains HK$40-80. Aroy Thai has friendly service and good-value (as opposed to authentic) Thai food, but if you can't wait till you get back to Hong Kong or Kowloon, this is an acceptable substitute.

Bookworm Café (☎ 2982 4838, 79 Main St) Dishes HK$35-65. This place is everything to everyone (except carnivores): a vegetarian cafe/restaurant with excellent breakfasts (HK$35-60) and fruit juices, a second-hand bookshop and an Internet cafe. A true oasis, this place.

Deli Lamma Café (☎ 2982 1583, 36 Main St) Starters HK$35-40, mains HK$70-110. This relaxed cafe-restaurant serves continental fare leaning towards the Mediterranean, with a fair few pasta dishes and pizzas (HK$58-76).

Espresso Banza (☎ 2982 0865, 67A Main St) Meals HK$15-48. This coffee shop has a tiny seating area, and serves sandwiches (HK$15-20), baguettes (HK$20-24) and pizzas (HK$30-48).

Pizza Milano (☎ 2982 4848, 2 Back St) Dishes HK$50-87. If you're looking for affordable pizzas (from HK$50/62/98 for small/medium/large) and pasta dishes (HK$50-70), Lamma's only Italian restaurant is the correct choice.

Spicy Island (☎ 2982 0830, 23 Main St) Meals HK$100. This relatively new place promises (and delivers, locals say) 'genuine Indian cuisine'.

Toochka's (☎ 2982 0159, 44 Main St) Meals HK$120-150. Toochka's has outside seating and is popular for its Indian food, although it offers a number of international dishes too.

Hung Shing Ye Above the beach at Hung Shing Ye is *Han Lok Yuen* (☎ 2982 0680, 16-17 Hung Shing Ye). Meals HK$150. This restaurant is famous territory-wide for its roast pigeon, but arrive early (it closes at 8.30pm, at 7pm on Sunday) or you'll have to settle for something else.

Concerto Inn (☎ 2982 1668, 28 Hung Shing Ye Beach) Dishes HK$33-57. The food is no great shakes at Lamma's only real hotel, but if you're on the beach at Hung Shing Ye and fancy rice or noodles (HK$33-55) or a sandwich (HK$34-49), you won't have to go far.

Sok Kwu Wan An evening meal at Sok Kwu Wan is an enjoyable way to end a trip to Lamma. The restaurants line the waterfront on either side of the ferry pier and will be chock-a-block on weekend nights with Chinese and expats who have arrived on company junks and the yachts known locally as 'gin palaces.' Most of the dozen or so restaurants offer the same relatively high-quality seafood at similar prices, but a few places stand out from the rest.

Rainbow Seafood Restaurant (☎ 2982 8100, 1A-1B & 16-20 First St) Meals HK$150-200. The Rainbow, with two waterfront locations, specialises in steamed grouper (or garoupa), fried lobster in butter sauce and steamed abalone. What's more, book a table (in advance) and you'll be

Green Turtles & Eggs

Sham Wan (Deep Bay) has traditionally been the one beach in the whole of Hong Kong where endangered green turtles *(Chelonia mydas)*, one of three species of sea turtles found in Hong Kong waters, still struggle onto the sand to lay their eggs from early June to the end of August. In September 2000, however, a late arrival laid over 100 eggs on the beach at Tai Long Wan (Big Wave Bay), north of Shek O on Hong Kong Island. Tai Long Wan is a popular beach and staff at the Agriculture, Fisheries and Conservation Department (AFCD) removed the eggs for artificial incubation. In November, 23 hatchlings were swimming in tanks at Ocean Park, awaiting release into the South China Sea during the warmer months.

The AFCD staff were not being overly cautious. On Lamma, the poor armoured creatures, which can grow to a metre in length and weigh 140kg, have been habitually repulsed in their attempts to deposit eggs by a nefarious alliance of property developers, pollution and greedy islanders.

Female green turtles take between 30 and 40 years to reach sexual maturity and always head back to the same beach where they were born to lay their eggs, which occurs about every three years. Fearing that Sham Wan would catch the eye of housing estate developers and that the turtles would swim away forever, the area was declared a Site of Special Scientific Interest and closed (and patrolled by the AFCD) between June and October. The other almost insurmountable hurdle for the long-suffering turtle is the appetite of Lamma locals for their eggs. In 1994 three turtles laid about 200 eggs, which were promptly harvested and consumed by villagers. Several years later villagers sold the eggs to Japanese tourists for HK$100 each. Kwai taan, or 'turtle egg', by the way, is one of the rudest things you can call a Cantonese-speaking person.

transported by yacht from Queen's Pier in Central (three to seven sailings on weekday evenings, 10 to 13 all day at weekends) or Aberdeen.

Lamma Hilton Shum Kee Seafood Restaurant (☎ 2982 8241, 26 First St) Meals HK$150-200. Some people consider this the best seafood restaurant in Sok Kwu Wan (and, no, it's not connected with the hotel chain).

Wan Kee Seafood Restaurant (☎ 2982 8548, 2982 8279, 28 First Street) Meals HK$150-200. This smaller establishment with the unfortunate name offers less frenetic service than most of the other places in Sok Kwu Wan.

Mo Tat Wan Surprisingly, in this relatively remote corner of Lamma there's an upmarket Mediterranean restaurant, *Cocabana* (☎ 2328 2138, 7 Mo Tat Wan). Meals HK$150-250. Not only is the food good, it's inventive.

Entertainment

Yung Shue Wan has several watering holes and boozers worth checking. You may have to sign a members' book; several operate on club licences.

Fountainhead (☎ 2982 2118, 17 Main St) This is the most popular bar in Yung Shue Wan, with a good mixture of Chinese and expats regularly in attendance. There's decent music, an amiable bar staff, free salted peanuts and beer at affordable prices.

Island Bar (☎ 2982 1376, 6 Main St) The Island remains the bar of choice for long-term expats living on Lamma so if you want the low-down on what's up, head here.

Diesel's Sports Bar (☎ 2982 4116, 51 Main St) This place, just beside Toochka's and under the same management, is the new kid on the block and attracts punters with its big-screen TV during football and rugby matches. Staff are friendly.

Y2K (☎ 2982 6196, 68 Main St) This place has the cheapest beer in the village and can often get pretty rowdy, particularly in the wee hours. Go in with a Chinese friend.

Getting There & Away

To/From Central Both Yung Shue Wan and Sok Kwu Wan are served by ferries run by the Hong Kong & Kowloon Ferry Co from pier 5 at the outlying islands ferry terminal in Central.

Ordinary and fast ferries depart Central for Yung Shue Wan approximately every hour (with additional sailings around 8am and 6pm) from 6.30am to 12.30am; the last fast ferry leaves at 7.30pm (2pm on Sunday and public holidays). The last boat to Central from Yung Shue Wan leaves at 11.30pm. The trip on the ordinary ferry takes 30 minutes, and the adult one-way fare is HK$10 (HK$14 on Sunday and public holidays). The fast ferries, which take just 20 minutes, cost HK$15 (HK$20 on Sunday and public holidays).

From Central, 'express' (ie, fast) ferries reach Sok Kwu Wan in 35 minutes and cost HK$13 (HK$18 on Sunday and public holidays). The ferries leave about every 1½ hours, with the first leaving Central at 7.20am and the last at 11.30pm. The last boat to Central from Sok Kwu Wan is at 10.40pm.

Ordinary ferries leave pier 5 at the outlying islands ferry terminal in Central for Pak Kok Tsuen, at Lamma's northern tip, at 7.30am, 8.30am, 6pm (with a stop at the North St Pier in Kennedy Town), 7pm and 8pm Monday to Saturday only. They return to Central at 7am, 8am (via Kennedy Town), 9am, 6.30pm and 7.30pm. The trip takes 25 minutes and costs HK$15.

To/From Aberdeen Express ferries link the pier at Aberdeen Promenade with Yung Shue Wan (HK$11) via Pak Kok Tsuen (HK$5.50) nine times a day, with the first ferry leaving Aberdeen at 6.30am and the last at 7pm Monday to Saturday. There are some 15 ferries on Sunday and public holidays, with the first leaving Aberdeen at 7.30am and the last at 7.30pm. The last ferry for Aberdeen leaves Yung Shue Wan at 7.30pm and Pak Kok Tsuen at 7.40pm Monday to Saturday. On Sunday and public

holidays, the last sailing times are 8pm and 8.10pm respectively.

There is also a smaller ferry – a kaido, really – run by Chuen Kee Ferry (☎ 2982 8225) between Aberdeen and Sok Kwu Wan via Mo Tat Wan. The journey between Aberdeen and Mo Tat Wan takes 25 minutes and it's another 10 minutes from there to Sok Kwu Wan. The fare for adults/children is HK$7/3.50 (HK$10/5 on Sunday and public holidays). There are eight departures from Aberdeen to Sok Kwu Wan from Monday to Saturday between 6.45am and 7.25pm, leaving roughly every 1½ hours. In the other direction there are seven departures from Monday to Saturday between 6.05am and 6.45pm. On Sunday and public holidays the service increases to 16 trips in each direction; the earliest and latest boats from Aberdeen are 8am and 7.55pm, departing approximately every 45 minutes. From Sok Kwu Wan, the earliest and latest trips are 6.15am and 7.15pm.

A sampan from Aberdeen to Yung Shue Wan will cost about HK$100 during the day and double that or more in the wee hours, when drunken revellers who have missed the last ferry back from Central are trying to get home. If you should be in the same boat, don't panic; there are always a number of people ready and willing to split the cost.

LANTAU

Lantau is a Cantonese word meaning 'broken head', but Chinese call Hong Kong's largest island Tai Yue Shan (big island mountain), a name that refers both to its size and elevation. At 142 sq km, Lantau is almost twice the size of Hong Kong Island, and its highest point, Lantau Peak (934m), almost double the height of Victoria Peak.

Amazingly, only about 45,000 people live on Lantau, compared with Hong Kong Island's 1.4 million. They are mainly concentrated in a couple of centres along the south coast, because the interior is so mountainous, though some 15,000 people have moved into the high-rises of Tung Chung opposite the airport at Chek Lap Kok in recent years. Not everyone on Lantau resides here of their own accord; the island is home to three prisons.

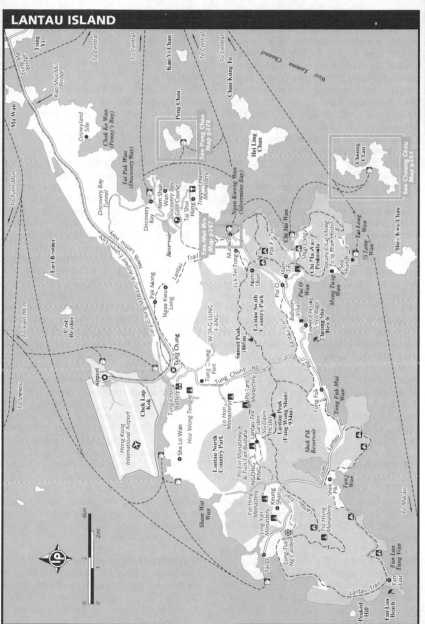

Rock carvings discovered at Shek Pik on the south-western coast of Lantau suggest that the island was inhabited as early as the Bronze Age 3000 years ago, before the arrival of the Han Chinese; a stone circle uncovered at Fan Lau may date from Neolithic times. The last Song dynasty emperor passed through here in the 13th century while fleeing the Mongol invaders. He is believed to have held court in the Tung Chung Valley to the north, which takes its name from a local hero who gave up his life for the emperor. Tung Chung is still worshipped by the Hakka people of Lantau, who believe he can predict the future.

Like Cheung Chau, Lantau was once a base for pirates and smugglers, and was one of the favourite haunts of Cheung Po Tsai. The island was also an important trading post for the British long before they showed any interest in Hong Kong Island.

Lantau is an excellent (some might say the best) island to escape from the city. Much of the island is designated country park and there are several superb mountain trails, albeit difficult at times, including the 70km Lantau Trail, which passes over both Lantau Peak and Sunset Peak (869m); some interesting traditional villages such as Tai O on the west coast; several important religious retreats, including the Po Lin Monastery and the adjacent Tian Tan Buddha, the largest outdoor Buddha statue in the world; and some excellent beaches including Cheung Sha, the longest and among the cleanest in Hong Kong.

Information

The Country & Marine Parks Authority (☎ 2420 0529) maintains an information kiosk to the left as you leave the main ferry pier at Mui Wo. It's open from 8.30am to noon on weekdays and to 4.30pm at the weekend.

HSBC (☎ 2984 8271) has a branch in Mui Wo on Mui Wo Ferry Pier Rd just south of the roundabout and before the turn up South Lantau Rd. There's another HSBC branch in Tai O on Tai O Market St. You'll see it as you cross the footbridge from the mainland to the island.

The main post office is on Ngan Kwong Wan Rd in Mui Wo, a short distance west of the footbridge, which crosses the Silver River.

Mui Wo

Mui Wo (plum nest), Lantau's 'capital', is on Silvermine Bay, so named for the silver mines that were once worked to the north-west along the Silver River. In fact, many foreign residents refer to Mui Wo as Silvermine Bay.

About a third of Lantau's population lives in the township of Mui Wo and its surrounding hamlets. Though there are several decent places to stay here, the options for eating and drinking are few – you'll find better options elsewhere on the island.

Silvermine Bay Beach has been cleaned up and rebuilt and is now an attractive place, with scenic views and opportunities for walking in the hills above. There's a complex with toilets, showers and changing rooms open from April to October.

If you have the time, consider hiking out to **Silvermine Waterfall**, the main feature of a picturesque, landscaped garden near the old abandoned Silvermine Cave north-west of the town. The waterfall is quite a spectacle during the rainy season when it swells and gushes. En route you'll pass the local **Man Mo Temple**, originally built during the reign of Emperor Shen Zong of the Ming dynasty (1368–1644). Like the Man Mo Temple on Hollywood Rd in Sheung Wan, it is dedicated to the civil and military deities.

Silvermine Cave was mined for silver in the latter half of the 19th century but it has now been sealed off for safety.

You can reach the temple, cave and waterfall by walking west along Mui Wo Rural Committee Rd and then following the marked path north. All in, the walk should take about an hour.

Trappist Haven Monastery

North-east of Mui Wo and south of Discovery Bay is the Trappist Haven Monastery at Tai Shui Hang. The monastery is known throughout Hong Kong for its cream-rich milk, sold in half-pint bottles everywhere,

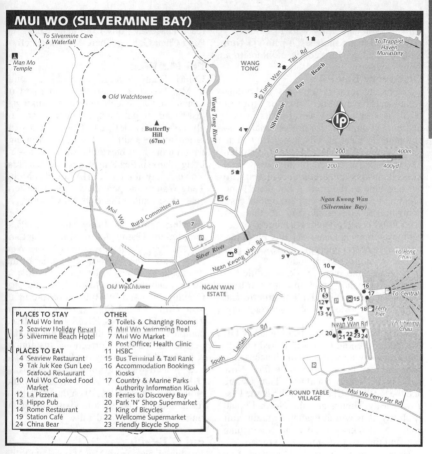

MUI WO (SILVERMINE BAY)

To Silvermine Cave & Waterfall

Man Mo Temple

WANG TONG

To Trappist Haven Monastery

● Old Watchtower

▲ Butterfly Hill (67m)

Wong Tong River

Silvermine Bay Beach

Tung Wan Tau Rd

Ngan Kwong Wan (Silvermine Bay)

Mui Wo Rural Committee Rd

Silver River

Ngan Kwong Wan Rd

Old Watchtower

NGAN WAN ESTATE

To Hong Chau

To Central

Lantau Rd

South

Ngan Wan Rd

To Cheung Chau

ROUND TABLE VILLAGE

Mui Wo Ferry Pier Rd

Ferry Pier

0   200   400m
0   200   400yd

PLACES TO STAY	OTHER
1 Mui Wo Inn	3 Toilets & Changing Rooms
2 Seaview Holiday Resort	6 Mui Wo Swimming Pool
5 Silvermine Beach Hotel	7 Mui Wo Market
	8 Post Office; Health Clinic
PLACES TO EAT	11 HSBC
4 Seaview Restaurant	15 Bus Terminal & Taxi Rank
9 Tak Juk Kee (Sun Lee)	16 Accommodation Bookings
Seafood Restaurant	Kiosks
10 Mui Wo Cooked Food	17 Country & Marine Parks
Market	Authority Information Kiosk
12 La Pizzeria	18 Ferries to Discovery Bay
13 Hippo Pub	20 Park 'N' Shop Supermarket
14 Rome Restaurant	21 King of Bicycles
19 Station Café	22 Wellcome Supermarket
24 China Bear	23 Friendly Bicycle Shop

but – alas – the cows have been moved to Yuen Long and Trappist Dairy Milk now comes from over the border in China.

The Trappist order, a branch of the Roman Catholic Cistercians, was founded by a converted courtier at La Trappe in France in 1662 and gained a reputation as one of the most austere religious communities in the Church. The Lantau congregation was established at Beijing in the 19th century.

Trappist monks take a vow of absolute silence, and there are signs reminding visitors to keep radios and cassette players turned off and to speak in low tones. There

is also the possibility of spending the night here (see Places to Stay later).

Getting There & Away You can reach the monastery on foot by following a rather difficult and steep trail just beyond the Mui Wo Inn on the northern side of Silvermine Bay Beach, but it's much easier to get here from Peng Chau, which is accessible direct from Central or from Mui Wo. Rental Kaito (☎ 9033 8102) sails sampans to Tai Shui Hang from the small pier just north of the main Peng Chau ferry pier between nine and 10 times daily from 7.45am to 5pm, with an extra sailing at 8.45pm on Saturday. Alternatively, you can easily walk to Discovery Bay by following the coastal path via Nim Shue Wan village for a couple of kilometres.

Discovery Bay

Lying on the north-eastern coast of Lantau, what locals have dubbed Disco Bay (or just 'DB') is very much a world of its own, a bedroom community for professionals who commute to Central. Discovery Bay (Yue Ging Wan in Cantonese) has a fine stretch of sandy beach ringed by high-rises and more luxurious condominiums clinging to the headland to the north – but there is no pressing need to visit except to ogle at residents in their converted golf carts that cost HK$200,000 each. There is a handful of decent restaurants in Discovery Bay Plaza just up from the ferry pier and an 18-hole golf course in the hills to the south.

A Disneyland theme park, scheduled to open in 2005 and attract up to five million visitors a year, is under construction at Penny's Bay north-east of Discovery Bay.

Getting There & Away Until recently DB existed in splendid isolation, linked only to the outside by ferry and all but inaccessible from the rest of Lantau even on foot. Now buses make the run to and from Tung Chung and the airport at Chek Lap Kok via the Discovery Bay Tunnel and the North Lantau Highway. A new trail leading from the golf course will take you down to Silvermine Bay and the rest of Lantau in no time.

High-speed ferries run by Discovery Bay Transportation Services (☎ 2987 7351) leave the Star Ferry terminal in Central every 10 to 30 minutes between 6.30am and 1am, and from then there are three trips (five on Saturday and Sunday) until the daytime schedule resumes. Similar services run from Discovery Bay to Central. Tickets are HK$25 and the trip takes 25 minutes.

There are five high-speed ferry departures on weekdays from Discovery Bay to Mui Wo at 7.25am, 11am, 3pm, 4.10pm and 6.10pm, with between five and seven sailings at the weekend and on public holidays. Tickets cost HK$11 and the trip takes

between 12 and 15 minutes. You can also reach Discovery Bay from Peng Chau; see Peng Chau Getting There & Away later.

Chi Ma Wan

Chi Ma Wan, the large peninsula due south of Mui Wo, is a relatively remote part of Lantau and an excellent area for hiking – just be sure to get a map as the trails are not always clearly defined. There's a decent beach to the south at Tai Long Wan and fringing the next bay to the south-west – Yi Long Wan – is Sea Ranch, a residential area. You can stay at the HKYHA hostel at Mong Tung Wan on the peninsula's south-western coast. See Lantau Places to Stay later.

Getting There & Away The inter-island ferry linking Cheung Chau, Mui Wo on Lantau and Peng Chau calls at the Chi Ma Wan ferry pier on the north-eastern corner of the peninsula six times a day (with the first at 6.15am and the last at 8.30pm) heading for Cheung Chau and five times a day going to Mui Wo and Peng Chau (first 6.55am, last 7.05pm). The fare is HK$8.40. The large complex just south of the pier is *not* a hostel but the Chi Ma Wan Correctional Institution.

Some 14 ferries a day run from Central to Sea Ranch from Monday to Saturday (HK$25) and 16 times a day on Sunday and public holidays (HK$30). You must be a resident or invited guest to visit Sea Ranch; ring ☎ 2989 2128 for details.

Pui O Beach

Just under 5km from Mui Wo is Pui O, the first of several coastal villages along South Lantau Rd. Pui O has a decent beach, but since it's the closest one to Mui Wo it's always crowded. The village has several restaurants, holiday flats and stalls renting bicycles. There's a privately run camping ground on the beach.

Bus No 7 to Pui O leaves from Mui Wo roughly every half-hour from 7.10am to 7.25pm on weekdays, till 10.30pm on Saturday and 7.55pm on Sunday and public holidays. The last No 7 bus back from Pui O leaves at 7pm (7.20pm on Sunday and holidays).

Cheung Sha Beach & Tong Fuk

Cheung Sha (Long Sand), at over 3km Hong Kong's longest beach, is divided into 'upper' and 'lower' sections; a trail over a hillock links the two. Upper Cheung Sha, with occasional good surf, is the prettier and longer stretch and boasts a modern complex with changing rooms, toilets, showers and a snack bar. Lower Cheung Sha has a fine little guesthouse and a beachfront restaurant (see Places to Stay and Places to Eat later in this section).

The beach at Tong Fuk is not as nice, but the village has several shops and – wait for it – a South African-style restaurant (see Places to Eat). To the west is the rather 'scenic' sprawl of Ma Po Ping Prison.

Cheung Sha Beach and Tong Fuk can be reached from Mui Wo on the No 4 bus. It departs from Mui Wo roughly every half-hour to an hour from 5.45am (6.40am on Sunday and public holidays) till 10.30pm (10.20pm on Sunday). The last No 4 bus back from Tong Fuk leaves at 7pm (9.30pm on Sunday and holidays).

Shek Pik Reservoir

West of Tong Fuk, South Lantau Rd begins to climb the hills inland before crossing an enormous dam holding back the Shek Pik Reservoir (completed in 1963), which provides Lantau as well as Cheung Chau and parts of Hong Kong Island with drinking water. Just below the dam is the granddaddy of all Lantau's prisons, Shek Pik Prison.

The trail along the water catchment area just east of the reservoir, with picnic tables and barbecue pits, offers some of the easiest and most peaceful walking on Lantau. From here you can also pick up the switchback trail to Dog's Tooth Peak (539m) from where another trail heads north to Lantau Peak.

Bus No 1 and night bus No N1 between Mui Wo and Tai O (see that section later in this chapter) will drop you off at the reservoir. You can also catch bus No 2 linking Mui Wo with Ngong Ping.

Ngong Ping

Perched 500m up in the western hills of Lantau is the Ngong Ping Plateau, a major drawcard for Hong Kong day-trippers and foreign visitors alike, especially since 1993 when one of the world's largest statues of Buddha was unveiled.

Po Lin Monastery Po Lin, or 'precious lotus', is a large Buddhist temple complex originally built in 1924. Today it is a fairground as much as religious retreat, attracting many visitors. Most of the buildings you'll see on arrival are new, with the older, simpler ones tucked away behind them.

The lotus is a significant emblem in Buddhist iconography as it symbolises the ability of every person to attain enlightenment. The lotus flower grows from the mud of a pond, and from such base material evolves a thing of great beauty. This is a metaphor for transformation and lotus-like motifs decorate the monastery.

The monastery (open 6am-5.30pm daily) is very photogenic. The Ngong Ping Plateau, covered in mist in the early morning, and Lantau Peak to the south-east, create a sublime backdrop and the rows and rows of huge, pollen-yellow incense sticks arrayed in front of the temple fill the air with the scent of sandalwood.

On a hill above the monastery is the Tian Tan Buddha statue (open 10am-5.30pm daily), a seated representation of the Lord Gautama some 22m high (or 34m if you include the podium). There are bigger Buddha statues elsewhere – notably the 71m-high Grand Buddha in Leshan in China – but apparently these are not seated, outdoors or made of bronze. The statue was cast in a factory in Nanjing, and then shipped in more than 200 pieces to Hong Kong in 1993. The large bell within the Buddha is controlled by computer and rings 108 times during the day to symbolise escape from what Buddhism describes as the 108 'troubles of mankind'.

The podium is composed of separate chambers on three levels. In the first level are six statues of bodhisattvas, or Buddhist 'saints', each of which weighs two tonnes. On the second level is a small museum (☎ 2985 5248; admission HK$28; open 10am-5.30 daily) containing oil paintings

KELLI HAMBLET

The Tian Tan Buddha statue is said to be the largest outdoor seated bronze Buddha.

and ceramic plaques of the Buddha's life and teachings. Entry is free if you eat at the monastery's vegetarian restaurant (see Lantau Places to Eat later).

It's well worth climbing the 271 steps for a closer look at the statue and surrounding views. The Buddha's Birthday, usually celebrated in May, is a lively time to visit when thousands make the pilgrimage. Try to avoid Sundays or public holidays when the entire complex is awash in families with radios blaring. Visitors are requested to observe some decorum in dress and behaviour. It is forbidden to bring meat into the grounds.

Lantau Tea Garden A footpath to the left of the Buddha statue leads to the Lantau Tea Garden (☎ 2985 5484), the only one in Hong Kong. The tea bushes are in desperate shape, not worth even a short detour, but the garden is on the way to the SG Davis Youth Hostel and Lantau Peak.

Getting There & Away Bus No 2 leaves Mui Wo for Ngong Ping every 20 minutes to a half-hour from 7.50am (8am on Sunday) to 6.40pm (6.20pm on Sunday). The last bus leaves Ngong Ping at 7.20pm.

If carrying on to Tai O from Ngong Ping, catch bus No 21, with between eight and nine departures a day (first 7.30am, last 5pm). Bus No 23 links Ngong Ping and the centre of Tung Chung, from where you can catch the Tung Chung MTR line back to Kowloon or Central. Departures are frequent – up to every 10 minutes on Sunday – from 8.10am to 7.10pm.

A taxi to/from the ferry pier at Mui Wo will cost you about HK$125 one way.

Lantau Peak

Known as Fung Wong Shan, or Phoenix Mountain in Cantonese, this 934m-high peak is the second-highest in Hong Kong after Tai Mo Shan in the New Territories. The views from the summit are absolutely stunning; on a clear day it is possible to see Macau 65km to the west.

The easiest and most comfortable way to make the climb is to spend the night at the SG Davis Hostel, get up at the crack of dawn and pick up the signposted trail at the hostel that runs south-east to the peak. Many climbers get up earlier to reach the summit for the sunrise; take a torch and wear an extra layer of clothes as it can get pretty chilly at the top in the early hours.

Another signposted trail leading east from the hostel will take you along the northern slopes of Lantau Peak to **Po Lam Monastery** at Tei Tong Tsai and then south through a valley leading to Tung Chung, from where you can catch the MTR back to Kowloon or Hong Kong or the No 3 bus (hourly departures from 6am to 11.30pm daily) to Mui Wo. This charming walk – if you ignore the airport – also takes you past **Lo Hon Monastery**, which has a canteen serving vegetarian food, as well as Tung Chung Fort and Tung Chung Battery. See Tung Chung later.

Lantau Trail

This 70km-long footpath follows the mountain tops from Mui Wo and then doubles back at Tai O along the coast to where it started. It takes about 24 hours, but the trail is divided into a dozen manageable stages ranging from 45 minutes to three hours.

A realistic approach is to do the trail's first four stages, which take in the highest and most scenic parts and can be accessed from Mui Wo or, conversely, from the Po Lin Monastery and SG Davis Hostel at Ngong Ping (see that section earlier). The walk between Ngong Ping and Mui Wo via both Lantau and Sunset Peaks is 17.5km long. It will take at least seven hours and can be treacherous in the steep sections. Note that stage No 1 (45 minutes, 2.5km) of the Lantau Trail from Mui Wo follows South Lantau Rd. There's an alternative, more scenic path from Mui Wo to Nam Sham, where stage No 2 begins, via Luk Tei Tong.

The western part of the trail, which follows the south-western coast of Lantau from Tai O to Fan Lau and then up to Shek Pik, is also very scenic.

The most important things to take are a map (see Information at the start of this chapter), drinking water and some food supplies. Depending on the weather, equip yourself with rain gear and sunscreen. Shops are few and far between. After Tai O, for example, the next opportunity to buy anything to eat or drink is at Fan Lau three hours later.

Lung Tsai Ng Garden

This magical place – a garden with a lotus pond crossed by a zigzag bridge – was built by a wealthy merchant in the 1930s in a small valley near where the village of Lung Tsai once stood. The site is rather derelict, but atmospheric nonetheless. You can reach here via a trail from the Tai O Rd, a continuation of South Lantau Rd just west of Keung Shan (bus No 1 from Mui Wo to Tai O or bus No 21 from Ngong Ping to Tai O); alight when you see the sign for the country park management centre. There's a camping ground a short distance to the south-west.

Tai O

A century ago this village on the west coast of Lantau was an important trading and fishing port, exporting salt and fish to China. As recently as the 1980s it traded in IIs (illegal immigrants) brought from China under cover of darkness by 'snake heads' in long narrow boats, sending back contraband such as refrigerators, radios and televisions.

Today Tai O is in decline except perhaps as a tourist destination. A few of the salt pans still exist, but most have been filled in to build high-rise housing. Older people still make their living from duck farming, fishing, making the village's celebrated shrimp paste and processing salt fish, but the younger generation have left in droves. It remains a popular place for locals to buy seafood, both fresh and dried.

Tai O is built partly on Lantau and partly on a tiny island about 15m from the shore. Until the mid-1990s the only way to cross was via a rope-tow ferry pulled by elderly Hakka women. That and the large number of sampans in the small harbour earned Tai O the nickname 'the Venice of Hong Kong'. Today a narrow iron bridge spans the canal.

Some of the traditional-style village houses still stand in the centre. A fire in 2000 destroyed many of Tai O's famed stilt houses on the waterfront, but when the government tried to raze the rest and relocate residents elsewhere, the move was strongly opposed. What few escaped the fire remain. There are also a number of shanties, their corrugated iron walls held in place by rope, and houseboats that haven't set sail for years – they'd capsize immediately if they tried. The stilt houses and the local temple dedicated to Kuan Tai, the God of War, are on Tai O Market St. To reach them, cross the bridge from the mainland to the island and go right at the Fook Lam Moon restaurant.

Getting There & Away Bus No 1 leaves Mui Wo for Tai O every 20 minutes to a half-hour from 6am (6.30am on Sunday and public holidays) to 1.10am. The last No 1 bus leaves Tai O at 12.10am, though bus No N1 leaves for Mui Wo at 2.50am, returning from there at 3.45am. Bus No 11 links Tai O with Tung Chung and bus No 21 with Ngong Ping. See those sections for details.

A ferry run by Lee Tat Passenger Service (☎ 2985 5868) links Tai O with Tuen Mun in the New Territories, via Sha Lo Wan on Lantau's north coast, at 8am and 4.30pm on weekdays, at 8am, 3pm and 5.30pm on

Saturday and 8am, 10.15am, 2pm, 4pm and 6pm on Sunday. The fare is HK$28.

Fan Lau

Fan Lau (Divided Flow), a small peninsula on the south-western tip of Lantau, has a couple of good beaches and the remains of **Fan Lau Fort**, built in 1729 to guard the channel between Lantau and the Pearl River estuary from pirates. It remained in operation until the end of the 19th century and was restored in 1985. The sea views from here are sterling.

To the south-east of the fort is an **ancient stone circle**. The origins and age of the circle are uncertain, but it probably dates from the Neolithic or early Bronze Age and may have been used in rituals.

The only way to reach Fan Lau is on foot. To get here from Tai O, walk south from the bus station for 250m and pick up the coastal Lantau Trail. It then carries on to the north-east and Shek Pik, where you can catch the No 1 bus back to Mui Wo. You may manage to flag down a passing sampan that will take you back to Tai O for about HK$300.

Tung Chung

In recent years change has come to Tung Chung on Lantau's northern coast at a pace that can only happen in Hong Kong. This previously all but inaccessible farming region, with the small village of Tung Chung at its centre, has seen Chek Lap Kok, the mountain across Tung Chung Bay, flattened to build Hong Kong's new airport and a 'New Town' served by the MTR rises up a short distance to the north-east.

As part of the territory's plans to solve the housing crisis, Tung Chung New Town has now become a huge, residential estate of 15,000 people and growing. It is essentially part of the airport project (some houses are for those who work there).

These developments and transportation improvements have spelled the end of Tung Chung as a peaceful and secluded spot. But efforts have been made to protect Tung Chung Old Village. Buildings may rise no higher than three storeys and each floor can be no larger than 70 sq metres.

Seeing Pink Dolphins

About 200 partly misnamed Chinese White Dolphins (Sousa chinensis) – they are actually bubble-gum pink – inhabit the coastal waters around Hong Kong, finding the brackish waters of the Pearl River estuary to be the perfect habitat. Unfortunately these glorious, ever-smiling mammals, which also called Indo-Pacific Humpback Dolphins, are being threatened by environmental pollution, and their numbers are dwindling.

The threat comes in many forms, but the most prevalent – and direct – dangers are sewage, chemicals, over fishing and boat traffic. Over 150,000 cu metres of raw sewage are dumped into the western harbour every day, and high concentrations of chemicals such as DDT have been found in tissue samples taken from some of the dolphins. Several dead dolphins have been entangled in fishing nets and, despite the dolphins' skill at sensing and avoiding surface vessels, some have collided with boats.

The dolphins' habitat has also been diminished by the erosion of the natural coastline of Lantau Island during the construction of the new airport, which required land reclamation of approximately 9 sq km of seabed and the destruction of many kilometres of natural coastline. The North Lantau Highway also consumed about 10km of the natural coastline.

Hong Kong Dolphinwatch (☎ 2984 1414, ⓦ www.zianet.com/dolphins, 1528A Star House, 3 Salisbury Rd, Tsim Sha Tsui) was founded in 1995 to raise awareness of these wonderful creatures and promote responsible ecotourism. It offers 2½-hour cruises (HK$320/160 for adults/children) to see the pink dolphins in their natural habitat every Wednesday, Thursday, Saturday and Sunday. Coaches leave the Mandarin Oriental Hotel in Central at 8.30am and the Kowloon Hotel in Tsim Sha Tsui at 9am for Tung Chung via the Tsing Ma Bridge and return at 1pm. About 96% of the cruises result in the sighting of at least one dolphin; if none is spotted, passengers are offered a free trip.

Yuen Po St Bird Garden

A cheerful market vendor

Mischievous smiles in the streets of Hong Kong.

Women peeling prawns on Cheung Chau island.

Mid-Autumn Festival cakes

Catching some rays on the beach, Repulse Bay.

The view from atop Tai Mo Shan.

Shenzhen seen from Lok Ma Chau border.

It's a hive of activity: boats on the water and buildings on the hills above Stanley Market.

Annals record a settlement at Tung Chung as early as the Ming dynasty. There are several Buddhist establishments in the upper reaches of the valley, but the main attraction here is **Tung Chung Fort** (☎ 2721 2326 for information, Tung Chung Rd; admission free; open 9am-1pm & 2pm-4pm Wed-Mon), which dates back to 1832 when Chinese troops were garrisoned on Lantau. The Japanese briefly occupied the fort during WWII. Measuring 70m by 80m and enclosed by granite-block walls, it retains six of its muzzle-loading cannons pointing out to sea.

About 1km to the north are the ruins of **Tung Chung Battery**, a much smaller fort built in 1817. All that remains is an L-shaped wall with a gun emplacement in the corner. The ruins were only discovered in 1980, having been hidden for about a century by scrub.

Facing Tung Chung Bay to the southwest in the village of Sha Tsui Tau is **Hau Wong Temple**, founded at the end of the Song dynasty. The temple contains a bell inscribed by the Qing dynasty emperor, Qian Long, and the interior walls are also adorned with his musings on life in Lantau.

Getting There & Away Once one of the most difficult places to reach, the Tung Chung MTR line will now get you here from Central in about 23 minutes.

Bus Nos 3 and 13 connect Mui Wo with Tung Chung New Town. Departures from Mui Wo are roughly every hour between 5.45am and 11pm; the last No 13 bus from Tung Chung back to Mui Wo is at midnight. Departures are more frequent on Sunday and public holidays. Tung Chung and Tai O are connected by bus No 11, with half-hourly departures from Tai O between 5.20am and midnight. Bus No 21 links Tung Chung with Ngong Ping; see that section earlier for details.

A host of other buses connect Tung Chung with Kowloon and the New Territories via the Tsing Ma Bridge and Tsing Yi Island: bus No E31 runs from Tung Chung to Tsuen Wan (where you can pick up the Tsuen Wan MTR line); bus No E32 runs to

Kwai Fong MTR station; and bus No E33 runs to Tuen Mun. There are also a few overnight routes that serve the airport and run through Tung Chung.

Fast ferries run by Airport Ferry Services (☎ 2987 7351) link Tung Chung New Town with Tuen Mun in the New Territories, sometimes calling at the airport at Chek Lap Kok along the way. Ferries depart from Tuen Mun at 7.20am, 11.20am, 1.20pm, 4pm, 5.10pm and 5.50pm, with the return boats leaving Tung Chung between 20 and 30 minutes later. The trip take 17 minutes and costs HK$15 (HK$10 for children and seniors).

Activities

Bicycles are available for hire in Mui Wo a short distance from the ferry pier: **Friendly Bicycle Shop** (☎ 2984 2278, Shop 12, Mui Wo Centre, 1 Ngan Wan Rd), opposite Wellcome, and the nearby **King of Bicycles** (☎ 2984 9761, Shop 14, Mui Wo Centre, 1 Ngan Wan Rd). They cost HK$10 per hour and HK$25/35 per day during the week/at the weekend.

In summer at the weekend bikes can also be hired from stalls in front of the Silvermine Beach Hotel in Mui Wo and in Pui O village.

Places To Stay

Camping The Country & Marine Parks Authority (W www.info.gov.hk/afcd/parks) maintains a total of nine free *camp sites* along the Lantau Trail. These are clearly labelled on the *Countryside Series: Lantau Island* and *Lantau Trail* maps and listed in the *Camp Sites of Hong Kong Country Parks* brochure available from the tourist office. The closest sites to Mui Wo are at Pak Fu Tin, about 2km south-east of the ferry pier along South Lantau Rd (stage No 1 of the Lantau Trail), and at Nam Shan on the alternative stage No 1 of the trail. The site at Shap Long on the northern edge of the Chi Ma Wan Peninsula is also within easy striking distance of Mui Wo. Other sites include those at Lo Kei Wan and Shek Lam Chau, south-west of Tong Fuk; Kau Ling Chung and Tai Long Wan, both to the east along the coast from Fan Lau; Tsin Yue Wan

HONG KONG

(along the coast between Fan Lau and Tai O); and Man Cheung Po, near the Tsz Hsing Monastery south-west of Lung Tsai Ng Garden. You can also camp at the *SG Davis Hostel* and the *Jockey Club Mong Tung Wan Hostel* for HK$16 (HK$25 for nonmembers); see Hostels & Dormitories below for details.

Private Rooms & Apartments During the summer months and at weekends, you'll find kiosks set up to rent *holiday rooms* and *apartments*, including Brilliant Holiday (☎ 2984 2662, Shop KC, Lower Deck, Mui Wo Pier). The holiday apartments can be readily identified by the photos on display. Expect to pay HK$120/200 weekdays/ weekend for a double room and from HK$200 for a studio. Be warned that not all the places are in Mui Wo – many are along Cheung Sha Beach and in Pui O village.

Hostels & Dormitories The HKYHA has two hostels on Lantau Island, one a stone's throw from the Tian Tan Buddha in Ngong Ping and the other in a remote area of the Chi Ma Wan Peninsula. The hostels are open to HKYHA/HI card-holders only, but membership is available if you pay the nonmember rate for a total of six nights. See Hostel Cards under Visas & Documents in the Hong Kong Facts for the Visitor chapter.

SG Davis Hostel (☎ 2985 5610, fax 2788 3105, W www.yha.org.hk/sgdavis.html, Ngong Ping) Beds for juniors/senior members HK$25/35, camping for members/nonmembers HK$16/25. This 52-bed hostel, open seven days a week year-round, is a 10-minute walk from the bus stop in Ngong Ping (see Getting There & Away in the earlier Ngong Ping section) and is the ideal place to stay if you want to catch the sunrise at nearby Lantau Peak. Check-in is from 7am to 10am and again from 4pm (2pm on Saturday) to 11pm. From the bus stop, take the paved path to your left as you face the Tian Tan Buddha, pass the public toilets on your right and the Lantau Tea Garden on your left and follow the hostel signs. If you visit in winter be sure to bring warm clothing for the evenings and early mornings.

Jockey Club Mong Tung Wan Hostel (☎ 2984 1389, fax 2788 3105, W www.yha .org.hk/mongtung.html, Mong Tung Wan) Beds for juniors/senior members HK$25/35, camping for members/nonmembers HK$16/25. This tranquil 88-bed, waterfront property on the south-eastern side of the Chi Ma Wan Peninsula is jointly operated by the HKYHA and the Jockey Club. In the past it's been open at the weekend and on the eve of public holidays only, so telephone the HKYHA (☎ 2788 1638) in advance. From Mui Wo, take bus No 7 (or bus A35 from Hong Kong International Airport) and alight at Pui O. Take the footpath across the fields from the bus stop and continue along Chi Ma Wan Rd until it leaves the sea edge. At a sharp bend in the road at Ham Tin, turn right onto the footpath by the sea and follow it to the hostel – about 45 minutes. Alternatively, you can take a ferry to Cheung Chau and hire a sampan (about HK$50) to the jetty at Mong Tung Wan. A sampan carries about 10 people and their luggage.

Trappist Haven Monastery (☎ 2987 6286, 2914 2933, Tai Shui Hang) You can stay at this Roman Catholic monastery where the monks have taken a vow of silence, but applications must be made in writing or by telephone. Write to the Grand Master, Trappist Haven Monastery, PO Box 5, Lantau, Hong Kong. Men and women sleep in separate dorms. For directions on how to reach the monastery see Getting There & Away under Trappist Haven Monastery earlier in this Lantau section.

Guesthouses Along Lower Cheung Sha Beach you'll find the self-proclaimed 'smallest hotel in Hong Kong', *Babylon Villa (☎ 2980 3145, fax 2980 3024, e babylon@wlink.net, W babylon-villa-hotel.com, 29 Lower Cheung Sha Village)*. Doubles HK$650 including breakfast, one-night weekday/weekend package with breakfast and dinner from HK$1350/ $1450. This is a cute retreat with three non-smoking rooms (pink, blue and yellow) right on the water and next to The Stoep Restaurant (see Places to Eat). To reach Babylon Villa, take bus No 4 from Mui Wo.

Hotels There are three decent accommodation options in Mui Wo lining Silvermine Bay Beach.

Seaview Holiday Resort (☎ 2984 8877, fax 2984 8787, 11 Tung Wan Tau Rd) Doubles/triples HK$250/300 Sun-Thur, HK$300/350 Fri, HK$500/600 Sat. The Seaview is by far the cheapest place to stay along the beach, but is not as nice as the other two hotels.

Mui Wo Inn (☎ 2984 7225, fax 2984 1916, Tung Wan Tau Rd) Doubles from HK$280 Sun-Fri, HK$450-550 Sat, twins from HK$400 Sun-Fri, HK$650 Sat; breakfast included. This is the last hotel on the beach and can be identified by the ring of faux-classical statues in front.

Silvermine Beach Hotel (☎ 2984 8295, fax 2984 1907, e sbh@hdkf.com, Tung Wan Tau Rd) Doubles HK$880 1380. This 'Savoy Hotel' of Mui Wo has some good discount packages for long-term stayers: weekly HK$2000-4200, monthly HK$6000-15,000.

Places to Eat

Mui Wo The food isn't great, but it is cheap, at **Mui Wo Cooked Food Market**. This covered area north-west of the ferry pier harbours a large number of food stalls.

Rome Restaurant (☎ 2984 2311, Shop A-B, Grand View Mansion, Mui Wo Ferry Pier Rd) Meals HK$100. The food is not the best and you may have trouble being understood, but it is convenient to the ferry pier and open when many other places are shut.

Seaview Restaurant (☎ 2984 8327, 2 Tung Wan Tau Rd) Dishes HK$30-60. This cheapie, not to be confused with the Seaview Holiday Resort farther north, is right on the beach.

Tak Juk Kee (Sun Lee) Seafood Restaurant (☎ 2984 1265, 1 Chung Hao Rd) Dishes HK$55-80. This friendly restaurant catches delightful sea breezes from Silvermine Bay and is arguably the best Chinese restaurant in Mui Wo. Try the chilli prawns (HK$80), squid with vegetables (HK$55) or the chicken with cashew nuts (HK$55).

Silvermine Beach Hotel (☎ 2984 8295, Tung Wan Tau Rd) Meals about HK$150.

The restaurant at this relatively flashy hotel is no great shakes, but can be recommended for its South-East Asian and barbecue dinner buffet available on Saturday from 6.30pm to 9.30pm (HK$178/88 adults/children).

China Bear (☎ 2984 7360, Ground floor, Mui Wo Centre, Ngan Wan Rd) Mains HK$55-85, snacks HK$25-65. The China Bear is the most popular expatriate pub/restaurant in town, with a wonderful open bar facing the water. Among the pub-grub offerings are fish and chips (HK$85), an all-day breakfast (HK$58) and 250g fillet steak (HK$75).

Hippo Pub (☎ 2984 9876, Shop D, Grand View Mansion, Mui Wo Ferry Pier Rd) Mains HK$55-80. This Western-style bar-restaurant is hidden in an alley behind the Rome Restaurant. Old faithfuls include the Hippo British breakfast (HK$55) and fish and chips (HK$60).

La Pizzeria (☎ 2984 8933, Ground floor, Grand View Mansion, 11C Mui Wo Ferry Pier Rd) Mains HK$60-110, small/ medium/ large pizzas from HK$35/48/68. Most people come here for the pizzas, but there are lots of pasta choices (HK$45-60) and main courses such as fajitas (HK$78) and barbecued spare ribs (HK$110).

Station Café (☎ 2984 1919, Shop 19, Mui Wo Centre, 3 Ngan Wan Rd) Mains HK$30-90. This pleasant and very popular cafe/restaurant has set lunches (HK$32-48) and pizzas (HK$50-88).

Mui Wo Market (Ngan Shek St) is to the west after you cross the footbridge over the Silver River. You'll find both a **Park 'N' Shop** (Mui Wo Ferry Pier Rd) and a **Wellcome** (Ngan Wan Rd) supermarket in the centre of Mui Wo.

Discovery Bay The restaurants in the circular plaza opposite the ferry pier at Discovery Bay offer a wide variety of cuisines.

Brezza (☎ 2914 1906, Shop G01, Discovery Bay Plaza) Sandwiches HK$35-50. Though it does more substantial dishes, this Italian place is a good choice for lunch, with decent sandwiches and pastries.

Chili 'N' Spice (☎ 2987 9191, Shop 102F, Discovery Bay Plaza) Meals HK$150-200.

This branch of the popular chain is a pot-pourri of spicy Singaporean, Thai and Indonesian flavours.

Jo Jo Indian Restaurant (☎ 2987 0122, *Shop 101A, Discovery Bay Plaza*) Meals HK$150. This sister restaurant of the popular Jo Jo Mess in Wan Chai has punters lining up for its lamb dishes.

Shogun (☎ 2987 9299, *Shop G07, Discovery Bay Plaza*) Mains HK$50-80. The Korean food here might not be as authentic as what you'd find in Sheung Wan, but it's good nonetheless.

Pui O The only Indian restaurant on 'real' Lantau (ie, Discovery Bay excluded) is *Namaste Indian Restaurant* (☎ 2984 8491, *31 South Lantau Rd*). Dishes HK$38-88. Namaste has curries (HK$65-88) of every hue and type, a range of vegetarian dishes (HK$38-43) and a set lunch for HK$39.

Cheung Sha Beach & Tong Fuk Facing Lower Cheung Sha Beach is *The Stoep Restaurant* (☎ 2980 2699, *32 Lower Cheung Sha Village*) Mains HK$55-150. Open Tues-Sun. This Mediterranean-style restaurant has fish dishes (HK$55-85) and a South African barbecue (HK$80-150).

The Gallery (☎ 2980 4966, 2980 2582, *26 Tong Fuk Village*) Mains HK$90-130. Open Wed-Sun & public holidays. This South African restaurant with Middle Eastern overtones (go figure) has steaks for HK$130 and *boervors* sausages for HK$95.

Ngong Ping The car park at the Po Lin Monastery is awash with *snack bars* and *kiosks* selling vegetarian edibles.

Po Lin Vegetarian Restaurant (☎ 2985 5248, *Ngong Ping*) Set meals HK$60-100. The monastery has a good reputation for its cheap vegetarian food. This simple restaurant is in the covered arcade to the left of the main monastery building.

Tea Garden Restaurant (☎ 2985 5161, *Lantau Tea Garden, Ngong Ping*) Meals HK$100. If you'd prefer to eat fish, head for this place. It's down the path to the left of the Buddha statue just before the SG Davis Hostel.

Tai O This village is famous for its seafood restaurants, many of which display their names in Chinese only.

Fook Lam Moon (☎ 2985 7071, *29 Market St*) Meals HK$100. This relatively upmarket (for Tai O) restaurant serves tasty and not-over-refined dishes.

Getting There & Away

Bus With the opening of the Tung Chung MTR line and the two Lantau Link bridges connecting the island to the New Territories you can travel to Lantau by bus and MTR. It takes about the same time as by ferry but the trip isn't as scenic – apart from the thrill of crossing the Tsing Ma Bridge on a double-decker.

A number of buses connect Tung Chung with Kowloon and the New Territories via the Tsing Ma Bridge and Tsing Yi Island; see Getting There & Away under Tung Chung earlier in this Lantau section for details. For information on buses that link Hong Kong Island and Kowloon with the airport at Chek Lap Kok and the ferry from Tuen Mun to the airport, see the Hong Kong Getting Around chapter.

Boat This section deals with getting to and from Mui Wo in Silvermine Bay, the main entry port for Lantau Island. See Getting There & Away in the Trappist Haven Monastery, Discovery Bay, Chi Ma Wan and Tai O sections for specifics on reaching those destinations by boat without going to Mui Wo first.

To/From Central Both ordinary and fast ferries depart for Mui Wo about every half-hour between 6.10am (7am on Sunday and public holidays) and 12.30am from pier 7 at the outlying islands ferry terminal in Central. Between those times there's a 3am fast ferry to Mui Wo via Peng Chau. The last ferry from Mui Wo to Central is at 11.30pm though there is a fast ferry at 3.40am, which calls at Peng Chau first. The journey on the ordinary ferry takes 48 minutes, and the adult one-way fare is HK$10.50/16.80 in ordinary/deluxe class (HK$15.70/25 on Sunday and public holidays). The fast ferries, which take just 31 minutes, cost HK$21 (HK$31 on Sunday and public holidays). Some ferries (the 3am from Central and three early-morning boats from Mui Wo) stop at the neighbouring island of Peng Chau, adding 20 minutes to the trip.

To/From Tsim Sha Tsui At the weekend and on public holidays *only*, ferries depart for Mui Wo from the Tsim Sha Tsui Star Ferry pier in Kowloon. Ordinary ferries leave Tsim Sha Tsui at 2pm, 2.15pm, 3.15pm and 4.15pm on Saturday and fast ferries at 9.15am, 11.15pm, 1.15pm and 3.15pm on Sunday and public holidays. The return ferries from Mui Wo are at 2.40pm, 3.15pm, 4.40pm and 5.15pm on Saturday and 10.15am, 12.15pm, 2.15pm and 4.15pm on Sunday and public holidays.

The one-way fare on the ordinary ferry is HK$15.70/25 in ordinary/deluxe class and HK$31 on the fast ferry.

Inter-Island Services An ordinary inter-island ferry links Mui Wo with Cheung Chau (via Chi Ma Wan in most cases) and Peng Chau some 18 times a day. The first ferry leaves Mui Wo for Cheung Chau via Chi Ma Wan at 6am and for Peng Chau at 6.35am; the last ferry to Cheung Chau is at 10.20pm and to Peng Chau at 11.20pm. Boats leave approximately every 1½ hours. From Mui Wo it takes 20 minutes to reach Peng Chau, 15 minutes to Chi Ma Wan and 50 minutes to Cheung Chau. The flat fare is HK$8.40.

Getting Around

Bus The New Lantao Bus Company (☎ 2984 9848, W www.kcm.com.hk/nlb) runs a total of 16 lines (including two night buses) to destinations on the island, including Hong Kong International Airport at Chek Lap Kok. Buses, often with a choice of ordinary or air-conditioned buses, run daily on all routes, though frequencies are increased on Sunday and public holidays to handle the flood of visitors. Bus No 23 runs on weekends and public holidays only. There is a complicated pricing system for Lantau buses – weekday buses cost from HK$2.50/3.40 to HK$8/16 on ordinary/air-conditioned buses and

Sunday buses range from HK$4.30/5.20 to HK$13/25.

Buses from Mui Wo depart from the terminus just opposite the ferry pier. For buses to specific destinations around the island see the individual listings. Bus No A35 leaves Mui Wo for the airport at Chek Lap Kok via Tong Fuk every half-hour from 6am to midnight. The first bus leaves the airport for Mui Wo at 6.30am, the last at 12.05am. After that, the N35 runs about once an hour.

Taxi Lantau taxis, which are blue, cost HK$12 at flag fall and HK$1.20 for each additional 200m. It's not easy to get one and the drivers don't like to pick fares up on country roads. It's easiest to find taxis at the stands in Mui Wo and Tong Fuk – elsewhere, taxis are a rare item. You could try the call service (☎ 2984 1328, 2984 1368), but don't hold your breath.

PENG CHAU

Shaped vaguely like a horseshoe, tiny Peng Chau is just under 1 sq km in area. It is inhabited by around 8000 people, making it far more densely populated than its larger neighbour Lantau.

Peng Chau is fairly flat and not especially beautiful, but it has its charms. It is perhaps the most traditionally Chinese – narrow alleys, crowded housing, a good indoor wet market near the ferry pier, heaps of closet-sized restaurants and shops, and everywhere the sound of mahjong tiles being slapped on tables. There are also a couple of small but interesting temples.

Until recently the island's economy was supported by fishing and some cottage industries, notably the manufacture of furniture, porcelain and metal tubing. However, these manufacturing industries are now all but dead, having moved to mainland China where cheap labour is plentiful and laws governing industrial safety and pollution are less stringent. Nowadays, weekend tourists contribute significantly to Peng Chau's coffers.

There are no cars on Peng Chau, and you can walk around it easily in an hour.

PENG CHAU

Commercial Radio Station

Bridge to Tai Lei Island

TAI LUNG TSUEN

Tung Wan

KAM PENG ESTATE

BBQ Area

PENG LAI COURT

SHAN TING TSUEN

Kam Fa Temple

Tin Hau Temple

To Discovery Bay & Trappist Haven Monastery

Po Peng St

Lo Peng St

Wing On St

Lung Mo Temple

Service Reservoir

Ferry Pier

Pier

Graves

Finger Hill (95m)

Shing Ka Rd

WAI TSAI TSUEN

Nam Shan Rd

TAI WO

YUEN LING TSAI

Yuen Tong Monastery

NAM WAN SHAN TING SAN TSUEN

NAM WAN SAN TSUEN

NAM WAN

To Mui Wo & Cheung Chau

To Central

1 Wellcome Supermarket
2 Peng Chau Indoor Recreation Centre & Market
3 Post Office
4 HSBC
5 Sea Breeze Club
6 Jungle Restaurant & Pub

0   150   300m
0   150   300yd

Climbing the steps up to **Finger Hill** (95m), the island's highest point and topped with a winged Chinese-style pavilion, offers some light exercise and excellent views. To get to it, turn right at the Tin Hau Temple at the end of Lo Peng St just up from the ferry pier and walk south along Wing On St. This gives way to Shing Ka Rd, and Nam Shan Rd leads from here east up to Finger Hill. Unfortunately, most of Peng Chau's sewage, plastic bags and other debris wind up in the sea, making otherwise pleasant Tung Wan Beach on the eastern side of the island too dirty for swimming.

Information

There's an HSBC branch (☎ 2983 0383) at 1-3 Wing Hing St. The post office is on the opposite side of the street a few steps to the south.

Places to Eat

Peng Chau has a couple of popular pub/restaurants worth checking. Both are closed on Monday.

Sea Breeze Club (☎ 2983 8785, 38 Wing Hing St) Starters HK$38-68, mains HK$48-148. The Sea Breeze is known for its fine T-bone steaks, which aren't cheap at HK$148.

But the place is so popular that Discovery Bay residents hop on the kaido to dine here.

Jungle Restaurant & Pub (☎ 2983 8837, *38A-C Wing Hing St*) Mains HK$49-69 This small but cosy place next door serves popular pub grub like fish and chips (HK$69), bangers and mash (HK$65), all-day breakfast (HK$65) and six draught beers. It also has a snooker and three pool tables.

The *indoor market* is housed in the same block as the Peng Chau Indoor Recreation Centre near the ferry pier on the corner of Lo Peng and Po Peng Sts. Enter from the rear. There's a *Wellcome* supermarket at the northern end of Lo Peng St just up from the ferry pier.

Getting There & Away
Ordinary and fast ferries leave for Peng Chau approximately once an hour between 7am (7.50am on Sunday and public holidays) and 12.30am from pier 7 at the outlying islands ferry terminal in Central. There's also a 3am fast ferry to Peng Chau that carries on to Mui Wo on Lantau. The last ferry from Peng Chau to Central is at 11.30pm (11.35pm on Sunday) though there is a fast ferry at 3.25am, which stops at Mui Wo before heading for Central.

The journey on the ordinary ferry takes 38 minutes, and the adult one-way fare is HK$10.50/16.80 in ordinary/deluxe class (HK$15.70/25 on Sunday and public holidays). The fast ferries, which take just 25 minutes, cost HK$21 (HK$31 on Sunday and public holidays).

An inter-island ferry links Peng Chau with Mui Wo and (frequently) Chi Ma Wan on Lantau as well as Cheung Chau up to 11 times a day. The first ferry leaves Peng Chau at 5.40am for all three destinations; the last ferry to Mui Wo is at 11.40pm. Boats leave every 1½ to two hours and take 20 minutes to reach Mui Wo, 35 minutes to Chi Ma Wan and one hour to Cheung Chau. The flat fare is HK$8.40.

Peng Chau is the main springboard for the Trappist Haven Monastery, with up to 10 sailings a day. See Getting There & Away in that earlier section for details.

The same kaido company, Rental Kaito (☎ 9033 8102), links Peng Chau with Discovery Bay every 30 minutes to an hour, with up to 19 sailings a day (up to 21 on Sunday). Boats leave from a small jetty just north of the main ferry pier.

TUNG LUNG CHAU
Guarding the eastern entrance to Victoria Harbour is Tung Lung Chau (East Dragon Island), whose position was once considered strategic for protection.

Tung Lung Fort, on the north-eastern corner of the island, was built in the late 17th or early 18th century and was attacked a number of times by pirate bands before being abandoned in 1810. Little remains of the fort except the outline of the exterior walls, but the views are great and there's an **information centre** (*open 9am-4pm Wed-Mon*). There's a camp site a short distance to the west of the fort.

The north-west tip of the island boasts an important rock carving of what is thought to be a dragon. It is probably the oldest such carving in the territory and certainly the largest, measuring 2.4m by 1.8m.

Getting There & Away
It is difficult to reach Tung Lung Chau at any time other than the weekend when ferries run by Lam Kee Kaido (☎ 2560 9929) heading for Joss House Bay in the New Territories from Sai Wan Ho, just east of Quarry Bay on Hong Kong Island, stop at Tung Lung Chau along the way. On Saturday, boats sail from Sai Wan Ho at 9am, 10.30am, 3.30pm and 4.45pm, departing from Tung Lung Chau about a half-hour later. On Sunday and holidays there are boats from Sai Wan Ho at 8.30am, 9.45am, 11am, 2.15pm, 3.30pm and 4.45pm with returns from Tung Lung Chau at 9am, 10.20am, 1.45pm, 3pm, 4pm and 5.30pm.

The trip takes a half-hour, and the one-way fare is HK$28/14 for adults/children under 12.

To catch the ferry, take the MTR to Sai Wan Ho and then Exit A to Tai On St. Turn right and then keep on going till you reach the quayside. The ride to Joss House Bay from Tung Lung Chau is significantly shorter than the trip from Sai Wan Ho, and you could even go by one route and return by the other. From Joss House Bay there are buses to the Choi Hung MTR station in Kowloon.

PO TOI

Po Toi is a rocky island off the south-eastern coast of Hong Kong Island and a favourite of weekend junk party-goers who frequent the few seafood restaurants beyond the jetty at Tai Wan in the south-west. There's some decent walking on Po Toi, a tiny Tin Hau Temple across the bay from the pier and some mysterious rock carvings resembling stylised animals and fish on the southern coast. There's no accommodation here, but you can pitch a tent.

Place to Eat

Ming Kee Seafood Restaurant (☎ *2849 7038*) Meals HK$100. This is one of three restaurants in Po Toi village and by far the most popular with day-trippers. Make sure you book if you're a crowd.

Getting There & Away

A ferry run by Po Toi Kaido Services (☎ 2554 4059) leaves Aberdeen for Po Toi on Tuesday, Thursday and Saturday at 9am, returning from the island at 10.30am. If you're not just there for the ride, you may have to spend the night. On Sunday a single boat leaves Aberdeen at 8am, but there are several more departures from Stanley (at 10am, 11.30am, 3.30pm and 5pm). Boats return from Po Toi at 9.15am, 10.45am, 3pm, 4.30pm and 6pm. The fare is HK$20.

China Excursion – Shenzhen

If you've visited Hong Kong, you've been to China. Just have a look at the territory's postage stamps, the official seal, the chop in your passport – they all say 'Hong Kong SAR, China'. But it's not really China. The only way to say you've really visited China is to cross the border with the mainland at Lo Wu and enter Shenzhen.

Shenzhen, a 'Special Economic Zone' full of five-star hotels, beggars, shopping malls and hookers that has to be seen to be believed, is not a true reflection of China either, but it will give you a brief glimpse of how different a SEZ is from a 'Special Administrative Region' – a SAR – like Hong Kong.

In many ways, all of Shenzhen – and not just the tacky theme park to the west that bears a similar name – could be called 'China in miniature'. Along the roads, congregating in hotel lobbies and outside the train and bus stations, you'll spot young Muslim Uighurs from Xinjiang Province grilling kebabs on makeshift braziers, heavily made-up prostitutes from Shanghai, minority people from Kunming in the south-west selling mouse deer antlers, snake bile, tortoise shells and other 'medicinal' items, and cadres in black Mercedes, their windows blacked out lest the proletariat catch a glimpse of their pampered and privileged world.

This is a place where almost four million Chinese people, the vast majority from elsewhere in the country, have paid their toll and see themselves as finally having arrived on the road to riches. For them Shenzhen is mesmerising for all its opportunities.

Shenzhen is a restricted zone; Chinese nationals require a special internal passport even to enter it, much less live and work here. The northern part of the SEZ is walled off from the rest of China by an electrified fence to prevent smuggling and to keep back the hordes of people trying to emigrate illegally. The frontier with Hong Kong to the south is equally fortified for the same reasons. At the moment, if you buy your visa at the border with Hong Kong

Highlights

- A visit to Minsk World, a decommissioned Soviet aircraft carrier open to the public in Dapeng Bay
- A night out in the raucous bars of Shekou
- Shopping in the Dongmen Market area
- A massage in Luohu Commercial City

(see Visas under Information later in this chapter), your stay will be limited to the confines of the Shenzhen SEZ *only*. Without a proper Chinese visa, you cannot travel north into the rest of China, even to Guangzhou.

Thousands of Hong Kong Chinese cross the border into Shenzhen every day. With prices of everything at least half of what they are in Hong Kong, they come to shop, eat, take massage, have clothing tailored, even have an evening out on the town. There's more to Shenzhen than those things, of course, but don't come here in search of Chinese history and culture. Shenzhen's past doesn't stretch that far and its god is not Kuanti or Kwun Yam but Mammon.

HISTORY

Shenzhen was no more than a tiny village on Pearl River estuary when it won the equivalent of a national lottery and became a Special Economic Zone in 1980 along with three others: Zhuhai, across the border from Macau; Shantou in the eastern part of Guangdong Province; and Xiamen in Fujian Province.

Developers added a stock market, a stand of glittering hotels, office blocks and a population of two million (which has since almost doubled) to this fishing village and the world as Shenzhen knew it came to an end. Indeed, the only fishnets you're likely to see in these parts nowadays will be on the legs of Shenzhen's formidable hordes of whores.

SHENZHEN

Like many fortune winners, Shenzhen has attracted a lot of undesirables over the past couple of decades: up to two-thirds of its residents have no permit to live there, beggars and touts throng the streets, and its morals have gone flaccid, with prostitution, drugs and sleaze endemic. A surging crime rate is another of its less appealing aspects. But it's a simpler, more wide-eyed and definitely cheaper place than Hong Kong.

The pulsating boomtown of Shenzhen is where Chinese go to get rich which, according to the late Premier Deng Xiaoping, is a 'glorious' endeavour.

Borders make a big difference in a lot of ways, including basic ones like language. Shenzhen is in Guangdong county, where the most prevalent language is Cantonese. But since the vast majority of the people there are from other parts of China, the most commonly used language is *putonghua* (called Mandarin in English), which is the official language of the People's Republic of China. See the Language chapter at the back of this book for background and key phrases.

ORIENTATION

Shenzhen (Shumchun in Cantonese) actually refers to three places: Shenzhen City, just north of the Hong Kong border crossing at Lo Wu; the Shenzhen Special Economic Zone (SEZ); and Shenzhen county, which extends for many kilometres north, east and west of the SEZ. Most of the hotels, restaurants and shopping centres are in Shenzhen City, along Jianshe Lu, Renmin Nan Lu and Shennan Lu.

In the western part of the SEZ are a string of theme parks and resorts as well as Shenzhen University. To the south-west is the port of Shekou, which is a nightlife and entertainment area in its own right. The main attraction in the eastern part of the zone is the beach and the attractions around Xiaomeisha.

Most people reach Shenzhen from Hong Kong by taking the Kowloon-Canton Railway (KCR) to Lo Wu and walking across the border, though you can also get here by the high-speed ferry that links Hong Kong with Shekou. See the China section under

Sea in the Hong Kong Getting There & Away chapter for details.

The border between Hong Kong and Shenzhen is open from 6.30am until 11.30pm daily.

Maps

Most of the maps on sale at shops and stalls near Shenzhen train station and the Luohu Commercial City shopping centre are in Chinese characters only. Universal Publications' *Shenzhen Touring Map* (HK$20) covers the entire country, with large-scale insets of the districts in Shenzhen City. Clearer and more useful is the *Map of Shenzhen in Detail* (HK$22), which concentrates on Shenzhen City. In Hong Kong, you can pick up a copy of either map at the Joint Publishing Company bookshop (☎ 2525 0105), 9 Queen Victoria St, Central.

INFORMATION
Tourist Offices

The Shenzhen Tourist Information Centre (☎ 232 1533, 232 1633) on the ground floor of the train station is open from 6am to 9pm daily. Don't expect to collect much from here beyond a few brochures, however; the staff are linguistically limited to Mandarin. There's another branch (☎ 668 7691) in the Shekou ferry terminal.

Travel Agencies

There are several branches of the China Travel Service (CTS), where you can make inquiries and buy tickets. The most convenient branch is the one in the lobby of the Guangxin Hotel (☎ 217 6615) at 2069 Renmin Nan Lu, which sells train and plane tickets; those with more general tourist inquiries should go to room 1102 (☎ 218 2660) on the 11th floor of the same building. You may find the staff at the China International Travel Service (CITS; ☎ 229 1897) in room 1110 down the hall more helpful. CTS has another branch (☎ 366 7808, 366 7898) in the lobby of the Wah Chung International Hotel at 3041 Shennan Dong Lu. The CTS Shekou branch (☎ 681 9090, 681 9091) is at 45 Taizi Lu near Xihai (West Ocean) Park.

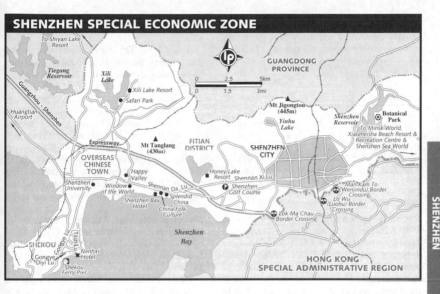

SHENZHEN SPECIAL ECONOMIC ZONE

You should not abuse the privilege, but the business centres at many top-end hotels have flight, bus, rail and ferry schedules, and staff there should be able to help with queries and bookings, even if you're not a hotel guest. If you buy tickets from these business centres, expect to pay a little more.

The Shenzhen Greenland International Travel Agency (☎ 222 3838, W www .5155555.com) in the lobby of the Shenzhen Hotel, 3085 Shennan Dong Lu, is a good place to buy plane tickets.

Visas

Holders of Canadian, American, Australian, New Zealand and most European Union passports (along with many others) can buy a visa valid for the Shenzhen SEZ *only* for five days at the border with Hong Kong for HK$100. Visas are available on the 1st floor of the immigration and customs building. You can get a similar visa when you debark from the ferry at Shekou but *not* after 6pm.

Everyone else, including *British nationals* at the moment, must have a Chinese visa obtained in Hong Kong, Macau or elsewhere in advance. Those wanting to leave the confines of the Shenzhen SEZ – even to

visit Guangzhou – must also have such a visa. They are available from Chinese embassies and consulates, CTS branches and local travel agents. See the Hong Kong Facts for the Visitor chapter for a list of Chinese consular representatives overseas and the Hong Kong Getting There & Away chapter for recommended travel agents.

In any case, it is strongly advised that you get your visa in advance. The queues to buy them at the border are serpentine and the wait interminable. At weekends, the eve of public holidays, special festivals like the goddess Tin Hau's birthday and other times, you can wait in line for up to two hours.

Money

Currency China's official currency is the renmenbi, literally, 'people's money', but is more commonly called the yuan and shown in this book by a 'Y' before amounts. The yuan is divided into 100 fen and, confusingly, 10 jiao. Paper notes are issued in denominations of one, two, five, 10, 50 and 100 yuan; one, two and five jiao; and one, two and five fen. Coins are in denominations of one yuan; five jiao; and one, two and five fen.

Exchange Rates The renmenbi is a strictly controlled currency and generally not convertible outside the country. Leave it all behind when you depart.

Some exchange rates are:

country	unit		yuan
Australia	A$1	=	Y4.42
Canada	C$1	=	Y5.35
European Union	€1	=	Y7.59
Hong Kong	HK$1	=	Y1.06
Japan	¥100	=	Y6.9
New Zealand	NZ$1	=	Y3.64
UK	UK£1	=	Y12.02
USA	US$1	=	Y8.28

Exchanging Money Shenzhen operates on a dual currency system: Chinese renmenbi and Hong Kong dollars. Most shops, restaurants and hotels will gladly accept Hong Kong dollars and usually make change in that currency. However, in smaller shops, food stalls and at the market, your change will come back in renmenbi, and you will lose a little on the exchange rate.

The Bank of China, with branches at 23 Jianshe Lu and 1197 Heping Lu, is open from 8.30am to 11.30am and 2pm to 5pm weekdays and 9.30am to 3.30pm Saturday. HSBC has a branch at the Century Plaza Hotel at the corner of Renmin Nan Lu and Chunfeng Lu. These banks have ATMs linked to several international money systems, including Cirrus and Plus, and they accept certain international bank cards (Visa, American Express and MasterCard). There's a Jetco ATM in the lobby of the Far East Grand Hotel at 2097 Shennan Dong Lu.

Black market moneychangers may approach you as you emerge from the customs and immigration building on the border or on the street asking for *gǎngbì* (Hong Kong dollars). It's best to avoid them.

Post & Communications
The main Shenzhen post office is at 3013 Jianshe Lu, just north of the junction with Shennan Lu. There's another post office at 2016 Chunfeng Lu. For express delivery of letters or packages, contact EMS (Speedpost; ☎ 222 7299), which has an office next door to the main post office at 3010 Jianshe Lu.

The China Telecom office, where you can make long-distance calls and buy phonecards, is east of the main post office on Shennan Dong Lu. Most hotels now offer IDD service from guestrooms.

Phonecards are also available from large hotels and China Telecom kiosks around the city in eight denominations, from Y20 to Y300.

China's country code is 86. For direct dialling to Shenzhen, the area code is 0755 within China and 755 from abroad, including Hong Kong and Macau.

Email & Internet Access There's an Internet service available at the China Telecom office (enter from 1001 Dongmen Nan Lu), open from 9am (10am at the weekend) to 5pm. The charge is Y20 an hour. A cheaper place with longer hours and a friendly younger crowd is the 24-hour Net Bar (☎ 218 0288) on the 5th floor of Gold Hotel, 2098 Shennan Dong Lu. Accessing the Net costs Y5 from 6am to 6pm and Y7 at other times. The Landmark Hotel (☎ 217 2288), 3018 Nanhu Lu, has an Internet cafe open 7am to 3am daily.

Bookshops
Shenzhen Book City (☎ 207 3030) is a massive, four-floor emporium near the Shenzhen Stock Exchange with books (mostly in Chinese) for computer geeks, language students and children. There are a few English-language titles too.

Medical Services
The Outpatient Department of the Shenzhen People's Hospital (☎ 222 3303) is at the corner of Jianshe Lu and Shennan Dong Lu, just south of the main post office.

Emergency
The Shenzhen branch (☎ 557 6355) of the Public Security Bureau (PBS), the section of the police force that deals with foreigners, can be found at 174 Jiefang Lu.

The medical emergency number is ☎ 120.

Dangers & Annoyances

Traffic congestion is a major problem in Shenzhen, and you'll be taking your life in your hands every time you try to cross the road, even when the light is in your favour. In particular watch out for cyclists (who seldom use the bike lanes provided and motor scooters. Use the pedestrian walkways wherever possible.

Shenzhen is a mecca for beggars from all over the country. They mainly congregate on Jianshe Lu and Renmin Nan Lu, tenaciously following foreigners in search of alms. If you do give them money, this is usually the green light for the rest of them to pursue you.

Prostitution is rife in Shenzhen and if you're a single male spending the night at virtually any hotel with the exception of the very top-end ones, you're bound to get at least one phone call from a *xiǎojiè* (literally, 'miss', but often used in association with prostitutes) asking you if you want company. (Someone at the front desk always tips them off.) Prostitutes congregate at the southern end of Renmin Nan Lu, on the pedestrian walkways and elsewhere.

Spitting is a major annoyance in Shenzhen as it is throughout China, despite attempts by the authorities to stop this disgusting and unhealthy practice. You'll see people expectorating on the pavement, in the market and even in shops.

The worst time is the early morning, when half the city is hacking and coughing in an attempt to give the sputum in their lungs an exit visa. Wear earplugs and stay in bed.

SHENZHEN CITY 深圳市

There isn't a whole lot in Shenzhen City to see, but it can be an interesting place to explore. The area near the border is a good place for walking. Most visitors spend their time exploring the shopping arcades, restaurants and markets along Renmin Nan Lu and Jianshe Lu.

The most popular place for locals and travellers alike is the **Luohu Commercial City** shopping centre (*Renmin Nan Lu*), five storeys of madness to the left as you emerge from the customs and immigration building. Here you'll find clothing and craft shops,

massage parlours and restaurants of every shape and hue.

EAST SHENZHEN
Botanical Park 植物园

Though hardly spectacular, the gardens of the 590-hectare Botanical Park (*Zhíwù Gōngyuán*) are spacious, green and one of the few places in the area free of concrete, skyscrapers or factories. The park is northeast of the centre, on the eastern shore of the Shenzhen Reservoir in Luohu District and can be reached by bus No 220.

Minsk World 明思克航母世界

Minsk World (*Míngsīkè Hángmǔ Shìjiè;* ☎ 535 5333, 525 1427, Dapeng Bay, Yantian District; adult/child Y100/50; open 9.30am-6pm daily) has got to be one of the world's most unusual attractions: a 40,000-ton decommissioned Soviet aircraft carrier, complete with choppers and MiG fighter planes parked on the deck. You can scramble up and down the Minsk's five levels, viewing sailors' bunks, old propaganda posters, exhibits on space travel (including the stuffed corpse of first-dog-in-space Strelka) and missiles, missiles and more missiles. There's even a Russian restaurant. Bus Nos 103 and 205 will take you here. A taxi from the centre will cost about Y80.

Shenzhen Sea World

Shenzhen Sea World (*Shēnzhèn Hǎiyáng Shìjiè;* ☎ 506 2986, W www.szxms.com.cn, Xiaomeisha Recreation Centre, Yantian District; adult/child Y100/50; open 9.30am-8.30pm daily), near the holiday resort of the same name, is chock-a-block with aquariums and tanks filled with creatures from the deep, but most people come to see the shows and performances: trapeze acts, dancing with sharks, dolphin synchronised swimming and so on. This place is about 30km from the centre. Bus Nos 103 and 430 both go here.

WEST SHENZHEN
Theme Parks

If Paris can have a version of Disneyland, why can't Shenzhen have half a dozen home-grown ones to call its own?

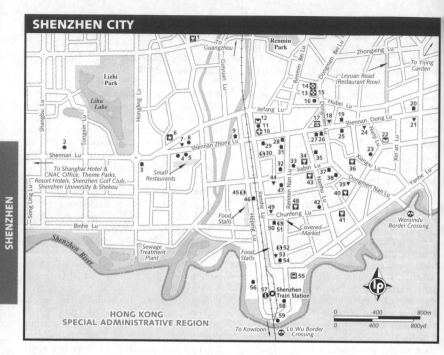

SHENZHEN CITY

Over in what is called Overseas Chinese Town, 15km west of the centre and about halfway to Shekou, you'll find four of these parks. They're naff in the extreme, but it's always fun to see other people having a good time and the kids just love them.

Splendid China This park *(Jiù Zhōnghuá;* ☎ *660 2043,* Ⓦ *www.chinafcv.com, Shennan Da Lu, Overseas Chinese Town; adult/child Y70/35 summer & holidays; open 8.30am-6pm daily, 10.30am-10pm summer)*, or more descriptively 'Splendid China Miniature Scenic Spot', is an assembly of China's sights at 1/15 of their normal sizes that allows you to 'visit all of China in one day'.

China Folk Culture Villages Contiguous to Splendid China and part of the same group, China Folk Culture Villages *(Zhōngguó Mínzú Wénhuà Cūn;* ☎ *660 2315,* Ⓦ *www.chinafcv.com, Shennan Da Lu, Overseas Chinese Town; adult/child Y85/45,*

combined ticket with Splendid China Y145/70, Y155/80 summer; open 8.30am-6pm daily, 10.30am-10pm summer) gives you the chance to see real-life examples of the 56 ethnic minorities of China wandering around. On display are re-creations of two-dozen minority villages, including a cave, as well as a lama temple, a drum tower, a rattan bridge and a 1000-eyed statue of Kuanyin (Kwun Yam in Cantonese), the Goddess of Mercy. There are performances throughout the day at the Central Theatre and the Carnival Parade Ground to the north-east.

Food Street at China Folk Culture Villages has a number of restaurants and food stalls to choose from.

Window of the World This place *(Shìjiè Zhīch-uāng;* ☎ *660 0447, Shennan Da Lu, Overseas Chinese Town; adult/child Y100/50, Y110/55 summer & holidays; open 9am-10pm daily, 9am-11.30pm summer & holidays)* takes the concept of Splendid China

SHENZHEN CITY 深圳市

PLACES TO STAY
- 3 Oriental Regent Hotel
  晶都酒店
- 9 Yat Wah Hotel
  日华宾馆
- 19 Gold Hotel; Net Bar
  富丽华大酒店；网吧
- 20 South China International Hotel
  中南国际大酒店
- 25 Far East Grand Hotel
  远东大酒店
- 26 Shenzhen Airlines Hotel
  深圳航空大酒店
- 27 Guangdong Hotel
  粤海酒店
- 28 Wah Chung International Hotel; CTS
  华中国际酒店；中国旅行社
- 29 Shenzhen Hotel; Shenzhen Greenland International Travel Agency
  深圳大酒店
- 31 CTS Dahua Hotel
  深圳中旅大华酒店
- 32 Petrel Hotel; Petrel Watching Restaurant
  海燕大酒店；
  海燕观光大酒楼
- 35 Landmark Hotel; Piazza Café; Piazza Café; Chao Zhou Restaurant
  富苑酒店；广场西餐厅；
- 37 Sunshine Hotel; JJ Disco
  阳光酒店
- 38 Furong Hotel; Polka No 1 Club
  芙蓉宾馆
- 46 Shen Tie Hotel; Tiecheng Restaurant
  深铁大酒店；铁城食街
- 47 Guangxin Hotel; CITS; CTS
  广信酒店；
  中国国际旅行车；
  中国旅行社
- 50 Century Plaza Hotel; Laurel Restaurant; Jade Garden Restaurant
  新都酒店；丹桂轩

- 54 Shangri-La Hotel; Henry J Bean's Bar & Grill; Shang Palace
  香格里拉大酒店；泮溪酒家；亨利酒吧
- 56 Forum Hotel
  富临大酒店

PLACES TO EAT
- 7 Friday Café
  星期五西餐厅
- 18 KFC
  肯德基
- 21 Muslim Hotel Restaurant
  穆斯林宾馆与餐馆
- 24 McDonald's
  麦当劳
- 39 Charwphraya Thai Restaurant
  昭帕耶泰国餐馆
- 44 Pizza Hut
  必胜客
- 49 Luohu Restaurant
  罗湖餐厅
- 53 Panxi Restaurant
  泮溪酒家

OTHER
- 1 Wall Street Disco
  华尔街迪斯科
- 2 Shenzhen City Hall
  深圳市政府
- 4 Shenzhen Stock Exchange
  深圳证券交易所
- 5 Shenzhen Book City
  深圳书城
- 6 Public Security Bureau
  公安局
- 8 Shunhing Square; Shops; Genroku Sushi
  信兴广场；商店
- 10 Shenzhen People's Hospital
  深圳人民医院
- 11 EMS (Speedpost)
  特快专递
- 12 Post Office
  邮局

- 13 Dongmen Market (area)
- 14 Mong Kok Commercial Centre
- 15 Kowloon City Plaza
- 16 Moi Department Store
- 17 China Telecom Office
  中国电信
- 22 Post office
  邮局
- 23 Electronic Shops
  电子商店
- 30 Bank of China
  中国银行
- 33 International Trade Centre; ITC Revolving Restaurant
  国际贸易中心；
  深圳国贸旋转餐厅
- 34 Power 2 Disco
- 36 Better Ole Club
- 40 1897 Club
- 41 Feelings Club
- 42 Park 'N' Shop
- 43 New York, New York Club
- 45 Bank of China
  中国银行
- 48 Jungle Jungle Café/Bar
- 51 HSBC
  汇丰银行
- 52 Bank of China
  中国银行
- 55 Local Bus & Minibus Station
  公共汽车站和中巴车站
- 57 Shenzhen Tourist Information Centre
  深圳旅游信息中心
- 58 Luohu Commercial City; Laurel Restaurant; Shops; Massage Parlours; Long-Distance Bus Station
  罗湖商业城；
  长途汽车站
- 59 Border Crossing Building (Customs & Immigration)
  联检大楼（海关）

one step further by providing models of sights from around the world. Thus you can admire miniature versions of the Eiffel Tower, the Golden Gate Bridge, Mt Fuji, the Kremlin and even a Maori village. Musical,

dance and other cultural performances – Japanese zither solo, changing of the guard at the Arc de Triomphe, even a full wedding in white in a church on International St – take place at various locations during the day.

Happy Valley No, not where you go to the races on Hong Kong Island on Wednesday evening...This Happy Valley *(Huānlè Gǔ; ☎ 694 9168,* W *www.oct-tour.com/park/happy, Shennan Da Lu, Overseas Chinese Town; adult/child Y90/45; open 9.30am-9pm daily)* is more of an amusement than theme park, but there's also a Happywood Studio where you too can be 'a hero in the Anti-Japanese War' (read WWII) and performances at the Happy and Cartoon theatres (seats cost an extra Y15 and Y20 for adults and children respectively).

Happy Valley is just across Shennan Da Lu from Eye of the World. Entrance includes admission to **Maya Beach** *(open Apr–mid-Oct)*, a re-created Caribbean strand with a smoke-belching volcano towering above and artificial waves. If you want to just visit the beach, admission costs Y50/25 for adults/children.

Safari Park 野生动物园

Safari Park *(Yěshēng Dòngwùyuán; ☎ 662 2888, Xili Lake, Nanshan District; admission Y80, Y90 summer & holidays; open 8am-6.30pm)* features some 3000 animals representing 150 species, including lions, tigers, baboons, giraffes and zebras on an area of some 120 hectares. There have been some ghastly reports of animal abuse here in the past; see the boxed text It's a Jungle out There.

Getting There & Around

Bus Nos 101 and 423 from the centre will take you to all four theme parks listed previously. A taxi cab should cost about Y50 one-way.

You can walk between the four theme parks easily enough, but a mini-monorail run by the Shenzhen Happy Line Tour Co (☎ 690 6777) links all four as well as the Shenzhen Bay Hotel and several other sights. The monorail (adult/child Y35/18) operates between 9.30am and 7pm or 8pm weekdays, depending on the season, and 9am to 8.30pm at weekends and holidays.

To get to the Safari Park, you should take bus No 101, 236 or 434. A taxi will cost about Y80.

It's a Jungle out There

A few years ago, the Shenzhen Tourism Corporation tried to boost declining tourist figures at its Safari Park by taking desperate measures – it began staging sadistic animal shows. This was not surprising in a land where animal rights is a concept as foreign as blue eyes and the freedom to say what you *really* think. The audience was waiting with bear-baiting breathlessness.

Spicing up the normally 'bland' show (ie, seeing animals act and respond naturally) were savage fights between two stallions that had been goaded into a frenzy after being placed in front of a mare. The horses gouged chunks out of each other and left the ring bloodied and crippled. A sideline attraction featured Malayan bears being made to walk upright in bright little costumes, encouraged by tugging on the rings ventilating their nostrils.

In 1999 the park said it had cleaned up its act after reports in the foreign press of this barbaric treatment and abuse of animals, and the Safari Animal Protection Station (☎ 559 2885) was set up. They have, in fact, stopped selling live chickens and rabbits for kids to throw into the tiger cages, but reports keep filtering through of drugged animals being kept behind electric fences. You may want to check the situation as it exists before making the trip out to this place.

SHEKOU 野生动物园

The port of Shekou, or 'snake mouth', lies on a small peninsula jutting into the Pearl River estuary about 30km south-west of the city centre. Shekou has no sights as such, but it is an easy and more relaxed way to enter the Shenzhen SEZ and its nightlife, particularly the European-style pubs and bars (see Entertainment later in this chapter), are something of a draw. Bus Nos 204 and 226 connect Shekou with Shenzhen City.

ACTIVITIES

Hong Kong residents with a passion for golf often head to Shenzhen, where there were a dozen courses at last count. In most cases green fees are lower and the golf courses

Taking a leisurely cruise around Peng Chau.

Fish farming at Sam Mun Tsai, New Territories.

Dried pickings at the seafood market.

Fish farming is the main industry in the fishing village of San Mun Tsai, in the New Territories.

Ferry to isolated Mo Tat Wan, Lamma Island.

The tiny but charming island of Peng Chau.

Po Lin (Precious Lotus) Monastery, Lantau Island

Wow! Paragliding at Shek O, Hong Kong Island.

more spacious. Some of the resort hotels, including the one at Xili Lake, have a course, but the most popular and accessible is **Shenzhen Golf Club** (*Shēnzhèn Gāoěrfū Qiúhuì;* ☎ *330 8888, Shennan Xi Lu, Futian District*). The club has a contact office in Hong Kong (☎ *2890 6321*). The **Century Plaza Hotel** (☎ *232 0888, Renmin Nan Lu*) can also arrange golf packages.

There are a number of legitimate massage places in Luohu Commercial City, including **Jian Fu Mei Health & Beauty Centre** (☎ *232 2835*) on the 4th floor and **Nan Chang Massage Health Care** (☎ *232 1703*) on the 2nd floor. Expect to pay between Y60 and Y110 for an hour.

If you want more upmarket surrounds head for the **Sunshine Hotel Sauna** (☎ *223 3888 ext 5456, 1 Jiabin Lu*), where sauna plus massage for 45/90 minutes costs Y298/456.

PLACES TO STAY – BUDGET

There's quite a choice of hotels at the budget end of the spectrum in Shenzhen, where a cheap room means anything around or under Y300. Still, you'll get a much larger and more luxurious room here than you would for the same amount of money in Hong Kong. You could try your luck with the hotel touts at the train station, but they will usually take you to rather less-than-salubrious sleaze joints.

Hotels in Shenzhen discount deeply during the week, slicing as much as 40% off the regular rack rate. This is partially reduced by the 10% or 15% tax/service charge levied by many hotels.

CTS Dahua Hotel (*Zhōngyoǔdàhuá Jiǔdiàn;* ☎ *220 2828, fax 220 2828, 3023 Renmin Nan Lu*) Singles/doubles Y238/310. This rather dark, gloomy hotel is about the cheapest deal you'll find in the centre of town.

Guangxin Hotel (*Guāng Xìn Jiǔdiàn;* ☎ *223 8945, fax 225 5849, 2069 Renmin Nan Lu*) Singles & doubles/triples/quads Y288/385/465. The Guangxin is a very centrally located place popular with overseas Chinese travellers. It's a bit scruffy, but the staff are friendly and helpful.

Petrel Hotel (*Hǎiyàn Dàjiǔdiàn;* ☎ *223 2828, fax 222 1398, Haiyan Building, Jiabin Lu*) Singles/doubles Y280/380. This hotel has 283 rooms spread over 29 floors and a number of outlets, including the charmingly named Petrel Watching Restaurant (see Places to Eat).

Shentie Hotel (*Shēntiě Dàshà;* ☎ *558 4248, fax 556 1049, 1076 Heping Lu*) Singles & doubles Y258-298, triples/quads Y380/448. This hotel has relatively upmarket rooms for the price and a decent location, apart from the railway line it backs on to. For once, request a room in the front, overlooking the busy main road. It will be quieter.

Shenzhen Hotel (*Shēnzhèn Jiǔdiàn;* ☎ *225 1666, fax 222 4922, 3085 Shennan Dong Lu*) Standard/deluxe rooms Y328/348, triples Y378. This place isn't much to look at from the outside, but has a newly renovated interior. And at the corner of Shennan Dong Lu and Jianshe Lu, it's about as central as you're going to find.

Wah Chung International Hotel (*Huázhōng Guójì Jiǔdiàn;* ☎ *223 8060, fax 222 1439, 3041 Shennan Dong Lu*) Singles/doubles/triples Y300/380/480. This hotel has a central location and 170 spacious rooms. It had been feeling a bit tired, but was under extensive renovation the last time we visited.

Yat Wah Hotel (*Rìhuá Bīnguǎn;* ☎ *558 8530, fax 558 8535, 4006 Shennan Dong Lu*) Singles & doubles/triples/quads Y150/250/280. The Yat Wah, just to the west of the railway tracks, is in a low-rise building next to a colourful kindergarten playground. The outside looks slightly tattered, but the rooms are large, bright and airy.

PLACES TO STAY – MID-RANGE

In Shenzhen, a mid-range room should cost anywhere between Y400 and Y700.

Far East Grand Hotel (*Yuǎndōng Dà Jiǔdiàn;* ☎ *220 5369, fax 220 0239, 2097 Shennan Dong Lu*) Singles Y478, doubles Y498-588. This is yet another mid-range option along the Shennan Dong Lu hotel row.

Gold Hotel (*Fùlìhuá Dà Jiǔdiàn;* ☎ *218 0288, fax 217 7436, 2098 Shennan Dong Lu*) Singles Y480-680, doubles Y680-850, suites from Y1180. This is quite a good deal for what is actually a top-end hotel. Conveniently located to a lot of nightlife spots as well.

Guangdong Hotel *(Yuèhǎi Jiǔdiàn;* ☎ *222 8339, fax 223 4560, 3033 Shennan Dong Lu)* Doubles Y660-869, suites from Y1078. This 200-room hotel in a sparkling glass-and-steel tower has won awards for its service. It is popular with Japanese business travellers for whom there is a floor of traditional Japanese-style rooms.

South China International Hotel *(Zhōngnánguójì Dà Jiǔdiàn;* ☎ *225 6728, fax 225 6936, Shennan Dong Lu)* Singles Y580-630, doubles Y630-690. This is a very flash place, with Hong Kong-style service.

Shenzhen Airlines Hotel *(Hángkōng Dà Jiǔdiàn;* ☎ *223 7999, fax 223 7866, 3027 Shennan Dong Lu)* Singles/doubles Y480/638. This is an attractive, newly renovated hotel with friendly staff – so friendly, in fact, that you can rent a room by the half-day (Y200/300).

PLACES TO STAY – TOP-END

You can get a better deal at most of the top-end hotels in Shenzhen by booking through CTS in Hong Kong. During the week, however, rates are so deeply discounted that you can probably do just as well on your own.

Century Plaza Hotel *(Xīndū Jiǔdiàn;* ☎ *232 0888, fax 233 4060,* W *www.szcentury plaza.com, Renmin Nan Lu)* Rooms Y1320-1430, suites from Y1980. This is an excellent, extremely well-run hotel with fabulous bars and restaurants, including the Laurel (see Places to Eat later in this chapter).

Forum Hotel *(Fùlín Dà Jiǔdiàn;* ☎ *558 6333, fax 556 1700, 1085 Heping Lu)* Rooms from Y1200. This 541-room palace is less glitzy than most equivalent top-end hotels in Shenzhen and has a lovely Chinese art gallery.

Oriental Regent Hotel *(Jīngdū Jiǔdiàn;* ☎ *224 7000, fax 224 7290,* W *www.jindow .com, Financial Centre Building, Shennan Zhong Lu)* Rooms Y880-1280, suites from Y1380. This 400-room property is the latest five-star one to land in the SEZ. It's a wee

bit off the track, but perhaps it is all the more attractive for that.

Shangri-La Hotel *(Xiānggé Lǐlā Dà Jiǔdiàn;* ☎ *233 0888, fax 233 9878,* W *www .shangri-la.com, Jianshe Lu)* Rooms Y1750-2000, suites from Y3150. Despite all the competition this place still keeps its prices up there in the stars. And it can: it faces the train station, is topped by the fabulous Tiara revolving restaurant (see Places to Eat), and service is excellent.

Shenzhen Bay Hotel *(Shēnzhèn Wān Dà Jiǔdiàn;* ☎ *660 0111, fax 660 0139, Shennan Da Lu)* Rooms Y860-1030, suites from 1300. This 308-room hotel is a bit of a ways out and wedged between the Window of the World and the China Folk Culture Villages theme parks. Overlooking Shenzhen Bay on a large plot of land, it offers all the recreational amenities you'd want or need, including one of the largest pools in China. Bus No 101 or 423 will drop you off outside.

Shenzhen Landmark Hotel *(Shēnzhèn Fùyuàn Jiǔdiàn;* ☎ *217 2288, fax 229 0473,* W *www.szlandmark.com, 3018 Nanhu Lu)* Rooms Y1540-2008, suites from Y2420. This hotel is one of Shenzhen's premier 'face' properties and has especially well-trained English-speaking staff. Memorable outlets too.

Sunshine Hotel *(Yáng Guāng Jiǔdiàn;* ☎ *223 3888, fax 222 6719, 1 Jiabin Lu)* Rooms from Y1600-1800, suites from Y2600. This good but over-priced five star is very popular with Japanese travellers.

PLACES TO STAY – RESORT HOTELS

As unlikely as it may sound, given that Thailand and the Philippines are a hop, skip and/or a jump away from southern China, you may be interested in staying at one of Shenzhen's numerous resort hotels. Generally of interest to locals and Hong Kong Chinese yearning to breathe freely in the wide-open spaces, the resorts offer everything from swimming pools and golf courses to horseback riding and boating. The huge dim sum restaurants become nightclubs in the evening, with Las Vegas-style floor shows.

Expect to pay about Y400 for a double at most resort hotels in Shenzhen. As with the hotels, resorts offer discounts of at least 20% during the week.

The easiest way to reach the resort hotels is to catch one of the resort-operated minibuses that leave from the local bus station just north of the Luohu Commercial City shopping centre, but they are also served by local buses and minibuses.

Honey Lake Resort *(Xiāngmì Hú Dùjià Cūn;* ☎ *370 8988, fax 370 5045, Shennan Xi Lu)* Rooms from Y300, weekend packages from Y560. This is the closest resort to town, situated next to a little lake in the Futian district of West Shenzhen and just opposite the Shenzhen Golf Course. The Honey Lake China Amusement Park and Honey Lake Water Park are also here. Take bus No 113, 204 or 423.

Shiyan Lake Resort *(Shíyán Dùjià Cūn;* ☎ *776 0341, 776 0106, Shiyan Lake, Bao'an District)* Rooms from Y380. This 380-villa resort can be found on the shores of Shiyan Lake, 40km to the north-west of Shenzhen. It is famous for its Yulu hot springs, a 1000-year-old natural wonder renowned for its therapeutic qualities. Take bus No 532.

Xiaomeisha Beach Resort *(Xiǎoméishā Dà Jiǔdiàn;* ☎ *506 0000, fax 506 1003, Xiaomeisha, Yantian District)* Rooms from Y380. This place is about 30km to the east of Shenzhen on the coast, and despite being just down the road from China's nuclear power station at Daya Bay, is a popular resort packed with aquatic amusements, beach activities and a 4m-high bungee jump. Shenzen Sea World (see East Shenzhen earlier in this chapter) is here too. Take bus No 103 or 430.

Xili Lake Resort *(Xīlì Hú Dùjià Cūn,* ☎ *662 6888, fax 666 0521, Xili Lake, Nanshan District)* Rooms from Y270 Mon-Fri, Y330 Sat & Sun. This 365-room resort is on the shores of antler-shaped Xili Lake. Camping facilities can be found at the resort. Take bus No 101, 226 or 442.

PLACES TO EAT

Though it's going the way of the dodo in Hong Kong, eating at *dai pai dong* (food stalls) is still very common in Shenzhen. There are some excellent ones serving dishes cooked in clay pots just up from the train station on the west side of Jianshe Lu and to the north-west on Heping Lu.

Dim sum is available for breakfast or lunch in all but the scruffiest hotels. Usually dim sum restaurants are on the 2nd or 3rd floor, never the lobby. Prices are considerably lower than those in Hong Kong.

You'll find a slew of attractive, reasonably priced restaurants behind Book City and the Shenzhen Stock Exchange on Shennan Lu. Another good place for restaurants is Leyuan Lu, which runs north of Shennan Dong Lu.

Fast-food places – **McDonald's**, **Pizza Hut**, **KFC** and the like – litter Shenzhen (literally). If you do want fast food, try **Fairwood** *(Dà Kuàihuó; 1st floor, Luohu Commercial City)*, which is part of a Hong Kong chain.

There's a lively **covered wet market** *(Cnr Chunfeng Lu & Renmin Nan Lu)* opposite the Century Plaza. **Park 'N' Shop** supermarket has branches in Shenzhen City *(3012 Chunfeng Lu)*, which is open from 8.30am to 11pm daily, and in Shekou *(Crystal Garden Centre, 8 Taizi Lu)*.

Chao Zhou Court *(☎ 217 2288 ext 588, 3rd floor, Shenzhen Landmark Hotel, 3018 Nanhu Lu)* Meals about Y150. This posh restaurant is an excellent choice for Chiu Chow food, a cuisine not as common as you'd think in this part of Guangdong Province. Try the shark's fin with rice.

Charwphraya Thai Restaurant *(Zhāopàyē Tàiguó Cānguǎn;* ☎ *225 9988, 45 Dongmen Nan Lu)* Dishes from Y30. Don't expect Bangkok-standard cuisine, but if you need a fix of *tom yom gung* or *pad thai* noodles, the Charwphraya can oblige.

Friday Café *(Xīngqīwǔ Xī Cāntīng;* ☎ *246 0757, Ground floor, Shunhing Square, Jiefang Lu)* Dishes from Y25. This attractive cafe in one of the most striking modern buildings in Shenzhen attracts a lot of foreign businesspeople at lunch time.

Genroku Sushi *(Yuánlù Huízhuǎn Shòusī;* ☎ *246 2117, Lower ground floor, Shunhing Square, Shennan Zhong Lu)* Sushi

Y8, dishes Y28-58, set meals Y80-158. This is one of eight Shenzhen branches of a popular Hong Kong sushi fast-food chain. Sushi comes on a conveyor belt, of course.

Henry J Bean's Bar & Grill (*Hēnglì Jiŭbā;* ☎ 233 0888 ext 8270, 2nd floor, Shangri-La Hotel, Jianshe Lu) Meals about Y150. This place does a fine spread of American favourites: burgers, fries, ribs, etc.

ITC Revolving Restaurant (*Shēnzhèn Guómào Xuánzhuàn Cāntīng;* ☎ 225 1464, 49th floor, International Trade Centre, Cnr Renmin Nan Lu & Jiabin Lu) Dishes about Y100. No longer the highest restaurant in China, but still up there with the stars. Rather expensive, but worth it for the views.

Jade Garden (☎ 232 0888 ext 328, Ground floor, Century Plaza Hotel, Renmin Nan Lu) Lunch/dinner buffet Y88/128 adults, Y68/98 children. This is a popular spot for Hong Kong Chinese visiting Shenzhen with their families.

Laurel Restaurant (*Dānguìxuān;* ☎ 232 3666, Shop 5010, Luohu Commercial City; ☎ 232 3888, 2nd floor, Century Plaza Hotel, Renmin Nan Lu) Dim sum Y16-18, dishes from Y48. This is one of the finest Chinese restaurants in town, and you'll realise that as you wait in the queue. Dim sum is served from 7am daily.

Luohu Restaurant (*Luóhú Dà Jiŭjiā;* ☎ 225 2827, 223 9325, Jianshe Lu) Meals about Y100. Opposite the Century Plaza Hotel, this is one of the most popular restaurants in the city centre. At night it's noticeable a long way off for its brightly lit Chinese temple-style roof.

Muslim Hotel Restaurant (*Mùsīlín Bīnguǎn Yǔ Cānguǎn;* ☎ 222 8207, Ground floor, Muslim Hotel, 2013 Wenjin Nan Lu) If you fancy trying *huí* (Chinese Muslim) food (eg, various beef and mutton dishes, onion cakes) head for this hotel done up like a mock mosque. What's more, it's all halal.

Panxi Restaurant (*Bànxī Jiŭjiā;* ☎ 233 4589, 1038 Jianshe Lu) Dishes Y28-58. This restaurant, next to the Shangri-La Hotel, is one of Shenzhen's most popular, reasonably priced Chinese restaurants.

Petrel Watching Restaurant (*Hǎiyàn Guānguāng Dà Jiŭlóu;* ☎ 222 2823, 29th floor, Petrel Hotel, Haiyan Building, Jiabin Lu) Meals about Y100, dim sum Y5-9. This charmingly named restaurant may not be the highest in Shenzhen, but the views are just fine. This is a popular spot with locals.

Piazza Café (*Guǎngchǎng Xī Cāntīng;* ☎ 217 2288, 1st floor, Shenzhen Landmark Hotel, 3018 Nanhu Lu) Lunch/dinner buffet Y113/188. This is more than a hotel coffee shop, with nice decor and good, reasonably priced food. Brunch on Sunday (11.30am to 2.30pm) features a live band.

Shang Palace (☎ 233 0888 ext 8230, 2nd floor, Shangri-La Hotel, Jianshe Lu) Meals about Y250, lunch/dinner buffet Y113/188. This restaurant cooks up the very best in Cantonese cuisine.

Tiara Revolving Restaurant (☎ 233 0888, ext 8310, 31st floor, Shangri-La Hotel, Jianshe Lu) Lunch/dinner buffet Y168/238. For more sedate entertainment, one of the best venues is this revolving restaurant on the top of the Shangri-La Hotel. It serves meals and afternoon tea.

Tiecheng Restaurant (*Tiěchéng Shíjiē;* ☎ 558 4248, 1080 Heping Lu) Dishes from Y20. This is one of the best places if you are sticking to a budget yet want to sample some good food. What's more, the staff are helpful (although not many of them speak English) and prices are very low.

ENTERTAINMENT

While it's generally 'early to bed and early to rise' in Zhuhai, Shenzhen after dark is a happening SEZ, and you'll find any number of entertainment options. Don't go looking for high culture, though; this is definitely clubbing and pubbing territory.

Shenzhen City has the preponderance of clubs and mainstream discos while Shekou, the port to the south-east, is littered with Western-style bars. You'll find examples in both areas, however.

Serious clubbers should look at the schedules in *HK Magazine* and *bc Magazine*, which advertise upcoming events in Shenzhen.

Do remember that if you plan to make a night of it, you'll have to do just that. The border with Hong Kong closes at 11.30pm and doesn't reopen until 6.30am. Don't worry, though; you'll have plenty of company on that first KCR train back to Hung Hom.

Shenzhen City

Most of the top-end hotels have international style bars and even clubs. You'll find quite a few nightlife venues along Chunfeng Lu. Most clubs charge a cover of Y30 to Y80.

1897 Club (☎ 225 2888, Chunfeng Lu) This is a popular watering hole for businessmen looking for company.

Better Ole (☎ 222 6666, Xiangxi Lu) This enormous club on two floors has an Egyptian theme – pharaohs and sphinxes galore – with a disco floor, a nightclub floor and a karaoke room. Where the name comes from is anyone's guess.

Feelings Club (☎ 239 111, 3007 Chunfeng Lu) Competition for Better Ole, Feelings is a self-styled 'entertainment plaza' spread over three floors.

Henry J Bean's Bar & Grill (☎ 233 0888 ext 8270, 2nd floor, Shangri-La Hotel, Jianshe Lu) This hotel restaurant is a low-key sort of place, though it periodically has live music.

JJ Disco (☎ 223 3888, ext 3008, 1st floor, B block, Sunshine Hotel, 1 Jiabin Lu) This club is a perennial favourite of the expat and local mature crowd.

Jungle Jungle (☎ 518 3388, 2002 Renmin Nan Lu) More of a cafe/bar than a club, Jungle Jungle, with its vines and ferocious animal heads, is where to go if you've eschewed the Safari Park.

New York, New York (☎ 228 5888, Top floor, Nanguo Cinema Building, 2063 Nanhu Lu) This massive and quite cheesy Vegas-style disco opposite the International Trade Centre is popular with Hong Kong young bloods.

Polka No 1 Club (☎ 223 3911, 1st floor, Furong Hotel, Dongmen Nan Lu) Less flashy, more – can we say? – underground than other clubs in Shenzhen.

Power 2 Disco (☎ 220 9982, Jiabin Lu) This place, popular with locals, pulsates until dawn.

Wall Street Disco (Huáěrjiē Dísīkē; ☎ 589 0388, Xihu Building, 16 Bao'an Nan Lu) The cavernous Wall Street north-west of the centre attracts a mixed clientele.

Shekou

Shekou harbours a large number of expatriates lured to the mainland by cheaper rents and the easy commute to Hong Kong. Consequently a variety of popular watering holes with names like Half Tooth and Lost Angel might make the trip out to the port worthwhile. Be advised that many of them are girlie bars, though.

The vast majority of the pubs and bars line Taizi Lu, north of the ferry pier, and Gongye Diyi Lu, which runs to the east of Taizi Lu down to the Nanhai Hotel. You can reach Shekou from the city centre on bus No 204, which goes to the ferry pier, and the No 226, which stops at Times Plaza, Shekou's landmark skyscraper. Minibus No 49 or 439, which leave from the Shenzhen train station, also serve Shekou.

Cheers (☎ 667 5922, Shop 125, Crystal Garden, 8 Taizi Lu) Cosy with a tropical theme and disco, this friendly place burns the midnight oil till 7am.

Goodfellas Bar (☎ 669 0382, Shop 101-103, Crystal Garden, 8 Taizi Lu) This is one of the best clubs in Shekou, with an eclectic crowd and rock and roll played full blast.

Firkin Tavern (☎ 669 6375, Yinzhao Building, 6 Taizi Lu) This Irish pub's happy hour (5pm to 8pm) draws in the crowds parched for Guinness and Boddington.

Joe Bananas (☎ 668 0690, Gongye Diyi Lu) Another Chinese imitation, Joe Bananas has no connection with the bar in Hong Kong's Wan Chai district. It's a disco and karaoke club rolled into one.

Sailor Bar (☎ 884 8688, Shop D7, Taizi Square) This tiny place, once the local of foreign sailors docking in Shekou, is in a little square north of the main strip.

SHOPPING

Like Mrs Ho (see the boxed text Tally, Ho Tai Tai!), many people make the trip up from Hong Kong to shop – everything else is peripheral.

SHENZHEN

Your first port of call should be Luohu Commercial City, which greets you as you emerge from customs and immigration (see the Shenzhen City section earlier in this chapter). Here there are corridors of stalls selling ceramics, curios for souvenir and antique hunters, knockoff handbags and clothing.

Popular for tailored suits and skirts, electronic goods, custom-made drapes and cheap ready-to-wear is the area around the **Dongmen Market** on Hu Bei Lu, just off Dongmen Lu. Be warned that this is pickpocket territory so keep your valuables safe.

Nose around the outdoor market itself or head for one of the multistorey shopping malls: the **Mong Kok Commercial Centre** *(2031 Dongmen Lu)*, or the **Kowloon City Plaza**, a few steps to the south. The **Moi department store** *(☎ 220 000, 2047 Dongmen Lu)* is good for cosmetics and well-made fakes. There are a number of cut-price **electronics shops** along Nanji Lu and Huaqiang Lu, but *caveat emptor*.

If you're looking for the real thing at international prices, head for **Shunhing Square** on Shennan Zhong Lu. This towering building is a great piece of architecture and also the focus of top-notch shopping, hosting a medley of such famous brand names as Hugo Boss, Bally, D'Urban, Max-Mara and Escada.

GETTING THERE & AWAY
Air
Shenzhen's Huangtian Airport (hotline ☎ 777 6789, flight information ☎ 589 1020) is now one of the busiest in China. There are flights to most major domestic destinations as well as international ones such as Bangkok, Singapore and Jakarta. It is often significantly cheaper to fly from Guangzhou, however.

Air tickets can be purchased from CTS and various travel agents in top-end hotels; see Travel Agencies under Information earlier in this chapter. If you don't mind trekking out there, CNAC (☎ 336 5288),

---

Tally, Ho Tai Tai!

Mrs Ho is a tai tai. *Taìtai*, literally, 'great great', simply means 'Mrs', and every married Chinese woman is a tai tai. But tai tai in Hong Kong has a further meaning, a somewhat different connotation. Tai tais are the well-to-do, leisured wives of successful businessmen. They lunch, take tea in the lobby of Hong Kong's Peninsula Hotel, gossip with their friends (mostly via mobile phone) and play mahjong. And they shop, increasingly in Shenzhen, for tai tais – however wealthy – are *always* in search of a bargain.

Mrs Ho and I went to Shenzhen together. Well, not exactly…The incomparable *HK Magazine* (see Listings under Entertainment in the Hong Kong Facts for the Visitor chapter) had recently run a cover story about a tai tai who would board the KCR for Lo Wu in the morning at least once a week, spend the day shopping, nibbling and being pampered and return at the end of the day thoroughly relaxed, satiated and clothed – at half the price it would have cost her in Hong Kong.

Mrs Ho 'took' me shopping at Luohu Commercial City, then for lunch at the Laurel (well, I ate at the one in the Century Plaza Hotel – Mrs Ho prefers the one in the mall, where she has contacts and never has to wait for a table) and to her favourite (legitimate – Mrs Ho is a married women with children, after all) massage parlour for an hour's worth of foot rubbing after pounding the pavements of the SEZ all day. I did stop short of following her into the manicurist's where, 'feeling particularly whimsical' one day, she had tiny flowers, butterflies, birds and Chinese characters painted on each fingernail.

Some people in Hong Kong – foreigners and Chinese alike – are snide about tai tais, dismissing them as lazy, self-indulgent creatures whose main concern is the quality of the oolong and the price of the knock-off Gucci handbag. But I – and now you – know differently. Tai tais have got something to teach us all.

which handles all Chinese airlines, is in the Shanghai Hotel west of the centre on Shennan Xi Lu. Take bus No 3, 201 or 204.

If you've come to Shenzhen expressly to fly on to other destinations in China, you won't pay much less on flights to Beijing, Shanghai or Guilin than you would directly from Hong Kong. Flights to Chengdu, Kunming and Xian, however, can be between 20% and 30% cheaper.

Departure Tax Departure tax is Y50 for domestic flights and Y100 for international flights. Ticketing agents will often try to sell you flight insurance which is *not* compulsory, no matter what they say. Just refuse.

Bus
You cannot reach Shenzhen from Hong Kong or Kowloon proper by bus, though there are buses to Shenzhen airport. Buses also link Hong Kong International Airport at Chek Lap Kok with major hotels in Shenzhen City. See China under Land in the Hong Kong Getting There & Away chapter.

Long-distance buses leave from the bus station (☎ 233 7378) beneath the Luohu Commercial City shopping centre. Destinations include Guangzhou (Y60), Zhongshan (Y70), Zhuhai (Y90) and Shantou (Y150), among many more.

Train
The KCR offers the fastest and most convenient transport to Shenzhen from Hong Kong. Trains to the border crossing at Lo Wu depart from Hung Hom station in Tsim Sha Tsui every three to 10 minutes throughout the day. For more information see Train in the Land section of the Hong Kong Getting There & Away chapter and Train under Public Transport in the Hong Kong Getting Around chapter.

There are frequent local trains from Shenzhen train station (☎ 232 6560) to Guangzhou, and the journey takes 2½ hours. Ticket prices are Y45 for a hard (ie, 2nd-class) seat and Y65 for a soft (1st-class) one. There is also an express service that takes 1½ hours and costs Y70. Queues can be appalling at the train station at weekend and on

holidays. If you're spending the night before moving on, try to book a ticket through your hotel or a travel agency.

Car & Motorcycle
It is possible to drive across the Hong Kong–Shenzhen border, but it makes little sense to do so given the convenience of public transport. There is also a long queue of vehicles at the border checkpoints.

The original border crossing is at Man Kam To (Wenjindu on the mainland side) just east of Lo Wu. There's another crossing to the west at Lok Ma Chau.

Boat
Hong Kong Ferries link Shenzhen airport and the port of Shekou with Central on Hong Kong Island and Tsim Sha Tsui in Kowloon. For schedules and fares, see the China section under Sea in the Hong Kong Getting There & Away chapter.

Macau There is a daily ferry connecting the port of Shekou with Macau. The boat leaves Shekou at 11.15am and arrives at 12.45pm. The fare is Y95.

Zhuhai Ferries also operate between Shekou and Zhuhai and the journey takes about one hour. There are departures every 15 to 30 minutes from 7.30am to 6.30pm. The fare is Y55 to Y65.

GETTING AROUND
To/From the Airport
Shenzhen's Huangtian Airport is 35km south-west of Shenzhen City. The best way to reach it from Hong Kong is to take the ferry to Fuyong ferry terminal, where a free shuttle bus will transfer you to the airport. See the China section under Sea in the Hong Kong Getting There & Away chapter for details.

Airport shuttle buses leave from outside the Hualian Hotel to the east of Lizhi Park on Shennan Zhong Lu. Tickets cost Y20 and the trip takes about 40 minutes. Bus No 330 (Y20) makes the run to the airport between 6am and 7pm daily as do minibus Nos 501 and 507.

Getting to Shenzhen airport by direct bus from Hong Kong is also possible. See Bus in the Land section of the Hong Kong Getting There & Away chapter.

Bus & Minibus

Government-run city buses and local minibuses depart from the station north-east of Luohu Commercial City.

Shenzhen's buses are not as crowded as those elsewhere in China, but the destinations are written only in Chinese. Fares range from Y1 to Y4 (or Y2 to Y12 for air-conditioned ones), depending on the destination. If you think you're going to be doing a lot of travel by bus in Shenzhen, IC travel cards are available at kiosks throughout the city in denominations from Y35 to Y300.

Minibuses are faster, privately run and cheap (Y2 to Y5), but if you can't read the destination in Chinese, you will need help.

Taxi

Taxis are abundant and metered in Shenzhen. The flag fall is Y12.50 for the first 3km and Y0.60 for every additional 250m. It costs 30% extra to catch a cab between 11pm and 6am and if the distance exceeds 30km.

Taxi drivers will be more than happy to take you long distances. Sample fares are Y280 to Y320 to Guangzhou, Y550 to Zhongshan and Y700 to Zhuhai, which will take about four hours. You should be able to rent a taxi for the day for about Y300.

ORGANISED TOURS

You could see Shenzhen quite comfortably by taking a series of local buses, but you have to be able to read the destination panels in front.

Shenzhen Pengyun International Travel Agency (☎ 243 5057, 239 3888) Fare Y10. Easier than catching a local bus is to catch one of the purple-coloured double-decker buses. They run from the local bus station north-east of Luohu Commercial City and make a continuous loop throughout the day around Shenzhen City and the theme parks to the west.

Facts about Macau

Lying only 65km west of Hong Kong but predating that territory's colonisation by almost 300 years, Macau was the first European enclave in Asia. When China resumed sovereignty over what is now called the Special Administrative Region of Macau in 1999, it was by far the oldest.

Macau is a fascinating mix of cultures – a fusion of Mediterranean and Asian architecture, food, lifestyles and temperaments. It is a city of cobbled back streets, baroque churches, ancient stone fortresses and exotic street names etched on *azulejos*, the distinctive Portuguese blue enamel tiles. There are a heap of interesting (and important) Chinese temples and restored colonial villas, and the cemeteries of Macau are the final resting places of many European and American missionaries, painters, soldiers and sailors who died at what was once called 'Macao Roads'. You will also find many good-value hotels, excellent restaurants and lively casinos here.

Most travellers who visit Macau spend just a few hours there on a whistle-stop tour, and many who travel to Hong Kong don't bother going to Macau at all. That's a pity, because it's one of those 'treasure chest' sort of places where something new can be found at every step and on every visit.

Macau was (and remains) a popular destination for Hong Kong residents. In general, Hong Kong Chinese go to gamble at the casinos while foreigners make the trip to enjoy a little bit of the Mediterranean on the South China Sea.

Compared to how it was 10 years ago, Macau is hard to recognise today. Hong Kong Chinese had always looked down upon Macau as a sleepy, dirty, impoverished backwater, with nothing to recommend it except legalised gambling and cheap dim sum. It is now so tidy that it is ranked second only to Singapore as the cleanest city in Asia. Before the Portuguese colonial government departed in 1999, it had spent some M$70 million on renovating and refurbishing civil buildings, churches, gardens and public squares; the place is now a colourful palette of pastels and ordered greenery. There are several new museums, two of which are world-class, a glittering multilevel cultural centre and a nightlife strip built on reclaimed land. The increase in the number of Portuguese and Macanese restaurants has been nothing short of phenomenal, particularly on the two islands.

Getting to Macau from Hong Kong has never been difficult, and with high-speed ferries now running between the two territories virtually every half-hour it has become even easier. Go to Macau and stay a night or two (or even longer), and you'll discover something pretty or old or curious or tasty around every corner.

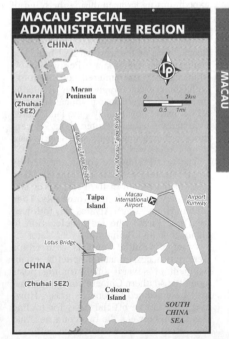

HISTORY
Early Settlement

Archaeological finds from digs around Hác Sá Bay on Coloane Island suggest that Macau has been inhabited since Neolithic times.

Like Hong Kong before the British came, Macau before the arrival of the Portuguese was home to a relatively small number of inhabitants, mainly Cantonese-speaking farmers and Fujian fisherfolk. From the early 16th century, Macau's history became intertwined with that of Portugal and its other overseas territories and colonies.

Arrival of the Portuguese

On voyages to India in the 15th century, Portuguese mariners and explorers such as Vasco da Gama (1460–1524) learned of a curious, light-skinned people known as the Chin, whose huge ships had also called on Indian ports. We now know that these were reports of the enormous Chinese maritime expeditions undertaken during the reign of the second Ming emperor, Yong Le, between 1405 and 1433.

In 1510–11 the Portuguese routed Arab fleets at Goa on the west coast of India and Malacca on the Malay Peninsula. At Malacca they encountered several junks with Chinese captains and crews. Realising that the Chins were not a mythical people at all but natives of 'Cathay', the land Marco Polo had visited and written about 2½ centuries earlier, a small party sailed northward to open trade with the Chinese.

The first Portuguese contingent, led by Jorge Álvares, set foot on Chinese soil in 1513 at the mouth of the Pearl River at a place they called Tamaõ (probably Tuen Mun in Hong Kong). Álvares was followed by Tomé Pires, who led a delegation to Guangzhou and Beijing four years later.

Portugal's initial contacts with China were not successful and, despite the establishment of several small trading posts along the southern Chinese coast, a permanent base seemed beyond its grasp. However, in 1553 an official basis for trading was set up between the two countries, and the Portuguese were allowed to settle on Shangchuan (or Sheungcheun), a small island about 80km south-west of the mouth of the Pearl River. The exposed anchorage at Shangchuan forced the Portuguese traders to abandon the island that same year, and they moved to Lampacau, an island closer to the Pearl River estuary, where they were able to purchase silks for re-sale to Japan.

To the north-east of Lampacau was a small peninsula where the Portuguese had frequently dropped anchor. Known variously as Amagau, Amacau, Amaquoa, Aomen and Macau (see the boxed text What's in a Name?), the peninsula had two natural harbours – an inner one on the Qianshan waterway facing the mainland and an outer one in a bay on the Pearl River – and two sheltered islands to the south. In 1557 officials at Guangzhou allowed the Portuguese to build temporary shelters on the peninsula in exchange for customs dues and

What's in a Name?

The name 'Macau' is derived from A-Ma Gau, or the 'bay of A-Ma', a reference to the goddess A-Ma, better known as Tin Hau. At the south-western tip of Macau peninsula, and facing the Inner Harbour, stands the A-Ma Temple, which dates back to the early 16th century. Many people believe that when the Portuguese first arrived and asked the name of the place, 'A-Ma Gau' was what they were told.

According to legend, A-Ma, a poor girl looking for a passage to Guangzhou, was turned away by wealthy junk owners. Instead, a poor fisherman took her on board. A storm blew up and wrecked all the junks but not the fishing boat. When it returned to the Inner Harbour, A-Ma walked to the top of nearby Barra Hill and, in a glowing aura of light, ascended to heaven. The fisherman built a temple on the spot where they had landed (which was, in fact, on the water's edge until land reclamation early in the last century pushed it farther inland).

In modern Cantonese, 'Macau' is Ou Mun (Aomen in Mandarin), meaning 'gateway of the bay'.

rent, as well as an agreement to rid the area of the pirates endemic at the time.

A Trading Powerhouse

Macau grew rapidly as a trading centre, largely because Chinese merchants wanted to trade with foreign countries but were forbidden to leave the country by imperial decree. The most lucrative trade route for the Portuguese was the long circuit from Goa on the west coast of India to Japan and back, with Macau the essential link between the two.

Acting as agents for Chinese merchants, Portuguese traders took Chinese goods such as porcelain and silks to the west coast of India and exchanged them for cotton and textiles. The cloth was then taken to Malacca to trade for spices and sandalwood. The Portuguese would then carry on to Nagasaki in Japan, where the cargo from Malacca was exchanged for Japanese silver, swords, lacquerware and fans that would be traded in Macau for more Chinese goods.

In the late 16th century the Portuguese were the carriers of all large-scale international commerce between China and Japan, via Macau. But the territory was not just gaining in economic strength. Such was Macau's growing status and importance that when the Holy See established the bishopric of Macau in 1576, it included both China and Japan. By 1586, Macau was large and important enough for the crown to confer upon it the status of a city: *Cidade de Nome de Deus*, or 'City of the Name of God'.

The Golden Years

By the beginning of the 17th century Macau supported several thousand permanent residents, including about 900 Portuguese. The rest were Christian converts from Malacca and Japan and a large number of slaves from Portuguese outposts in Africa, India and the Malay Peninsula. Large numbers of Chinese had moved into Macau and worked there as traders, craftspeople, hawkers, labourers and coolies.

Trade was the most important activity in the new town, which was concentrated on the lower half of the peninsula between the

Praia Grande and the Inner Harbour. At the same time, Macau had become a centre of Christianity in Asia. Priests and missionaries accompanied Portuguese ships, although the interests of traders and missionaries frequently conflicted.

Among the earliest missionaries was Francis Xavier (later canonised) of the Jesuit order, who spent two years (1549–51) in Japan attempting to convert the local population before turning his attention to China. He was stalled by the Portuguese, who feared the consequences of his meddling in Chinese affairs, but made it as far as Shangchuan, where he caught a fever and died in December 1552. Subsequently it was Jesuit missionaries, not traders, who were able to penetrate China beyond Macau and Guangzhou.

The Portuguese who stayed in Macau, along with their Macanese descendants, created a home away from home. Their luxurious villas overlooking the Praia Grande and splendid baroque churches were paid for with the wealth generated by their monopoly on trade with China and Japan. These buildings included the Jesuit Church of Madre de Deus (or São Paulo, built in 1602), hailed as the greatest monument to Christianity in Asia.

Portuguese Decline

Portugal's decline as an imperial power came as quickly as its rise. In 1580 Spanish armies occupied Portugal and for more than 60 years three Spanish kings were to rule over the country – and Macau. In the early years of the 17th century the Dutch, embroiled in the Thirty Years' War with Spain, moved to seize the rich enclaves of Macau, Nagasaki and Malacca. In June 1622 some 13 Dutch warships carrying 1300 men attacked Macau but retreated when a shell fired by a Jesuit priest from one of the cannons on Monte Fort hit a stock of gunpowder and blew the Hollanders out of the water. Many of the enclave's forts were built or strengthened after this attack.

The Japanese soon became suspicious of Portuguese and Spanish intentions. Japan began closing its doors to foreign trade and locked them tight in 1639. Two years later, Dutch harassment of Portuguese commerce and trading interests ended with the capture of Malacca. The Portuguese could no longer provide the Chinese with the Japanese silver needed for an exchange of silk and porcelain, or with spices from the Malay Peninsula, since the spice trade was now in the hands of the Dutch.

A Change of Status

The overthrow of the moribund Ming dynasty in 1644 saw a flood of refugees unleashed on Macau. Henceforth the enclave would have to deal with the victorious Manchus. In 1684 the most corrupt of them, the *hoppo* (*hoi poi* in Cantonese), the customs superintendent who held the monopoly on trade with foreigners, set up an office in the Inner Harbour.

At the same time religious infighting weakened the status of Macau as a Christian centre. In what became known as the Rites Controversy, the Jesuits maintained that central parts of Chinese belief – ancestor worship and Confucianism, for example – were not idolatrous or incompatible with the Christian faith. The Dominicans and Franciscans, equally well represented in Macau and elsewhere in Asia, disagreed. It took an edict by Pope Clement XI condemning the rites in 1715 to settle the matter. That stopped further missionary expansion into China.

In the mid-18th century Chinese authorities created the *co hong,* a mercantile monopoly based in Guangzhou for dealing with foreign trade. Numerous restrictions were placed on Western traders, including limitations on the amount of time they could reside in Guangzhou (November to May). Macau in effect became an outpost for all European traders in China, a position it held until the British took possession of Hong Kong in 1841. When other Chinese ports were opened to foreign trade, most non-Portuguese Westerners left Macau. One foreigner who did remain behind was the Irish-born painter George Chinnery, who continued working in Macau until his death in 1852 (see the boxed text George Chinnery: Chronicler of Macau, in the Macau Peninsula chapter).

Until the mid-19th century the history of Macau was a long series of incidents involving the Portuguese, Chinese and British as the Portuguese attempted to maintain a hold on the territory. But as time progressed and the troublesome British wrestled concession after concession out of China, the Portuguese grew bolder.

The Treaty of Nanking (1842) had ceded the island of Hong Kong in perpetuity to the British; the Treaty of Tientsin (1860) gave them Kowloon on the same terms. The Portuguese felt they too should take advantage of China's weakness and push for sovereignty over the territory they had occupied for three centuries. Negotiation began in 1862, although it was not until 1887 that a treaty was signed in which China effectively recognised Portuguese sovereignty over Macau in perpetuity.

With the advent of the steamship and then other motorised vessels, there were fewer transhipments from Chinese ports through Macau and more direct transactions between those ports and Hong Kong. Macau's economy was greatly assisted by the legalisation of gambling, which came into effect during the administration of Governor Isidoro Francisco Guimarães (1851–63), but by the close of the 19th century the ascent of the British colony and the decline of the Portuguese territory had become irreversible.

Macau in the 20th Century

By the turn of the 20th century Macau was little more than an impoverished backwater, its glory days all but forgotten. It did, however, continue to serve as a haven for Chinese refugees fleeing war, famine and political oppression. Among them was Sun Yat Sen, founder of the republic of China, who lived here for a short time before the 1911 Revolution. The birth of the Portuguese republic in 1910 seemed to have little effect on this sleepy outpost.

There was little change in Macau's population figures until the mid-1920s when large numbers of Chinese immigrants doubled the number of residents to 160,000. A steady stream of refugees from the Sino-Japanese War meant that by 1939 the population reached 245,000. During WWII many Europeans took refuge in Macau as the Japanese honoured Portugal's neutrality, and refugees from China and Hong Kong poured into the enclave. By 1943 the population stood at 500,000. There was another influx of Chinese refugees in 1949 when the Communists took power in China, and from 1978 until about 1981 Macau was a haven for Vietnamese boat people. Macau was made an overseas province of Portugal in 1951.

Macau's last great upset occurred in 1966–67, when China's Cultural Revolution spilled over into the territory. Macau was stormed by Red Guards, and violent riots resulted in a few of them being shot and killed by Portuguese troops. The governor at the time reportedly proposed that Portugal should leave Macau forever but, fearing the loss of Macau's foreign trade, the Chinese backed off.

In 1974 a revolution restored democracy in Portugal and the new left-wing government began to divest Portugal of the last remnants of its empire, including Mozambique and Angola in Africa and East Timor in the Indonesian archipelago. Powerbrokers in Lisbon tried to return Macau to China as well, but the word from Beijing was that China wished Macau to remain as it was – for the time being.

Most observers agree that China knew it had neither the ability nor the desire to administer such a developed and complex territory while in the throes of the Cultural Revolution. Others, however, see a more ominous reason behind the rejection: At the time the Portuguese enclave was being used to launder vast amounts of Nazi bullion destined for China (see the boxed text The Führer's Gold). In any case, Macau became a 'special territory' with greater autonomy than ever before.

The End of Portuguese Rule

Once the Joint Declaration over Hong Kong was signed by Britain and China in 1984, it was inevitable that China would seek a similar agreement with Portugal on Macau's future. Talks began in 1986 and an agreement was signed the following April.

The Führer's Gold

Generally unknown to the weekend stampede of cash-rich punters and tourists bewitched by Macau's casinos and historical charms is the foul-smelling reason why many people believe China allowed Portugal to continue administering Macau for so long.

During WWII, 'neutral' Portugal had received vast quantities of gold in payment for supplies shipped to the Third Reich. This bullion, bearing the unmistakable stamp of an eagle and Nazi swastika, was difficult to offload on world markets and China, in effect closed off to the world, was the ideal 'laundry'. The gold was shipped to China via Macau as late as the 1970s. China denies the allegations, but former employees of Macau's Gold Import Commission point an accusing finger.

Under the so-called Sino-Portuguese (or simply Macau) Pact, Macau too would become a 'Special Administrative Region' (SAR) of China. The date set was 20 December 1999, ending 442 years of Portuguese rule. Like Hong Kong, the Macau SAR would enjoy a 'high degree of autonomy' for 50 years in all matters except defence and foreign affairs – under the slogan 'one country, two systems'.

Unlike the uncertainty and panic that preceded the return of Hong Kong to China, Macau approached the handover with relatively little anxiety, and on the whole the enclave was able to avoid the prickly issues that dogged the Hong Kong handover negotiations.

Prior to the handover Macau was not a colony per se, but a 'territory under the temporary administration of Portugal'. In any case, Macau had always taken its cue from China in matters regarding the administration of the territory, while Hong Kong existed quite independently, administered according to the dictates of an independent, colonial set of laws.

The Basic Law for Macau differed from its Hong Kong equivalent in that holders of foreign passports were not excluded from holding high-level posts in the post-handover administration (apart from the position of chief executive). There was also no stipulation that China would station troops of the People's Liberation Army (PLA) in Macau after the return of the territory to China, though it did just that and today they are more evident than they are in Hong Kong.

Macau had directly elected some of the members of its Legislative Assembly since the Assembly's founding in 1976, but unlike Hong Kong did not rush through proposals to widen the franchise or speed up democratisation at the last minute. The existing legislature continued to serve throughout the handover, unlike that in the British territory.

But not everything went smoothly. Macau residents were pleased when Portugal gave everyone born in Macau a Portuguese passport, which would allow them the right to live anywhere in the European Union. The UK had refused to do the same thing for Hong Kong Chinese people. However not everyone in Macau benefited by Portugal's move. Until 1975, any Chinese refugee reaching Macau could obtain residency (after that anyone caught sneaking into the territory was considered an illegal immigrant and sent back). Thus, as much as 70% of the population had not actually been born in Macau and therefore didn't qualify for Portuguese citizenship.

As in Hong Kong, Macau SAR passports are only issued to those of Chinese descent. China also does not permit dual citizenship. What that means in effect is that it will not offer any consular protection to Macau SAR residents who travel abroad with a Portuguese passport or recognise that nationality of a Macau SAR resident holding dual citizenship when they are travelling on the mainland.

Up to and during the transition, Portugal had dragged its heels on sweeping the upper echelons of the bureaucracy of non-Chinese. As the eve of the handover approached, civil servants were bought out, retired or paid lump-sum gratuities and a flood of Portuguese left the territory, leaving behind a less-than-saddened population of Chinese and mixed-blood Macanese. The Portuguese, it is said, were never very popular rulers.

In the mid-1990s over-enthusiastic speculation in housing and property left a huge glut of unoccupied buildings and offices. Property prices tumbled and by the close of the decade there were 30,000 vacant apartments in Macau (one for every 14 residents). The economy, largely dependent on tourism and gambling, was faltering across the board, due not only to the regional economic downturn but also to a staggering increase in violent crime.

The years 1996 to 1998 were a grim showdown for Macau's all-important tourist industry, with an escalating number of gangland killings (see the boxed text Dicing with Death in the Macau Facts for the Visitor chapter). Tourist arrivals fell by some 36% in August 1997, compared with the same month the year before, and looked poised to drop even lower under the inertia of Hong Kong's equally palsied tourism figures. However, since the handover and China's less-than-lenient stand on organised crime (at least where it hurts its own interests) crime figures have dropped and tourist figures have almost reached pre-1997 levels.

The Handover

The handover ceremony on 20 December 1999 was as stage-managed as the one held 2½ years before in Hong Kong. Once again a beaming Premier Jiang Zemin shook hands with the head of state of an outgoing colonial power, and once again the latter bore a rather stoic expression. The following day 500 PLA soldiers drove down from Zhuhai. There are now 10,000 stationed here.

The ceremony took place in a purpose-built, glass and steel structure financed by both China and Macau on the eastern edge of the reclaimed NAPE area (pronounced 'NA-pay'; short for Novos Aterros do Porto Exterior, or 'New Reclaimed Land of the Outer Harbour'). As if to illustrate how less than smooth the road to the handover had been, the two sides could not agree what purpose the hall should serve after the handover and in 2000 it was pulled down.

GEOGRAPHY
Macau is divided into three main sections: the Macau Peninsula, which is attached to mainland China to the north; the middle island of Taipa, directly south of the peninsula and linked to it by the 2.5km-long Macau-Taipa Bridge and the new 4.5km-long Friendship Bridge; and Coloane Island, south of Taipa and connected to it by a wide causeway.

Macau is a tiny place. It has a total land area of only 23.8 sq km, which takes in the peninsula (7.8 sq km), Taipa Island (6.2 sq km) and Coloane Island (7.6 sq km). Recent land reclamation around the causeway, Praia Grande and NAPE areas has added more then 2 sq km to the territory's total land area.

GEOLOGY
Macau's territory consists of small granite hills surrounded by a limited amount of level ground. The highest point is Alto de Coloane (176m) on Coloane Island.

CLIMATE
Macau's climate is similar to Hong Kong's (see the Climate section in the Facts about Hong Kong chapter) with one major difference: There's a delightfully cool sea breeze on warm summer evenings. The best time to visit Macau is between October and December, as the humidity is low and the days are bright and sunny. Winter (January to March) is cool but also bright, with an average temperature of about 16°C. Conditions become humid from about April, building up through the rainy season beginning in May and tapering off in late September. The average temperature in summer is 27°C. Between 1020mm and

2540mm of rain falls between April and September. The typhoon season lasts from May to October.

GOVERNMENT & POLITICS
The executive branch of the Macau SAR government is led by the chief executive, who is chosen by an electoral college made up of 300 local representatives. The post is currently filled by Edmund Ho Hau Wah, a locally born banker who is popular with most Macau residents.

The Legislative Assembly, which sits in the new Rotunda da Baia da Praia Grande on reclaimed land in the Nam Wan Lakes area, consists of 23 members, 16 of whom are directly elected and seven chosen by the executive branch. At the time of writing there were plans to expand the Legislative Assembly at the next elections in October 2001.

Like Hong Kong, Macau has a Court of Final Appeal, which is the highest court in the territory and has the power of final adjudication.

There are currently two mayors: one for peninsular Macau and one for the islands.

ECONOMY
Tourism and the spin of the roulette wheel still drive Macau's economy. In the past, gambling was Macau's *raison d'être*, and although that's not as true as it once was, it's still the major cash cow. The gaming industry has been monopolised by a small and wealthy Chinese business syndicate that trades under the name of STDM (Sociedade de Turismo e Diversões de Macau, meaning Macao travel & amusement co). It has been owned by magnate Stanley Ho since 1962.

STDM's licence is due to expire in 2002. At present STDM contributes 40% of government revenue through its payment of betting tax.

Tourism usually generates more than 40% of GDP, and almost a third of the labour force works in some aspect of it. There has been a strong push in recent years to develop alternative tourist facilities throughout the territory to shake off the strong association between holidays in Macau and gambling. The plan is to make

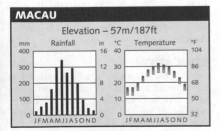

Macau more of a family destination, based on its history, charm and beauty.

Recent government objectives, many of them successful, have been to encourage a diverse service sector to diminish the economic reliance on gambling. Macau welcomes about 7.5 million tourists a year, which is more than 17 times its population. More than half of the tourists are Hong Kong residents, with most of the balance coming from China, Japan, South Korea, Taiwan, Thailand, the UK and the USA.

Macau has various light industries, such as fireworks, textile and toy production, but factories have slowed down and many companies have moved across the border to take advantage of the lower labour costs of southern China. The main reason wages have remained low relative to Hong Kong is that Macau allows a large number of Chinese workers to cross the border daily from Zhuhai to work. The agreement is controversial, since it weakens the position of Macau's workers to demand better wages, but it greatly benefits workers living in Zhuhai. Unemployment in Macau is currently around 6%.

Macau closely follows the formula for economic success employed in Hong Kong. It is a duty-free port and the maximum rate of salary taxation is 15%.

In the past decade Macau has launched a series of enormous public works projects. The completion of Macau's US$11.8 billion airport in 1995 was one of the most ambitious. This freed business travellers from having to use Hong Kong as the gateway to and from Macau, though it has been competing for customers with the Zhuhai airport to the south-west ever since it opened. Another big project was the construction of a deep-water port on the north-eastern side of Coloane Island. But keeping the port open will be a challenge – Macau's shallow harbour gets choked with mud flowing down from the Pearl River. Ships that berth there are limited in size to about 4000 tonnes.

Land reclamation projects have been equally ambitions. The one along the Praia Grande (Macau's historic waterfront), buffeted by the NAPE reclaimed area, has created the two large freshwater lakes, an area also known as the Docas (docks). The causeway linking the two islands, once a narrow two-lane raised road, is now a six-lane highway.

Heading west from the causeway is the US$25 million Lotus Bridge, which opened in 2000, linking Macau with Hengqing Island in the Zhuhai Special Economic Zone. To handle the anticipated increase in motor vehicle traffic brought on by the new airport and the Taipa City high-rise housing development on Taipa, a second bridge was built between the island and peninsular Macau. There are plans to build a third covered span between the two that could be crossed during a typhoon. At present the existing bridges are closed during such storms.

The plan to link either Macau or Zhuhai with a US$1.7 billion bridge to Hong Kong is another indication of the level of credence given to huge infrastructure projects in this part of the world. The idea is to enmesh the whole Pearl River Delta into an economic axis fully supported by modern communications. If it makes it off the drawing board – and it almost certainly will – the new bridge will make Tsing Ma Bridge in Hong Kong look like a plank thrown across a stream.

POPULATION & PEOPLE

Macau's population is currently 438,000, with an annual growth rate of about 1.6%. About 95% of people live on the peninsula, making it one of the most densely populated areas on earth. Coloane Island has remained essentially rural, but Taipa Island is rapidly becoming an urban extension of peninsular Macau.

The population is about 95% Chinese. Less than 2% of Macau residents are Portuguese and the rest are Macanese: people with mixed Portuguese, Chinese and/or African blood.

EDUCATION

Since 1997 10 years' free education has been guaranteed to all children up to the age of 15. As in Hong Kong, there are a large number of private schools but only one Portuguese-language school remained after the handover, Escola Portuguesa de Macau on Avenida do Infante Dom Henrique.

Macau University (☎ 831 622) on Taipa Island is the largest of Macau's 10 institutes of higher learning. It was once the privately owned University of East Asia but has since been taken over by the government, re-named and opened as a public university with a student body of around 5000. The university is still rapidly expanding, attracting students from Hong Kong and overseas.

The Macau Polytechnic Institute (☎ 578 722), Rua de Luís Gonzaga Gomes, offers industrial and technical training.

ARTS

For such a tiny place, Macau has spawned or influenced a number of writers and artists. Their work is on display at the Macau Museum and in the Gallery of Historical Pictures in the Macau Museum of Art.

In literature, first and foremost was Portugal's national poet, Luís de Camões (1524–80), who was banished from Portugal to Goa and then, it is said, to Macau in the 16th century. He is reputed to have written part of his epic poem *Os Lusiadas*, which recounts the 15th-century voyage of Vasco da Gama to India, during two years spent in the enclave (in fact, there is no firm evidence that he ever set foot in Macau).

The teacher, judge, opium addict and Symbolist poet (eg, *Clepsidra*) Camilo Pessanha (1867–1926) lived and worked in Macau for the last 30 years of his life. Locally born writers include Henrique de Senna Fernandes (1923–), author of the *Nam Wan* collection of short stories and the novel *The Bewitching Braid*, and the much beloved Macanese writer José dos Santos Ferreira (1919–93), known as Adé, who wrote in *patuá*, a dialect forging Portuguese and Cantonese. A statue in honour of Adé, who wrote plays, operettas and poems, has been erected in the Jardim des Artes along Avenida da Amizade opposite the Macau Landmark building.

The most important painter to have graced the shores of Macau was George Chinnery (1774–1852), who spent a quarter of a century in Macau, from 1825 until his death, and is remembered for his paintings and sketches of the territory's landscape, architecture and people (see the boxed text George Chinnery: Chronicler of Macau in the Macau Peninsula chapter). Other influential European painters who spent time in Macau include the Scottish physician Thomas Watson (1815–60), who was a student of Chinnery and lived in Macau from 1845 to 1856, the Frenchman Auguste Borget (1808–77), who spent 1836 painting Macau's waterfront and churches, and the watercolourist Marciano António Baptista (1856–1930), who was born in Macau.

One of the finest Chinese artists who painted in a Western style was Guan Qiaochang (1830–50). He worked under the name of Lamqua and was another of Chinnery's pupils. His oil portraits of mandarins and other Chinese worthies are particularly fine.

SOCIETY & CONDUCT
Traditional Culture

Traditional culture among the Chinese of Macau is by and large indistinguishable from that of Hong Kong. For more details see Traditional Culture under the Society & Conduct section in the Facts about Hong Kong chapter.

The Portuguese minority have a vastly different culture, one that has evolved under a number of different influences, including the Roman, Moorish, French, Spanish, Flemish and Italian cultures. Portuguese architectural styles reflect a variety of forms from Romanesque and Gothic through Baroque to Neoclassical; it is to the churches of Macau that one looks for the pageantry of Portuguese building style. The colourful religious festivals are signs of a healthy and vibrant Portuguese culture in Macau and of course, Portuguese food is to be found in abundance.

Macanese culture is different still, with a unique cuisine, set of festivals and traditions, and even its own dialect or patois called *patuá*. The *do*, the traditional woman's outfit, has long disappeared, though you may catch a glimpse of it at certain festivals.

MACAU

Dos & Don'ts

If you follow the advice given in the same section in the Facts about Hong Kong chapter, you should get along fine in Macau. Make sure you dress appropriately when entering the territory's churches and temples, and casinos enforce a rather relaxed dress code. See Gambling, under Entertainment in the Macau Facts for the Visitor chapter.

RELIGION

For the vast majority – more than 90% – of Macau Chinese, Taoism and Buddhism are the dominant religions (see Religion in the Facts about Hong Kong chapter). Four and a half centuries of Portuguese Christian rule left its mark, however, and the Roman Catholic Church is very strong in Macau, with an estimated 30,000 (7% of the population) adherents. Macau consists of a single diocese, directly responsible to Rome.

LANGUAGE

Portuguese and Chinese are the official languages of Macau, with the Cantonese dialect the more widely spoken. For key phrases and words in both, see the Language chapter at the end of this book.

Facts for the Visitor

HIGHLIGHTS

The fine colonial architecture and excellent walks, particularly along the waterfront, are what make this enclave unique. Macau is a city of variegated shades, textures and moods, best appreciated on a slow wander through its narrow streets.

There are a few attractions that stand head and shoulders above the rest. The ruins of the Church of St Paul are a must-see. Although only the facade remains of this edifice, it possesses such majesty that it has become an icon of Macau. Above the facade and now accessible by escalator is the Monte Fortress and the incomparable Museum of Macau.

The A-Ma Temple is a wonderful snapshot of Chinese religious life, especially during festivals. The Chinese New Year sees the temple resounding to music and crackers. The Kun Iam Temple in the north of the peninsula is an intriguing complex of temples dedicated to the Goddess of Mercy. The Church of St Lawrence is a metaphor for the whole decaying nobility of the city. Other highlights include the Lou Lim Ioc Garden, the Old Protestant Cemetery, the cable car ride to the Guia Fortress, the gloriously renovated (and illuminated at night) Largo do Senado, the Clube Militar de Macau (now open as a restaurant to the public), the Avenida da Praia and its villa museums on Taipa, the Chapel of St Francis Xavier in Coloane Village, and Macanese food everywhere.

PLANNING
When to Go

Macau is an easy breakaway for Hong Kong residents, who account for more than half of all arrivals in the territory, and weekends and public holidays in Hong Kong generate a flood of tourists. You'd be wise to avoid these times, since hotels double their prices and rooms of any sort can be hard to find.

Chinese New Year (late January/early February) is chaotic in Macau and hotel rooms are a prized commodity. Still, it's a

> ### Note
>
> Much of the advice given for Hong Kong applies to Macau as well. If you find any sections missing here, refer to the ones in the Hong Kong Facts for the Visitor chapter for more details.

colourful time to visit as the city literally explodes with bangers and fireworks, which are legal here, and the streets have a carnival atmosphere.

The Macau Grand Prix, held in the third week of November, is also a peak time for visitors. See the Public Holidays & Special Events section later in this chapter for details of other festive occasions.

Maps

The Macau Government Tourist Office distributes two versions of the *Macau Tourist Map*. Both have major tourist sights and streets labelled in Portuguese and Chinese characters, and include small inset maps of Taipa and Coloane. The larger one is much more detailed, however, with bus routes and other useful information for travellers.

There are other maps of the territory on sale at bookshops in Macau and Hong Kong, including *Map of Macau, Zhongshan and Zhuhai in Detail* (HK$22), but most of them are totally useless.

If you really want to know where you're going, pick up a copy of the *Atlas de Macau* (M$99), which divides the entire territory into 80 large-scale maps. The bookshop at the Macau Museum (☎ 357 911) stocks copies.

TOURIST OFFICES
Local Tourist Offices

The Macau Government Tourist Office (MGTO; ☎ 315 566, 513 355, fax 510 104, e mgto@macautourism.gov.mo), 9 Largo do Senado, is a well-organised and helpful source of information. It's open from 9am to

6pm daily. It has a large selection of free pamphlets on everything from Chinese temples and Catholic churches to fortresses, gardens and walks. Especially good are the *Walking Tours* and *Cultural Heritage Tours of Macau* pamphlets. The MGTO's Web site (Ⓦ www.macautourism.gov.mo) should win awards, if it hasn't already done so.

The MGTO has information counters at the Guia Lighthouse (☎ 569 808), open 9am to 5.30pm; the Macau Cultural Centre (☎ 751 718), open 9.15am to 6pm daily; the facade of the Church of St Paul (☎ 358 444), open 9am to 6pm; Macau International Airport (☎ 861 436), open according to incoming flights; and the ferry terminal (☎ 726 416), open 9am to 10pm. There are also computer terminals with information on the territory placed at strategic locations, including the ferry terminal, the lobby of the Leal Senado, the Lisboa Hotel, the New Yaohan department store, the Grand Prix and Wine museums and, on Taipa, the Hyatt Regency Hotel.

The MGTO runs a tourist assistance unit to help travellers who may have run into trouble during their stay. The hotline is ☎ 340 390, fax 510 104; it operates from 9am to 6pm daily.

Tourist Offices Abroad

On Hong Kong Island there's a useful branch of the MGTO (☎ 2857 2287, fax 2559 0698) en route to the Macau ferries in room 336–337, Shun Tak Centre, 200 Connaught Rd in Sheung Wan. There's another branch (☎ 2769 7970, fax 2261 2971) at counter 3B in the Arrivals Hall of Hong Kong International Airport at Chek Lap Kok.

Other MGTO representative offices around the world include:

Australia
Icon Group Services (☎ 02-9285 6856, fax 9264 7046, Ⓔ macau@icongsa.com.au) Level 17, 456 Kent St, Sydney NSW 2000

France
Investment Tourism & Trade of Portugal (ICEP; ☎ 01 53 83 75 95, fax 01 42 89 30 74) 135 Boulevard Haussmann, 75008 Paris

Germany
MGTO (☎ 069 350 046, fax 350 040, Ⓔ k.siegmund@discover-fra.com) Eiffelstrasse 14A, 60529 Frankfurt am Main

Italy
ICEP (☎ 02-795 228, fax 794 622) Largo Augusto 3, 200122 Milan

Japan
Mile Post Consultations (☎ 03-5275 2537, fax 5275 2535, Ⓔ mpc-bara@pa2.so-net.ne.jp) 3rd floor, Sanden Building, 5-5, Kojimachi 3-chome, Chiyoda-ku, Tokyo 102

Malaysia
Pacific World Travel (☎ 03-241 3899, fax 248 1357, Ⓔ pwt@melewar.com) 2/5–6 Bangunan Angkasa Raya, Jalan Ampang, 50450 Kuala Lumpur

Philippines
MGTO (☎ 02-817 2644, fax 813 4781, Ⓔ mgtophil@info.com.ph) 9th floor, PDCP Bank Building, Alfaro Corner Herrera St, Sacedo Village, Makati City

Portugal
Delegacao de Macau em Lisboa (☎ 01-793 6542, fax 796 0956, Ⓔ turmacau@esoterica.pt) Ground floor, 115 Avenida Cinco de Outubro, 1050 Lisboa

Singapore
MGTO (☎ 732 3239, fax 732 3205, Ⓔ cti_network@pacific.net.sg) #09-01 Orchard Shopping Centre, 321 Orchard Rd, 238866 Singapore

South Korea
Glocom Korea (☎ 02-778 4402, fax 778 4404, Ⓔ glocomco@chollian.net) Suite 1105, Paiknam Building, President Hotel, 188-3, Eulchiro 1-ka, Chung-ku, Seoul

Taiwan
MGTO (☎ 02-2546 6086, fax 2546 6087, Ⓔ mgtottwn@ms27.hinet.net) 3rd floor, 150 Tun Hwa North Rd, Taipei

Thailand
Pacific Leisure (☎ 02-255 5989, fax 652 0509, Ⓔ pl_group@loxinfo.co.th) 8th floor, Maneeya Center Building, 518/5 Ploenchit Rd, Bangkok 10330

UK
CiB Representation (☎ 020-7771 7000, fax 7771 7059, Ⓔ bernstein@cibgroup.co.uk) 1 Battersea Church Rd, London SW11 3LY

USA
MGTO (☎ 310-568 6407, fax 338 0708, Ⓔ mgto@itr-aps.com) Suite 660, 5757 West Century Blvd, Los Angeles, CA 90045-6407

VISAS & DOCUMENTS
Visas

The vast majority of travellers, including citizens of the European Union (EU), Australia, New Zealand, the USA, Canada and

South Africa, can enter Macau with just their passports and stay one month. Hong Kong residents with a Hong Kong identity card, permanent identity card or re-entry permit, and Portuguese nationals, get 90 days.

Travellers who do require them can get visas valid for 20 days on arrival in Macau. They cost M$100/50 for adults/children under 12 years of age. If you're part of a tour group of 10 people or more, visas are M$50 each, and family visas (one couple plus children under 12) cost M$200.

Travellers from countries that do not have diplomatic relations with China should apply for visas in advance at a Chinese embassy or consulate in a third country.

Visa Extensions Once your permitted length of stay has expired, you can obtain one only one-month extension. To do this you must go in person to the Macau Immigration Office (☎ 725 488), ground floor, Travessa da Amizade, which is opposite the Palace Floating Casino near the Macau ferry terminal. It's open from 9am to 12.30pm and 2.30pm to 4pm Monday to Saturday.

Driving Licence & Permits

Under the *ancien régime* Macau honoured only International Driving Permits (IDPs), which are available from your local automobile association for a relatively small fee. Nowadays your local license will be fine, though it's always a good idea to carry an IDP as well. Holders of Hong Kong driving licences may have to have them validated by the Macau traffic police (☎ 374 214).

Hostel Card

You must have a Hostelling International (HI) card or equivalent if you want to stay at either of the official hostels on Coloane Island.

Macau Museums Pass

A pass allowing you entry to a half-dozen museums over a five-day period is available for M$25/12 for adults/children under 18 and seniors over 65. Participating museums are the Grand Prix Museum, the Wine Museum, the Maritime Museum, the Lin Xezu

Museum, the Macau Museum of Art and the Museum of Macau. Also, check the Web site (W www.macaumuseum.gov.mo).

EMBASSIES & CONSULATES

Like its counterpart Hong Kong, the Macau Special Administrative Region (SAR) is not a country but a part of China. Therefore, if you need to get a visa in advance to visit Macau you must apply to a Chinese embassy or consulate beforehand. For a list, see the Embassies & Consulates section in the Hong Kong Facts for the Visitor chapter.

Consular representatives with responsibility for Macau are almost always based in Hong Kong. Again, see the Embassies & Consulates section in the Hong Kong Facts for the Visitor chapter. One notable exception is Portugal, which has a consulate general (☎ 335 100) in an exquisite colonial mansion at 45 Rua de Pedro Nolasco da Silva.

CUSTOMS

Customs formalities are very few and it's unlikely you'll ever be bothered by them. You're allowed to bring in a reasonable quantity of tobacco, alcohol and perfumes, but remember that when returning to Hong Kong the customs authorities will only allow you to take 1L of spirits, 200 cigarettes, 50 cigars or 250g of tobacco (Hong Kong residents are only allowed one bottle of table wine or port, 100 cigarettes or 25 cigars). There are no restrictions on the amount of foreign currency that can be taken in or out of Macau – which is either good or bad news for those with a severe addiction to gambling – and no export duties on any goods, including antiques.

Like their Hong Kong equivalents, Macau customs officials take a very dim view of drugs. Note that you aren't allowed to take fireworks bought in Macau back to Hong Kong.

MONEY
Currency

Macau's currency is the pataca, normally written as M$, which is divided into 100 avos. Bills are issued in denominations of M$20, M$50, M$100, M$500 and M$1000.

There are little copper coins worth 10, 20 and 50 avos and silver-coloured M$1 and M$5 coins.

Exchange Rates

The Macau pataca is pegged to the Hong Kong dollar at the rate of M$103.20 to HK$100, with a permissible variation rate of up to 10%. As a result exchange rates for the pataca are virtually the same as for the Hong Kong unit (eg, US$1 = M$8). For a table of exchange rates see the Money section in the Hong Kong Facts for the Visitor chapter.

Exchanging Money

Cash & Travellers Cheques Hong Kong dollars, including coins, are readily accepted throughout Macau; when you spend HK$ in big hotels, restaurants and department stores your change will be returned in that currency. Although you might make a tiny saving by using patacas, it's not really worth changing your Hong Kong dollars into the Macau currency as most money-changers and banks will refuse to change them back if you get stuck with a handful of bills. You would be wise to use up all your patacas before departing Macau.

ATMs Macau ATMs are usually linked up to international money systems like Cirrus, Maestro, GlobalAccess or Plus, and many (including the HSBC and Banco Nacional Ultramarino ATMs at the Macau ferry terminal) accept certain international bank cards issued by Visa, American Express and MasterCard. The Jetco network, used by Standard Chartered and a host of smaller banks, accepts Cirrus ATM cards as well as MasterCard and American Express. There's a wealth of ATMs outside the Lisboa Hotel facing Avenida do Infante Dom Henrique. Most ATMs allow you to choose between patacas and Hong Kong dollars.

There's a HSBC bank (☎ 553 669) at 639 Avenida da Praia Grande with an ATM. HSBC's ATM hotline is ☎ 599 2123. The Bank of America (☎ 568 821) has a useful branch with an ATM near the Largo do Senado at 70 Avenida de Almeida Ribeiro. It's open from 9am to 5pm weekdays and to

1pm on Saturday. The Standard Chartered Bank (☎ 786 111) is on the 8th floor of the Macau Landmark on Avenida de Amizade.

Credit Cards Major credit cards are readily accepted at Macau's hotels, larger restaurants and casinos. Theft or loss of a credit card should be reported to police and then the company's representative office in Hong Kong. See Lost or Stolen Credit Cards under Money in the Hong Kong Facts for the Visitor chapter for the telephone numbers of major credit card companies there.

American Express (AmEx) has several representative offices in Macau where you can get cash on your card, exchange money and seek other credit card services. The main office (☎ 363 262), 23B Rua de São Paulo, is at the foot of the ruins of the Church of St Paul and is open from 9am to 5.30pm daily. Another branch (☎ 579 898) is in the Lisboa Hotel in shop G3 of the Old Wing, 2–4 Avenida de Lisboa, and is open 24 hours.

Citibank (☎ 378 188) has a branch at 251–253 Avenida da Praia Grande and is open from 9.30am to 4pm on weekdays and till noon on Saturday.

International Transfers HSBC (☎ 553 669, fax 315 421), 639 Avenida da Praia Grande, does international money transfers as does Banco Nacional Ultramarino (BNU; ☎ 355 111, fax 371 748), 22 & 38 Avenida de Almeida Ribeiro, and Banco Comercial de Macau (BCM; ☎ 791 0000), 572 Avenida da Praia Grande. The AmEx offices listed in the previous Credit Cards section can also arrange for cash transfers, but you have to have a cardholder's account.

Moneychangers You'll find money-changers open 24 hours in the arrivals hall of Macau International Airport and in shop G3 of the Lisboa Hotel's Old Wing, 2–4 Avenida de Lisboa.

You can also change cash and travellers cheques at the banks lining Avenida da Praia Grande and Avenida de Almeida Ribeiro as well as major hotels, though the latter seldom offer optimum rates.

Costs

As long as you stay away from the hostess clubs and the casinos, your trip should be reasonably cheap and you'll spend much less than the HK$250 budget mentioned in the Costs section of the Hong Kong Facts for the Visitor chapter. Accommodation in the area of cheap guesthouses near the Inner Harbour can be had for as little as M$70 a night for a single, and cheap eats abound.

Try to avoid travelling to Macau on weekends and public holidays, as hotels and transport are more expensive at these times.

Tipping & Bargaining

Most large hotels and many restaurants add a 10% service charge to the bill. Hotels also levy a 5% government tax. Like Hong Kong, Macau is not gratuity driven and there is no obligation to tip, say, taxi drivers; just round the fare up.

Most shops have fixed prices, but if you buy clothing, trinkets and so on from the street markets there is some scope for bargaining. It's a different story at the pawnshops, where you should bargain ruthlessly.

You can lose your shirt – literally – while gambling in Macau; the pawnbrokers will buy and sell just about everything. Of course, a second-hand shirt isn't worth an avos; even a decent camera won't get you much more than the price of a ferry ticket back to Honkers. The upper stretches of Avenida de Almeida Ribeiro have a cluster of pawnshops, their windows glistening with engagement and wedding rings, gold Rolexes and expensive cameras.

POST & COMMUNICATIONS

Correios de Macau, Macau's postal system, is efficient and inexpensive. It also produces some startlingly beautiful postage stamps for collectors; see the Shopping section at the end of this chapter for details.

Postal Rates

Domestic letters cost M$1/1.50 for up to 20/50g. Surface mail weighing up to 20/50g costs M$1.50/3 to China and Hong Kong, M$2/3.50 to Portugal and M$3.50/5.50 to elsewhere.

For international mail, Macau divides the world into two zones: zone 1 (M$4.50/7.50 for up to 20/50g) is East and South-East Asia; zone 2 (M$6/10.50 for up to 20/50g) is everywhere else. There are special rates for China and Portugal.

Printed matter receives a discount of about 30% off these rates. To register a letter costs an extra M$12.

Sending Mail

The service at post offices is efficient, and the staff usually speak English. The main post office (☎ 574 491), open 9am to 6pm weekdays and to 1pm on Saturday, is on Avenida de Almeida Ribeiro facing the Largo do Senado. There are other post office branches in peninsular Macau (including the ferry terminal, open from 10am to 7pm Monday to Saturday) as well as on the islands. There are also little red booths that dispense stamps from vending machines. Large hotels sell stamps and postcards and can post letters and parcels.

EMS (Speedpost; ☎ 596 688) is available at the main post office. Other companies that can arrange express forwarding are DHL (☎ 372 828), Federal Express (☎ 703 333) and UPS (☎ 963 535).

Receiving Mail

Poste restante service is available at counter Nos 1 and 2 at the main post office on Avenida de Almeida Ribeiro. You can collect letters from 9am to 6pm on weekdays and to 1pm on Saturday.

Telephone

Macau's telephone service provider is Companhia de Telecomunicações de Macau (CTM; inquiry hotline ☎ 1000, ☎ 891 3822). In general, the phone service is good – you'll seldom have trouble with broken public phones and noisy lines. Public pay phones are mostly concentrated around the Largo do Senado and the Lisboa Hotel. Large hotels have public phones in the lobby, and there is a courtesy phone at MGTO's main office in the Largo do Senado. ·

Local calls are free from private or hotel telephones, while at a public pay phone they cost M$1 for five minutes. All pay phones permit International Direct Dialling (IDD). Rates are cheaper from 9pm to 8am during the week and all day Saturday and Sunday.

The international access code for every country *except* Hong Kong is ☎ 00. If you want to phone Hong Kong, dial ☎ 01 first, then the number you want; you do *not* need to dial Hong Kong's country code (☎ 852). To call Macau from abroad – including Hong Kong – the country code is ☎ 853.

Remember you'll need lots of change to make an IDD call – unless you buy a phonecard from CTM. These are sold in denominations of M$100, M$200 and M$300 and most public phones accept them. If you're carrying a mobile phone, CTM will sell you a rechargeable SIM chip to 'localise' your service for M$260.

There are seven CTM branches in Macau. The following, all of which can be reached on ☎ 1000, are the most convenient for travellers.

CTM Building 25 Rua Pedro Coutinho (two blocks north-east of the Lou Lim Ioc Garden; open 9am to 6pm daily)
Nam Kwong Building 245 Avenida do Doutor Rodrigo Rodrigues (four blocks north-east of the Lisboa Hotel; open 9am to 6pm daily)
Mobile Zone 18 Rua de São Domingos (two blocks east of the Largo do Senado; open 10am to 8pm daily)
Tele-One Macau 22 Rua do Doutor Pedro José Lobo (just north of the Lisboa Hotel; open 10am to 8pm daily)

Another option is to make use of the 'country direct' service, described in the telephone section of the Hong Kong Facts for the Visitor chapter. The following are the access numbers in Macau:

Australia	(Optus)	☎ 0 800 611
	(Telstra)	☎ 0 800 610
Canada		☎ 0 800 100
Hong Kong		☎ 0 800 852
New Zealand		☎ 0 800 640
UK	(BT)	☎ 0 800 440
	(CWC)	☎ 0 800 444
USA	(AT&T)	☎ 0 800 1111
	(MCI)	☎ 0 800 131
	(Sprint)	☎ 0 800 121

Useful Numbers The following table lists some important telephone numbers. For numbers to call at more difficult times, see Emergencies later in this chapter.

Local directory assistance	☎ 185
International directory assistance	☎ 101
Time in English	☎ 140
Macau ferry terminal	☎ 790 7240
TurboJet	☎ 790 7039
Hong Kong & Yaumatei Ferry Co (HYFCO)	☎ 726 301

Fax
Most mid-range and top-end hotels have fax services. Charges vary but may be a fixed rate per page or according to the time taken to send the fax. If your hotel doesn't have a fax, you can send and receive faxes at the main post office on Avenida de Almeida Ribeiro.

Email & Internet Access
Email services are not very well developed in Macau and there are no commercial cybercafes at present. The business centres in the more expensive hotels offer email services, and some don't mind non-guests using the facilities.

CTM's Mobile Zone branch at 18 Rua de São Domingos has three terminals on the first floor where you can access email and surf the Web for free (provided you can log on). It's open from 10am to 8pm daily. You can also check emails at the UNESCO Centre (☎ 727 220) on Alameda Doutor Carlos d'Assumpção in NAPE, which is diagonally opposite the Macau Landmark, and on the ground floor library of the Macau Museum of Art.

INTERNET RESOURCES
Lonely Planet's Web site (W www.lonely planet.com) links to Macau sites via Sub-WWWay and covers travel news at Scoop. Other useful Macau sites include:

Cityguide Anything and everything about Macau: transport, accommodation, restaurants, bars etc.
W www.cityguide.gov.mo
Government Statistics Department The details behind the facts and figures.
W www.dsec.gov.mo

Macau Cultural Institute Information on Macau's cultural offerings and events.
W www.icm.gov.mo

Macau Government Information Statistics and basic information about the territory.
W www.macau.gov.mo

Macau Government Tourist Office The best Web site on Macau, bar none.
W www.macautourism.gov.mo

Macau Museums Interlinked site on Macau's museums and galleries.
W www.macaumuseum.gov.mo

Macau Yellow Pages Telephone directory on the Web.
W www.yp.com.mo

BOOKS

Most of the best books on Macau are published in Portuguese, but there are a few good titles in English. You'll probably do better sourcing books on Macau in Hong Kong, but for a selection of the possible outlets in the territory see Bookshops under Information in the Macau Peninsula chapter.

Lonely Planet

Travellers heading to the mainland should get Lonely Planet's comprehensive *China* guide, which includes a chapter on Macau as well as Hong Kong. Macau is also covered briefly in Lonely Planet's *South-East Asia*. The *Cantonese phrasebook* is a complete guide to the primary language of Macau. *World Food: Hong Kong* includes a section on Macau's unique cuisine.

Travel

Shann Davies' *Macau Miscellany* and *More Macau Miscellany* are entertaining looks at Macau's cultural, historical and sociological ephemera. *Macau: A Cultural Janus* by Christina Miu Bing Cheng is a very dry, academic look at what sets Macau apart from other places in the region.

Picture books worth looking out for include *Macau Watercolours* by Murray Zanoni and *Macau Streets* by César Guillén-Nuñez and Leong Ka Tai. *Colours of Macau*, published by the Foundation for the Cooperation and Development of Macau, is a lovely album with text in three languages.

Macau Contemporary Architecture, published by the Architects' Association of Macau, and *Macau Gardens & Landscape Art*, by Francisco M Caldeira Cabral, Annabel Jackson and Leong Ka Tai, are esoteric but beautiful volumes nonetheless. *George Chinnery: Images of 19th Century Macau* is a well-illustrated catalogue of a special exhibit held in the territory in 1997.

History & Politics

A Macao Narrative by the Hong Kong novelist Austin Coates is a slim but comprehensive and highly readable history of the territory until the mid-1970s. His *Macao and the British: Prelude to Hong Kong, 1637-1842* focuses on the decline of both Portuguese supremacy and Macau and the ascent of the British and Hong Kong in the region.

Macau by César Guillén-Nuñez is rather dull and dry but can be read in one sitting. *Macau 2000*, edited by JA Berlie, examines the territory from a historical and political standpoint on the eve of the 21st century. *Macau Remembers* by Jill McGiverins is an up-to-date series of political portraits and interviews of Macau's movers and shakers.

General

Novels set in Macau are rare but Austin Coates' *City of Broken Promises*, a fictionalised account of the 18th-century Macanese trader Martha Merop (1766–1828) set in peninsular Macau and Taipa is a classic. *Macau* by Daniel Carney is trash.

Macau: Mysterious Decay and Romance, edited by Donald Pittis and Susan J Henders, is an anthology of writings on Macau and an excellent introduction to the territory.

FILMS

The first feature produced in Macau was *The Bewitching Braid* (1995), a bittersweet romantic comedy focusing on Macau's cultural and racial mix, set in the 1930s and based on the novel by Henrique de Senna Fernandes (see Arts in the Facts about Macau chapter).

Two films partly shot in Macau are the James Bond classic *The Man with the Golden Gun* (1974), starring Roger Moore and Christopher Lee, and *Indiana Jones and*

MACAU

the Temple of Doom (1984) with Harrison Ford. In the latter, Macau (including the unmistakable arcades of Avenida de Almeida Ribeiro) masquerades as 1930s Shanghai.

NEWSPAPERS & MAGAZINES
Macau has eight daily newspapers, two of them in Portuguese *(Macau Hoje, Jornal Tribuna de Macau)* and the rest in Chinese. There are also a couple of weeklies, including *Ponto Final*.

There are no English-language daily newspapers in Macau but *Ponto Final* includes a synopsis of local news in English every week. The two Hong Kong English-language dailies, the *South China Morning Post* and *iMail*, are both available from newsagents around town. If you want a copy of the *International Herald Tribune* or *Newsweek*, *Time* or *Asiaweek* magazine, your best bets are the bookshops of the top-end hotels.

The MGTO publishes the monthly tourist newspaper *Macau Travel Talk*; it's usually available at its office on the Largo do Senado.

RADIO & TV
Radio Macau has three stations, two of which broadcast in Cantonese and one, called Ilha Verde (green island), in Portuguese. There are no local English-language radio stations, but you should be able to pick up broadcasts from Hong Kong.

Teledifusão de Macau (TdM) is a privately owned station that broadcasts on two channels: Cantonese and Portuguese. While TdM does produce some of its own programs, most broadcasts in the evening are relays from RTPE, Portugal's national TV station.

It's easy to pick up Hong Kong stations in Macau (but not the other way around) and you can also receive stations from China. Many hotels have access to TV Cabo Macau (Macau cable TV), which broadcasts on some 20 to 30 channels.

VIDEO SYSTEMS
Like Hong Kong, Macau uses the PAL standard for TV broadcasting and video tapes.

PHOTOGRAPHY & VIDEO
You can find virtually any type of film, camera and accessory in Macau, and photo processing is cheap and of a high standard. A good shop for all photographic services, including visa photos, is Foto Princesa (☎ 575 959), 55–59 Avenida de Infante Dom Henrique.

Another street with a concentration of camera shops is Rua do Campo west of the Vasco da Gama Garden. Two good shops are Lua Prata (☎ 308 175) at 351 Rua do Campo and Foto Maxim's (☎ 376 850) at 301–303 Rua do Campo. The latter's branch at 11–11A Largo do Senado next to the MGTO office will develop 36 exposures in one hour for M$48.

TIME
Like Hong Kong, Macau is eight hours ahead of GMT/UTC and does not observe daylight saving.

ELECTRICITY
Macau's system is the same as that in Hong Kong and China: 220V, 50 Hz (cycles per second) AC. The electric outlets accept plugs with three round pins, the same as Hong Kong's older design.

WEIGHTS & MEASURES
Macau uses the international metric system. You'll see no sign of British imperial measure, but wet markets and traditional medicine shops sell things by the *leung*, or *tael* (37.5g), and the *gan* (600g).

LAUNDRY
All hotels offer a laundry service, but it is usually quite expensive. Hidden in the alleyways of Macau are many hole-in-the-wall laundries that charge much more reasonable prices; just look for the word *lavandaria*. A road with a cluster of laundries is Rua dos Mercadores, to the north of Largo do Senado and just off Avenida de Almeida Ribeiro.

One relatively central place, tried and tested and smelling like roses, is Lavandaria Guia (☎ 352 876) at 85 Rua Nova à Guia, just south of the Royal Hotel. It's open 9.30am to 7pm Monday to Saturday.

Another laundry that's relatively easy to find is Lavandaria Macau, which is in the same building as the San Va Hospedaria, 67 Rua de Felicidade.

LEFT LUGGAGE
You can store your bags in electronic lockers (M$20 or M$25, depending on the size) on both the arrivals and departure levels of the Macau ferry terminal. There is also a left-luggage office on the departures level open from 6.45am to midnight daily.

Another option is to leave your luggage with the concierge at a hotel. Hotels will generally allow you to store a bag when you check out, a big convenience if you must vacate your room by noon but don't want to return to Hong Kong until the evening.

HEALTH
The advice given in the Health section of the Hong Kong Facts for the Visitor chapters applies equally to Macau.

Medical Services
Macau has two hospitals, both of which have 24-hour emergency services. The Conde São Januário Central Hospital (☎ 313 731) is on Estrada do Visconde de São Januário, which is south-west of the Guia Fort. The Kiang Wu Hospital (☎ 371 333), Rua Coelho do Amaral, is north-east of the ruins of the Church of St Paul.

If you require less urgent medical assistance, contact the Tap Seac Health Centre (☎ 569 011) at 89 Avenida do Conselheiro Ferreira de Almeida.

WOMEN TRAVELLERS
Macau differs little from Hong Kong in its attitudes and treatment of women, both local and foreign. For details see the Women Travellers section in the Hong Kong Facts for the Visitor chapter.

GAY & LESBIAN TRAVELLERS
Despite intensive research, your long-suffering author found not a single venue specifically for gays and/or lesbians in the Macau SAR. With Hong Kong and its clubs, bars and saunas a one-hour ferry ride

away, there doesn't appear to be a lot of motivation to start something up here.

TRAVEL WITH CHILDREN
On the second floor of the New Wing of the Lisboa Hotel, 2–4 Avenida de Lisboa, is Children's World (☎ 569 229, 577 666), where kids can play video games or snooker while mum and dad impoverish themselves at the blackjack tables or feed the 'hungry tigers' (slot machines).

If you want to 'lose' the kids for a day or two the Hyatt Regency Hotel (☎ 831 234 ext 1856) on Taipa Island has activities such as scuba diving, water polo, tennis, wind-surfing, ice skating, canoeing and rock climbing to keep the little terrors constructively occupied. Less strenuous activities include theatre, picnics, barbecues and visits to the Maritime and Fire Department Museums. The programs are available from mid-July to late August and over the Easter weekend, and children must be aged between five and 12. A day's worth of activities should cost between M$55 and M$85 for registered guests and M$65 and M$105 for non-guests in summer. Four/six hours of activities at Easter costs M$55/85.

USEFUL ORGANISATIONS
For those wishing to do business in Macau, any of the following organisations will be of help.

Associação Comercial de Macau (Macau Business Association; ☎ 576 833, fax 594 513) 175 Rua de Xangai. This is Macau's chamber of commerce.
Instituto de Promoção do Comércio e do Investimento de Macau (Macau Trade and Investment Promotion Institute; ☎ 710 528, fax 590 309) 4th and 5th floors, World Trade Center, 918 Avenida da Amizade. The institute promotes investment and trade in Macau.
World Trade Center Macau (☎ 727 666, fax 727 633) 17th floor, World Trade Center, 918 Avenida da Amizade. The centre offers trade information services and arranges conferences and exhibitions.

DANGERS & ANNOYANCES
Macau's three-year stint as Dodge City (1996–98), with gangland violence taking

MACAU

to the streets and international hotels being sprayed with semi-automatic gunfire, are well and truly over. Triads have tentacles though, and in March 2001 the best-known Portuguese lawyer residing in Macau was kidnapped, ostensibly on the orders of the imprisoned Broken Tooth Koi (see the boxed text Dicing with Death), and was

only freed after a SWAT team, acting on a tip-off, raided the central Macau flat where he was being held.

As in most tourist destinations, burglaries and pickpocketing can be problems. Most hotels are well guarded, and if you take reasonable care with your valuables you should avoid trouble. Be on guard in very

---

Dicing with Death

The years 1996 to 1998 were a grim showdown for apparently sleepy, Portuguese-run Macau. Some 40 people were killed as senior Triad leaders jostled for control of the lucrative gambling rackets and at least one international hotel was raked with AK47 gunfire. On 8 May 1998 alone, 14 cars and motorcycles and a couple of shops were engulfed in flames when Triad members, protesting the arrest of their boss, Wan Kwok 'Broken Tooth' Koi, let off a string of firebombs. Needless to say, the violence scared tourists off in a big way.

The Triad violence resulted from a tug-of-war between gangs eager to grab what they could of shrinking profits from Macau's gambling indrustry, aided and abetted by lax and corrupt law enforcement. Big money was to be made from chaperoning high rollers from mainland China, who cruised into town with a cartload of dosh in tow. The police seemed powerless to stop the knifings and shootings; some residents blamed them for corruption and even collusion. With nothing like Hong Kong's Independent Commission Against Corruption (ICAC) in Macau, there was a lot of room for salary top-ups.

The Triad turf-cum-civil war dated back to the late 1980s when Ng Wai, nicknamed 'Wet Market' because he allegedly once ran the protection rackets in Mong Kok market, arrived from Hong Kong. He quickly fell out with Wan, a former employee, and soon the Shui Fong (water room) gang, backed by Ng, and Wan's 10,000-strong 14K were warring openly on the streets. Posters accusing Ng of being a drug trafficker would appear all over the territory, and he and his mob would retaliate with bullets, knives and letters to the editor. 'Warning', read one, 'from this day on it is forbidden to mention Broken Tooth Koi in the press; otherwise bullets will have no eyes and knives will have no feelings.'

As the time of the 1999 handover approached and China had put sufficient pressure on Portugal to clean up its act, the government issued a new anti-Triad law calling for a lengthy prison term for anyone found to be a senior leader. Ng took refuge in his New Century Hotel on Taipa, Koi was arrested and sentenced to 15 years and many other Triad members, including post-1997 imports from Hong Kong, fled overseas, particularly to Bangkok. They obviously had got the message from China loud and clear. Just hours before Broken Tooth was jailed in November 1999, three of his partners in crime were meted out Chinese-style justice just over the border in Zhuhai: a bullet to their heads.

The culture of violence is unlikely to disappear overnight, however. Hong Kong films, as popular in Macau as they are at home, promote and glorify violence – swelling the Triad ranks with young recruits fed on a diet of savage cinema. Youngsters often see violence as a way of life and a channel to respect. Even Broken Tooth Koi has his own homage on celluloid, a film imaginatively named Casino (1998), which traces his rise through the K14 ranks to the top.

But while it may be difficult to admire a cut-throat like Koi, it's hard not to acknowledge his sheer gall. From within the confines of the maximum-security prison in Coloane he was able to stage-manage the kidnapping of lawyer Jorge Neto Valente in early 2001, and planned to demand M$20 million ransom for his release. And when Broken Tooth's appeal was turned down by Macau's Court of Final Appeal he did what any criminal, guilty as the day is long, would do: he threatened to go to the World Court in The Hague.

crowded places, such as the ferry terminal, around the ruins of the Church of St Paul and the Largo do Senado. Cheating at gambling is a serious criminal offence in Macau and gorillas roam through the halls to make sure it doesn't happen.

Traffic is especially heavy and can be dangerous; quite a few tourists have been hit while jaywalking. Be especially careful of the ubiquitous motor scooters and mopeds, which seem to take particular delight at cutting you off or forcing you back on the pavement. Crossing the road can be difficult as cars don't always come to a halt at pedestrian crossings, which are marked by black and white stripes as in the UK.

Macau has just as many prostitutes as Zhuhai and if you are a single man checking into one of the cheaper hotels, especially in the western district near the Inner Harbour, expect to have regular phone calls asking if you want a *xiaojie* (young girl). This can get very annoying as they don't take no for an answer and eventually come knocking on your door. Some budget hotels have a welcoming committee of hookers loitering by the main entrance or even in the lobby, so it's pretty obvious what's what. The East Asia Hotel and the Villa Capital are the two worst offenders, but some of the places around Praça Ponte e Horta to the south are just as bad.

EMERGENCIES

In the event of an emergency phone ☎ 999 for the fire services, police or an ambulance.

Other important numbers include:

Fire	☎ 572 222
Police	☎ 573 333
Maritime police	☎ 559 944
Ambulance	☎ 371 333, 313 731
Tourist Assistance Unit (9am to 6pm daily)	☎ 340 390

BUSINESS HOURS

Most government offices are open from 9am to 1pm and 2.30pm to 5.30pm or 5.45pm on weekdays. Private businesses keep longer hours and most casinos are open 24 hours. Banks are normally open 9am to 5pm weekdays and to 1pm on Saturday.

PUBLIC HOLIDAYS & SPECIAL EVENTS
Public Holidays

As in Hong Kong, Macau hits pay dirt when it comes to public holidays, with a full 20 dates marked in red on the calendar each year. This, of course, is the result of two very different cultures mixing their cultural and religious traditions over more than 400 years and mother China arriving with a couple of days of her own.

The following are public holidays in Macau:

New Year's Day (called the Day of Universal Brotherhood) 1 January
Chinese New Year (three days) late January/early February
Easter late March/early April
Ching Ming early April
Buddha's Birthday April/May
Labour Day 1 May
Dragon Boat Festival June
Mid-Autumn Festival September/October
China National Day 1 & 2 October
Cheung Yeung mid/late October
All Souls' Day 2 November
Feast of the Immaculate Conception 8 December
Macau SAR Establishment Day 20 December
Winter Solstice 22 December
Christmas Eve & Christmas Day 24 & 25 December

Half-days are allowed on the day before the start of Chinese New Year and on New Year's Eve day.

Traditional Festivals

In addition to the holidays above, the Chinese in Macau celebrate the same religious festivals as their counterparts in Hong Kong. Temples come to life at this time, with bundles of bangers and clips of crackers exploded throughout the day. There are several important Catholic festivals as well. The tourist newspaper *Macau Travel Talk*, available from the MGTO, has regular listings of events and festivals. The following are just some of the more important festivals that are *not* public holidays.

MACAU

Lantern Festival This entertaining festival occurs in mid to late February, about two weeks after Chinese New Year.

Procession of Our Lord of Passion A colourful procession, bearing a statue of Jesus Christ, begins in the evening in February/March at St Augustine Church and proceeds to Macau Cathedral. The statue is kept in the cathedral overnight and the procession returns to St Augustine's the following day. The tradition goes back more than four centuries.

Feast of Tou Tei A minor holiday held in honour of the Earth God in March or early April.

A-Ma Festival This festival in late April/early May honours Macau's patron goddess and namesake. The main A-Ma Temple in the south-west of peninsular Macau comes alive with worshippers.

Feast of the Drunken Dragon & Feast of the Bathing of Lord Buddha Celebrated on the same day in late April/May, these festivals see dancing dragons in the streets of the Inner Harbour and the washing of Buddhist images in temples throughout Macau.

Procession of Our Lady of Fatima Celebrated on 13 May, this commemorates the series of appearances made by the Virgin Mary to three peasant children at Fatima in Portugal in 1917. A procession, which first took place in 1929, begins at the Cathedral and ends at Penha Church.

Festival of Tam Kong This holiday honouring the Taoist god of seafarers is celebrated in May.

Camões Day & Portuguese Communities Day Held on 10 June, this day commemorates Portugal's national poet and is celebrated by Portuguese around the world.

Feast of St Anthony of Lisbon This event on 13 June marks the feast day of the patron saint of Lisbon. A small parade is held from the Church of St Anthony.

Procession of St John the Baptist The procession for St John the Baptist, the patron saint of Macau, is held on 24 June.

Battle of 13 July Celebrated only on the island of Coloane, this holiday commemorates the final defeat of pirates in 1910.

Maidens' Festival This minor holiday in mid-August, also known as Seven Sisters Day, is reserved for girls and young lovers.

Hungry Ghosts Festival This festival in late August/early September marks the start of a two-week period honouring the dead.

Special Events

The Macau Arts Festival kicks off the cultural year in March and features music, drama and dance from both Asia and the West. The International Music Festival, held for two weeks in late October and early November, is a mix of opera, musicals, visiting orchestras and other musical events. Concerts are generally held in the new Macau Cultural Centre. The International Jazz Festival takes place at the Cultural Centre in mid-May.

Annual sporting events include the Macau Open Golf Tournament in April/May, the Women's Volleyball Grand Prix in August, the Formula 3 Grand Prix in November and the Macau International Marathon in December. In September and October the International Fireworks Festival adds a splash of colour to the Macau night sky.

ACTIVITIES

Activities for the most part are centred on the islands. There are two hiking trails on Taipa, the possibility of horse riding at the Macau Jockey Club, and a number of shops in and around Taipa Village rent bicycles. In addition to two decent beaches and related water sports, Coloane offers four trails, a go-karting track, an 18-hole golf course and more bikes. The Hác Sá Sports and Recreation Park at Hác Sá Beach has as many sporting and recreational facilities as you care to name – from tennis and badminton courts to an Olympic-size swimming pool. For details, see the Activities section in the Taipa & Coloane Islands chapter.

Peninsular Macau is not just about museums, ancient churches and cobbled backstreets. The Future Bright Amusement Park (☎ 953 399) at 1B-C Rua de Coelho do Amaral, on the south-eastern side of the Camões Grotto and Garden, has an ice-skating rink, bowling alley, indoor children's playground, a video games arcade and a McDonald's.

The Vitória Sport Centre (☎ 580 762, 574 484), near the Royal Hotel at 19 Estrada da Vitória, has an Olympic-size swimming pool and two tennis courts. Adjacent to the pool is a gymnasium where local clubs get together to practice martial arts, basketball and other sports. There's a billiards room on the 2nd floor of the New Wing of the Lisboa Hotel (☎ 577 666), 2-4 Avenida de Lisboa.

The best jogging track on the peninsula is up around the Guia Fort. It's also the venue for early morning tai chi *(taijiquan)*. Another attractive route for runners is along the Avenida da República on the waterfront around the south-western tip of the peninsula.

WORK

Finding employment in Macau is difficult. The few foreign residents (ie, Portuguese) speak English so there is little need to import English-language teachers. Average monthly wages are less than US$500, less than a third of what they are in Hong Kong. Unemployment in Macau is currently around 6%.

ACCOMMODATION

Macau's hotels are much cheaper than those in Hong Kong. For the same price you'd pay for a room in Hong Kong's Chungking Mansions you can get a comfortable room in Macau with air-conditioning, private bath and TV. At the very bottom end of the market, you can still find a few places that have ultra cheap singles and doubles.

A few words of advice: Visiting Macau at the weekend, on public holidays or during the summer high season should be avoided if possible, as rooms are scarce and hotel prices double or even treble. For definition purposes, 'weekend' really means only Saturday night; Friday night is usually not a problem unless it's also a holiday. There's usually a Hong Kong–bound exodus from the territory on Sunday afternoon. During special events and at festivals, such as the Macau Grand Prix or the Chinese New Year, rooms can be virtually impossible to obtain.

Substantial discounts (30% or more) are available if you book through a travel agency, but this usually only applies to hotels of three stars and above. In Hong Kong you'll find a lot of these agents at the Shun Tak Centre, 200 Connaught Rd, Sheung Wan, from where the ferries to Macau depart. If you haven't booked your room before your arrival, you can do it at the ferry pier in Macau.

If you're staying at accommodation that is two stars or lower, you'll have to bargain your own discount.

Camping

There's quite a nice camping site with toilets and showers at Hác Sá Beach. Whether it's worth travelling that far to save some money on a night's accommodation is something you'll have to decide. See Places to stay under Coloane Island in the Taipa & Coloane Islands chapter.

Hostels

Macau now has two hostels on Coloane Island – one at Cheoc Van Beach and a newer one at Hác Sá Beach – and they are run by the government's Education & Youth Services Department (☎ 344 340, fax 317 307) based at 43 Rua de São Tiago da Barra. A night's stay costs from M$40 to M$100, depending on the type of accommodation and the day of the week. A Hostelling International card (or equivalent) is required. Again, for details see Places to Stay under Coloane Island in the Taipa & Coloane Islands chapter.

Guesthouses

All guesthouses (and other businesses, for that matter) must have their signs in both Chinese and Portuguese. Guesthouses in Macau are denoted by several names, including *vila*, *hospedaria* and *pensão*.

There are a few old classic guesthouses remaining in Macau, with dirt cheap prices and plenty of dirt (not to mention cockroaches and other things that crawl and bite in the night – of both the four and two-legged variety). Prices start at as little as M$70, and for that sort of money you're about one step up from the pavement in terms of comfort.

If you can't handle the rice-paper walls and all the torn linoleum at the lower end of the business, the middle ground of Macau's guesthouse world offers accommodation from M$300 and up. These are generally much cleaner and more comfortable than the places in Hong Kong's Chung King Mansions and Tsim Sha Tsui district, where you'll pay more or less the same price.

Hotels

Not surprising for a place driven by tourism, Macau has an amazing number and variety of hotels. The more than four dozen hotels in the territory range from fully renovated architectural museum pieces to modern high-rise glass-and-concrete blocks and cylinders. And then there's always the unspeakable Lisboa Hotel: imagine a squat tin can the colour of egg yolk, topped with a pin cushion.

The mid-range market offers hotels that are all reasonably comfortable but pretty much the same in terms of what they offer. The best way to get a room at this level is to book through one of the travel agencies at the Shun Tak Centre in Hong Kong or at the ferry pier on arrival in Macau. At the top end, there are hotels that offer facilities and service to outmatch Hong Kong.

Mid-range and top-end hotels levy a 5% government room tax and a 10% service charge.

FOOD

Eating – be it Portuguese or Macanese 'soul food', Chinese dim sum or the special treats available from street stalls and night markets – is one of the most rewarding aspects of a visit to Macau. Indeed, some people make the trek over from Hong Kong just to have lunch at Fernando's on Coloane Island or dinner at the Pousada de São Tiago in peninsular Macau. When going out for dinner, it's worth remembering that people eat relatively early here. In some restaurants the dining room is clear and the chef has left by 9pm.

It's important to understand the difference between Portuguese and Macanese food. Portuguese cuisine is heavy, meat-based and not particularly refined. It makes great use of a viscous form of olive oil, garlic and *bacalhau* (dried salted cod), which can be prepared in many different ways. It sometimes combines meat and seafood in one dish, such as *porco à Alentejana*, which is a tasty casserole of pork and clams. Some favourite dishes are *caldo verde*, a green vegetable soup thickened with potatoes; *pasteis de bacalhau* (codfish croquettes), *sardinhas grelhadas* (grilled sardines) and *feijoada*, a casserole of beans, pork, spicy sausages, potatoes and cabbage – not unlike French *cassoulet* – that is actually Brazilian in origin but was expropriated long ago by the Portuguese. There's also oxtail and veal dishes and rabbit prepared in various ways.

Macanese food is much more interesting. It borrows a lot of its ingredients and tastes from Chinese and other Asian cuisines, as well as from those of former Portuguese colonies in Africa and Indian. It is redolent of coconut, tamarind, chilli, jaggery (palm sugar) and shrimp paste.

The most famous Macanese speciality is African chicken, with the bird done in coconut and chillies. Apart from cod, there's plenty of other fish and seafood: shrimp, prawns, crab, squid and white fish. Sole, a tongue-shaped flat fish, is a Macanese delicacy. The contribution from the former Portuguese enclave of Goa on the west coast of India is spicy prawns.

Other Macanese favourites include *casquinha*, or stuffed crab; *porco balichão*, an unforgettable savoury dish of pork cooked with tamarind and shrimp paste; *minchi*, minced beef or pork cooked with potatoes, onions and spices; and baked rice dishes made with cod, prawns or crab. A Macanese dessert is *serradura*, a calorie-rich 'sawdust' pudding made with crushed biscuits or cookies, cream and condensed milk. Eat a dish of that and you'll never leave the table.

Dining in Macau is a quarterly advertorial freebie, but a good source nonetheless for information about some three dozen restaurants. Check out the Web site at www.dininginmacau.com.

DRINKS
Nonalcoholic Drinks

Macau doesn't produce any local specialities. The soft-drink market is dominated by brands imported from the West and Hong Kong. Green and jasmine tea predominate at Chinese restaurants, but Macau's supermarkets stock Twinings and Lipton.

Alcoholic Drinks

Wine & Spirits The Portuguese influence on the drinks market in Macau is most visible in the many fine imported Portuguese red and white wines, ports and brandies on offer. The most popular tipple in Macau is *vinho verde*, a crisp, dry, slightly effervescent 'green' wine that goes down a treat with salty Portuguese food and spicy Macanese dishes. Mateus Rosé, in its distinctive oval-shaped bottle, is one of the better-known Portuguese wines and sells for around M$40 a bottle – but it's raspberry-flavoured plonk. Eschew it in favour of many of the fine vintages from Dão, Douro or Alenquer. Wine lovers should visit the Macau Wine Museum (see the Macau Peninsula chapter) to learn more about the Portuguese varieties.

Portugal is famous for its ports – and why not? They were the ones who invented the fortified wine. All sorts of 'ruby' ports are available – Parador (about M$80 a bottle) is particularly fine. For a little something different, try the evocatively named Lágrima do Christo (tears of Christ), an unusual white port. Some Portuguese aguardentes (brandies) are worth trying, including Adega Velha and Antigua VSOP Aliança.

Wine and spirits are much cheaper in Macau than in Hong Kong – even less expensive than at Hong Kong's so-called 'duty-free shops'. Part of the reason has to do with Hong Kong's 90% import tax on alcoholic beverages. In Macau, Portuguese wine carries no import duty, and other imported alcohols are taxed at around 22%.

One of the best places to buy Portuguese wines, ports and brandies is Provinhos (☎ 353 401), 183 Rua à Nova Guia, though you'll find quite a good selection at large supermarkets.

Beer While Carlsberg and San Miguel from Hong Kong and China's Tsingtao dominate the market, Macau Beer produces four of its own brews, and very good they are too: Super Dry, Golden Ale, Amber Ale and Stout.

ENTERTAINMENT
Discos & Nightclubs
The club scene in Macau has yet to reach the level of sophistication that it has in Hong Kong, and nightlife here is largely limited to tacky nightclub floorshows and hostess clubs patronised by visiting Hong Kong, Chinese and Japanese tourists. If you're a fan of feather boas, cheesy chorus lines and two beads and a feather (or was it

two feathers and a bead?) covering vital parts, this sequined world will be right up your, well, alley.

Gambling
At last count, Macau had 10 casinos, all of which operate round the clock. Although the games in Macau are somewhat different from those in Las Vegas, the same basic principles apply.

No matter what the game, the casino enjoys a built-in mathematical advantage. In the short-term, anyone can hit a winning streak and get ahead, but the longer you play, the more certain it is that the odds will catch up with you. The best bet (as it were) is to gamble for fun only. Don't put down more than you can afford to lose and don't think you can 'make up your losses' by gambling more. If you win, consider yourself lucky and leave the table.

For casino games that are more sophisticated than the slot machines, what the Chinese call 'hungry tigers', see the boxed text Some Fun & Games in Macau.

The legal gambling age in Macau is 18 years for foreigners and 21 years for Macau residents. Photography is absolutely prohibited inside the casinos. All casinos also have a dress code. Men cannot wear shorts, even relatively long ones, or a singlet (undershirt) unless they have a shirt over it. Women wearing shorts or vests are refused entry, as is anyone wearing thongs (flip-flops).

In the unlikely event that you make an absolute packet at a Macau casino, transporting the cash safely to wherever you want it can be arranged for you by Securicor (☎ 718 601, fax 718 616, W www .securicor.com.hk), 185–191 Avenida Venceslau de Morais. They're on call 24 hours.

Despite the surfeit of casinos, the most popular form of gambling in Macau is in reality mah jong, played not in the casinos but in private homes. Down any side street you'll hear the rattle of mah jong tiles being thrown on the table till late in the night.

SPECTATOR SPORTS
The Macau Stadium (☎ 838 208), Avenida Olímpica, next to the Macau Jockey Club

Some Fun & Games in Macau

Baccarat Also known as *chemin de fer*, or 'railroad', this has become the card game of choice for the upper crust of Macau's gambling elite. Baccarat rooms are always the classiest part of any casino, and the minimum wager is high – at least M$100, and up to M$1000 at some casinos.

Two hands are dealt simultaniously – a player hand and a bank hand. Players can bet on either hand (neither is actually the house hand) and the hand that scores closest to nine is the winner. The casino deducts a percentage if the bank hand wins, which is how the house makes its profit.

If the player understands the game properly, the house only enjoys a slightly better than 1% advantage over the player.

Blackjack Also known as 21, this card game is easy to play, although it requires some skill to play it well. The dealer takes a card and gives another to the players. Face cards count as ten, aces as one or 11. Cards are dealt one at a time – the goal is to get as close as possible to 21 (blackjack) without going over. If you go over 21 you 'bust', or lose. Players are always dealt their cards before the dealer, so if they bust they will always bust before the dealer does. This is what gives the casino the edge over the player. If the dealer and player both get 21, it's a tie and the bet is cancelled. If players get 21, they get even money plus a 50% bonus. Dealers must draw until they reach 16, and stand on 17 or higher. The player is free to decide when to stand or when to draw.

Boule Boule is very similar to roulette, except that it's played with a ball about the size of a billiard ball, and there are fewer numbers. Boule has 24 numbers plus a star. The payoff is 23 to one on numbers. On all bets (numbers, red or black, odd or even) the casino has a 4% advantage over players.

Dai Siu Cantonese for 'big small', this game is also known as *sik po* (dice treasure) or *cu sik* (guessing dice). It's extremely popular in Macau.

The game is played with three dice. The dice are placed in a covered glass container, the container is then shaken and you bet on whether the toss will be from three to nine (small) or 10 to 18 (big). However, you lose on combinations where all three dice come up the same, such as 2-2-2, 3-3-3 and so on – unless you bet directly on three of a kind.

For betting dai siu the house advantage is 2.78%. Betting on a specific three of a kind gives the house a 30% advantage.

Fan Tan This is an ancient Chinese game practically unknown in the West. The dealer takes an inverted silver cup and plunges it into a pile of porcelain buttons, then moves the cup to one side. After all bets have been placed, the buttons are counted out in groups of four. You have to bet on how many will remain after the last set of four has been taken out.

---

on Taipa Island, seats 15,000 but is being enlarged and will accommodate 30,000 by the time the Asian Games are held there in 2005.

Throughout the year the stadium hosts international soccer meets and track and field competitions. On the first Sunday in December the Macau International Marathon starts there and makes its way around Taipa Island before crossing to the Macau Peninsula and then returning to the stadium. The stadium has synthetic and natural grass football pitches, as well as facilities for volleyball and basketball.

Another organisation that may be worth contacting for details of forthcoming events is the Macau Sports Institute (☎ 580 762) at the Tourist Activities Centre on Rua de Luís Gonzaga Gomes.

Grand Prix

The biggest sporting event of the year is the Formula 3 Macau Grand Prix held in the

Some Fun & Games in Macau

Keno Although keno is played in Las Vegas and other casinos around the world, it is thought to have originated in China more than 2000 years ago. Keno was introduced to the USA by Chinese railroad workers in the 19th century.

The game is basically a lottery, which is why some European countries call their national lottery just that. There are 80 numbers, of which 20 are drawn in each game. You are given a keno ticket and the object is to list the numbers you think will be drawn. You can bet on four numbers and, if all four are among those drawn in the game, you're a winner. You can play five numbers, six, seven and so on. You have about one chance in nine million of guessing all 20 winning numbers. With only about two drawings per hour, it's a slow game to play.

Pai Kao This is a form of Chinese dominoes similar to mah jong. One player is made banker and the others individually compare their hands against the banker's. The casino doesn't play, but deducts a 3% commission from the winnings for providing the gambling facilities.

Roulette This is a very easy game to play. The dealer simply spins the roulette wheel in one direction and tosses a ball the other way. Roulette wheels have 36 numbers plus a zero, so your chance of hitting any given number is one in 37. The payoff is 35 to one, which is what gives the casino its advantage.

Rather than betting on a single number, it's much easier to win if you bet odd or even, or red versus black numbers. If the ball lands on zero, everyone loses to the house (unless you also bet the zero). If you bet red or black, or odd or even, the casino's advantage is 2.7%.

Slot Machines These 'one-armed bandits' or 'hungry tigers' are the classic sucker's games in any casino. Maybe the reason why slot machines are so popular is because it takes no brains to play – just put the coin in the slot and pull the handle. Some machines allow you to put in up to five coins at a time, which increases your chance of winning fivefold. Contrary to popular belief, how hard or gently you pull the handle has no influence on the outcome. There are many small payoffs to encourage you to keep playing, but the goal of every slot player is to hit the grand jackpot (or 'megabucks' as it is called in Macau).

The odds for winning on a slot machine are very low. Machines are usually designed to give the casino a 25% advantage over the player. It's like spinning five roulette wheels at once and expecting them all to land on number seven. The more reels on the machine, the more unlikely it is they will line up for the ultimate pay-off. Three-reel machines give you one chance in 8000 of hitting the jackpot. You have one chance in 160,000 of lining up four reels. If you play a five-reel machine, your chances of lining up all five winning numbers is one in 3.2 million.

MACAU

third week of November. As in Monaco, the streets of the town make up the race track. The 6km circuit starts near the Lisboa Hotel and follows the shoreline along Avenida da Amizade, going around the reservoir and back through the city.

The Grand Prix, which began in 1954, consists of two major races – one for cars and one for motorcycles. Both races attract many international contestants as well as spectators; more than 50,000 people flock to

see it and accommodation is tight. Be sure to book a return ticket on the ferry if you have to get back to Hong Kong right after the race.

Certain areas in Macau are designated as viewing areas for the races. Streets and alleys along the track are blocked off, so it's unlikely you'll be able to find a decent vantage point without paying for it. Prices for seats in the Reservoir Stand are M$200/350 for a single day/package (which includes practice days and qualifying events before the start of the actual races) and M$400/700 at the Lisboa, Mandarin Oriental and Grand Stands. To watch just the practice days and qualifying events costs M$30/40 for one/two days. For ticket inquires and bookings call ☎ 555 555, or Hong Kong ☎ 7171 7171.

Horse Racing

Horse racing has a long history in Macau. In the early 1800s horse races were held outside the city walls on an impromptu course. The area around Estrada Marginal do Hipódromo in the northern part of the peninsula was a popular racecourse in the 1930s, but it has now been taken over by apartment blocks and factories.

Regular horse races are held at the Macau Jockey Club (☎ 821 188, racing information hotline ☎ 820 868, Hong Kong ☎ 800-967 822), Estrada Governador Albano de Oliveira, on Taipa Island. For more details, see the Taipa Island section of the Taipa & Coloane Islands chapter.

Dog Racing

Macau's Canidrome (☎ 261 188, W www.macaudog.com), Avenida do General Castelo Branco, is the largest facility for greyhound racing in Asia. Greyhound races are held four times a week on Monday, Thursday and Saturday and Sunday, starting at 8pm. There are 14 races per night, with six to eight dumb dogs chasing a mechanical rabbit around the 455m oval track. Admission to the Canidrome costs M$2 or M$5 in the members' stand. For racing information call Macau hotline ☎ 333 399 or ☎ 800-903 888 in Hong Kong.

Off-course betting centres in the Lisboa Hotel and the Kam Pek and Jai Alai Casinos accept bets from 5pm onwards.

The annual event at the Canidrome, usually held at the end of summer, is the Slot Greyhound Derby.

SHOPPING

The main shopping area is along the Avenida do Infante Dom Henrique and Avenida de Almeida Ribeiro. Other shopping zones can be found along Rua da Palha, Rua do Campo and Rua Pedro Nolasco da Silva.

The St Dominic Market is in the alley just behind the Central Hotel and northwest of the MGTO. It's a good place to pick up cheap clothing.

While exploring Macau's back lanes and streets you'll stumble across bustling markets and traditional Chinese shops selling bird cages, dried herbs and medicines, and seafood places, bakeries and shops festooned with colourful paper offerings to burn to honour the dead. Rua de Madeira is a charming market street selling chickens, dried meats, sausages and fruit, with many shops selling carved Buddhas and other religious items.

Rua dos Mercadores, which leads up to Rua da Tercena, will lead you past tailors, wok sellers, tiny jewellery shops, incense and mah jong shops and other traditional businesses. At the far end of Rua da Tercena, where the road splits, is a flea market where you can pick up old Macanese coins. There's another flea market near the ruins of the Church of St Paul.

Great streets for antiques, ceramics and curios are Rua de São Paulo, Rua das Estalagens and Rua de São António, and the lanes off them. Buy cautiously, and be aware that a large number of forgeries – especially moulded cement Buddha heads buried in the back garden for a few months and passed off as ancient stone carvings – make their way into Macau from Zhuhai and points beyond in China. Rua das Estalagens is also good for cheap clothing.

The largest department store in Macau is the Japanese-owned New Yaohan opposite the ferry terminal. Central Plaza on Avenida de Almeida Ribeiro just down from the Leal Senado has a concentration of top-end shops.

Macau produces some wonderful postage stamps, real collector's items that include images of everything from key colonial landmarks to roulette tables and high-speed ferries. Mint sets and first-day covers are available at a special outlet at the main post office; enter from Avenida de Almeida Ribeiro between the post office's main entrance and the Bank of America at No 70.

The MGTO distributes a useful pamphlet called *Shopping in Macau*, which highlights neighbourhoods and their specific wares.

Getting There & Away

AIR

Airport & Airlines

Ultra-modern Macau international airport, built on reclaimed land off Taipa Island at a cost of US$11.8 billion and partly financed by the People's Republic of China, opened to great fanfare in December 1995 – but it all went pear-shaped almost immediately. Today it is one of the least busy airports in Asia, partly because of the economic downturn that knocked Asia sideways in the late 1990s and partly because of neighbouring Zhuhai's decision to build its own airport a relatively short distance away in Doumen county. Even TAP Air Portugal no longer flies to Macau.

On the plus side, the small volume of passenger traffic means that immigration, customs and baggage-handling procedures are fast and efficient.

Though many airlines have offices in Macau, only a few actually fly into the territory and those are listed below. Please note that the China National Aviation Corporation (CNAC) contact numbers are also good for a number of smaller Chinese carriers, including China Eastern Airlines (code MU), China Northern Airlines (CJ), China Northwest Airlines (WH), China Southern Airlines (CZ), China Southwest Airlines (SZ), Shanghai Airlines (FM) and Yunnan Airlines (3Q).

You can check flight schedules on the Hong Kong & Macau Airline Timetable Web site (W www.hktimetable.com).

Air Koryo (JS; ☎ 356 634; airport ☎ 861 329) 20th floor, Hoi Wong Commercial Centre, 55 Rua da Praia Grande

Air Macau (NX; ☎ 396 5555; airport ☎ 898 3300) Ground floor, Dynasty Plaza Building, Avenida da Amizade, NAPE

CNAC (☎ 788 034; airport ☎ 861 299) Ground floor, Iat Teng Hou Commercial Centre, Avenida de Dom João

EVA Airways (BR; ☎ 726 848; airport ☎ 861 330) 21st floor, ground floor, Dynasty Plaza Building, Avenida da Amizade, NAPE

Singapore Airlines (SQ; ☎ 711 728; airport ☎ 861 321) Room 1001, 10th floor, Luso International Building, 1–3 Rua Dr Pedro Jose Lobo

Trans Asia Airways (GE; ☎ 701 556; airport ☎ 862 200) 11th floor, Macau Finance Centre, 244–246 Rua de Pequim

Xiamen Airlines (MF; ☎ 780 663; airport ☎ 861 335) 5th floor, I Tak Commercial Centre, 126 Rua de Pequim

Buying Tickets

The situation for buying tickets to or in Macau is much the same as for Hong Kong (see the Hong Kong Getting There & Away chapter). As always, better deals on discount fares are found through travel agencies than directly through the airlines.

If you're flying from a city that is directly linked by air with Macau, check as it could well be cheaper to fly straight to Macau rather than entering via Hong Kong. Macau is linked to a limited number of cities around the world, though there are quite a few flights from cities in China, and from Taipei and Kaohsiung in Taiwan.

Travel Agencies Travel agencies in Macau selling discounted tickets include the following:

Amigo Travel (☎ 337 333, fax 378 383) Shop G35, ground floor, New Wing, Lisboa Hotel, 2–4 Avenida de Lisboa

Estoril Travel (☎ 710 361, fax 710 353) Ground floor, Kingsway Commercial Centre, 192 Rua de Luís Gonzaga Gomes

New Sintra Tours (☎ 377 666, fax 710 116) Ground floor, New Wing, Lisboa Hotel, 2–4 Avenida de Lisboa

Departure Tax

Airport departure tax is M$130/80 for adults/children aged two to 12 for international destinations and M$80/50 for destinations in China.

Hong Kong

East Asia Airlines (☎ 727 288; in Hong Kong ☎ 2108 4838, W www.helihongkong

.com) runs an eight-passenger helicopter shuttle service between Macau and Hong Kong that takes 16 minutes and costs HK$1206/1310 on weekdays/weekends. There are up to 22 flights daily between 9.30am and 11pm from Hong Kong, and between 9am and 10.30pm from Macau. In Hong Kong departures are from the helipad at the Shun Tak Centre (☎ 2859 3359), 200 Connaught Rd in Sheung Wan; in Macau they leave from the roof of the ferry terminal (☎ 790 7240). There are no ordinary flights between Macau and Hong Kong.

Canada

Trans Asia Airways and EVA Airways have at least one flight per day to and from Vancouver via Taipei.

Australia

You can fly to Perth, Melbourne and Sydney on Tuesday and Saturday with Singapore Airlines via Singapore.

Continental Europe

Singapore airlines has a weekly flight on Friday to Madrid via Singapore.

China

Macau is connected to a large number of cities in China. Air Macau and a number of Chinese carriers (see the earlier Airport & Airlines entry) fly to Beijing (daily), Chongqing (three times a week), Fuzhou (daily), Guilin (daily), Haikou (four times a week), Kunming (daily), Nanjing (twice a week), Shanghai (three times daily), Xiamen (twice daily) and Xian (daily).

North-East Asia

There are more flights between Macau and Taiwan than any other place, since Taiwan businesspeople use the territory as a gateway to the mainland. Most passengers just remain on the plane as the flight number is changed.

EVA Airways, Trans Asia Airways and Air Macau each have up to six flights a day to and from Taipei. Air Macau and Trans Asia Airways each fly to Kaohsiung twice a day while EVA Airways has a daily flight.

Air Macau has flights to Seoul on Thursday and Sunday.

There are no regularly scheduled flights between Macau and Japan, but Japan Air System has occasional charters.

South-East Asia

Singapore Airlines flies between Macau and Jakarta via Singapore and Kuala Lumpur twice a week on Tuesday and Saturday. Air Macau offers direct flights to Bangkok on Monday, Wednesday and Friday and to Manila on Tuesday and Saturday.

LAND
China

The Zhuhai Special Economic Zone (SEZ) in mainland China just across Macau's northern border makes for an interesting day or overnight trip. (See the China Excursion – Zhuhai chapter for details.) Take bus No 3, 5 or 9 to the Border Gate (known as the Portas de Cerco, or 'gates of siege', in Portuguese) and simply walk across. A second crossing into the mainland has now been opened on the causeway linking Taipa and Coloane. The Cotai Frontier Post allows passengers to cross over the new Lotus Bridge linking Macau and the Zhuhai SEZ from 9am to 5pm daily – but apart from those heading for Zhuhai airport it is of little use to most visitors. Bus No 26 will drop you off here.

Holders of most passports will be able to purchase their visas at the border, but it will ultimately save you time (if not money) to buy one in advance (for details see the Visas section, under Information in the Zhuhai chapter). If you do plan to return the same day, remember that the border gate closes from midnight to 7am.

If you want to travel farther afield in China, buses run by the Kee Kwan Motor Road Co (☎ 933 888) leave the small station on Rua das Lorchas, 100m south-west of the end of Avenida de Almeida Ribeiro, for Guangzhou (M$55, every 15 minutes) and Zhongshan (M$20, every 20 minutes) throughout the day. But the bus to Guangzhou, which is 130km to the northwest, takes about six hours and often gets bogged down at customs. It's probably easier to take a bus to the border, walk across and catch a train or minibus to Guangzhou from the other side.

SEA
Departure Tax
Macau levies a departure tax of M$19 on anyone leaving the territory by sea for China or Hong Kong, but it's almost always included in the price of the ticket.

Hong Kong
Hong Kong is far and away the most popular gateway to and from Macau. Although Macau is separated from Hong Kong by 65km of water, the journey can be made in about an hour. Sometimes queues at customs and immigration can add another 30 minutes to the journey. There are frequent departures throughout the day. The schedule is somewhat reduced between midnight and 7am, but boats run virtually 24 hours. There is talk about starting up services between Tuen Mun in the New Territories and Macau.

Two ferry companies operate services to and from Macau. TurboJet (☎ 790 7039; in Hong Kong ☎ 2859 3333 for information, ☎ 2921 6688 for bookings, ⓦ www.turbojet.com.hk) runs three types of vessels from the Macau ferry pier at the Shun Tak Centre (☎ 2859 3359), 200 Connaught Rd in Sheung Wan on Hong Kong Island, and from the Macau Ferry Terminal (☎ 790 7240) in Macau. Jetfoils (single-hull jet-powered hydrofoils) and foil-cats (catamaran-jetfoils) take about 55 minutes to make the crossing while turbocats (jet-powered catamarans) take 65 minutes. You no longer choose the type of vessel you take; just buy your ticket and board the vessel. Economy/super class tickets cost HK$130/232 on weekdays, HK$141/247 at the weekend and on holidays and HK$161/260 at night (ie, from 5.45pm to 6.30am). They are M$1 more expensive travelling from Macau.

The Hong Kong & Yaumatei Ferry Co (HYFCO; ☎ 726 301; in Hong Kong ☎ 2516 9581, ⓦ www.nwff.com.hk) operates catamarans (433 seats on two decks) from the China ferry terminal on Canton Rd in Tsim Sha Tsui 14 times a day, with departures on the hour from 8am to 9pm. They depart Macau hourly from 9.30am to 10.30pm but the 9.30pm and 10.30pm services terminate at the Macau ferry pier in Sheung Wan and *not* in Tsim Sha Tsui. The trip takes about 75 minutes and tickets cost HK$113/154 on weekdays during the day/night (ie, after 6pm from Hong Kong and 6.30pm from Macau), and HK$134/154 at weekends and on public holidays.

Tickets can be booked up to 28 days in advance and are available at the ferry terminals, all China Travel Service (CTS) branches (see under Organised Tours later in this chapter) and many travel agents. There is a standby queue before each sailing for passengers wanting to travel before their ticketed sailing. On weekends and public holidays you'd be wise to book your return ticket in advance because the boats are often full.

You need to arrive at the pier at least 15 minutes before departure, but you should allow 30 minutes because of occasional long queues at the immigration checkpoint, especially on the Hong Kong side.

Luggage space on the jetfoils and turbocats is limited; some boats have small overhead lockers while others have storage space at the bow and stern. You are theoretically limited to 10kg of carry-on luggage in economy class (you can probably get away with more if it's not too bulky), but oversized or overweight bags can be taken on as checked luggage. There is more luggage space on the HYFCO catamarans.

China
A daily ferry run by the Yuet Tung Shipping Co (☎ 574 478, 331 067) connects Macau with the port of Shekou in the Shenzhen SEZ north of Hong Kong. The boat departs from Macau at 2.30pm and arrives in Shekou at 4pm. The fare is M$100/57 for adults/children, and tickets can be bought up to three days in advance from the point of departure, which is not the main ferry pier in Macau but pier No 14 just off Rua das Lorchas, 100m south-west of the end of Avenida de Almeida Ribeiro.

Sampans and ferries make the short trip across the Inner Harbour to Wanzai (M$12) on the mainland throughout the day from a small pier to the south-west, where Rua das Lorchas meets Rua do Dr Lourenço Pereira Marques.

ORGANISED TOURS

Tours booked on the ground in Macau are generally much better value than those booked in Hong Kong, though the latter include transportation to and from Macau and usually a side trip across the border to Zhuhai. Tours from Hong Kong are usually one-day whirlwind tours, departing for Macau in the morning and returning to Hong Kong on the same evening. Such a tour typically costs about HK$750.

A typical tour is a one-day affair that takes you to the port of Shekou in the Shenzhen SEZ, then by boat to Zhuhai. From there it carries on to Cuiheng, birthplace of Dr Sun Yat Sen, in Zhongshan county, then by bus to Macau, and back by jetfoil to Hong Kong by 7.30pm. Such an escapade would cost HK$1180/1000 for adults/children, frayed nerves included.

Finding a tour is easy. In Hong Kong, the Macau Government Tourist Office (☎ 2857 2287, fax 2559 0698) in room 336 of the Shun Tak Centre, 200 Connaught Rd, Sheung Wan (where the Macau ferries depart) has heaps of information on tours, as do the numerous travel agents in the same building. One company that organises tours of Macau and China is Gray Line (☎ 2368 7111, fax 2721 9651, W www.grayline .com.hk). China Travel Service (CTS; in Hong Kong ☎ 2851 1788; in Macau ☎ 709 888) is another agent worth checking out for a range of tours.

For tours from within Macau, see the Organised Tours section in the following Getting Around chapter.

Getting Around

TO/FROM THE AIRPORT

Airport bus AP1 (M$6) leaves the airport and first zips around Taipa, passing the Macau Jockey Club and the New Century and Hyatt Hotels. It then crosses the Macau-Taipa Bridge and stops at the Lisboa Hotel as well as several other hotels in the centre (Nam Yue Hotel, Kingsway Hotel, New World Emperor Hotel, Holiday Inn, Grandeur Hotel and Fortuna Hotel) before proceeding to the Macau Ferry Terminal and the Portas do Cerco (border gate), where it terminates. The fare is M$6 and the bus departs every 15 minutes from 6.30am to 1.20am.

A taxi from the airport to the centre of town should cost about M$40.

BUS

Public buses and minibuses run by TCM (☎ 850 060) and Transmac (☎ 271 122) operate on some 40 routes throughout the day from 6.45am till midnight. Buses display their ultimate destination in Portuguese and in Chinese. Fares, using either pataca or Hong Kong dollar coins, are dropped into a box upon entry; there's no change.

The *Macau Tourist Map*, distributed for free by the Macau Government Tourist Office (MGTO), has a full list of both bus companies' routes. You will also find them on the MGTO (W www.macautourism.gov.mo) and the Cityguide (W www.cityguide.gov.mo) Web sites.

Macau Peninsula

Buses on peninsular Macau cost a flat M$2.50. The two most useful buses for travellers are probably Nos 3 and 3A, which run between the ferry terminal and the city centre, near the main post office. The No 3 also goes up to the border crossing with the mainland, as does the No 5. The following are the most useful bus routes on the peninsula:

No 3 From the ferry terminal, past the Macau Forum and Lisboa Hotel, along Avenida Almeida Ribeiro and up to the border gate

No 3A Follows the same route as the No 3 but goes west from Avenida Almeida Ribeiro over to the budget hotel district and terminates on Praça Ponte e Horta

No 10 From the border gate to the ferry terminal, past the Macau Forum and the Lisboa Hotel, along part of Avenida Almeida Ribeiro and down to the A-Ma Temple (bus No 10A follows a similar route)

No 12 From the ferry terminal, past the Macau Forum and the Lisboa Hotel and then up to the Lou Lim Ioc Garden and Kun Iam Temple

The Islands

From Macau peninsula, the fare to Taipa is M$3.30, to Coloane Village M$4 and to Hác Sá Beach on Coloane M$5. Some of the most useful bus routes to the islands are:

No 21 From the A-Ma Temple and along Avenida Almeida Ribeiro to the Lisboa Hotel, over the bridge to Taipa Village and on to Coloane (bus No 21A follows the same route but carries on to Cheoc Van and Hác Sá beaches)

No 22 From the Kun Iam Temple, past the Hotel Lisboa to Taipa Village, and then the Macau Jockey Club

No 25 From the border via Lou Lim Ioc Garden, past the Lisboa Hotel to Taipa Village and Macau University, then on to Cheoc Van and Hác Sá beaches on Coloane

No 26A From Avenida Almeida Ribeiro, past the Lisboa Hotel and through Taipa to the airport and the Lotus Bridge and Cotai Frontier Post and then to Coloane Village (and Cheoc Van and Hác Sá beaches in summer)

CAR & MOTORCYCLE

The streets of peninsular Macau are a gridlock of cars plastered with go-faster stripes and stickers and mopeds that will cut you off at every turn. While driving here might look like it could be fun, it's strictly for the locals. That said, a rental car or Moke, which is a brightly coloured Jeep-like convertible (see the following Rental section), can be a convenient way to explore the islands. Motorcycles are not available for rent in Macau.

MACAU

Road Rules

As in Hong Kong but *not* China, vehicles drive on the left-hand side of the road. Drivers and front-seat passengers are in theory required to wear seat belts. It's illegal to beep the horn in built-up areas of Macau (ie, most of the peninsula).

For information about driving licences and permits, see that section under Visas & Documents in the Macau Facts for the Visitor chapter.

Rental

Happy Mokes (☎ 439 393, fax 727 888), in room 1025 of the arrivals hall at the ferry terminal, has four-person Mokes available to rent for M$450/500 per day during the week/weekends and six-person vehicles for HK$500/600. The rate is for 24 hours. Your Moke comes with a full tank of fuel, and you have to return it with a full tank or pay over the odds for them to do so.

You can also rent Mokes from Avis Rent A Car (☎ 336 789, fax 314 112), which has an office in the shopping arcade of the Mandarin Oriental Hotel. Avis also rents cheap Subarus that cost M$400 a day during the week and M$520 at the weekend. You can book in advance through the Avis Hong Kong office (☎ 2890 6988, fax 2895 3686), Bright Star Mansion, 93 Leighton Rd, Causeway Bay.

TAXI

Taxis in Macau have meters and drivers are required to use them. Flag fall is M$10 for the first 1.5km and M$1 for each additional 250m. There is a M$5 surcharge to go to Taipa and Coloane; travelling between Taipa and Coloane is M$2 extra. Journeys starting from the airport incur an extra charge of M$5. Large bags cost an extra M$3. Taxis can be dispatched by radio by ringing ☎ 519 519, ☎ 939 939 or ☎ 398 8800. Not many taxi drivers know streets and other destinations by their Portuguese names, so it is handy to have your destination written out in Chinese characters beforehand.

It should cost you about M$300 to hire a taxi for the day. Both the itinerary and the price should be agreed upon in advance. Any large hotel will be able to help you to arrange this.

BICYCLE

Bikes can be rented in Taipa Village; see the Taipa & Coloane chapter for details. They are available in a wide variety of classes – from light 10-speed racers to heavyweight clunkers – and cost M$10 to M$12 per hour.

You are allowed to cross the Macau-Taipa Bridge on foot but not on a bicycle; the only way to get a bike across to the island is in the boot of a car. Bikes are allowed on the causeway linking Taipa and Coloane, however.

PEDICAB

These three-wheeled trishaws, called *triciclos* in Portuguese, seat two people and are really only for tourists. They are not the cheap form of transport they are elsewhere in Asia. The main place to find one is outside the Lisboa Hotel. Pedicabs don't have meters, of course, and you must agree on a fare beforehand. Expect to pay anything from M$30 to M$50 for a single ride and M$150 per hour of a very slow tour of Macau. Pedicabs cannot negotiate hills, so you'll be limited to touring the waterfront and some of the narrow alleys.

ORGANISED TOURS

It's cheaper to book tours in Macau than in Hong Kong. A typical bus tour of peninsular Macau booked through the MGTO (☎ 315 566, fax 510 104) or any of the agents listed below takes three to 3½ hours and costs M$180 per person, including lunch. By limousine it costs M$500 for one person and M$350 per person for two or more passengers. Bus tours to the islands lasting 1½ to two hours cost about M$100 per person. You can also book a one-day bus tour across the border into Zhuhai, which usually includes a trip to the former home of Dr Sun Yat Sen in Zhongshan county.

Some Macau-based tour operators to try include:

Asia Tours & Travel (☎ 355 633, fax 565 060) 1st floor, 225 Avenida da Praia Grande
China Travel Service (CTS; ☎ 709 888, fax 706 611) Xinhua Building, Rua de Nagasaki
Guangdong Macau Tours (☎ 726 728, fax 726 722) 12th floor, Nam Yue Building, Avenida do Doutor Rodrigo Rodrigues
Hi-No-De Caravela (☎ 726 995, fax 726 997) 5th floor, Block D, 1142M Avenida do Doutor Rodrigo Rodrigues
Macau Zhuhai (☎ 552 739, fax 552 735) Room 406, Presidente Hotel, Avenida da Amizade
South China Macao Travel (☎ 706 620, fax 706 624) 5th floor, Nam Fong Building, Avenida da Amizade

Air

Companies offering helicopter sightseeing tours over Hong Kong can offer the same thing over Macau. See Air under Organised Tours in the Hong Kong Getting Around chapter for details.

Bus

If you're on a very brief visit to Macau the Tour Machine, run by Avis Rent A Car

(☎ 336 789), might be an option. It's a replica 1920s-style English bus, complete with leather upholstery, that seats nine people and runs on fixed routes in about two hours past some of Macau's most important sights. You're allowed to disembark, stretch your legs and take photos along the way. There are two departures a day – at 11am and 3pm – from the Macau Ferry Terminal. Tickets cost M$150/80 for adults/children. The Tour Machine can also be chartered for M$300 per hour for trips in Macau.

Boat

A motorised junk (☎ 595 481), moored at the little pier next to the Maritime Museum and opposite the A-Ma Temple on Rua de São Tiago da Barra, offers 30-minute rides (M$10) around the Inner Harbour with taped commentary. Departures are daily at 10.30am, 11.30am, 3.30pm and 4pm; and there are up to six additional sailings between 11am and 5pm when six or more tickets are sold.

MACAU

Macau Peninsula

The lion's share of Macau's museums, churches, gardens, ancient cemeteries, colonial buildings and cobbled back streets are on the peninsula. If you're after more active pursuits like cycling, hiking or swimming, head for the islands (see the following Taipa & Coloane Islands chapter).

Since 1992 more than half of all buildings of historic significance in Macau have been restored. Particularly good examples of this energetic renovation campaign are the Largo do Senado, the splendid villas lining the Avenida da Praia Grande and the Rua da Felicidade, with its red-and-white shuttered shop houses. The Macau Museum in the Monte Fort and the Macau Museum of Art in the Cultural Centre are just two new world-class attractions that alone make a visit to the territory worthwhile.

INFORMATION
Tourist Offices

For details about tourist offices, see Local Tourist Offices in the Macau Facts for the Visitor chapter.

Bookshops

Hong Kong is a much better bet for English-language books about Macau, but the bookshops at the major hotels usually stock a decent selection of Macau-related titles, and the gift shop at the Macau Museum (☎ 357 911) in the Monte Fort has a very good choice. It's open 10am to 6pm from Tuesday to Sunday.

For Portuguese-language publications and music CDs, check out Livraria Portuguesa (☎ 515 915), 18–22 Rua de São Domingos, open from noon to 8pm Monday to Saturday and to 7pm on Sunday. It has a coffee shop in the basement and an art gallery upstairs.

Just around the corner, Livraria São Paulo (☎ 374 029), at 11 Travessa do Bispo, mainly has books in Portuguese and oriented towards Catholicism, but there are some general-interest English-language books.

Highlights

- A visit to the ruins of the Church of St Paul and a quick escalator ride up to the Monte Fort and the Macau Museum

- A Formula 3 test drive on one of the simulators at the Grand Prix Museum

- A stroll along the Praia Grande and a visit to the A-Ma Temple

- A walk around the evocative Old Protestant Cemetery

- A visit to the Kun Iam Temple, especially during a Buddhist religious festival, and a rest in the cool and shady Lou Lim Ioc Garden

- A night at the Lisboa Casino

The Plaza Cultural de Macau bookshop (☎ 338 561), in the basement at 32G Avenida do Conselheiro Ferreira de Almeida, has a fair amount of stock in English. It's open from 10am to 7pm Monday to Saturday.

CENTRAL MACAU PENINSULA (MAP 14)

Avenida de Almeida Ribeiro (San Ma Lo, or 'new St', in Cantonese) is Macau's main thoroughfare. It starts at the delightful Avenida da Praia Grande and ends at the Inner Harbour, effectively dividing the narrow southern peninsula from central and northern Macau. Its extension, Avenida do Infante Dom Henrique, runs south of Avenida da Praia Grande to the Outer Harbour, just below the landmark Lisboa Hotel.

Jorge Álvares Monument

This smallish statue of the first Portuguese mariner to land on Chinese soil (1513), located on Avenida da Praia Grande a short distance to the south-west of where Avenida de Almeida Ribeiro begins, is as good a place as any to start a tour of peninsular

Macau. Opposite the statue is the **Supreme Court building** (Tribunais), the 19th-century residence of Macau's governors.

Largo do Senado

'Senate square', with its wavy black-and-white cobbles and its breathtakingly beautiful colonial buildings, is the heart and soul of Macau. The lovely **Santa Casa da Misericordia**, on the southern side of the square, was a home for orphans and prostitutes in the 18th century. The patron was the Macanese trader Martha Merop (1766–1828), heroine of Austin Coates' *City of Broken Promises* (see Books in the Macau Facts for the Visitor chapter). The square and its buildings are illuminated at night.

Leal Senado

Facing the square to the west is Macau's most important historical building, the 18th-century Leal Senado *(163 Avenida de Almeida Ribeiro)*, which now houses the Provisional Municipal Assembly of Macau. The Leal Senado is the main seat for city administration but once had much greater powers and dealt on equal terms with Chinese officials during the last century. It's called the 'loyal senate' because the body sitting here refused to recognise Spain's sovereignty during the 60 years that Spain occupied Portugal.

In 1654, a dozen years after Portuguese control was re-established, King João IV ordered a heraldic inscription to be placed inside the Senate's entrance hall, which can still be seen today. To the right of the entrance hall is an **art gallery** *(☎ 387 333; admission free; open 9am-9pm daily)* with rotating exhibits, usually relating to the history of Macau.

Above the wrought-iron gates leading to the garden is an interesting bas-relief that some say depicts the Virgin Mary Misericordia sheltering rich and poor under her cloak while others hold that it represents the 16th-century Portuguese queen Doña Leonor. The angels that once graced these walls were removed shortly after the handover.

On the 1st floor is the **Senate Library** *(☎ 387 333; admission free; open 1pm-7pm weekdays)*, which has an extensive collection of books on Asia and wonderful wood-carved furnishings and panelled walls.

Church of St Augustine

South-west of the Leal Senado via Rua Central is the Church of St Augustine *(Igreja de São Agostinho; Largo de São Agostinho; open 10am-6pm daily)*. Though its foundations date from 1586, the present church was built in 1814. The high altar contains a statue of Christ bearing the cross, which is carried through the streets during the Procession of Our Lord of Passion on the first Sunday of Lent (see Public Holidays & Special Events in the Macau Facts for the Visitor chapter).

Dom Pedro V Theatre

Opposite the Church of St Augustine is the Dom Pedro V Theatre *(Teatro Dom Pedro V; ☎ 939 646, Calçada do Teatro)*, a colonnaded, cream-coloured building built in the neo-classical style in the early 19th century. It is occasionally used for performances and other events (see Theatre in the Entertainment section).

Church of St Lawrence

If you proceed south-west along Rua de São Lourenço, you'll come to the Church of St Lawrence *(Igreja de São Lourenço; Rua de São Lourenço; open 10am-6pm Tues-Sun, 1pm-2pm Mon)*. It is considered the most fashionable church in Macau. The original church was built of wood in the 1560s and was eventually reconstructed in stone in the early 19th century. One of the two towers of the church formerly served as an ecclesiastical prison. The church has a magnificent painted ceiling.

Stone steps lead to the ornamental gates, but if you want to go inside the church use the entrance on Rua da Imprensa Nacional.

Government House

South of the Chapel of St Joseph's Seminary is the monumental Government House *(Cnr Avenida da Praia Grande & Travessa do Padré Narciso)*, a pillared, rose-coloured building. Originally built for a Portuguese

MACAU

noble in 1849, the building was acquired by the government at the end of the 19th century and is now headquarters of various branches of the Macau SAR government, including the Secretariat for Security.

Macau Cathedral

East of the Largo do Senado is the Cathedral *(Sé Catedral; Largo da Sé; open 10am-6pm daily)*, a not particularly attractive structure built in 1850 to replace an earlier one badly damaged in a typhoon 14 years earlier. The cathedral, which has some notable stained-glass windows, is the focus for most major religious festivals and holy days in Macau.

Church of St Dominic & Treasury of Sacred Art

A fine example of ecclesiastical baroque architecture, the imposing Church of St Dominic *(Igreja de São Domingos; Largo de São Domingos; open 10am-6pm daily)*, north-east of the Largo do Senado, is a 17th-century replacement of a chapel built by the Dominicans in the 1590s. The church has an impressive multi-tiered altar with images of Our Lady of the Rosary flanked by St Dominic and St Catherine of Sienna. A small chapel on the left contains a statue Our Lady of Fatima, the very one carried in a procession of the faithful every year on 13 May. The church, with its distinctive cream-coloured facade and green shutters, underwent extensive renovations from 1994 to 1997.

The Treasury of Sacred Art *(Tresouro de Arte Sacra;* ☎ *572 401; admission free; open 10am-6pm daily)* is a treasure-trove of ecclesiastical art and liturgical objects exhibited on three floors that reach up to the loft of the church tower. Among the most valuable and interesting objects are a 17th-century portrait of St Augustine and an ivory statuette of St John the Baptist wearing a hair shirt the wrong way round.

Ruins of the Church of St Paul

The facade is all that remains of a Jesuit church built in the early 17th century. But with its wonderful statues, portals and engravings, some consider the ruins of the Church of St Paul *(ruinas de Igreja de São Paulo; Rua de São Paulo)* to be the greatest monument to Christianity in Asia.

Built on one of Macau's seven hills, the church was designed by an Italian Jesuit and built by early Japanese Christian exiles and Chinese craftsmen. It was completed in 1602, and the crowned heads of Europe of the time competed to present it with the most prestigious gifts. The church was abandoned after the expulsion of the Jesuits in 1762 and a military battalion was stationed here. In 1835 a fire erupted in the kitchen of the barracks, destroying everything but the facade, the impressive stone steps leading to it and the magnificent mosaic floor. Renovation work was completed in 1995.

The facade has been described as a 'sermon in stone' and a *Biblia pauperum*, a 'Bible of the poor' to help the illiterate understand the Passion of Christ and the lives of the saints.

At the very top is a dove, representing the Holy Spirit, surrounded by stone carvings of the sun, moon and stars. Beneath the Holy Spirit is a statue of the Infant Jesus surrounded by stone carvings of the implements of the crucifixion (eg, the whip, crown of thorns, spear). In the centre of the 3rd tier stands the Virgin Mary as she is being assumed bodily into heaven along with angels and two types of flower: the peony, which represents China, and the chrysanthemum, a symbol of Japan. To the right of the Virgin is a carving of the apocalyptic woman (Mary) slaying a seven-headed hydra; the Chinese characters next to her read 'the holy mother tramples the heads of the dragon'. To the left of the central statue of Mary a 'star' guides a ship (the Church) through a storm (sin).

The 4th tier has statues of Jesuit doctors of the church (from left to right): Blessed Francisco de Borja; St Ignatius Loyola, the founder of the order; St Francis Xavier, the apostle of the Far East; and Blessed Luís Gonzaga.

On the northern side is a stairway leading to the former choir loft, which affords excellent views across central Macau.

Museum of Sacred Art & Crypt The small Museum of Sacred Art *(Museu de*

Arte Sacra; ☎ 387 333; Rua de São Paolo; admission free; open 9am-6pm daily) was opened in the chancel of the Church of St Paul to the north-west of the facade in 1996 after archaeological excavations had been completed. It contains polychrome carved wooden statues, silver chalices and monstrances and oil paintings.

To the east of the museum is the church crypt, which now contains the remains of the Nagasaki martyrs as well as those of Vietnamese and other Japanese Christians killed in the 17th century.

Monte Fort

On a hill and accessible by escalator just east of the ruins of the Church of St Paul, Monte Fort *(Fortaleza do Monte; open daily 6am-7pm May-Sept, 7am-6pm Oct-Apr)* was built by the Jesuits between 1617 and 1626 as part of the College of the Mother of God. Barracks and storehouses were designed to allow the fort to survive a siege of up to two years, but the cannons were fired only once: during the aborted attempt to invade Macau by the Dutch on 24 June 1622, the feast of St John the Baptist. Since then, Christ's baptiser has been the patron saint of Macau.

Macau Museum This museum *(Museu de Macau; ☎ 357 911, Monte Fort, adult/ child & senior M$15/8; open 10am-6pm Tues-Sun)* tells the story of the hybrid territory of Macau, with a host of CD-ROMs, videos and holograms. This place is highly recommended.

The 1st level, called the Genesis of Macau, takes you through the early history of the territory, with parallel developments in the East and the West compared and contrasted. The section devoted to religions (1st floor) is excellent. Equally fascinating is the recreated Macau street, with its architecture, and holograms of people going about their business or playing mahjong.

On the 2nd level (Popular Arts & Traditions of Macau) you'll see and hear everything from a recreated firecracker factory and the recorded cries of street vendors, to the poet Adé reading from his work in Macanese dialect.

The top floor illustrates 'Contemporary Macau' – its contributions to literature, urban development and plans for the future. Interesting exhibits cover the history of the Bela Vista Hotel and some of the entries for the Macau SAR flag and seal submitted before the 1999 handover. The stylised white lotus against a green background and topped with five gold stars was the winner.

The easiest way to reach the Macau Museum is via the escalator just east of the ruins of the Church of St Paul, though a small path also links the two. You can also get here by following Calçada do Monte north from Rua de Pedro Nolasco da Silva, which is the extension of Rua de São Domingos.

Hong Kung Temple

The Hong Kung Temple *(Cnr Rua das Estalagens & Rua de Cinco de Outubro; open 10am-6pm daily)*, in a market district west of the Church of St Paul and the Monte Fort, was built in 1750 and dedicated to Kwan Tai (or Kuanti), the God of War, Literature and Wealth. His image is the one in the middle of the main altar, flanked by his son and standard bearer. The temple gets particularly busy in May and June, when two festivals in Kwan Tai's honour take place.

Church of St Anthony

A couple of blocks north of the ruins of the Church of St Paul at the end of Rua de São António is the modern Church of St Anthony *(Igreja de São António; Largo de São António; open 10am-6pm daily)*. The church was the first to be founded in Macau (1558) and is memorable for having been burned three times: in 1809, 1874 and 1930. Saint Anthony had military connections, and on the occasion of his feast day (13 June), an image of the saint is taken on a tour of inspection of the remnants of the city's battlements.

Cemetery of St Michael the Archangel

The Cemetery of St Michael the Archangel *(Cemitério de São Miguel Arcanjo; Estrada do Cemitério; open 10am-6pm daily)*, east

MACAU

of the Church of St Anthony, is almost exactly in the centre of the Macau Peninsula. Although a few of the tombs are plain, the vast majority are baroque ecclesiastical works of art. This is peninsular Macau's largest cemetery.

Near the main entrance on Estrada do Cemitério is the **Chapel of St Michael** (*Capela de São Miguel; open 10am-6pm daily*), a doll-size lime green church with a tiny choir loft. For something you'll only get to see while travelling, walk quietly around to the back of the church (ie, the northern side), climb up the metal stairs and have a look at what's drying in the warm air. They are the remains of people buried seven or eight years ago, and the bones will now be stored in large urns to save space in the cemetery.

Chinese Reading Room
This octagonal structure (*Rua de Santa Clara*), with its double stone staircase and little round tower, is a wonderful mix of Chinese and Portuguese influences that could only be found in Macau. The Chinese Reading Room is opposite the lovely **St Francis Garden** (*Jardim de São Francisco*).

SOUTHERN MACAU PENINSULA (MAP 13)
Southern Macau encompasses three areas: around the Macau Forum and Tourist Activities Centre, halfway between the ferry terminal and the Lisboa Hotel; the rectangle of reclaimed land called NAPE to the south; and the south-western tip of the Macau Peninsula.

Macau Forum & Tourist Activities Centre
The Macau Forum (*Forum de Macau*) and the Tourist Activities Centre (*Centro de Actividades Turísticas; CAT*) sit side by side on Rua de Luís Gonzaga Gomes to the south-east of central Macau. The former is a conference and exhibition space; the latter houses the Macau Sports Institute as well as two worthwhile museums.

Grand Prix Museum Cars from the Macau Formula 3 Grand Prix, including the Triumph TR2 that won the first Grand Prix in 1954, as well as the motorcycles that have taken top awards over the years, can be seen at the Grand Prix Museum (*Museu do Grande Prémio;* ☎ 798 4108, *Basement floor, CAT, 431 Rua de Luís Gonzaga Gomes; adult/child under 19 M$10/5, child under 11 free; open 10am-6pm Wed-Mon*). A fun feature are the simulators, which allow you to test your racing skills. If you'd rather not get behind the wheel, you can play with the TV monitors that let you choose any part of the circuit and see how it was covered.

Macau Wine Museum Oenophiles will no doubt make a beeline for the Macau Wine Museum (*Museu do Vinho de Macau;* ☎ 798 4188, *CAT, 431 Rua de Luís Gonzaga Gomes; adult/child under 19 M$10/5, child under 11 free; open 10am-6pm Wed-Mon*). For the most part, the museum is a rather inert display of wine racks, barrels, presses and a few simple tools used by winemakers, but some of the more recent wines on display are available for tasting, which is included in the entry fee.

NAPE
The rectangular area of reclaimed land called NAPE (Novos Aterros do Porto Exterior, or 'new reclaimed land of the outer harbour') separates the Outer Harbour from what was once Praia Grande Bay but is now a large artificial lake. NAPE is primarily an area of warehouses, bars and restaurants, but there are a couple of important sights here as well. Reclaimed land often has that cheap, burnt rubber smell of artificiality and NAPE is no exception. When you're as small a place as Macau is, though, you have to grab what you can where you can.

The Macau Cultural Centre This new centre (*Centro Cultural de Macau;* ☎ 797 7418, W *www.ccm.gov.mo; Avenida Xian Xing Hai, NAPE*) is an imaginative and much-needed addition to Macau's cultural landscape. Located south of the World Trade Center, in the south-western corner of NAPE, the US$100-million centre designed by Bruno Soares is the territory's prime

Kun Iam Temple, Macau. The first treaty of trade between China and the USA was signed here, 1844.

The bright lights of the Casino Lisboa, Macau.

Macau's magnificent Largo do Senado

Musicians play their shiny tubas in Macau.

The ruins of the epic Church of Saint Paul.

Historic A-Ma Temple, Macau

Baroque Church of St Dominic

Pedicab in Largo do Senado

Portuguese influence in Macau can be seen in the architecture.

venue for theatre, concerts, operas and other cultural performances. The Macau Museum of Art (see following) is part of the centre, and a walkway connects it with a large tower standing in the harbour, which affords wonderful views of the harbour.

Macau Museum of Art This museum *(Museu de Arte de Macau; ☎ 791 9800, Avenida Xian Xing Hai, NAPE; adult/concession M$5/3; open 10am-7pm Tues-Sun)* is an enormous, five-story complex with more than 10,000 sq metres of floor space, housing a library with art-related titles, Internet access, ticket offices, lecture halls, temporary exhibits, a Gallery of Historical Paintings (mostly Western and including works of all the artists mentioned in the Arts section of the Facts about Macau chapter), and Chinese painting, calligraphy and porcelain.

Kun Iam Statue Though it sounds naff in the extreme, this 20m-high bronze monument to the Goddess of Mercy emerging, Venus-like, from a lotus in the Outer Harbour is actually quite attractive and restful once you've entered her 'blossom'. This is the two-level **Kun Iam Ecumenical Centre** *(Centro Ecuménico Kun Iam; ☎ 751 516, Avenida Doutor Sun Yat Sen; admission free; open 10.30am-6pm Sat-Thur)*, which is open to people of all faiths for conferences, meetings or just contemplation. The statue sits on an artificial island in the harbour and is connected to the mainland by a 60m-long causeway.

South-West Corner

The south-western tip of the Macau Peninsula has a number of interesting sights, and so it should: it was the first area to be settled in Macau.

Avenida da República From the centre of town, Avenida da Praia Grande and Rua da Praia do Bom Parto form an arc that leads into Avenida da República, one of the most beautiful avenues in the territory. In the not-too-distant past, this promenade followed the shoreline of Praia Grande Bay;

land reclamation has turned the bay into two artificial lakes.

This stretch is lined with beautiful colonial villas and civic buildings. Have a look at the **Mateus Ricci College** *(17 Avenida da Praia do Bom Parto)*, one of the oldest schools in Macau. A short distance to the south-west and towering above Avenida da República is the **former Bela Vista Hotel**, which holds enough stories and secrets to fill several volumes. It is now the residence of the Portuguese consul-general.

A short distance to the south-west is a superb villa called the **Santa Sancha Palace** *(Palacete de Santa Sancha; Estrada de Santa Sancha)*, erstwhile residence of Macau's Portuguese governors.

Penha Hill Towering above the colonial villas along Avenida da República is Penha Hill *(Colina da Penha)*, from where you'll get an excellent view of the central area of Macau and across the Pearl River into China. The **Bishop's Palace** (1837) is here as is the **Chapel of Our Lady of Penha** *(Capela de Nostra Señora da Penha; open 9am-5.40pm daily)*, an ugly cement block of a church built on the site of a 17th-century church in 1935.

Macau Tower The tall structure on the narrow isthmus of land south-east of Avenida da República is the Macau Tower, which, at almost 339m, is the 8th-tallest such structure in the world. When the tower is completed, a series of four lifts will take you to the observation decks in 45 seconds and allow views as far away as Hong Kong on a clear day. The tower will also have a revolving restaurant. Next to the tower is the new **Macau Convention Centre**.

Farther west along the isthmus is a grey granite monument called the **Gates of Understanding** *(Portas de Entendimento)*, looking not unlike an open book with a frilly top. It was erected in 1994.

Barra Hill Above the point where Avenida da República turns north into Rua de São Tiago da Barra, the oldest street in Macau, stands 732m-high Barra Hill *(Colina da*

MACAU

Barra). A fort was built at the foot of the hill in 1629. Much of the fort was demolished over the years to make room for roads and in the 1980s the government converted the ruins into a Portuguese-style inn. The **Pousada de São Tiago** (see Places to Stay – Top End), with its tunnel-like entrance, loopholes and **Chapel of St James** *(Capela de São Tiago)*, is worth seeing even if you aren't staying there.

A-Ma Temple North of Barra Hill is the A-Ma Temple *(Rua de São Tiago da Barra; open 10am-6pm daily)*, known as 'Ma Kok Miu' in Chinese. It is dedicated to the goddess A-Ma, who is better known as Tin Hau (see the boxed text What's in a Name? in the Facts about Macau chapter).

The original temple on this site was probably already standing when the Portuguese arrived, although the present one may only date back to the 17th century. The temple is built into the foot of a hill and is made up of a warren of prayer halls and pavilions, some dedicated to A-Ma and others to Kun Iam. Behind the temple is a climbing network of small gardens.

At the main entrance to the temple is a large boulder with a *lorcha*, a traditional sailing vessel of the South China Sea, engraved into it and painted. The boat people of Macau make a pilgrimage here during the A-Ma Festival held in late April or early May, when the hillside and the tiled roofs of the complex resound to the deafening sound of firecrackers and a lion dance is performed.

Maritime Museum Just opposite the A-Ma Temple, the Maritime Museum *(Museu Marítimo; ☎ 595 481, Largo do Pagode da Barra; adult/child & senior M$10/5 Mon & Wed-Sat, M$5/3 Sun; open 10am-5.30pm Wed-Mon)* is not Macau's biggest or best museum but is interesting nonetheless and has a collection of boats and other artefacts related to Macau's seafaring past. Particularly good are the mock-ups of a Hakka fishing village and the displays of the long narrow boats that are raced during the Dragon Boat Festival in June. There's also a small aquarium.

A motorised junk moored next to the museum offers 30-minute rides around the Inner Harbour daily. For details, see the Organised Tours section of the Macau Getting Around chapter.

NORTHERN MACAU PENINSULA (MAP 13)

The northern part of the peninsula was more recently developed than the southern and central areas. Nevertheless, there are quite a few important historic sites in this region of Macau and some lovely gardens.

Luís Camões Garden & Grotto

The Camões Garden *(Jardim de Luís de Camões; Praça de Luís de Camões; open 6am-9pm daily)* is a pleasant, cool and shady place popular with local Chinese, who use the open space to 'walk' their caged songbirds, play Chinese checkers or just stroll. There are good views from the Chinese pavilion at the top of the hill.

In the centre of the park is the Camões Grotto, which contains a bust of the one-eyed national poet of Portugal. Luís de Camões (1524–80) is said to have written part of his epic *Os Lusiadas* by the rocks in Macau, but there is no firm evidence that he was ever in the territory. Two stanzas of the masterpiece are carved on the pedestal.

Casa Garden

The restored colonial villa east of the Camões Garden is called the Casa Garden and was the headquarters of the British East India Company when it was based in Macau in the early 19th century. Today the villa houses the **Fundação Oriente**, or Oriental Foundation, an organisation founded in 1996 to promote Portuguese culture worldwide, and an **exhibition gallery** *(☎ 398 1126, 13 Praça de Luís de Camões; admission free; open 10am-6pm daily)* with both permanent and temporary exhibits of Chinese antiques.

Old Protestant Cemetery

Opposite the Casa Garden to the south-east is the Old Protestant Cemetery *(15 Praça de Luís de Camões)*, the final resting place of

George Chinnery: Chronicler of Macau

Though George Chinnery may enjoy little more than footnote status in the history of world art, as a chronicler of his world (colonial Macau) and his times (the early 19th century) he is without peer. In the absence of photography, taipans and mandarins turned to trade art (commissioned portraiture), and Chinnery was its king. But today he is known less for his formal portraits and paintings of factory buildings and clipper ships than his landscapes and sometimes fragmentary sketches of everyday life in the Asia of two centuries ago.

Chinnery was born in Ireland in 1774 and studied at the Royal Academy of Arts before turning his hand to portrait painting in Dublin. He sailed for India in 1802 and spent the next 23 years working and painting in Madras and Calcutta. He fled to Macau in 1825 to escape Calcutta's 'cranky formality' and the attentions of his wife (who he described as 'the ugliest woman I ever saw in my life') and took up residence at 8 Rua de Ignácio Baptista, just south of the Church of St Lawrence, where he lived (bags packed just in case he had to flee in a hurry) until his death in 1852. He is buried in the Old Protestant Cemetery.

Although Chinnery is sometimes 'claimed' by Hong Kong (the Mandarin Oriental Hotel even has a bar named after him, with reproductions of his works on the walls) he visited the crown colony only once during the hot summer of 1846. Although he was unwell and did not like it very much, he managed to execute some vivid sketches of the place. Chinnery is portrayed as a somewhat buffoonish and money-grasping drunkard in Austin Coates' *City of Broken Promises*.

Chinnery's paintings and sketches are also on display in the Historical Pictures Gallery of the Hong Kong Museum of Art, the Tokyo Bunko and, in London, the Tate Britain and the National Portrait Gallery, which owns a striking self-portrait of him in front of a landscape.

many early non-Portuguese residents of Macau, including English, Scots, Americans and Dutch.

As church law forbade the burial of non-Catholics on hallowed ground, there was nowhere to inter Protestants who died in the community. The territory beyond the city walls was considered Chinese soil, and the Chinese didn't much approve of foreigners desecrating their land either. The unhappy result was that the Protestants had to bury their dead in the nearby hills, hoping the Chinese wouldn't notice.

The governor finally allowed a local merchant to sell some of his land to the British East India Company, and the cemetery was established in 1821 (the date '1814' above the gate refers to when the cemetery committee was formed). A number of old graves were then transferred to the cemetery, which explains the earlier dates (eg, 1811) on some of the tombstones.

Among the better-known people buried here is the Irish-born artist George Chinnery, noted for his portrayals of Macau and its people (see the boxed text above). His tomb is in the northern part of the cemetery.

To the east the tombstone of Robert Morrison, the first Protestant missionary to China, records that he 'for several years laboured alone on a Chinese version of the Holy Scriptures which he was spared to see completed'.

Lin Fung Temple

Diagonally opposite the Canidrome greyhound racetrack is Lin Fung (Lotus) Temple *(Avenida do Almirante Lacerda; open 10am-6pm daily)*. Built in 1592 as a Taoist temple, the main hall is now dedicated to Kun Iam while other shrines honour A-Ma and Kwan Tai.

The temple complex is where Mandarins from Guangdong province would stay when they visited Macau. The most celebrated of these visitors was Lin Zexu, the commissioner charged with stamping out the opium trade, who stayed here in September 1839. A 2m-high granite statue of the commissioner recalls the visit as does the **Lin Zexu**

Memorial Hall (☎ *580 166, Avenida do Almirante Lacerda; adult/child & senior M$10/3; open 9am-5pm daily*). The exhibits are rather dull, with old photographs, a model of a Chinese war junk and opium-smoking paraphernalia. Amusing is the life-size tableau of the famous 1839 meeting, with Lin Zexu and his interpreter looking upright and determined and the Westerners looking debauched and rather shifty.

Kun Iam Temple

The Buddhist Kun Iam Temple (*Avenida do Coronel Mesquita; open 10am-6pm daily*), opposite Avenida do Almirante Costa Cabral, was originally founded in the 13th century, but the present buildings date from 1627. It's really a complex of temples, the most interesting in Macau, and is dedicated to Kun Iam, the Goddess of Mercy. Rooms adjacent to the main hall celebrate the goddess with a collection of pictures and scrolls, and there are bonsai trees whose trunks have been trained to form the characters for 'good luck' and 'prosperity'.

The terraced gardens behind the temple are very attractive. The first treaty of trade and friendship between the USA and China was signed at a stone table here in 1844 and a tablet marks the spot. Also here are four ancient banyan trees with intertwined branches; lovers come hear to pray before the 'Sweetheart Tree'.

Farther to the west and opposite Rua da Madre Terezina is another **Kun Iam Temple** (*Avenida do Coronel Mesquita*). Though a lot smaller, it is a hive of activity and colour and well-worth visiting.

Lou Lim Ioc Garden

The cool and shady Lou Lim Ioc Garden (*10 Estrada de Adolfo de Loureiro; admission M$1 Sat-Thur, free Fri; open 6am-9pm daily*) was once the property of a wealthy Chinese merchant called Lou Kau and the family's ornate mansion to the north, with its colonnades and arches, is now the Pui Ching Secondary School. The gardens are a mixture of European and Chinese plants, with huge shade trees, lotus ponds, bamboo groves, grottoes and a bridge with nine

turns (since evil spirits can only move in straight lines). The ornamental mountains and stones, one of which is said to resemble Kun Iam, are built to suggest a Chinese painting and are modelled on those in the famous gardens of Suzhou. You can often hear people practising Chinese musical instruments and singing in the garden.

The Victorian-style **Lou Lim Ioc Garden Pavilion** (*Pavilhão do Jardim Lou Lim Ioc; ☎ 387 333; admission free; open 9am-6pm daily*), which is in the centre of the pond and connected to the mainland by little bridges, is used for temporary exhibits and for recitals during the International Music Festival in late October and on into early November.

Sun Yat Sen Memorial Home

Around the corner from the Lou Lim Ioc Garden and opposite the police station is a memorial home dedicated to Dr Sun Yat Sen (*Casa Memorativa de Doutor Sun Yat Sen; ☎ 574 064, 1 Rua de Silva Mendes; admission free; open 10am-5pm Wed-Mon*), the founder of the Chinese Republic. Sun practised medicine at the Kiang Wu Hospital on Rua Coelho do Amaral for some years before turning to revolution and seeking to overthrow the Qing dynasty. The house, built as a memorial to Dr Sun in the pseudo-Moorish style, contains a collection of flags, photos and documents relating to the life and times of the 'Father of the Nation'. It replaces the original house, which blew up while being used as an explosives store.

Flora Garden

The Flora Garden (*Jardim da Flora; Travessa do Túnel; open 9am-6pm daily*), Macau's largest, was once the grounds of the Flora Palace, an aristocratic Portuguese family mansion that burned to the ground in 1931 after a nearby firecracker factory exploded.

This attractive garden, on a street off Avenida de Sidónio Pais, has been refurbished and contains a miniature zoo, aviary and a couple of tennis courts. This is also where you catch the mini cable car to the top of Guia Hill (see the following section).

KELLI HAMBLET

The Guia chapel and lighthouse, atop Guia Hill.

Guia Fort & Lighthouse

The fortress built in 1638 atop Guia Hill (Colina da Guia), the highest point on the Macau Peninsula, was originally designed to defend the border with China, but it soon came into its own as a lookout post and storm warnings were sounded from the bell in the **Chapel of Our Lady of Guia** (*Capela de Nostra Señora da Guia; open 9.30am-5.30pm daily*) built in 1622. The walls of the little church have interesting drawings, and there's a colourful choir loft above the main entrance.

The 15m-tall Guia Lighthouse (*Farol da Guia*) next to the chapel is the oldest on the China coast. When it was first lit in 1865, it was powered by paraffin and could be seen for 40km in clear weather. It has been electrically powered since 1909.

There are two hiking trails on Guia Hill, which are also good for jogging. One trail circles the mountain, a total distance of 1.7km, and is called the Walk of 33 Curves. Inside this loop is the shorter Fitness Circuit Walk, along which are 20 exercise stations. You can't help noticing all the old bunkers strewn around the hilltop, relics of both WWII and the so-called Cold War.

Getting There & Away The easiest way to reach the top of Guia Hill is to hop on the little Guia Cable Car (Teleférico da Guia) that runs from Rua do Túnel near the entrance to

the Flora Garden. The cable car runs continuously from 9am to 6pm Tuesday to Sunday and costs M$3/5 one-way/return for adults and M$1/3 concession. To reach the Guia Lighthouse and the chapel, turn south after getting off the cable car, walk up the hill and continue on for another 10 minutes.

PLACES TO STAY

Hotels in Macau are generally split geographically into price constituencies, with many cheap guesthouses and hotels occupying the western reaches of the peninsula, around Rua das Lorchas and Avenida de Almeida Ribeiro, and top-end hotels in the east and centre of town. There are a few exclusive options with excellent views in the south of the peninsula as well.

Most people arriving from Hong Kong book their hotels in advance, often at the booking offices in the Shun Tak Centre in Sheung Wan, from where the ferries to Macau depart. Doing this saves a considerable amount off the walk-in rate, but you can do the same thing at the ferry terminal in Macau.

If you've booked a mid- or top-range hotel room, follow the crowds out to the front of the terminal and under the overpass from where the hotel shuttle buses depart. Even if you just want to check out the hotel, jump on board. This saves a lot of time and effort.

Places to Stay – Budget (Map 14)

The key to finding a good, cheap and clean room in Macau is patience. If one place charges too much, just try another. Many inexpensive guesthouses and hotels are clumped together in specific areas, so don't worry if you want to compare prices.

Prices for accommodation in Macau have dropped dramatically in recent years and may continue to do so. Don't take the prices quoted in this section as necessarily the lowest, and bargain hard. As long as you haven't arrived on a Saturday or public holiday, you should be able to find something acceptable within a half-hour or so of beginning your search.

MACAU

Macau's true budget accommodation is not far from the centre of town. Generally these hotels form a cluster to the north-west of the Largo do Senado, a lively area between Rua da Caldeira and Rua das Lorchas of narrow lanes, food stalls and shops, which was once known as Chopsticks. Though many of the places are pretty grotty, there are a few cosy retreats that won't cost too much and you'll be within easy walking distance of most of the major sights.

In this section, 'budget' means anything under about M$300 for a room.

Central Hotel (☎ *373 888, 264 Avenida de Almeida Ribeiro*) Singles M$150-188, doubles M$160-280. This place is in bad repair but is just what its name says, a short hop north-west of the Largo do Senado.

Man Va Hotel (☎ *388 655, 3rd floor, 30 Travessa da Caldeira*) Singles/doubles from M$172/230. To the east of the Floating Casino is a street called Travessa da Caldeira, where you'll find this rather scuzzy place; the more expensive rooms have a fridge.

San Va Hospedaria (☎ *573 701,* e *sanva@hongkong.com, 67 Rua de Felicidade*) Singles/doubles M$70/140. On the 'street of happiness' that was once the hub of the red light district, this traditional-style place has a great deal of character, though the rooms are like cupboards, not very clean and separated by flimsy cardboard partitions. The atmosphere is good and the place has a homey feel about it; you should be able to hammer the price down if it's quiet.

Ko Wah Hotel (☎ *375 599, 4th floor, 71 Rua de Felicidade*) Singles/doubles M$150/170. This 27-room hotel just a block north of the San Va is not very nice or clean but the management seems friendly. Take the lift to reception on the 4th floor.

Vila Universal (☎ *573 247, 1st floor, Cheng Peng Building, 73 Rua de Felicidade*) Singles/doubles M$147/216. This place is arguably one of the best, but certainly not the Ritz.

Hou Kong Hotel (☎ *937 555, fax 338 884, 1 Travessa das Virtudes*) Singles/doubles M$220/280 Mon-Fri, M$309/389 Sat & holidays. This place is at the bottom of a lively street and has reasonable rooms.

Vila Tai Loy (☎ *939 315, 1st floor, 20 Travessa das Virtudes*) Singles/doubles from M$300/380, M$150/190 for stays of five nights or more. The rooms at this place are relatively attractive and the manager is friendly, but the place has a frayed feeling that is less than welcoming.

East Asia Hotel (☎ *922 433, fax 922 430, 1A Rua da Madeira*) Singles M$260-340, doubles M$400-500, triples M$500. If you can force your way through the scrum of women loitering with intent outside this place, it just might be worth it. The hotel is housed in a classic colonial-style building and, though it's been remodelled, has not lost all its charm. The 98 rooms are spacious and have private bath. There's a fine restaurant on the 2nd floor that serves dim sum for extremely reasonable prices.

Vila Capital (☎ *920 154, 920 157, 3 Rua Constantino Brito*) Singles/doubles M$230/250. This place must be the headquarters of the Macau Prostitutes' Union. It's seedy and tacky but has good-value rooms.

Another part of Macau that has a few budget places is the area between the Lisboa Hotel and Rua da Praia Grande. Most of the owners speak little English, and are not really used to dealing with foreigners. Many are from the mainland.

Pensão Nam In (☎ *710 024, 3 Travessa da Praia Grande*) Singles/doubles M$110/230. This place has singles with a shared bath and pleasant doubles with a private bath.

Mondial Hotel (☎ *566 866, fax 514 083, 8-10 Rua de António Basto*) **Map 13** Rooms HK$200 Mon-Fri, HK$300 Sat & Sun. This hotel, in the northern part of the Macau Peninsula, has two wings and is on the eastern side of peaceful Lou Lim Ioc Garden, overlooking the Sun Yat Sen Memorial House. Don't expect much in the way of facilities, however.

Places to Stay – Mid-Range (Map 14)

Many mid-range hotels in Macau are three star, and a few are even four star. Again the prices listed are for the most part rack rates and are sometimes halved during the week and in the off season. Expect to pay anything from M$400 to almost M$1000 for a mid-range room.

Beverly Plaza Hotel (☎ 782 288, fax 780 684, Ⓦ www.beverlyplaza.com, 70 Avenida do Doutor Rodrigo Rodrigues) Rooms M$820-1100, suites from M$1800. This rather flash hotel is very popular with weekend visitors from Hong Kong.

Fortuna Hotel (☎ 786 333, fax 786 363, 63 Rua da Cantão) Rooms M$720-1180, suites from M$1888. This place is in a useful position if you want to frequent the casino in the Lisboa Hotel but don't actually want to stay there.

Fu Hua Hotel (☎ 553 838, fax 527 575, 98-102 Rua de Francisco Xavier Pereira) Map 13 Singles/doubles/triples M$730/830/830, suites from M$1380. If for some reason you want to stay in the northern part of the Macau Peninsula, choose this modern and bright hotel a stone's throw from the Kun Iam Temple.

Guia Hotel (☎ 513 888, fax 559 822, 1-5 Estrada do Engenheiro Trigo) Map 13 Rooms M$470-600. If you want something smaller and a bit 'isolated' (if there is such a thing in Macau), choose this place at the foot of Guia Hill.

Kingsway Hotel (☎ 702 888, fax 702 828, 230 Rua de Luís Gonzaga Gomes) Map 13 Rooms M$780-980, suites from M$1180. You might consider this hotel, which boasts its own casino, if you want to be that much closer to the ferry terminal. It has a massive sauna and Jacuzzi open from 1pm to 7am daily.

Macau Masters Hotel (☎ 937 572, fax 937 565, 162 Rua das Lorchas) Singles/doubles M$440/550, triples M$1000. This place right on the Inner Harbour has modern rooms and facilities.

Metropole Hotel (☎ 388 166, fax 330 890, Ⓔ mhhotel@macau.ctm.net, 493-501 Avenida da Praia Grande) Singles/doubles M$530/700, suites from M$1200. You couldn't get any more central than the Metropole but it's in desperate need of a face-lift.

Pousada de Mong Há (☎ 561 252, fax 519 058, Ⓦ www.ift.edu.mo) Map 13 Singles/doubles M$400/500 Mon-Fri, M$500/600 Sat & Sun, suites M$900, including breakfast. This traditional-style Portuguese inn with Asian touches sits atop Mong Há Hill and is run by students at the Institute for Tourism Studies. The restaurant here is open weekdays for lunch and for dinner on Friday night only, when a Macanese buffet costs M$130.

Hotel Presidente (☎ 553 888, fax 552 735, Ⓦ www.hotelpresident.com.mo, 355 Avenida da Amizade) Rooms M$660-920, suites from M$2280. The Presidente is on a busy road within easy walking distance of the centre and the NAPE nightlife area.

Royal Hotel (☎ 552 222, fax 563 008, Ⓔ royalmcu@macau.ctm.net, 2-4 Estrada da Vitória) Rooms M$750-1100, suites from M$2200. This place is a bit removed from the action but attractive for that reason, and has some great (and cheap) weekday packages.

Sintra Hotel (☎ 710 111, fax 567 769, Ⓔ bcsintra@macau.ctm.net, Avenida de Dom João IV) Rooms M$860-1260, suites from M$1860. Recent renovations have turned this hotel south of the Avenida da Praia Grande into a palace. Service is among the best in Macau.

Sun Sun Hotel (☎ 939 393, fax 938 822, Ⓔ sunsun96@macau.ctm.net, 14-16 Praça Ponte e Horta) Rooms M$600-980, suites from M$1650. This modern-looking and clean place usually offers rooms for much less than its advertised price. The rooms on the upper floors have excellent views of the Inner Harbour.

Places to Stay – Top End

Macau doesn't have quite the array of luxury hotels that Hong Kong does, but there are a few gems that will make your stay special. During the summer season, many of the top-end places get solidly booked, even on weekdays. Expect to pay anything over M$1000 for a room in this category.

Grandeur Hotel (☎ 781 233, fax 781 211, Ⓦ www.hotelgrandeur.com, 199 Rua de Pequim) Map 14 Rooms M$1000-1200,

MACAU

suites from M$1850. This 26-storey hotel east of the centre has a revolving restaurant on the top floor.

Holiday Inn Macau (☎ 783 333, fax 782 321, w www.holiday-inn.com, 82-86 Rua de Pequim) Map 14 Rooms M$1000-1480, suites from M$3300. It's not up to the usual Holiday Inn standards and service is somewhat erratic, but the location is excellent.

Lisboa Hotel (☎ 377 666, fax 567 193, e lisboa@macau.ctm.net, 2-4 Avenida de Lisboa) Map 14 Rooms M$1350-2000, suites from M$3800. This is Macau's most famous (and unsightly) landmark, with both an old and a new wing and more than 1000 rooms. The Lisboa has probably the best shopping arcade in Macau, and for many its casino is the only game in town.

Mandarin Oriental (☎ 567 888, fax 594 589, w www.mandarinoriental.com, 956-1110 Avenida da Amizade) Map 13 Rooms M$1800-2100, suites from M$4600. This superb five-star hotel has a huge pool at the harbour's edge. There may be special packages available, and try to book your room through an agent to take advantage of weekday specials.

Pousada de São Tiago (☎ 378 111, fax 552 170, w www.saotiago.com.mo, Fortaleza de São Tiago da Barra, Avenida da República) Map 13 Rooms M$1580-1920, suites from M$2200. The 'St James Inn', built into the ruins of a 17th-century fort, commands a splendid view of the harbour (as does the pool), and the interior decor, with its flagstones and wooden beams, is a delight. Even if you don't stay, it's worth stopping for a drink on the terrace. It only has 23 rooms so book well in advance.

Ritz (☎ 339 955, fax 317 826, e ritz htlm@macau.ctm.net, Rua Comendador Kou Ho Neng) Map 13 Rooms M$980-1380, suites from M$2080. This palace of a place, in a quiet street high above Avenida da República, is as close as you'll get to staying at the legendary Bela Vista across the road.

PLACES TO EAT
Portuguese & Macanese

Alfonso III (☎ 586 272, 11A Rua Central) Map 14 Soups M$18, mains M$65-75. This basic Portuguese restaurant, a short stroll south-west of the Leal Senado, has won a well-deserved reputation among the Portuguese community in Macau (particularly for its *feijoada*, M$75), but tables can often be in short supply, so phone to book ahead.

Ali Curry House (☎ 555 865, 4K Avenida da República) Map 13 Mains M$38-68. This place serves inexpensive Macanese curries and has outside tables along the waterfront.

Barra Nova (☎ 965 118, 287 Rua do Almirante Sérgio) Map 13 Mains M$38-64, fish dishes M$40-158. This small restaurant, nestled in a row of excellent local eateries, serves excellent Macanese specialities like *porco balichão* (pork cooked with tamarind and shrimp paste; M$48), and spicy *piri-piri* prawns (M$50). It's just south of Rua do Peixe Salgado – 'street of the salt fish'.

Clube Militar de Macau (☎ 714 000, 975 Avenida da Praia Grande) Map 14 Starters M$55-70, mains M$95-220, set dinner M$90. The Portuguese and other dishes may not be the best in town, but the restaurant at the Military Club, once strictly open to members only, is housed in one of Macau's most distinguished colonial buildings, well worth a visit in itself.

Comida a Portuguesa Carlos (☎ 751 838, Vista Magnífica Building, Rua Cidade de Braga, NAPE) Map 13 Mains M$50-70. Carlos, which has some of the warmest service in town and serves good Portuguese food, has moved from its original site near the Lou Lim Ioc Garden in central Macau to the NAPE nightlife and restaurant area.

Dom Galo (☎ 751 383, Avenida Sir Anders Ljungstedt, NAPE) Map 13 Mains from M$40. This pleasant little place, done up the way a child would imagine a Macanese or Portuguese town square, is a sister-restaurant to Galo in Taipa Village. Try the stir-fried clams with parsley and garlic.

Henri's Galley (☎ 556 251, 4G/H Avenida da República) Map 13 Meals about M$150. This place is on the waterfront at the southern end of the Macau Peninsula. An old-timer on the Macau restaurant scene, Henri's feels a bit tired and prices are relatively high.

Restaurante Litoral (☎ *967 878, 261A Rua do Almirante Sérgio*) **Map 13** Meals about M$120. This restaurant is just a short walk north of the Maritime Museum.

A Lorcha (☎ *313 193, 289A Rua do Almirante Sérgio*) **Map 13** Meals about M$150. Some people refer to this place, not far from the A-Ma Temple, as the 'quality benchmark' of Portuguese food in Macau. Among the fine dishes are chicken with onion and tomato, feijoada and raw codfish salad.

Platão (☎ *331 818, 3 Travessa São Domingos*) **Map 14** Starters M$26-36, mains from M$50. This place is a knock-off Portuguese restaurant staffed by Filipinos, but the seafood fried rice (M$52) and courtyard tables make it worth a visit.

O Porto Interior (☎ *967 770, 259B Rua do Almirante Sérgio*) **Map 13** Meals about M$150. You shouldn't have much trouble finding this place with the over-the-top Portuguese. It's just where its name says it is: at the 'Inner Harbour'.

Solmar (☎ *574 391, 512 Avenida da Praia Grande*) **Map 14** Meals about M$150. Despite the gloomy interior, Solmar is quite an institution in Macau, and serves excellent seafood dishes (try the seafood soup) and grilled chicken with pepper and chillies.

Restaurante Vela Latina (☎ *356 888, 201 Rua do Almirante Sérgio*) **Map 14** Meals about M$150. This bizarre place serves 'Portuguese cuisine in a new way to perform' on the ground floor, Japanese on the 1st and Thai on the 2nd. They obviously can't get them all right, so stick to the bottom.

Chinese

Rua da Felicidade, or 'Street of Happiness', was the old red-light district and it's a good part of town to start hunting for both established and hole-in-the-wall Chinese restaurants, though a number of the latter don't have English menus.

Fat Siu Lau Restaurant (☎ *573 580, 64 Rua da Felicidade*) **Map 14** Meals about M$150. The 'house of the smiling Buddha', established in 1903, is without a doubt

Macau's most famous Chinese restaurant, though there is a decent selection of Portuguese and other Western dishes. The house speciality is roast pigeon.

Sai Nam (☎ *574 072, 36 Rua da Felicidade*) **Map 14** Abalone & shark's fin plate about M$380. If you want to sample abalone at its freshest, try this small restaurant which specialises in the shellfish and has quite a reputation in Macau.

Abalone Ah Yat Restaurant (☎ *780 807, Basement floor, Fortuna Hotel, 63 Rua da Cantão*) **Map 14** Meals about M$200. This is another place specialising in dishes made from the 'king of clams'. For around M$800, four people can share a set meal of abalone, a small hotpot, crispy garlic chicken and an array of seafood, plus a bottle of Portuguese wine. Another recommended dish is the bird's nest soup.

Dynasty Chinese Restaurant (☎ *793 3821, 2nd floor, Mandarin Oriental Hotel, 956-1110 Avenida da Amizade*) **Map 13** Meals about M$200. This hotel restaurant serves sophisticated Cantonese cuisine and has some interesting goose, fish, frog, turtle and (in season) snake specialities.

Fook Lam Moon (☎ *786 622, Cam Va Cac Building, 259 Avenida da Amizade*) **Map 14** Meals about M$200. This place has superb seafood dishes.

Long Kei (☎ *589 505, 7B Largo do Senado*) **Map 14** Dishes from M$45. Open 11am-11pm. This landmark place with a neon cow out front is a straightforward Cantonese restaurant. There are more than 350 Cantonese dishes on offer.

Pan-Asian

Kruatheque (☎ *330 448, Rua Henrique de Macedo*) **Map 14** Meals about M$250. This place near the Vasco da Gama Garden and in something of a Thai neighbourhood, serves rather expensive Sino-Thai food to appreciative families. There's live music here some nights.

Silla Korean Restaurant (☎ *569 039, Mezzanine floor, Hotel Presidente, Avenida da Amizade*) **Map 14** Meals about M$200. For those with a craving for *bulgogi* and *gimchi*, the Korean can oblige.

MACAU

New Furusato (☎ 388 568, *Ground floor, New Wing, Lisboa Hotel, 2-4 Avenida de Lisboa*) **Map 14** Meals from M$300. Not quite Tokyo prices for the sushi but on the way there.

Other Cuisines

Frascati Restaurant (☎ 783 333, *4th floor, Holiday Inn, Rua de Pequim*) **Map 14** Meals about M$300. This restaurant serves Italian favourites along with a medley of Spanish and Portuguese dishes.

Monster Island Italian Restaurant (☎ 752 239, *483-495 Rua Cidade de Santarem*) **Map 13** Meals about M$120. This place looks like something a group of unbalanced Sicilians would have created if they cared deeply about Halloween. Come here for the novelty, not the food.

Mezzaluna (☎ 567 888, *2nd floor, Mandarin Oriental Hotel, 956-1110 Avenida da Amizade*) **Map 13** Meals M$250-300. This restaurant serves *la cucina italiana* in classy surroundings. The pasta is fresh and the pizzas piping hot from wood-fired ovens. Try either the pigeon roasted with polenta and porcini mushrooms or the open ravioli of baby lobster with spinach and basil.

Ritz Dining Room (☎ 339 955, *Ground floor, Ritz Hotel, 2 Rua da Boa Vista*) **Map 13** Starters M$38-138, mains M$118-198, set meals M$338. For those who want to indulge, the Ritz's main restaurant is the place to come. The high prices belong more to Hong Kong than Macau, but the menu is expansive, with the stress on continental grills. The wine list is equally extensive (and pricey).

Restaurante Safari (☎ 322 239, *14 Patio do Cotovelo*) **Map 14** Soups M$14, mains M$22-60, set menus M$50. This friendly hybrid of a place, serving coffee-shop food as well as spicy chicken, steak and fried noodles, is at the end of a small alleyway just off Avenida de Almeida Ribeiro.

Yes Brazil (☎ 358 097, *6A Travessa Fortuna*) **Map 14** Mains M$38-68. This tiny, friendly place near the ruins of the Church of St Paul serves an excellent feijoada (M$70) and other Brazilian dishes and has a daily set menu for just M$38.

Pizzeria Toscana (☎ 726 637, *Apaia do Grande Premio de Macau, Avenida da Amizade*) **Map 13** Meals about M$100. This pizzeria near the ferry terminal has some fine pastas and pizzas.

Vegetarian Cuisine

Fruitarian (☎ 355 726, *117B Rua de Francisco Xavier Pereira*) **Map 14** Snacks about M$40. Macau doesn't offer much in the way of vegetarian restaurants or even snack bars but this place, with fruit juices, ice cream and yoghurt, might do for a snack or in a pinch.

Cafes

Bolo de Arroz (☎ 339 089, *11 Travessa de São Domingos*) **Map 14** Cake & coffee M$20. This *pastelaria*, or pastry shop, is in a small street with several other eateries. It has a splendid range of Portuguese and Macanese pastries (try the coconut tart), cakes, sandwiches and aromatic coffees.

Caravela (☎ 712 080, *Kam Loi Building, 7 Rua do Comandante Mata e Oliveira*) **Map 14** This excellent pastry shop north-east of the Sintra Hotel is a bit hard to find but the delectable pastries, snacks and simple Macanese dishes make it worth the search.

Petisco Fernandes (☎ 563 865, *4F Avenida da República*) **Map 13** Mains M$23-38. This little cafe near Henri's Galley has simple and cheap one-platers.

Fast Food (Map 14)

Macau's street stalls sell excellent stir-fried dishes; try any of the *dai pai dong* along Rua do Almirante Sérgio near the Inner Harbour. There are a few *food stalls* in Rua da Escola Commercial, a tiny lane one block west of the Lisboa Hotel and next to a sports field.

Yuk gon, dried sweet strips of pork and other meats, are a Macau speciality, as are the *hung yan bang*, delightful almond-flavoured biscuits or cookies sprinkled with powdery white sugar. The best places to find both are around Rua da Caldeira and Travessa do Matadouro, which are at the northern end of Avenida de Almeida Ribeiro near the Inner Harbour.

O Barril 2 (☎ 370 533, 14A/B Travessa de Santo Domingos) Mains from M$50. This little place opposite the Bolo de Arroz pastry shop is where to head if you want something fast and savoury Portuguese.

Papatudo (☎ 703 117, 68G/F Rua de Luís Gonzaga Gomes) Snacks about M$50. This little place serves sandwiches and snacks.

Self-Catering

Macau has about a half-dozen markets *(mercados)* selling fresher-than-fresh fruit, vegetables, meat and fish. Two of the largest are the *Almirante Lacerda City market* (Map 13) *(Mercado Municipal Almirante Lacerda; 130 Avenida do Almirante Lacerda)* in northern Macau and the *St Lawrence City market* (Map 14) *(Mercado Municipal de São Lourenço; Rua de João Lecaros)* in the south.

The *New Yaohan department store* (Map 13), opposite the ferry terminal, has the largest supermarket in Macau. *Pavilions Supermercado* (Map 14) *(421 Avenida da Praia Grande)*, has a wide selection of imported food and drinks, including items from Portugal. The *Supermercado San Miu* (Map 14) *(248 Avenida do Doutor Rodrigo Rodrigues)* is centrally located.

Park 'N' Shop (Map 13) *(69B Avenida de Sidónio Pais)* is a branch of the Hong Kong chain of supermarkets in northern Macau.

ENTERTAINMENT
Pubs & Bars

NAPE (Map 13) The main place for a pub crawl is the Docks – the reclaimed NAPE area – with a row of attractive theme bars lining the waterfront area to the south-east around the Kun Iam statue. Don't expect Hong Kong's Lan Kwai Fong though; at times this area can feel distinctly dead. These places are typically open till the wee hours: 3am or 4am.

Casablanca Cafe (☎ 751 281, Vista Magnífica Court, Avenida Doutor Sun Yat Sen) This elegant watering hole has photos of Hollywood and Hong Kong film icons decorating the walls and large red velvet cinema curtains draped over the main bar.

Rio Cafe (☎ 751 306, Vista Magnífica Court, Avenida Doutor Sun Yat Sen) If you're in a former Portuguese colony, why not take your cue from another one? The orange-and-blue decor and the outside seating by the Outer Harbour may just conjure up images of Ipanema.

Sanshiro Pub (☎ 751 238, Vista Magnífica Court, Avenida Doutor Sun Yat Sen) This is the poor kid on the block and attractive for that, with beer by the pitcher, two-for-one happy hour from 4pm to 8pm and outside tables.

Signal Cafe (☎ 751 052, 1st floor, Vista Magnífica Court, Avenida Doutor Sun Yat Sen) This very posh upstairs bar is for Macau's trend-setters.

Bar Why Not (☎ 751 930, 27-31 Avenida Sir Anders Ljungstedt) This place just up from the waterfront has loud music that often leads to spontaneous dancing.

Central Macau (Map 14) Beyond the NAPE area, your best bet for pubs and bars is Macau's hotels, though there are one or two independent places worth checking out.

Embassy Bar (☎ 567 888, Mandarin Oriental Hotel, 956-1110 Avenida da Amizade) Map 13 This very popular ground-floor bar, which opens at 5pm, features a live band nightly at 10.30pm and has a small dance floor.

Fortuna Lounge (☎ 786 333, Ground floor, Fortuna Hotel, 63 Rua da Cantão) Not to be confused with the nightclub on the 5th floor, the Fortuna Lounge has live bands and is popular with young people. Most everyone out on the town shows up here at some point during the evening.

Oskar's Pub (☎ 783 333, Holiday Inn Macau, 82-86 Rua de Pequim) This pub off the main lobby draws a large number of local expats. Happy hour is from 5pm to 9pm.

The Rotunda (☎ 781 233, 26th floor, Grandeur Hotel, Rua de Pequim) If you enjoy revolving while you drink, well, have another one. No, really, this bar on top of the Grandeur affords a slowly circling view of China and points south.

Shanghai KTV Lounge (201 Avenida de Almeida Ribeiro) This very central karaoke

MACAU

bar and club attracts Generation X (or even Y) local Chinese.

Discos & Nightclubs

Much of the nightlife in Macau is targeted at those who've come to gamble or spend money on prostitutes; there's not too many places with what could be called style or good taste. If you want to go clubbing, you'd better do it in Hong Kong and get it out of your system before you visit Macau. There is a clump of *discos* frequented by young Chinese on Rua Filipe Ó Costa just behind the old Estoril Hotel and north of the Vasco da Gama Garden with names like Devil & Angel, Disco.com and DNA. They flash in the dark but don't look very welcoming somehow.

Most hotels have some sort of disco, where you'll pay a cover charge (often steep) entitling you to one or two drinks, or a nightclub with a floorshow.

Crazy Paris Show (☎ 377 666, *Lisboa Hotel, 2-4 Avenida de Lisboa*) **Map 14** Admission M$300. Shows 8pm & 9.30pm nightly. This show, similar to the revues so popular in Las Vegas, is performed in the Lisboa's Mona Lisa Hall. Buy your tickets in the lobby of the New Wing. No-one under 18 years of age is allowed entry.

Deluxe Club Savoy (☎ 377 666, *3rd floor, Lisboa Hotel, 2-4 Avenida de Lisboa*) **Map 14** Entry M$200. This huge, brightly lit place appeals to visitors from Hong Kong and mainland China and features a Filipino band and floor show.

Fortuna Nightclub (☎ 785 678, *5th floor, Fortuna Hotel, 63 Rua da Cantão*) **Map 14** Entry before/after 10pm M$368/488. This enormous warehouse of a place is patrolled by hostesses and reverberates to the sounds of karaoke.

Skylight Nightclub (☎ 553 888, *2nd floor, Hotel Presidente, 355 Avenida da Amizade*) **Map 14** This place has no cover charge, but you have to buy at least one drink for about M$85; it's more of a hostess bar than a dance club.

China City (☎ 726 633, *Jai Alai Complex, Travessa do Reservatório*) **Map 13** Entry M$488-899. This nightclub near the

ferry terminal is a girlie club, with hostesses that circulate and keep the clientele smiling (or whatever). The cover charge varies depending on the time of entry. There may be additional charges on top of the admission for the time spent simply talking with the hostesses. The complex is also home to two cinemas (the *Jai Alai UA1* and *UA2*), the *UFO Disco* on the 2nd floor (see next entry), the *Darling Thai Massage & Sauna* and the *Taipan Health Spa*, where a sauna and 45-minute massage costs M$288.

Also at the Jai Alai Complex is *UFO Disco* (☎ 728 131, *2nd floor, Jai Alai Palace & Casino, Jai Alai Complex, Travessa do Reservatório*) **Map 13** It's pulsating disco in the sleaziest building in Macau. Should you get into any trouble, the ferry terminal (and escape) is a five-minute run away.

Jazz

Macau Jazz Club (☎ 596 014, *The Glass House, Avenida Doutor Sun Yat Sen, NAPE*) **Map 13** Open 6pm-late Wed-Sun. The Jazz Club has now taken up residence in a lovely little glass building on the waterfront in NAPE. There's live jazz at 10.30pm on Friday and Saturday nights (perhaps an hour earlier in summer), and it's hard to imagine any place more magical to listen to good music in Macau at the moment.

Classical Music

Macau Cultural Centre (☎ 797 7418, *Avenida Xian Xing Hai, NAPE*) **Map 13** This is the territory's premier venue for classical music concerts, though other places (such as the Lou Lim Ioc Garden Pavilion and the Chapel of St Joseph's Seminary) are also used occasionally. To book tickets ring ☎ 555 555 or in Hong Kong ☎ 7171 7171. You can book packages, including ferry tickets, hotel accommodation and concert tickets, in Hong Kong on ☎ 2540 6333.

Cinemas

Macau does not offer much in the way of foreign (ie, non-Hong Kong or mainland Chinese films), and cinemas lack the sophistication and variety offered in Hong Kong.

MACAU

Cineteatro Macau (☎ 572 050, *Rua de Santa Clara*) **Map 14** This three-screen cinema north-west of St Francis Garden is one exception and shows good quality films in English, as well as Hong Kong movies.

Theatre

Dom Pedro V Theatre (☎ 939 646, *Calçada do Teatro*) **Map 14** The Macau Cultural Centre (see Classical Music earlier) is the main venue used for theatre, but this stunning theatre is used for occasional staged performances, including drama and small concerts.

Casinos

None of the casinos in Macau offer the atmosphere or level of service considered minimal in Las Vegas. There are no seats for slot machine players or cocktail waiters offering free drinks to gamblers. The casinos don't have 'change girls' walking the casino floor and breaking bills for slot players so they can keep feeding the 'hungry tigers'. A most obnoxious custom is the automatic tip: Dealers and croupiers take 10% of your winnings for themselves without even asking.

Yet Macau's casinos have no trouble attracting punters and are usually jam-packed. All casinos in Macau stay open 24 hours.

Macau has 10 casinos, with most of them in big hotels such as the *Holiday Inn* (☎ 786 424), the *Kingsway* (☎ 701 111), the *Lisboa* (☎ 375 111) and the *Mandarin Oriental* (☎ 564 297) on the peninsula and the *Hyatt Regency* (☎ 831 536), the *New Century* (☎ 831 111 ext 1946) and the *Pousada Marina Infante* (☎ 838 333) on Taipa Island. Independent casinos include the *Macau Palace Floating Casino* (☎ 346 701) moored in the Outer Harbour south-west of the ferry terminal; the *Jai Alai Casino* (☎ 726 086, *Jai Alai Complex, Travessa do Reservatório*) and the *Kam Pek Casino* (☎ 780 168, *Rua de Foshan*), close to (and accessible from) the Lisboa Hotel.

The classiest casinos with the highest minimum bets are the ones at the Kingsway and Mandarin Oriental Hotels, though the latter has the reputation of being rather stuffy. The Floating Casino is in an old converted ferry and attracts the lower end of the gambling strata as does the little Kam Pek Casino. The Jai Alai Casino, in the building where they used to play *pelota basca*, essentially handball played with a wicker 'mitt', is popular for its location: across from the ferry terminal.

That leaves the Lisboa, a casino in a class (if that's not an oxymoron here) of its own. By no means the newest or the best casino in town, the Lisboa is still the largest and liveliest. When typhoon signal eight is hoisted and all the other casinos shut down, only this one stays open. The Lisboa, with four storeys of spacious gambling halls, feels more comfortable than the other casinos. Maybe it's because this is the only place in town where you can't see the ghastly Lisboa building.

Taipa & Coloane Islands

A visit to Macau's two islands perfectly rounds off a trip to the territory. While peninsular Macau is where the vast majority of the territory's population lives, works and makes merry, Coloane and, to a lesser extent nowadays, Taipa are oases of calm and greenery. Striking pastel-coloured colonial villas and civic buildings preside over quiet lanes and a couple of delightful beaches, there's ample opportunity for walking and cycling, and the Portuguese and Macanese restaurants of Taipa Village are alone worth the trip.

In recent years, a few large-scale projects have threatened to shake the islands from their torpor, however. Once rural Taipa now boasts four major hotels, a university, a racecourse and stadium, high-rise apartments and an airport. At the same time, the advent of a luxury resort hotel, golf course and deepwater port have heralded an era of change on Coloane. The causeway connecting the two islands has been widened by landfill to such an extent that the two are now almost one and a US$25 million bridge links the lot with the island of Hengqin in the Zhuhai SEZ to the west.

All of this has failed to remove the essential ingredients of what make these two little islands so charming.

INFORMATION

The Islands Provisional Municipal Council has an information centre (☎ 827 882) on Rua do Governador Tamagnini Barbosa just south of the Pak Tai Temple on Taipa Island. It is open from 9am to 5pm daily.

The Macau Government Tourist Office (MGTO; ☎ 315 566) has a branch at Macau International Airport (☎ 861 436), which is open for each incoming flight. There's a computer terminal with information about Macau at the Hyatt Regency Hotel on Taipa.

GETTING THERE & AWAY

The most useful buses from peninsular Macau to both Taipa and Coloane are Nos

21, 21A, 25 and 26A. Bus Nos 22 and 28A travel to and around Taipa only and terminate at the Macau Jockey Club.

TAIPA ISLAND

When the Portuguese first sighted Taipa (Tam Chai in Cantonese, Tanzai in Mandarin) it was actually two islands. Over the centuries the pair were joined together by silt pouring down from the Pearl River. Landfill and reclamation no doubt will do the same thing to Taipa and Coloane eventually.

Traditionally an island of duck farms and boat yards, with enough small fireworks factories to satisfy the insatiable demand for bangers and crackers, Taipa (population 18,000) is rapidly becoming urbanised. The construction of Taipa City, a large high-rise housing development in the centre of the island, is a major ongoing project and the rural charm that existed here in the past is well and truly gone.

Resisting the onslaught, however, is a parade of baroque churches and buildings, Taoist and Buddhist temples, overgrown esplanades and lethargic settlements. It's still easy to experience the traditional charms of the island almost anywhere but Taipa City.

TAIPA ISLAND

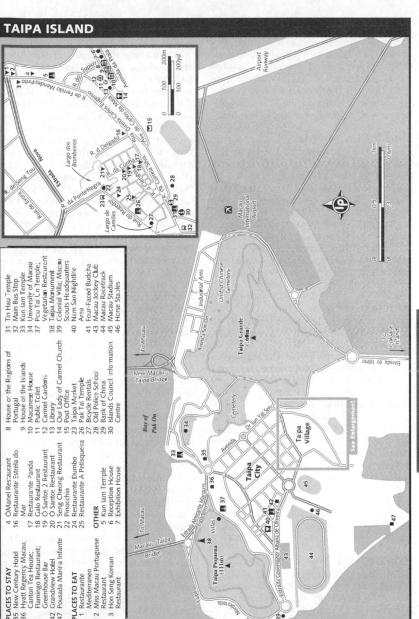

PLACES TO STAY
35 New Century Hotel
36 Hyatt Regency Macau;
   Canton Tea House;
   Flamingo Restaurant;
   Greenhouse Bar
42 Grandview Hotel
47 Pousada Marira Infante

PLACES TO EAT
1 Restaurante
   Mediterraneo
2 Miss Macau Portuguese
   Restaurant
3 Hon Seng Korean
   Restaurant
4 OManel Restaurant
16 Restaurante Estrela do
   Mar
17 Restaurante Panda
18 Galo Restaurant
19 O Santos 2 Restaurant
20 O Santos Restaurant
21 Seng Cheong Restaurant
22 Pinocchio
24 Restaurante Dumbo
25 Restaurante A Petisqueira

OTHER
5 Kun Iam Temple
6 Reception House
7 Exhibition House
8 House of the Regions of
   Portugal
9 House of the Islands
10 Macanese House
11 Public Toilet
12 Carmel Gardens
13 Library
14 Our Lady of Carmel Church
15 Post Office
23 Taipa Market
26 Pak Tai Temple
27 Bicycle Rentals
29 Bank of China
30 Old Police School
   Islands Council Information
   Centre
31 Tin Hau Temple
32 Main Bus Stop
33 Kun Iam Temple
34 University of Macau
37 Pou Tai Un Temple;
   Vegetarian Restaurant
38 Taipa Monument
39 Colonial Villa; Macau
   Scouts Headquarters
40 Nam San Nightlife
   Area
41 Four-Faced Buddha
43 Macau Jockey Club
44 Macau Racetrack
45 Macau Stadium
46 Horse Stables

MACAU

Taipa Monument

Greeting you from the foot of **Taipa Pequena** (112m) hill as you cross the Macau-Taipa Bridge is this zigzag-shaped marble monument erected in 1985 above Estrada de Sete Tanques. The three levels show aspects of Chinese, Portuguese and Macanese culture as well as Macau landmarks in relief.

Pou Tai Un Temple

Some 200m south-west of the Hyatt Regency Hotel on Estrada Lou Lim Ieok is Pou Tai Un, the largest temple on the islands. The main hall, dedicated to the Three Precious Buddhas, contains an enormous bronze statue of Lord Gautama, and there are brightly coloured prayer pavilions scattered around the complex. If you're visiting at lunchtime, the temple operates a vegetarian restaurant, the vegies grown in the temple's extensive gardens. See Places to Eat later in this section for details.

Kun Iam Temple

Perched on a ledge below the University of Macau is this tiny temple dedicated to Kun Iam, the Goddess of Mercy. A figure of Kun Iam sits on a pink-tiled altar. Reach the temple by taking the set of stone steps running off Estrada da Ponte de Pac On.

United Chinese Cemetery

This cemetery in the north-eastern corner of the island along Estrada da Ponta da Cabrita is the final resting place for the followers of the triumvirate of Chinese religions: Buddhism, Taoism and Confucianism. The graves face the open sea, a propitious vista for these permanent residents. Among the graves is a 10m-high **statue of Tou Tei**, the Earth God, and gardens filled with Buddhist and Taoist images, pavilions and moon gates.

Taipa Village

This village to the south of the island and in the shadow of the Hong Kong-style 'New Town' of Taipa City has somehow managed to retain its storybook charm. It is a tidy sprawl of traditional Chinese shops and some excellent restaurants, punctuated here

and there by grand colonial villas, churches and ancient temples.

Down along what was once the seafront and is now an artificial lake is the **Avenida da Praia**, a tree-lined esplanade with wrought-iron benches and old-world charm that is perfect for a leisurely stroll. The five verdigris-coloured villas facing the water were built in 1921 by wealthy Macanese as summer residences and now collectively form the **Taipa House Museum** (*☎ 827 012, Avenida da Praia; admission free; open 10am-8pm daily*). The two houses to the east of where Avenida da Praia meets Rua do Supico are used for receptions and special exhibitions; the three to the west house permanent collections.

The first of the houses, the **House of the Regions of Portugal**, contains costumes and examines traditional ways of life around the country. The **House of the Islands** looks at the history of Taipa and Coloane, with some interesting displays devoted to the islands' traditional industries: fishing and the manufacture of oyster sauce, shrimp paste and fireworks.

The last (and best) is the **Macanese House**, a residence done up in traditional Macanese style that looks like the *dom* and *doña* residing here left just yesterday. The mix of furnishings – heavy blackwood furniture and Chinese cloisonné with statues and pictures of saints and the Sacred Heart – is fascinating and the house offers a snapshot of life in the early 20th century.

From the western end of Avenida da Praia walk up the steps to the **Church of Our Lady of Carmel** built in 1885. The colonial **library** opposite the church is a recent reproduction, replacing the original that had been pulled down illegally. Surrounding it are the pretty **Carmel Gardens**.

Following Avenida de Carlos da Maia will take you past an **old police school** that may be the future home of PLA soldiers and into Rua da Correia Silva, which leads to a small **Tin Hau Temple** some 170 years old and partly occupied by a primary school on the Largo Governador Tamagnini Barbosa. Close by is the main bus stop and several bicycle rental shops. To the north-east just

RICHARD I'ANSON

MICHAEL AW

Acrobats perform at a Lion Dance in Macau.

Western music in a Chinese setting, Macau.

OLIVER STREWE

Decorations for the Mid-Autumn Festival stand before St Francis Xavier Chapel, Coloane Village.

OLIVER STREWE

Narrow back streets of Macau.

RICHARD I'ANSON

St Michael's Cemetery, Macau, is adorned with monuments.

OLIVER STREWE

Shop on Rua da Felicidade (Street of Happiness), once Macau's red-light district.

OLIVER STREWE

Sharing a private joke in the cool and shady Lou Lim Ioc Garden, Macau.

off Rua do Regedor is **Pak Tai Temple**, dedicated to the guardian of peace and order. The village **market** is housed in a building at the end of Rua do Regedor.

There's a tiny **Kun Iam Temple** along Rua de Fernão Mendes Pinto, a narrow, walled road along which cars just manage to squeeze their way.

Macau Stadium

East of Taipa Village on Avenida Olímpica is the 15,000-seat Macau Stadium (☎ 838 208), which opened in 1997 and is used for local and international sporting events, festivals and pop concerts. It is currently being expanded and its capacity will be doubled in time for the Asian Games, to be held here in 2006.

Macau Jockey Club & Racetrack

The Macau Jockey Club (☎ 821 188, W www .macauhorse.com, Estrada Governador Albano de Oliveira; admission M$20, minimum bet M$10), also known as the Hippodrome, has been Macau's venue for horse racing since 1991. If you know your quinellas from your trifectas and six-ups, this is the place to go.

Races are held twice weekly, on Sunday afternoon from 12.30pm and at night midweek (usually Tuesday, but not always) from 7.30pm. For information about meetings and starting times, call either the Macau (☎ 820 868) or the Hong Kong (☎ 800-967 822) hotline.

North-east of the Macau Jockey Club's main entrance on Estrada Governador Albano de Oliveira is a **Four-Faced Buddhist shrine**. Guarded by four elephants and festooned with Thai-style floral bouquets, it looks just like the Erawan shrine in Bangkok. Praying at this shrine is supposed to bring good fortune, which is undoubtedly why it's located here.

Activities

Taipa has two hiking trails. The **Little Taipa Trail** (Trilho de Taipa Pequena) is a 2km-long circuit around a hill of that name in the north-western part of the island. The 2.2km-long **Big Taipa Trail** (Trilho de Taipa Grande) rings Taipa Grande, a 160m hill at the eastern end of the island.

Bicycles (from M$10 an hour) can be rented at several locations in Taipa Village, including **Iao Kei Bicicleta** (☎ 827 975, 36 Largo Governador Tamagini Barbosa) as well as in Rua do Regedor near the market and in Largo de Camões. The **A Wah Hardware Shop** (☎ 820 652, 73B Avenida de Kwong Tung) in the Nam San district also rents bikes.

The **MGTO** (☎ 315 566) can help you organise horse riding at the **Macau Jockey Club** (☎ 821 188) and also use the golf driving range there.

Special Events

A fair is held in Largo de Camões and the narrow streets east of Rua do Regedor from noon to 9pm every Sunday. Up to 125 stalls sell traditional crafts, clothing, toys, food and drinks and there are cultural performances held from 4pm to 5pm.

Places to Stay

Grandview Hotel (☎ 837 788, fax 837 777, e hotelgdv@macau.ctm.net, 142 Estrada Governador Albano de Oliveira) Rooms M$350/550 on weekdays/weekends. This rather tasteful hotel is a short gallop northeast of the Macau Jockey Club and close to the Nam San nightlife area (see Entertainment later in this section). If you don't want to watch the nags or bend your elbow, you can take advantage of the hotel's swimming pool, sauna and badminton courts. A real bargain.

Hyatt Regency Macau (☎ 831 234, fax 830 195, W www.macau.hyatt.com, 2 Estrada Almirante Marques Esparteiro) Rooms M$850-1800, suites from M$2800. More of a resort than a hotel as such, this place has four tennis courts, two squash courts, a nearby golf course, a fully equipped gymnasium, play areas for the kiddies, a huge heated swimming pool and a casino. Restaurants in the hotel dish up Cantonese, Macanese and Portuguese, and there's a decent delicatessen if you want to make yourself a picnic. For information about summer programs for children, see

MACAU

Travel with Children in the Macau Facts for the Visitor chapter.

New Century Hotel (☎ *831 111, fax 832 222,* e *nch@macau.ctm.net, 889 Avenida Padre Tomás Pereira*) Rooms M$1300-2000, suites from M$3500. This Chinese baroque caravanserai is owned by Ng 'Wet Market' Wai, a rival of Broken Tooth Koi (see the boxed text Dicing with Death in the Macau Facts for the Visitor chapter). When the New Century first 'launched' Koi's boys shot up the facade with machine guns just to show Wet Market who was boss. It seems Wet was; Koi's in the slammer. Showy, over the top, ostentatious and boasting a 'Las Vegas-style casino', the 554-room New Century is very popular with some Hong Kong Chinese.

Pousada Marina Infante (☎ *838 333, fax 832 000, Marina da Taipa Sul, Cotai*) Rooms M$880-1180, suites from M$1680. This new property with the cosy name is actually a huge 312-room structure built on reclaimed land south of the Macau Jockey Club. It has Macau's newest casino, but it's hard to imagine why anyone would want to stay here unless they were crossing nearby Lotus Bridge to and from Zhuhai regularly.

Places to Eat
The number of restaurants in Taipa, particularly in the village, has grown by leaps and bounds in just a few short years. While much of the choice is restricted to Portuguese and Macanese cuisine, you'll also find some excellent Cantonese, vegetarian and even Korean places.

Canton Tea House (☎ *831 234, Hyatt Regency Macau, 2 Estrada Almirante Marques Esparteiro*) Meals M$200-250. The Hyatt's upmarket Chinese restaurant has very good (though pricey) Cantonese fare and serves dim sum from 8am to 3pm at the weekend. There are a fair few vegetarian options on the menu.

Restaurante Dumbo (☎ *827 888, Rua do Regedor*) Meals about M$120. This attractive restaurant with *azulejos* (Portuguese blue tiles) on the walls serves decent Portuguese dishes like prawns with garlic and salt and roast suckling pig.

Restaurante Estrela do Mar (☎ *825 025, 12 Rua Direita Carlos Eugénio*) Mains from M$40. The long-established 'Star of the Sea', now relocated from the Macau Peninsula, serves some of the best old-style Portuguese food in Macau.

Flamingo (☎ *831 234 ext 1874, Hyatt Regency Macau, 2 Estrada Almirante Marques Esparteiro*) Meals M$300. Overlooking a duck pond and surrounded by lush tropical growth, this restaurant serving Portuguese seafood and classic Macanese dishes is probably the most romantic on the island.

Galo (☎ *827 423, 45 Rua da Cunha*) Meals about M$120. This place, easily recognised by the picture of a red-combed rooster above the door, is a quaint addition to the string of eateries along Rua da Cunha.

Hon Seng Korean Restaurant (☎ *827 205, 673 Rua de Fernão Mendes Pinto*) Meals M$150-200. Korean-style barbecue might be a welcome alternative to pork with clams and dried cod.

Ó Manel (☎ *827 571, 90 Rua de Fernão Mendes Pinto*) Meals M$80-90. This small but friendly place should be your first choice for classic Portuguese dishes, like *caldo verde* (vegetable and potato soup) and *bacalhau* (dried cod), be it baked, grilled, stewed or boiled. Portions are huge.

Restaurante Mediterraneo (☎ *825 069, Chuen Yuet Garden, 108 Rua de Fernão Mendes Pinto*) Mains M$68-80. This place, with its cool Mediterranean interior and modern cuisine, is a cut above the other restaurants on Rua de Fernão Mendes Pinto.

Miss Macau Portuguese Restaurant (☎ *827 957, 102 Rua de Fernão Mendes Pinto*) Mains M$60-75. Tacky does not begin to describe this scarlet establishment, whose owner can boast not one but *four* former Miss Macaus in his family. The food (really Macanese) is quite good, and a bill of over M$500 earns you a free bottle of wine.

A Petisqueira (☎ *825 354, 15 Rua de São João*) Meals about M$120-150. This excellent restaurant is in a little alley that is easy to overlook. It has a decent wine list and serves its own home-made cheese.

Pinocchio (☎ *827 128, 4 Rua do Sol*) Meals M$120-150. This is the place that started the Taipa Village restaurant phenomenon, and you should at least make a visit to pay your respects (provided you can get in). Recommended dishes include grilled squid and fresh sardines. The roast lamb is always a treat.

Pou Tai Un Temple Restaurant (☎ 811 038, Estrada Lou Lim Ieok) Meals about M$70. This restaurant in the Buddhist Pu Tai Un Temple is strictly vegetarian. It's just around the corner from the Hyatt Regency Macau.

Ó Santos (☎ 827 508, 20 Rua da Cunha) Mains M$62-68. This tiny place is famous for its stuffed pork loin. Its nearby branch *Ó Santos II* (☎ 825 236, 28 Rua dos Clérigos) has a weekend buffet for M$65.

Seng Cheong (☎ 827 589, 30 Rua da Cunha) Meals M$100. This Cantonese restaurant is celebrated for its fried fish balls and steamed eel.

Entertainment
The area within the Nam San complex of buildings just north of the Macau Jockey Club has become something of a nightlife area in recent years, with a half-dozen or so late-night pubs and bars opening their doors. Among the most popular are *Pátio das Cantigas* (116B Avenida de Kwong Tung) and the *Irish Pub* (☎ 820 708, 116C Avenida de Kwong Tung) next door, which is where most evenings that begin at the Mandarin Oriental's Embassy Bar and descend into the Fortuna Lounge end up. Other places to try include: the *Bar dos Namorados* (85E Avenida de Kwong Tung); the *Café La Marseille* (☎ 822 920, 73D Avenida de Kwong Tung); and the *Island Pub* (☎ 822 781, 85A Avenida de Kwong Tung).

The Greenhouse Bar (☎ 831 234, Hyatt Regency Macau, 2 Estrada Almirante Marques Esparteiro) This is where you go if you want a quiet drink. Cocktails are expensive, but there's a happy hour from 5pm to 7pm.

COLOANE ISLAND
A haven for pirates till the start of the 20th century, Coloane (Lo Wan in Cantonese, Luhuan in Mandarin; population 2500) fought off the last assault by buccaneers on the South China Sea in 1910, and islanders still celebrate the anniversary of the victory on 13 July. Happily the island's beaches no longer resound to the whistle of cannonballs or the clash of broadswords. Instead, Coloane attracts large numbers of visitors to its sleepy main village and sandy coastline.

Seac Pai Van Park
About a kilometre south of the expanded causeway, now lined with images of Chinese mythological animals and astrological symbols, is 20-hectare Seac Pai Van Park (☎ 870 277, Estrada Seac Pai Van; open 8am-6pm in summer, 9am-5pm in winter). Built in the wooded hills on the western side of the island, it has well-tended gardens, with hundreds of species of plants and trees from around the world, a **Garden of Medicinal Plants**, a children's playground and zoo, a lake with swans and so on, but the most notable feature is the walk-in **aviary** (admission M$5; open 10.30am-4.30pm Tues-Sun), which contains a number of rare birds, including Palawan peacocks and crested white pheasants. The recently opened **Museum of Nature & Agriculture** (☎ 827 012; admission free; open 10.30am-4.30pm Tues-Sun) has traditional farming equipment, dioramas of Coloane's ecosystem and displays cataloguing a wide range of the island's fauna and flora.

A-Ma Statue
This colossal 20m statue of the goddess who gave Macau its name (see the boxed text What's in a Name? in the Facts about Macau chapter) atop **Alto de Coloane** (176m) was hewn from a form of white jade quarried in Fangshang near Beijing and erected in 1998. A cable car will soon link Hác Sá Beach with the 'summit' and the statue. At present you can reach it by following Estrada do Alto de Coloane south-west from Estrada Seac Pai Van or by walking along the Coloane Trail (Trilho de Coloane) from the park (see Activities later in this chapter).

Coloane Village
The only real settlement on the island, this is still largely a fishing village in character

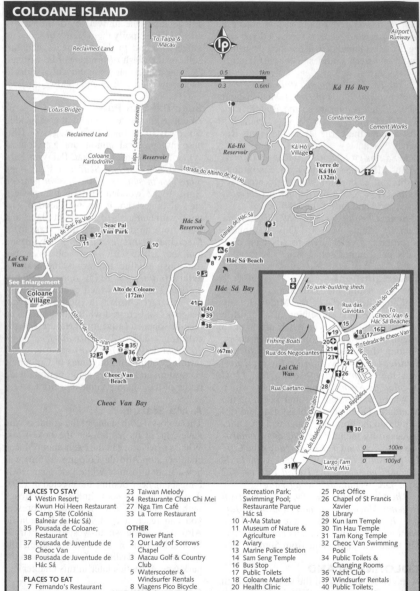

COLOANE ISLAND

PLACES TO STAY
4 Westin Resort;
  Kwun Hoi Heen Restaurant
6 Camp Site (Colónia
  Balnear de Hác Sá)
35 Pousada de Coloane;
  Restaurant
37 Pousada de Juventude de
  Cheoc Van
38 Pousada de Juventude de
  Hác Sá

PLACES TO EAT
7 Fernando's Restaurant
15 Caçarola Restaurant
19 Lord Stow's Bakery

23 Taiwan Melody
24 Restaurante Chan Chi Mei
27 Nga Tim Café
33 La Torre Restaurant

OTHER
1 Power Plant
2 Our Lady of Sorrows
  Chapel
3 Macau Golf & Country
  Club
5 Waterscooter &
  Windsurfer Rentals
8 Viagens Pico Bicycle
  Rental
9 Hác Sá Sports &

Recreation Park;
  Swimming Pool;
  Restaurante Parque
  Hác sá
10 A-Ma Statue
11 Museum of Nature &
  Agriculture
12 Aviary
13 Marine Police Station
16 Sam Seng Temple
16 Bus Stop
17 Public Toilets
18 Coloane Market
20 Health Clinic
21 Asian Artefacts Shop
22 Bus Stop

25 Post Office
26 Chapel of St Francis
  Xavier
28 Library
29 Kun Iam Temple
30 Tin Hau Temple
31 Tam Kong Temple
32 Cheoc Van Swimming
  Pool
34 Public Toilets &
  Changing Rooms
36 Yacht Club
39 Windsurfer Rentals
40 Public Toilets;
  Showers
41 Bus Stop

(particularly at the northern end), although in recent years tourism has given the local economy a boost. The village is a fascinating relic of the Macau that was, and strolling along the narrow lanes, flanked by pastel-coloured shops and restaurants, is a joy. Just east of the village is Macau's only prison, where Broken Tooth Koi (see the boxed text Dicing with Death in the Macau Facts for the Visitor chapter) is currently in residence.

The bus will drop you off in the village's attractive **main square**; the **market** is on the eastern side. To the west is the waterfront; China is just across the channel. From here a sign points the way north to the **Sam Seng Temple** on Rua dos Navegantes, which is so small it's not much more than a family altar. Just past the temple is the village pier and beyond that to the north-east several **junk-building sheds**. Junks are still built here (it takes about two months to make one), but a fire in 1999 destroyed many of the sheds and the industry is dying.

If you walk south along Avenida de Cinco de Outubro, you'll soon reach the village's main attraction, the **Chapel of St Francis Xavier**. This delightful little church was built in 1928 to honour St Francis Xavier, who died on Shangchuan Island, the Portuguese colonisers' first port of call, in 1552. He had been a missionary in Japan, and Japanese Catholics still come to Coloane to pay their respects.

A fragment of St Francis' arm bone used to be kept in the chapel, along with the relics of Portuguese and Japanese Christians martyred in Nagasaki in 1597, Vietnamese Christians killed in the early 17th century and Japanese Christians massacred in a rebellion in Japan during the 17th century. In 1996 many of these bones were moved to the crypt of the ruined Church of St Paul (see the Macau Peninsula chapter).

In front of the Chapel of St Francis Xavier is a **monument** surrounded by cannonballs commemorating the successful – and final – routing of pirates in 1910.

South of the chapel and opposite the village library is the small **Kun Iam Temple**, an altar inside a little walled compound on Travessa da República. Although there are no signs to indicate the path, if you walk to the south-east just a little farther past the stone wall, you'll find a considerably larger and more interesting **Tin Hau Temple** in Largo Tin Hau Miu. At its entrance is a traditional hand-powered fire engine.

At the very southern end of Avenida de Cinco de Outubro in Largo Tam Kong Miu is the **Tam Kong Temple**, dedicated to the Taoist God of Seafarers. To the right of the main altar is a whale bone, more than a metre long, which has been carved into a model of a ship, complete with a dragon's head and a crew of men in pointed hats.

Cheoc Van Beach

About 1.5km down the Estrada de Cheoc Van, which runs east and then south-east from the village, is Cheoc Van – 'bamboo bay' – Beach. You can swim in the ocean (there are public changing rooms and toilets) or in the **outdoor pool** *(adult/child under 17 M$15/5; open 8am-9pm Mon-Fri, 8am-midnight Sat & Sun)* just up from the beach. The beach also has a **yacht club** (☎ 882 252) where you can inquire about renting boats and windsurfing boards.

Hác Sá Beach

Hác Sá (black sand) is a much larger and more popular beach then Cheoc Van. The sand is indeed a grey to blackish colour and makes the water look somewhat dirty, but actually it's perfectly clean and fine for swimming. Hác Sá Bay is beautiful, and on a clear day you can just make out the mountaintops on Hong Kong's Lantau Island.

The **Hác Sá Sports and Recreation Park** (☎ 882 296, Estrada Nova de Hác Sá; open 8am-9pm Sun-Fri, 8am-11pm Sat) by the bus stop seems to have just about everything on offer: swimming pool (adult/child M$15/5), three tennis courts (M$30 per hour, M$60 after 7pm; racquet & ball hire available), a five-a-side football ground (M$70 per hour, M$100 after 7pm), a mini-golf course (M$10 per hour), ping pong tables (M$5 per hour) and badminton courts (M$10 per hour). There are places to rent windsurfing boards and jet skis at both ends of Hác Sá Beach.

KELLI HAMBLET
Church of Our Lady of Sorrows of Ká Hó

Ká Hó Village

At the eastern end of Coloane is the traditional village of Ká Hó, now spoiled by the neighbouring cement and power plants and a deepwater container port. Part of the village is given over to a leprosarium, whose few residents live in tumbledown old villas and grow their own vegetables. The most interesting sight in the area is the modern **Church of Our Lady of Sorrows of Ká Hó** built in 1966, which has a large bronze crucifix above the north door sculpted by the Italian artist Francisco Messima.

Activities

Coloane has several walking and fitness trails. The longest, which begins at Seac Pai Van Park, is the **Coloane Trail** (Trilho de Coloane), and the entire loop is just over 8km. The shorter **North-East Coloane Trail** (Trilho Nordeste de Coloane) is near Ká Hó and runs for about 3km. Other trails include the 1.5km-long **Mount Ká Hó Trail** (Trilho do Altinho de Ká Hó) and the 1.5km-long **Hác Sá Reservoir Circuit** (Circuito da Barragem de Hác Sá), which both loop around the reservoir north-west of Hác Sá Beach.

The **Coloane Kartodrome** (☎ 882 126, 580 762, Estrada de Seac Pai Van; open 10am-6.30pm daily), which is on the southern end of the causeway on Coloane's northern shore, is the territory's most popular venue for go-karting. It costs M$100/300 for 10/25 minutes in a 3½HP or 9HP go-kart, M$500/800 for a half-hour/hour in a 20HP one. There are all sorts of packages available (eg, 25 minutes in a 9HP go-kart

plus return ferry tickets from/to Hong Kong for M$430 or the same deal plus one night's accommodation for M$650). Races are held here on Sunday.

The 18-hole, par-71 **Macau Golf & Country Course** (☎ 871 111, 1918 Estrada de Hác Sá), which is connected to the Westin Resort hotel by walkway on the 9th floor, is open to nonguests. Green fees are M$700/1400 on weekdays/weekends, and you must have a handicap certificate to tee off. The driving range and putting course (☎ 870 041) is open to the public from 7am to 5pm daily.

Bicycles are available for rent for M$20 per hour from **Viagens Pico** (☎ 882 531) next door to (and owned by) Fernando's restaurant on Hác Sá Beach.

Places to Stay

Camping There's a *camping site* at the Colónia Balnear de Hác Sá (☎ 825 170, Estrada Nova de Hác Sá), a recreational area for youth. The site is equipped with toilets and showers.

Hostels Coloane has both of Macau's hostels. In the past, staying at either was a complicated procedure as you couldn't just show up but had to reserve ahead and pay at the hostel booking office on the Macau Peninsula. That's all about to change, with travellers welcome on arrival, but it is strongly recommended that you call the hostel(s) or the MGTO (☎ 315 566) before you set out to verify that this is indeed the case. You must have a Hostelling International card or equivalent to stay at either hostel. There are separate quarters for men and women.

Pousada de Juventude de Cheoc Van (☎ 882 024, Rue de António Francisco) Bed in double/quad/dorm M$70/50/40 Mon-Fri, M$100/70/50 Sat & Sun. This very clean hostel is on the eastern side of Cheoc Van Bay below the Pousada de Coloane. During the off season (basically winter) it's pretty easy to get in here, but during peak season (summer and holidays) competition for beds is keen. Big youth groups tend to book this place out during school holidays. The hostel has a small kitchen and garden.

Pousada de Juventude de Hác Sá (☎ 882 701, *Estrada Nova de Hác Sá*) Bed in double/quad/dorm M$70/50/40 Mon-Fri, M$100/70/50 Sat & Sun. This circular, grey-tiled building at the southern end of Hác Sá Beach is more modern than the Cheoc Van hostel.

Hotels For a relaxed and appealing atmosphere try *Pousada de Coloane* (☎ 882 143, *fax 882 251, Estrada de Cheoc Van*). Singles & doubles M$680-750, triples M$880-950. This cosy, 22-room hotel overlooking Cheoc Van Beach was looking a bit frayed around the edges until a recent make-over. It has its own little sauna and swimming pool, and is well known for its excellent Sunday lunch buffet. If two of you spend more than M$600 at the hotel's restaurant (see Places to Eat), you get one night's free accommodation.

Westin Resort (☎ 871 111, *fax 871 122*, Ⓦ *www.westin.com, 1918 Estrada de Hác Sá*) Rooms M$2000-2350, suites from M$5000. This five-star 'island resort' complex is on the eastern side of Hác Sá Beach. Each of the 208 rooms has a large terrace and the overall atmosphere is that of a country club, with an attached 18-hole golf course, eight tennis courts, two squash courts, badminton courts, billiard tables, swimming pools, an outdoor spa, sauna and gymnasium. This is the perfect getaway if you want a resort break.

Places to Eat

Coloane is not the treasure-trove of restaurants and other eateries that is Taipa Island, but there are a few decent options offering a variety of cuisines at all price levels.

Caçarola (☎ 882 226, *8 Rua dos Gaivotas*) Starters M$20-50, mains M$45-80. This rather claustrophobic place just up from the pretty main square in Coloane Village, is a popular place with simple and honest Portuguese cuisine and Filipino staff.

Restaurante Chan Chi Mei (☎ 882 086, *1 Rua Caetano*) Meals about M$60-80. The Nga Tim Café's upmarket big sister restaurant serves exquisite fish dishes for far less than you'd pay on Taipa or the peninsula.

Fernando's (☎ 882 531, *house No 9 Hác Sá Beach*) Soups M$22-26, fish & seafood M$55-148, meat dishes M$50-128, rice dishes M$60-66. This place deserves honourable mention for some of the best Portuguese food and fish dishes in Macau. The atmosphere is also pleasant, but it can get crowded in the evening. Famed for its seafood, Fernando's has a devoted clientele and an almost legendary profile in good-dining circles. The eponymous owner/manager is straight out of Central Casting. Make sure you book ahead, though it's not possible to do so at the weekend.

Kwun Hoi Heen (☎ 871 111, *Westin Resort, 1918 Estrada de Hác Sá*) Set lunch M$280/360 for two/three courses. The Kwun Hoi Heen stands out among the hotel restaurants on Coloane Island for its sumptuous views and superb Cantonese cuisine. The set lunch served from Monday to Friday is excellent value.

Lord Stow's Bakery (☎ 882 534, *1 Rua da Tassara*) Sandwiches M$13-15. OK, so this establishment on the main square produces the *pasteis de nata*, a warm egg custard tart. What Chinese bakery on the south China coast doesn't? Still, they're a cut above, and the Lord's bread is, well, heavenly.

Nga Tim Café (☎ 882 086, *8 Rua Caetano*) Meals about M$80. The food at this little place next to the Chapel of St Francis Xavier is Sino-Portuguese, and while the restaurant is certainly no work of art, the view outside is. If it's a sunny day, take a seat in the square and savour both the scenery and the food.

Restaurante Parque Hác Sá (☎ 882 297, *Hác Sá Sports & Recreation Park, Estrada Nova de Hác Sá*) Buffet M$120. This is a pleasant place for lunch or dinner by the beach at Hác Sá.

Pousada de Coloane Restaurant (☎ 882 143, *Cheoc Van Beach*) Meals about M$200. This restaurant has decent hotel Portuguese food and seating on a veranda overlooking Cheoc Van Beach. The Sunday lunch and the Saturday night barbecue buffets (both M$98) are particularly good value. The hotel usually offers free accommodation during the off season for couples and groups eating and drinking at the restaurant (see Places to Stay for details).

Taiwan Melody (☎ *881 218, 3A Rua dos Negociantes*) Meals about M$60. This touchy-feely tearoom and shop just up from the Chapel of St Francis Xavier is a New Age oasis in an old age village.

La Torre (☎ *880 156, Praia de Cheoc Van*) Pizza M$45-66, pasta M$60-65, mains M$65-185. Next to the swimming pool at Cheoc Van Beach is this fine Italian restaurant, which has some excellent pastas and pizzas and outside seating.

Shopping

The back streets of Coloane Village, especially Rua dos Negociantes, are lined with shops selling antiques, bric-a-brac and traditional goods like incense and hell money. ***Taiwan Melody*** (see Places to Eat), which can also be entered from Rua dos Negociantes, has a good selection of books, tea and teaware.

Asian Artefacts (☎ *881 022, 25 Rua dos Negociantes*) Open 10am-7pm daily. Asian Artefacts sells some of the best-quality antiques in Macau.

China Excursion – Zhuhai

Like Shenzhen, Zhuhai is a 'Special Economic Zone'. But Zhuhai, or 'pearl of the sea', has never reached the level of success (or excess) of its well-heeled step-sister across the Pearl River estuary to the northeast. So much the better for residents and travellers, for the city of Zhuhai, with almost 700,000 people just over the border from Macau, is one of the cleanest and greenest metropolises on the mainland.

To be sure, Zhuhai is a boom town and doing well out of its position on the 'gold coast' of southern China. In true rags to riches style, Zhuhai was built from the ground up on what was not long ago rice fields and other farmland. Travellers who visited here in the early (or even late) 1980s will remember a small agricultural town with a few rural industries and a peaceful beach, a place to stop for lunch on the way to Cuiheng, where Dr Sun Yatsen, the founder of the Republic of China, was born in 1866.

That's all history now. The Zhuhai of today not only has the usual SEZ skyline of glimmering five-star hotels and big factories, bargain shopping and pulsating discos and clubs, it also has its own spotless and ultramodern airport.

Zhuhai is mainly a business destination or, like Shenzhen, a place where people come from south of the border to shop, take massage, eat cheaply and rent karaoke rooms for Y600 a night, including beer and female 'company'. But if you're looking for an easy getaway from Macau (or Hong Kong for that matter) with all the modern conveniences, the city is worth a visit. Zhuhai is close enough to the border with Macau for a day trip; alternatively, you can use Zhuhai as an entry or exit point for the rest of China (provided you have the right visa).

Zhuhai is not only prettier and cleaner than Shenzhen, it is also friendlier and more laid-back. There's more of a sense of community in Zhuhai as well. Here you'll see school children on the streets – a rarity in Shenzhen.

Highlights

- A lavish cultural performance at New Yuan Ming Palace
- A walk around delightful Mingting Park on Yeli Island
- A meal at Youyi Lu and Yingbin Dadao, Zhuhai's unofficial restaurant strip
- An early morning visit to Gongbei Market

As in Shenzhen, the lingua franca in Zhuhai is *putonghua*, or Mandarin, which is China's official language (see the Language chapter at the back of this book). You will hear a great deal more Cantonese here than in Shenzhen, however.

ORIENTATION

The Special Economic Zone of Zhuhai extends from the border with the Macau Special Administrative Region in the south, Zhongshan county to the north and incorporating riverine Doumen county to the west and south-west. With a total land area of 1300 sq km, it is larger than Hong Kong but has only about a tenth of its population.

The municipality of Zhuhai, which hugs the eastern side of the peninsula just north of Macau, has three main districts. Gongbei, which abuts the Macau border, is the main tourist district, with lots of hotels, restaurants and shops but few sights as such. To the north-east is Jida, which contains some large waterfront hotels and resorts as well as Jiuzhou Harbour, where passenger ferries to Hong Kong, Shenzhen (Shekou) and Guangzhou arrive and depart. Xiangzhou is the northernmost part of Zhuhai City and has many government buildings, housing blocks and a busy fishing port.

Less than ten years ago, the flat and fertile delta of Doumen county to the west and south-west of Zhuhai City was given over almost entirely to agriculture, but land

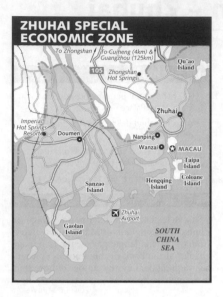

ZHUHAI SPECIAL ECONOMIC ZONE

reclamation, an airport and the new Lotus Bridge linking the Zhuhai Special Economic Zone's Hengqing Island with Macau has changed the face of all that.

Maps

There's not a lot of choice if you need a map with at least some of the street and places names in English. *The Tour and Transportation Map of Zhuhai* (Y5) is badly drawn, hard to read and not to scale but can be purchased relatively easily at bookshops and hotels. The Zhuhai inset of the *Map of Macau, Zhongshan and Zhuhai in Detail* (HK$22) is hardly what you'd call detailed but it is clearer. In Hong Kong, you can buy it at the Joint Publishing Company bookshop (☎ 2525 0105), 9 Queen Victoria St, Central.

INFORMATION
Travel Agencies

Some of the staff at the China Travel Service (CTS) office (☎ 888 6748, fax 815 6464) next to the Zhuhai Overseas Chinese Hotel on Yingbin Dadao speak English and are anxious to be of assistance. The office is open 8am to 9.30pm weekdays and 9.30am to 5.30pm at the weekend. The

business centres at many top-end hotels have flight, bus, rail and ferry schedules and should be able to help with queries and bookings. If you buy tickets from these business centres, expect to pay a little more.

Visas

Holders of Canadian, American, Australian, New Zealand and most European Union passports, as well as many others, can buy a visa valid for the Zhuhai SEZ *only* for 72 hours on arrival at Gongbei Port. The visa costs M$100 and is available on the 2nd floor; go through the door marked 'Visas' on the right side of the immigration hall and walk up the steps. These are also available if you arrive from Hong Kong by ferry.

Everyone else, *including* British nationals at the moment, must have a Chinese visa obtained in Hong Kong, Macau or elsewhere in advance. Those wanting to leave the confines of the Zhuhai SEZ, even to visit Sun Yatsen's birthplace at Cuiheng or the Zhongshan Hot Springs, must also have such a visa. They are available from Chinese embassies and consulates, CTS branches and local travel agencies. See the Hong Kong Facts for the Visitor chapter for a list of Chinese consular representatives overseas and the Hong Kong and Macau Getting There & Away chapters for a list of travel agencies.

Money

China's currency, the renmenbi, is more commonly called the yuan and shown as a 'Y' before figures in this chapter.

Three currencies are effectively in circulation in Zhuhai, and most shops, restaurants and hotels will gladly accept Hong Kong dollars and Macau patacas along with renmenbi. The Macau pataca is worth slightly less than the Hong Kong dollar (HK$1 = M$1.04 at the time of writing) and is pegged to the Hong Kong unit. See the Money section under Information in the Shenzhen chapter for more details and a table of exchange rates.

Exchanging Money If you pay for things in Hong Kong dollars or patacas at hotels, big restaurants and large stores, you will usually get change back in those currencies. In smaller shops, food stalls and the like, it will probably come back in renmenbi, and you will lose a little on the exchange rate.

There's a Bank of China (BOC) branch in Gongbei Port just after immigration, where you can change foreign currency into renmenbi. It's open 8.30am to 5pm weekdays and 10am to 4pm at the weekend. The towering main BOC branch (☎ 888 3333) is next to the Yindo Hotel at the corner of Yingbin Dadao and Yuehai Dong Lu and opens the same hours. The ATMs at both BOC branches are linked to several international money systems, including Cirrus and Plus, and they accept Visa, American Express and MasterCard as long as you have a PIN code.

You can also change money in most hotels. The moneychangers at the border crossing, both before and after you enter China, should be avoided.

Post & Communications

The most useful post offices are on Yuehai Dong Lu, from where you can make long-distance telephone calls and buy phonecards, and at 18 Qiaoguang Lu. Both are open 8am to 8pm daily. You can make IDD calls from your room in most hotels.

China's country code is 86. For direct dialling to Zhuhai, the area code is 0756 within China and 756 from abroad, including Hong Kong and Macau.

Email & Internet Access You can access your email and surf the Web at the Internet Bar (813 4965) on the 4th floor of the Guangdong Regency Hotel's West Tower, 30 Yuehai Dong Lu. It opens 11am till midnight daily and charges Y10 per hour.

Toilets

You'll find toilets everywhere in Zhuhai, on the street, in malls and even in the market, but they are inevitably à la turque (ie, squat) toilets.

Emergency

Branches of the Public Security Bureau (PBS), the section of the police force that deals with foreigners, can be found on Guihua Lu in Gongbei (☎ 864 2114) and at the corner of Anping Lu and Kangning Lu in Xiangzhou (☎ 822 2459).

The tourist complaint hotline is ☎ 336 6061.

Dangers & Annoyances

While many of Zhuhai's streets are admirably lined with palm and other oxygen-creating trees and plants, the pavements are full of cracked slabs and gaping holes that could potentially disable you if you fell into one. Watch where you step, especially after dark.

Spitting is a major annoyance in Zhuhai as it is throughout China. See Dangers & Annoyances in the Shenzhen chapter for the delightful details.

Prostitution is not so in-your-face here as it is in Shenzhen and the hookers themselves hardly as persistent, but there is a constant parade – both day and night – of young women strutting their stuff along the eastern end of Yuehai Dong Lu. Unless you're into it, it's best to avoid the area, especially after nightfall. Be advised that the 'barber shops' and 'salons' being advertised by twirling, pastel-coloured poles are usually fronts for massage parlours and brothels.

JIDA

The bulk of Zhuhai's most interesting sights and activities are in Jida, the district to the north-east of Gongbei.

Zhuhai Holiday Resort

Zhuhai Holiday Resort (Zhūhǎi Dùjià Cūn; ☎ 333 2038), south-west of Jiuzhou Harbour, has the best beach in Zhuhai – which isn't really saying much. The beach is largely disappearing to the developers, and there isn't much open sand left.

Have a look around the resort itself. It's not an unattractive place, landscaped and boasting a slew of recreational pastimes (see Places to Stay – Top End for details).

Bus Nos 4, 9 and 13 will take you to the resort.

Bailian Cave & Park 白莲洞公园

Bailian (White Lotus) Cave is in the park of that name (Báilián Dòng Gÿngyuán; Bailian

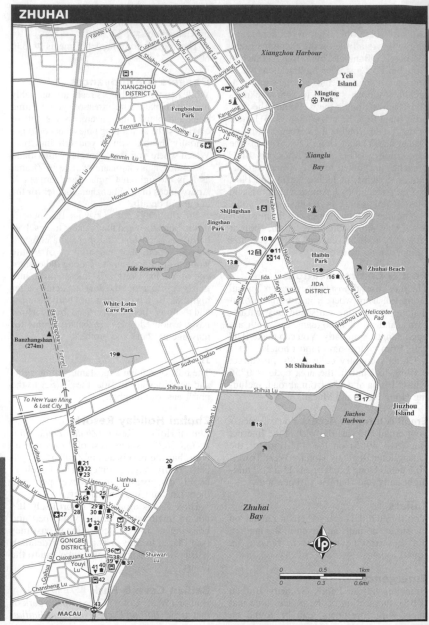

ZHUHAI

ZHUHAI 珠海

PLACES TO STAY

10 Paradise Hill Hotel
13 Zhuhai Hotel
    珠海宾馆
16 Harbour View Hotel &
    Resort
    怡景湾大酒店
18 Zhuhai Holiday Resort
20 Grand Bay View Hotel
21 Overseas Chinese
    Hotel
    华侨大酒店
24 Yindo Hotel
    银都酒店
29 Guangdong Regency
    Hotel
    (West Tower);
    Internet Bar
    珠海粤海酒店
    （西楼）；
    网吧
30 Good World Hotel
32 Hualigong Hotel
    华丽宫酒店
33 Guangdong Regency
    Hotel
    (East Tower); Big
    Dipper Revolving
    Restaurant
    珠海粤海酒店（东楼）
35 Popoko Hotel
    步步高大酒店
37 Gongbei Palace Hotel
    拱北宾馆
40 Friendship Hotel
    友谊宾馆

PLACES TO EAT

2   Floating Restaurant
23 Indian Restaurant
    印地安复合式餐厅
25 Maxim's
38 May Flower
    Restaurant
41 Restaurant Row

OTHER

1   Xiangzhou Bus Station
    香洲汽车站
3   Fishing Boats
4   Post Office
    邮局
5   Revolutionary Martyrs'
    Memorial
    革命烈士陵园
6   Xiangzhou Public
    Security Bureau
    香洲公安局
7   Zhuhai People's
    Hospital
    珠海人民医院
8   Shijingshan Cable Car
    石景山缆车
9   Zhuhai Fisher Girl Statue
11 Zhuhai Trade &
    Exhibition Centre
12 Zhuhai Museum
    珠海市博物馆
14 Duty-Free Shopping
    Centre
    免税购物中心
15 Haibin Amusement Park
    海滨娱乐园

17 Jiuzhou Harbour
    Passenger Terminal
    (Boats to Hong
    Kong & Shenzhen)
    九洲港客运站
    （乘船至香港和深圳）
19 Bailian Cave & Park
    白莲洞公园
22 China Travel Service
    中国旅行社
26 Bank of China
    中国银行
27 Gongbei Public
    Security Branch
    拱北公安分局
28 CNAC Building
31 Gongbei Market
    拱北市场
34 Post Office
    邮局
36 Post Office
    邮局
39 Gongbei Bus Station;
    Yongtong Hotel
    拱北公共汽车总站
42 Local Bus Station;
    Entrance to Gongbei
    Port Commercial Plaza
    公共汽车站；
    拱北港商城入口
43 Gongbei Port
    (Customs &
    Immigration); Portas
    do Cerco
    拱北港
    （海关与出入境）

Lu; admission Y1; open 9am-5pm daily), fanning out below several peaks, including Banzhangshan (Camphor Mountain). Features of the park include the Huatuo Temple and the adjacent Dashi and Liujiao pavilions. There is also the **Jidan Gardens** and two central lakes with rowing boats and a small junk with sails.

Bailian Cave and Park is on the northern side of Jiuzhou Dadao, running between Gongbei and Jida districts. Bus No 2 passes right by and can drop you off at the park entrance.

Haibin Park

Once only trees, Haibin Park *(Hăibīn Gÿngyuán; ☎ 333 2562; Jida Lu; open 10am-7pm daily)* now contains amusement rides in the south, a swimming pool, shooting range, roller-skating rink, barbecue pits and picnic areas. The park is attractive and a great relief from the streets.

To the east of Haibin Park is a small **beach** and in the harbour to the north you will find the **Zhuhai Fisher Girl statue**, a mermaid-like creature that has become the city's symbol.

ZHUHAI

Bus Nos 2, 4, 9 and 20 can drop you off by the park entrance.

Zhuhai Museum 珠海市博物馆

Zhuhai Museum (*Zhūhǎi Shì Bówùguǎn;* ☎ 334 1085, 191 Jianshan Lu; admission Y10; open 9am-5pm daily) is housed on two floors of what was until recently Jiuzhou Cheng, a fashionable shopping centre that looks like some kind of restored Ming dynasty village, with lotus ponds, zigzag bridges and bamboo in the courtyards. The museum contains a small but interesting collection of copperware (drinking vessels, temple bells, figurines etc), some of which date back 5000 years; Tibetan art and artefacts, including gilded cups formed from human skulls; and scroll paintings and calligraphy. The photo mural of modern Zhuhai with Macau in the background is interesting.

Bus Nos 2, 20, 26 and 205 stop in front of the museum.

Jingshan Park 景山公园

Jingshan Park (*Jǐngshān Gōngyuán;* ☎ 222 2630, Haibin Bei Lu; admission Y1; open 10am-7pm daily) is noted for its 'boulder forest' covering 'Paradise Hill' behind it and the **Shijingshan Cableway**, which will take you to the top (Y40). Miniature go-karts just beyond the entrance cost Y25/40 for five/10 minutes.

Bus Nos 2, 13, 20, 205 and 206 will drop you off at the park.

XIANGZHOU 香洲

There's not a heck of a lot to see or do in Zhuhai's northernmost district, but **Yeli Island** and its delightful **Mingting Park**, accessed by footbridge from Xiangwan Lu, provide a backdrop for the fleet of **fishing boats** bobbing up and down in Xiangzhou Harbour.

The austere **Revolutionary Martyrs' Memorial** (*Lièshi Língyuán; Fenghuang Bei Lu*) at the entrance to Fengboshan Park is dedicated to local victims of the Japanese, who were executed during WWII. Walk towards the pagoda at the top of the steps to reach the park.

NEW YUAN MING PALACE & LOST CITY 圆明新园

New Yuan Ming Palace (*Yuánmíng Xīnyuán;* ☎ 861 0388, fax 862 7350, Jiuzhou Dadao; adult/child Y100/60; open 9am-9pm daily), a massive theme park built at a cost of Y600 million at the foot of Dashilin mountain north-west of Gongbei, is Zhuhai's most popular tourist sight. It is a reproduction of the original Yuan Ming Palace in Beijing, which was torched by British and French forces during the Second Opium War (1856–58) and is marginally less tacky than the theme parks in Shenzhen.

The impressive entrance, straight out of Tiananmen Square in Beijing, leads to an enormous playground of sights from around China and the world, including the Great Wall, Italian and German castles, halls, restaurants, temples and a lake covering 80,000 sq m.

There are lavish, 30-minute performances (eg, Emperor's Ascension to the Throne, Imperial Wedding Ceremony, the Pearl of China dance) scheduled at 11am, 3pm and 7.30pm as well as daylong demonstrations by craftspeople and artisans.

Lost City (☎ 861 0388, fax 862 7350, Jiuzhou Dadao; adult/child Y140/90, including admission to New Yuan Ming Palace; open 9am-9pm Apr-Oct) This vast adventure and water park is just next door to the New Yuan Ming Palace and a great place to take kids on a hot summer day. Activities and rides at extra cost include bungee jumping (Y150), bungee rocket (Y100), super swing (Y30) and rocket man (Y50); Y250 gets you a go on the lot.

You can reach both parks directly on bus Nos 13 and 25. Bus Nos 30, 40, 201, 202 and 206 will drop you off a little to the south.

IMPERIAL HOT SPRING RESORT 御温泉

This massive resort (*Yù Wēnquán Dùjià Cūn;* ☎ 579 7128, fax 579 8541, ⓦ www .imperial-hot-spring.com), west of Zhuhai City in Doumen county, has a number of thermal pools (outdoor/indoor Y98/280) where you can soak away the fatigue and grime of touring a Chinese SEZ or have one of three types of massage (Hong Kong/ Shanghai/Thai at Y180/198/230). Bus No 209 (Y6 or Y7) from Zhuhai City will take you to the resort in 80 minutes.

PLACES TO STAY – BUDGET

Though hotel prices are generally lower than those in Shenzhen, budget accommodation is pretty scarce on the ground in Zhuhai. There is one option, however.

Gongbei Palace Hotel (*Gŏngbĕi Bīnguăn;* ☎ 888 6833, fax 888 5686, *21 Shuiwan Lu, Gongbei*) Single Y150, doubles Y150-280, villa suites with/without sea view Y480/330. This over-the-top hotel, with golden, pagoda-like roof and turrets and once the most luxurious place close to the Macau border, has taken a beating from all the competition and rooms cost less than a third of what they did a couple of years ago. It's about a minute's walk from the Gongbei Port and by the waterfront, but the 'beach' is just for looking – it's too rocky to swim here.

PLACES TO STAY – MID-RANGE

Hotel prices usually rise by 10% or 20% on weekends and public holidays, but hotel rates in Zhuhai are almost always negotiable.

Friendship Hotel (*Yŏuyì Jiŭdiàn;* ☎ 813 1818, fax 813 5505, *2 Youyi Lu, Gongbei*) Singles/doubles from Y368/388. This reasonably priced modern hotel is opposite the border crossing and a pretty park and around the corner from an interesting old market street filled with food stalls and hawkers.

Good World Hotel (*Hăo Shìjiè Jiŭdiàn;* ☎ 888 0222, fax 889 2061, *82 Lianhua Lu, Gongbei*) Doubles/triples Y300/440. Central and almost upmarket, the Good World is one of the best deals in Zhuhai. A 30% discount is sometimes available.

Hualigong Hotel (*Huálìgōng Jiŭdiàn;* ☎ 813 1828, fax 813 1299, *116 Yuehua Lu, Gongbei*) Singles/doubles from Y368/438. This small hotel is bare-bones in the extreme but reasonably clean and in the centre of the action. Expect something in the region of 50% off the asking price during the week.

Zhuhai Overseas Chinese Hotel (*Huáqiáo Bīnguăn;* ☎ 888 6288, fax 888 5119, ⓦ *www.hb-hotel.com, Yingbin Dadao,*

Gongbei) Doubles from Y368, suites from Y498. This friendly, 197-room hotel is a block north of Yuehai Lu and has a decent international-style outlet called the Poly Coffee Shop.

Popoko Hotel (*Bùbùgāo Dà Jiŭdiàn;* ☎ 888 6628, fax 888 9992, *2 Yuehai Dong Lu, Gongbei*) Doubles from Y388. This 218-room hotel overlooking the waterfront has a number of decent outlets, including Taiwan Cuisine Street, but it's a bit worn at the edges.

Yongtong Hotel (*Yŏngtōng Jiŭdiàn;* ☎ 888 8887, fax 888 9342, *20 Youyi Lu, Gongbei*) Singles & doubles/triples/quads Y338/438/498. The 102-room Yongtong is nothing special but is attached to the Gongbei bus station and opposite Gongbei Port and thus very central. Because of its good location and relatively affordable prices, it's a favourite of backpackers.

PLACES TO STAY – TOP-END

Most hotels add a 10% service charge to the bill in Zhuhai but the top-end places usually tack on an extra 15%.

Grand Bay View Hotel (*Zhūhăi Hăiwān Dàjiŭdiàn;* ☎ 887 7998, fax 887 8998, ⓦ *www.gbvh.com, Shuiwan Lu, Gongbei*) Rooms Y830-980, suites from Y1180. This new, 242-room hotel, overlooking the sea but close to the centre, is a favourite of business travellers, with the top three floors reserved for them. It has all the amenities you'd expect, including the fine Harbour Cafe, a Western restaurant with some of the best views in town.

Guangdong Regency Hotel (*Zhūhăi Yuèhăi Jiŭdiàn;* ☎ 888 8128, fax 888 9433, ⓔ *zhgdrhtl@pub.zhuhai.gd.cn, 1145 Yuehai Lu, Gongbei*) Doubles from Y730, suites from Y1500. The hotel's 361 guestrooms and the Big Dipper revolving restaurant are in the East Tower. A walkway leads to the West Tower, where you'll find the Recreation Centre, with bowling, squash, gym, billiards and Internet cafe on the 4th and 5th floors and a rooftop pool.

Harbour View Hotel & Resort (*Yíjǐngwān Dà Jiŭdiàn;* ☎ 332 2888, fax 337 1365, ⓔ *hvhbc@pub.zhuhai.gd.cn, 47 Haijing Lu, Jida*) Rooms Y880-980, suites from

ZHUHAI

Y1380. This 383-room pile on the waterfront is more a hotel than a resort and has all the mod-cons as well as four bowling lanes, tennis courts and indoor games.

Paradise Hill Hotel (*Shíjǐngshān Lǚyóu Zhōngxīn;* ☎ 333 7388, fax 333 3508, W *www.paradisehillhotel.com, Jingshan Lu, Jida*) Doubles Y738-1180, suites from Y1380. From the outside this hotel looks like a cross between a Victorian manse and a Thai palace, but the 215 rooms are tastefully done, most have verandas and views of Jingshan Park.

Yindo Hotel (*Yíndū Jiǔdiàn;* ☎ 888 3388, fax 888 3311, Cnr Yingbin Dadao & Yuehai Lu, Gongbei*) Rooms from Y860, suites from Y1360. The Yindo, with 299 rooms, next to the main Bank of China branch, is one of the best places to stay within striking distance of the border. Along with restaurants and the Tea Palace, which serves traditional Chinese brews, it has a swimming pool, massage centre, sauna, bowling alley and billiards.

Zhuhai Hotel (*Zhūhǎi Bīnguǎn;* ☎ 333 3718, fax 333 2339, W *www.zhuhai-hotel .com, Jingshan Lu, Jida*) Doubles Y688-888, villas from Y980. While not as flash as some of its competitors in Jida, the Zhuhai has a lot of traditional touches, a lovely back courtyard ringed with villas and lots of recreational facilities.

Zhuhai Holiday Resort (*Zhūhǎi Dùjià Cūn;* ☎ 333 3838, fax 333 3311, W *www .zhuhai-holitel.com, 9 Shihua Dong Lu, Jida*) Rooms Y880-980, suites from Y1380, villas Y2280-4980. This five-star complex, with spacious grounds and some eight restaurants, hugs the coast north-east of Gongbei near Jiuzhou Harbour. Its amenities include a bowling alley, tennis courts, clubhouse, go-kart racing, the Star Club disco, karaoke and sauna.

PLACES TO EAT

Zhuhai is brimming with places to eat. The area of Gongbei closest to the Macau border crossing has most of everything – restaurants, bakeries, night markets and street vendors. The north-eastern corner of Youyi Lu and Yingbin Dadao is Zhuhai's unofficial food alley. There is a good collection of restaurants there plus a few street vendors.

Try Lianhua Lu for bakeries and a couple of cheap restaurants serving Cantonese food; there are a few of these on Yuehai Dong Lu as well. In warm weather many restaurants set up tables outside. There's a collection of these places opposite the Zhuhai Overseas Chinese Hotel on Yingbin Dadao, most of which sell seafood. Many of the top-end hotels have decent bakeries.

May Flower Restaurant (☎ 333 0000, Shuiwan Lu*) Meals about Y100-120. This place opposite the Gongbei Palace Hotel specialises in Cantonese seafood (Y100 to Y120 for fish and shellfish) and clay pot dishes (Y15 to Y28).

Big Dipper Revolving Restaurant (☎ 888 8128, 29th floor, Guangdong Regency Hotel, East Tower, Yuehai Lu*) Meals Y150-200. If you want to splash out in Zhuhai this is the ideal place, with some of the best views in town.

Indian Restaurant (*Yìndì'ān Fùhéshì Cāntīng;* ☎ 815 0615, 2100 Liannan Lu, Cnr Yingbin Dadao*) Meals Y60. No, nothing to do with curries, but wigwams, tomahawks and waitresses dressed up as cowgirls. Lots of bison burgers and buffalo fries, too.

Maxim's (☎ 888 5209, 4 Lianhua Lu*) Meals Y40. If you must eat imported fast food, try this branch of the Hong Kong chain not far from the border crossing. It's a good place for breakfast and for cakes any time of the day.

SHOPPING

Gongbei's modern *market* (*Yuehua Lu*) is primarily a food market, with fruit and vegetables on the 1st floor and meat and fish on the 2nd, and will give you a chance to compare what's on offer here with the fare at markets in Hong Kong and Macau. On the ground floor there are shops selling clothing and on the 3rd floor stalls with Chinese bric-a-brac.

The best shopping stretch, with loads of clothing shops, is on the west side of Yingbin Dadao, between Yuehua Lu and Qiaoguang Lu. For more clothing, as well as shoes and luggage, go to Lianhua Lu.

Branded in the SEZ

It's easy to mock the prose of non-native speakers of English, but when it comes to Chinese brand names it becomes almost compulsory.

Fancy a pair of Pansy Y-fronts, lads? If you're feeling frisky, refresh yourself with Horse Head facial tissues. Wake up in the morning with a Golden Cock (that's an alarm clock) and take your pleasure with a Imperial Concubine cup of tea (not forgetting to light up a Long Life cigarette). For your faithful Golden Cock you should avoid White Elephant batteries, but the Moon Rabbit variety should have it going like a, well, bunny. Rambo toilet paper must be the toughest stuff around and definitely preferable to the Thumbs Up variety. No-one is sure what the ginseng product with the name of Gensenocide is supposed to do exactly – revive or annihilate us all.

Gongbei Port Commercial Plaza, a huge shopping mall at the border crossing, has duty-free shops and plenty of stalls selling pirated tapes, CDs, video cassettes and DVDs.

GETTING THERE & AWAY
Air
Zhuhai's airport serves destinations in China, including Beijing (Y1700), Shanghai (Y1280) and Hangzhou (Y1110). There are also regular flights to Guangzhou (Y980).

Departure Tax In China, departure tax for domestic flights is Y50 and Y100 for international flights.

Border Crossings
Travellers from Macau cross the border at the Portas do Cerco, not the original border gate, an archway built in 1870 that is now a monument shunted to the side, but a modern complex with duty-free shops. After completing customs and immigration formalities on the Macau side, proceed across a large, open area to Gongbei Port, a similar complex on the Zhuhai side built for the 1999 Macau handover, were you go through the same procedures. Yingbin Dadao, Zhuhai City's main thoroughfare, runs north from Gongbei Port. The border gate between Macau and Zhuhai is open from 7am until midnight daily.

A second crossing to the mainland has now been opened on the causeway linking Taipa and Coloane. The Cotai frontier post allows passengers to cross the new Lotus Bridge linking Macau and the Zhuhai SEZ from 9am to 5pm daily. Apart from those heading for Zhuhai airport, the new crossing is of little use to most visitors.

Bus
Macau Travellers to and from Macau simply walk across the border between Gongbei Port in Zhuhai and Portas do Cerco in Macau. In Macau, bus Nos 3, 5 and 9 will take you to the border gate while bus No 26 goes to the new Cotai frontier post. A taxi from the ferry terminal costs about M$20. In Zhuhai, bus Nos 8, 9 and 31 go to and from Gongbei Port.

Buses from the Guangdong Regency Hotel (☎ 888 8128) link Zhuhai with Macau International Airport five times a day. The fare is Y50.

Guangzhou Buses for Guangzhou leave Gongbei bus station (☎ 225 1957) next to the Yongtong Hotel on Youyi Lu every 15 minutes from 6.30am to 8pm, and air-conditioned services cost Y50. The journey takes about 2½ hours.

Normal buses (Y35) to Zhuhai depart from the Liuhua bus station in Guangzhou opposite the main train station on Huanshi Xilu every half-hour. The air-conditioned minibuses here leave according to a posted schedule.

Other Destinations in China Buses to other points in China leave from either the main Gongbei bus station or the one below Gongbei Port Commercial Plaza (☎ 811 8687) on the border. Destinations include: Zhongshan (Y16), Dongguan (Y50), Foshan (Y55), Zhaoqing (Y64), Haikou (Y151) and Shantou (Y180).

Boat

Hong Kong Jetcats between Zhuhai and Hong Kong and operated by the Chu Kong Passenger Transportation Co (Hong Kong ☎ 2858 3876) do the trip in about 70 minutes. From the China ferry terminal on Canton Rd in Tsim Sha Tsui, boats depart at 7.45am, 9.30am, 11am, 2.30pm and 5pm. Boats from the Macau ferry terminal in Central depart at 8.40am, 10am, noon, 2pm, 4pm, 7.30pm and 9.30pm. The economy class fare is HK$177.

From Zhuhai the boats leave Jiuzhou Harbour (☎ 333 3333 for information) in Jida for Tsim Sha Tsui at 8am, 9.30am, 1pm, 3pm and 5pm to Tsim Sha Tsui, with an additional one at 5.30pm on Sunday and public holidays. They go to Central at 8.30am, 10.30am, 11.30am, 2pm, 6pm, 7.30pm and 9.30pm. An economy-class ticket in Zhuhai costs HK$160 from hotel business centres or HK$150 at Jiuzhou Harbour.

Shenzhen Ferries operate between the port of Shekou in the Shenzhen SEZ and Jiuzhou Harbour in Zhuhai and the journey takes about one hour. There are departures every 15 to 30 minutes from 7.50am to 6pm. The return from Shekou is at the same frequency from 7.30am to 6.30pm. The fare is Y65 through hotels and Y55 at the port.

GETTING AROUND
To/From the Airport

Zhuhai's airport is 43km south-west of the city centre in Doumen county, so travel to and from is a hassle unless you go via the new Lotus Bridge linking that part of the Zhuhai SEZ with Macau. A taxi costs around Y100. A CNAC shuttle bus (☎ 889 5494) runs reasonably regularly to the airport from the CNAC building on Yuehua Lu (Y20).

Bus & Minibus

Zhuhai has a clean, efficient and cheap bus system, with fares at Y1/2 for normal/air-conditioned buses. Minibuses ply the same routes as the larger buses and cost Y2 for any place in the city.

Taxi

Zhuhai taxis have no meters and fares are strictly by negotiation. A fair price from the Macau border to Jiuzhou Harbour is around Y20. You should be able to rent a taxi for the day, going wherever you like for as long as you like, for Y300.

ORGANISED TOUR

A ferry cruise that will take you down through Zhuhai Bay and around Macau and back in about an hour leaves Jiuzhou Harbour at 9.10am, 9.15am, 11.40am, 2pm and 3.15pm daily and costs Y30.

Language

HONG KONG

Hong Kong's two official languages are English and Cantonese. While Cantonese is used in Hong Kong in everyday life by the vast majority of the population, English remains the *lingua franca* of commerce, banking and international trade and is used in the law courts. There has been a noticeable decline in the level of English-speaking proficiency in the territory, however, due to emigration and the switch by many secondary schools, which previously taught all their lessons in English, to Chinese vernacular education.

On the other hand, the ability to speak Mandarin is on the increase due to the new political realities. For a Cantonese native speaker, Mandarin is far easier to learn than English. It's not uncommon these days to hear Cantonese and Mandarin being spoken in a sort of fusion-confusion.

MACAU

Cantonese is the language of about 95% of the population, though Portuguese enjoys special status after having been spoken here for almost half a millennium. That said, most Chinese in Macau are unable to speak Portuguese – English is more commonly understood. With Macau's return to Chinese sovereignty and so many immigrants from north China working in Macau, Mandarin is becoming an essential tool for business.

English is now the main language of instruction within the Macau educational system. If you're having trouble communicating, your best bet is to ask a young person.

GUANGDONG PROVINCE (CHINA)

While the Chinese have about eight main dialects, around 70% of the population of China speaks the Beijing dialect (commonly known as Mandarin in English) which is the official language of the People's Republic of China (PRC). In Guangdong Province, which includes the Special Economic Zones of Shenzhen and Zhuhai as well as the provincial capital, Guangzhou, Cantonese is still the most popular mode of expression though everyone also speaks Mandarin.

SPOKEN CHINESE

Cantonese differs from Mandarin to a greater degree than French differs from Spanish. Speakers of both dialects can read Chinese characters, but a Cantonese speaker will pronounce many of them differently from a Mandarin speaker. For example, when Mr Ng from Hong Kong goes to Beijing, he will be called Mr Wu. If Mr Wong goes from Hong Kong to Fujian Province the character for his name will be read as Mr Wee, and in Beijing he is Mr Huang.

WRITTEN CHINESE

Written Chinese has about 50,000 pictographs or 'characters'. While many of the basic Chinese characters are in fact highly stylised 'pictures' of what they represent, around 90% of the 6000 in common usage are actually compounds of a 'meaning' element and a 'sound' element.

The written language allows Chinese people from around the country to overcome the barrier posed by dialect. However, Hong Kong also has 150 of its own characters that are used to represent colloquial Cantonese words and slang. These are not understood by speakers of other dialects, or even some Cantonese speakers from the mainland.

Hong Kong, like Taiwan, uses the original 'complicated' set of characters as opposed to the system of 'simplified' characters adopted by China in the 1950s to increase literacy. In Hong Kong, Chinese characters can be read from left to right, right to left, or top to bottom; it's immediately apparent to speakers of the language. In China the government has been trying to get everyone to read and write from left to right.

Cantonese

Romanisation

China's own romanisation system, while very accurate, only works for Mandarin. You cannot use it to romanise Cantonese anymore than you can accurately write Russian in the Roman alphabet.

For Cantonese there are several competing romanisation systems and no official one. Hong Kong pupils and students are not required to learn romanisation at school, so asking a Cantonese native speaker to write a Chinese character in the Roman alphabet produces mixed results.

A number of romanisation schemes have come and gone, but at least three have survived and are currently used in Hong Kong: Meyer-Wempe, Sidney Lau and Yale. The Yale method is used in this book to transliterate all words except places names, surnames and the like. The table below illustrates the notable differences between the three major romanisation systems.

The use of spaces and hyphens can also be confusing as the way they are employed differs in Cantonese and Mandarin. While 'Hong Kong' can be written 'Hongkong', you'll never see 'Shang Hai' or 'Bei Jing'. Cantonese Chinese often hyphenate their given names.

In Mandarin there is a standard rule – names are kept as one word (thus 'Shanghai', 'Beijing', Mao Zedong). Cantonese has not adopted any such standard, however; this book uses what is most commonly accepted (eg, 'Hong Kong') and what appears in maps and atlases published by the government. The hyphenation of names appears to be falling into disuse.

Pronunciation

The following romanisation system is a simplified version designed to help you pronounce the Cantonese words and phrases in this book as quickly and easily as possible. Note that the examples given reflect British pronunciation.

Vowels

a	as in 'father'
ai	as the 'i' in 'find', but shorter
au	as the 'ow' in 'cow'
e	as in 'let'
ei	as the 'a' in 'say' but without the 'y' sound
eu	somewhat as the 'ur' in 'urn' with lips pursed
i	as the 'ee' in 'see'
iu	similar to vowels in the word 'you'
o	as in 'got'; as in 'go' when at the end of a word
oi	as the 'oy' in 'boy'
oo	as in 'soon'
ou	as in the word 'owe'
u	as in 'put'
ue	separate, as the 'ue' in 'suet'
ui	separate, as in 'oo' and 'ee'

Consonants

In general, consonants are pronounced as in English. Two that may give you a little trouble are:

j	as the 'ds' in 'suds'
ng	as in 'sing'

Tones

Chinese languages are rich in homonyms (ie, words that sound alike) and much of their superstitious beliefs, poetry and humour is based on this wealth. The Cantonese word for 'silk', for example, sounds the same as the words for 'lion', 'private', 'poem', 'corpse' and 'teacher'. What distinguishes the meaning of each word are changes in a speaker's pitch or 'tone' and the context of the word within the sentence; say *mai dan* in a restaurant and everyone will know you're asking for 'the bill'. Say the same thing in

Cantonese Romanisation

Meyer-Wempe	Sydney Lau	Yale
p'	p	p
p	b	b
t'	t	t
t	d	d
k'	k	k
k	g	g
ch'	ch	ch
ts	j	j
k'w	kw	kw
kw	gw	gw
s, sh	s	s
i, y	y	y
oo, w	w	w
oeh	euh	eu
ui	ui	eui
un	un	eun
ut	ut	eut
o	o	ou
oo	oo	u
ue	ue	yu

a market and people will come up to ask how much the 'eggs' you are 'selling' cost. Cantonese has seven tones (although you can easily get by with six).

The Yale romanisation system is designed to make pronunciation of Cantonese tones as simple as possible and may not necessarily reflect what you come across where official transliteration systems are used.

In the Yale system six basic tones are represented: three 'level' tones, which do not noticeably rise or fall in pitch (high, middle and low), and three 'moving' tones, which either rise or fall in pitch (high rising, low rising and low falling). Remember that it doesn't matter whether you have a high or low voice when speaking Cantonese as long as your intonation reflects relative changes in pitch. The following examples show the six basic tones. Note how important they can be to your intended meaning:

high tone: represented by a macron above a vowel, as in *fōo* (husband)
middle tone: represented by an unaccented vowel, as in *foo* (wealthy)
low tone: represented by the letter 'h' after a vowel, as in *fooh* (owe); note that 'h' is only pronounced if it occurs at the start of a word; elsewhere it signifies a low tone
middle tone rising: represented by an acute accent, as in *fóo* (tiger)
low falling tone: represented by a grave accent followed by the low tone letter 'h', as in *fòoh* (to lean)
low rising tone: represented by an acute accent and the low tone letter 'h', as in *fóoh* (woman)

Getting Started
The following list should help get you started; for a more in depth guide to Cantonese, with loads of information on grammar and pronunciation as well as phrases, pick up a copy of Lonely Planet's *Cantonese phrasebook*.

Pronouns

I	*ngóh*	我
you	*néhìh*	你
he/she/it	*kúhìh*	佢
we/us	*ngóh dēìh*	我哋
you (plural)	*néhìh dēìh*	你哋
they/them	*kúhìh dēìh*	佢哋

Greetings & Civilities

Hello, how are you?
néhìh hó ma? 你好嗎?
Fine, and you?
géìh hó, néhìh nē? 幾好,你呢?
Good morning.
jó sàhn 早晨
Goodbye.
bāàhìh baàhìh/joìh gin 拜拜/再見
Thank you very much.
dōh jē saàhìh/ 多謝晒/
m gōìh saàhìh 唔該晒
Thanks. (for a gift or special favour)
dōh jē 多謝
Thanks. (making a request or purchase)
m gōìh 唔該
You're welcome.
m sáìh haàhk hēìh 唔使客氣
Excuse me. (after bumping into someone)
duìh m juhèh 對唔住
I'm sorry.
m hó yi si 唔好意思
Don't worry about it.
m gán yiùh 唔緊要
Excuse me. (calling someone's attention)
m gōìh 唔該

Small Talk

What is your surname? (polite)
chéng mahn gwaìh sing?
請問貴姓?
My surname is ...
síùh sing ...
小姓 ...
My name is ...
ngóh giùh ...
我叫 ...
This is Mr/Mrs/Ms (Lee).
nì wáìh hahìh (léhìh) sìn sāàhng/
taàhìh táàhìh/síùh jé
呢位係(李)先生/太太/小姐
Glad to meet you.
hó gō hing yihng sìk néhìh
好高興認識你
Can you please help me take a photo?
hóh m hóh yíh bōng ngóh yíng
jēùhng séùhng a?
可唔可以幫我影張相呀?

Is it OK to take a photo?
hóh m hóh yíh yíng séuhng a?
可唔可以影相呀？

Language Difficulties

Do you speak English?
néhìh sìk m sìk góng yìng mán a?
你識唔識講英文呀？

Do you understand?
néhìh mìhng m mìhng a?
你明唔明？

I understand.
ngóh mìhng
我明

I don't understand.
ngóh m mìhng
我唔明

Can you repeat that please?
chéng joìh góng yat chi?
請再講一次？

What is this called?
nì goh giùh māt yéh a?
呢個叫乜嘢呀？

Getting Around

airport	*gēih chèhùhng*	機場
bus stop	*bā sí jahàhm*	巴士站
pier	*máh tàhùh*	碼頭
subway station	*dēih tit jahàhm*	地鐵站
north	*bāk*	北
south	*nàhàhm*	南
east	*dūng*	東
west	*sāih*	西

I'd like to go to ...
ngóh séuhng huìh ...
我想去 ...

Where is the ...?
... háih bìn doh a?
... 喺邊度呀？

Does this (bus, train etc) go to ...?
huìh m huìh ... a?
去唔去 ... 呀？

How much is the fare?
géih dōh chín a?
幾多錢呀？

I want to get off at ...
ngóh séuhng háih ... lohk ch?
我想喺 ... 落車

Stop here please. (taxi, minibus)
m gōìh, nì doh yáhùh lohk
唔該，呢度有落

How far is it to walk?
hààhng loh yiùh géih nohìh a?
行路要幾耐呀？

Where is this address please?
m gōìh, nì goh dēìh jí háìh bìn doh a?
唔該，呢個地址喺邊度呀？

Please write down the address for me.
m gōìh sé goh dēìh jí béìh ngóh
唔該寫個地址俾我

Accommodation

Do you have any rooms available?
yáhùh mó fóng a?
有冇房呀？

I'd like a (single/double) room.
*ngóh séuhng yiùh yāt gāàhn
(dāàhn yàhn/sēùhng yàhn) fóng*
我想要一間(單人/雙人)房？

I'd like a quiet room.
*ngóh séuhng yiùh yāt gāàhn
jihng dì gē fóng*
我想要一間啲嘅房？

How much per night?
géih dōh chín yāt máhàhn a?
幾多錢一晚呀？

Can I get a discount if I stay longer?
juhèh nohìh dī yáhùh mó jit kaùh a?
住耐啲有冇折扣呀？

Food

Do you have an English menu?
yáhùh mó yīng mán chāàhn páàhih a?
有冇英文餐牌呀？

Can you recommend any dishes?
yáhùh māt yéh hó gaàhìh siùh a?
有乜嘢好介紹呀？

I'm a vegetarian.
ngóh sihk jāàhìh
我食齊

I'd like the set menu please.
ngóh yiùh goh to chāàhn
我要個套餐

Please bring me a knife and fork.
m gōìh béìh ngóh yāt foòh dō chā
唔該俾我一副刀叉

Please bring the bill.
m gōìh, màahìh dāàhn
唔該，埋單

Shopping

How much is this?
nī goh géih dōh chín a?
呢個幾多錢呀？

That's very expensive.
hó gwaìh
好貴

Can you reduce the price?
pèhng dī dāk m dāk a?
平啲得唔得呀？

I'm just looking.
ngóh sīn táih yāt táih
我先睇一睇

Health

I'm sick.
ngóh yáhùh bēng
我有病

My friend is sick.
ngóh pàhng yáhùh yáhùh bēng
我朋友有病

I need a doctor.
ngóh yiùh táih yī sāng
我耍睇醫生

It hurts here.
nī doh m sùèh fuhk
呢度唔舒服

I have asthma.
ngóh hāàhùh chúèhn
我哮喘

I have diarrhoea.
ngóh tó ngōh
我肚痾

I'd like to see a female doctor.
ngọh yiùh wún yāt wáìh núhìh yī sāng
我要搵一位女醫生

I'm allergic to (antibiotics/penicillin).
ngóh duìh (kong sāng so/
pòòhn nèhìh sāìh làhm) gwoh mán
我對(抗生素/盤尼西林)過敏

Numbers

0	*lihng*	零
1	*yāt*	一
2	*yih (léhùhng)*	二(兩)
3	*sāàhm*	三
4	*sèìh*	四
5	*ng*	五
6	*luhk*	六
7	*chāt*	七
8	*baàht*	八
9	*gáùh*	九
10	*sahp*	十
11	*sahp yāt*	十一
12	*sahp yih*	十二
20	*yih sahp*	二十
21	*yih sahp yāt*	二十一

Help!
gaùh mēng a!
救命呀！

Watch out!
siùh sām!
小心！

Thief!
chéùhng yéh a!
搶嘢呀！

Call the police!
giùh gíng chaàht!
叫警察！

Call an ambulance!
giùh gaùh sēùhng chē!
叫救傷車！

100	*yāt baàhk*	一百
101	*yāt baàhk lìhng yāt*	一百零一
110	*yāt baàhk yāt sahp*	一百一十
120	*yāt baàhk yih sahp*	一百二十
200	*yih baàhk*	二百
1000	*yāt chīn*	一千
10,000	*yāt mahàhn*	一萬
100,000	*sahp mahàhn*	十萬

one million
yāt baàhk mahàhn　一百萬

Mandarin

Most foreigners are more successful at learning to speak Mandarin than Cantonese for two reasons: tones are much clearer, making the language easier to speak and understand, and in China you really don't have much of a choice. Getting a grasp on the written form is another story altogether.

Romanisation

In 1958 the Chinese officially adopted a system known as *pinyin* literally, 'same sound') as a method of rendering Mandarin into the Roman alphabet. The original idea was to do away with characters altogether at some stage and use only pinyin with accent marks showing tones. Most people resisted this and the plan was eventually abandoned.

Pinyin is often used on shop fronts, street signs and advertising billboards in China, but don't expect most people to be able to use it, as it never really took off as the main form of written Chinese.

Pronunciation

The following is a rough description of the sounds you'll hear in spoken Mandarin

Chinese. In pinyin, apostrophes are sometimes used to separate syllables, eg, writing *ping'an* prevents the word being pronounced *pingan*.

Vowels

Most pinyin vowels and consonants are pronounced as they would be in English, but a few may cause difficulty.

a	as in 'father'
ai	as the 'i' in 'high'
ao	as the 'ow' in 'cow'
e	as the 'u' in 'fur'
ei	as the 'ei' in 'weigh'
i	as the 'ee' in 'meet' or as the 'oo' in 'book' after **c, ch, r, s, sh, z** or **zh**
ian	as the word 'yen'
ie	as the word 'yeah'
o	like 'or' but with no 'r' sound
ou	as the 'oa' in 'boat'
u	as in 'flute'
ui	as the word 'way'
uo	as 'w' followed by the 'o' in 'or'
yu	as the German 'ü'; purse your lips and say 'ee'
ü	as the German 'ü'

Consonants

The English 'v' sound doesn't occur in Chinese. For beginners, the trickiest consonants are **c**, **q** and **x** because their pronunciation isn't remotely similar to English. Other than **n**, **ng** and **r**, consonants never occur at the end of a syllable.

c	as the 'ts' in 'bits'
ch	as in English, but with the tongue curled back
h	as in English, but articulated from the throat as in the 'ch' of 'loch'
q	as the 'ch' in 'chicken'
r	a difficult letter pronounced very vaguely as the 's' in 'pleasure'
sh	as in English, but with the tongue curled back
x	as the 'sh' in 'shine'
z	as the 'ds' in 'suds'
zh	as the 'j' in 'judge' but with the tongue curled back

Tones

Four basic tones are used in Mandarin, which makes the language easier to learn than Cantonese. As in Cantonese, changing the tone changes the meaning. For example, in Mandarin the word *ma* can have distinct different meanings, depending on which tone is used:

high tone	*mā* (mother)
rising tone	*má* (hemp, numb)
falling-rising tone	*mǎ* (horse)
falling tone	*mà* (scold, swear)

Getting Started

The following list of phrases in Mandarin will help get you started. If you want something more in-depth, arm yourself with a copy of Lonely Planet's *Mandarin Chinese phrasebook*.

Pronouns

I	*wǒ*	我
you	*nǐ*	你
he, she, it	*tā*	他/她/它
we, us	*wǒmen*	我们
you (plural)	*nǐmen*	你们
they, them	*tāmen*	他们

Greetings & Civilities

Hello.
   nǐ hǎo   你好

Goodbye.
   zàijiàn   再见

Thank you.
   xièxie   谢谢

You're welcome.
   búkèqi   不客气

I'm sorry.
   duìbùqǐ   对不起

Small Talk

May I ask your name?
   nín guìxìng?   您贵姓？

My (sur)name is ...
   wǒ xìng ...   我姓 ...

Where are you from?
   nǐ shì cōng   你是从 ...
   nǎr láide?   哪儿来的？

I'm from ...
   wǒ shì cōng ... láide   我是从 ... 来的

No. (don't have)
   méi yǒu   没有

No. (not so)
   búshì   不是

It doesn't matter.
méishì 没事

I want ...
wǒ yào ... 我要 ...

No, I don't want it.
búyào 不要

Language Difficulties

Do you understand?
dǒng ma? 懂吗？

I understand.
wǒ tīngdedǒng 我听得懂

I don't understand.
wǒ tīngbudǒng 我听不懂

Could you speak
more slowly please?
qǐng nǐ shuō màn 请你说慢
yīdiǎn, hǎo ma? 一点，好吗？

Getting Around

I want to go to ...
wǒ yào qù ... 我要去 ...

I want to get off.
wǒ yào xiàchē 我要下车

What time does it
depart/arrive?
jǐdiǎn kāi/dào? 几点开/到？

How long does the
trip take?
zhècì lǚxíng yào huā 这次旅行要花
duōcháng shíjiān? 多长时间？

Which platform?
dìjǐhào zhàntái? 第几号站台？

Please use the meter.
dǎ biǎo 打表

ticket office
shòupiào chù 售票处

one ticket
yìzhāng piào 一张票

two tickets
liǎngzhāng piào 两张票

one way ticket
dānchéng piào 单程票

return ticket
láihuí piào 来回票

buy a ticket
mǎi piào 买票

taxi
chūzū chē 出租车

microbus taxi
miànbāo chē, miàndī 面包车、面的

bus
gōnggòng qìchē 公共汽车

minibus
xiǎo gōnggòng qìchē 小公共汽车

train
huǒchē 火车

subway (underground)
dìxiàtiě 地下铁

Directions

Where is the ...?
... zài nǎlǐ? ... 在哪里？

I'm lost.
wǒ mílùle 我迷路了

Turn right.
yòu zhuǎn 右转

Turn left.
zuǒ zhuǎn 左转

Go straight ahead.
yìzhí zǒu 一直走

Turn around.
wàng huí zǒu 往回走

Toilets

Men/Women 男/女

toilet (restroom)
cèsuǒ? 厕所

toilet paper
wèishēng zhǐ 卫生纸

bathroom (washroom)
xǐshǒu jiān 洗手间

Money

How much is it?
duōshǎo qián? 多少钱？

Is there anything
cheaper?
yǒu piányi yìdiǎn 有便宜一点
de ma? 的吗？

That's too expensive.
tài guìle 太贵了

Bank of China
zhōngguó yínháng 中国银行

change money
huàn qián 换钱

Accommodation

Is there a room vacant?
yǒu méiyǒu kōng fángjiān?
有没有空房间？

Yes, there is/No, there isn't.
yǒu/méiyǒu
有/没有

Can I see the room?
wǒ néng kànkan fángjiān ma?
我能看看房间吗？

I don't like this room.
wǒ bù xǐhuan zhèijiān fángjiān
我不喜欢这间房

Are there any messages for me?
yǒu méiyǒu liú huà?
有没有留话？

May I have a hotel namecard?
yǒu méiyǒu lǚguǎn de míngpiàn?
有没有旅馆的名片？

hotel	
lǚguǎn	旅馆
tourist hotel	
bīnguǎn/fàdiàn/ jiǔdiàn	宾馆/饭店/ 酒店
reception desk	
zǒng fúwù tái	总服务台
dormitory	
duōrénfáng	多人房
single room	
dānrénfáng	单人房
twin room	
shuāngrénfáng	双人房
bed	
chuángwèi	床位
economy room (no bath)	
pǔtōngfáng	普通房
standard room	
biāozhǔn fángjiān	标准房
deluxe suite	
háohuá tàofáng	豪华套房

Time

What's the time?
jǐ diǎn?	几点？
... hour ... minute	
... diǎn ... fēn	... 点 ... 分
3.05	
sān diǎn wǔ fēn	3点5分
now	
xiànzài	现在
today	
jīntiān	今天
tomorrow	
míngtiān	明天
day after tomorrow	
hòutiān	后天
yesterday	
zuótiān	昨天

Emergencies – Mandarin

I'm sick.	
wǒ shēng bìng	我生病
I'm injured.	
wǒ shòushāng	我受伤
Fire!	
huǒ zāi!	火灾
Help!	
jiùmìng a!	救命啊
Thief!	
xiǎo tōu!	小偷
emergency	
jǐnjí qíngkuàng	紧急情况
police	
jǐngchá	警察
foreign affairs police	
wàishì jǐngchá	外事警察
pickpocket	
páshǒu	扒手
rapist	
qiángjiānzhě	强奸者

Health

hospital	
yīyuàn	医院
emergency room	
jízhěn shì	急诊室
laxative	
xièyào	泻药
anti-diarrhoea medicine	
zhǐxièyào	止泻药
aspirin	
āsīpǐlín	阿斯匹林
antibiotics	
kàngjūnsù	抗菌素
condom	
bìyùn tào	避孕套
tampon	
wèishēng mián tiáo	卫生棉条
sanitary napkin (Kotex)	
wèishēng mián	卫生棉
sunscreen (UV) lotion	
fáng shài yóu	防晒油
mosquito coils	
wénxiāng	蚊香
mosquito pads	
diàn wénxiāng	电蚊香

Numbers

0	*líng*	零
1	*yī, yāo!*	一、幺
2	*èr, liǎng*	二、两
3	*sān*	三

4	sì	四
5	wǔ	五
6	liù	六
7	qī	七
8	bā	八
9	jiǔ	九
10	shí	十
11	shíyī	十一
12	shí'èr	十二
20	èrshí	二十
21	èrshíyī	二十一
100	yìbǎi	一百
200	liǎngbǎi	两百
1000	yìqiān	一千
2000	liǎngqiān	两千
10,000	yíwàn	一万
20,000	liǎngwàn	两万
100,000	shíwàn	十万
200,000	èrshíwàn	二十万

Portuguese

Although there's no compelling reason for you to learn Portuguese for travelling in Macau, there are a few words that are useful to know for reading street signs, maps and menus.

almirante	admiral
alto/monte	hill
amizade	friendship
avenida	avenue
baía	bay
bairro	district
beco	alley
biblioteca	library
calçada	steep street
caminho	path
casa de cambio	moneychanger
casa de chá	teahouse
casa de pasto	restaurant (small)

Days – Portuguese

Monday	a segunda-feira
Tuesday	a terça-feira
Wednesday	a quarta-feira
Thursday	a quinta-feira
Friday	a sexta-feira
Saturday	o sábado
Sunday	o domingo

casa de penhores	pawn shop
colina	small hill
correios	post office
da, do	of
edificio	building
escola	school
estrada	road
farol	lighthouse
fortaleza	fortress
grande	big
guia	guide
hospedaria/vila	guesthouse
igreja	church
ilha	island
jardim	garden
largo	square (small)
mercado	market
miradouro	lookout point
museu	museum
paragem	bus stop
pátio	courtyard
penha	rock, crag
polícia	police
ponte	bridge
ponte-cais	pier
pousada	hotel
praça	square
praia	beach
rua	street
sé	cathedral
travessa	lane

Glossary

Refer to the Chinese Food special section in the Hong Kong Facts for the Visitor chapter for a detailed glossary of menu items.

amah – literally, 'mummy'; a servant, traditionally a woman, who cleans houses, sometimes cooks and looks after the children. Unmarried Chinese women from the countryside used to find work as amahs, but in Hong Kong the job is mostly done by Filipinos and other South-East Asian migrant workers nowadays.

bodhisattvas – deified Buddhists

chau – Cantonese for 'island'
cheongsam – a fashionable tight-fitting Chinese dress with a slit up the side
chim – bamboo sticks shaken out of a cylindrical box usually at a temple and used to divine the future
chop – see *name chop*
congee – rice porridge served with savoury titbits, usually eaten at breakfast (Cantonese: *jūk*)

dai pai dong – open-air street stalls, especially popular at night but fast disappearing in Hong Kong
dim sum – literally, 'to touch the heart'; a Cantonese meal of various titbits eaten as breakfast, brunch or lunch and offered from wheeled steam carts in restaurants; see also *yum cha*
dragon boat – a long, narrow skiff in the shape of a dragon used in the races on Dragon Boat Day in June

fleecy – a sweet cold drink usually containing red or green mung beans, and sometimes pineapple and other fruit; fruit smoothie or shake
fung shui – English spelling for the Cantonese *fung sui* (*feng shui* in Mandarin) meaning 'wind-water'; the Chinese art of geomancy that manipulates or judges the environment to produce good fortune

gam bei – literally, 'dry glass'; Chinese for 'cheers' or 'bottoms up'
godown – a warehouse, originally on or near the waterfront but now anywhere
gongfu – Chinese for kung fu
gwailo – literally, 'ghost person'; a derogatory word for 'foreigner', especially a Caucasian Westerner. Although some Hong Kong expatriates claim the term no longer has negative connotations, it does and is best avoided
gwaipo – female equivalent of *gwailo* (see previous)

Hakka – a Chinese ethnic group who speak a different Chinese language from the Cantonese; some Hakka people still lead traditional lives as farmers in the New Territories
HKTA – Hong Kong Tourist Association; former name of the Hong Kong Tourism Board (HKTB)
HKTB – Hong Kong Tourism Board
hong – a major trading house or company, often used to refer to Hong Kong's original trading houses, such as Jardine Matheson or Swire

II – illegal immigrant

joss – luck or fortune
joss sticks – incense
junk – originally Chinese fishing boats or war vessels with square sails; it now applies to the diesel-powered, wooden pleasure yachts that can be seen on Victoria Harbour

kaido – a small to medium-sized ferry that makes short runs on the open sea, usually used for non-scheduled services between small islands and fishing villages; also spelled kaito
karaoke – literally, 'empty music'; a popular Hong Kong pastime originating in Japan that allows you to sing along to the recorded melody of songs
KCR – Kowloon-Canton Railway

KMB – Kowloon Motor Bus Company
kung fu – the basis of many Asian martial arts (Chinese: *gongfu*)

LRT – Light Rail Transit

mahjong – popular Chinese game played among four persons with tiles engraved with Chinese characters
mai dan – 'bill' or 'check' (in a restaurant)
makee learnee – Anglo-Chinese pidgin for 'apprentice' or 'trainee'; very rarely heard in Hong Kong today

name chop – carved seal that acts as a signature
nullah – specifically Hong Kong word referring to a gutter or drain and occasionally used in place names

oolong – high-grade, partially fermented Chinese tea

PLA – People's Liberation Army
PRC – People's Republic of China

sampan – a motorised launch that can only accommodate a few people and is too small to go on the open sea; mainly used for inter-harbour transport
SAR – Special Administrative Region of China; both Hong Kong and Macau are now SARs
SEZ – Special Economic Zone of China that allows more unbridled capitalism but not political autonomy; Shenzhen and Zhuhai both enjoy SEZ status
shroff – Anglo-Indian word meaning 'cashier' and still commonly used in Hong Kong
snakehead – a smuggler of illegal immigrants

tai chi – slow-motion shadow boxing, a form of exercise; commonly shortened; also spelled *t'ai chi*
taijiquan – Mandarin for *tai chi*; usually shortened to *taiji*
taipan – 'big boss' of a large company
tai tai – leisured woman; businessman's wife
Tanka – Chinese ethnic group that traditionally lives on boats
Triad – Chinese secret society originally founded as patriotic associations to protect Chinese culture from the influence of usurping Manchus but today the Hong Kong equivalent of the Mafia

walla walla – a motorised launch used as a water taxi and capable of short runs on the open sea
wan – Chinese for 'bay'
wet market – local word for an outdoor market selling fruit and vegetables, fish and meat

yum cha – literally, 'drink tea'; common Cantonese term referring to the act of eating dim sum

LONELY PLANET

ON THE ROAD

Travel Guides explore cities, regions and countries, and supply information on transport, restaurants and accommodation, covering all budgets. They come with reliable, easy-to-use maps, practical advice, cultural and historical facts and a rundown on attractions both on and off the beaten track. There are over 200 titles in this classic series, covering nearly every country in the world.

 Lonely Planet Upgrades extend the shelf life of existing travel guides by detailing any changes that may affect travel in a region since a book has been published. Upgrades can be downloaded for free from **www.lonelyplanet.com/upgrades**

For travellers with more time than money, **Shoestring** guides offer dependable, first-hand information with hundreds of detailed maps, plus insider tips for stretching money as far as possible. Covering entire continents in most cases, the six-volume shoestring guides are known around the world as 'backpackers bibles'.

For the discerning short-term visitor, **Condensed** guides highlight the best a destination has to offer in a full-colour, pocket-sized format designed for quick access. They include everything from top sights and walking tours to opinionated reviews of where to eat, stay, shop and have fun.

CitySync lets travellers use their Palm™ or Visor™ hand-held computers to guide them through a city with handy tips on transport, history, cultural life, major sights, and shopping and entertainment options. It can also quickly search and sort hundreds of reviews of hotels, restaurants and attractions, and pinpoint their location on scrollable street maps. CitySync can be downloaded from **www.citysync.com**

MAPS & ATLASES

Lonely Planet's **City Maps** feature downtown and metropolitan maps, as well as transit routes and walking tours. The maps come complete with an index of streets, a listing of sights and a plastic coat for extra durability.

Road Atlases are an essential navigation tool for serious travellers. Cross-referenced with the guidebooks, they also feature distance and climate charts and a complete site index.

LONELY PLANET

ESSENTIALS

Read This First books help new travellers to hit the road with confidence. These invaluable predeparture guides give step-by-step advice on preparing for a trip, budgeting, arranging a visa, planning an itinerary and staying safe while still getting off the beaten track.

Healthy Travel pocket guides offer a regional rundown on disease hot spots and practical advice on predeparture health measures, staying well on the road and what to do in emergencies. The guides come with a user-friendly design and helpful diagrams and tables.

Lonely Planet's **Phrasebooks** cover the essential words and phrases travellers need when they're strangers in a strange land. They come in a pocket-sized format with colour tabs for quick reference, extensive vocabulary lists, easy-to-follow pronunciation keys and two-way dictionaries.

Miffed by blurry photos of the Taj Mahal? Tired of the classic 'top of the head cut off' shot? **Travel Photography: A Guide to Taking Better Pictures** will help you turn ordinary holiday snaps into striking images and give you the know-how to capture every scene, from frenetic festivals to peaceful beach sunrises.

Lonely Planet's **Travel Journal** is a lightweight but sturdy travel diary for jotting down all those on-the-road observations and significant travel moments. It comes with a handy time-zone wheel, a world map and useful travel information.

Lonely Planet's eKno is an all-in-one communication service developed especially for travellers. It offers low-cost international calls and free email and voicemail so that you can keep in touch while on the road. Check it out on **www.ekno.lonelyplanet.com**

FOOD & RESTAURANT GUIDES

Lonely Planet's **Out to Eat** guides recommend the brightest and best places to eat and drink in top international cities. These gourmet companions are arranged by neighbourhood, packed with dependable maps, garnished with scene-setting photos and served with quirky features.

For people who live to eat, drink and travel, **World Food** guides explore the culinary culture of each country. Entertaining and adventurous, each guide is packed with detail on staples and specialities, regional cuisine and local markets, as well as sumptuous recipes, comprehensive culinary dictionaries and lavish photos good enough to eat.

OUTDOOR GUIDES

For those who believe the best way to see the world is on foot, Lonely Planet's **Walking Guides** detail everything from family strolls to difficult treks, with 'when to go and how to do it' advice supplemented by reliable maps and essential travel information.

Cycling Guides map a destination's best bike tours, long and short, in day-by-day detail. They contain all the information a cyclist needs, including advice on bike maintenance, places to eat and stay, innovative maps with detailed cues to the rides, and elevation charts.

The **Watching Wildlife** series is perfect for travellers who want authoritative information but don't want to tote a heavy field guide. Packed with advice on where, when and how to view a region's wildlife, each title features photos of over 300 species and contains engaging comments on the local flora and fauna.

With underwater colour photos throughout, **Pisces Books** explore the world's best diving and snorkelling areas. Each book contains listings of diving services and dive resorts, detailed information on depth, visibility and difficulty of dives, and a roundup of the marine life you're likely to see through your mask.

OFF THE ROAD

Journeys, the travel literature series written by renowned travel authors, capture the spirit of a place or illuminate a culture with a journalist's attention to detail and a novelist's flair for words. These are tales to soak up while you're actually on the road or dip into as an at-home armchair indulgence.

The range of lavishly illustrated **Pictorial** books is just the ticket for both travellers and dreamers. Off-beat tales and vivid photographs bring the adventure of travel to your doorstep long before the journey begins and long after it is over.

Lonely Planet **Videos** encourage the same independent, tough-minded approach as the guidebooks. Currently airing throughout the world, this award-winning series features innovative footage and an original soundtrack.

Yes, we know, work is tough, so do a little bit of deskside dreaming with the spiral-bound Lonely Planet **Diary** or a Lonely Planet **Wall Calendar**, filled with great photos from around the world.

TRAVELLERS NETWORK

Lonely Planet Online. Lonely Planet's award-winning Web site has insider information on hundreds of destinations, from Amsterdam to Zimbabwe, complete with interactive maps and relevant links. The site also offers the latest travel news, recent reports from travellers on the road, guidebook upgrades, a travel links site, an online book-buying option and a lively travellers bulletin board. It can be viewed at **www.lonelyplanet.com** or AOL keyword: lp.

Planet Talk is a quarterly print newsletter, full of gossip, advice, anecdotes and author articles. It provides an antidote to the being-at-home blues and lets you plan and dream for the next trip. Contact the nearest Lonely Planet office for your free copy.

Comet, the free Lonely Planet newsletter, comes via email once a month. It's loaded with travel news, advice, dispatches from authors, travel competitions and letters from readers. To subscribe, click on the Comet subscription link on the front page of the Web site.

Lonely Planet Guides by Region

Lonely Planet is known worldwide for publishing practical, reliable and no-nonsense travel information in our guides and on our Web site. The Lonely Planet list covers just about every accessible part of the world. Currently there are 16 series: Travel guides, Shoestring guides, Condensed guides, Phrasebooks, Read This First, Healthy Travel, Walking guides, Cycling guides, Watching Wildlife guides, Pisces Diving & Snorkeling guides, City Maps, Road Atlases, Out to Eat, World Food, Journeys travel literature and Pictorials.

AFRICA Africa on a shoestring • Botswana • Cairo • Cairo City Map • Cape Town • Cape Town City Map • East Africa • Egypt • Egyptian Arabic phrasebook • Ethiopia, Eritrea & Djibouti • Ethiopian Amharic phrasebook • The Gambia & Senegal • Healthy Travel Africa • Kenya • Malawi • Morocco • Moroccan Arabic phrasebook • Mozambique • Namibia • Read This First: Africa • South Africa, Lesotho & Swaziland • Southern Africa • Southern Africa Road Atlas • Swahili phrasebook • Tanzania, Zanzibar & Pemba • Trekking in East Africa • Tunisia • Watching Wildlife East Africa • Watching Wildlife Southern Africa • West Africa • World Food Morocco • Zambia • Zimbabwe, Botswana & Namibia
Travel Literature: Mali Blues: Traveling to an African Beat • The Rainbird: A Central African Journey • Songs to an African Sunset: A Zimbabwean Story

AUSTRALIA & THE PACIFIC Aboriginal Australia & the Torres Strait Islands •Auckland • Australia • Australian phrasebook • Australia Road Atlas • Cycling Australia • Cycling New Zealand • Fiji • Fijian phrasebook • Healthy Travel Australia, NZ & the Pacific • Islands of Australia's Great Barrier Reef • Melbourne • Melbourne City Map • Micronesia • New Caledonia • New South Wales • New Zealand • Northern Territory • Outback Australia • Out to Eat – Melbourne • Out to Eat – Sydney • Papua New Guinea • Pidgin phrasebook • Queensland • Rarotonga & the Cook Islands • Samoa • Solomon Islands • South Australia • South Pacific • South Pacific phrasebook • Sydney • Sydney City Map • Sydney Condensed • Tahiti & French Polynesia • Tasmania • Tonga • Tramping in New Zealand • Vanuatu • Victoria • Walking in Australia • Watching Wildlife Australia • Western Australia
Travel Literature: Islands in the Clouds: Travels in the Highlands of New Guinea • Kiwi Tracks: A New Zealand Journey • Sean & David's Long Drive

CENTRAL AMERICA & THE CARIBBEAN Bahamas, Turks & Caicos • Baja California • Belize, Guatemala & Yucatán • Bermuda • Central America on a shoestring • Costa Rica • Costa Rica Spanish phrasebook • Cuba • Cycling Cuba • Dominican Republic & Haiti • Eastern Caribbean • Guatemala • Havana • Healthy Travel Central & South America • Jamaica • Mexico • Mexico City • Panama • Puerto Rico • Read This First: Central & South America • Virgin Islands • World Food Caribbean • World Food Mexico • Yucatán
Travel Literature: Green Dreams: Travels in Central America

EUROPE Amsterdam • Amsterdam City Map • Amsterdam Condensed • Andalucía • Athens • Austria • Baltic States phrasebook • Barcelona • Barcelona City Map • Belgium & Luxembourg • Berlin • Berlin City Map • Britain • British phrasebook • Brussels, Bruges & Antwerp • Brussels City Map • Budapest • Budapest City Map • Canary Islands • Catalunya & the Costa Brava • Central Europe • Central Europe phrasebook • Copenhagen • Corfu & the Ionians • Corsica • Crete • Crete Condensed • Croatia • Cycling Britain • Cycling France • Cyprus • Czech & Slovak Republics • Czech phrasebook • Denmark • Dublin • Dublin City Map • Dublin Condensed • Eastern Europe • Eastern Europe phrasebook • Edinburgh • Edinburgh City Map • England • Estonia, Latvia & Lithuania • Europe on a shoestring • Europe phrasebook • Finland • Florence • Florence City Map • France • Frankfurt City Map • Frankfurt Condensed • French phrasebook • Georgia, Armenia & Azerbaijan • Germany • German phrasebook • Greece • Greek Islands • Greek phrasebook • Hungary • Iceland, Greenland & the Faroe Islands • Ireland • Italian phrasebook • Italy • Kraków • Lisbon • The Loire • London • London City Map • London Condensed • Madrid • Madrid City Map • Malta • Mediterranean Europe • Milan, Turin & Genoa • Moscow • Munich • Netherlands • Normandy • Norway • Out to Eat – London • Out to Eat – Paris • Paris • Paris City Map • Paris Condensed • Poland • Polish phrasebook • Portugal • Portuguese phrasebook • Prague • Prague City Map • Provence & the Côte d'Azur • Read This First: Europe • Rhodes & the Dodecanese • Romania & Moldova • Rome • Rome City Map • Rome Condensed • Russia, Ukraine & Belarus • Russian phrasebook • Scandinavian & Baltic Europe • Scandinavian phrasebook • Scotland • Sicily • Slovenia • South-West France • Spain • Spanish phrasebook • Stockholm • St Petersburg • St Petersburg City Map • Sweden • Switzerland • Tuscany • Ukrainian phrasebook • Venice • Vienna • Wales • Walking in Britain • Walking in France • Walking in Ireland • Walking in Italy • Walking in Scotland • Walking in Spain • Walking in Switzerland • Western Europe • World Food France • World Food Greece • World Food Ireland • World Food Italy • World Food Spain **Travel Literature:** After Yugoslavia • Love and War in the Apennines • The Olive Grove: Travels in Greece • On the Shores of the Mediterranean • Round Ireland in Low Gear • A Small Place in Italy

Lonely Planet Mail Order

Lonely Planet products are distributed worldwide. They are also available by mail order from Lonely Planet, so if you have difficulty finding a title please write to us. North and South American residents should write to 150 Linden St, Oakland, CA 94607, USA; European and African residents should write to 10a Spring Place, London NW5 3BH, UK; and residents of other countries to Locked Bag 1, Footscray, Victoria 3011, Australia.

INDIAN SUBCONTINENT & THE INDIAN OCEAN Bangladesh • Bengali phrasebook • Bhutan • Delhi • Goa • Healthy Travel Asia & India • Hindi & Urdu phrasebook • India • India & Bangladesh City Map • Indian Himalaya • Karakoram Highway • Kathmandu City Map • Kerala • Madagascar • Maldives • Mauritius, Réunion & Seychelles • Mumbai (Bombay) • Nepal • Nepali phrasebook • North India • Pakistan • Rajasthan • Read This First: Asia & India • South India • Sri Lanka • Sri Lanka phrasebook • Tibet • Tibetan phrasebook • Trekking in the Indian Himalaya • Trekking in the Karakoram & Hindukush • Trekking in the Nepal Himalaya • World Food India **Travel Literature:** The Age of Kali: Indian Travels and Encounters • Hello Goodnight: A Life of Goa • In Rajasthan • Maverick in Madagascar • A Season in Heaven: True Tales from the Road to Kathmandu • Shopping for Buddhas • A Short Walk in the Hindu Kush • Slowly Down the Ganges

MIDDLE EAST & CENTRAL ASIA Bahrain, Kuwait & Qatar • Central Asia • Central Asia phrasebook • Dubai • Farsi (Persian) phrasebook • Hebrew phrasebook • Iran • Israel & the Palestinian Territories • Istanbul • Istanbul City Map • Istanbul to Cairo • Istanbul to Kathmandu • Jerusalem • Jerusalem City Map • Jordan • Lebanon • Middle East • Oman & the United Arab Emirates • Syria • Turkey • Turkish phrasebook • World Food Turkey • Yemen **Travel Literature:** Black on Black: Iran Revisited • Breaking Ranks: Turbulent Travels in the Promised Land • The Gates of Damascus • Kingdom of the Film Stars: Journey into Jordan

NORTH AMERICA Alaska • Boston • Boston City Map • Boston Condensed • British Columbia • California & Nevada • California Condensed • Canada • Chicago • Chicago City Map • Chicago Condensed • Florida • Georgia & the Carolinas • Great Lakes • Hawaii • Hiking in Alaska • Hiking in the USA • Honolulu & Oahu City Map • Las Vegas • Los Angeles • Los Angeles City Map • Louisiana & the Deep South • Miami • Miami City Map • Montreal • New England • New Orleans • New Orleans City Map • New York City • New York City City Map • New York City Condensed • New York, New Jersey & Pennsylvania • Oahu • Out to Eat – San Francisco • Pacific Northwest • Rocky Mountains • San Diego & Tijuana • San Francisco • San Francisco City Map • Seattle • Seattle City Map • Southwest • Texas • Toronto • USA • USA phrasebook • Vancouver • Vancouver City Map • Virginia & the Capital Region • Washington, DC • Washington, DC City Map • World Food New Orleans **Travel Literature:** Caught Inside: A Surfer's Year on the California Coast • Drive Thru America

NORTH-EAST ASIA Beijing • Beijing City Map • Cantonese phrasebook • China • Hiking in Japan • Hong Kong & Macau • Hong Kong City Map • Hong Kong Condensed • Japan • Japanese phrasebook • Korea • Korean phrasebook • Kyoto • Mandarin phrasebook • Mongolia • Mongolian phrasebook • Seoul • Shanghai • South-West China • Taiwan • Tokyo • Tokyo Condensed • World Food Hong Kong • World Food Japan **Travel Literature:** In Xanadu: A Quest • Lost Japan

SOUTH AMERICA Argentina, Uruguay & Paraguay • Bolivia • Brazil • Brazilian phrasebook • Buenos Aires • Buenos Aires City Map • Chile & Easter Island • Colombia • Ecuador & the Galapagos Islands • Healthy Travel Central & South America • Latin American Spanish phrasebook • Peru • Quechua phrasebook • Read This First: Central & South America • Rio de Janeiro • Rio de Janeiro City Map • Santiago de Chile • South America on a shoestring • Trekking in the Patagonian Andes • Venezuela **Travel Literature:** Full Circle: A South American Journey

SOUTH-EAST ASIA Bali & Lombok • Bangkok • Bangkok City Map • Burmese phrasebook • Cambodia • Cycling Vietnam, Laos & Cambodia • East Timor phrasebook • Hanoi • Healthy Travel Asia & India • Hill Tribes phrasebook • Ho Chi Minh City (Saigon) • Indonesia • Indonesian phrasebook • Indonesia's Eastern Islands • Java • Lao phrasebook • Laos • Malay phrasebook • Malaysia, Singapore & Brunei • Myanmar (Burma) • Philippines • Pilipino (Tagalog) phrasebook • Read This First: Asia & India • Singapore • Singapore City Map • South-East Asia on a shoestring • South-East Asia phrasebook • Thailand • Thailand's Islands & Beaches • Thailand, Vietnam, Laos & Cambodia Road Atlas • Thai phrasebook • Vietnam • Vietnamese phrasebook • World Food Indonesia • World Food Thailand • World Food Vietnam

ALSO AVAILABLE: Antarctica • The Arctic • The Blue Man: Tales of Travel, Love and Coffee • Brief Encounters: Stories of Love, Sex & Travel • Buddhist Stupas in Asia: The Shape of Perfection • Chasing Rickshaws • The Last Grain Race • Lonely Planet … On the Edge: Adventurous Escapades from Around the World • Lonely Planet Unpacked • Lonely Planet Unpacked Again • Not the Only Planet: Science Fiction Travel Stories • Ports of Call: A Journey by Sea • Sacred India • Travel Photography: A Guide to Taking Better Pictures • Travel with Children • Tuvalu: Portrait of an Island Nation

LONELY PLANET

You already know that Lonely Planet produces more than this one guidebook, but you might not be aware of the other products we have on this region. Here is a selection of titles that you may want to check out as well:

Mandarin phrasebook
ISBN 0 86442 652 6
US$7.95 • UK£4.50

Cantonese phrasebook
ISBN 0 86442 645 3
US$6.95 • UK£4.50

China
ISBN 0 86442 755 7
US$29.99 • UK£17.99

World Food Hong Kong
ISBN 1 86450 288 6
US$13.99 • UK£8.99

Healthy Travel Asia & India
ISBN 1 86450 051 4
US$5.95 • UK£3.99

Read This First: Asia & India
ISBN 1 86450 049 2
US$14.95 • UK£8.99

Hong Kong Condensed
ISBN 1 86450 253 3
US$11.99 • UK£6.99

CitySync
ISBN 1 86450 228 2
US$49.99 • UK£29.99

Hong Kong City Map
ISBN 1 86450 007 7
US$5.95 • UK£3.99

Chasing Rickshaws
ISBN 0 86442 640 2
US$34.95 • UK£19.99

Available wherever books are sold

Index

Text

Bold indicates maps.

Bold indicates maps.

Bold indicates maps.

Boxed Text

Places to Stay

Places to Eat

MAP 1 – LOCATOR

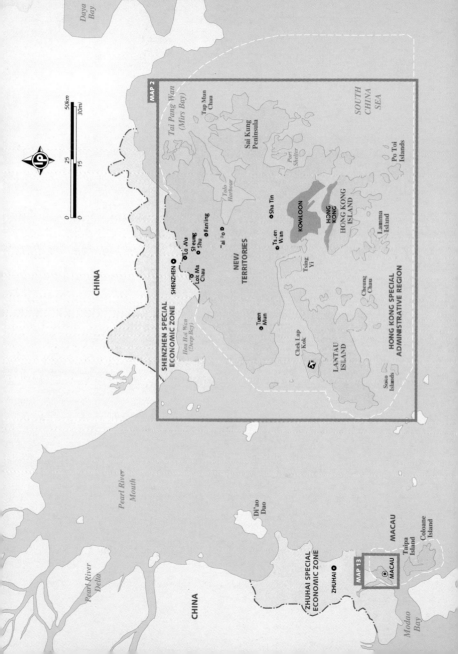

MAP 2 – HONG KONG SPECIAL ADMINISTRATIVE REGION

SHENZHEN SPECIAL ECONOMIC ZONE

To Guangzhou

SHENZH

CHINA

Lo Wu

Lok Ma Chau

Sheung Shui

San Tin

Fanl

Hau Hoi Wan (Deep Bay)

Mai Po Marsh

Shekou

Lau Fau Shan

Lam Tsuen North Country Park

NEW TERRITORIES

Yuen Long

Kam Tin

Nim Wan

LRT

Tai Mo Shan Country Park

Tai Mo S (957m)

Tai Lam Country Park

MacLehose Trail

Shing M Country I

Castle Peak (583m)

Tuen Mun

Tai Lam Chung Reservoir

Sham Tseng

Tsuen

Lung Kwu Chau

Tsing Yi

Ch

Sha Chau

Ma Wan

Tsing Yi

Lai Chi

East Brother

Chek Lap Kok

West Brother

Disneyland Site

Airport

Discovery Bay Tunnel

Hong Kong International Airport

Tau Pak Wan (Discovery Bay)

Airport Express

Discovery Bay

Tung Chung

Lantau Trail

Pak Mong

Peng Chau

Tung Chung Fort

LANTAU ISLAND

Lantau North Country Park

NGONG PING

Sunset Peak (869m)

Mui Wo

Ngan Kwong Wan

Tai O

Trail

Lantau Peak (934m)

Lantau South Country Park

Hei Ling Chau

Pak Kok Tsuen

Lantau Trail

Cheung Sha

Yung Shue Wan

Shek Pik Reservoir

Cheung Sha Beach

Chi Ma Wan Peninsula

Fan Lau

West Lamma Channel

Cheung Chau

So

La Isl

To Macau

Shek Kwu Chau

Lantau Channel

Soko Islands

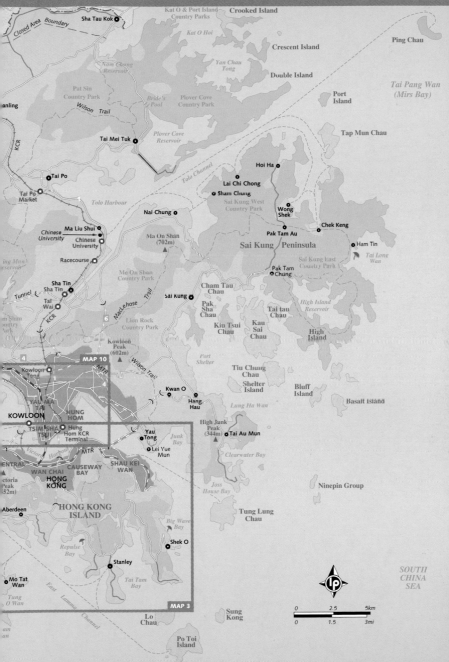

MAP 3 – HONG KONG ISLAND

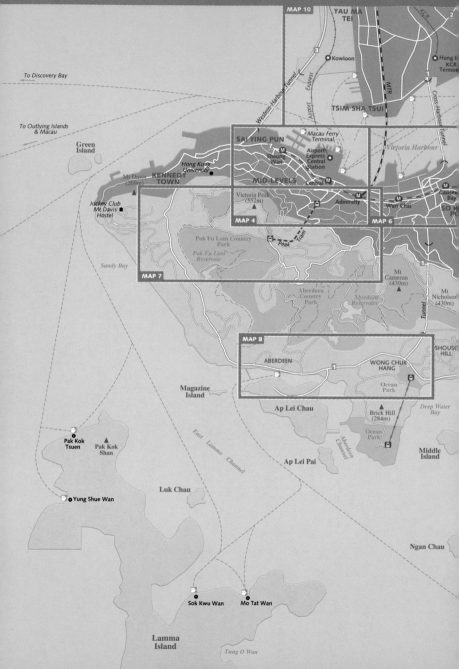

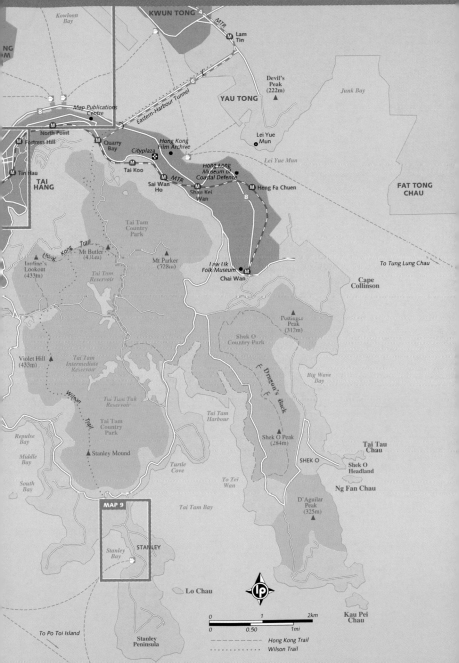

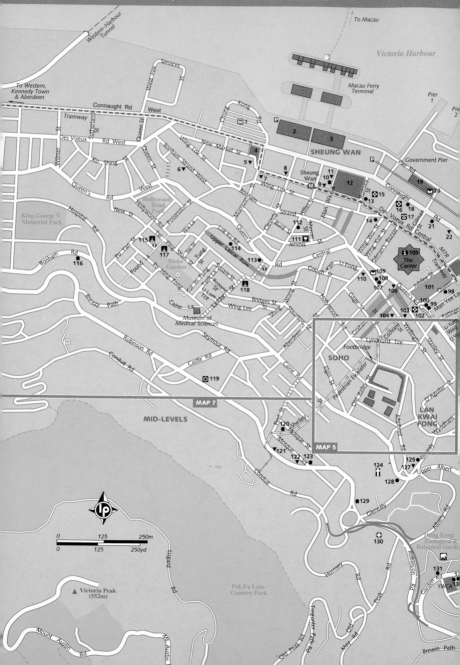

MAP 4 – SHEUNG WAN, CENTRAL & ADMIRALTY

To Macau

Victoria Harbour

Western Harbour Tunnel

Services

West Ferry

Kong

Macau Ferry Terminal

Pier 1

Pier 2

To Western, Kennedy Town & Aberdeen

Connaught Rd West

Tramway

Queen's

Rd West

Des Voeux

Ko Shing St

Wing Lok St

New Market St

Bonham Strand West

SHEUNG WAN

Government Pier

Pier Rd

1

2

3

4

5

6

7

8

9

10

11

12

13

14

15

16

17

18

19

20

21

22

Connaught

Des Voeux Rd Central

Sheung Wan

Bonham

Wing Lok St

Hillier

Strand

Morrison

Mercer St

Jervois

Wing Wo St

Wing Kut St

Cleverly St

Chinatown Bazaar

Queen's Rd Central

MTR

King George V Memorial Park

Hospital Rd

Queen's Rd West

New St

Hollywood Rd Park

Possession St

Tai Ping Shan St

Water La

Tung

Lok Ku Rd

Upper Lascar Row

111

114

113

112

Jervois

Central

Gough St

U Fong

105 The Center

109

108

107

106

110

101

100

99

98

103

102

104

Queen's Rd

Man Yee

Pottinger

D'Aguilar

Stanley

Li Yuen West

Li Yuen

Bonham Rd

Po Yan St

115

117

116

Bridges St

Shing

Tank

Rozario

U Lam Tce

Ladder

118

Square St

Caine

Wing Lee

Staunton

Aberdeen

Hollywood

Cage St

Graham

Elgin

Cochrane

Lyndhurst Tce

Wellington

Peel St

SOHO

Footbridge

Pedestrian Escalator

LAN KWAI FONG

Wyndham

Albert

Blake Garden

Po Hing Fong

Museum of Medical Sciences

Caine Rd

Robinson Rd

Seymour Rd

Castle Rd

119

Conduit Rd

MAP 7

MID-LEVELS

Breezy Path

Shelley

Mosque

120

121

122

123

MAP 5

124

125

127

128

129

130

Clenealy

Upper Albert

Glenealy

Conduit Rd

0   125   250m
0   125   250yd

▲ Victoria Peak (552m)

Pok Fu Lam Country Park

Mount Austin Rd

Mt Austin Rd

Lugard Rd

Hornsey Rd

Old Peak Rd

Peak Rd

Tregunter Path

May Rd

Hong Kong Zoological & Botanical Gardens

Robinson

Garden Rd

131

YWCA 13

Albany Rd

Brewin Path

To Jordan

Airport Express

Pier 3

Pier 4

Pier 5

23

Pier 6

24

Pier 7

25

Man Kwong St

Man To St

Bus Terminus

Blake Pier

To Tsim Sha Tsui

To Discovery Bay

Airport Express Central Station

Shuttle Bus

Man Cheung St

Harbour View St

International Finance Centre

26

To Hung Horn

Victoria

77

28

29

30

Exchange Square

31

32

Connaught Rd

35

Star Ferry Pier

To Tsim Sha Tsui East

Edinburgh

Queen's Pier

Luna Wui Rd

96

97

33

Memorial Gardens

City Hall (Lower Block)

Prince of Wales Building

95

91

94

Central

Connaught Rd

36

Central

Pedder St

Theatre La

7G

Prince's Bldg

37

Lister Rd

39

40

41

86

87

58

79

Pedder Bldg

80

77

Statue Square

71

Chater Garden

42

Lambeth Walk

Bank of America Tower

Helicopter Landing Ground

Pier

De Voeux Rd

MTR Town Hall Stn

43

82

83

81

74

75

73

72

70

Queen's Rd Central

66

Murray Rd

44

Central Harcourt Rd

Citic Tower

CENTRAL

Bank of China Tower

Lippo Centre

63

Admiralty

M

45

MTR Island Line

To Wan Chai & Causeway Bay

69

Garden Rd

Cotton Path

67

Citibank Plaza

65

64

Queensway Plaza

United Centre

56

Kennedy Rd

Harcourt Gardun

Police Headquarters

Former Government House

US Consulate

68

Murray Building

Peak Tram Terminus

Supreme Court

62

57

55

54

Queensway

Hennessy

46

50

49

48

Arsenal St

Lockhart

Queen's

51

52

Cotton Tree Dr

Peak Tram

Hong Kong Visual Arts Centre

Greenhouse

Aviary

Hong Kong Park

Kennedy Rd

61

ADMIRALTY

58

60

59

53

Star

Supreme Court Rd

Justice Dr

MacDonnell Rd

Barrett Rd

Kennedy Dr

Monmouth Tce

Bowen Dr

Bowen Rd

Bowen Rd

MAP 5

MAP 4 – SHEUNG WAN, CENTRAL & ADMIRALTY

PLACES TO STAY
- 10 The Bauhinia
- 34 Mandarin Oriental Hotel; Vong; Captain's Bar ; The Café
- 39 Ritz-Carlton Hotel
- 40 Furama Hotel; La Ronda; Island Restaurant; The Wine Room; Valet Shop
- 48 The Wesley
- 54 JW Marriott Hotel
- 58 Conrad International Hotel
- 61 Island Shangri-La Hotel; Petrus; Cyrano's
- 116 YWCA Building
- 120 Daisy Court (Hanlun Habitats)
- 123 Lily Court (Hanlun Habitats)
- 129 Bishop Lei International House

PLACES TO EAT
- 5 Golden Dragon & Golden Snow Garden Restaurants
- 6 Leung Hing Seafood Restaurant Delifrance
- 8 Ho Choi Seafood Restaurant
- 9 Korea Garden
- 11 Lee Fa Yuen Korea House Restaurant
- 22 Shalom Grill
- 26 Spaghetti House; Pacific Coffee Company; Eating Plus
- 29 Le Fauchon; Hunan Garden; Oliver's Super Sandwiches
- 42 Bull & Bear Pub
- 43 Secret Garden Korean Restaurant
- 47 Tan Ta Wan Thai Restaurant
- 49 Yoshinoya Noodles
- 50 Baccus
- 51 Shinta Indonesian Restaurant
- 52 Patong Thai Restaurant
- 53 Cine Città
- 65 Oliver's Super Sandwiches; Godown
- 84 Tandoor Indian Restaurant; Landau
- 85 Bistrot de Paris
- 86 Delifrance; Bookazine
- 87 Jimmy's Kitchen
- 88 China Tee Club; Blanc de Chine; Shanghai Tang
- 103 Mak's Noodle
- 104 Habibi
- 106 Dai Pai Dong
- 110 Lin Heung Tea House
- 121 Rico's
- 122 Phukets Seafood Grill Club; Brown
- 127 Mozart Stub'n

OTHER
- 1 Macau Ferry Terminal Bus Terminus
- 2 Shun Tak Centre; Macau Government Tourist Office
- 3 Wing On Centre
- 4 Western Market
- 12 Wing On Department Store
- 13 Wing On Annexe
- 14 Aero International Travel
- 15 Vicwood Plaza; Cobra International
- 16 Sincere Department Store
- 17 PCCW-HKT i.Shops
- 18 China Travel Service
- 19 Government Offices
- 20 Post Office
- 21 Hong Kong Jockey Club
- 23 Pier 5 (Ferries to Lamma)
- 24 Pier 6 (Ferries to Cheung Chau)
- 25 Pier 7 (Ferries to Lantau & Peng Chau)
- 27 Tower Three, Exchange Square
- 28 Forum Shopping Mall
- 30 Tower Two, Exchange Square
- 31 Exchange Square Bus Terminus
- 32 Tower One, Exchange Square
- 33 Jardine House; Jasmine Restaurant
- 35 Hong Kong General Post Office
- 37 City Hall, Public Library
- 37 Cenotaph
- 38 Hong Kong Club Building; Times Bookshop
- 41 HSBC
- 44 Far East Finance Centre
- 45 Admiralty Centre
- 46 Post Office
- 55 UA Pacific Place
- 56 Hong Kong General Chamber of Commerce
- 57 Pacific Place Shopping Mall; Kelly & Walsh Bookshop; Le Fauchon; Yè Shanghai; Dan Ryan's Chicago Grill; Grappa's; Seibu & Lane Crawford Department Stores; Chinese Arts & Crafts; Hong Kong Records; Galerie du Monde
- 59 British Consulate
- 60 British Council
- 62 Government Publications Office
- 63 La Café
- 64 Flagstaff House Museum of Teaware; KS Lo Gallery
- 66 Cheung Kong Centre
- 67 St John's Cathedral
- 68 St John's Building

- 69 SAR Government Headquarters
- 70 Sin Hua Bank (Former Bank of China Building)
- 71 Old Supreme Court (Legislative Council Building)
- 72 HSBC Building
- 73 Standard Chartered Bank Building; Sotheby's; Ocean Optical
- 74 Henley Building; Hanart T Z Gallery; American Express
- 75 Galleria Shopping Centre
- 76 Alexandra House; Christie's; Professional Bookshop
- 77 The Landmark; Hong Kong Book Centre; Oliver's Super Sandwiches; Miu Miu
- 78 Gloucester Tower
- 79 Central Building; Liuligongfang Shop
- 80 HMV
- 81 Edinburgh Tower
- 82 Uncle Eric's Vintage Wine Bar
- 83 Concorde Travel
- 89 Watson's Wine Cellar
- 90 Natori Travel
- 91 Queen's Theatre; Queen's Bar & Bistro
- 92 Tse Sui Luen Jewellers
- 93 Yue Hwa Chinese Products Emporium
- 94 World Wide House; Delifrance
- 95 Hong Kong Book Centre
- 96 Chinese Chamber of Commerce
- 97 King Fook Jewellers
- 98 JPC Bookshop
- 99 China Travel Service
- 100 New Wing Hing Dispensary
- 101 Central Market
- 102 CRC Department Store
- 105 HKTB Information Centre
- 107 Galerie Martini
- 108 Eu Yan Sang Herbalist
- 109 Post Office
- 111 Rice Bar
- 112 Po Kee Fishing Tackle
- 113 Lock Cha Tea Shop
- 114 Cat Street Galleries
- 115 Pak Sing Temple
- 117 Kuan Yin Temple
- 118 Man Mo Temple
- 119 Ohel Leah Synagogue
- 124 Roman Catholic Cathedral
- 125 Martinizing Drycleaners
- 126 Hong Kong Central Hospital
- 128 Caritas House
- 130 Canossa Hospital
- 131 Greenhouses
- 132 Park 'N' Shop Supermarket
- 133 Plum Blossoms Gallery

SOHO & LAN KWAI FONG – MAP 5

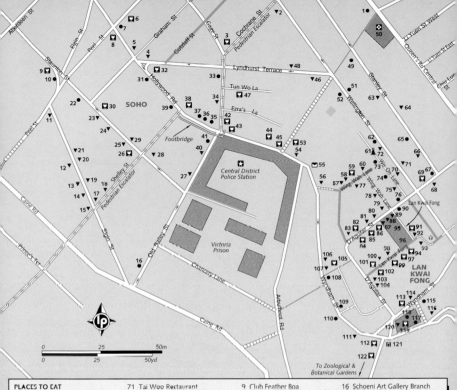

MAP 6 – WAN CHAI & CAUSEWAY BAY

To Kowloon

To North Point,
Quarry Bay &
Chai Wan

Fortress
Hill

Cross-Harbour Tunnel

Causeway Bay
Typhoon Shelter

Royal Hong
Kong Yacht
Club

Oil St

Fook Yum Rd

Wing On Rd

Electric Rd

Watson Rd

Shell St

Mercury St

Eastern Corridor

King Ming Rd

Whitfield Rd

Wing Hing St

Gordon Rd

Electric Rd

Tin Hau Temple Rd

Tsing Fung St

Lau Li St

Victoria Park Rd

Swimming
Pool

Tin Hau

Tennis Stadium

Tin Hau
Temple

Victoria Park

MTR Island Line

Noonday
Gun

Gloucester Rd

Cleveland St

97

85
86
87
84

90
92 93
91

95
96

90

Hoiston St

Paterson St

Kingston St

Cleverley St

World
Trade
Centre

89

88

100

99

Causeway Rd

Causeway Bay
Sports
Ground

CAUSEWAY
BAY

101

Lockhart Rd

102

103

105

104

Pearl
City
Mansion

Island
Beverley

Great George St

Windsor
House

Causeway
Bay Plaza

Causeway
Bay

106

111

112

107

108

Jardine's Bazaar

109

110

Yun Ping Rd

Sugar St

113

Tramway

Morrison Terrace

Shelter

St

Tung Lo Wan Rd

King St

Shing St

Wun Sha St

Chun St

114

115

121
122
123 120
124

Russell St

119

Irving St

Wan Rd

138
137
136

135

125

117

118

126

127
129

128

130

Hysan Ave

Lan Fong
Rd

Sun Wui Rd

Leighton Rd

Yee Wo St

Haven St

Matheson St

Jardine's Cres

Kai Chiu Rd

132

131

Leighton Rd

134

Lee Theatre
Plaza

133

Leighton Rd

St Paul's
Hospital

Caroline Path

Cotton Path

Kennedy Path

Eastern Hospital Rd

TAI HANG

Tai Hang Rd

Tiger Balm
Gardens

CAROLINE
HILL

Caroline Hill Rd

Broadwood Rd

116

South China Athletic
Association Stadium

Tung Wah
Eastern Hospital

LEIGHTON HILL

Wong Nai Chung Rd

Happy View Tce

Ventris Rd

Stadium Path

Stadium Path

Sports Stadium
Park House

Hong Kong Stadium

Tai Hang Dr

TAI HANG

To Happy Valley

0   150   300m
0   150   300yd

MAP 6 – WAN CHAI & CAUSEWAY BAY

PLACES TO STAY

5 Renaissance Harbour View Hotel; Dynasty Restaurant; Club ing
7 Grand Hyatt Hotel; One Harbour Road; Champagne Bar; JJ's
16 Harbour View International House (YMCA)
32 Wharney Hotel
39 Empire Hotel
55 Luk Kwok Hotel
63 Century Hong Kong
85 Alisan Guest House
88 Central Building; Lung Poon Villa; Lung Tin Guest House
93 Excelsior Hotel; Dickens Bar
100 Jetvan Travellers' House
102 Wang Fat Hostel
103 Noble Hostel; Kai Woo Hung Wan Guesthouse
104 Park Lane Hotel
114 New Cathay Hotel
115 Regal Hongkong Hotel
125 Phoenix Apartments; Wah Lai Villa; Dragon Inn; Yee Woo Guest House
132 Emerald House
133 Causeway Bay Guest House
144 South Pacific Hotel
146 Charterhouse Hotel

PLACES TO EAT

1 Port Cafe
9 East Ocean Seafood Restaurant
11 Victoria City; Saigon Vietnamese Restaurant; Viceroy Indian Restaurant; Punchline Comedy Club
15 La Bella Donna
19 American Restaurant
20 Portucale Restaurant & Pub
22 Pepperoni's Pizza & Cafe
24 Louis' Steak House
25 Cinta-J
28 China Town
30 Rigoletto's
34 Saigon Beach Vietnamese Restaurant
38 Cinta
40 Healthy Mess Vegetarian Restaurant
42 Simply Healthy
43 Coyote Bar & Grill
46 Chili Club
47 Yin King Lau Restaurant
50 Tim's Kitchen
51 Beijing Shui Jiao Wong
56 Delifrance
57 369 Shanghai Restaurant
58 Oliver's Super Sandwiches
65 Vegetarian Court; Liu Yuan Restaurant; Oliver's Super Sandwiches
67 Carriana Chiu Chow Restaurant
68 Shabu Shabu
70 Suikenkan
71 Food Stalls; Noodle Shops
75 Sze Chuen Lau Restaurant
76 Saint's Alp Teahouse
77 Tai Woo Seafood
79 Tomokazu
81 La Festa
82 Banana Leaf Curry House
89 Yin Ping Vietnamese Restaurant
92 Oliver's Super Sandwiches
94 King Heung Northern Chinese Restaurant
95 Vegi Food Kitchen
96 Nanking Kitchen
99 Paper Moon American Restaurant
113 Kung Tak Lam
119 Food Stalls; Tang Lung Chau Market
120 Dining Area Restaurant
122 Tai Ping Koon
123 Hangzhou Restaurant
124 Red Pepper
126 Queen's Cafe
127 Irene's Restaurant
129 Global Forever Green Taiwanese Restaurant
131 Korea Restaurant
134 Indonesian Restaurant
135 Chuen Cheung Kui
136 Sorabol Korean Restaurant
137 Perfume River Vietnamese Restaurant
138 Indonesia Padang Restaurant
145 Ichiban
147 Shaffi's Malik
155 Lung Moon Restaurant
156 Vegetarian Garden
159 Steam & Stew Inn
160 Jo Jo Mess Club
161 Harry Ramsden's
163 Oliver's Super Sandwiches

BARS/CLUBS

21 The Wanch
23 Charlie Luciano's
26 Joe Bananas
27 Royal Arms
29 Dusk till Dawn
31 Carnegie's
33 Tango Martini
35 Devil's Advocate Pub
37 Neptune Disco
44 Old China Hand
45 New Makati
48 Horse & Carriage
52 Neptune Disco 11
53 Delaney's; Kublai's Cyber Diner; Cat Street Bar & Restaurant
54 Big Apple
59 Horse & Groom
66 New Tonnochy Nightclub
80 Mine Disco
86 Royal's Pub
90 Shakespeare Pub
97 Stix
117 Brecht's Circle
128 King's Arms
139 Area Bar

OTHER

2 Wan Chai Ferry Pier
3 Harbour Road Indoor Games Hall
4 Wan Chai Ferry Pier Bus Terminus
6 Cyber Cafe
8 Hong Kong Trade Development Council
10 Cine-Art House
12 Visa Office of People's Republic of China
13 Chinese Arts & Crafts
14 Hong Kong Immigration & Transport Departments
17 Lim Por Yen Theatre; Pao Sui Loong Galleries; Goethe Institute; The Open Kitchen
18 Hong Kong Academy for the Performing Arts
36 Avanti Network Cybercafe
41 Alliance Française
49 POV 2 Bookshop
60 Tung Sun Commercial Centre; Hong Kong Society for the Aged
61 Lockhard Rd Market
62 Hong Kong Jockey Club
64 HSBC
69 Sunny Paradise Sauna
72 Hong Kong Sauna
73 New Paradise Health Club
74 HSBC
78 Causeway Bay Plaza Two
83 Post Office
84 Wellcome Supermarket
87 Zone-3 Sporting Goods Shop
91 Times Bookshop; Oscar's
98 Wellcome Supermarket
101 Excelsior Plaza; Cash On-Line Cyber Cafe
105 JP Cinema
106 Sogo Department Store

MICHEAL LAANELA

High flying against a backdrop of high rise – basketball courts in Wan Chai, Hong Kong Island

MAP 7 – THE PEAK

To Central

LUNG FU SHAN

Chiu Yuen Cemetery

Pok Fu Lam Rd

Hatton Rd

0 250 500m
0 250 500yd

To Jockey Club Mt Davis Hostel

Mt Davis Rd

Chinese Christian Cemetery

Lookout

Lookout

Sai Ko Shan (High West) (493m)

Hong Kong Trail

To Jockey Club Mt Davis Hostel

Sandy Bay Rd

Pisley Rd

Sassoon Rd

Pok Fu Lam Rd

Victoria Rd

Sha Wan Dr

Sandy Bay

To Aberdeen

To Buses

Pok Fu Lam Reservoir

Pok Fu Lam Country Park

Governor's

Harlech Rd

VICTORIA GAP

Pok Fu Lam Reservoir

Hong Kong Rd

Lugard Rd

Wireless Station

Lookout

Victoria Peak (552m)

Victoria Peak Garden

Walk

MAP 8 – ABERDEEN

Pok Fu Lam Country Park

Hong Kong Trail Section 2

Peel Rise

Aberdeen Country Park

To Pok Fu Lam Country Park & Aberdeen Country Park Entrances & Hong Kong Trail

Aberdeen Lower Reservoir

Aberdeen

Aberdeen Reservoir Rd

Aberdeen Bus Station

To Kennedy Town

Shek Pai Wan Rd

Wan St

Chinese Cemetery

Aberdeen Main Rd

Aberdeen Centre

Tin Hau Temple

Tin Wan Praya Rd

Aberdeen Praya Rd

Aberdeen Promenade

Fung Shing Rd

Old Main St

Yue Kwong Rd

Aberdeen Main Rd

Aberdeen Praya Rd

3

2

4

Nam Ning St

Hung Shing Shrine

12

11

13

5

6 7 8 9 10

Aberdeen Harbour

Ap Lei Chau Bridge

SOUTH HORIZONS

South Horizons Dr

Lee Nam Rd

Ap Lei Chau Bridge Rd

AP LEI CHAU

Lei Tung Estate Rd

Floating Restaurants

Sham Wan

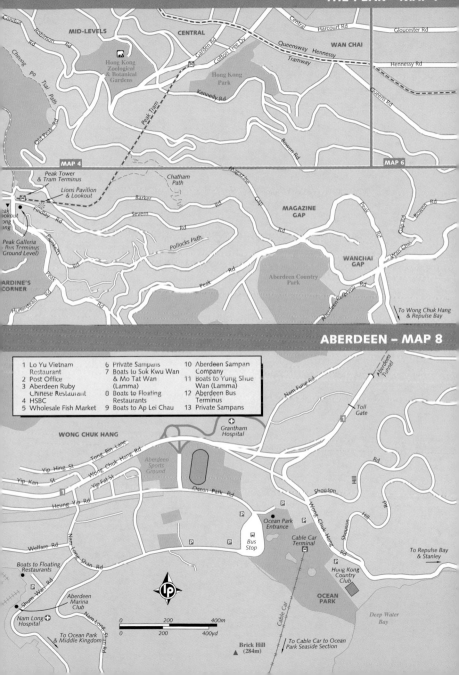

THE PEAK – MAP 7

Conduit Rd
Robinson Rd
MID-LEVELS
CENTRAL
Central
Harcourt Rd
Gloucester Rd
Cheung
Cotton Tree Dr
Garden Rd
Queensway
Hennessy
WAN CHAI
Po
Robinson Rd
Tsai Path
Hennessy Rd
Hong Kong Zoological & Botanical Gardens
Tramway
Old Peak Path
Hong Kong Park
Kennedy Rd
Queens Rd
Peak Tram
MAP 4
MAP 6

Peak Tower & Tram Terminus
Chatham Path
Lions Pavilion & Lookout
Barker Rd
Magazine Gap
Findlay Rd
Severn Rd
Rd
MAGAZINE GAP
Peak Lookout
Pollocks Path
Rd
Peak Rd
Bowen Rd
Peak Galleria Bus Terminus (Ground Level)
Plunketts Rd
Rd
WANCHAI GAP
Wan Chai Gap Rd
JARDINE'S CORNER
Peak Rd
Aberdeen Country Park
Aberdeen Reservoir Rd
Rd
Homestead Rd
Peak Rd
To Wong Chuk Hang & Repulse Bay

1 Lo Yu Vietnam Restaurant
2 Post Office
3 Aberdeen Ruby Chinese Restaurant
4 HSBC
5 Wholesale Fish Market
6 Private Sampans
7 Boats to Sok Kwu Wan & Mo Tat Wan (Lamma)
8 Boats to Floating Restaurants
9 Boats to Ap Lei Chau
10 Aberdeen Sampan Company
11 Boats to Yung Shue Wan (Lamma)
12 Aberdeen Bus Terminus
13 Private Sampans

Aberdeen Tunnel
Nam Fung Rd
Toll Gate
WONG CHUK HANG
Grantham Hospital
Nam Fung Rd
Yip Hing St
Tong Bin Lane
Aberdeen Sports Ground
Wong Chuk Hang Rd
Yip Kan St
Yip Fat St
Ocean Park Rd
Shouson Hill
Heung Yip Rd
Ocean Park Entrance
Welfare Rd
Bus Stop
Cable Car Terminal
Wong Chuk Hang Rd
To Repulse Bay & Stanley
Boats to Floating Restaurants
Nam Long Shan Rd
Hong Kong Country Club
Aberdeen Marina Club
Shum Wan Rd
OCEAN PARK
Nam Long Hospital
Nam Long Shan Rd
To Ocean Park & Middle Kingdom
0   200   400m
0   200   400yd
Brick Hill (284m)
To Cable Car to Ocean Park Seaside Section
Cable Car
Deep Water Bay

MAP 9 – STANLEY

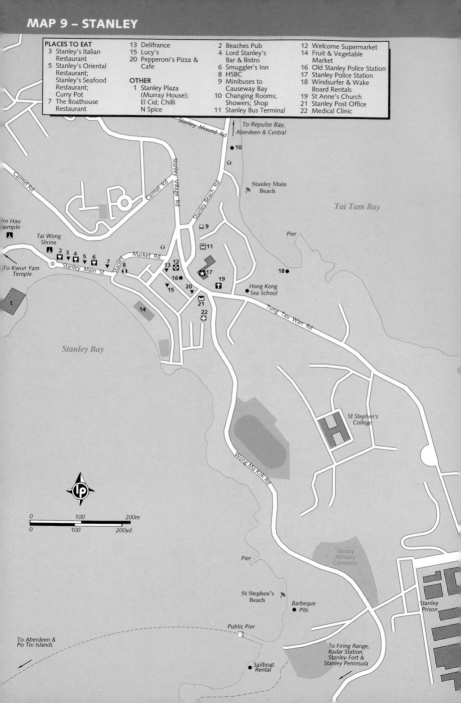

PLACES TO EAT
3 Stanley's Italian Restaurant
5 Stanley's Oriental Restaurant; Stanley's Seafood Restaurant; Curry Pot
7 The Boathouse Restaurant
13 Delifrance
15 Lucy's
20 Pepperoni's Pizza & Cafe

OTHER
1 Stanley Plaza (Murray House); El Cid; Chilli N Spice
2 Beaches Pub
4 Lord Stanley's Bar & Bistro
6 Smuggler's Inn
8 HSBC
9 Minibuses to Causeway Bay
10 Changing Rooms; Showers; Shop
11 Stanley Bus Terminal
12 Welcome Supermarket
14 Fruit & Vegetable Market
16 Old Stanley Police Station
17 Stanley Police Station
18 Windsurfer & Wake Board Rentals
19 St Anne's Church
21 Stanley Post Office
22 Medical Clinic

To Repulse Bay, Aberdeen & Central

Stanley Mound Rd

Carmel Rd

Stanley Village Rd

Stanley Beach Rd

Stanley Main Beach

Tai Tam Bay

Tin Hau Temple

Tai Wong Shrine

To Kwun Yam Temple

Market Rd

Stanley Main St

Stanley

Pier

Hong Kong Sea School

Stanley Bay

Tung Tau Wan Rd

Wong Ma Kok Rd

St Stephen's College

0   100   200m
0   100   200yd

Stanley Military Cemetery

Pier

St Stephen's Beach

Barbeque Pits

Stanley Prison

To Aberdeen & Po Toi Islands

Public Pier

Sailboat Rental

To Firing Range, Radar Station, Stanley Fort & Stanley Peninsula

A woman rows her sampan in Aberdeen Harbour, well-known for the junks moored in its waters.

MAP 10 – KOWLOON

To Hong Kong
Festival Walk
Lai Chi Kok M
City University of Hong Kong
Kowloon Tong M
To Hong Kong Baptist University
Lei Cheng UK Han Tomb Museum
Cheung Sha Wan M
MTR Tsuen Wan Line
Cheung Sha Wan Rd
SHEK KIP MEI
YAU YAT TSUEN
See Enlargement
Woh Chai St
Shek Kip Mei M
2
West Kowloon Corridor
Lai Chi Kok Rd
Yen Chow St
Sham Mong Rd
Sham Shui Po M
KCR East
SHAM SHUI PO
Airport Express & Tung Chung MTR Line
West Kowloon Hwy
MAP 11
Mong Kok Stadium
Boundary St
Prince Edward M
Prince Edward Rd West
Tung Chau St
Bedford Rd
Argyle St
3
MONG KOK
Mong Kok Rd
TAI KOK TSUI
Olympic O
Hoi Fai Rd
Anchor St
Cherry St
Mong Kok M
Argyle St
Nathan Rd
Dundas St
Hoi Wang Rd
YAU MA TEI
Ferry St
Yau Ma Tei M
Hamilton Rd
Pitt St
Waterloo Rd
KING'S PARK
Meteorological Station
Tung Kun St
King's Park Rise
Public Square St
Kowloon Central Post Office
King's Park Sports Ground
Gascoigne Rd
Temple St Night Market
Jordan Road Bus Terminal
Jordan Rd
Jordan M
Kowloon Cricket Club
Kowloon O
Shuttle Bus
Austin Rd
Hillwood Rd
China Ferry Terminal
Kimberley Rd
Granville Rd
TSIM SHA TSUI
Harbour City
Tsim Sha Tsui M
Ocean Terminal
Star Ferry Bus Terminal
Clock Tower
To Wan Chai
Victoria Harbour
To Central

Legend

1 New Capital Computer Plaza
2 HSBC
3 Post Office
4 Golden Shopping Centre
5 Dragon Centre; Sky Rink; Bus Depot
6 Police Station
7 Apliu Street Market
8 Sam Tai Ji Temple
9 Covered Market

Sham Shui Po (enlargement)

To Lei Cheng Uk Han Tomb Museum
Castle Peak Rd
Cheung Sha Wan Rd
Fuk Wa St
Fuk Wing St
Un Chau St
Tai Po Rd
Berwick St
Pak Tin St
To Mong Kok
1
2
4
3
5
Yen Chow St
Kweilin St
Pei Ho St
Ki Lung St
Apliu St
Sham Shui Po M
9
8
7
Tai Nan St
Nam Cheong St
Lai Chi Kok Rd
Yu Chau St

SHAM SHUI PO

MAP 12

0   0.5   1km
0   0.25   0.5mi

0   100   200m
0   100   200yd

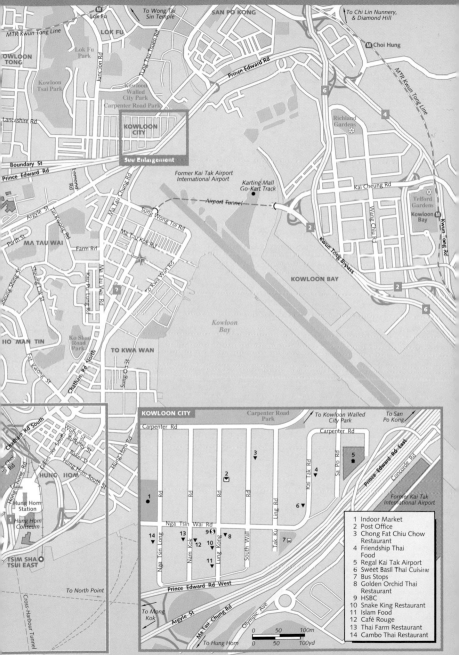

MTR Kwun Tong Line
Lok Fu
To Wong Tai Sin Temple
SAN PO KONG
To Chi Lin Nunnery, & Diamond Hill
M Choi Hung
KOWLOON TONG
Lok Fu Park
Junction Rd
Tseng Tong Kuen Rd
Prince Edward Rd
MTR Kwun Tong Line
Kowloon Tsai Park
Kowloon Walled City Park
Carpenter Road Park
Richland Gardens
Lancashire Rd
KOWLOON CITY
Telford Gardens
Kowloon Bay
Boundary St
Prince Edward Rd
See Enlargement
Former Kai Tak Airport International Airport
Karting Mall Go-Kart Track
Airport Tunnel
Kai Cheung Rd
Wang Chiu Rd
M Kwun Tong
Tonnochy Rd
Ma Tau Chung Rd
Tak Kwok St
Sung Wong Toi Rd
MA TAU WAI
Farm Rd
Ma Fu Kok Rd
Kwun Tong Byass
Purth St
Kwun Tong Rd
Argyle St
Tin Kwong Rd
Ma Tau Wai Rd
To Kwa Wan Rd
KOWLOON BAY
Jaume Shang Rd
Chatham Rd North
HO MAN TIN
Ko Shan Road Park
Sung On St
TO KWA WAN
Kowloon Bay

KOWLOON CITY

Carpenter Road Park
To Kowloon Walled City Park
To San Po Kong
Carpenter Rd
Carpenter Rd
Chatham Rd South
Wuhu St
Bulkeley St
Baker St
Gillies Ave South
HUNG HOM
Hung Hom Rd
Hong Chong Rd
3
2
5
Kai Tak Rd
Sa Po Rd
Prince Edward Rd East
Concorde Rd
4
Former Kai Tak International Airport
Hung Hom Station
1
Nga Tsin Long Rd
Nga Tsin Wai Rd
Nam Kok Rd
South Wall Rd
Ling Kong Rd
Tak Ku Rd
6
Hung Hom Coliseum
14
13
9
8
TSIM SHA TSUI EAST
12
10
7
11
Prince Edward Rd West
To North Point
Argyle St
To Mong Kok
Ma Tau Chung Rd
Olympic Ave
To Hung Hom
Cross Harbour Tunnel

1 Indoor Market
2 Post Office
3 Chong Fat Chiu Chow Restaurant
4 Friendship Thai Food
5 Regal Kai Tak Airport
6 Sweet Basil Thai Cuisine
7 Bus Stops
8 Golden Orchid Thai Restaurant
9 HSBC
10 Snake King Restaurant
11 Islam Food
12 Café Rouge
13 Thai Farm Restaurant
14 Cambo Thai Restaurant

0   50   100m
0   50   100yd

MAP 11 – YAU MA TEI & MONG KOK

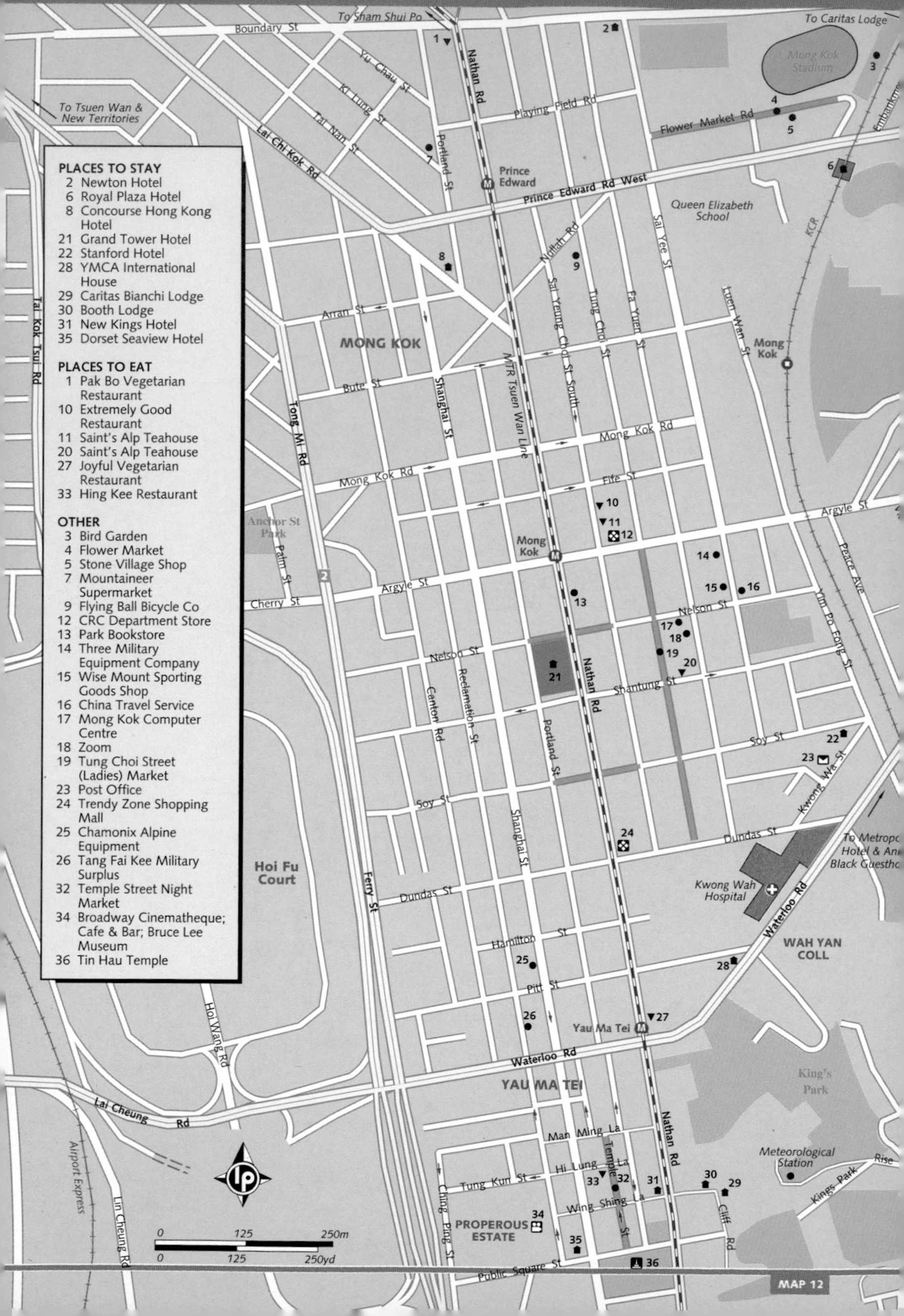

PLACES TO STAY
2 Newton Hotel
6 Royal Plaza Hotel
8 Concourse Hong Kong Hotel
21 Grand Tower Hotel
22 Stanford Hotel
28 YMCA International House
29 Caritas Bianchi Lodge
30 Booth Lodge
31 New Kings Hotel
35 Dorset Seaview Hotel
PLACES TO EAT
1 Pak Bo Vegetarian Restaurant
10 Extremely Good Restaurant
11 Saint's Alp Teahouse
20 Saint's Alp Teahouse
27 Joyful Vegetarian Restaurant
33 Hing Kee Restaurant
OTHER
3 Bird Garden
4 Flower Market
5 Stone Village Shop
7 Mountaineer Supermarket
9 Flying Ball Bicycle Co
12 CRC Department Store
13 Park Bookstore
14 Three Military Equipment Company
15 Wise Mount Sporting Goods Shop
16 China Travel Service
17 Mong Kok Computer Centre
18 Zoom
19 Tung Choi Street (Ladies) Market
23 Post Office
24 Trendy Zone Shopping Mall
25 Chamonix Alpine Equipment
26 Tang Fai Kee Military Surplus
32 Temple Street Night Market
34 Broadway Cinematheque; Cafe & Bar; Bruce Lee Museum
36 Tin Hau Temple
To Sham Shui Po
To Caritas Lodge
Boundary St
Mong Kok Stadium
To Tsuen Wan & New Territories
Yu Chau St
Ki Lung St
Tai Nan St
Lai Chi Kok Rd
Nathan Rd
Playing Field Rd
Flower Market Rd
Embankment
Portland St
Prince Edward
Prince Edward Rd West
Queen Elizabeth School
KCR
Nullah Rd
Sai Yee St
Sai Yeung Choi St
Tung Choi St
Fa Yuen St
Luen Wan St
Tai Kok Tsui Rd
Arran St
MONG KOK
Mong Kok
MTR Tsuen Wan Line
Sai Yeung Choi St South
Bute St
Shanghai St
Tong Mi Rd
Mong Kok Rd
Fife St
Argyle St
Anchor St Park
Palm St
Cherry St
Nelson St
Peace Ave
Yim Po Fong St
Shantung St
Canton Rd
Reclamation St
Portland St
Soy St
Kwong Wa St
Dundas St
To Metropole Hotel & Anne Black Guesthouse
Kwong Wah Hospital
Hoi Fu Court
Ferry St
Waterloo Rd
WAH YAN COLL
Hamilton St
Pitt St
Yau Ma Tei
Hoi Wang Rd
Waterloo Rd
YAU MA TEI
King's Park
Lai Cheung Rd
Man Ming La
Temple St
Hi Lung La
Tung Kun St
Wing Shing La
Ching Ping St
PROPEROUS ESTATE
Airport Express
Lin Cheung Rd
Meteorological Station
Kings Park Rise
Cliff Rd
0 125 250m
0 125 250yd
Public Square St
MAP 12

Repulse Bay's long beach is the most popular on Hong Kong Island.

CHRIS MELLOR

MAP 12 – TSIM SHA TSUI & HUNG HOM

To Yau Ma Tei
& Mong Kok

To Central

Star Ferry
Terminal

To Wan Chai

TSIM SHA TSUI & HUNG HOM – MAP 12

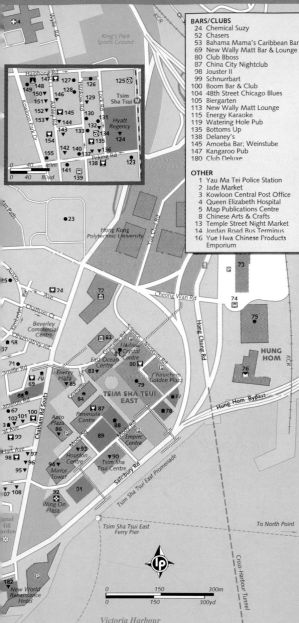

BARS/CLUBS
24 Chemical Suzy
52 Chasers
53 Bahama Mama's Caribbean Bar
69 New Wally Matt Bar & Lounge
80 Club Bboss
87 China City Nightclub
98 Jouster II
99 Schnurrbart
100 Boom Bar & Club
104 48th Street Chicago Blues
105 Biergarten
113 New Wally Matt Lounge
115 Energy Karaoke
119 Watering Hole Pub
135 Bottoms Up
138 Delaney's
145 Amoeba Bar; Weinstube
147 Kangaroo Pub
180 Club Deluxe

OTHER
1 Yau Ma Tei Police Station
2 Jade Market
3 Kowloon Central Post Office
4 Queen Elizabeth Hospital
5 Map Publications Centre
8 Chinese Arts & Crafts
13 Temple Street Night Market
14 Jordan Road Bus Terminus
16 Yue Hwa Chinese Products
   Emporium
18 Hong Kong Council of Women
23 Gun Club Hill Barracks
25 Onitsuka Shop
27 Hong Kong Observatory
29 Tse Sui Luen Jewellers
32 Cross-Border Bus Station (Buses to
   China)
33 China Hong Kong City
34 China Hong Kong City Bus Station
   (Buses to China)
40 HSBC
41 Kowloon Mosque & Islamic Centre
42 Wellcome Supermarket
43 HSBC
45 Burlington Arcade & Milton Mansion;
   Opal Mine; Sam's Tailor; Phoenix
   Services Agency
46 Cosmos Books
49 Yue Hwa Chinese Emporium
50 King Fook Jewellers; i.t Shop
67 American Express
71 K*facto.2y Shop
72 Hong Kong Museum of History
73 Hung Hom Station; Kowloon-Canton
   Railway Terminus
74 CTS Buses to China
75 Hong Kong Coliseum
76 Hong Kong International Mail Centre
81 New Mandarin Plaza
81 Crystal Spa
82 Hong Kong Science Museum
84 Hilton Towers
92 Wing On Department Store; Tai Ping
   Carpets
110 Ocean Boutique
114 Om International Jewellers
116 Citibank
123 China Travel Service; Wu Kong
    Shanghai Restaurant
125 Cash On-Line Cyber Cafe
126 Curio Alley
127 Ming's Sports Co
128 Hong Kong Jockey Club
130 Wellcome Supermarket
131 Swindon Books
133 Gulf Creation
134 Shadowman Cyber Cafe
139 Eternal East Bus Company (Buses to
    China)
140 HMV Record Store
141 Cohen Optical
148 Fuk Tak Temple
149 Haiphong Road Market
154 Ned Kelly's Last Stand
155 Yue Hwa Chinese Emporium
156 Park 'N' Shop Supermarket
158 Silvercord Towers & Shopping Centre;
    Traveller Services; Park 'N' Shop
159 Silvercord Cinema
162 i Cable Station; Lane Crawford
    Department Store; Shops & Restaurants
163 Shopping Arcade; Silk Road; Eastern
    Palace Chiu Chow Restaurant
165 Ocean Theatre
166 Sincerity Travel/Hong Kong Student
    Travel; Jade Garden Restaurant; Star
    Computer City; Chinese Arts &
    Crafts; King Sing Jewellers;
    Hong Kong Dolphinwatch
167 Hong Kong Tourism Board Information
    Centre
168 Star Ferry Bus Terminal
169 Hong Kong Cultural Centre
171 Ahluwalia & Sons Sporting Goods
173 HSBC
175 Hong Kong Space Museum
176 Hong Kong Museum of Art; Tai Yip
    Book Company
178 Kowloon General Post Office;
    PCCW-HKT Phone Centre
179 Mariners' Club

MAP 13 – MACAU PENINSULA

CHINA

Sun Yat Sen
Memorial Park

Ilha Verde

Inner Harbour

To Taipa, Airport
& Coloane

Reservoir

MAP 14

MAP 13 – MACAU PENINSULA

PLACES TO STAY
15 Fu Hua Hotel
24 Mondial Hotel
28 Guia Hotel
44 Kingsway Hotel
45 Mandarin Oriental Hotel;
   Dynasty Chinese Restaurant;
   Mezzaluna Restaurant;
   Embassy Bar
63 Pousada de São Tiago
69 Ritz Hotel;
   Ritz Dining Room

PLACES TO EAT
32 Pizzeria Toscana
50 Monster Island Italian
   Restaurant
55 O Porto Interior
56 Restaurante Litoral
57 Barra Nova
58 A Lorcha
66 Ali Curry House
67 Henri's Galley
68 Petisco Fernandes
74 Comida a Portuguesa
   Carlos
76 Dom Galo

OTHER
1 Portas de Cerco (Border
   Gate)
2 Police Station
3 Lin Fung Temple
4 Lin Zexu Memorial Hall
5 Canidrome
6 Mong Há Fort; Pousada de
   Mong Há
7 Kun Iam Temple
8 Almirante Lacerda City
   Market
9 Luis Camões Garden & Grotto
10 Casa Garden; Fundação
   Oriente Exhibition Gallery
11 Old Protestant Cemetery
12 Future Bright Amusement
   Park
13 King Wu Hospital
14 Fire Department Museum
16 CTM Shop
17 HSBC
18 Kun Iam Temple
19 Our Lady of Piety
   Cemetery
20 Montanha Russa Garden
21 Park 'N' Shop Supermarket
22 Flora Garden
23 Guia Cable Car
25 Lou Lim Ioc Garden
26 Sun Yat Sen Memorial
   Home
27 Police Station
29 Guia Fort & Lighthouse;
   MGTO
30 Jai Alai Complex; China City
   Nightclub; UFO Disco
31 New Yaohan Department
   Store; McDonald's; Pokka
   Coffee; Supermarket
33 Grand Prix Control Tower;
   Stands
34 Heliport
35 Macau Ferry Terminal;
   MGTO Branch
36 Macau Palace Floating Casino
37 Immigration Department
38 Tourist Activities Centre;
   Grand Prix Museum; Wine
   Museum
39 Macau Forum
40 Eternal Lotus Reunification
   Monument
41 Macau Polytechnic Institute
42 Arch of the Orient
   Monument
43 PLA Post
46 World Trade Center
47 Central People's Government
   Macau SAR Liaison Office
48 Macau Landmark; Standard
   Chartered Bank
49 José dos Santos Ferreira
   (Adé) Statue
51 UNESCO; Internet Access
52 Macau Cultural Centre;
   Macau Museum of Art
53 Mateus Ricci College
54 Chapel of Our Lady of
   Penha; Bishop's Palace
59 A-Ma Temple
60 Maritime Museum
61 Education & Youth Services
   Department
62 Gates of Understanding
   Monument
64 Barra Hill
65 Santa Sancha Palace
   (Ex Governor's Residence)
70 Residence of the Portuguese
   Consul-General
   (formerly Bela Vista Hotel)
71 Cybernetic Fountain
72 Macau Tower; Macau
   Convention Centre
73 Rotunda da Baia de Praia
   Grande
75 Bar Why Not
77 Rio Cafe
78 Signal Cafe
79 Casablanca Cafe
80 Sanshiro Pub
81 Macau Jazz Club
82 Kun Iam Statue &
   Ecumenical Centre

OLIVER STREWE

Macau's Portugese influence is most visible in the many imported Portugese wines, port and brandy.

The fountain in the magnificent Largo do Senado in Macau. The Senate Square is the city's focal point.

MAP 14 – CENTRAL MACAU

PLACES TO STAY
10 Royal Hotel
23 East Asia Hotel
24 Vila Capital
28 Macau Masters Hotel
29 Hou Kong Hotel
30 Sun Sun Hotel
31 Pensão Kuan Heng
32 Vila Tai Loy
33 Man Va Hotel
34 Vila Universal; Ko Wah Hotel
35 San Va Hospedaria; Lavandaria Macau
38 Central Hotel
59 Metropole Hotel
73 Sintra Hotel
76 Pensão Nam In
83 Lisboa Hotel (Old Wing); Shopping Arcade; American Express
84 Lisboa Hotel (New Wing); New Furusato Japanese Restaurant; Crazy Paris Show; Deluxe Club Savoy
86 Beverly Plaza Hotel
87 Fortuna Hotel; Abalone Ah Yat Restaurant; Fortuna Lounge; Fortuna Nightclub
89 Hotel Presidente; Silla Korean Restaurant; Skylight Nightclub
93 Holiday Inn Macau; Frascati Restaurant; Oskar's Pub
94 Grandeur Hotel; The Rotunda Bar

PLACES TO EAT
14 Kruatheque Restaurant
18 Yes Brazil Restaurant
36 Fat Siu Lau Restaurant
37 Sai Nam Restaurant
39 Restaurante Safari
40 Restaurant Vela Latina
43 Long Kei Restaurant
47 Platão Restaurant
48 Bolo de Arroz; Fruitarian O Barrilz Papatudo
62 Alfonso III
70 Solmar Restaurant
75 Caravela Cafe
80 Food Stalls
81 Clube Militar de Macau
88 Fook Lam Moon Restaurant

OTHER
1 Church of St Anthony
2 Ruins of the Church of St Paul; Museum of Sacred Art; Crypt
3 Escalator to Monte Fort & Macau Museum
4 Monte Fort; Macau Museum
5 Cemetery of St Michael the Archangel
6 Chapel of St Michael
7 Plaza Cultural de Macau; Bookshop
8 Old Estoril Hotel; Discos
9 Vitória Sport Centre; Swimming Pool
11 Vasco da Gama Garden
12 Provinhos Wine Shop
13 Lavandaria Guia
15 Lua da Prata Photo Shop
16 Foto Maxim's
17 Portuguese Consulate-General
19 American Express
20 Traditional Shops
21 Bird Cage Shop
22 Hong Kung Temple
25 Traditional Oyster Sauce Shop
26 Macau-Shenzhen Ferry Pier
27 Kee Kwan Motor Road Co (Buses to Guangzhou)
41 Shanghai KTV Lounge
42 Leal Senado; Exhibition Hall; Library
44 MGTO; Foto Maxim's
45 GPO
46 Church of St Dominic; Treasury of Sacred Art
49 Livraria Portuguesa
50 Internet Access; Mobile Zone CTM Shop
51 Livraria São Paulo
52 Macau Cathedral
53 Watson's Drugstore
54 Cineteatro Macau
55 Chinese Reading Room
56 HSBC
57 Bank of America
58 Bank of China
60 Supreme Court Building
61 Pavilions Supermercado
63 Church of St Augustine
64 Dom Pedro V Theatre
65 Chapel of St Joseph's Seminary
66 St Lawrence City Market
67 Church of St Lawrence
68 Government House
69 Citibank
71 Banco Comercial de Macau (BCM)
72 Foto Princesa
74 Tele-One Macau CTM Shop
77 Escola Portuguesa de Macau
78 Bank of China
79 Buses to Airport & Islands
82 Lisboa Casino
85 Kam Pek Casino
90 Main Police Station
91 CTM Telephone Office
92 Supermercado San Mui

RICHARD I'ANSON

Penha Church, on a hill above the Bela Vista. The views of central Macau from here are excellent.

MAP 15 – HONG KONG TRAIN SYSTEM

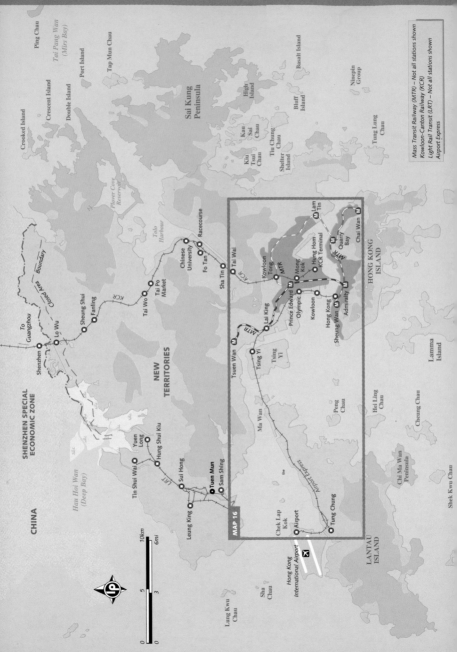

Mass Transit Railway (MTR) – Not all stations shown
Kowloon-Canton Railway (KCR)
Light Rail Transit (LRT) – Not all stations shown
Airport Express

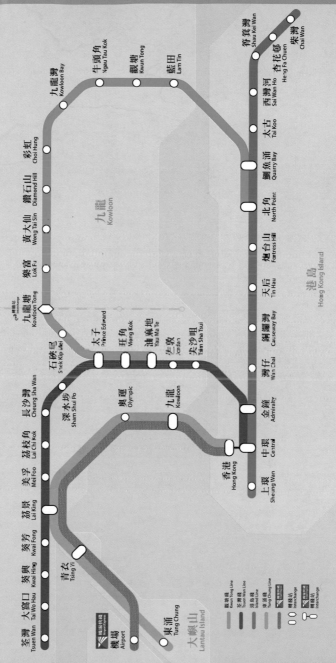

MAP LEGEND

CITY ROUTES

Hwy .... Primary Road	⟩═══ .... Tunnel
Rd ..... Secondary Road	.... Footbridge
St .... Street	La .... Lane

REGIONAL ROUTES

.... Tollway, Freeway
.... Primary Road
.... Secondary Road

BOUNDARIES

──·─·── .... International
──··─·── .... State
▬▬▬▬ .... Fortified Wall

HYDROGRAPHY

.... River, Creek	.... Marsh
.... Canal	.... Spring; Rapids
.... Lake	.... Waterfalls

TRANSPORT ROUTES & STATIONS

─O─ .... Train	─── ⚓ .... Ferry
─Ⓜ─ ....Metro, Tsuen Wan Line	──── .... Walking Trail
─Ⓜ─ ...... Metro, Island Line	▬ ▬ ▬ .... Tram
Ⓜ─ ...... Metro, Kwun Tong Line	┝─┥─Ⓔ─┝─ ... Cable Car, Chairlift

AREA FEATURES

▬▬▬ .... Building	.... Hotel
❀ .... Park, Gardens	.... Sports Ground
.... Market	.... Campus
.... Cemetery	.... Forest

POPULATION SYMBOLS

✪ **CAPITAL** ....National Capital	● **CITY** .... City	● Village .... Village
◉ **CAPITAL** ....State Capital	● **Town** ....Town	▬ .... Urban Area

MAP SYMBOLS

■ .... Place to Stay	▼ .... Place to Eat	● .... Point of Interest

✈ 🛩 ...... Airport, Airfield	⊞ .... Cinema	🏛 .... Museum	✿ ..... Shopping Centre
⑤ .... Bank	🏛 ... Confucian Temple	⛰ .... National Park	🏊 ...... Swimming Pool
🏖 .... Beach	✉ .... Embassy	⛩ .... Pagoda	🏛 .... Stately Home
☯ ...... Border Crossing	⌐ .... Gate	Ⓟ .... Parking	☯ .... Taoist Temple
🔔 🏯 .... Buddhist Temple	⛳ .... Golf Course	≍ .... Pass	☎ .... Telephone
🚌 🚏 .. Bus Terminal, Stop	✚ .... Hospital	🏠 🏛 ..... Pavillion, Shelter	🎭 .... Theatre
⛺ ....Camping Ground	🅰 .... Internet	❶ .... Police Station	☉ .... Toilet
🏰 .... Castle	☼ ☼ .... Lookout	✉ .... Post Office	■ .... Tomb
⌂ .... Cave	🎗 .... Monument	♨ .... Pub/Bar/Club	❶ .. Tourist Information
⛪ ✟ ....Church, Cathedral	▲ .... Mountain	⛩ .... Shinto Shrine	🐘 .... Zoo

Note: not all symbols displayed above appear in this book

LONELY PLANET OFFICES

Australia
Locked Bag 1, Footscray, Victoria 3011
☎ 03 8379 8000 fax 03 8379 8111
email: talk2us@lonelyplanet.com.au

UK
10a Spring Place, London NW5 3BH
☎ 020 7428 4800 fax 020 7428 4828
email: go@lonelyplanet.co.uk

USA
150 Linden St, Oakland, CA 94607
☎ 510 893 8555 TOLL FREE: 800 275 8555
fax 510 893 8572
email: info@lonelyplanet.com

France
1 rue du Dahomey, 75011 Paris
☎ 01 55 25 33 00 fax 01 55 25 33 01
email: bip@lonelyplanet.fr
www.lonelyplanet.fr

**World Wide Web: www.lonelyplanet.com *or* AOL keyword: lp
Lonely Planet Images: lpi@lonelyplanet.com.au**